THE SELECTION PROCESS FOR CAPITAL PROJECTS

ETM WILEY SERIES IN ENGINEERING & TECHNOLOGY MANAGEMENT

Series Editor: Dundar F. Kocaoglu

THE SELECTION PROCESS FOR CAPITAL PROJECTS

HANS J. LANG
DONALD N. MERINO

A WILEY-INTERSCIENCE PUBLICATION
JOHN WILEY & SONS, INC.
NEW YORK   CHICHESTER   BRISBANE   TORONTO   SINGAPORE

To our wives, Ruth and Rosemarie, who bore the burden of our long absences to prepare this book.

To Alexander Crombie Humphrey, William D. Ennis, and Arthur Lesser, Jr., Stevens pioneers in Engineering Economics, in whose footsteps we have sought to tread.

This text is printed on acid-free paper.

Copyright © 1993 by John Wiley & Sons, Inc.

All rights reserved. Published simultaneously in Canada.

Library of Congress Cataloging in Publication Data:

Lang, Hans J.
     The selection process for capital projects / Hans J. Lang, Donald
N. Merino.
          p.   cm. — (Wiley series in engineering & technology
management)
     "A Wiley-Interscience publication."
     Includes index.
     ISBN 0-471-63425-5
     1. Engineering economy.   2. Capital investments — Decision-making.
I. Merino, Donald N., 1937–   . II. Title. III. Series: Wiley
series in engineering and technology management.
TA177.4.L42   1993
658.15 — dc20   92-40500

Printed in the United States of America

10 9 8 7 6 5 4

CONTENTS

PREFACE

This book was designed as a text not only for the teacher-assisted student but for the self-study student. Its overall objective is to provide the reader with the conceptual and mathematical tools required for the selection of capital investments, particularly those that deal with capital projects. The selection of the most effective and the most efficient capital projects is one of the most important factors impacting our economy and our competitiveness in the global marketplace.

The selection process for capital projects is presented in four parts.

Part I covers the topics generally considered as basic engineering economics. A chapter on accounting is included because readers need to understand the sources and uses of cash flows on which the selection process depends and how these flows are generated within our economic system.

Part II applies the basics presented in Part I to economic analyses in which estimates of cash flows are assumed deterministic, that is, single-valued.

Part III covers risk analysis and uncertainty analysis and thus breaks away from the deterministic models of Part II by introducing risk measures and principles of choice for both risk and uncertainty.

Part IV presents the techniques generally used for incorporating non-monetary factors or attributes into the decision-making process. A summary of each of the four parts is at the end of each part.

Two types of readers are potential users of this book: (1) undergraduate and graduate students, and (2)self-study or independent students. The latter includes executives, managers, and managers-to-be in the manufacturing, engineering, product/marketing development, financial, and project functions of business and nonbusiness organizations. Multifunctional teams would find this text helpful in scoping and justifying product/process designs.

For undergraduate business, engineering management, and engineering programs, the text is adaptable to the following one-quarter, one-semester, and one-year courses.

Junior, one-quarter course	Parts I and II
Senior, one-quarter course	Parts III and IV
Junior, one-semester course	Parts I and II
Senior, one-semester course	Parts III and IV
Junior or senior, one-year course	Parts I to IV

For graduate engineering, management, and financial courses, the book could be used as a one-semester course with selections from Parts I to IV or as a one-year course which would include the entire text.

Elements from the text could also find application as supplementary material for courses in engineering economics, project management, and decision theory. In addition, the text could serve as a supplementary text for a variety of courses in areas of engineering (including industrial, engineering management, electrical, mechanical, chemical, computer, and civil) and business (including operations, financial, cost accounting, and project management).

There are problems at the end of each chapter that allow the self-study and teacher-assisted student to develop the skills needed to use the methodology presented. An appendix provides answers to selected problems.

We are forever grateful to the many people who contributed their time and effort in helping us prepare this text. They include Donald W. Merino, Anjali Ganeriwala, Norton Smith, Michael Antonucci, Thomas Popeck, Mark Troller, and Alex Depaoli.

HANS J. LANG
DONALD N. MERINO

Hoboken, New Jersey
August 1993

TO THE READER

Why read this book, or, rather, why study it? What will you learn? Will the effort be worth it? What will you be able to do that you cannot do now?

> Our hope is that you will be able to understand and critique economy studies for the proper allocation of capital spending and, if need be, carry out such studies yourself.

That's it in a nut shell. You'll function better as a citizen, as an employee, and as an employer in seeing that you and your family, your company, and your local, state, and federal governments use the resources available for capital investment wisely.

——1

CAPITAL PROJECTS IN THE NATIONAL ECONOMY

1.1 INTRODUCTION

There's an old adage that a penny saved is a penny earned. What should you do with this saving? Should you hide it under a floorboard or put it into a safety deposit box? This is hoarding, not saving. Hoarding won't help the economy or, in the long run, you—particularly if the purchasing power of savings declines. Should it go into a savings account or a certificate of deposit or a Treasury note or stocks and bonds? This is an improvement over hoarding, since, ultimately, your penny and other savings will find their way into updating and adding to your stock of capital, that is, your real or tangible wealth. If they don't, none of your savings will be worth much, since real wealth can't be created just by shuffling pieces of paper.

The object of this book is to describe the selection process—often called the *capital allocation process*—on which decisions for updating and adding to our stock of wealth are or should be based. This process has evolved over many years and has reached a high degree of sophistication. It will continue to evolve as new and better decision-making tools are discovered and applied.

We begin with an introductory chapter in which the U.S. stock of capital is briefly described. Of what does it consist? Who owns it? Who is responsible for its upkeep? Who decides how and when it should be retired, replaced, or added to? We then describe the significant part capital investment plays in the U.S. economy. Lastly, we "walk" you through the contents of the book ("run you through" might be more descriptive) and follow up this "walkathon" with an outline of the selection process for capital projects.

1.2 OUR STOCK OF CAPITAL

Our stock of capital includes our real or tangible wealth—our land, our natural resources, our infrastructure, our production facilities, our institutional structures and buildings, our office buildings, our houses and apartment buildings, or, in brief, all assets that economists and accountants lump together as property, plant, and equipment (PPE) or refer to as long-lived assets or fixed assets or tangible property. It is property, the cost of which, except for land, is spread over its service life. How this is done is something with which you will have to become familiar, since it plays an important part in determining the cash flow streams on which the selection process depends.

> *COMMENT:* The balance sheets of profit and not-for-profit organizations also show billions of dollars invested in intangible assets such as patents, trademarks, licenses, franchises, and copyrights. The selection process described herein also applies to such intangible (nonphysical) assets.

Ownership of the stock of capital is widespread and is vested in federal, state, and local governments and bodies, in partnerships and corporations, and in people such as you and I. Accountants refer to all of these owners as "entities." Decisions on retiring, replacing, and adding to capital stock are the responsibility of the owners of entities. In many instances, the power to make such decisions is delegated to professional managers accountable to the owners. Shareholders, for example, delegate this power to corporate managements, and the public delegates it to the managers of governmental entities.

1.3 OUR NATIONAL ECONOMY

Our economy is a mixed economy; that is, it consists of both a private and a public sector. Both sectors produce goods and services. The private sector does so for profit; the public sector, to fill needs that are seen by many of us as best performed by governmental bodies.

The yardstick for measuring the performance of the national economy is the gross national product (GNP). This is the total dollar value of the goods and services produced annually by the public and private sectors. It is also the total dollar value of all the earnings and costs—wages, salaries, rents, interest, and profit—that produced these goods and services (1).

The GNP is currently (1992 estimates) about $6 trillion. Its major components are tabulated below in billions of dollars.

	Billions of Dollars
Personal consumption expenditures	$4,010
Nonresidential fixed investment	513
Residential fixed investment	216
Federal, state, and local government expenditures	1,190
Net exports	−7
Inventory adjustments	−10
Gross national product	$5,912

These figures are in current dollars, that is, 1992 dollars. Such dollars cannot be directly compared with similar figures for previous years without adjusting for inflation, that is, for changes in the purchasing power of the dollar. We shall be concerned with the effect of inflation on cash flow projections and on capital investment decisions throughout this text.

The largest number in the previous tabulation—$4,010 billion—is for personal consumption expenditures, such as food, clothing, and health care. These do not add to the stock of tangible wealth, although they do, of course, govern our well-being—at least for the immediate present.

The two investment items for nonresidential and residential capital expenditures total $729 billion, or 12% of the GNP. These items are capital expenditures by the private sector to replace, upgrade, and augment its capital stock, that is, the production, institutional, residential, and other facilities held in private hands.

Expenditures by the public sector account for $1,190 billion, or about 20% of the GNP. This sum includes both capital and noncapital expenditures. Governments do not, in their bookkeeping, distinguish between moneys invested in new highways, public buildings, parks, and other capital projects and moneys spent to pay expenses, such as the salaries of educators, police officers, fire fighters, and other public employees, including those in the armed forces. An off-the-cuff estimate is that at least 20–25% of government expenditures, that is, about 5% of the GNP, is spent on maintaining, replacing, and adding to the capital stock owned by government entities.

With this estimate of capital expenditures for the public sector and with the data given earlier for the private sector, we come up with the following rounded totals for 1992.

	Capital Expenditures	
	Billions of Dollars	Percent of GNP
Private sector	730	12
Public sector	300	5
Total	1030	17

Many among us argue that the proportion of the GNP that we should allocate to public expenditures should be significantly larger; others say it should be lower; and still others feel it is about right.

What this proportion should be to best serve our long-term interests is not our concern in this text. It is, rather, to study a selection process that for both the private and public sectors channels the limited funds available for capital expenditures to best serve private investors and public concerns.

Funds for the public sector come from taxes and borrowings that ultimately depend on taxes for repayment. Taxpayers have an interest in seeing that such funds are spent properly. Funds for the private sector come from savings and borrowings. Investors have an interest in seeing that these funds are used to produce profits commensurate with their assumption of risk. The general public has an interest in seeing that the quest for profit does not compromise environmental, health, safety, educational, and other public needs.

1.4 CAPITAL EXPENDITURES

Annual capital expenditures of $1 trillion for updating and augmenting our stock of wealth or, to use accounting terminology, our stock of fixed assets, deserve respect as a serious commitment of human resources and materials. This commitment is usually the result of selecting projects for implementation from a much larger group, many of which also deserve attention, but all of which could not be implemented without straining the resources required for producing consumption goods and services. A decision-assisting or selection process to help decide where funds for capital investment should be allocated is therefore needed.

Capital expenditures take many forms. There are those for which the concept of the time value of money, which is central to the selection process described herein, is seldom applied and seldom need be. Studies for such expenditures are often called "present economy studies" (2). Although we will not neglect them, our main concern is with "future economy studies." These can be classified into three groups:

1. Studies that involve only monetary attributes and in which risk can be neglected. We refer to such studies as "economic analyses."
2. Studies in which economic analyses are supplemented and supported by a risk analysis.
3. Studies in which nonmonetary factors or attributes also take part.

The third group requires a multiattribute analysis (also called a multifactor analysis), in which both monetary and nonmonetary attributes are combined to produce figures of merit with which one alternative can be directly compared with another.

Asset retirement and replacement studies are typical candidates for the first group. So are many capital investment opportunities for new facilities and major additions to existing facilities for which nonmonetary attributes are not significant and risk analysis need go no further than sensitivity analysis, that is, no further than examining the ranges within which cash flow estimates may fall.

The second and third groups relate to projects for which the selection process must go beyond economic analysis into probability (risk) analysis and, more and more frequently, into multiattribute analysis.

1.5 A PREVIEW OF THE TEXT

The selection process for capital facilities is grounded on estimates of future cash flows. Cash flows occur when money changes hands. Money received is a positive cash flow; money disbursed is a negative cash flow. The more common positive cash flows arise from revenues (sales) and from borrowings. The more common negative cash flows arise from expenses, from repayment of debt, and from "first cost" or "investment cost," that is, the cost of the facility or project that, if implemented, will add to the nation's stock of capital.

Cash flow estimates are single-valued or multivalued. Consider the estimate for a future cash flow from selling a service or a product. If this estimate is given as $1,000,000 for a given year, the estimate is single-valued. If it is given as falling within a range of -20% to $+10\%$, that is, between $800,000 and $1,100,000, it is multivalued.

In this text, economic analysis refers to studies based on single-valued estimates (also called deterministic estimates) and risk analysis to studies based on multivalued estimates (also called probabilistic estimates). This limitation on the scope of the term "economic analysis" is one not usually made but is convenient for presenting the selection process as consisting of three more or less distinct types of analyses.

The three types of analyses—economic, risk, and multiattribute—are covered in Parts II, III, and IV of this text, respectively. All three parts require input from a discipline known as *engineering economy* or *engineering economics*. This input is presented in Part I.

1.5.1 Part I: Basic Engineering Economy

Part I consists of 11 chapters on basic engineering economics. The engineering profession led the way in recognizing that, in the analysis of capital investment opportunities, a dollar from a future cash flow is not worth as much as a dollar from a current cash flow. To add or subtract cash flows without allowing for "the time value of money" is like adding feet to inches without first converting one unit of length into the other. One thousand dollars in hand is worth more than the promise of $1,000 in the future, no matter how secure that future may be. None of us would accept a future cash flow in lieu of a present cash flow unless the future cash flow was greater. How much greater depends on our assessment of risk and our immediate need for cash.

This simple truth or fact of life led to the discipline of engineering economy under which investment opportunities, which depended on engineering input—as most investments in tangible wealth and many in intangible wealth do—are compared by discounting and/or compounding their life cycle cash flows to make them commensurable.

> *COMMENT:* Discounting, you will recall, is finding the value today of a cash sum to be realized in the future. At 10% interest, a cash receipt of $1,000 one year from now is worth—that is, is equivalent to—$909 today ($1,000/1.10). Compounding is the reverse. $909 invested today at 10% will grow to $1,000 ($909 × 1.10) in one year.

The rate of return used for discounting is known as the minimum attractive rate of return (MARR) and is set by what investors judge will compensate them for risk. The lower their assessment of risk, the lower is the return that they will accept.

The discounted cash flow method for comparing capital investment opportunities has become the cornerstone of engineering economy and is today the methodology generally used for studies involving the capital selection process.

The first chapter in Part I, Chapter 2, is an introduction to the basics of accounting, which are applied and referred to throughout the text. The emphasis is on income statements and how these can be used to develop cash flow forecasts for the life cycles of projects.

Chapter 3 presents cash flow patterns that frequently appear in a wide variety of capital investment situations. Rate-of-return formulas have been developed with which whole sets of cash flows can be made commensurable and thus avoid the need for discounting or compounding each individual cash flow.

Chapter 3 also discusses the "present economy studies" mentioned earlier for which future cash flows do not have to be discounted. These studies serve as a convenient introduction to "future economy studies," since it is usually worthwhile to see if the cash flowing in to a proposed investment during its life cycle exceeds the cash flowing out.

Chapter 4 is a necessary aside on methods for comparing investment opportunities that do not discount cash flow but are important because they are still with us as investment criteria. The most important of these is the payback period, that is, the length of time it takes to recover the first cost of an investment from future net cash flows. The two other methods described compare the accountant's viewpoint with the engineering economist's viewpoint in analyzing investment opportunities. Both viewpoints have their place, but the accountant's, which is geared to net income, is more pertinent for judging past performance, whereas the economist's, which is geared to cash flow, is more directly linked to expected future performance.

The equivalence relationships by which future cash flows—or, rather, cash flows at any point in time—are converted to equivalent cash flows at any other point in time are developed in Chapters 5 and 6. The most common conversion is discounting future cash flows to obtain equivalent present cash flows. The equivalence formulas cover not only single cash flows but sets of uniform cash flows and sets in which cash flows increase or decrease linearly or geometrically over all or part of a project's life cycle. Geometric gradients are particularly important for analyzing the effect of inflation on investment criteria.

These criteria—also called *figures of merit*—are developed in the remaining five chapters of Part I, Chapters 7–11. They are commonly used to compare the monetary consequences of capital investment opportunities with one another.

Present value (PV), also known as present worth (PW)

Annual worth (AW), which, if negative, is also known as equivalent uniform annual cost (EUAC) or simply annual cost (AC)

Future value (FV), also known as future worth (FW)

Internal rate of return (IRR)

Benefit-cost ratio (BCR)

The first three figures of merit are referred to as "the three worths" in this text. The cash flow factors for computing these worths for the most common cash flow patterns are derived in Chapter 7. Two concepts related to the three worths are then developed in Chapter 8. The first is "capitalized cost," a present value, and the second is capital recovery, an annual cost. The internal rate of return is discussed in Chapter 9 and how to surmount some of the problems associated with it in Chapter 10. Chapter 11 presents the last figure of merit, the benefit-cost ratio (BCR), which is commonly applied to projects in the public sector but is equally adaptable to projects in the private sector.

You should leave Part I with an understanding of the tools needed to carry out a capital investment study, namely, cash flow analyses and equivalence formulas based on the time value of money. In addition, you should have an appreciation for the figures of merit with which alternative investment opportunities are compared.

1.5.2 Part II: The Selection Process: Economic Analysis

The outputs from Part I serve as inputs for the eight chapters in Part II. The first two chapters, Chapters 12 and 13, deal with ranking mutually exclusive investment opportunities. Chapter 12 covers technological exclusivity, that is, ranking competing alternatives for which the selection of one precludes the selection of any other. It also introduces the important concept of marginal or incremental ranking. Chapter 13 covers financial exclusivity, in which we seek to optimize the set of projects on which the limited funds available should be expended.

Chapter 14 takes us to capital funding and to the selection of the MARR, the minimum attractive (or acceptable) rate of return on which the time-value-of-money calculations are based.

Replacement studies have their own vocabulary, and procedures and are covered in Chapter 15. For these, it is seldom necessary to go into risk and multiattribute analyses to arrive at a recommendation.

Up to this point, the examples presented in the text are based on before-tax cash flows. This is usually the first step in analyzing an investment opportunity. If the results are favorable, an after-tax analysis is made. However, to do so requires an understanding of such expenses as depreciation, which are not cash flows but which impact on income taxes, which are cash flows. Depreciation expenses and income taxes are brought into capital investment studies in Chapter 16.

> *COMMENT:* The practice of first carrying out a before-tax analysis and following up with an after-tax analysis is no longer as prevalent as it once was. Computer programs are available with which we can go directly to an after-tax analysis. However, most students of engineering economics find it helpful to begin with a thorough grounding in before-tax studies before launching into after-tax studies. This is, therefore, the approach commonly adopted and the one applied in this text.

Chapter 17 is devoted to the special topic of public projects. In one respect, these are simpler to analyze than private-sector projects, since depreciation and income taxes play no part. In other respects, however, the analysis of such projects is more difficult because of benefits and disbenefits, that is, estimates of cash flows into and out of the pockets of the public in addition to the cash flows into and out of the public projects themselves. A new toll-free highway link, for example, that reduces the mileage between points A and B is an effective cash flow (a reduction in travel expenses) into the pockets of those of us who travel the new route. It must therefore be included along with other monetary benefits and disbenefits in a cash flow analysis.

Equivalent rates of return and how such rates are used in analyzing price level effects are the leading topics of Chapter 18. You will find that inflation is not difficult to handle. Higher figures of merit are often obtained in an inflationary atmosphere. However, adjusting the results obtained to the decline in the purchasing power of the dollar may prove the results disappointing.

The last chapter in Part II is a critique of the criticisms that have been leveled against cost studies based on the time value of money and, in particular, against the high rates of return used for discounting cash flows for private-sector investment opportunities. High discount rates can crowd out investments that, from a long-range viewpoint, are highly desirable. The conclusion reached is that the analytical procedures developed in Part II are sound—no one has yet come up with a better approach—but that more attention needs to be paid to the selection of the parameters, such as the discount rate, on which the analytical procedures are based, on realistic estimates for what it really costs to do nothing, and on including and properly weighting noneconomic consequences.

1.5.3 Part III: The Selection Process: Risk Analysis

With the completion of Part II, we leave single-valued estimates for cash flow and other parameters, such as planning horizons, and replace them with multivalued estimates. How to extend the procedures developed in Part II to such estimates is the major topic of Part III.

Part III consists of five chapters, the first of which, Chapter 20, is on estimation. The topics cover how estimates are usually classified, the ranges of accuracy that can be expected for each class, and the cost categories that are used in analyzing business operations to determine break-even points and other concepts important to economic analysis.

Chapter 21 on sensitivity analysis is a bridge between economic analysis and risk analysis. Sensitivity analysis computes figures of merit, not for a single value of each parameter that takes part in the selection process (for example, cash flows, rates of inflation, rates of return, planning horizons), but for the ranges within which the estimates for these parameters may fall.

Risk analysis, in its more sophisticated aspects, is covered in Chapters 22, 23, and 24. Such analyses depend on the sound application of probability theory. Chapter 22 begins with a discussion of the rules that underlie this theory and then develops equations for the laws of expected value and variance as applied to discrete probability distributions. Expected values serve as surrogates or substitutes for single-valued estimates. Variance provides us with an additional figure of merit—one that measures risk. The chapter concludes with a decision tree analysis. Such trees are a convenient way to display the impact of probability distributions on cash flow patterns.

The bulk of Chapter 23 is an introduction to continuous probability distributions. The laws of expected value and variance for discrete distributions are modified to include continuous distributions and are then applied to uniform and normal distributions, both of which find application in the project selection process. The chapter concludes with a discussion of certain "principles of choice" with which the risk propensities of alternatives are often compared.

Chapter 24 covers beta distributions and Monte Carlo simulation. Beta distributions are a useful tool for approximating expected values and variances when only a limited amount of data are available, for example, an optimistic, most likely, and pessimistic estimate for each key parameter. Monte Carlo simulation is a technique that has come into its own with the advent of the computer. It uses random number tables to select numerical values for the parameters that enter into selection studies and produces profiles from which the probability of reaching any given figure of merit is obtained.

Chapter 25, which discusses uncertainty, has been included under risk analysis, although logically it belongs in a separate section. There are many situations in which it is not possible to assign a likelihood to happenings or "states of nature" over which we have no control. Examples are competitive pressures, possible tax reform legislation, more stringent Environmental Protection Agency (EPA) rulings, the outcome of labor arbitration, and unpredictable weather patterns (several years of drought or exceptionally severe winters) on long-term construction projects. Cash flow estimates are prepared for each state, and a selection is made with the help of certain principles of choice, which should not be confused with the principles presented in Chapter 23 for risk analysis.

1.5.4   Part IV: The Selection Process: Multiattribute Analysis

Throughout Parts II and III, we repeatedly emphasize that monetary criteria are often insufficient for decision making but must usually be satisfied, at least in the private sector, before nonmonetary consequences are introduced. How to meld monetary and nonmonetary attributes into figures of merit that reflect both sets of attributes is the subject matter of Part IV.

Part IV consists of three chapters of which the first, Chapter 26, is a general introduction to the selection of nonmonetary candidates for multiattribute analyses and to the concept of cost effectiveness in which one nonmonetary attribute (e.g., chemical pollution, loss of life, social roads, social electric transmission lines) is singled out for comparison with the costs required to reduce disbenefits or to enhance benefits. The chapter concludes with a much neglected attribute, namely, equity.

> *COMMENT:* A social road or a social electric transmission line is a facility that is justified, not on short-term gains, but on the benefits it will ultimately bring in improving the lives and incomes of hitherto isolated populations.

Chapter 27 begins with the simpler techniques and then moves on to the more sophisticated techniques for handling any number of nonmonetary attributes and incorporating them into figures of merit that include the monetary attributes. The simpler techniques include graphical presentations, such as score cards and polar graphs. The more sophisticated techniques use ranking and weighting of attributes and alternatives.

Chapter 28 has two major topics. The first takes the techniques described in Chapter 27 one step further with a methodology known as the analytical hierarchy process (AHP). The second acquaints you with one more nonmonetary attribute, which fittingly belongs at the end of a text on the capital selection process. This topic is the risk preference of investors and how such preferences affect their decisions.

Each of the four parts concludes with a summary of the leading topics covered therein. For Part IV, this summary serves the entire text.

1.6 AN OUTLINE OF THE SELECTION PROCESS

The selection process for capital projects begins with the recognition of an investment opportunity. It then proceeds as follows.

- A study team is assembled, whose size and makeup depend on the complexity and magnitude of the proposed project. The objective of this team is to make a recommendation to a decision maker to proceed or not to proceed with the investment under review.
- The set of mutually exclusive alternatives on which the study is to be based are identified, and the figures of merit to be used are selected.
- The noneconomic consequences, if any, that should be brought into the study are identified. The number and variety of these will influence the data-gathering function.
- The economic consequences are examined first. This part of the selection process usually begins with single-valued cash flow estimates. The cash flows are discounted to make future cash flows commensurate with current cash flows. The discount or interest rate used is the minimum attractive rate of return (MARR) selected by the ultimate decision maker.
- If the results are favorable, a risk analysis using multivaried estimates is made. This can take the form of a sensitivity analysis, for which probability distributions are not required, or a risk analysis, for which they are.
- If the economic consequences appear favorable and there are nonmonetary factors that must be considered, a multiattribute analysis is made.
- A recommendation on the results of the study is given the decision maker.
- If recommended, the project becomes a candidate for inclusion in a capital expenditures budget.

1.7 SUMMARY

The major points covered in this chapter are highlighted below.

- Annual expenditures for replacing and adding to our nation's stock of capital projects are currently on the order of $1 trillion. This includes projects in both the public and the private sectors.

- Funding for capital projects is limited. Therefore, a selection process is needed to pick those projects that best serve public and private interests. We refer to this process herein as "the selection process for capital projects."
- The selection process consists of three distinct parts: an economic or deterministic analysis, a risk or probabilistic analysis, and a multiattribute analysis.
- Economic and risk analyses are concerned primarily with monetary attributes, such as present worths, rates of return, and benefit-cost ratios.
- A multiattribute analysis goes beyond monetary attributes to include nonmonetary attributes, such as equity, quality, safety, appearance, serviceability, risk preference, and others.
- Asset retirement and replacement cost studies, and many studies for new facilities, require only an economic analysis. However, others—and particularly the larger and more complex projects—require a risk analysis or both a risk and a multiattribute analysis.

REFERENCES

1. Paul A. Samuelson and William D. Nordhaus, *Economics*, 13th ed. (New York: McGraw-Hill, 1989), pp. 102–121. This is an excellent introduction to the GNP for those of you who are not familiar with this concept and its significance as a yardstick for the performance of our economy.
2. E. Paul DeGarmo, John R. Canada, and William G. Sullivan, *Engineering Economy*, 8th ed. (New York: Macmillan, 1988). The author of the first edition of this book, E. Paul DeGarmo, labeled studies in which it is not necessary to consider the time value of money "present economy studies."

PROBLEMS

Stock of Capital

1-1   Do you think our stock of capital should include such human resources as you (the reader), we (the authors), and the millions of other people who consider themselves to be a part of the United States? If so, how would you assign a dollar value to this resource?

National Economy

1-2   The distribution of income is skewed toward high incomes in the United States and other industrial economies. The ownership of capital is even more so. How would this affect the selection process for capital projects?

1-3 In discussing the gross national product, we were a little loose in defining it. We should have said that it is the value of the **final** goods and services produced annually, that is, those sold for consumption or production. It does not include **intermediate** goods and services, since the salaries, wages, rents, interest, and profit that produced these goods are included in the price of the final goods. With this in mind, see if you can determine which of the goods and services below are, or are not, included in the GNP:

a) The loaf of bread you buy

b) The loaf of bread a restaurant buys

c) A home meal produced by a master chef

d) A restaurant meal

e) A home meal produced by you

f) The steel that went into your car

g) The tires on your car

h) The gasoline you purchase to drive to work

i) The gasoline a trucking firm buys to transport goods

j) Your purchase of an original Van Gogh oil painting

1-4 As mentioned, the GNP is both the dollar value of the final goods and services produced in any year and the sum total of the salaries, wages, rents, interest, and profit that produced these goods and services. Can you explain why these two aggregates must be the same?

1-5 The GNP is broken down in considerable detail by both areas and products. In forecasting cash flows for a particular investment opportunity, how would such a breakdown help you?

1-6 What is the net national product? Why is it a better measure of what is happening to our stock of wealth than the GNP? (See Reference 1.)

1-7 The gross domestic product (GDP) is now replacing the GNP in many discussions of our economy. What is it, and why do we now see it so frequently? (You may have to do a little research on this. There is nothing on the GDP in Reference 1.)

Capital Expenditures and Engineering Economics

1-8 Consider an investment in a training program to upgrade the skills of unemployables. How could such a program be justified economically? Would nonmonetary attributes also play a part?

1-9 What is the difference between a present economy study and a future economy study? Is shopping for best buys a present economy study?

1-10   What are the three types of analyses that comprise the project selection process? How do they differ from one another? Do they usually proceed sequentially as described in the text? Can you give examples in which they may not proceed in this way?

1-11   What is your individual "time value of money"; that is, what sum of money one year from now would make you reject an offer of $1,000 now?

1-12   What is the relationship between risk and the minimum acceptable rate of return (the MARR)? Sketch a graph showing this relationship.

1-13   Suppose the risk of recovering the investment in a given opportunity is zero. Does this mean that investors will require no rate of return? Justify your answer, but, in doing so, don't forget inflation.

1-14   An example of a cash flow that bypasses the capital project responsible for producing it was given in this chapter. Can you give other examples that share this characteristic?

1-15   In comparing the sales price of two comparable products, what non-monetary attributes do you consider?

PART I
BASIC ENGINEERING ECONOMY

___2
ACCOUNTING

2.1 INTRODUCTION

You don't have to be an accountant or an estimator to make an economic analysis, but a practitioner of engineering economics is expected to understand at least the fundamentals of both disciplines. We mentioned in Chapter 1 that economic studies for the capital selection process depend on estimates of cash flow. The data on which such forecasts are based come from many sources, of which one of the most important is accounting records. This chapter therefore provides an overview of the accounting process and how useful cash flow data are extracted from financial statements. A later chapter (Chapter 20) provides a similar overview of estimation.

2.2 ACCOUNTING

We begin with a definition of accounting:

Accounting is the management science that deals with the **financial condition** and the **financial performance** of **entities** by recording, analyzing, and reporting the **transactions** in which they engage in order to assess their current performance and to forecast their future performance.

Four terms are boldfaced. We will now examine these.

2.2.1   Entities

Entities are the bounded systems whose innards accountants examine to determine their state of health. They are of two types: for-profit or not-for-profit. A convenient classification follows.

For-profit (business) entities
    Sole proprietorships
    Partnerships
    Corporations

Not-for-profit entities
    Private-sector organizations
    Public-sector organizations

We have not included ourselves or you in the preceding list, but, when an accountant helps you prepare the income statement that will become your tax return, you are, as far as he or she is concerned, an entity.

The capital selection process applies to both profit (business) and not-for-profit entities. Business entities are found in the private sector of our economy. However, there are public-sector entities that compete with and function much like their private counterparts. Utility companies owned by counties, cities, and towns are one of many examples. For these and other not-for-profit entities, the terms "profit" and "loss" are replaced with "surplus" and "deficit," respectively.

The business entities include sole proprietorships, which are owned by one individual; partnerships, which are owned by two or more individuals; and corporations, which are owned by few or many shareholders. The sole proprietorship is the most common form of business organization, but corporations are dominant in terms of business activity. The following tabulation compares the three forms for 1991 (1).

	Businesses		Annual Receipts	
	Number (millions)	Percent	Dollars (billions)	Percent
Proprietorships (nonfarm)	13.1	71	611	6
Partnerships	1.6	9	411	4
Corporations	3.6	20	9,186	90
	18.3	100	10,208	100

Proprietorships and partnerships are not legal persons in the eyes of the law. Therefore, their owners are fully responsible for their acts and obligations, and creditors can, if necessary, go beyond the assets of the businesses to the assets of the owners in order to satisfy their claims.

Corporations, on the other hand, are legal persons. Their shareholders have limited liability, which means that corporations are responsible for their own acts and obligations. Creditors can rely only on corporate assets for the satisfaction of their claims.

Proprietorships and partnerships are managed by their owners; corporations are not. The shareholders elect a board of directors, which appoints executives to serve as managers. In short, ownership and management are divorced, and the interests of the managers may conflict with those of the shareholders.

Examples of not-for-profit entities in the private sector include universities, schools, hospitals, museums, and charitable organizations. Examples are also found in the public sector, but these function under the aegis of federal, state, and local governments, which are themselves accounting entities, as are school districts, water and sanitary districts, public utility and transit authorities, and all other governmental bodies subject to accounting review.

Thus, accounting entities can be as large as the federal government or as small as a school district; as large as a megacorporation or as small as the corner delicatessen. They can be an entire organization or one of its parts, and, as mentioned, they can also include you and this text's authors.

In what follows, our attention will be focused on corporations and governmental entities, since these are the major disbursers of moneys for capital outlays.

2.2.2 Transactions

A transaction is a piece of business—a sale, a purchase, a borrowing, the repayment of a loan, the payment for a service, the issuance of stock, the repurchase of stock, and so on. Transactions make entities function. Without them there would be stagnation and, ultimately, death. Transactions when properly recorded, analyzed, and reported give us both the financial condition and the financial performance of entities.

2.2.3 Financial Condition

The financial condition of an entity is its state of health or well-being at any given point in time. This is reported in a financial statement, called the "balance sheet" or, more formally, "the statement of financial condition." The points of time usually selected for issuance are the end of each month, of each quarter, and of each year. Monthly issues are for the benefit of management. Quarterly and annual issues are for those outsiders who need to know or wish to know an entity's current condition—bankers, suppliers, creditors, and shareholders.

2.2.4   Financial Performance

An entity can be in good health and perform badly—although not for long—
by living off what it has accumulated in the past. It can be in poor health and
perform well, indicating that its health is improving and, if good performance
continues, that it will eventually get well. Financial performance over a period
of time—a month, a quarter, a year—is recorded, analyzed, and reported
in the "statement of income" and in two additional statements that supplement
this statement and the balance sheet—the "statement of owner's equity" and
the "statement of cash flow."

Not-for-profit entities use similar statements with somewhat different names.
The income statement, for example, is often called the "statement of receipts
and expenditures." The owner's equity statement is the "statement of fund
balances." For many such entities, it is not possible to prepare balance sheets,
because there is no way of determining the value of their assets. This applies
particularly to federal, state, and local governments. How, for example, do
you set a dollar value on Yellowstone National Park?

2.3   BALANCE SHEETS

The financial condition of an entity is given by its assets (what it owns) and
its liabilities (what it owes). The difference between the two is "owner equity"
which is also referred to as "net worth," "capital," "net assets," or just
"equity."

Assets, liabilities, and owner equity are tied together by the basic equation
of accounting—as fundamental to accounting as the law of conservation of
mass and energy is to the natural sciences.

$$\text{Assets} - \text{Liabilities} = \text{Owner Equity}$$

or, as it is usually written,

$$\text{Assets} = \text{Liabilities} + \text{Owner Equity}$$

which, in equation format, becomes

$$A = L + E \tag{2.1}$$

You can see and touch assets. You can see and touch the pieces of paper
that document liabilities. However, you can't touch equity, because it is
nothing more than the difference that brings balance sheets into balance.
Consider the house you just bought for $100,000 with a $75,000 mortgage.
The house is an asset; the mortgage is a liability. Your equity is the difference
of $25,000. You can't see, hear, smell, or touch this difference, but you can
see the house and you can touch the mortgage note in your desk drawer.

A typical balance sheet is given in Figure 2.1. The assets total $620,000 and the liabilities, $210,000. The difference of $410,000 is the equity.

Assets are broken down into three categories—current, fixed, and other. Current assets consist of cash and items that can quickly be converted into cash. Fixed assets (PPE) consist of land (property), which cannot be depreciated, and plant and equipment, which can, that is, which are depreciable. Other assets include intangibles such as patents and any other asset that is not classified as current or fixed.

Liabilities are broken down into two major categories—current and long-term. Current liabilities are due in one year or less. Long-term liabilities are due in one year and a day or more.

One important balance sheet term you should be familiar with is "working capital." This is simply the difference between current assets and current liabilities. Estimates of cash flow for working capital enter into the capital project selection process.

ABC COMPANY
BALANCE SHEET AS OF DECEMBER 31, 199X

ASSETS

Current assets	
Cash	$ 40,000
Accounts receivable	120,000
Inventories	180,000
Total current assets	340,000
Property, plant, and equipment	
At cost	400,000
Less accumulated depreciation	150,000
Total property, plant, and equipment	250,000
Other assets	30,000
Total assets	$620,000

LIABILITIES AND EQUITY

Current liabilities	
Accounts payable	$ 70,000
Notes payable	20,000
Total current liabilities	90,000
Long-term note	120,000
Total liabilities	210,000
Paid-in capital	150,000
Retained earnings	260,000
Total equity	410,000
Total liabilities plus equity	$620,000

Figure 2.1. A typical balance sheet.

Equity is also broken down into two major accounts. The first, paid-in capital, is that portion of the difference between the assets and liabilities that was contributed by owners both initially and whenever an infusion of capital was needed. The second, retained earnings, is that portion of the difference between assets and liabilities coming from the production of goods and services, that is, from earnings that were retained in the business and not distributed as dividends to shareholders or as drawings to sole proprietors or partners.

Managers strive to make the difference between the assets and liabilities at the end of an accounting period larger than it was at the beginning of the accounting period. We can formulate this objective very simply, as follows.

Let A_1, L_1, and E_1 be the assets, liabilities, and equity at the beginning of the period and A_2, L_2, and E_2 the assets, liabilities, and equity at the end of the period. By the balance sheet equation,

$$A_1 - L_1 = E_1$$

and

$$A_2 - L_2 = E_2$$

Subtracting the first equation from the second gives

$$(A_2 - A_1) - (L_2 - L_1) = (E_2 - E_1)$$

or

$$\Delta A - \Delta L = \Delta E$$

If ΔE is positive, management has succeeded in increasing the difference between assets and liabilities over the time period under study.

2.4 INCOME STATEMENTS

Suppose a service produced by a business or not-for-profit entity is sold and either paid for or billed. An asset on the left side of the balance sheet equation, "cash" or "accounts receivable," goes up by the amount of the sale. No other asset account and no liability account take part in the transaction. Therefore, an owner equity account on the right side of the balance sheet equation—in this instance, sales revenue—must go up by the same amount; otherwise, the balance sheet would not remain in balance.

The expenses of producing goods or services are either immediately paid for or, what is more common, booked as a liability (accounts payable) to be paid later. If paid immediately, this is a decrease in the asset account "cash," which is matched by a corresponding decrease in an owner equity account for expenses. If, on the other hand, the expenses are not paid for immediately, the liability account "accounts payable," on the right side of the balance sheet equation is increased and the proper equity account for expenses is decreased. Either way, the balance sheet remains in balance and the equity accounts accurately reflect the difference between the assets and the liabilities that belongs to the owners.

If revenues exceed expenses during any given period, the earnings for the period are positive. If the difference is substantial (or, occasionally, even if it is not), management may decide to distribute some of the difference to the owners. These distributions, which are called *dividends* for shareholders and *drawings* for sole proprietorships and partnerships, reduce the equity of the accounting entity but increase that of the owners.

The extent to which earnings are kept in the business or are distributed to owners is of no concern to the capital selection process. The concern is rather with total earnings, since the portion that is not distributed to owners accrues to their benefit as an increase in the owner equity account, retained earnings.

The statement of income equation for any given accounting period can be expressed as follows:

$$\text{Revenues} - \text{Costs} = \text{Earnings}$$

Letting R stand for revenue, C for costs or expenses, and ΔE for the increase in equity over the period before any distribution to owners gives us

$$R - C = \Delta E \tag{2.2}$$

Equation (2.2) is the model for statements of income. A typical example is given in Figure 2.2.

The revenues for the period are $900,000. The total expenses before taxes are $782,000 ($550,000 + $220,000 + $12,000), and the earnings before taxes, often referred to as the net income before taxes, are the difference, or $118,000. The net earnings or income after taxes are $90,000.

The total expenses of $782,000 are broken down into three categories: the cost of goods and services sold, which total $550,000; the operating expenses (also, unfortunately, called overhead), which total $220,000; and the non-operating expenses, such as interest payments on borrowed funds, which total $12,000. The note on depreciation at the bottom of Figure 2.2 will mean more to you as we proceed.

You should note that neither the balance sheet nor the statement of income shows the distribution of dividends or drawings to owners. This is left to the statement of retained earnings, which, for reasons mentioned earlier, is of little concern to us.

ABC COMPANY
INCOME STATEMENT FOR YEAR ENDING DECEMBER 31, 199X

Revenues	$900,000
Less cost of goods and services sold	550,000
Gross profit	350,000
Less operating expenses	
Selling expenses	110,000
General and administrative expenses	110,000
Total operating expenses	220,000
Operating income	130,000
Less nonoperating expenses (interest)	12,000
Net income before income taxes (NIBT)	118,000
Less income taxes	28,000
Net income after income taxes (NIAT)	90,000

Notes:

Earnings before and after income taxes are synonomous with net income before and after income taxes.

Depreciation expenses may be included both in the
cost of goods and services sold and in operating expenses. If so, these and other noncash expenses need
to be identified in order to obtain the net cash flow from
operations.

Figure 2.2. A typical income statement.

2.5 STATEMENT OF CASH FLOW

Financial management probably spends more time recording, analyzing, and
forecasting cash flow than any other accounting parameter. The reporting is
summarized in a statement of cash flow in which the cash on hand at the end
of the review period is compared with the cash on hand at the beginning of
the period. The difference, which is either positive or negative (or by happenstance zero), is analyzed by breaking it down into three parts:

Cash flow from operating activities
Cash flow from financing activities
Cash flow from investing activities

For economic studies on project selection, estimates of future cash inflows
and outflows from operating activities are prepared with the help of pro forma
income statements (forecasts of income). These statements are discussed more
fully in section 2.7.

Cash flows from financing activities include cash receipts or disbursements
from one or all of the following—the sale of stock by a corporation to provide
paid-in capital, entering into a long-term loan, repaying the loan, and dis-
tributing dividends or drawings. Interest payments on borrowed funds are
not treated as financial activities but as operating activities.

Cash flows from investing activities include cash receipts and disbursements from the purchase of fixed assets and the disposal of such assets when retired or replaced.

In the selection process, we usually start with the assumption that the first cost and the working capital (the funds needed to "set up shop" before cash flows in from sales) for a new venture are supplied by equity financing, that is, by investors rather than creditors. If the results are favorable, we then examine a mixture of equity and creditor financing or even consider leasing to conserve cash.

The three groups of activities that produce cash flows—operations, financing, and investing—are all involved in the cash flow patterns developed in Chapter 3 to help analyze capital investment opportunities.

2.6 THE ACCOUNTING PROCESS

The accounting process is a systematic and logical methodology for processing a myriad of transactions to produce the financial statements on which managements, bankers, creditors, suppliers, and shareholders rely. We highlight this process below but suggest that you also go to one or more of the suggested references at the end of this chapter.

The process begins with the journal or daily record of transactions. We know that every transaction must be recorded in at least two accounts; otherwise, balance sheets would not balance. One of these accounts is debited, and the other is credited. The words *debit* and *credit* stand for left and right, and that is all they stand for. Their abbreviations are *dr.* and *cr.* Each simple journal entry (a simple entry is one that affects just two accounts) is therefore recorded as follows:

	Dr.	Cr.
Name of first account	XXXX	
Name of second account		XXXX

Not shown are the number of the transaction, its date, and, if needed, a brief description. These items are also recorded in the journal.

What do we post on the left side and what on the right? Since assets are on the left side of the balance sheet equation, an increase to an asset account is posted under the debit column. Similarly, since liabilities and equities are on the right side of the balance sheet equation, an increase in a liability or equity account is posted under the credit column. It follows that a deduction to an asset account is a credit posting and a deduction to a liability or equity account is a debit posting. Figure 2.3 will help you remember these rules. Consider their application to the following transactions.

1. An asset is exchanged for an asset—cash for a new truck costing $25,000. One asset account, cash, decreases by the same amount that another asset

WHERE TO RECORD JOURNAL ENTRIES

DEBIT SIDE		CREDIT SIDE
ASSETS	=	LIABILITIES + EQUITY
Increase in asset accounts		Decrease in asset accounts
Decrease in liability accounts		Increase in liability accounts
Decrease in owner equity accounts (expenses)		Increase in owner equity accounts (paid–in capital and revenue)

Figure 2.3. Rules for recording accounting entries.

account, property, plant, and equipment (PPE), increases. Liability accounts and equity accounts are not affected. The journal entry is

Property, plant, and equipment	$25,000	
Cash		$25,000

As shown, a credit to cash is a cash outflow. It follows that debits to cash are cash inflows.

2. A second truck costing $25,000 is purchased for $10,000 cash and a $15,000 note. The asset account, property, plant, and equipment, increases by $25,000. A liability account, notes payable, increases by $15,000, and an asset account, cash, decreases by $10,000. No revenue and expense (owner equity) accounts are involved. The compound journal entry is

Property, plant, and equipment	$25,000	
Cash		$10,000
Notes payable		$15,000

We refer to this entry as a compound entry, since more than two accounts are involved.

3. Consulting services worth $10,000 were completed and paid for in cash or charged to accounts receivable. The asset account, cash or accounts receivable, is debited $10,000. The liability accounts are not affected. The difference between assets and liabilities is increased by the amount of the sale. The increase is recorded in an owner equity account, namely, revenue or sales.

Cash or accounts receivable	$10,000	
Revenue (sales)		$10,000

COMMENT: Why are revenues entered on the credit side along with liabilities? They have to be to keep the balance sheet equation in balance. Since a cash sale increases the asset "cash," a debit entry, the source of the cash, a sale, must be a credit entry to show the increase in owner equity. The same argument, in reverse, applies to the owner equity accounts covering expenses or costs.

4. The expenses incurred for consulting services amounted to $7,000. These were paid for in cash or charged to accounts payable. Either way, appropriate owner equity accounts for the expenses incurred have decreased by $7,000. Lumping all the expenses together, the journal entry is

| Expenses | $7,000 | |
| Cash or accounts payable | | $7,000 |

No matter what the transaction, no matter how many accounts are affected, the balance sheet always remains in balance, provided, of course, the accounts are properly identified and are properly entered as debits or credits.

What does the accounting process do with the hundreds of journal entries that pile up during an accounting period? It does the obvious; that is, it sets up a separate page for each account and assembles all these pages in one place, called the *ledger*. On each ledger page, the debit entries to an account are posted on the left side and the credit entries are posted on the right side. The two columns are summed up either continuously to give the current balance in the account or at the end of each accounting period to give the balance at the end of the period. The procedure is illustrated in Figure 2.4.

Account Name	Account No.
Debit (left)	Credit (right)
Balance for asset accounts at beginning of period	Balance for liability and equity accounts at beginning of period
An increase in an asset account is posted on this side of the form because assets are on the left side of the balance sheet equation.	An increase in a liability or equity account is posted on this side of the form because liabilities and equity are on the right side of the balance sheet equation.
A decrease in a liability or equity account is posted on this side.	A decrease in an asset account is posted on this side.
Balance for asset accounts at end of period	Balance for liability and equity accounts at end of period

Note: The ledger pages used in the accounting process include references to the number and date of the journal entries from which the postings on these pages are derived. They may also include columns in which the account balances are kept current.

Figure 2.4. Ledger page makeup.

In the four journal entries just discussed, there were recordings to the following seven accounts:

Cash

Accounts receivable

Property, plant, and equipment

Notes payable

Accounts payable

Revenues

Expenses

Each account has its own ledger page. The page for cash, assuming that only these four transactions occurred, that sales and expenses were cash transactions, and that the beginning cash balance was $80,000, is shown below. The numbers in parentheses refer to the four transactions described earlier.

CASH

Dr			Cr	
Beginning balance	$80,000	(1)		$25,000
(3)	10,000	(2)		10,000
		(4)		7,000
	$90,000			$42,000
Ending balance	$48,000			

The same conventions are followed as for recording entries in the journal: cash inflows on the left, cash outflows on the right. Each posting is identified by a reference to the page and transaction number in the journal.

Liability accounts have their beginning and ending balances on the right side. An increase in a liability account is therefore posted on the right and a decrease on the left.

For equity accounts, there is a separate ledger page for paid-in capital, for each source of revenue and gain, and for each type of expense or loss. Revenues and gains are posted on the right side and losses on the left.

At the end of each accounting period, a trial balance is prepared from the account balances in the ledger to make sure that there are no errors in the ledger postings. Next, certain adjustments are made, one of which, for depreciation, will be covered later. The adjusted trial balance is then used to prepare the financial statements described earlier.

2.7 PRO FORMA INCOME STATEMENTS

Pro forma income statements serve as a framework or structure for organizing cash flow estimates for operating activities. Consider Table 2.1, in which the

TABLE 2.1   Income Statement for the Month Ending 7/31/9X

Revenue	$100	Cash inflows
Less:		
Cash outflow excluding interest payments	65	Cash outflows
Interest payments	5	Cash outflows
Noncash expenses	5	
	$ 75	—
Net income (earnings) before taxes	25	—
Less: Income taxes (40%)	10	Cash outflows
Net income (earnings) after taxes	$ 15	—
Add back noncash expenses	5	—
Net cash flow from operations	$ 20[a]	—

[a]($100 − $65 − $5 − $10 = $20)

major cash flows due to operating activities are identified with the help of an income statement.

The income statement proper ends with the net income after taxes. Two additional lines have been added to obtain the net cash flow from operations, which equals, as you can easily verify, the net income after taxes plus noncash expenses, such as depreciation.

There are three assumptions that, with few exceptions, are always made for the selection process for capital projects when forecasting the cash flow from operations.

The first assumption is that revenues are matched by cash payments at the end of each accounting period; that is, the ending balance in accounts receivable is zero or—what amounts to the same thing—the same at the end as at the beginning of the accounting period. If this were not the case, we could not use the credit entries in the revenue accounts as surrogates for the cash inflow from sales, since some of these entries would be matched by debit entries to accounts receivable.

The second assumption is that all expenses on open account have been paid by the end of each accounting period; that is, the ending balances in accounts payable are also zero or are also the same at the end as at the beginning of each accounting period.

The third assumption is that the only noncash expenses of any significance are depreciation expenses and two expenses related to depreciation: amortization and depletion. Amortization is the term used for depreciating intangible assets, such as patents and goodwill. Depletion refers to noncash expenses for depleting natural resources.

For convenience, pro forma income statements are often turned on their side and amputated to avoid unnecessary detail. This is done in Table 2.2, which begins with the net cash flow before taxes of $30,000 from Table 2.1.

TABLE 2.2 Abbreviated Income and Cash Flow Statement

Year	Net Cash Flow Before Taxes	Depreciation	Net Income Before Taxes	Income Taxes	Net Cash Flow After Taxes
(1)	(2)	(3)	(4)	(5)	(6)
			(2) − (3)		(2) − (5)
1	30	5	25	10	20
2					
3	(To be filled in with the estimated cash flows for the remainder of the life cycle.)				
—					
—					
N					

You should have no trouble matching the figures in Table 2.2 with those in Table 2.1. We will use a format such as this for after-tax analyses. At times, we will have to enlarge it to separate the cash flows for interest payments from other expenses. How and why we do this will become apparent later.

Depreciation expenses and gains and losses on the disposition of assets play such an important role in economic analyses that we need to know how the accounting process is applied to such transactions. This is done in the two subsections that follow.

2.7.1 Depreciation

The cost of a depreciable asset is expensed over a substantial portion or over all of its estimated useful life. The tax authorities allow various depreciation methods, which will be discussed in Chapter 16. The accounting process is the same for all methods. Example 2.1 is for the most common method, namely, straight-line depreciation.

Example 2.1 Depreciation Assume that the truck in Transaction 1 on page 25 is to be depreciated over a five-year period, at the end of which time it will have no appreciable salvage value. Its cost was $25,000. Each of the next five years should therefore pick up an expense of $5,000 ($25,000/5). The balance sheet at any point in time will show the truck and other fixed assets at their original price (refer to Figure 2.1) but will also show, at the end of each accounting period, the depreciation accumulated on these assets since their purchase. The difference between the purchase price of a fixed asset and its accumulated depreciation is its book value.

Accumulated depreciation is a right-hand entry in the accounting process, since it represents a deduction from the worth of a fixed asset. The left-hand entry, which keeps the balance sheet in balance, is depreciation expense, an owner equity account that, like all other expenses whether cash or noncash, is a debit account because it reduces owner equity.

Although accumulated depreciation is a right-hand entry in journals and ledgers, it is shown on the left side of balance sheets by changing its sign. This is a convenience to provide in one place what fixed assets originally cost, how much they have been depreciated, and their current book value.

At the end of the first month of ownership of the truck, the following adjusting entry is made prior to the preparation of the financial statements:

Depreciation expense	$417	
Accumulated depreciation		$417

For a depreciable life of five years or 60 months, the annual depreciation expense is $5,000 ($25,000/5) and the monthly expense is $417 ($25,000/60). If the truck is the only asset in the property, plant, and equipment account, it would show up as follows on the asset side of the balance sheet at the end of the first month of ownership:

Property, plant, and equipment	$25,000
Less accumulated depreciation	417
Book value	$24,583

The income statement for the month would show a noncash expense for depreciation of $417. The journal entry shown above would be recorded each month for 60 months. At that time, the accumulated depreciation on the truck would be $25,000 and its book value would be zero.

There is much more on depreciation in Chapter 16. However, at this time you should be aware that the depreciable life of an asset (the period of time over which its cost is prorated) does not have to be, and often is not, the same as its useful life. Accelerated depreciation and inflation often bring the book value of an asset far below its market value, which is why the discussion that follows on gains and losses from the disposal of assets is important.

COMMENT: As an aside, you may be interested in knowing that the IRS allows accounting entities to keep two sets of books. One set, prepared for the IRS, can be based on accelerated depreciation, that is, rapid write-offs of fixed assets. The other set, prepared to show financial performance, can be based on more realistic estimates of useful life and often favors straight-line rather than accelerated depreciation.

2.7.2 Gains and Losses from the Disposal of Assets

Gains and losses from the disposal of assets result from differences between market value and book value. If market value exceeds book value, there is a gain; if it is less, there is a loss. Consider the following example.

Example 2.2 Gains and Losses The truck bought for $25,000 is sold for a cash payment of $18,000 at the end of two years, at which time its book value is $15,000 ($25,000 less two years of accumulated depreciation at $5,000 per year). Its market value on the day of sale is therefore $3,000 more than its book value. The compound journal entry for recording this transaction involves four accounts.

Cash	$18,000	
Accumulated depreciation	$10,000	
Fixed assets (truck)		$25,000
Gain		$ 3,000

The debit entry to cash is obvious. So, after a few moments reflection, are all the others. We no longer own the truck and must therefore delete it from the accounting records. We do this with a credit entry of $25,000, since it is in the ledger as a debit entry of $25,000 for its first cost. The balance in the account is now zero. The same argument applies to the accumulated depreciation. At the time of sale, there is a credit entry of $10,000 for accumulated depreciation in the ledger, which is closed out by a debit entry for the same amount. The difference between the book value and the market value, which brings both the entry and the balance sheet into balance, is a gain of $3,000. This gain is not a cash flow but an increase in owner equity and is treated in the same way as a revenue account, although it is usually identified separately so that the revenue earned from operations, that is, from the sale of goods and services, is clearly identified. That the gain is not a cash flow is obvious from the preceding journal entry. It is, however, subject to a capital gains tax, which is a cash outflow and which would be recorded as follows for a tax rate of 30%:

Capital gains tax ($3,000 × 0.30)	$900	
Cash		$900

The net cash flow from the sale is therefore $17,100 ($18,000 − $900).

If the truck were sold below its book value, say for $13,000, the journal would show the following entry:

Cash	$13,000	
Accumulated depreciation	$10,000	
Loss	$ 2,000	
Fixed assets (truck)		$25,000

You should have no trouble seeing where these figures come from. Just remember that the resulting loss is debited to an equity account for gains and losses due to the disposal of assets (a gain would, of course, be credited). Since it is usually possible to offset losses such as the ones just mentioned against the taxable income from operations, there may be a tax saving. For a tax rate of 30%, this would be $600 ($2,000 × 0.30), which makes the cash flow from the sale equal to $13,600 ($13,000 + $600).

This completes our overview of accounting. The concepts presented here will be applied throughout the text. We hope you have found this discipline a more conceptual and stimulating subject than its image as "bookkeeping" usually conveys.

2.8 SUMMARY

In Chapter 2, we introduced you to accounting as the science that records, analyzes, and reports on the financial condition and the financial performance of entities. These include for-profit and not-for-profit organizations. The major points covered are itemized below.

- The financial statement that reports on the financial condition of an accounting entity at a given point in time is the balance sheet. The equation on which this sheet is based is the fundamental equation of accounting, namely

$$\text{Assets} = \text{Liabilities} + \text{Equity}$$

- The statement that reports on the financial performance of an accounting entity over a given period of time is the income statement. The equation of this statement is

$$\text{Revenues} - \text{Expenses (Costs)} = \text{Earnings}$$

- The earnings (the net income after taxes) are before owner withdrawals as dividends (for corporations) or drawings (for proprietorships and partnerships). The split between withdrawals by owners and the earnings retained in the business is of little interest to the capital selection process, since all earnings whether withdrawn or not accrue to the benefit of owners.
- Cash flow estimates over the life cycle of projects are inputs for the capital project selection process. They stem from three sources—operating activities, financing activities, and investing activities.
- The accounting process by which the numerous transactions in which entities take part are recorded, analyzed, and reported begins with recording journal entries, posting these entries into the ledger, and from there to the preparation of the financial statements.
- Two transactions that are particularly important to the selection process are depreciation and gains and losses on the disposal of assets. Depreciation, although a noncash operating expense, must, like other such expenses, be brought into after-tax cash flow analyses for its effect on income taxes.
- The disposal of assets results in gains and losses due to differences between the market and book values of the assets sold. These gains and losses are noncash flows, which also impact on income taxes.

REFERENCE

1. U.S. Bureau of the Census, *Statistical Abstract of the United States, 1991*, Table 861. (Washington, DC: U.S. Government Printing Office, 1991).

SUGGESTED READINGS

1. Charles T. Horngren and Walter T. Harrison, Jr., *Accounting*, 2nd ed. (Englewood Cliffs, NJ: Prentice-Hall, 1992). The first five chapters on the basic structure of accounting are an excellent introduction to accounting concepts and the accounting process.
2. Robert F. Meigs and Walter B. Meigs, *Accounting: The Basis for Business Decisions*, 8th ed. (New York: McGraw-Hill, 1990). This book is also recommended for its clear exposition of the fundamentals of accounting.
3. James A. Cashin and Joel J. Lerner, *Accounting I*, 3rd ed. (New York: Schaum's Outline Series, McGraw-Hill, 1987). Another good source on accounting theory, with numerous practice problems.

PROBLEMS

COMMENT: This problem set gives students an understanding of how accounting concepts and principles are used to manage a business and as financial performance measures.

Entities

2-1   Identify some of the profit and not-for-profit entities with which you are in daily contact.

2-2   Although proprietorships and partnerships are not separate legal entities in the eyes of the law, accountants treat the owners and their businesses as separate entities. Why do they do this?

Transactions

2-3   Which of the following "happenings" would be deemed transactions by accountants and which would not? For those that you identify as transactions, which accounts would be affected?

a) Your firm has just been told that it will be awarded a construction contract for $5 million.

b) Your firm has applied for a loan of $200,000.

c) Your firm has donated $10,000 to the Salvation Army.

d) Your firm has decided to sponsor a "Carnival Day" for its employees and has "budgeted" $25,000 for this event.

e) Your firm has paid an advance of $500,000 on a supercomputer to be delivered in one year.

f) Your firm has been awarded a settlement of $1 million on a lawsuit, which the other party has decided to appeal.

Financial Condition and Performance

2-4 Fill in the last column in the table below with the words *good*, *fair*, or *poor*.

Financial Condition		
Today	*One Year Later*	*Financial Performance*
good	better	
good	good	
good	fair	
fair	good	
fair	fair	
fair	worse	
bad	fair	

Financial Statements

2-5 (a) Identify the following as balance sheet or income statement accounts and (b) as asset, liability, equity, revenue, or expense accounts. Which are point-in-time accounts, and which are period-of-time accounts? What are the dimensions of point-in-time accounts? Of period-of-time accounts?

- Cash
- Salaries payable
- Salary expense
- Retained earnings
- Sales
- Depreciation expense
- Gains and losses on disposal of assets
- Paid-in-capital
- Accumulated depreciation (*see* Problem 2-7)
- Prepaid (unexpired) rent (*see* Problem 2-13)
- Contract advance
- Accounts payable
- Office equipment
- Land
- Buildings
- Processing machinery
- Accounts receivable

2-6 Why are revenue and expense accounts often referred to as equity accounts?

2-7 Accumulated depreciation is a credit or right-hand entry because it reduces the book value of a fixed asset. However, it is neither a debt nor an equity account but a contra-asset account, that is, an asset account with a credit entry. How and why did it get this name? (*Hint*: To answer this question, consider where it appears on a balance sheet.)

2-8 Why do we need the delta (Δ) in front of E in the income statement equation?

2-9 The income statement does not show the distribution of earnings to owners. Where is this shown? What effect do such distributions have on the balance sheet?

2-10 Revise equation (2.2) to show the distribution of earnings (D) and the earnings retained in the business (ΔE_r).

2-11 Why is the split between the distribution of earnings to owners and the earnings retained in the business not a concern of the project selection process?

2-12 The statement of cash flows identifies cash flows as originating from operating (O), investing (I), and financing (F) activities. Identify each of the following transactions as one or the other of these activities or as a noncash (NC) activity.

a) Payment of part of the principal on a long-term investment
b) Payment of wages to employees
c) Cash sale of land
d) Acquisition of equipment by issuing a note
e) Acquisition of a building by issuing common stock
f) Payment of an account payable
g) Payment of a cash dividend
h) Collection of an account receivable
i) Depreciation of equipment
j) Issuing common stock for cash
k) Cash sale of merchandise
l) Sale of merchandise on account
m) Payment of interest on an outstanding debt

2-13 Many expenses are prepaid, for example, rent and insurance. The unused (unexpired) portion of such expenses belongs to an asset account called "prepaid expenses." Assume a corporation pays $12,000 for one year's rent of office space. Prepare journal entries for (a) the day the rental contract was signed and (b) the rental expense for the first month. (*Hint*: Use Example 2.1 on depreciation as a guide.)

The Accounting Process

2-14 Corporation ABC was founded on April 1, 19X2 with an initial capital infusion of $50,000 in cash and of land with a fair market value of

$25,000. Record the journal entry, post the ledger, and prepare a balance sheet as of the day of founding.

2-15 During April 19X2, the following transactions took place at Corporation ABC (*see* Problem 2-14 for beginning balances). Record the journal entries, post the ledger, prepare a balance sheet for April 30, 19X2, and an income statement for April 19X2.

a) Performed a service for a customer and received $5,000 in cash.

b) Performed a service for a customer for $3,000 to be paid next month.

c) Bought construction supplies on account for $10,000.

d) Paid the following expenses in cash: rent, $1,500; salaries, $3,200; janitor services, $200.

e) Received a utility bill for $200 due next month.

f) Sold the land for $30,000.

g) Bought office furniture and equipment for $6,000 with $3,000 cash and a $3,000 note.

h) Paid $5,000 to the seller of the construction supplies.

i) Took one month's depreciation on the office equipment using straight-line depreciation, a depreciable life of five years, and no salvage value.

j) Recorded one month's interest due on the $3,000 note to the office equipment supplier. The monthly interest charge is $30.

k) Recorded income taxes payable at 40% of the taxable income for the month.

2-16 What was the cash flow, if any, from operating, investing, and financing activities for the ABC Corporation during April 19X2? How does the total cash flow compare with the difference in cash on hand on 4/1/19X2 and on 4/30/19X2?

2-17 A computer installation was purchased for $100,000. Its depreciable life was taken as four years. For straight-line depreciation, what is the annual depreciation expense, assuming no salvage value? What was the journal entry on the day of purchase and at the end of each year to record depreciation?

2-18 What is the journal entry for removing the computer in Problem 2-17 from the books of account at the end of the fourth year, assuming no net salvage value at that time?

2-19 The computer is sold at the end of its third year for $30,000. What is the journal entry? What would the journal entry be if it were sold for $15,000?

2-20 You are looking at an income statement and see the following:

• Depreciation expense, $20,000
• Amortization expense, $10,000

- Gain on disposal of an asset, $5,000
- Depletion expense, $20,000
- Loss on disposal of an asset, $7,000

Using these figures, what adjustments would you make to net income before taxes to arrive at net cash flow before taxes?

2-21   The cash flows for the four transactions recorded in section 2.6 were posted to the cash account in the ledger. Do the same for the other accounts using $XXX for the beginning balances. (Assume all transactions are cash.)

2-22   The GNP for 1992 was approximately $5.5 trillion. The annual receipts from business in 1991 were about $10.2 trillion. How do you explain this difference? (*Hint*: Go back to Chapter 1 and see the definition of GNP for the answer.)

____3
CASH FLOW PATTERNS

3.1 INTRODUCTION

We know from Chapter 1 that the selection process for capital projects is grounded on estimates of cash flows. It follows that we need to identify the cash flows that will stream into and out of a proposed capital project during its life cycle. Furthermore, we need to become familiar with the cash flow patterns that appear over and over again in the analysis of capital investment opportunities. Both of these topics are covered in this chapter.

In addition, this chapter introduces you to "present economy studies." These were defined in Chapter 1 as studies in which it is not necessary to allow for the time value of money. Although such studies are not the major concern of this text, they do bring out the importance of comparing net cash flows before discounting or compounding in order to see whether a proposed investment has any possibility of earning a return. It can only do so if cash receipts over its life cycle exceed cash disbursements.

3.2 CASH FLOW STREAMS

The cash flow streams into and out of a capital facility that are significant for the capital selection process are identified below:

- Cash flows in from sales of goods and services
- Cash flows out for expenses incurred in producing goods and services
- Cash flows out for interest payments on borrowed funds

- Cash flows out for income tax payments to federal, state, and local governments
- Cash flows in from the disposal of assets throughout the life cycle and at its termination
- Cash flows out for replacing assets throughout the life cycle
- Cash flows in from borrowed funds
- Cash flows out to pay back the principal on borrowed funds

This list identifies all the important cash flows except first cost, working capital, and the imputed cash flows from benefits and disbenefits that flow directly into and out of the pockets of the public.

First cost is also called "initial cost," "investment cost," "initial investment," "capital investment," and "capital expenditure." It includes land, which is not depreciable, and depreciable assets such as plant and equipment.

Working capital is the funds needed to operate a capital facility before revenues become available for covering expenses. In economy studies, we usually assume it is recovered at the end of the life cycle, at which time it becomes a cash inflow. Additions to, and deductions from, working capital can occur throughout the life cycle. Working capital is not a depreciable item.

As mentioned, the cash flows used in economy studies also include the "imputed cash flows" from the benefits and disbenefits produced by not-for-profit entities. In the example mentioned in Chapter 1, highway improvements were justified in part by reduced travel expenses for highway users.

In economy studies, we assume initially that the first cost of a capital facility plus the working capital requirements are cash outflows from owner-investors on which they expect a return. If such studies prove favorable, further studies may be made in which all or part of the funding is furnished by creditors or lessors, or both.

Throughout Parts I and II of this text, estimates for the magnitude of cash flow streams are assumed to be single-valued, that is, deterministic. This simplification serves us well in our discussion of basic engineering economy in Part I and its application to economic analysis in Part II. Once we have mastered the basics, we replace single-valued with more realistic multivalued estimates. A description of such estimates, their sources, and the ranges of accuracy that can be expected from them is therefore deferred to Chapter 20, the first chapter of Part III on risk analysis.

The cash flow estimates assembled for an economic analysis are usually portrayed in a diagram in which each cash flow is shown at its proper location on a time-value line. The conventions used for drawing these diagrams are discussed in the next section.

3.3   CASH FLOW CONVENTIONS

All cash flows are discrete; that is, they occur at distinct points in time, namely, the moments at which cash (or checks) are transferred. However, for the selection process, we assume that cash flows are either discrete or continuous and, if discrete, that they occur at end-of-period, that is, at the end of each month or each quarter or each year throughout the life cycle. The end-of-period assumption simplifies the discounting and compounding computations, which will be discussed in Chapter 5. The continuous cash flow convention is fully discussed in Chapter 6.

The conventions for drawing diagrams with discrete cash flows are shown in Figure 3.1. Comments on these conventions follow.

- The time scale is shown along the x-axis. This is the time-value line or simply the time line. The line is broken up into periods representing months or quarters or years. The location of zero is arbitrary but usually represents the present, that is, "today." The future is to the right of zero, and the past is to the left of zero.
- For finite life cycles, the last time period is period N. For infinite life cycles (for reasons that will become clear in later chapters, it is often convenient to assume a project will last forever), the symbol for infinity is used as shown.

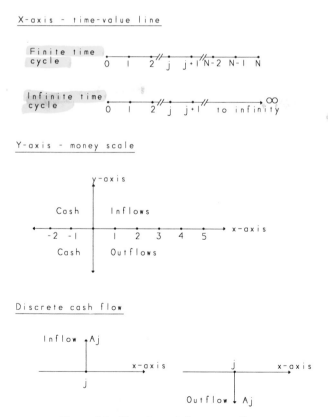

Figure 3.1. Discrete cash flow conventions.

- The y-axis is the monetary scale along which cash flow estimates are measured. This axis is often omitted unless monetary quantities are drawn to scale.
- End-of-period (discrete) cash flows are indicated by arrows pointing up for cash inflows and down for cash outflows. A "present" or "current" cash flow is identified as an arrow occuring at zero.
- The letter A is commonly used to label arrows. If A has no subscript, it usually represents the end-of-period cash flows of a uniform series (to be defined) in which every cash flow has the value A. If A has a subscript, it defines the location of A on the time line. Thus, A_0 is the cash flow at zero (or, as we usually say, at the end of period zero, A_1, the cash flow at the end of period 1, and so on). However, the letters P and F are also used to designate present and future cash flows, that is, cash flows at the end of periods 0 and N, respectively.
- The following abbreviations are used throughout the text: EOP, EOM, EOQ, EOY (end of period, end of month, end of quarter, end of year, respectively) and EOP 0, EOY 1, and so on (discrete cash flows at end of period 0, end of year 1, and so on).
- The magnitudes of the cash flows are shown either at the arrowheads or close to the arrows. The arrows are seldom drawn to scale.

Figure 3.2 shows the conventions used to depict continuous cash flows. Such flows are a useful abstraction and, as mentioned, are fully described in Chapter 6. Until we arrive there, the following example will help you understand what we mean when we say that a cash flow is continuous.

Consider a loan on which interest payments of $1,200 have to be made annually. These payments are discrete yearly cash flows. For the debtor, they are represented by arrows pointing downward at the end of each year during the term of the loan. If interest has to be paid monthly rather than annually, there are 12 discrete cash flows per year, each amounting to $100, and, if it has to be paid daily, there are 365 discrete cash flows per year, each amounting to $3.28 ($1,200/365). The more frequent the payments are, the smaller each discrete cash flow is until, finally, or, as the mathematicians say, "as we approach the limit," there are an infinite number of cash flows, each representing an infinitesimal amount.

Figure 3.2. Continuous cash flow conventions.

COMMENT: Many of you will recall from calculus that the product of infinity (∞) multiplied by an infinitesimal (zero) can equal a finite number, which in our example is $1,200.

You may wonder why, since all cash flows are discrete, we concern ourselves with continuous cash flows. The answer is that it is often simpler to assume continuous cash flows than discrete cash flows occurring daily, weekly, or even monthly throughout an entire life cycle or a substantial portion of it. We don't ask you to accept the value of this concept now, but we think you will as we proceed into the text.

In Figure 3.2,

- Continuous cash flows are shown as prisms; that is, they are "roofed." The roofs extend from the end of one period (in this case, period j) to the end of the next period [in this case, period $(j + 1)$]
- The cash flows are labeled with bars placed over the numbers representing their magnitudes. In Figure 3.2, the total cash inflow for the period from j to $(j + 1)$ is an estimated $1,200 flowing uniformly and continuously throughout this period. A cash outflow is shown in the same way but below the time line.

Preliminary studies for capital project selection are usually made using discrete end-of-period cash flows for all cash flow streams, including first cost. If, for example, the period is one year, all cash flows are assumed to occur at year-end. This simplifying assumption may strike you as being totally unrealistic. It is, but you will soon see that it works, and one reason it works is that it gives conservative answers that are badly needed to overcome the undue optimism in many cash flow estimates. In more definitive studies, some of the discrete cash flows may be replaced with continuous cash flows. As we proceed, you will understand the reasons for choosing one type of cash flow or another and how to handle both types.

Cash flow diagrams are often supported by cash flow tabulations in which all of the cash flows at the end of each period in the life cycle are identified and the net cash flow at the end of each period is determined. These net cash flows become the inputs for the cash flow diagrams.

3.4 COMMON CASH FLOW PATTERNS

Certain cash flow patterns occur over and over again in the selection of capital projects. The most common—really the building blocks from which many of the more complicated patterns we encounter later are developed—are illustrated in the figures listed below.

A description of each pattern follows.

3.4.1 Single Payments

In Figure 3.3, as in the figures that follow, the symbol P is used for a cash outflow or inflow at the end of period zero (EOP 0) and the symbol F for a cash inflow or outflow at the end of period N (EOP N). In many studies, the period of time is years, and we often use the word *year* as a synonym for *period*.

The left side of Figure 3.3 applies to a creditor from whom a sum P is borrowed, to be recovered at the end of period N by payment of a single sum F, including interest. It also applies to an investor who invests P now (now is EOP 0) and expects to get back his or her investment plus a return at the end of period N. If the arrows are reversed in direction (turned 180 degrees around the time line), the diagram is that of a debtor who borrows P and is obligated to pay back F, as shown in the right half of Figure 3.3.

If only one arrow is shown, the diagram represents a donation or gift. An arrow pointing downward at EOP 0 or any other time is a cash outflow from a donor. Similarly, an arrow pointing upward is a current cash inflow to a donee.

3.4.2 Annuities or Uniform Series

The next most common cash flow pattern is one involving a uniform series of payments over a given period of time. Such series are called "annuities."

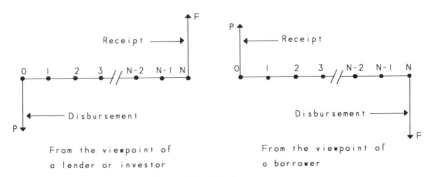

Figure 3.3. Single payments.

Cash flow diagrams are given in Figures 3.4 and 3.5. In each figure, both a normal and a simplified format are shown. We usually use the simplified format.

The diagrams in the left of Figure 3.4 are for a cash outflow P at EOP 0 by an investor or a creditor who recovers his or her investment or loan with a uniform series of cash inflows A, starting at EOP 1 and ending at EOP N. The diagrams in the right half of Figure 3.4 are those of a debtor who borrows a sum P and repays it with a uniform series of cash outflows A.

An annuity for which the first cash inflow or outflow begins with EOP 1 is called an **ordinary annuity**. If the first member of the series occurs at EOY 0 and the last at EOP ($N − 1$), it is called an **annuity due**.

Annuities due do not appear as frequently in the capital selection process as ordinary annuities. When they do, you should have no trouble in seeing that they can be diagramed to resemble Figure 3.4 by letting the cash flow at EOP 0 equal ($P − A$). However, the last payment is at EOP ($N − 1$), not at EOP N.

The diagrams in the left half of Figure 3.5 are those of an investor or an annuitant who invests A dollars every period for N periods and recovers this investment in one lump sum F at EOP N. The diagrams in the right half of Figure 3.5 represent N cash inflows of a sum A by a creditor to a debtor that are repaid with one lump sum payment F at EOP N.

3.4.3 Arithmetic Gradient Series

An arithmetic gradient series is one in which cash flows increase or decrease by a uniform amount, G, from one period to the next. The first cash flow is

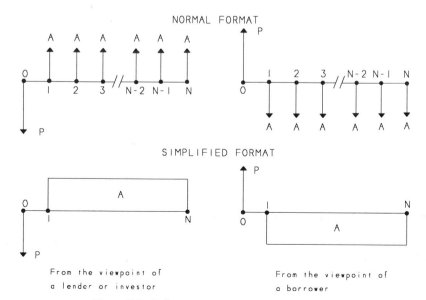

Figure 3.4. Ordinary annuities with current payment.

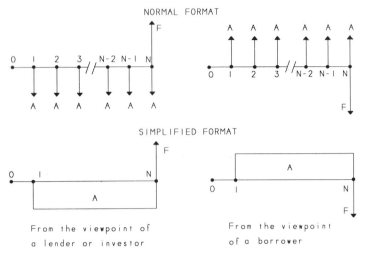

Figure 3.5. Ordinary annuities with future payment.

at EOP 2. The diagrams in Figure 3.6 show both a normal and a simplified format for a positive gradient. The gradient can also be negative.

Arithmetic gradients find application in a wide variety of cash flow situations. One of the most common is replacement studies, in which operating and maintenance expenses are assumed to increase by a fixed amount each year. Loan repayment schedules and building up a nest egg for the years to come may also take this form. In the top left diagram of Figure 3.6, the sums shown are invested starting with G at EOP 2 and ending with $G(N - 1)$ at EOP N. At EOP N the sum F is withdrawn. In the middle left diagram, a sum P is invested at EOP 0 and the sums shown are withdrawn starting with G at EOP 2. The bottom left figure shows a uniform series superimposed on an arithmetic gradient. The cash inflow at EOP 1 is A, at EOP 2 is $(A + G)$, and so on up to EOP N, for which it is $[A + G(N - 1)]$.

COMMENT: Why does the first cash flow for the gradient series occur at EOP 2? The answer is, it makes it easier to combine a uniform series A with a gradient series G to come up with the cash flow pattern at the bottom left of Figure 3.6.

3.4.4 Geometric Gradient Series

A geometric progression or gradient is one in which periodic cash flows increase or decrease by a constant rate or percentage. Estimates of increases and decreases in revenues, costs, and other cash flows due to inflation, productivity gains, technological innovations, and changes in sales volume and

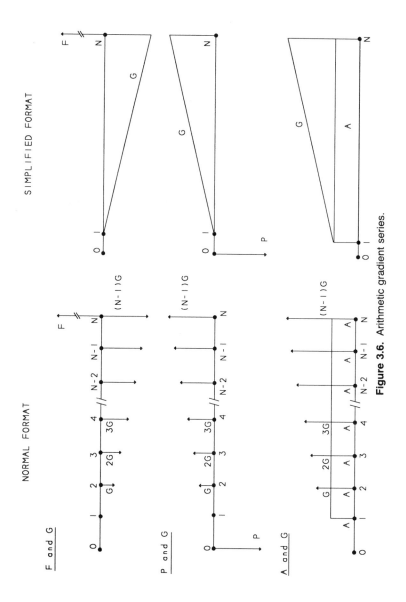

Figure 3.6. Arithmetic gradient series.

47

prices independent of price level effects can often be represented as geometric gradients.

Figure 3.7 illustrates a cash flow diagram for a geometric gradient series. Such curves can show very rapid rises for high inflation rates and illustrate a major problem in forecasting cash flows, which will be discussed in subsequent chapters. If a high rate of inflation is assumed over the entire life of a long-lived project, the resulting curve is shaped like a hockey stick and the fore-casting for such curves is sometimes called the "hockey stick" approach.

Inflation and the other factors mentioned earlier may affect all of the diverse monetary elements that enter into an economic study in different ways. Because of the difficulty of peering even a few years into the future, it is common in preliminary cost studies to assume no inflation, to use current prices for all revenue and cost items, and to use rates of return for discounting that do not include inflationary effects. However, these assumptions should not be carried into the more definitive cost studies that may be called for after preliminary analyses have been completed.

Throughout the text, the terms "rate of return" and "interest rate" are used interchangeably. Rate of return is the broader term. "Interest rate" commonly refers only to the return on credit instruments, such as mortgages or notes. "Rate of return" embraces such returns but also includes the returns that owners receive as dividends or drawings and as capital appreciation.

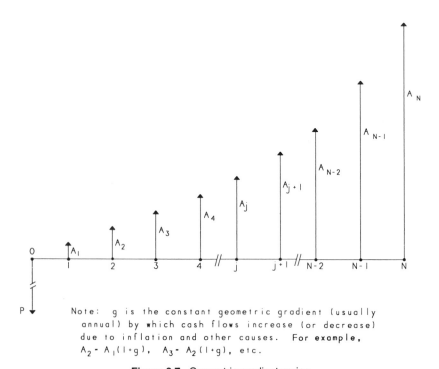

Note: g is the constant geometric gradient (usually annual) by which cash flows increase (or decrease) due to inflation and other causes. For example, $A_2 = A_1(1+g)$, $A_3 = A_2(1+g)$, etc.

Figure 3.7. Geometric gradient series.

3.4.5 Continuous Cash Flow

There are three continuous cash flow diagrams in Figure 3.8. The first shows a future cash flow $\overline{F}$ spread continuously over year N, representing the recovery on an investment P at EOY 0. The second shows a present investment $\overline{P}$ for which the cash flow is spread continuously over year 1. The recovery from this investment is the single-sum cash inflow F at EOY N. The third shows an annuity representing N continuous cash inflows, $\overline{A}$, resulting from a single sum investment, P.

These diagrams and modifications of them will be applied to capital investment opportunities as we proceed.

3.5 TYPICAL APPLICATIONS

Many of the cash flow patterns that appear in the selection process for capital projects are combinations of the patterns described previously. A small sampling of their utility is given in the following figures:

Loans	Figure 3.9
Funding	Figure 3.10
Replacements	Figure 3.11

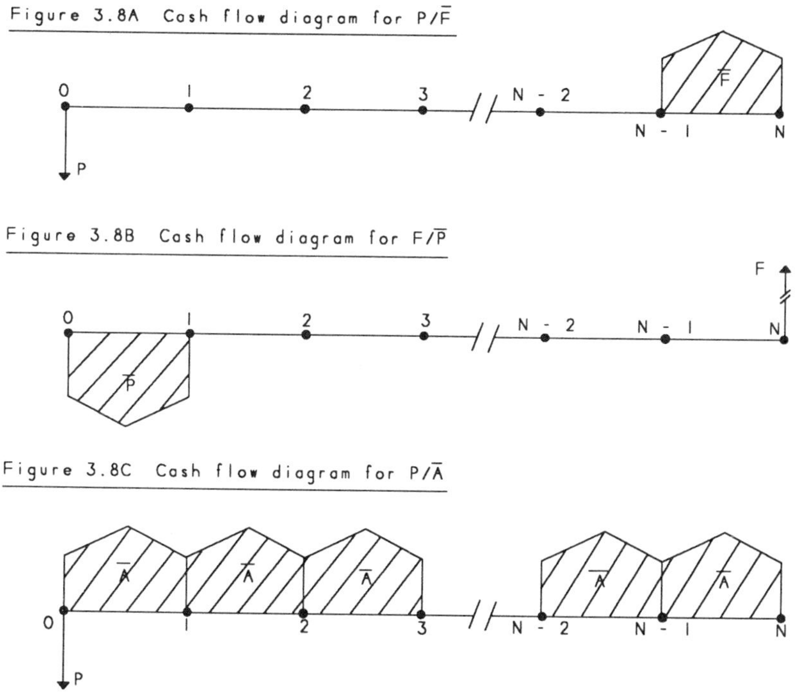

Figure 3.8A   Cash flow diagram for $P/\overline{F}$

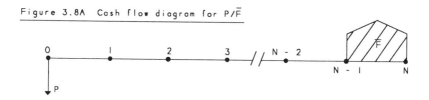

Figure 3.8B   Cash flow diagram for $F/\overline{P}$

Figure 3.8C   Cash flow diagram for $P/\overline{A}$

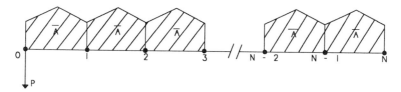

Figure 3.8. Continuous cash flow diagrams.

3.5.1 Loans

Most loans are not single-payment loans, such as those shown in Figure 3.3, but are loans that require periodic payments of interest and/or principal over the term of the loan. Examples are mortgages, car loans, installment loans, and borrowed funds for capital expansion.

The cash flow diagrams in Figure 3.9 illustrate three common loan repayment schemes. In the first diagram, only the interest is paid each year on the outstanding principal P. The principal is repaid at the end of the term—in this case, five years. The sum F is equal to the sum P, since it excludes the

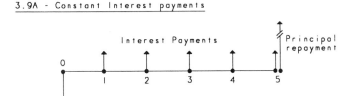

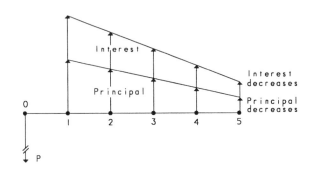

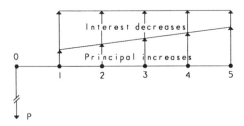

Figure 3.9. Loans.

last interest payment. This cash flow pattern is a combination of the patterns shown in Figures 3.3 and 3.4.

The second cash flow diagram shows a portion of the principal plus the interest on the outstanding balance being repaid at the end of each of five years. If the principal portion of the repayment schedule is an arithmetic gradient, the interest portion will also be an arithmetic gradient. The cash flow pattern is a combination of an arithmetic gradient superimposed over an annuity, as shown in Figure 3.6.

The third repayment scheme has a pattern that is identical with that of Figure 3.4. It is the most common repayment scheme for loans and is also widely used in preliminary project selection studies to show uniform cash inflows from an investment. For debt repayment, the sum to be repaid is "amortized"; that is, the payments A at the end of each time period are equal, but the proportion of interest and principal changes with each payment. Initially, the interest portion is large and the principal portion small. Near the end of the loan, the portions are reversed, with the interest portion being small and the principal portion large.

As discussed in Chapter 2, interest is an expense that is deducted to arrive at taxable income and income tax payments. However, the repayment of the principal is not an expense and does not affect taxable income or income taxes. It is simply a transaction in which an asset account, cash, is credited and a liability account, notes payable, is debited. Owner equity accounts are not affected.

How a loan is repaid is an important feature of cash flow analyses and makes it necessary to treat the principal and interest portions of debts separately.

3.5.2 Funding

Capital projects are funded by owners and creditors, that is, by equity capital and creditor capital.

Figure 3.10A illustrates the use of equity capital. The sum P represents the first cost. This may include estimates for the cost of land, for the project facility itself, and for the working capital requirements.

The net cash flows shown for the remaining years of the life cycle are the differences between cash receipts and disbursements. These differences may be a uniform series as shown, a composite of a uniform series and a gradient, or a set of discrete cash flows that form no identifiable pattern and for which each cash stream must therefore be handled individually. At the end of the cycle, there may or may not be a salvage value. In Figure 3.10A, a salvage value is shown as a future sum S. The similarity between this cash flow pattern and that for an annuity with an added future gift (the salvage value) should be noted.

The cash flow diagram in Figure 3.10B differs from that in Figure 3.10A in that all of the funds needed for the capital investment are borrowed. There is no present sum P, but there is a cash outflow for debt repayment in addition to the net cash flows just described.

<u>3.10A Funding by owners (internal funding)</u>

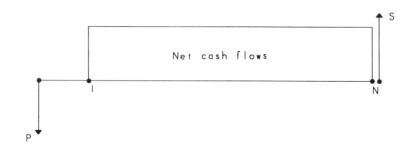

<u>3.10B Funding by creditors (external funding)</u>

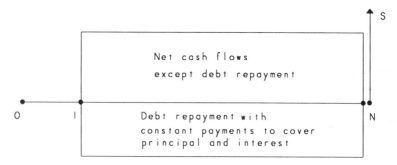

Figure 3.10. Internally and externally funded projects.

Why doesn't Figure 3.10B show a present sum, *P*, for the estimated first cost? The cash inflow from borrowed funds equals the cash outflow to buy or construct the capital investment opportunity under study. Two cash flows of the same magnitude but pointing in different directions could have been shown. Since they cancel each other out, the net cash flow at EOY 0 is zero.

Many projects are financed with both owner (equity) capital and borrowed (creditor) capital. For these, the present sum *P* is the equity financing only, that is, the investment from ownership funds. The external financing would be represented by one of the debt repayment schemes previously discussed.

Most private companies make their capital allocation decisions on the self-financed (100% owner equity) model. However, once a project is chosen, various financing alternatives (leveraging a part or all of the project with debt, leasing equipment rather than outright purchase, etc.) are often examined before a decision on how to proceed with the actual implementation is made. The rationale for this approach is to prevent confusion between the basic economics of competing alternatives, on the one hand, and financing alternatives, on the other.

3.5.3 Replacements

Studies that deal with replacements and retirements outnumber all other capital project selection studies.

Figure 3.11 illustrates a typical cash flow diagram for a replacement study. The estimated market value of the item considered for replacement (in the jargon used for replacement studies, this item is the defender) is represented by a cash outflow, P, and its estimated value, N years from today as a cash inflow F or S (for salvage). Operating and maintenance expenses are shown as periodic cash outflows. In Figure 3.9, A is assumed constant for the period of time under study. However, it is as likely to be an arithmetic or geometric gradient superimposed over a uniform series. Similar diagrams are drawn for each proposed replacement (the challengers). Time-value calculations are then made to determine whether the existing equipment should or should not be replaced.

The cash flow patterns of Figures 3.3 to 3.11 will be replicated again and again in the examples that are interspersed throughout this text. Most capital project selection problems (if we were bold, we would say 90%) can be approximated with these patterns or with combinations of them.

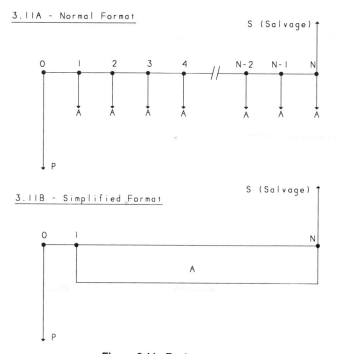

Figure 3.11. Replacements.

3.6 PRESENT ECONOMY STUDIES

We are not going to spend much time on the topic of present economy studies—just enough to show that there are numerous studies involving the flow of cash for which the time value of money need not be considered. Such studies were christened "present economy studies" by DeGarmo (1). We introduce them to make you aware that such problems exist and that you should not confuse them with "future economy studies," for which the time value of money must be considered.

Many present economy studies involve cost comparisons in which capital expenditures play no significant part. Some common examples are as follows:

- *The selection of materials for fabricating parts sold to other manufacturers or used internally in later stages of production.* If the existing production line can handle any of the proposed materials and if no additional operating labor is required, the selection will depend primarily on the cost of the material and, for each material, on the rate at which parts can be produced on the production line. Other factors that may have to be considered are shipping costs, scrap production, and differential maintenance costs.
- *The speed at which a production line should be operated.* This will involve a balance between higher production, on the one hand, and possibly more downtime and higher maintenance and tool replacement costs, on the other.
- *The economical lot size for batch operations.* These studies require a balance between length of run and setup and shutdown costs. The longer the run is, the lower these costs are, but, if excessive quantities are produced, this may increase expenses for warehousing and may interfere with production schedules for other operations performed on the same equipment or on the same production line.
- *The most economical crew size.* Downtime for a given task often varies directly with the size of the crew, since some subtasks may not require a full crew. The total hours paid, including downtime, must be examined for crews of various sizes.
- *Labor incentives to improve productivity.* Here the cost of the incentives must be compared with the estimated savings due to productivity gains.

The preceding examples share the following similarities:

- For each alternative, the figure of merit is the net cash flow—the algebraic sum of the estimated cash flow streams for receipts and disbursements. The selection process is therefore based on comparing these sums without regard to the time value of money.

- The answers obtained today may not hold six months or one year from now. This means that such studies should be reviewed at regular intervals to determine if the assumptions on which they were based still hold.
- Many of the problems can be quite complex, and the more difficult ones in which many combinations of cash flow streams impact on each other are often solved using management science techniques, such as linear programming.

If capital expenditures are introduced into any of the preceding problems, they may metamorphose into future economy studies. However, this is not necessarily the case. Consider a company at which a given product made of mild steel may be replaced with one made of plastic. The existing production line will have to be replaced. If its market value (the net estimated recovery cost if sold) is higher than or equal to the quoted price of a new production line for handling plastic and if the estimated operating and maintenance costs throughout the life cycle are lower for plastic than for mild steel, the study is complete, because all of the cash flow estimates favor plastics. There is, however, an important caveat that applies to many of the types of problems outlined earlier. The alternatives for which costs are being compared should be functionally equivalent as far as waste production, serviceability, length of service, customer satisfaction, and other nonmonetary attributes are concerned.

Consider one more example, which illustrates this warning. In mining, petroleum refining, and chemical operations, it is often possible to balance higher processing costs associated with increased recoveries against lower costs with lower recoveries. In mining particularly, it is not unusual to compare two alternatives, for one of which the capital expenditure for the process facility, the operating and maintenance costs, and the cost to produce one pound of metal are all lower than for the other. The first alternative is a clear choice for optimizing the return on investment. No time-value-of-money calculations are needed for a decision on this criterion alone. Assume, however, that the residue from this alternative contains minerals that could be recovered if the second alternative were selected but that may be lost forever if the first alternative were selected. With this given, the comparison of the two alternatives lacks functional equivalence and may therefore not be valid.

In conclusion, although present economy studies far outnumber future economy studies, they play a relatively small part in the capital selection process. Their milieu is operations and particularly manufacturing processes. If you would like to know more about them, you should turn to the Reference and Suggested Reading at the end of this chapter.

We have mentioned the time value of money many times in this and the preceding chapters. However, before we deal with this concept, we are going to describe several of the more common figures of merit that do not depend on discounting but that are still in use today. These lead us into Chapter 4.

3.7 SUMMARY

In this chapter, we identified the cash flows that are significant in economic analyses for selecting capital projects. These include revenues, cash costs and expenses (see Chapter 2), capital expenditures, working capital, salvage values, benefits, and disbenefits.

In carrying out such analyses, cash flow estimates are presented in the form of diagrams and tables that identify the times during a project's life cycle during which cash flows occur.

The cash flow diagrams fall into common patterns, which are referred to as single payments, uniform series (annuities), arithmetic gradients, and geometric gradients. These, singly or in combination, represent most of the situations encountered when capital expenditures are compared. Examples given include loans, funding, and replacements.

The last topic covers studies for which the time value of money need not be considered to arrive at a choice among alternatives. They fall into two broad groups.

1. Studies in which there are no significant capital expenditures.
2. Studies in which there may be such expenditures but higher capital costs are not offset by lower periodic costs or higher savings throughout the life cycle.

REFERENCE

1. E. Paul DeGarmo, John R. Canada, and William G. Sullivan, *Engineering Economy*, 6th ed. (New York: Macmillan, 1988). Chapter 2 in this text covers the topic of present economy studies with many numerical examples.

SUGGESTED READING

1. John A. White, Marvin H. Agee, and Kenneth E. Case, *Principles of Engineering Economic Analysis*, 3rd ed. (New York: John Wiley & Sons, 1989). Chapter 1 of this text offers several examples of present economy studies.

PROBLEMS

Cash Flow Diagrams

COMMENT: For the first 11 problems, draw the time-value-of-money line, locate zero, divide the line into periods, and diagram the cash flows. Where dollar values are not given, use symbols such as P, F, A,

$\overline{A}$, A_j, $\overline{A}_j$, and so on. Do not draw the cash flow arrows to scale but at least indicate their relative size. Assume EOP discrete cash flows, unless continuous cash flows are asked for.

3-1 You expect a lump sum inheritance of $30,000 three years from today.

3-2 The inheritance in Problem 3-1 will be disbursed over five years at $6,000 per year. The first payment occurs when you reach age 45. You are now 35 years old.

3-3 You have borrowed P dollars but have a grace period of six months before you start repaying the principal and interest in equal quarterly installments of A dollars up to EOQ N.

3-4 In your capacity as a bank loan officer, you have approved a car loan for $9,000 to be amortized with 30 monthly payments of $350 each.

3-5 You decide to lease a car for a 30-month period. There is no initial payment. The lease payments are A dollars per month. The payments start on the day the lease is signed. An additional payment of $2A$ dollars is also required now. You will recover it at the termination of the lease, depending on the condition of the car.

3-6 One of the five lottery tickets you bought for $1 each came through. You will be receiving $50,000 per year for 35 years, starting now.

3-7 Your company is considering the purchase of a new piece of testing equipment that is expected to contribute $6,000 to net cash flow the first year. After that, the net cash flow will decrease by $500 annually. The equipment costs $25,000, has a useful life of ten years, and has a salvage value at that time of $9,000.

3-8 A proposed improvement in an assembly line will have an initial purchase and installation cost of $50,000. The annual maintenance costs are estimated at $2,500 over the useful life of 12 years, at which time the salvage value is zero. Periodic overhauls will be required every 3 years, which are estimated to cost $4,800.

3-9 BALLOONS-R-US invested $3,000 in a new air compressor seven years ago. During the first year of operation, $100 was spent on maintenance, and this cost increased by $25 each year. The company has just sold the compressor for $150. Draw the cash flow diagram for the life cycle of the machine.

3-10 Your firm has decided to invest P dollars in a major chemical facility to be bought from one of its competitors. One-half of the sum will be borrowed and repaid with 20 equal annual installments of A_1 dollars to cover amortization of the debt. The working capital requirements are estimated at $0.1\,P$, and the net cash flow, not including debt amortization, is estimated at A_2 dollars annually for 25 years. At that time, the salvage value of the plant is estimated at 0.05 P.

Present Economy Studies

3-11 Rotors for small irrigation pump units can be manufactured at plant X by two different machining sequences, S1 and S2. Sequence S1 consists of three machines—M1, M2, and M3. Sequence S2 consists of four machines—A, B, C, and D. The scrap rates for the machines are as follows:

M1	5%	A	4%
M2	8%	B	4%
M3	4%	C	5%
		D	1%

The batch size for each sequence is 1,000 units. Raw materials cost $2 per unit. The batch processing costs for S1 are $7,000 and for S2, $5,000. Which sequence produces the lowest unit cost?

3-12 In an assembly line for DC motors, workers can typically produce between 125 and 175 motors during an eight-hour shift. For a production rate of 125 motors, defects average 2%; for a rate of 150 motors, 5%; and for a rate of 175 motors, 10%. The total cost of the material in the finished product is $24.75, and the workers on the assembly line are paid $2.50 per acceptable motor. The material in the defective units has no scrap value.

a) What rate achieves the lowest unit cost?

b) At what rate would the workers prefer to work?

3-13 At an independent automobile parts manufacturer, the plant manager has the choice of using either machine A or machine B to stamp out front and rear fenders. Because the fender market is not predictable, orders for different fenders are received on a recurring basis but for different quantities. Machine A requires four setup operations of 0.25 hours each. Machine B requires six setup operations of 0.15 hours each. Once set up, machine A takes 0.50 hours to finish a fender and machine B, 0.55 hours. The hourly wages for the machine operators are $15 and $17 for machines A and B, respectively, and the hourly overhead rates are $10 and $9, respectively.

a) Which machine is preferred for order sizes of 100 fenders?

b) Which machine is preferred for order sizes of 500 fenders?

c) What is the break-even order size?

3-14 A manufacturing company is considering leasing a fleet of new cars for their salespeople. The final choices have narrowed down to three models.

	Alternatives		
	Model A	Model B	Model C
Monthly lease	$250	$375	$550
Miles per gallon	30	27	33
Maintenance, $/mile	$0.17	$0.15	$0.07

Salespeople travel an average of 3,000 miles per month. Gas prices are estimated at $1.25 per gallon.

a) Based on total monthly costs, what is the most economical car for the company?

b) What nonmonetary attributes might also influence the decision?

3-15 Two methods of developing a mine are under review. Method A recovers 60% of the ore at a cost of $25 per ton. Method B recovers 50% of the ore at a cost of $15 per ton. The cost of processing the recovered ore is $50 per ton. The ore yields 350 pounds of metal per ton, which will sell for an estimated $1 per pound. Which method should be used?

4

UNDISCOUNTED FIGURES OF MERIT

4.1 INTRODUCTION

In selecting capital projects, decision makers rely on certain well-accepted financial criteria or, as they are often called, figures of merit. The figures of merit chosen are influenced by many factors, including simplicity, familiarity, data requirements, and theoretical correctness.

The major figures of merit applied to the project selection process fall into two broad categories: those that consider the time value of money by discounting cash flows and those that do not. We refer to the latter as "undiscounted figures of merit."

Surveys of business and financial executives indicate that figures of merit from both categories are commonly used to assist in making capital investment decisions. However, the figures of merit that do not discount cash flows are considered approximate at best, and by many practitioners, incorrect at worst.

Why do we consider methods that are defined as approximate or incorrect? As mentioned, these methods are still in current use and still have appeal for certain audiences because they are often quite simple to use. You may, therefore, at some time be faced with having to compare the more sophisticated methods with those described in this chapter. This you cannot do without a knowledge of the latter. Furthermore, you may yourself use one of them— the payback period—for a "quick and dirty" approach to a very preliminary culling of available investment candidates and for very rough risk assessments whenever cash flow problems loom.

The three most common undiscounted figures of merit still applied today are

- Payback period
- Return on total investment (ROI)
- Return on average investment (ROAI)

Each of these will be discussed in the following sections.

4.2 PAYBACK PERIOD

The payback period still serves as a convenient tool for a very rough and preliminary screening of the many candidates that offer themselves for consideration as capital investment opportunities. This is particularly true for replacement studies and generally for cost studies that involve relatively small first costs ($250,000 or less) and relatively short life cycles (eight to ten years, but usually less).

Payback is the length of time, usually expressed in years, needed to recover the initial cost of a capital investment. A more precise definition is the number of years it takes for the sum of the annual net cash flows to equal zero.

The cash flows involved were described in Chapter 3. They include the first cost, P, for which the symbol A_0 is often used for symmetry with other cash flows, for example, cash flows $A_1, A_2, \ldots A_{j-1}, A_j \ldots A_N$.

4.2.1 Payback with Equal Cash Flows

If the annual net cash flows are equal, then the payback period is the first cost, P, divided by the annual cash flow, A; that is,

$$\text{Payback} = \frac{\text{Investment}}{\text{Net cash flow}} = \frac{P}{A} \tag{4.1}$$

Equation (4.1) is applied in Example 4.1.

Example 4.1 Payback Period Comparison   You are evaluating three proposals— A, B, and C—for each of which the estimated first cost is $120,000. However, the estimated annual net cash flows differ markedly, as shown in the table below.

	Cash flows (in thousands of dollars)		
End of Year	A	B	C
0	− $120	− $120	− $120
1	40	—	—
2	40	60	—
3	40	60	—
4	40	60	240
Net life cycle cash flow	$40	$60	$120
Payback period (in years)	3.0	3.0	4.0

You are asked to evaluate the alternatives using the payback method and to choose the "best" alternative for your company.

The payback period is three years for alternative A ($120/40) and three years for alternative B [$120/(0 + $60 + $60)], but the size and timing of the cash flows are substantially different. Alternative A has a cash return of $80,000 in two years, as compared to $60,000 for alternative B. However, alternative B has a net life cycle cash flow that is $20,000 higher than alternative A ($60,000 versus $40,000). If cash forecasts for the firm as a whole show a possible cash shortage, management will select alternative A because of an earlier cash inflow; otherwise, they may prefer alternative B.

The payback period for alternative C was obtained by assuming that the entire cash flow of $240,000 for the fourth year came in at the end of that year. The investment is an attractive one, since it brings in twice the first cost in four years— an annual rate of return of almost 20%. However, many managers would shy away from it, because the cash flows are in a not-too-distant but nevertheless not-too-near future.

One of the more interesting conclusions that we can draw from Example 4.1 is that one can learn much by simply arraying cash flow figures to make comparisons without necessarily introducing any figures of merit, whether discounted or undiscounted.

4.2.2   Payback with Unequal Cash Flows

If the net cash flows are unequal, then the payback period is the number of years for the cumulative net cash flow to equal zero. Thus,

$$\sum_{0}^{N*} A_j = 0 \qquad (4.2)$$

where

$$A_j = \text{the net cash flow for any period } j$$

$$N^* = \text{the payback period}$$

In equation (4.2), A_0 is, of course, the net cash outflow for the proposed capital expenditure under review.

Calculations of the payback period with unequal cash flows is illustrated in Example 4.2. Problems of this type are usually set up on spreadsheets, and the results are then plotted as illustrated in Figure 4.1. The ubiquitous use of spreadsheet software with graphical capabilities makes such calculations and the resulting graphs easily accessible. However, in many situations, the calculations are relatively simple and can more easily and quickly be done with paper, pencil, and a hand calculator.

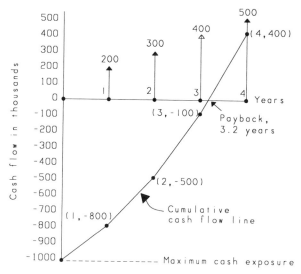

Figure 4.1. Graph of payback period.

Example 4.2 Payback with Unequal Cash Flows Your company is considering investing $1 million for a robot-welding machine to help fabricate office equipment. The yearly savings are estimated at $200,000 for the first year, escalating to $500,000 in four years. The escalation is assumed to be an arithmetic gradient.

How long will it take to recover the $1 million? A cash flow tabulation for the first four years of operations with all the figures in thousands of dollars shows the following:

End of Year	Outflow	Inflow	Net Cash Flow	
			Annual	Cumulative
0	$1,000	—	− $1,000	− $1,000
1	—	$200	200	− 800
2	—	300	300	− 500
3	—	400	400	− 100
4	—	500	500	400

The cumulative cash flow reaches zero between years 3 and 4. Interpolation gives a payback period of 3.2 years. A graphical presentation of Example 4.2 is given in Figure 4.1.

Graphs such as Figure 4.1 also give us a picture of the "project balance" based on undiscounted (0% rate of return) cash flows. A project balance tells us the extent to which we would be hurt if the project under review were terminated at any time before its full life cycle. For end-of-year cash flows, if the project in Example 4.2 died before EOY 1, we would lose $1 million; if before EOY 2, $800,000; and so on. Such balances are sometimes prepared using compounded cash flows. We do not mention them further in this text except in the Suggested Reading at the end of the chapter.

As mentioned in the Introduction, payback periods have their advantages and disadvantages. We will now look at these.

4.2.3   Payback Advantages and Disadvantages

Although the payback method has many critics, it is still widely used. Furthermore, it is often wisely used (1). To understand why this is so, we need to review the reasons businesspersons defend it in spite of the criticisms leveled against it.

The major criticisms are that the payback method is theoretically incorrect because

- no consideration is given to cash flows after the payback period
- the cash flows are not discounted, thus ignoring the time value of money
- it is possible for the payback period to be greater than the project life cycle

The first error is serious and can lead to incorrect decisions. This is especially true if there are significant net cash inflows in the years after the payback period or if salvage values are substantial. For this reason, we should always look at the cash flows for all of the life cycle and not just at the flows that reduce equation (4.2) to zero.

The second error is correctable, and a number of companies have modified the traditional undiscounted payback method to a discounted payback method. However, it does nothing to correct the first error.

The third error is a trivial one, since a project whose payback period is longer than its project life cycle is obviously not viable.

The reasons businesspersons still use the payback method are that

- it is easy to understand
- it is sometimes a useful device for quickly screening candidates out of the selection process
- it serves as a risk indicator, especially when very short paybacks are desired to ease cash shortage forecasts

The first reason appeals to all lovers of simplicity and efficiency.

The second reason is an accepted use of the payback method in industry and government for short-term investments concerned with replacements and relatively small in-house or in-plant improvements. Many firms, for example, have a policy that such capital expenditures must have a payback of three years or less.

The third reason is a reaction to the not uncommon experience of having everything that could go wrong, go wrong. Managers are wary of the future and for that reason alone favor short payback periods. Most decision makers feel more comfortable with a two- to three-year payback than a four-year or longer payback, even though discounted figures of merit show substantial returns.

4.3   RETURN ON TOTAL INVESTMENT (ROI)

The ROI and ROAI criteria are favored by financial executives who feel comfortable with accounting data and see project evaluation in traditional accounting and financial terms. Both criteria use book values and the accounting concepts of profit and net income discussed in Chapter 2. You will recall that book value at a given point in time is the original or first cost of an investment less the accumulated depreciation up to that point in time and that net income or profit after taxes is the so-called bottom line, which seldom (and then only by happenstance) is equal to the annual net cash flow from operations.

The definition of ROI is given by the following equation:

$$\text{ROI} = \frac{\text{Average net income per year}}{\text{Original book value or first cost}} \qquad (4.3)$$

The denominator of equation (4.3) is, as shown, the original book value of the investment. The numerator is the average annual net income after taxes over the life cycle, although net income before taxes is also used. To obtain this average, pro forma income statements are prepared for each year of the expected life cycle. The average net income per year is then calculated. Example 4.3 illustrates this procedure.

Example 4.3   Return on Original Investment   A new plastics mold is under consideration. The installed first cost is estimated at $1 million. The pro forma income statements on which the cost study is based show sales averaging $500,000 annually for ten years and expenses, excluding depreciation, averaging $300,000 per year. Depreciation expense is estimated at $100,000 per year based on straight-line depreciation over a useful life of ten years and on the assumption that the entire capital expenditure is depreciable. The net salvage value is estimated as zero and the income tax rate as 30%. Your financial vice-president wants to determine the ROI for this investment, as well as the life cycle cash flow. A combination pro forma income statement and cash flow statement representing average performance over ten years follows. You will recognize the format from Chapter 2.

	Average Annual Forecasts for Ten-Year Period (in thousands of dollars)	
Revenues	$500	Cash inflow
Less all costs except depreciation	300	Cash outflow
Less depreciation	100	—
Net income before taxes	100	—
Income taxes (30%)	30	Cash outflow
Net income after taxes	70	—
Plus depreciation	100	—
Net cash flow from operations	170	—

The ROI for this investment is given by equation (4.3), in which the numerator is $70,000 (not $170,000) and the denominator is $1,000,000.

$$\text{ROI} = \frac{\$70,000}{\$1,000,000} = 7.0\%$$

The net cash flow for the ten-year period is $700,000, that is, the difference between the net cash flow from operations of $1,700,000 ($170,000 × 10) for ten years and the initial investment of $1,000,000. You will shortly be able to determine that the return based on discounted cash flows is 11%.

The limitations of ROI as a figure of merit are that

— the time value of money is ignored.
— noncash flow streams, such as depreciation, participate in sizing this figure of merit.
— using an average pro forma income statement is not realistic. If cash flows are not discounted, this understates the contribution of the earlier years and overstates that of the later years.

Several variations of equation (4.3) exist:

— Using average net cash flows per period instead of profit per period. In Example 4.3, this would give a return of 17.0%.
— Reducing the size of the denominator by deducting the estimated salvage value at the end of the life cycle. This increases the return.
— Including an estimate for working capital in the denominator, thus decreasing the return.
— Applying a geometric gradient to revenues and costs to allow for inflation. This increases the return.

COMMENT: If you are faced with comparing the results of a cost study using discounted figures of merit with the results obtained by using ROI, you need to know which variation, if any, is used by financial management. Our recommendation is to avoid the use of ROI or ROAI entirely.

4.4 RETURN ON AVERAGE INVESTMENT (ROAI)

This figure of merit is a further refinement of the ROI in that the book value of the first cost is averaged over the life of the project. The rationale for this approach is that book value decreases over time by the allowance for depreciation. For many, if not most, investments, the book value at the end of an investment's life cycle is a small percentage of its original book value. However, there are some investments that retain their value and even appreciate over time. Luxury automobiles, jewelry, and paintings are examples.

   Those who favor ROAI argue that the return on investment should be based on the average book value of the investment over its life cycle. This value is given by

$$\text{Average book value} = \frac{P + S}{2} \tag{4.4}$$

where P is the original book value or first cost and S is the estimated final book value or net salvage value.

   Example 4.4 illustrates how the ROAI approach differs from the ROI approach. However, its limitations are the same as those of ROI.

Example 4.4 Return on Average Investment For the data in Example 4.3 and for zero salvage value the ROAI is 14.0% as shown below.

$$\text{Average book value} = \frac{\$1,000,000 + 0}{2} = \$500,000$$

and

$$\text{ROAI} = \frac{\$70,000}{\$500,000} = 14.0\%$$

This concludes our discussion of undiscounted cash flow figures of merit. We will have little occasion to refer to them in the remainder of this text.

4.5 SUMMARY

The three most common undiscounted figures of merit still in use today for comparing capital investment opportunities are

- Payback period
- Return on investment (ROI)
- Return on average investment (ROAI)

The payback period is popular because of its simplicity. It also serves as a surrogate for more sophisticated risk analyses by telling managers how quickly they will recover their investment. Since the future is always uncertain, the shorter the payback is, the greater the confidence level a decision maker assigns to an investment opportunity.

The ROI and ROAI are accounting methods based on the initial or average book value of the investment and on the average annual net income over its life cycle. They are still applied to the selection process because they produce results with which many managers feel comfortable.

The payback period has some merit as an investment criterion (1). This cannot be said for ROI and ROAI.

REFERENCE

1. D. J. Leech, *Economics and Financial Studies for Engineers* (New York: Halsted Press, John Wiley & Sons, 1982). Chapter 8 on the payback period is worth reading. The following quotation from page 98 sums up the author's and our attitude toward its use:

> . . . if we appreciate the quick and easy nature of payback calculations, we will not complain that they ignore the time value of money. Payback period is a coarse filter. We will accept a project with a short payback if subsequent positive cash flows are likely to be large enough for us to believe that . . . a good project [will not turn] into a bad one.

SUGGESTED READING

2. G. J. Thuesen and W. J. Fabrycky, *Engineering Economy*, 7th ed. (Englewood Cliffs, NJ: Prentice-Hall, 1989). Chapter 6 of this text has an extended discussion on "project balance," in which cash flows are compounded using the MARR to determine the balance at any period throughout the life cycle.

PROBLEMS

Payback Period

4-1 Go back to Example 4.1. What would the payback period be for alternative C if the net cash flow for year 4 had been evenly distributed over the year?

4-2 Hampton Ventures, a venture capital firm, invested $150,000 in International Networks, Inc., a start-up firm, with the following cash flow results:

EOY	Cash Flow
1	$20,000
2	40,000
3	80,000
4	80,000
5 to 7	90,000

What was the payback period for Hampton's investment?

4-3 A manufacturing company is considering two projects, code named Pegasus and Zeus. Each project will result in additional revenues of $10,000 for five years. Pegasus will cost the company $35,000 and will have no salvage value. Zeus will cost the company $45,000 and will have a 50% salvage value at the end of year 5. What are the payback periods for Pegasus and Zeus?

4-4 Gatehouse, Inc., is considering upgrading the HVAC system currently installed in its facility. A contractor has suggested the following three alternatives, with their estimated yearly savings in energy costs:

EOY	A	B	C
0	− $30,000	− $35,000	− $40,000
1–5	12,000	10,000	9,500

What are the payback periods for each system?

4-5 Alternative A has an initial cost of $65,000, and alternative B has an initial cost of $32,000. The expected revenues less costs are $14,000 each year for five years for A and $8,000 each year for five years for B. At the end of this period, the salvage value for A is zero, while B is expected to be sold for 100% of its initial cost. All values are EOY. Which alternative is preferable using the payback method? What does your answer tell you about the shortcomings of the payback period?

4-6 The anticipated monthly EOP cash flows for two mutually exclusive alternatives are

EOM	Alternative I	Alternative II
0	− $200	− $420
1	120	240
2	120	205
3	120	205
4	120	205
5	180	205

Determine the payback period in months for both alternatives.

4-7 The anticipated annual cash flows, in thousands of dollars, for two mutually exclusive alternatives are

EOY	Alternative I	Alternative II
0	− $300	− $300
1	100	150
2	150	125
3	400	100
4	200	500

Determine the payback periods for both alternatives.

4-8 A project has the following characteristics:

Useful life	10 years
First cost	$30,000
Benefits	$20,000 annually
Maintenance	$2,000 in year 1, rising by $2,000 per year for 10 years
Salvage value	$4,000

Draw the cash flow diagram for the project and calculate the payback period.

4-9 A firm is considering two mutually exclusive alternatives for its plant.

	A	B
Initial cost	$6,000	$4,000
Annual net cash flow	$1,500	$ 750
Life (years)	7	7

Which alternative should be selected based on the payback period?

4-10 A proposed investment is expected to save $2,000 annually for 7 years. The payback period is 2.5 years. What is the first cost of the investment?

4-11 A proposed investment is expected to save $2,000 the first year. These savings are expected to increase by $500 per year for the next five years. If the payback period is three years, what is the first cost of the investment?

Return on Investment

4-12 Rework Example 4.4 for a salvage value of $200,000. In doing so, the depreciation expense will have to be revised. Use straight-line depreciation on the difference between the first cost and the estimated salvage value.

4-13 Gillmore, Inc., is considering two mutually exclusive alternatives—A and B. Each alternative requires an initial capital investment of $11

million. The after-tax cash flows and net income in thousands of dollars over the life cycles are tabulated below. Take salvage values to be zero.

Year	Cash Flows		Net Income	
	A	B	A	B
1	$3,800	$ 500	$2,700	$ – 600
2	3,400	900	2,300	– 200
3	3,000	1,300	1,900	200
4	2,600	1,700	1,500	600
5	2,200	2,100	1,100	1,000
6	1,800	2,500	700	1,400
7	1,400	2,900	300	1,800
8	1,000	3,300	– 100	2,200
9	600	3,700	– 500	2,600
10	200	4,100	– 900	3,000

For each alternative, what is (a) the payback period, (b) the return on total investment (ROI), and (c) the return on average investment (ROAI)?

___5
RATES OF RETURN

5.1 INTRODUCTION

Money has time value. Its value depends on the rate of return that creditors and investors will accept for giving up current purchasing power for future purchasing power. This rate is known as the MARR, or minimum attractive (or acceptable) rate of return. How investors decide on an MARR is the subject of a later chapter. For the time being, we accept it as a given.

This chapter presents the essential background for understanding the terminology commonly used in discussing rates of return and interest rates, including the MARR. We have already said that these two terms will be used interchangeably but that the term "rate of return" has a broader meaning. For this reason, this chapter carries the title shown.

Our subject breaks down into four parts:

1. Simple and compound interest rates
2. Nominal and effective interest rates
3. Continuous compounding
4. Compounding and discounting

5.2 SIMPLE AND COMPOUND INTEREST

With simple interest, you do not earn interest on interest; with compound interest, you do.

Suppose you deposit a sum P in a savings account paying $i\%$ simple interest and let the interest accumulate for a number of years. If P were $1,000 and i were 5%, you would earn $50 on your deposit the first year, $50 the second year, $50 the third year, and so on for as long as your deposit remained in the bank. For each year, the interest earned is the product Pi, which in this case equals $50 (1,000 $\times$ 0.05). At the end of one year, your bank account would show $1,050; at the end of two years, $1,100; and at the end of N years, $1,000 plus N times $50.

The formula for simple interest that relates a future bank balance F to a present deposit P is easily derived with the help of the following table.

End of Year (EOY)	Bank Balance F at End of Year	
0	P	
1	$P + Pi$	$= P(1 + i)$
2	$P + Pi + Pi$	$= P(1 + 2i)$
3	$P + Pi + Pi + Pi$	$= P(1 + 3i)$
.		
.		
.		
N	$P + PiN$	$= P(1 + iN)$

The equation for simple interest for any combination of F, P, i, and N is therefore

$$F = P(1 + iN) \tag{5.1}$$

For comparison, the equation for compound interest, which will be derived shortly, is

$$F = P(1 + i)^N \tag{5.2}$$

Although the two equations look alike, appearances can be and, in this instance, are deceiving. This becomes apparent in the discussion that follows.

No bank today offers simple interest. It could not compete unless the rate if offered was substantially higher than that for banks offering compounding. However, simple interest is still used for calculating interest earned on fractional periods. If, for example, the principal and interest on a loan were to be repaid in five years and two months, the interest for the five years would be compounded but interest for the two months would often be treated as simple interest.

If you had been offered 5% compounded annually on an investment of $1,000, there would be $1,050 in your account at the end of one year, that is, the same amount as with simple interest. During the next year, however, you would earn 5% on $1,050, not on the original deposit of $1,000. At the end of two years, your bank balance would therefore be $1,102.50 ($1,050 + $1,050 $\times$ 0.05) as compared with $1,100 for simple interest. The difference of $2.50 is not great (it might buy a few candy bars), but it grows geometrically rather than arithmetically with time. For higher interest rates and longer periods of time, the "force" of compound interest, as it is sometimes called, can be staggering. This is shown below for a deposit P of $1,000 and a rate of 12% compounded annually.

| | Bank Balance F at End of | | |
	10 Years	20 Years	40 Years
Simple interest	$2,200	$3,400	$ 5,800
Compound interest	3,106	9,646	93,051

You can check any or all of these figures with equations (5.1) and (5.2).

The equation for compound interest is also easily derived. Let P be the original deposit in a bank that offers $i\%$ compounded annually. The bank balances—the future sums—at the end of each year for N years, assuming no withdrawals, are tabulated below.

End of Year (EOY)	Bank Balance F at End of Year	
0	P	
1	$P(1 + i)$	$= P(1 + i)$
2	$P(1 + i)(1 + i)$	$= P(1 + i)^2$
3	$P(1 + i)(1 + i)(1 + i)$	$= P(1 + i)^3$
.		
.		
N	$P(1 + i)^N$	$= P(1 + i)^N$

You will recognize the last line in this tabulation as equation (5.2). If any three of its four terms—F, P, i, and N—are known, the fourth can be calculated.

Simple interest never did make sense except to the banks that held your deposits. Example 5.1 will provide you with the practice you need in appreciating the difference, not only between simple and compound interest, but also between annual compounding and compounding periods shorter than one year.

Example 5.1   Simple and Compound Interest   You have just moved to a new town with $1,000 in your pocket, for which you have no immediate need. You decide to deposit it in a savings account at one of the local banks. There are five of these, all of which are offering 12% interest. However, each bank quotes its rate differently, as shown in the following tabulation.

Bank	Interest Rate Quotation
A	12% simple interest
B	12% compounded annually
C	12% compounded quarterly
D	12% compounded monthly
E	12% compounded continuously

You decide to compare what your deposit of $1,000 would earn at the end of one year and at the end of ten years, assuming no withdrawals. The results are shown in Table 5.1.

For the end of year 10 (EOY 10), you obtained the results for bank A from equation (5.1) and those for bank B from equation (5.2), as shown below:

$$\text{Bank A: } F = P(1 + iN) = \$1,000 (1 + 0.12 \times 10) = \$2,200$$

$$\text{Bank B: } F = P(1 + i)^N = \$1,000 (1 + 0.12)^{10} \quad = \$3,106$$

Next you decide how banks C, D, and E compare with bank B. Bank C quotes 12% with quarterly compounding. This means that, at the end of each quarter, your deposit earns 3%, that is, one-fourth of 12%, on the current balance. Bank D quotes monthly compounding, which means that, at the end of each month, your deposit earns 1% on the current balance. We will discuss bank E later.

A deposit earning 12% compounded quarterly produces bigger bank balances than a deposit earning 12% compounded annually, because it earns interest on interest at the end of each quarter rather than at the end of each year. At the end of the first year, a bank balance of $1,000 grows to $1,125.51 for quarterly compounding, as compared to $1,120 for annual compounding. We used equation (5.2) to obtain this figure, letting M be the number of compounding periods per year—in this case, four—and letting i_M be the interest rate for each quarterly compounding period—in this, case 3% (12%/4).

$$F = P(1 + i_M)^M = \$1,000 (1 + 0.03)^4 = \$1,125.51$$

For monthly compounding, M is 12 and i_M is 1%. The sum F then equals

$$F = P(1 + i_M)^M = \$1,000(1 + 0.01)^{12} = \$1,126.82$$

The difference between quarterly and monthly compounding is small for one year. For ten years, however, it is not negligible. For quarterly compounding, the number of compounding periods for ten years is MN, or 40 (4×10). For monthly compounding, MN is 120 (12×10). The bank balances or future sums at that time are then

$$\text{Bank C: } F = P(1 + i_M)^{MN} = \$1,000(1 + 0.03)^{40} \quad = \$3,262$$

$$\text{Bank D: } F = P(1 + i_M)^{MN} = \$1,000(1 + 0.01)^{120} = \$3,300$$

TABLE 5.1 Future Value F of Present Sum P

Bank	Frequency of Compounding	End of Year 1	End of Year 10
A	Simple (no compounding)	$1,120	$2,200
B	Annual	1,120	3,106
C	Quarterly	1,126	3,262
D	Monthly	1,127	3,300
E	Continuous	1,127	3,320

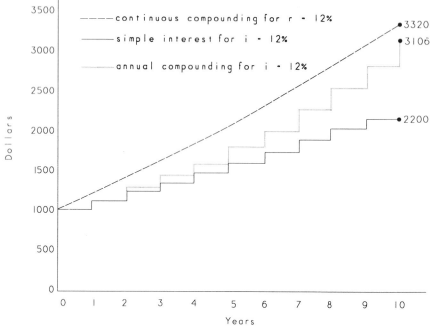

Figure 5.1. The "force" of compound interest.

You tentatively decide on bank D but not before checking what you could earn at bank E. This was given as $3,320 in ten years in Table 5.1. We leave the proof for a later section of this chapter.

The results for simple, annual, and continuous compounding are graphed in Figure 5.1, which shows the growth in the bank balance for the 10-year period for banks A, B, and E.

The conclusion we reach is that, as the frequency of compounding increases, so does the return for any given "nominal" interest rate. The word *nominal* brings us to the next section.

5.3   NOMINAL AND EFFECTIVE INTEREST RATES

We begin with definitions of "periodic," "nominal," and "effective" rates, followed by examples to help clarify the definitions.

The *periodic rate* is the rate for the specified compounding period. If compounding is done monthly, it is the rate for one month; if it is done daily, it is the rate for one day; and so on.

The *nominal rate* is the periodic rate multiplied by the number of compounding periods per year. It is thus an annual rate. If the periodic rate is 1.0% per month, the nominal rate is 12% per year.

The *effective rate* is the annual rate equivalent to the periodic rate compounded for the number of periods per year. For 1% per month, it is, as you will see, greater than 12% per year.

If you look back at Table 5.1, you will see that, for a deposit of $1,000 at 12%, you would have achieved one of the bank balances shown in the following table at the end of one year, depending on the number of compounding periods per year your bank was offering.

Compounding Frequency	Periods per Year	Future Sum, F
Annually	1	$1,120.00
Quarterly	4	1,125.51
Monthly	12	1,126.83
Continuous	—	1,127.50

COMMENT: In tabulations such as the one just given, we will generally avoid cents, since, throughout the selection process, we are dealing with estimates that are seldom, if ever, better than three significant figures. However, cents were shown to distinguish more clearly between monthly and continuous compounding.

A bank offering 12.7% interest compounded annually would produce the same bank balance at the end of each year as a bank offering 12% compounded monthly. Another way of saying this is that a nominal annual rate of 12% with monthly compounding is equivalent to an effective annual rate of 12.7%.

In what follows, we use the symbol r for the nominal annual rate and i for the effective annual rate. For annual compounding, r equals i. For compounding periods shorter than one year, r is less than i.

COMMENT: There are situations for which the compounding period is greater than one year and for which effective rates are therefore smaller than nominal rates. These are rare enough to justify not spending much time on them in this text. However, we do have one example of this in Chapter 8.

There are times when we need to convert nominal to effective rates, and vice versa. This is done with the help of two equations derived from equation (5.2).

For P equal to $1 and for an effective rate i, the future sum F at the end of one year is

$$F = P(1 + i) = (1 + i)$$

What nominal rate for any given compounding frequency will produce the same future sum? To answer this question, we use equation (5.2). The periodic interest rate i_M is the nominal rate, r, divided by the number of compounding periods per year, M. Therefore,

$$F = (1 + r/M)^M = (1 + i_M)^M$$

Solving for i gives

$$i = (1 + r/M)^M - 1 = (1 + i_M)^M - 1 \qquad (5.3)$$

and solving for r/M or i_M gives

$$r/M = i_M = (1 + i)^{1/M} - 1 \qquad (5.4)$$

To obtain r, we multiply i_M by M.

It is obviously important to recognize the difference between nominal and effective rates where business practices rely on this difference. Bond interest is paid semiannually. The effective rate is, by equation (5.3), higher than the nominal rate. Thus, a 12% bond paying 6% every six months produces a return of 12.35% $[(1.06)^2 - 1]$. Mortgage rates are quoted as nominal rates. The effective interest rate on a 12% mortgage amortized monthly is, as we just saw, 12.7%. Credit cards specify a monthly interest rate of, say, 1.5%. The nominal rate is 12 times this figure, or 18%. The effective rate is close to 20%. Banks in their advertisements usually quote two rates—the nominal and the effective—although, unfortunately, they do not use this terminology.

> *COMMENT:* If an investor is asked what rate of return, that is, what MARR, should be applied in an economic analysis and if he or she then answers 15%, we assume without further questioning and quite correctly that this is an effective annual rate.

Several examples on nominal, effective, and periodic interest rates follow. Examples on continuous compounding, including one on bank advertisements, are included in the next section of this chapter.

Example 5.2   Credit Cards   You notice that your credit card bill says that you are being charged 1.5% per month on the unpaid balance. What are the nominal and effective rates? The periodic rate, i_M, is 1.5%, and the number of compounding periods, M, is 12. Therefore, the nominal rate, r, is

$$r = i_M M = 1.5\% \times 12 = 18.0\%$$

The effective rate, i, is obtained from equation (5.3):

$$i = (1 + r/M)^M - 1 = (1.015)^{12} - 1 = 19.56\% \text{ /year}$$

The next example resembles Example 5.1. However, a little repetition in a subject as important as this one is healthy and does more good than harm, provided, of course, you follow through on checking each step in the computations.

Example 5.3   The Force of Compound Interest   As church treasurer, you are concerned about receiving the most from endowment funds. Since your financial objectives stress interest income, you have examined the interest rates of several banks and savings institutions.

The following table summarizes your findings.

Compounding Period	M	Interest rates, %		
		r	r/M	i
Annual	1	10.00	10.00	10.00
Semiannual	2	10.00	5.00	10.25
Quarterly	4	10.00	2.50	10.38
Monthly	12	10.00	0.833	10.47
Daily	360/365[a]	10.00	0.0277	10.51
Continuous	∞	10.00	0	10.52

[a]Sometimes 360 days are used, and sometimes 365 days are used. You will get the same answer for i to seven significant figures.

You knew that the effective rates would be higher than the nominal rates, but you had not realized that the largest increase would be from annual to semiannual (10% to 10.25%), and the next largest from semiannual to quarterly (10.25% to 10.38%). Furthermore, you had not realized that effective rates for monthly, daily, and continuous compounding would all be about the same and, in fact, would be the same—10.5%—if the results shown above were only carried to three significant figures.

You decide to work with the banks offering monthly, daily, or continuous compounding and then make a selection based on other factors that should also influence your decision, for example, which bank president is a member of the congregation and could be of help in securing a mortgage on a proposed church expansion.

COMMENT: We introduce the nonquantifiable factor—membership in the congregation—to remind you of the importance of nonmonetary consequences or attributes in decision making. In Chapter 1, we mentioned that monetary consequences are usually handled first but that, once this part of an analysis is completed, the nonmonetary are taken into account.

The previous calculations were based on equation (5.3). The substitutions for annual, semiannual, and quarterly compounding are shown in the following tabulation:

| | Formula | |
Compounding Period	$(1 + r/M)^M - 1$	Effective Rate, %
Annual	$(1 + 0.10) - 1$	10.00
Semiannual	$(1 + 0.05)^2 - 1$	10.25
Quarterly	$(1 + 0.025)^4 - 1$	10.38

We leave it to you to check the arithmetic and to do the same for monthly and daily compounding. Continuous compounding is covered in the next section.

5.4 CONTINUOUS COMPOUNDING

Annual, quarterly, monthly, and daily compounding are examples of discrete compounding for which the number of compounding periods per year is finite. With continuous compounding, we go "the limit" and let the compounding frequency be infinite. In other words, continuous compounding is an extension of discrete compounding for which the number of compounding periods per year is infinite and the time span of each period is therefore infinitesimal. Continuous compounding will produce effective interest rates close to discrete monthly and daily compounding. Why then do we bother with continuous compounding?

Continuous compounding is in common use today because it is no more difficult and, in some respects, simpler to apply than discrete compounding. Formulas for continuous compounding are derived directly from equation (5.3) by letting M, the number of compounding periods per year, approach infinity. The derivation is given in Appendix 5A, to which you should now turn. The two equations developed there are ones that we will use throughout the text to convert the nominal rate for continuous compounding to its effective discrete counterpart, and vice versa.

$$i = e^r - 1 \tag{5.5}$$

and

$$r = ln(1 + i) \tag{5.6}$$

For an application of these formulas, we turn back to Table 5.1 to check the value of \$3,320. For a nominal rate of 12% compounded continuously, the effective rate is

$$i = e^r - 1 = e^{0.12} - 1 = 1.1275 - 1 = 0.1275$$

For an effective rate of 12.75%, a sum P of \$1,000 will, in ten years, grow to a future sum F of \$3,320. You should check this figure by using equation (5.2).

Values of e^r are easily obtained from many hand calculators. You should have no problem showing that, for a nominal rate of 10%, the effective rate is 10.52%.

As mentioned, banks today quote two rates. Example 5.4 gives typical nomenclature used in their offerings.

Example 5.4 Bank Rates For savings accounts and certificates of deposit (CDs), banks state both a nominal and an effective rate, although they generally do not use these terms. The nominal rate is called the "current yield," or the "annual rate," or simply "today's rate." The effective rate is called the "effective yield" or the "annual yield." Consider the following quotations on 3-, 6-, and 12-month CDs.

	Today's Rates, %	Annual Yields, %
3-month	9.00	9.42
6-month	9.50	9.96
12-month	10.25	10.79

For a nominal rate of 9.00% compounded continuously, equation (5.5) gives an effective rate of 9.42%, as shown below:

$$i = e^r - 1 = e^{0.090} - 1 = 1.0942 - 1 = 9.42\%$$

Similar computations for 6-month and 12-month CDs should be carried out by you.

5.5 COMPOUNDING AND DISCOUNTING

We compound to find out what a single present sum, P, earning a rate of return, i, would be worth (i.e., would be equivalent to) at the end of a number of years (or periods), N. This future sum, F, is the future worth or future value of P.

We discount to find out what sum P would have to be set aside today to produce a given future sum F at the end of year N if invested at a rate of return i. This present sum P is called the present value or present worth of F.

The single-sum compounding formula is equation (5.2). It is called "single sum" because, with this formula, only one cash flow is compounded. The single-sum present worth or discounting formula is equation (5.2) rearranged as follows:

$$P = F(1 + i)^{-N} \qquad (5.7)$$

The ratio of F to P is called the "compound amount factor" and that of P to F, the "present worth factor." The first equals $(1 + i)^N$ and the second equals $(1 + i)^{-N}$. Each is the reciprocal of the other. Values of these factors

LIFE CYCLE

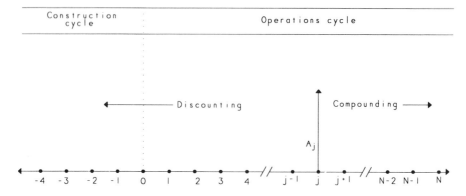

- To determine the equivalent value of a single sum at any location to the left of A_j, use the discount factor $(1+i)^{-N}$, where N is the number of periods between A_j and the new location, and i is the rate of return.

- To determine the equivalent value of a single sum at any point to the right of A_j, use the compound factor $(1+i)^{N}$, where N is the number of periods between A_j and the new location.

Figure 5.2. Compounding and discounting.

for interest rates varying from 1/2% to 50% can be found in Appendix B at the end of the text.

An example on discounting that complements Example 5.1 on compounding follows.

Example 5.5 Discounting Suppose you want a balance of $3,000 at the end of 10 years in one of the banks you examined in Example 5.1. What sum would you have to deposit today to withdraw $3,000 at EOY 10? Common sense tells you that you would have to make the largest deposit in bank A and the smallest in bank E. For a nominal rate of return of 12%, the sums that should be deposited today are given in Table 5.2.

For bank A, the result shown was derived from equation (5.1),

$$P = F/(1 + iN) = \$3,000/(1 + 0.12 \times 10) = \$1,363$$

TABLE 5.2 Present Value P of Future Sum F of $3,000 at EOY 10

Bank	Frequency of Compounding	Effective Rate, %	Deposit P at End of Year Zero
A	Simple interest	12.00	$1,363
B	Annual	12.00	966
C	Quarterly	12.55	920
D	Monthly	12.68	909
E	Continuous	12.75	904

For bank E, using equation (5.7), we get

$$P = F/(1 + i)^N = \$3{,}000/(1 + 0.1275)^{10} = \$904$$

You should have no trouble in verifying the present values for annual, quarterly, and monthly compounding.

In the four examples that follow (Examples 5.6–5.9), we use the single-sum compounding and discounting formulas, letting first F and then i, P, and N, respectively, be the unknowns. In each example, there is one cash inflow and one cash outflow. The cash flow diagram is Figure 3.3.

We also use these examples to introduce a new notation for rate-of-return factors and formulas that will be used throughout this text. For the compound amount factor $(1 + i)^N$, we substitute the notation $(F/P,i,N)$ and for the present worth factor $(1 + i)^{-N}$, $(P/F,i,N)$. Thus, instead of writing

$$F = P(1 + i)^N \qquad \text{and} \qquad P = F(1 + i)^{-N}$$

we write

$$F = P(F/P,i,N) \qquad \text{and} \qquad P = F(P/F,i,N)$$

This notation serves as a convenient model for replacing the more cumbersome rate-of-return formulas derived in Chapter 6 for application to the cash flow patterns of Chapter 3.

Example 5.6 Lending   A creditor lends a sum P of $1,000 at an effective interest rate of 12% for five years, at which time the sum F, representing the accumulated interest and principal, must be repaid. The cash outflow is $1,000 now, and the inflow is the sum F five years from now. To get F, we substitute in equation (5.2)

$$F = P(1 + i)^N = P(F/P,i,N) = \$1{,}000(F/P,12,5)$$
$$= \$1{,}000 \times 1.762 = \$1{,}762$$

Here we have substituted the notation $(F/P,i,N)$ for $(1 + i)^N$ and $(F/P,12,5)$ for $(1 + 0.12)^5$. The multiplier 1.762 is obtained from the interest rate table in Appendix B at the end of the text for 12%, and N equals 5.

Example 5.7 Investing   An investor purchases a piece of land for $10,000. At the end of five years, he sells it for $50,000. The cash outflow, P, is $10,000 now, and the inflow, F, is $50,000 five years from now. What was the rate of return on this investment? Here P, F, and N are known. The unknown is i. The compound amount factor is the ratio of F to P, which is 5 ($50,000/$10,000).

$$F/P = (1 + i)^N = (F/P,i,5) = 5$$

From Appendix B, the ratio of F/P for five years and a rate of return of 35% is $(1.35)^5$ or 4.8403; for five years and 40%, it is 5.378. Linear interpolation gives 37.9%. A hand calculator gives 38.0%. This answer is more accurate, since compounding and discounting are not linear relationships. However, the difference is not significant.

Example 5.8 Endowing You want to make a gift of $10,000 to your college three years from now, at which time you and your fellow alumni will celebrate your 25th reunion. CDs with three-year terms are being offered at 9.5%. The cash outflow now is P. The inflow, F, to you three years from now is $10,000. How big a CD would you have to purchase? The knowns are F, i, and N. The unknown is P. Substituting in equation (5.7), we get

$$P = F(P/F,i,N) = 10,000(P/F,9.5,3)$$

$$= \$10,000(1 + 0.095)^{-3} = \$10,000 \times 0.7617$$

$$= \$7,617$$

In this example, we have substituted the notation $(P/F,i,N)$ for the present worth factor $(1 + i)^{-N}$. To obtain this factor for an interest rate of 9.5%, we can interpolate between 9% and 10% using the tables in Appendix B. However, in this instance, we chose to compute the factor directly with a hand calculator.

Example 5.9 Doubling Your Money How long will it take to double your money for any given interest rate, i? The unknown is N. The ratio of F/P is 2. You have been told that dividing the interest rate expressed as a percentage into 74 (some texts use 70 and others 72) gives you a good approximation. You start with

$$F/P = 2 = (1 + i)^N$$

and then take the logarithm of both sides and rearrange the terms to solve for N:

$$N = \ln 2/\ln(1 + i) = 0.692 /\ln(1 + i)$$

Values of N for various values of i are tabulated below, together with a check on the "rule of 74."

$i(\%)$	$(1 + i)$	$\ln (1 + i)$	N,years	$N \times i(\%)$
1	1.01	0.00995	69.6	70
5	1.05	0.04879	14.2	71
10	1.10	0.09531	7.3	73
20	1.20	0.18232	3.8	76
30	1.30	0.26236	2.6	79

The approximation is not too bad. You can use it to dazzle your friends.

So much for rates of return and for the two single-sum formulas—one for compounding and one for discounting—that are presented in this chapter. The two formulas are the building blocks from which the rate-of-return formulas for the cash flow patterns of Chapter 3 are derived. Their derivations and their application to the capital project selection process are the leading topics of Chapter 6.

5.6 SUMMARY

To an investor or creditor, interest is compensation for giving up a certain present sum for an uncertain future sum. The greater the uncertainty is, the higher is the expected rate of return, that is, the MARR.

With rates of return, we need to distinguish between simple and compound interest, between periodic and annual rates, between nominal and effective rates, and between discrete and continuous compounding.

Compound interest earns interest on interest. Simple interest does not and plays little or no part in the selection process.

A periodic rate usually refers to the rate for a period shorter than one year, for example, one month or one quarter. If the period is one year, then the periodic rate and the annual rate are identical.

The nominal rate is an annual rate obtained by multiplying the periodic rate by the number of periods per year. It is not a true measure of return, since it does not include the return due to compounding more than once a year. The true measure is given by an annual rate referred to as the "effective rate."

For discrete compounding, the number of compounding periods per year is finite. For continuous compounding, the number is infinite. Most banks quote two rates of return: a nominal rate based on continuous compounding and the equivalent discrete, effective annual rate.

The rate of return that investors quote as their MARR, or minimum attractive rate of return, is, with few exceptions, an effective annual rate.

Two rate-of-return formulas were derived. One compounds a present single sum, P, into an equivalent future single sum, F. The other discounts a future single sum, F, into an equivalent present single sum, P. The two formulas are

$$\text{For compounding: } F = P(1 + i)^N = P(F/P,i,N)$$

$$\text{For discounting: } \quad P = F(1 + i)^{-N} = F(P/F,i,N)$$

$(F/P,i,N)$ is the single-sum compound amount factor, and $(P/F,i,N)$ is the single-sum present worth factor.

SUGGESTED READING

1. We have no reading suggestions other than the instruction manuals that accompany hand calculators for financial analysis. You will find such calculators more adaptable than the interest rate tables of Appendix B, since they avoid interpolating between rate-of-return factors and interest rates. Since hand calculators are constantly being improved, we suggest that you shop around before buying one.

PROBLEMS

Periodic Compounding

5-1   Go back to Example 5.1 and Table 5.1, and carry out similar calculations for semiannual, weekly, and daily compounding. For daily compounding, use both 360 and 365 days. You will find that the answers for weekly and daily compounding will not differ significantly from those for continuous compounding. For the capital project selection process, these differences are irrelevant.

5-2   Find the interest rate per month that corresponds to an effective annual rate of 16.5%.

5-3   Find the effective annual rate that corresponds to a rate of 0.5% per week.

5-4   The MARRs of investors are usually expressed as effective annual rates. What is the equivalent monthly rate for an MARR of 15%?

5-5   A sum of $1,000 is invested at the end of every quarter for 25 quarters. Interest on these funds is compounded at the rate of 1% per month.
 a) Find the equivalent rate per quarter.
 b) Find the nominal rate per year.
 c) Find the effective annual rate.
 d) Find the effective rate per year if interest were compounded continuously.

5-6   A $10,000 loan carries an interest rate of 2% per quarter, and the interest is compounded every quarter. What is (a) the nominal annual rate and (b) the effective annual rate?

5-7   Using equation (5.5), show that the single-sum compound amount equation [equation (5.2)] can be written as $F = P\,e^{rN}$ and the single-sum discount equation [equation (5.7)] as $P = F\,e^{-rN}$.

5-8   As N approaches infinity, what do the factors $(F/P,i,N)$ and $(P/F,i,N)$ approach? For interest rates of 1%, 5%, 10%, 15%, 20%, 25%, and 50%, what is the number of periods, N, that make the present value of the future sum, F, equal to or less than $0.0001\,F$? What does this tell you about the significance of future versus current flows in the capital project selection process?

5-9 For the following cash flow tabulation, find the value of X that makes the present value of the negative cash flow streams equal to the positive cash flow of $800 at EOY 0. The MARR is 15%.

EOY	Cash Flow
0	$800
1	− 100
2	− 150
3	− 200
4	X

5-10 Consider the following cash flow pattern:

EOY	Cash Flow
0	− $10,000
1	5,000
2	5,000
3	5,000

Using equation (5.7) and the interest rate tables in Appendix B, calculate the present worth for an MARR of (a) 15% and (b) 25%. Do the results indicate that there is some MARR that makes the present worth of the above cash flow pattern zero?

5-11 A person deposits $3,000 in a savings and loan institution that is advertising an annual interest rate of 6.2%, compounded monthly. What is the periodic rate and the effective annual rate? How much money will accumulate in the account at the end of two years?

5-12 A recent graduate is planning on investing $1,000 in a CD at 10% per year, compounded monthly. How much money will she have when she cashes in the CD after five years? How much money would she have if the interest were compounded quarterly?

5-13 You have just computed the present value of a cash flow pattern for a potential investor. He now asks for the future value. You can get it in two ways. What are they, and in which way would you proceed?

5-14 An investor purchased a painting by a local artist for $2,000. She sold it ten years later for $5,000. What was her rate of return?

5-15 A junior in college is planning ahead for a car when he graduates two years from now. He estimates that he will need $3,000 to make a 20% down payment. How much money should he deposit today in his savings account if his bank offers an effective annual interest rate of 9%?

5-16   An investor has requested that her investment counselor set up a trust fund that would be worth at least $100,000 in 15 years. If the investment counselor is able to invest funds at an effective annual rate of 10%, what amount is required to set up the fund?

5-17   How many years will be required for a sum of money to triple if the annual interest rate is 10%?

5-18   You have received an investment brochure that boldly proclaims that you can triple your money in six years. After reading the fine print, you discover that the investment instruments are currently earning between 12% and 15% annually. Will you triple your money in six years? What if the interest rate jumped up to 20%? What if the interest rate fell to 1%? Is there a general rule like the "rule of 74" for doubling your money that you can deduce?

5-19   Explain how the present value of any diagram with future cash flows—no matter how complicated and no matter how far it strays from any of the cash flow diagrams presented in Chapter 3—can be computed using equation (5.7).

APPENDIX 5A
CONTINUOUS COMPOUNDING

The formula for continuous compounding is derived from equation (5.3).

$$i = (1 + r/M)^M - 1 \qquad (5.3)$$

Since r/M equals $1/(M/r)$ and M equals Mr/r, we can, with the help of a little algebra, rearrange this formula as follows:

$$i = \{[1 + 1/(M/r)]^{M/r}\}^r - 1$$

As M/r approaches infinity, that is, as M gets larger and larger, the term inside the braces approaches e, the base of the natural system of logarithms. It follows that

$$i = e^r - 1 \quad \text{and} \quad r = \ln(1 + i)$$

The mathematician Leonard Euler (1707–1783) named e many years ago when he proved that $(1 + 1/x)^x$ approaches e as x approaches infinity. In the preceding derivation, x is M/r.

──6
EQUIVALENCE RELATIONSHIPS

6.1 INTRODUCTION

It's time to say more about equivalence. We used this term several times in talking about the equivalence of present and future cash flows. For a more complete understanding, consider the following.

You have a choice of one of two items—A or B. If you are indifferent to one or the other, that is, if you would as soon have A as B, we say that A and B are equivalent. If you are indifferent to accepting a dollar now or a greater sum one year from now or a still greater sum N years from now, we say that the dollar now and each of its two future values are equivalent to each other.

The notion of equivalence is a personal one. Present and future values are related through the minimum rate of return you will accept, that is, by your MARR. Under similar circumstances, your MARR may be different from someone else's. If you have a "risk prone" personality, you will accept a lower MARR for a given risk (or you will assess a given risk as less risky) than if you had a "risk neutral" or "risk adverse" personality.

The concept of equivalence will be with us throughout this text as we convert the cash flow patterns of Chapter 3 into single-sum equivalents or into equivalent uniform series. However, there are occasions when we cannot arrange cash flows into a convenient pattern. When this happens, it is well to remember that, no matter how complicated the cash flow diagram is, no matter how many cash inflows and outflows there are, and no matter how these differ in magnitude from one another, each cash flow stream can be considered separately and brought to a selected point on the time-value line with the two single-sum factors derived in Chapter 5.

6.2 EQUIVALENCE

In Chapter 3, cash flow patterns were illustrated for uniform series (annuities), arithmetic gradients, and geometric gradients. In this chapter, rate-of-return formulas and factors for these patterns will be derived from the formulas for compounding and discounting single cash flow streams. We begin with an investment opportunity for which the cash flow pattern is a combination of a single sum and a uniform series.

Example 6.1 Equivalence A capital investment opportunity is under review. The estimated first cash outflow of P_0 at EOY 0 is $10,000. The estimated net cash inflows (cash receipts less disbursements) at EOY 1, EOY 2, and EOY 3 are an ordinary annuity (uniform series) of $5,000 per year for three years, payable at the end of each year. There is no salvage value. The investors want a return of at least 15% (their MARR).

Figure 6.1A is the cash flow diagram. The present worth or present value P_A (the two terms are synonomous) of the uniform series using equation (5.7) and the rate of return tables in Appendix B is

$$P_A = A[(P/F,i,1) + (P/F,i,2) + (P/F,i,3)]$$
$$= A[(P/F,15,1) + (P/F,15,2) + (P/F,15,3)]$$
$$= \$5,000(0.8696 + 0.7561 + 0.6575) = \$5,000 \times 2.2832$$
$$= \$11,416$$

The net present value (NPV) or net present worth (NPW) of the cash flow pattern of Figure 6.1 is therefore

$$NPV = P_A - P_0$$
$$= \$11,416 - \$10,000 = \$1,416$$

COMMENT: The sum of the above three present worth factors, that is, of $(P/F,15,1)$, $(P/F,15,2)$, and $(P/F,15,3)$ is 2.2832. You will soon see that this is the (P/A) factor for converting a uniform series, A, to its present worth, P. Looking ahead, go to Appendix B and locate the (P/A) factor for 15% and three years. You will find that $(P/A,15,3)$ equals 2.2832. The present worth of the three $5,000 cash flows is then easily obtained by just multiplying $5,000 by this factor. Thus,

$$P_A = A(P/A,i,N) = A(P/A,15,3) = \$5,000 \ (2.2832)$$
$$= \$11,416$$

If this comment eludes you now, come back to it after you have reviewed Appendix 6A.

EQUIVALENT CASH FLOW DIAGRAMS FOR i = 15%

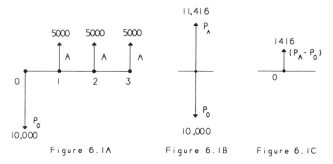

Figure 6.1A   Figure 6.1B   Figure 6.1C

EQUIVALENT CASH FLOW DIAGRAMS FOR i = 23.4%

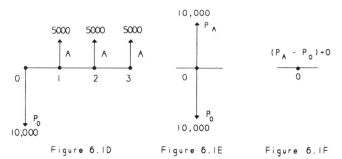

Figure 6.1D   Figure 6.1E   Figure 6.1F

Figure 6.1. Equivalence.

Since P_A is equivalent to the three \$5,000 cash flow streams for an MARR of 15%, Figure 6.1B is equivalent to Figure 6.1A. However, we can replace the two arrows in Figure 6.1B with their difference, which is \$1,416, as shown in Figure 6.1C. The three representations are equivalent, since the present value of any of the three diagrams for a rate of return of 15% is \$1,416.

It follows that a present sum of \$11,416 is equivalent to three end-of-year sums of \$5,000, since the three future sums have a present value of \$11,416.

Throughout this text, we will frequently compare the present worth (PW) of the cash inflow streams with the PW of the cash outflow streams, as we did in the preceding example. If the difference between PW_{in}, the present value of the arrows pointing upward, and PW_{out}, the present value of the arrows pointing downward, is positive, the investment will earn a higher rate of return than the MARR.

To see this more clearly, turn again to the interest rate tables of Appendix B. The higher the interest rate is, the smaller the discount factor, P/F, for any given N is. Thus, future sums of \$5,000 that are due in one, two, and three years, respectively, have the following present values for rates of return of 15%, 20%, and 25%.

Present Value of $5,000

i, %	Due in One Year		Due in Two Years		Due in Three Years	
	Factor	Sum	Factor	Sum	Factor	Sum
15	0.8696	$4,348	0.7561	$3,781	0.6575	$3,287
20	0.8333	4,167	0.6944	3,472	0.5787	2,894
25	0.8000	4,000	0.6400	3,200	0.5120	2,560

Obviously, if the difference between PW_{in} and PW_{out} is positive for any given MARR, there is some rate of return greater than the MARR for which PW_{in} will exactly equal PW_{out}. This rate of return is called the internal rate of return (IRR). It can be obtained by trial and error using Appendix B, as in Example 6.2.

Example 6.2   Internal Rate of Return   Go back for a moment to Example 6.1, but this time compute P_A and NPV for 20% and 25%. The results are

For 20%: $P_A = \$5,000 \,(0.8333 + 0.6944 + 0.5787) = \$10,530$

$$NPV = \$10,530 - \$10,000 = \$530$$

For 25%: $P_A = \$5,000 \,(0.8000 + 0.6400 + 0.5120) = \$9,760$

$$NPV = \$9,760 - \$10,000 = \$-240$$

Somewhere between 20% and 25% is a rate of return for which the present value P_A equals $10,000 and the difference between P_A and P_0 (the NPV) is therefore zero. Interpolation yields an IRR of 23.4%. (You could have obtained this answer directly with a hand calculator, but it is also important for you to learn how to use the tables in Appendix B.)

The equivalent cash flow diagrams are Figures 6.1D, 6.1E, and 6.1F. All that remains in Figure 6.1F is a dot at EOY 0.

COMMENT: Rather than accept the findings in Example 6.2, you should check the computations to become familiar with Appendix B. Furthermore, you should substitute 23.4% for 15% in Example 6.1 to corroborate that, except for possible rounding errors, you will get a present worth of $10,000 for the three cash flows of $5,000.

6.3   MULTISUM FORMULAS

In Chapter 3, we introduced two types of cash flow—discrete and continuous—and, in Chapter 5, we introduced two types of compounding—discrete and continuous. This implies four sets of rate-of-return formulas, of which only three have any practical applications. These are

- Discrete cash flows with discrete compounding
- Discrete cash flows with continuous compounding
- Continuous cash flows with continuous compounding

The fourth set—continuous cash flows with discrete compounding—is not feasible.

The rate-of-return factors that we require for the capital project selection process are given in Tables 6.2, 6.3, and 6.4, using the notation in Table 6.1. The equations for each factor are derived in Appendix 6A. We suggest that you take the time to go through at least some of the derivations, even if it means reconstituting your high school algebra classes.

The cash flow patterns for which rate-of-return factors are shown in Table 6.2 include single sums, uniform series (annuities), arithmetic gradients, and geometric gradients. Many of the factors also appear in Tables 6.3 and 6.4

A brief description of the factors follows.

- Use present worth factors to obtain equivalent present values of

future single sums	$(P/F,i,N)$
annuities	$(P/A,i,N)$
arithmetic gradients	$(P/G,i,N)$
geometric gradients	$(P/A_1,i,g,N)$

- Use future worth factors to obtain equivalent future values of

present single sums	$(F/P,i,N)$
annuities	$(F/A,i,N)$
arithmetic gradients	$(F/G,i,N)$

- Use annuity factors to obtain equivalent uniform series of

present sums	$(A/P,i,N)$
future sums	$(A/F,i,N)$
arithmetic gradients	$(A/G,i,N)$

In Table 6.3, the nominal rate, r, replaces i, and, in Table 6.4, bars are placed over those cash flows that are continuous.

Don't let this list of factors overwhelm you. A look at Appendix B will show you some simple relationships among them. Take any table, say the one for 10%, and find the line for N equals 5. Note that the following pairs of factors are reciprocals:

P/F and F/P	0.6209 and 1.611
P/A and A/P	3.791 and 0.2638
F/A and A/F	6.105 and 0.1638

TABLE 6.1   Variables for Rate-of-Return Equations

Variable	Symbol	Units
Receipts and Disbursements		
Present value	P	Dollars
Future value	F	Dollars
Annuities	A	Dollars per period
Arithmetic gradient	G	Increase/decrease in dollars per period
Rates		
Effective rate	i	Percent or ratio
Nominal rate	r	Percent or ratio
Geometric (general)	g	Percent or ratio
Geometric (inflation)	f	Percent or ratio
Time Periods		
Years	N	—
Compounding periods per year	M	—

Note: Continuous cash flows are identified by bars, as shown in Figure 3.2.

Also note that A/P equals A/F plus i, a relationship that is often used to simplify cash flow analyses in which both of these factors would otherwise appear. Thus, for 10% and N equals 5,

$$(A/P,10,5) = (A/F,10,5) + 0.10$$
$$0.2638 = 0.1638 + 0.10$$

COMMENT: A little algebraic manipulation of the factor formulas in Table 6.2 will prove this relationship.

Next note that, as N approaches infinity,

P/F and A/F approach zero
A/P approaches the interest rate i
P/A and A/G approach $1/i$
P/G approaches $1/i^2$

You should confirm these approaches to infinity by noting what happens to the factors in Appendix B for any i as N grows larger and larger. You should also note that the approaches become more pronounced the higher the rate

**TABLE 6.2 Factors for Rate-of-Return Formulas
Discrete Cash Flows—Discrete Compounding**

Name of Factor	Factor Symbol	Functional Format	Factor Formula
Present Worth Factors for Discounting			
Single payment	P/F	$(P/F,i,N)$	$\dfrac{1}{(1 + i)^N}$
Uniform series (annuity)	P/A	$(P/A,i,N)$	$\dfrac{(1 + i)^N - 1}{i(1 + i)^N}$
Arithmetric gradient	P/G	$(P/G,i,N)$	$\dfrac{(1 + i)^N - 1}{i^2(1 + i)^N} - \dfrac{N}{i(1 + i)^N}$
Geometric gradient	P/A_1	$(P/A_1,i,g,N)$	$\dfrac{1 - [(1 + g)/(1 + i)]^N}{(i - g)}$
Future Worth Factors for Compounding			
Single payment	F/P	$(F/P,i,N)$	$(1 + i)^N$
Uniform series (annuity)	F/A	$(F/A,i,N)$	$\dfrac{(1 + i)^N - 1}{i}$
Arithmetic gradient	F/G	$(F/G,i,N)$	$\dfrac{(1 + i)^N - 1}{i^2} - \dfrac{N}{i}$
Annuity Factors for Uniform Series			
Capital recovery	A/P	$(A/P,i,N)$	$\dfrac{i(1 + i)^N}{(1 + i)^N - 1}$
Sinking fund	A/F	$(A/F,i,N)$	$\dfrac{i}{(1 + i)^N - 1}$
Arithmetic gradient	A/G	$(A/G,i,N)$	$\dfrac{1}{i} - \dfrac{N}{(1 + i)^N - 1}$

of return. Compare, for example, the number of years it takes the factor A/P to approach i for rates of 10%, 25%, and 50%. For long-lived capital projects—dams, tunnels, bridges, highways—it is often more convenient to assume infinite rather than finite lives, due to the simplicity of the preceding relationships for infinite time periods.

Lastly, note that the formulas for many of the factors can be derived by simply multiplying the formulas for two other factors together. Thus, if the formulas for P/G, P/F, and A/P are known, those for F/G and A/G can be obtained as follows:

$$F/G = (P/G)(F/P) \quad \text{and} \quad A/G = (P/G)(A/P)$$

A brief description of each of the factor tables follows.

**TABLE 6.3 Factors for Rate-of-Return Formulas
Discrete Cash Flows—Continuous Compounding**

Name of Factor	Factor Symbol	Functional Format	Factor Formula
Present Worth Factors for Discounting			
Single payment	P/F	$(P/F,r,N)$	e^{-rN}
Uniform series (annuity)	P/A	$(P/A,r,N)$	$\dfrac{1-e^{-rN}}{e^r-1}$
Future Worth Factors for Compounding			
Single payment	F/P	$(F/P,r,N)$	e^{rN}
Uniform series (annuity)	F/A	$(F/A,r,N)$	$\dfrac{e^{rN}-1}{e^r-1}$
Annuity Factors for Uniform Series			
Capital recovery	A/P	$(A/P,r,N)$	$\dfrac{e^r-1}{1-e^{-rN}}$
Sinking fund	A/F	$(A/F,r,N)$	$\dfrac{e^r-1}{e^{rN}-1}$
Arithmetic gradient	A/G	$(A/G,r,N)$	$\dfrac{1}{e^r-1}-\dfrac{N}{e^{rN}-1}$

6.3.1 Discrete Cash Flow and Discrete Compounding

In Table 6.2, as in Tables 6.3 and 6.4, each rate-of-return factor is identified by (1) its symbol (P/F, P/A, etc.), which, except for the geometric gradient, locates the factor in the interest rate tables of Appendix B; (2) its functional format [$(P/F,i,N)$, $(P/A,i,N)$, etc.]; and (3) the formula for its rate-of-return factor. For the geometric gradient, we use Appendix C instead of Appendix B.

The cash flow patterns with which these factors are used are given in Chapter 3.

DISCRETE CASH FLOW

P/F and F/P	Figure 3.3	Single sum
P/A and A/P	Figure 3.4	Uniform series
F/A and A/F	Figure 3.5	Uniform series
P/G, F/G, and A/G	Figure 3.6	Arithmetic gradient
P/A_1	Figure 3.7	Geometric series

CONTINUOUS CASH FLOW

| $P/\overline{F}$, $F/\overline{P}$ | Figure 3.8 | Single sum |
| $P/\overline{A}$ | Figure 3.8 | Uniform series |

In Chapter 3, the situations to which these factors apply were also briefly described.

The only factor that needs special comment at this time is the present worth factor for the geometric gradient, $(P/A_1,i,g,N)$. It includes not only the interest rate, i, but also the geometric gradient, g. The cash flow, A_1, is the flow at EOP 1. The equation for this factor, as given in Table 6.2, is valid whether or not the rate of return, i, exceeds the geometric gradient, g. However, we usually work with i greater than g, since the major application of the formula is with inflation and investors will insist that the MARR stay ahead of the inflation rate. Where inflation is the only geometric series, we replace the symbol g with f.

There are, however, many situations that can be represented by geometric series, for example, productivity gains, technological innovations, and reve-

TABLE 6.4   Factors for Rate-of-Return Formulas
Continuous Cash Flow—Continuous Compounding

Name of Factor	Factor Symbol	Functional Format	Factor Formula r Format	Factor Formula i Format
Present Worth Factors for Discounting				
Single payment	$P/\overline{F}$	$(P/\overline{F},r,N)$	$\dfrac{e^r - 1}{re^{rN}}$	$\dfrac{i}{ln(1 + i)}(1 + i)^{-N}$
Uniform series (annuity)	$P/\overline{A}$	$(P/\overline{A},r,N)$	$\dfrac{e^{rN} - 1}{re^{rN}}$	$\dfrac{i}{ln(1 + i)} \cdot \dfrac{(1 + i)^N - 1}{i(1 + i)^N}$
Future Worth Factors for Compounding				
Single payment	$F/\overline{P}$	$(F/\overline{P},r,N)$	$\dfrac{e^{rN}(e^r - 1)}{re^r}$	$\dfrac{i(1 + i)^N}{[ln(1 + i)](1 + i)}$
Uniform series (annuity)	$F/\overline{A}$	$(F/\overline{A},r,N)$	$\dfrac{e^{rN} - 1}{r}$	$\dfrac{i}{ln(1 + i)} \cdot \dfrac{(1 + i)^N - 1}{i}$
Annuity Factors for Uniform Series				
Capital recovery	$\overline{A}/P$	$(\overline{A}/P,r,N)$	$\dfrac{re^{rN}}{e^{rN} - 1}$	$\dfrac{ln(1 + i)}{i} \cdot \dfrac{i(1 + i)^N}{(1 + i)^N - 1}$
Sinking fund	$\overline{A}/F$	$(\overline{A}/F,r,N)$	$\dfrac{r}{e^{rN} - 1}$	$\dfrac{ln(1 + i)}{i} \cdot \dfrac{i}{(1 + i)^N - 1}$

nues and costs impacted by sales volume, independent of price level effects. Formulas for combining such gradients into one gradient and using equivalent interest rates (i_{eq}) are developed in a later chapter. The present worth factor for a given geometric series then becomes $(P/A_1,i_{eq},N)$.

6.3.2 Discrete Cash Flow and Continuous Compounding

We don't need the rate-of-return equations in Table 6.3 for continuous compounding with discrete cash flows. If we are given a rate of return r for continuous compounding, we can always convert it to its equivalent effective rate and use the formulas in Table 6.2. However, as a practitioner of engineering economy, you are expected to be familiar with the equations and factors in Table 6.3, and we will occasionally use them to show you how easy they are to apply.

6.3.3 Continuous Cash Flows

You will recall that for continuous compounding (not to be confused with continuous cash flow) effective rates did not differ substantially from those for monthly, weekly, and daily compounding. We will also find this to be the case with comparisons of discrete and continuous cash flows.

The six rate-of-return formulas for continuous cash flows in Table 6.4 are in two formats—the r format and the i format. The two formats are equivalent, and the first format can be converted to the second by substituting e^r for $(1 + i)$ and $ln(1 + i)$ for r [see equations (5.5) and 5.6)]. The derivations of the equations in Table 6.4 are given in Appendix 6A.

The relationship between rate-of-return formulas for discrete and continuous cash flows is a simple one, as shown:

Present Worth Factors

$$P/\overline{F} = \frac{i}{ln(1 + i)}\,(P/F) \qquad \text{and} \qquad P/\overline{A} = \frac{i}{ln(1 + i)}\,(P/A)$$

Future Worth Factors

$$F/\overline{P} = \frac{i}{ln(1 + i)(1 + i)}\,(F/P) \qquad \text{and} \qquad F/\overline{A} = \frac{i}{ln(1 + i)}\,(F/A)$$

Annual Worth Factors

$$\overline{A}/P = \frac{ln(1 + i)}{i}\,(A/P) \qquad \text{and} \qquad \overline{A}/F = \frac{ln(1 + i)}{i}\,(A/F)$$

Five of the six factors are related through the ratio $i/ln(1 + i)$ or its reciprocal. The exception is $F/\overline{P}$. $\overline{A}/P$ and $P/\overline{A}$ are reciprocals, as are $\overline{A}/F$ and $F/\overline{A}$. However, $P/\overline{F}$ and $F/\overline{P}$ are not.

Appendix D lists values of $i/ln(1 + i)$, $ln(1 + i)/i$, and $i/(1 + i)ln(1 + i)$ for all of the rate tables in Appendix B.

After this surfeit of rate of return factors, it is best to stop and see where we are by means of an example.

Example 6.3   Comparison of Rate-of-Return Factors   Consider an investment of $25,000, which produces a net cash flow of $5,000 annually for ten years. The salvage value is zero. The cash flow diagram is given in Figure 6.2. The MARR is 12%.

You have been asked to examine six alternatives for obtaining the present value of the ten annual cash flow streams.

Alternative	Description
1	$5,000 per year at an effective annual rate of 12%
2	$5,000 per year at a nominal annual rate of 11.33% with continuous compounding
3	$1,250 per quarter ($5,000 annually) for ten years at an effective rate of 12%
4	$417 per month ($5,000 annually) for ten years at an effective rate of 12%
5	$5,000 per year for ten years at an effective rate of 12%, using the *i*-format
6	$5,000 per year for ten years at an effective rate of 12%, using the *r*-format

We already know how to handle alternative 1; that is, we could get our answer by dealing with each of the ten annual cash streams separately, as we did in Example 6.1. However, at that time, the only rate of return factors with which we were familiar were those for single sums. We are now ready to apply the *P/A* factor to make a wholesale conversion of all ten streams. From Appendix B, for *N* equals 10 and *i* equals 12%, this factor equals 5.650. The present value of the ten streams

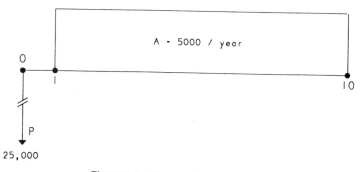

Figure 6.2. Diagram for Example 6.3.

is therefore

$$P_A = \$5,000 \ (P/A,i,N) = \$5,000 \ (P/A,12,10) = \$5,000 \times 5.650$$

$$= \$28,250$$

For alternative 2, we selected a nominal rate of 11.33% because this rate is equal to an effective rate of 12%, as shown below.

$$i = e^r - 1 = e^{0.1133} - 1 = 1.12 - 1 = 12\%$$

Furthermore, using the nominal rate gives us an opportunity to apply the rate-of-return factor for P/A found in Table 6.3.

$$(P/A,r,N) = \frac{1 - e^{-rN}}{e^r - 1} = \frac{1 - e^{-1.133}}{e^{0.1133} - 1} = 5.650$$

and

$$P_A = \$5,000 \times 5.650 = \$28,250$$

Alternatives 3 and 4 are a bit tricky. Note that the effective rate is given as 12%. However, the cash flows are not end-of-year. We therefore need the periodic rates for quarterly and monthly compounding. For quarterly compounding, i_M equals [see equation (5.4)]

$$i_M = (1 + i)^{1/M} - 1 = (1.12)^{0.25} - 1 = 1.0287 - 1 = 2.87\%$$

As shown, i_M is not one-fourth of 12% but, as we should have expected, somewhat less.

For quarterly net cash flows, M equals 4 and the number of compounding periods for ten years is 40. The present worth of the uniform series is then

$$P_A = \$1,250 \ (P/A,i_M,MN) = \$1,250 \ (P/A,2.87,40)$$

$$= \$1,250 \times 23.61 = \$29,510$$

The P/A factor of 23.61 for 2.87% is obtained from Appendix B by interpolating between 2.5% and 3% for N equals 40 or by using a hand calculator.

For monthly compounding,

$$i_M = (1 + i)^{1/12} - 1 = (1.12)^{0.08333} - 1 = 1.00949 - 1$$

$$= 0.949\%$$

For monthly cash flows of \$417 (\$5,000/12) for ten years (120 periods),

$$P_A = \$417(P/A,i_M,MN) = \$417 \ (P/A,0.949,120)$$

$$= \$417 \times 71.50 = \$29,790$$

Here the P/A factor lies between 0.75% and 1% and can be obtained by inter-polation from the tables in Appendix B or, as mentioned earlier, with a hand calculator.

Alternatives 5 and 6 are for continuous cash flow. For the i-format, we obtain the equivalent present value by multiplying P/A from alternative 1 by the ratio $i/ln(1 + i)$ found in Appendix D:

$$P_A = \$28{,}250\ (i/ln(1 + i)) = \$28{,}250 \times 1.059 = \$29{,}910$$

For alternative 6, using the r-format, the P/A factor is given by

$$(P/\overline{A}) = \frac{e^{rN} - 1}{re^{rN}} = \frac{e^{1.13} - 1}{0.113\ e^{1.13}} = \frac{2.106}{0.3526} = 5.983$$

and

$$P_A = \$5{,}000 \times 5.983 = \$29{,}910$$

The equivalent present values for the six alternatives are compared below:

Alternatives	Present Value
1 and 2	28,250
3	29,510
4	29,770
5 and 6	29,910

Note that the present value is highest for continuous cash flow. Why? The cash streams flow in earlier. Note, too, that the difference in present value between discrete cash flows compounded annually and continuous cash flows compounded continuously is about 6%. However, the difference between monthly discrete cash flows and continuous cash flows is less than 0.5%.

In working with effective annual rates, as we usually do, the continuous cash flow convention is, with the help of the factors in Appendix D, easier to apply than converting effective rates to periodic monthly or weekly rates and applying the discrete cash flow convention.

An important lesson to be learned from this example is illustrated by alternatives 3 and 4. A common mistake is simply to divide the effective rate of 12% by 4 to get a periodic rate of 3% for quarterly compounding and by 12 to get a periodic rate of 1% for monthly compounding. Both of these periodic rates will give you an effective rate higher than 12%, as we know from Example 5.1 on simple and compound interest.

This concludes our discussion of the rate-of-return factors that we will be applying throughout the text. We suggest once more that you review their derivations in Appendix 6A.

6.4   MANIPULATING RATE-OF-RETURN FACTORS

With few exceptions, we now have all of the formulas and factors that we need for the economic analyses carried out in this text. Unfortunately, we cannot do as much with them as we would like until we learn how to apply them to situations in which the formula time zone (FTZ) to which the rate factors are rigidly bound differ from the problem time zone (PTZ) on which our solutions ultimately depend. If the two time zones coincide, fine; if not, we have to take the steps outlined below.

The formula time zones (FTZs) on which the rate-of-return formulas are based are defined below:

- For uniform series, the formulas are based on the first cash flow, A, at the end of period 1 and the last cash flow at the end of period N.
- For arithmetic gradients, the formulas are based on the first cash flow, G, at the end of period 2 and the last cash flow $(N - 1)G$ at the end of period N.
- For geometric gradients, the formulas are based on the first cash flow, A_1, at the end of period 1 and the last cash flow, A_N, at the end of period N.

If the PTZ does not fall on the FTZ, we proceed as in Example 6.4.

Example 6.4   Formula Time Zones and Problem Time Zones   Consider Figure 6.3A, which is identical with Figure 6.1A, except that the first cash flow A is at the end of year 3. The time-value line shows the locations of zero for both the FTZ and the PTZ. The P/A factor gives the present value at EOY 0 for the FTZ, which is at EOY 2 for the PTZ. This value was $11,416 (see Example 6.1). To get the present value at EOY 0 of the PTZ, we have to move $11,416 two years to the left; that is, we have to discount it using the factor $(P/F,i,2)$. Thus,

$$P_A = A \ (P/A,i,N)(P/F,i,N)$$

$$= \$5,000 \ (P/A,15,3)(P/F,15,2)$$

$$= \$5,000 \times 2.28320 \times 0.7561 = \$11,416 \times 0.7561$$

$$= \$8,630$$

For this investment, the net present value $(P_{in} - P_{out})$ is a negative $1,370 ($8,630 − $10,000), indicating that the investment does not satisfy the MARR of 15%.

Assume now that the first cash flow A occurs as shown on Figure 6.3B, which you will recognize as an annuity due (see Chapter 3). The present value at zero on the FTZ is $11,416. To get the present value at zero on the PTZ, we move one year to the right. Therefore,

$$P_A = \$11,416 \ (F/P,i,N)$$

$$= \$11,416 \ (F/P,15,1)$$

$$= \$11,416 \times 1.150 = \$13,120$$

The same procedure is followed for arithmetic and geometric gradients. For arithmetic gradients, the first cash flow on the FTZ is at EOP 2 (see Figure 3.6). Consider Figure 6.4A, which shows an arithmetic gradient of $100 per year, with the first cash flow at EOY 1. The present value of this gradient at EOY 0 on the FTZ is, for an MARR of 15%,

$$P = G \ (P/G,i,N)$$
$$= \$100 \ (P/G,15,5) = \$100 \times 5.775$$
$$= \$578$$

However, since the PTZ is one time period to the left of the FTZ, we move to the right one year, as shown below, for the present value on the PTZ:

$$P = \$578 \ (F/P,15,1) = \$578 \times 1.15$$
$$= \$665$$

Another approach to reconciling PTZs and FTZs, is illustrated below. It consists of replacing one cash flow diagram with another that is more amenable to the application of the rate factors. Gradients, for example, can be negative as well as positive. In Figure 6.4B, the gradient is −$100. This diagram can be replaced with that of Figure 6.4C, which shows an annuity above the time-value line and a gradient below it. Figures 6.4B and 6.4C are equivalent. You can see this by noting that the net cash flows for each year are identical.

6.3A First payment after EOY 1 on PTZ

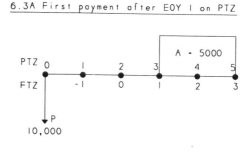

6.3B First payment before EOY 1 on PTZ

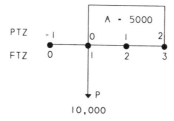

Figure 6.3. Manipulating annuities.

6.4A First payment on EOY I on PTZ

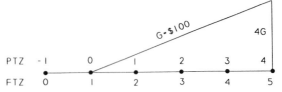

6.4B Negative gradient

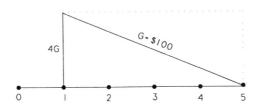

6.4C Equivalent diagram for Figure 6.4B

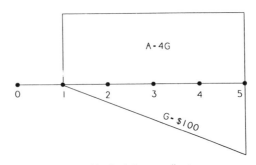

Figure 6.4. Manipulating gradients.

For the annuity, A equals $(N - 1)G$, which in this instance is $4G$ or \$400. At an i of 15%, its present worth is

$$PW_{in} = A\ (P/A,i,N)$$
$$= \$400\ (P/A,15,5)$$
$$= \$400 \times 3.352 = \$1,340$$

The present worth of the gradient is

$$PW_{out} = G\ (P/G,i,N)$$
$$= \$100\ (P/G,15,5)$$
$$= \$100 \times 5.775 = \$578$$

The net present value of the cash flow pattern of Figure 6.4B and its equivalent, Figure 6.4C, is therefore the difference, which is $762.

At times we also need to consider changes in the rate of return during the life cycle of a project. In 1981, the prime rate reached 20%; that is, prime corporate debtors had to pay 20% on borrowed funds. Since the prime rate is a bellwether for all rates of return, including the rates investors will demand, comparable MARRs were in the range of 30–40% and higher. At these rates, the present values of cash flows ten or more years in the future are close to worthless, as you can verify by checking the *P/F* factors in Appendix B.

If an investor were convinced that interest rates would not remain as high (or as low) as their current value, the time-value analysis would proceed as in Example 6.5.

Example 6.5 Rate-of-Return Zones The cash flow diagram of Figure 6.5 shows ten cash flow streams in three rate zones. Suppose you are asked to find the equivalent value of all streams at EOY 3.

You first compound all the cash flows in zone 1 at a rate of 20% and bring them to EOY 0. You then move them to the right another three years, that is, up to EOY 3, using a rate of 12%.

Similarly, you discount all the cash flows in zone 3 at a rate of 8%, bringing them to EOY 5. You then discount them further at 12% to bring them to EOY 3.

The cash flow streams in zone 2 are discounted or compounded at 12%, depending on whether they are to the right or the left of EOY 3.

The sum of the equivalent values of all of the cash flow streams at EOY 3 is their net present value. You should have no trouble with the calculations. The answer is $3,177.

This concludes our presentation of rate-of-return factors. In the next chapter, we begin our study of the five figures of merit that are commonly used to judge and rank the monetary attributes of capital investment opportunities.

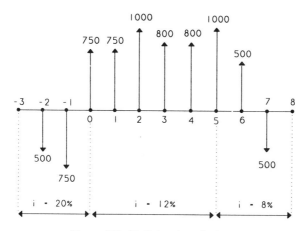

Figure 6.5. Multiple rates of return.

You already have some familiarity with two of these—the present value or present worth and the future value or future worth.

6.5   SUMMARY

You now know the following about any cash flow pattern, no matter how complex.

- The pattern can be converted into an equivalent single sum at the end of any given period of time
- The most common conversion is that which reduces a cash flow pattern to a single sum at EOP 0. This sum is referred to as the present value or present worth of the pattern.
- Another common conversion is that which reduces a cash flow pattern to a single sum at EOP N. This sum is referred to as the future value or future worth of the pattern.

COMMENT: Still another common conversion, which will be fully discussed in Chapter 7, is to reduce a cash flow pattern to a uniform series that runs from EOP 1 to EOP N. This is the annual worth.

The conversions are carried out by compounding and discounting cash flow streams using the MARR. Without such conversions, it would not be possible to compare investment opportunities whose cash flow patterns differ. With the conversions, all of the opportunities under review are reduced to a common denominator with which direct comparisons can be made.

Fortunately, many investment opportunities can be represented by cash flow patterns similar to those discussed in Chapter 3. For these, the conversion to a single present or future sum (or to a uniform series) is made with the aid of rate-of-return formulas and factors for discrete and continuous compounding and for discrete and continuous cash flows. Values of the factors are obtained from the appendixes at the end of this text or, often more convenient, directly with hand calculators programmed for business and financial analysis.

In applying the formulas, you must distinguish the PTZ from the FTZ if the two time zones are not coincident. The conversions are made by first applying the formulas based on the FTZ and then compounding or discounting the answers obtained to accommodate the PTZ.

SUGGESTED READINGS

1. Courtland A. Collier and William B. Ledbetter, *Engineering Economic and Cost Analysis*, 2nd ed. (New York: Harper & Row, 1988). Chapter 21 on double arith-

metic and geometric gradients adds several rate-of-return factors to those discussed in this chapter. These factors are convenient for economy studies involving double gradients. However, it doesn't take much longer to apply the formulas in Table 6.2.

2. Chan S. Park and Gunter P. Sharp-Bette, *Advanced Engineering Economics*. (New York: John Wiley & Sons, 1990). This book carries engineering economics into more advanced mathematics than conventional texts. It discusses the application of Z-transforms to discrete cash flow diagrams and Laplace transforms to continuous cash flow diagrams. We suggest that you imbibe our text, which has more mathematics than most, before treading into these waters, unless your hobby is advanced mathematics.

PROBLEMS

Using Appendices B, C, and D

6-1 Open this text to Appendix B, which contains discrete tables for rates of return of 0.50%–50%. For two or three of the tables (your pick), confirm the relationships discussed in this chapter, that is,

a) the reciprocity of F/P and P/F, of A/P and P/A, and of A/F and F/A

b) the fact that A/P equals A/F plus the rate of return.

6-2 Next, notice what happens to the factors in Appendix B as N gets larger and larger. For a rate of return of 10%, what are the values of F/P, P/F, A/P, P/A, F/A, A/F, and A/G for

a) N equal to 100 years?

b) N equal to infinity?

6-3 How would you obtain the present worth gradient factor, P/G, and future worth gradient factor, F/G, from the factors in Appendix B? Do so for $i = 12\%$ and $N = 5$ years.

6-4 For continuous cash flow computations, you need both Appendix B and Appendix D. Use both appendixes to compare the values of the following factors for discrete and continuous cash flow, using i equal to 8% and N equal to 10 years:

a) F/P and $F/\overline{P}$ **d)** P/F and $P/\overline{F}$

b) P/A and $P/\overline{A}$ **e)** A/P and $A/\overline{P}$

c) F/A and $F/\overline{A}$ **f)** A/F and $A/\overline{F}$

6-5 Notice that the A/G factor in Appendix B for N equals 1 is zero, no matter what the rate of return. Can you explain this?

6-6 Appendix C gives you the present worth factors for geometric series. Find the value of $(P/A_1,i,g,N)$ for the following factors:

a) $(P/A_1,5,2,5)$ e) $(P/A_1,10,2,20)$

b) $(P/A_1,5,5,5)$ f) $(P/A_1,15,3,10)$

c) $(P/A_1,10,5,10)$ g) $(P/A_1,15,15,15)$

d) $(P/A_1,10,5,\infty)$ h) $(P/A_1,15,5,\infty)$

6-7 Why do we have tables for rates of return as low as 0.50% in Appendix B?

Using Factor Formulas

COMMENT: The tables in Appendix B cover a wide span of interest rates. However, suitable tables are not always available. You will then have either to interpolate between two of the tables in Appendix B or use a hand calculator programmed for most of the above factor formulas, or go to the formulas themselves. Here we assume that you will do the latter in Problems 6-8 to 6-11 to become familiar with Tables 6.2, 6.3, and 6.4.

6-8 A municipality specifies that, in discounting cash flows, a rate of 8.5% should be used. Compute the following factors for this rate. (*Hint:* Notice that in Table 6.2 the formulas all contain $(1 + i)^N$. Therefore, by calculating F/P first, you have a good start on all the others.)

a) $(F/P,8.5,10)$ d) $(A/P,8.5,10)$

b) $(P/A,8.5,10)$ e) $(A/F,8.5,10)$

c) $(P/\overline{A},8.5,10)$

6-9 You are given $(A/P,11,10) = 0.1698$. What is the value of $(A/F,11,10)$? Extract the value of $(1 + i)^N$ from the factor formula for A/F and then calculate the values of P/F, P/A, F/A, and A/F. What is the value of $(P/A,i,\infty)$ and $(A/P,i,\infty)$?

6-10 What nominal annual interest rate for continuous compounding corresponds to an effective annual rate of 11%? Using this rate and the equations in Table 6.3, calculate the values of the following factors:

a) $(P/F,r,10)$ e) $(P/A,r,\infty)$

b) $(F/P,r,10)$ f) $(A/P,r,\infty)$

c) $(P/A,r,10)$ g) $(A/F,r,10)$

d) $(F/A,r,10)$

6-11 Compare the *r*-format and the *i*-format in Table 6.4. For any two of the *r*-formats (your pick), develop the *i*-format from the *r*-format, using the relationship between *i* and *r* for continuous compounding.

Factor Equations and Formulas

COMMENT: Problems 6-12 to 6-16 are intended to hone your algebraic skills, which, for some of you, may have gotten a little rusty.

6-12 Turn to Appendix 6A, section 6A.1.1 on uniform series. Note the formula for the sum of a geometric progression. Prove that for $a = (1 + i)^{-1}$ and the ratio $r = (1 + i)^{-1}$, the geometric sum equals the formula for the P/A factor in Table 6.2.

6-13 Add i to the formula for the A/F factor in Table 6.2, and show by algebraic manipulation that the sum equals the A/P factor.

6-14 Show that the factor formula for A/G equals the formula for A/F for $N = 2$.

6-15 Using the formula for P/G in Table 6.2, show that P/G approaches $1/i^2$ as N approaches infinity.

6-16 Prove that the present worth factor, P/A_1, for a geometric series equals $N/(1 + i)$ when $g = i$. *Hint:* If you substitute i for g in the formula for a geometric series in Table 6.2, the formula reduces to 0/0, which is an indeterminate; that is, the value of 0/0 depends upon the situation under review. To prove that the present worth factor equals $N/(1 + i)$, start with the formula for the sum of a geometric series or use your common sense.

Multisum Calculations

COMMENT: For the problems that follow, assume end-of-period cash flow unless otherwise noted.

6-17 For the cash flow diagram of Figure 6.1A, show that the net present value for a rate of return of 23.4% is zero.

6-18 What present sum is equivalent to annual payments of $5,000 for five years at 6%?

6-19 How would you compare the receipt of $8,000 for ten years and the receipt of $10,000 for seven years, if the interest rate is 8% compounded annually? Which would you prefer?

6-20 What is the single amount at EOY 3 that is equivalent to a uniform annual series of $10,000 for ten years at 8%, compounded annually?

6-21 Find the uniform annual series of eight payments that would be equivalent to the following gradient series: $5,000 initially with a $500 increment per year for seven years.

6-22 If you borrow $20,000 and agree to repay it in ten equal quarterly installments starting one year from the date of the loan, how much would each payment be if the effective annual interest rate on the loan is 12%?

6-23 What is the present worth of a series of $1,000 quarterly payments covering 20 years? The effective annual rate of return is 15%.

6-24 The first cost is $10,000. The estimated net cash flows at EOY1, EOY 2, and EOY 3 are $4,000. The MARR is 8%. Using Example 6.1 as a guide,

a) What is the NPV for the MARR?

b) What is the NPV for a rate of return of 10%?

c) What rate of return would make the NPV zero?

6-25 For the following annual discrete cash flows, calculate the present worth and the future worth at EOY 4 for an annual return of 8%:

EOY	Cash Flow
−2	$150
0	−200
1	200
2	25
5	−75
7	25

6-26 A rental property is for sale for $200,000. A prospective buyer intends to hold the property for 12 years, at the end of which time she expects to sell it for an estimated $180,000. During the ownership period, annual receipts are estimated at $30,000 and annual disbursements at $12,000. The prospective buyer wants a return of 9%. How high is she prepared to go with her offer?

6-27 What six-year uniform payment, starting one year from now, would be the same as spending $4,000 now, $3,000 three years from now, and $8,000 five years from now if the interest rate is 10% per year? Draw a cash flow diagram before attempting any calculations.

6-28 Hal's of Paris Declawing Service will require $21,000 in three years to purchase a new declawing machine. How much will Hal have to set aside each year if he can invest funds at 8% per year? Draw a cash flow diagram.

6-29 A small dam and irrigation system is expected to cost $500,000. Annual operating and maintenance costs are estimated at $50,000 for the first year and an additional $2,000 per year each year over the 25-year useful life of the investment. Assuming discrete cash flows, what is the present worth for an MARR of 10%?

6-30 For Problem 6-29, what would be the annual payments into a fund expected to pay for the dam and irrigation system, including the operation and maintenance costs, over the life of the system?

6-31 A drilling machine costs $15,000. Operating costs are expected to be $2,500 per year. Maintenance costs are estimated at $300 per year for the first year and are expected to increase by $50 per year for each year of the anticipated life of seven years. The estimated salvage value is $4,000, and the MARR is 15%. Draw the cash flow diagrams and calculate

a) the present worth of the machine

b) the annual worth of the machine

6-32 Under a leasing alternative to the purchase agreement, the drilling machine in Problem 6-31 may be leased for seven years at an annual cost of $4,500. The lease payments begin at EOY 0. Operating expenses are expected to be the same for the leased machine as for the purchased machine. However, maintenance costs under the lease will be the responsibility of the manufacturer. Draw cash flow diagrams and calculate

a) the present worth

b) the annual worth

Equivalence

6-33 The Introduction to this chapter tells you that the notion of equivalence is a personal one. What is the minimum sum of money four years from now that you would accept in lieu of $5,000 two years from now? What is the corresponding rate of return?

6-34 An initial investment of $25,000 produces net cash flows of $5,000 annually for ten years. What are the present values of the six alternative cash flow situations described in Example 6.3, using an MARR of 10% rather than 12%?

6-35 For what value of X are the following two cash flow series equivalent for an MARR of 10%?

EOY	A	B
0	− $10,000	$X
1	5,000	3,500
2	5,000	4,500
3	5,000	5,500
4	5,000	6,500
5	5,000	7,500

Manipulating Rate-of-Return Factors

6-36 Consider a uniform series of $8,000 annually for ten years. What are the present values for the following situations, for each of which you should draw a cash flow diagram showing both the FTZ and the PTZ?

a) The first cash flow is at EOY 1.

b) The last cash flow is at EOY 8.

c) The first cash flow is at EOY 5.

6-37 The gradient for an arithmetic gradient series is $100. The first annual flow is $500 and the last is $1,500. Using cash flow diagrams to show both the FTZ and PTZ, answer the following questions.

a) What is N?

b) What is the uniform series on which the gradient is superposed?

c) What is the present value if the first cash flow occurs at EOY 1?

d) At EOY −2?

e) At EOY 4?

6-38 The arithmetic gradient is −$100. The first cash flow is $1,200, and the flows continue for six years.

a) What is N?

b) What is the uniform series on which this gradient is superimposed?

c) What is the present value if the first cash flow occurs at EOY 1?

d) At EOY 3?

e) At EOY −1?

6-39 For the cash flow diagram of Figure 6.5, assume that the rates of return for the three time zones are 15%, 10%, and 6%, respectively. Compute the equivalent single sum at EOY 4.

6-40 Draw the cash flow diagram, and find the equivalent value of the following cash flow streams at EOY 6.

Year	Cash Flows
0	− $10,000
1–4	$1,500 rising by $500 annually
5	− $1,000
6	$1,000
7	$5,000
10	− $1,500
12	$6,000

For EOYs 0–4, use 12%, compounded annually; for EOYs 5–8, use 10%, compounded semiannually; for EOYs 9–12, use 8%, compounded continuously.

APPENDIX 6A
DERIVATION OF RATE-OF-RETURN FACTORS

6A.1 DISCRETE CASH FLOW WITH DISCRETE COMPOUNDING

The single-sum compound amount factor, $(1 + i)^N$, and the single-sum present worth factor, $(1 + i)^{-N}$, were derived in Chapter 5.

6A.1.1 Uniform Series Factors

For the cash flow diagram, see Figure 3.4. It follows that the ratio of P to A is

$$P/A = [(1 + i)^{-1} + (1 + i)^{-2} + \ldots (1 + i)^{-N}]$$

The term in brackets is a geometric progression for which the ratio between successive terms is less than 1. The sum of such a progression is

$$a(1 - r^N)/(1 - r)$$

The first term, a, and the ratio, r, are both equal to $(1 + i)^{-1}$. Substituting and rearranging gives the uniform series present worth factor $(P/A,i,N)$:

$$P/A = \frac{(1 + i)^N - 1}{i (1 + i)^N} = (P/A,i,N)$$

COMMENT: If you're a little rusty on your algebra, this is a good time to spruce up.

To find out what happens to P/A as N approaches infinity, we rearrange the previous equation as follows:

$$P/A = \frac{1}{i} - \frac{1}{i(1 + i)^N}$$

The last term approaches zero as N approaches infinity.

The uniform series future worth factor, F/A, is obtained by substituting $F(1 + i)^{-N}$ for P in the previous equation and solving for F. This gives

$$F/A = \frac{(1 + i)^N - 1}{i} = (F/A,i,N)$$

6A.1.2 Arithmetic Gradient Factors

Refer to Figure 3.6. Each step is an annuity, G, for which we obtain the future worth by using the F/A factor. The first annuity goes from EOP 2 to EOP N, the second from EOP 3 to EOP N, and so on. This gives

$$F/G = [(F/A,i,N - 1) + (F/A,i,N - 2) \ldots + (F/G,i,1]$$

Substituting the formula for F/A in each of the terms, simplifying, and rearranging gives

$$F/G = \frac{(1 + i)^N - 1}{i^2} - \frac{N}{i}$$

The present worth factor, P/G, equals $(F/G)(P/F)$. Therefore, P/G equals

$$P/G = \frac{(1 + i)^N - 1}{i^2(1 + i)^N} - \frac{N}{i(1 + i)^N}$$

As N approaches infinity, P/G approaches $1/i^2$.

6A.1.3 Geometric Series Factors

Refer to Figure 3.7. The present value of the series is

$$P = \frac{A_1}{(1 + i)} \left[1 + \frac{(1 + g)}{(1 + i)} + \frac{(1 + g)^2}{(1 + i)^2} + \ldots \frac{(1 + g)^N}{(1 + i)^N} \right]$$

The expression within the brackets is a geometric series in which the first term is 1 and the ratio between successive terms is $(1 + g)/(1 + i)$. The sum of the expression is therefore

$$\frac{1 - (1 + g)^N (1 + i)^{-N}}{1 - (1 + g)(1 + i)^{-1}}$$

Simplifying and rearranging gives

$$P/A_1 = \frac{1 - (1 + g)^N (1 + i)^{-N}}{(i - g)} = (P/A_1,i,g,N)$$

The future value is obtained by multiplying by the compound amount factor $(1 + i)^N$, and the equivalent uniform series is obtained by multiplying by the uniform series factor A/P.

6A.2 DISCRETE CASH FLOWS WITH CONTINUOUS COMPOUNDING

The relationship between the effective and nominal rates for continuous compounding was derived in Appendix 5A.

$$e^r = (1 + i)$$

Raising both sides to the nth power yields

$$(1 + i)^N = e^{rN}$$

Substituting e^r for $(1 + i)$ and $(e^r - 1)$ for i wherever these items appear in Table 6.2 produces the rate factors for continuous compounding in Table 6.3. Consider, for example, the F/A factor for discrete compounding:

$$F/A = \frac{(1 + i)^N - 1}{i}$$

Substituting e^{rN} for $(1 + i)^N$ and $(e^r - 1)$ for i gives

$$F/A = \frac{e^{rN} - 1}{e^r - 1}$$

You should, on your own, derive one or two of the other factors in Table 6.3, using the relationship between effective and nominal rates for continuous compounding.

6A.3 CONTINUOUS CASH FLOW

We begin with the rate-of-return formula for F/A based on discrete compounding:

$$(F/A,i,N) = \frac{(1 + i)^N - 1}{i}$$

To derive the equation for an annuity A in which the sum $\overline{A}$ is a continuous cash flow, we let M stand for both the number of compounding periods per year and the number of payments per year, which, when summed up, equal $\overline{A}$. It follows that, as the number of payments per year increases and ultimately approaches infinity, so will the number of compounding periods. Thus, continuous cash flow is directly linked to continuous compounding.

To derive the continuous cash flow formulas, we start with discrete cash flows and discrete compounding, letting MN equal the total number of compounding periods for N years, r/M the periodic interest rate for each period M, and A/M that portion of the total annual annuity received at the end of each period M.

Substituting in the formula for F/A gives

$$F = \frac{A}{M} \left[\frac{(1 + r/M)^{NM} - 1}{r/M} \right]$$

which equals

$$F = A \left[\frac{(1 + r/M)^{MN} - 1}{r} \right]$$

Rearranging as we did in Appendix 5A for continuous compounding formulas and substituting gives

$$F = A \frac{\{[1 + 1/(M/r)]^{M/r}\}^{rN} - 1}{r}$$

The term within braces approaches e as M/r approaches infinity. (Refer to Appendix 5A if this step is not clear.) Therefore,

$$F/\overline{A} = \frac{(e^{rN} - 1)}{r}$$

For converting to the i-format, we substitute $(1 + i)$ for e^r and $ln(1 + i)$ for r. This yields

$$F/\overline{A} = \frac{(1 + i)^N - 1}{ln(1 + i)}$$

which can be written

$$F/\overline{A} = \frac{i}{ln(1 + i)} (F/A)$$

For the derivation of the $P/\overline{A}$ factor, substitute $P (1 + i)^N$ for F:

$$F/\overline{A} = P(1 + i)^N/\overline{A} = \frac{i}{ln(1 + i)} F/A$$

Solving for P gives

$$P = \frac{i}{ln(1 + i)(1 + i)^N} F/A$$

However,

$$P/A = \frac{F/A}{(1 + i)^N}$$

so that

$$P/\overline{A} = \frac{i}{ln(1 + i)} P/A$$

This relationship can be converted to the r-format by substituting e^r for $(1 + i)$ and r for $ln(1 + i)$.

The $\overline{A}/P$ and $\overline{A}/F$ factors are reciprocals of those developed previously and need not be considered further. This leaves the $F/\overline{P}$ and $P/\overline{F}$ factors, which, as mentioned in the body of this chapter, are not reciprocals. The diagrams for deriving these two factors are given in Figure 3.8.

The $F/\overline{P}$ factor is derived by first asking what is the equivalent future sum at the end of year 1 of a present value P that is spread continuously over that year and then moving that sum to the right from the end of year 1 to the end of year N or $(N - 1)$ years.

In Figure 3.8B, a single-sum future value F_1 at EOY 1 would be that of a continuous cash flow annuity with an N of 1, that is,

$$F_1 = \overline{P} (F/\overline{A},i,N) = \overline{P} \frac{e^r - 1}{r}$$

The compound amount formula for moving to the right $(N - 1)$ years with continuous compounding gives

$$F = F_1 e^{r(N-1)} = F_1 e^{rN}/e^r$$

Simplifying and rearranging yields

$$F/\overline{P} = \frac{e^{rN}(e^r - 1)}{re^r}$$

The i-format is easily derived and leads to

$$F/\overline{P} = \frac{i}{(1 + i) ln(1 + i)} (F/P)$$

The *P/F* factor is derived by first asking what is the equivalent single sum at the end of $(N - 1)$ years of a future sum F that is spread continuously over year N and then moving this sum to the left $(N - 1)$ years. We leave this derivation to you. You should have no trouble in showing that

$$P/\bar{F} = \frac{i}{\ln{(1 + i)}} \, (P/F)$$

____7
THE THREE WORTHS

7.1 INTRODUCTION

Five figures of merit—all based on the equivalence relationships of Chapter 6—are commonly used for comparing and ranking alternative capital investment opportunities. They are

Present worth (PW) or present value (PV) or net present value (NPV)

Future worth (FW) or future value (FV) or net future value (NFV)

Annual worth (AW) or, if the annual worth is negative, annual cost (AC) or equivalent uniform annual cost (EUAC)

Internal rate of return (IRR) and its offshoot the external rate of return (ERR)

Benefit-cost ratio (BCR)

We cover the three worths—present worth, future worth, and annual worth—in this chapter, the IRR and its offshoot, the ERR in Chapters 9 and 10, and the BCR in Chapter 11.

The figures of merit give us numerical quantities that allow us to compare and rank alternatives, based on their monetary attributes. Since these attributes are usually considered before the nonmonetary attributes, this is an important first step in reaching a decision as to whether to proceed and, if so, with which alternatives.

We refer to the first three of the five criteria listed above as "the three worths." In discussing them, we also introduce a new topic—cotermination—

which deals with the procedures we have to follow when we compare alternatives whose life cycles differ.

7.2   THE THREE WORTHS

You are probably wondering why we need to consider all three worths. The equivalence equations in Chapter 6 showed that any present worth can be converted to a future worth by multiplying it by the proper compound amount factor (F/P) and to an ordinary annuity (annual worth) by multiplying it by the proper capital recovery factor (A/P). In other words, any one of the three worths can be readily converted to any of the other two. Why, if this is so, do we nevertheless consider all three? Two comments are worth noting.

1. Many decision makers find it easier to think in terms of uniform series, that is, annual worths or costs, rather than present worths. Furthermore, there are situations, particularly those involving cotermination, for which annual worths are more relevant than present worths.

2. There are circumstances that make it more convenient to evaluate future worths first for subsequent conversion to present worths or annual worths, or both. Furthermore, there is an entire class of problems that involve life insurance, pensions, and related benefits and costs for which future worth is often the preferred figure of merit.

As mentioned, the three worths—present, future and annual—are directly linked through the rate-of-return factors derived in Chapter 6. Of the three, the present worth is the most common figure of merit, with annual worth in second place and future worth in third place.

We listed the major cash flows into and out of capital projects during their life cycles in Chapter 3. A recapitulation of these is helpful at this time.

The major cash outflow at the beginning of the life cycle is the first cost. This may include not only the cost of the facility itself but also the cost of land and initial working capital.

During the life cycle, the significant cash inflows are revenues and the significant cash outflows are the expenses that have to be incurred in order to produce the goods and services from which revenues are derived. At the end of the life cycle, there may be sizable cash inflows from the disposal of assets and working capital and sizable cash outflows for the restoration activities that may have to be carried out for environmental, safety, and esthetic reasons. For projects that may be funded in part with borrowed capital (creditor equity), additional cash flows include inflows of borrowed cash to help construct or acquire a capital facility and outflows for repayment of principal and interest. The interest on borrowed money that would normally be due during the construction period is often deferred, that is, added to the debt and repaid during the operating cycle.

Some guidelines on how these cash flows are applied to obtain any of the three worths are given in the following paragraphs.

For preliminary studies, discrete compounding and end-of-period discrete cash flows are generally assumed for all cash flow estimates. The rate of return is the effective rate for the life cycle. For cycles of five years or more, the length of the period is usually one year. For life cycles of three or four years, the length of the period may also be one year but is often one quarter or one month. For life cycles of two years and less, the length of the period is usually one quarter or one month.

For more definitive studies, discrete compounding with discrete cash flows is used for some cash flow streams and continuous compounding with continuous cash flows for other cash flow streams, depending upon the nature of the streams. For revenues and expenses, continuous cash flow is usually more representative of how cash will flow once a project is implemented than discrete cash flow.

For first cost, cash payments for investing in existing facilities are discrete cash flows. However, for investments in new facilities that are still to be built, continuous cash flows or, better yet, monthly cash flows based on estimates of progress payments during the construction period are more realistic.

For salvage values and restoration costs, the discrete cash flow assumption is usually applied, even though these flows may, in some cases, cover a substantial period of time. The reason this is justified is that cash flows far into the future do not contribute substantially to present worth.

For both preliminary and definitive studies, additions to and deductions from working capital throughout the life cycle are usually treated as single sums. This is also the case for the disposal of assets no longer needed and for the replacement of assets that normally wear out before the end of the life cycle.

In this text, discrete compounding and discrete cash flows are usually assumed in the examples given. This is simply a convenience. We suggest that you rework some of the examples using continuous cash flow where this assumption seems more appropriate than discrete cash flow.

The end of year zero (EOY 0) in a cost study can be taken at any selected time. The two most commonly selected times are the beginning of the life cycle and the beginning of the operating period if a construction period precedes it (see Figure 5.2). The values obtained for the present worths (and, of course, the other two worths) will depend on the location of zero on the time line. However, it will not affect the ranking of the alternatives or the values of those figures of merit that are based on ratios rather than money sums, for example, the internal rate of return and the benefit-cost ratio.

7.2.1 Present Worth

The most widely used figure of merit based on discounted cash flow is the present worth. The American National Standards Institute (ANSI) Code

Z94.5 defines "present worth" as

- The monetary sum that is equivalent to a future sum when interest is compounded at a given rate, or as
- The discounted value of a future sum when discounted at a given rate.

The PW of a single cash flow stream is also referred to as its present value, or PV. For a set of such streams, the terms "net present worth" (NPW) or "net present value" (NPV) are often used. Usually the abbreviations PW or PV will serve for both single cash flow streams and sets of such streams, unless the context in which these terms are used is not clear.

For a study to proceed, the MARR and the alternatives to be reviewed must be selected. The estimates of cash flow are prepared and structured into cash flow tables and/or diagrams. The NPV of each alternative is then calculated, and the "winners"—those with the highest NPV—are reviewed with, or recommended to, the parties responsible for a "go," "no go," or "further study" decision. In cost studies, the NPVs are negative and the preferred alternatives are those with the smallest negative numbers, which are, of course, those with the highest NPV.

> *COMMENT:* If you have been away from algebra for a while, you may have forgotten that -2 is a larger number than -4 and that an NPV of $-\$1,000$ is larger than one of $-\$2,000$.

Before reviews or recommendations occur, two additional steps may need to be taken. The first step is introduced in this chapter and then is covered more fully in Chapter 9 on the internal rate of return. An alternative may pass the PW test in having a present worth equal to, or greater than, zero, but a pair-by-pair comparison of alternatives may indicate that its incremental cash flows will not produce a satisfactory return.

The second step deals with the nonmonetary attributes—the irreducibles. What is the impact of each alternative on soil, air, and water pollution? Is the distribution of the proposed benefits and disbenefits an equitable one? How can the nonmonetary attributes be combined with the monetary ones to produce figures of merit with which direct comparisons can be made? The answer to the last question is the major topic of Part IV on multiattribute analysis.

There is no need to review the mathematics involved in converting cash flow streams into their present worths. This was covered in Chapters 5 and 6. We therefore go directly to an example to apply what we learned there to a specific capital investment.

> *Example 7.1   Robot-welding Machine*   A study group in your company has proposed purchasing a robot-welding machine. The cost of the machine is $100,000. Its installation will cost an additional $15,000. The expected annual net cash flow

is $40,000 per year for five years. The net salvage value—the difference between what a used robot welder might sell for and the cost of removing it from the premises and preparing it for sale—is $10,000. The cash flow diagram is given in Figure 7.1.

The MARR before tax, established as company policy for this type of investment, is 20%. At an income tax rate of 30%, this is roughly equivalent to an after-tax return of 14% (70% of 20%).

> *COMMENT:* You will learn later that the relationship between before-tax and after-tax MARRs is not as simple as that used above. However, you will also learn that it often works quite well.

The present worth of this investment is easily calculated. The investment P is a cash outflow of $115,000. The return is a uniform series of $40,000 per year for five years (taken as end-of-year cash flows) plus the recovery of $10,000 at the end of five years from selling the used robot welder.

$$
\begin{aligned}
PW &= A(P/A,i,N) + S(P/F,i,N) - P \\
&= \$40,000 \ (P/A,20,5) + \$10,000 \ (P/F,20,5) - \$115,000 \\
&= \$40,000 \times 2.991 + \$10,000 \times 0.4019 - \$115,000 \\
&= \$119,640 + \$4,019 - \$115,000 \\
&= \$8,643
\end{aligned}
$$

Since the PW is positive, this capital expenditure will, if the estimates prove to be true, earn a return of more than 20%. You already know how to compute this return from Example 6.2, and you should do so. The answer is a little over 23%.

7.2.2 Annual Worth

We could obtain the annual worth of the investment just mentioned by simply multiplying the PW we have just calculated by the appropriate A/P factor. This, however, would not give you the practice you need in carrying out an annual worth analysis from scratch. We do this in Example 7.2.

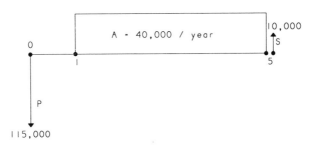

Figure 7.1. Cash flow diagram for robot welder.

Example 7.2   The Robot Welder Revisited   All of the data in Example 7.1 apply to this example. So does the cash flow diagram of Figure 7.1. The rate-of-return equation for finding the annual worth is

$$AW = A + S(A/F,20,5) - P(A/P,20,5)$$
$$= \$40,000 + \$10,000 \times 0.1344 - \$115,000 \times 0.3344$$
$$= \$40,000 + 1,344 - \$38,456$$
$$= \$2,888$$

The first term is the uniform series representing the net cash flow of $40,000 annually for five years. The second term converts the salvage value, S, into an equivalent uniform series by multiplying it by the A/F factor for 20% and five years. The third term is the initial investment of $115,000, converted to its equivalent uniform series by multiplying it by the A/P factor for 20% and five years. The answer is identical, except for rounding errors, to the answer that we will obtain by multiplying the PW obtained in Example 7.1 by the A/P factor for converting a single sum to an equivalent uniform series. Thus,

$$AW = PW (A/P,i,N) = \$8,643 \times 0.3344$$
$$= \$2,890$$

Example 7.2 demonstrates once again that any one of the worths can be converted to its equivalent value for any of the other two worths by application of the appropriate rate-of-return factors.

7.2.3   Future Worth

The future worth could be obtained by multiplying the present or annual worth by the proper F/P and F/A factors, respectively. However, we carry out an analysis in Example 7.3 in which all cash flows are converted to their equivalent future values for the same reason that we did for annual worth; that is, the practice in doing so won't hurt you and will help you in becoming familiar with equivalence relationships.

Example 7.3   Another Look at the Robot Welder   The cash flow diagram for this example is again that of Figure 7.1. The rate-of-return equation for the future worth is

$$FW = A(F/A,20,5) + S - P(F/P,20,5)$$
$$= \$40,000 \times 7.442 + \$10,000 - \$115,000 \times 2.488$$
$$= \$297,680 + \$10,000 - \$286,120$$
$$= \$21,560$$

This answer can also be obtained directly from the present or annual worth as shown:

$$FW = PW(F/P,20,5)$$
$$= \$8,643 \times 2.488$$
$$= \$21,500$$

and

$$FW = AW(F/A,20,5)$$
$$= \$2,888 \times 7.442$$
$$= \$21,500$$

Now that you know how to move from one worth to another, no matter which one you start out with, we will look at another common application of the time value of money, namely, financing. This is done in Example 7.4.

Example 7.4   Cash or Credit   The treasurer of your company has to decide how to pay for the new robot welder—cash or credit. The company's bank will lend $100,000 at 12% interest to be amortized with five end-of-year payments of $27,740 each. The supplier will accept a $20,000 down payment and installment payments of $4,000 per month for 24 months.

Cash flow diagrams for the two financing schemes are given in Figure 7.2. The treasurer now has to decide whether the supplier's offer is more attractive than the bank's offer.

How did the bank arrive at annual payments of $27,740? It did so by finding the annuity that at 12% and for five years is equivalent to $100,000.

$$A = \$100,000(A/P,12,5) = \$100,000 \times 0.2774$$
$$= \$27,740$$

COMMENT: If the bank's terms had called for monthly payments, the 12% rate quoted by it would be a nominal rate for which the periodic monthly rate i_M is 1%. The monthly payments would therefore be

$$A = \$100,000(A/P,1,60) = \$100,000 \times 0.02224$$
$$= \$2,224$$

These payments total $26,688 per year, which is about $1,000 less than annual payments of $27,740.

The treasurer also needs to know the split between principal and interest in the five annual payments. The bank would, of course, give her a schedule with these figures. However, it is important for you (and her) to understand how this split is computed. The following table summarizes the computations.

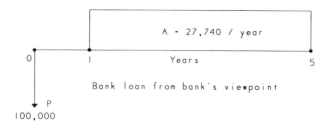

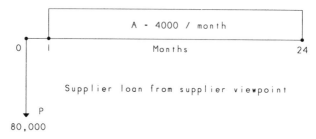

Figure 7.2. Financing options.

| Year | Principal Outstanding at Beginning of Year | Annual Payment | | Principal Portion | Principal Outstanding at End of Year |
		Interest Portion	Total Payment		
(1)	(2)	(3)	(4)	(5)	(6)
		12% of (2)		(4) − (3)	(2) − (5)
1	$100,000	$12,000	$27,740	$15,740	$84,260
2	84,260	10,111	27,740	17,629	66,631
3	66,631	7,996	27,740	19,744	46,887
4	46,887	5,626	27,740	22,114	24,773
5	24,773	2,973	27,740	24,767	6

The principal outstanding at the end of year 5 after the last payment is $6, due to a small rounding error that need not concern us. The schedule handed to the treasurer by the bank would adjust the last payment to avoid the $6 as a final payment.

What the treasurer now has to do is calculate the interest rate for the repayment schedule offered by the supplier that would make that schedule equivalent to a loan of $80,000 (the difference between the cash price of the robot welder and the down payment). P, A, and N are known. The unknown is i. The calculations are as follows:

$$P/A = (P/A, i, 24)$$

$$P/A = \$80,000/\$4,000 = 20 = (P/A, i, 24)$$

A hand calculator gives the answer very quickly—1.513%. It can also be found by interpolating between the tables in Appendix B for 1.5% and 1.75%. The nominal rate is 18.2% (12 × 1.513), and, as you can easily prove, the effective rate is 20%.

Since the cost of borrowing from the supplier (20%) is considerably higher than the cost from borrowing from the bank (12%), the treasurer decides that she will either pay cash or use bank credit. What she does will depend on her cash flow forecasts for the coming year and beyond. It may also depend on other available opportunities offering the same or better returns that she forgoes by using cash.

> COMMENT: Here we have introduced the concept of opportunity cost, that is, the cost of forgoing other opportunities for the opportunity at hand. There will be more on this important concept throughout the text.

In Example 7.4, we learned how to separate the principal and interest portions of periodic payments. This can be a cumbersome process. Some hand calculators are programmed for such calculations. The equations on which they are based and which will permit you to single out any one payment or any group of payments are given in Appendix 7A.

7.3 COTERMINATION

Valid comparisons using discounted cash flows require that each alternative participating in a project selection study have the same planning horizon. It makes no sense to compare the net present value of an alternative for which cash flows cover a span of N years with the net present value of another alternative for which the cash flows cover a shorter or a longer time span. An alternative with a long life span may show a higher NPV than one with a short life span, not because it is sounder economically, but because there are more cash flow streams to discount. In short, we need to "coterminate" to provide a common planning horizon for all of the alternatives participating in a study.

Consider, for example, two alternatives, one of which—alternative A— has a life span of three years and the other of which—alternative B— has a life span of six years. For a valid comparison based on discounted cash flows, we must either extend the planning horizon of alternative A to six years or shorten that of alternative B to three years so that the two alternatives share a common horizon of six or three years, respectively.

The cash flow diagrams for these two ways of equalizing life cycles to a common planning horizon are shown in Figures 7.3 and 7.4. The two methods will be referred to as the LCM (lowest common multiple) and the early-sale approaches. Both assume finite planning horizons, and both are examples of the methodology referred to as cotermination.

> COMMENT: Alternatives can also be coterminated by assuming infinite planning horizons for which each alternative is replicated an infinite

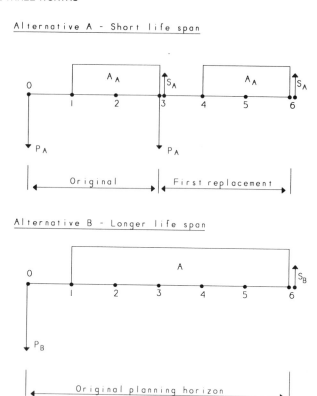

Figure 7.3. Cotermination with LCM approach.

number of times. This is a very practical approach in many cases and utilizes the concept of capitalized cost, which is developed in Chapter 8.

7.3.1 Lowest-Common-Multiple Cotermination

If you need a refresher on finding LCMs, you can go to any textbook on arithmetic. However, you will probably recall from your grammar or high school days that, to determine the LCM of a set of numbers, you first must factor each number into its prime numbers, that is, into numbers divisible only by 1 and themselves (2, 3, 5, 7, 11, 13, . . . , etc.). The LCM is the product of all of the primes in the set, with each prime raised to the highest power in which it appears in any one member of the set.

Most cost studies for which alternatives have to be coterminated are concerned with relatively short life cycles—less than ten years and often in the range of three to six years. The topics covered are usually equipment and materials subject to obsolescence (e.g., computers) and to erosion, corrosion, and heavy-duty service for which replacements are frequent and for which a

Alternative A - Short life span

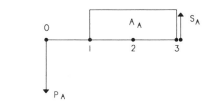

Alternative B - Longer life span

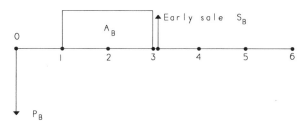

Figure 7.4. Cotermination with early-sale approach.

variety of options are available, differing in first cost, maintenance and repair costs, and useful service life.

For projects with relatively long life cycles, cotermination using finite life cycles is seldom applied, although there is no reason why it cannot be. Let us suppose that there are two alternatives—one with an estimated life cycle of 20 years and the other, of 25 years. For rates of return current today and likely to be for many years, present worths for cash flow streams 20 or more years in the future are often insignificant compared with the present worths of earlier cash flow streams. For this reason, a cost study for the two alternatives might as well be carried out for a 20-year life cycle rather than for an LCM of 20 and 25 years, which is 100 years.

In carrying out cost studies using the LCM approach for cotermination, it is assumed that the alternative with the shorter life span will be replaced by an identical unit and that all cash flows, including the first cost and the salvage value, remain unchanged as we proceed from one cycle to the next. Offhand, this assumption makes no sense, but it nevertheless serves us well. After all, we are only making a decision on what to do now, that is, at the beginning of the first cycle. The LCM approach allows us to reach a decision, but it is a decision we need not live with for more than one cycle. At the end of the first cycle, the same procedure will be gone through with cash flow estimates current at that time.

COMMENT: In Chapter 15 of Part II, you will work with studies for replacing existing equipment in which the assumption of identical replacements need not hold.

Example 7.5 involves cotermination using the LCM methodology. The preferred figure of merit for such problems is the equivalent uniform annual cost (EUAC or simply AC), which is, of course, a negative annual worth.

Example 7.5   The Trucking Industry   Trucking is a major industry in the United States, and much information is available on the costs of operating and maintaining a fleet of trucks. A trucking company—The Truck Transport Corporation, or TTC for short—is considering the purchase of 25 trucks. The selection has been narrowed down to two options, for which the cost estimates are tabulated as follows:

	Option 1	Option 2
Cost of truck	$40,000	$50,000
Annual O&M costs	35,000	30,000
Salvage value	4,000	5,000
Economic life in years	4	6

The operating and maintenance costs (O&M) are averages based on TTC's experience. They do not include driver costs, since this cost is the same for the two options and therefore would not affect the choice. Since the lives differ, the alternatives have to be coterminated. The LCM of 4 and 6 is 12, and, therefore, the planning horizon is 12 years ($2^2 \times 3$). This means option 1 must be replicated three times and option 2, twice.

A cash flow table for the two options follows. All figures are in thousands of dollars. Since the analysis will be carried out with annual cost as the figure of merit, costs are shown with plus signs and salvage values, which are cash inflows, with minus signs. The option with the lowest cost will therefore be the option with the highest worth and the preferred selection. The MARR before taxes is 20%.

The cash flow diagrams for the two alternatives are given in Figure 7.5. These were drawn from the last column in Table 7.1.

We begin by calculating the EUAC (or AC) for only one cycle of both the 4-year and 6-year alternatives. You will find out later why we do this first rather than go directly to a cash flow analysis for the entire planning horizon. The cash flow diagrams are given in Figure 7.6.

For the 4-year alternative,

$$AC = A + P(A/P,i,N) - F(A/F,i,N)$$

$$= \$35 + \$40(A/P,20,4) - \$4(A/F,20,4)$$

$$= \$35 + \$40 \times 0.3863 - \$4 \times 0.1863$$

$$= \$49.7 \text{ k}$$

and, for the 6-year alternative,

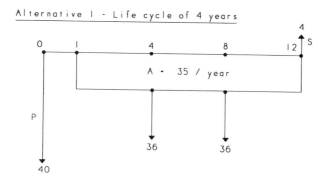

Alternative 1 - Life cycle of 4 years

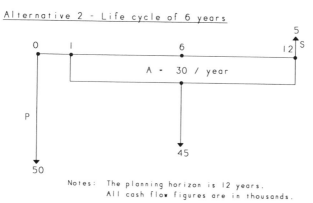

Alternative 2 - Life cycle of 6 years

Notes: The planning horizon is 12 years.
All cash flow figures are in thousands.

Figure 7.5. Multi-cycle cash flow diagram for Example 7.5.

TABLE 7.1 Cash Flows, Dollars Per Year (in thousands)

End of Year	First Cost	O&M	Salvage Value	Net Cash Flow
	Option 1: 4-Year Life Cycle			
0	$40	—	—	$40
1–4	—	$35	—	35
4	40	—	$ −4	36
5–8	—	35	—	35
8	40	—	−4	36
9–12	—	35	—	35
12	—	—	−4	−4
	Option 2: 6-Year Life Cycle			
0	$50	—	—	$50
1–6	—	$30	—	30
6	50	—	$ −5	45
7–12	—	30	—	30
12	—	—	−5	−5

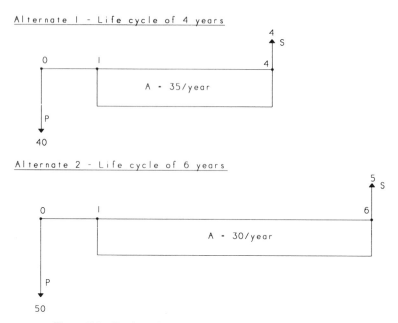

Figure 7.6. Single cycle cash flow diagram for Example 7.5.

$$AC = A + P(A/P,i,N) - F(A/F,i,N)$$
$$= \$30 + \$50\ (A/P,20,6) - \$5\ (A/F,20,6)$$
$$= \$30 + \$50 \times 0.3007 - \$5 \times 0.1007$$
$$= \$44.6\ k$$

The 6-year option looks like a clear winner. However, before we reach a decision, we should look at the annual costs for the coterminated life span of 12 years. For these computations, we need to go back to Figure 7.5.

The factor equations for the 4-year option for the full time span of 12 years is

$$AC = \$35 + \$36\ (P/F,20,4)(A/P,20,12)$$
$$+ \$36(P/F,20,8)(A/P,20,12) - \$4(A/F,20,12)$$
$$+ \$40(A/P,20,12)$$
$$AC = \$35 + \$36 \times 0.4823 \times 0.2253$$
$$+ \$36 \times 0.2326 \times 0.2253 - \$4 \times 0.0253$$
$$+ \$40 \times 0.2253$$
$$= \$49.7\ k$$

These equations look rather formidable (although they are really not). For this reason, an explanation of each term follows.

- The annual worth of the annuity in the cash flow diagram of Figure 7.5 is $35,000. This is the first term in the preceding equation.
- The single-sum payment of $36,000 at the end of the fourth year is the difference between the cash outflow of $40,000 for a new truck and the inflow of $4,000 for the estimated resale value of the old truck. This difference is first converted to its equivalent present worth with the P/F factor and then to its equivalent uniform series with the A/P factor.
- The single-sum payment of $36,000 at the end of year 8 is handled in the same way.
- The cash inflow of $4,000 at the end of year 12 is converted to its equivalent annual worth, using the A/F factor.
- The last term in the equation is the initial investment of $40,000 multiplied by the A/P factor to obtain its equivalent annual cost.

The factor equation for alternative 2 is derived in the same way, although here we deal with only two cycles.

$$AC = \$30 + \$45 \ (P/F,20,6)(A/P,20,12)$$
$$- \$5(A/F,20,12) + \$50(A/P,20,12)$$
$$AC = \$30 + \$45 \times 0.3349 \times 0.2253 - \$5 \times 0.0253$$
$$+ \$50 \times 0.2253$$
$$= \$44.5 \ k$$

We again conclude that alternative 2 is the better choice, because its annual cost of $44,500 is lower than that of alternative 1. Another way to express this conclusion is to say that the annual worth of $-\$44,500$ for alternative 2 is higher than that of $-\$49,700$ for alternative 1.

COMMENT: Before leaving this example, make sure that you understand the derivation of the factor equations for the 12-year span and confirm that our calculations are not in error.

You may now ask, "Why all this fuss about cotermination?" We obtained the same answer for the simple calculations involving only one cycle as we did for the much more complicated calculations involving multicycles. To understand the reason for the fuss, go back to the single-cycle solutions and convert them to their equivalent PWs.

For the 4-year option,

$$PW = -\$49,700(P/A,20,4) = -\$49,700 \times 2.589$$
$$= -\$129,000$$

and, for the 6-year option,

$$PW = -\$44,500(P/A,20,6) = -\$44,500 \times 3.326$$
$$= -\$148,000$$

How can this be? The PW of the 4-year option is higher than that of the 6-year option ($-\$129,000 > -\$148,000$), which is contrary to the results we obtained with the annual worth. The answer is that we used the P/A factors for 4 and 6 years, respectively, rather than the P/A factor for the coterminated planning horizon of 12 years. The correct computations for the PWs are therefore as follows:

For the 4-year alternative,

$$PW = -\$49,700(P/A,20,12) = -\$49,700 \times 4.439$$
$$= -\$220,000$$

and, for the 6-year alternative,

$$PW = -\$44,500(P/A,20,12) = -\$44,500 \times 4.439$$
$$= -\$197,000$$

Our results are now consistent.

We conclude that, if an economic analysis requires cotermination, the annual worth should be used as the figure of merit, since it has the same value no matter how many replications. If the present worth is required because it is customary to present budget requests with this figure of merit, the annual worth should be calculated first and then converted to its equivalent PW, using the P/A factor for the coterminated planning horizon.

7.3.2 Early-Sale Cotermination

As mentioned, the LCM approach to cotermination is more common than the early-sale approach. However, there are exceptions. Some secondhand goods have a large and well-publicized market. Mobile equipment, construction equipment, mechanical equipment such as pressure vessels and heat exchangers, machinery such as pumps, compressors, and conveyors, and construction materials such as piping and valving are examples. For these, reasonable estimates for resale value can be made. Early sale cotermination is also used when the life span of an alternative is subject contractually to a fixed length.

The early sale option is examined in Example 7.6.

Example 7.6 Early-Sale Cotermination The estimated resale value of the truck in alternative 2 of Example 7.5 is $10,000 after four years of operation. The cash flow diagram is given in Figure 7.7. The present worth calculations are straightforward. All figures are in thousands of dollars.

For alternative 1,

Alternate 1 - Life cycle of 4 years

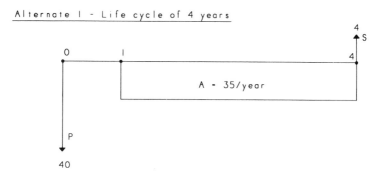

Alternate 2 - Life cycle of 6 years, early sale at 4 years

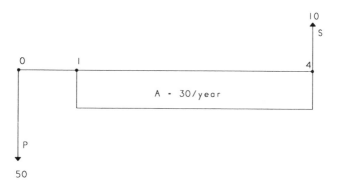

Figure 7.7. Cash flow diagram for Example 7.6.

$$PW = -\$35(P/A,20,4) - \$40 + \$4(P/F,20,4)$$
$$= -\$35 \times 2.589 - \$40 + \$4 \times 0.4823$$
$$= -\$128.7 \text{ k}$$

and, for alternative 2,

$$PW = -\$30(P/A,20,4) - \$50 + \$10(P/F,20,4)$$
$$= -\$30 \times 2.589 - \$50 + \$10 \times 0.4823$$
$$= -\$122.9 \text{ k}$$

Alternative 2 remains the preferred choice. However, this is happenstance. There is no assurance that the results reached with the two methods of cotermination will be the same.

7.4 A PREVIEW OF RANKING

The previous examples on the selection of a truck give us a convenient opening for previewing the ranking methodology that is the leading topic of Chapter 12. The selection of alternative 1 or 2 could have been made by considering the differential cash flow between the two alternatives. This is done in Example 7.7 and in Figure 7.8.

Example 7.7 Differential Cash Flow In Table 7.2, the three columns of dollar figures are, respectively, the net annual cash flows for alternative 2, the net annual cash flows for alternative 1, and the differential cash flows. The first two columns come from Table 7.1. However, we have gone back to using minus signs for cash outflows and plus signs for cash inflows, since most of the differential cash flows are positive.

The cash flow diagram of Figure 7.8 now resembles an investment situation in which an initial investment of $10,000 will produce an annuity of $5,000 annually for 12 years plus a lump sum of $36,000 at the end of years 4 and 8. However, it will be necessary to invest an additional $45,000 at the end of year 6 and $1,000 at the end of year 12 to benefit from the investment. Is it a good investment? The present worth equation in factor form is

$$PW = \$5(P/A,20,12) + \$36(P/F,20,4) + \$36(P/F,20,8)$$
$$- \$45(P/F,20,6) + \$1(P/F,20,12) - \$10$$

You should have no trouble verifying the equation or that the PW is $22,970. This indicates that the incremental investment of $10,000 will earn a return substantially greater than 20%. In short, alternative 2 is a good buy.

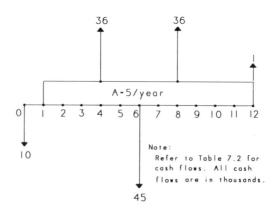

Figure 7.8. Differential cash flow analysis.

TABLE 7.2 Cash Flows, Dollars Per Year (in thousands)

End of Year	Option 2	Option 1	Option 2 Less Option 1
0	$-50	$-40	$-10
1-4	-30	-35	5
4	—	-36	36
5-6	-30	-35	5
6	-45	—	-45
7-8	-30	-35	5
8	—	-36	36
9-12	-30	-35	5
12	+5	+4	1

7.5 UNPATTERNED SETS OF CASH FLOWS

We have already mentioned that there are occasions when cash flow streams do not fit into a convenient pattern. For such unpatterned sets, each cash flow stream must be handled separately, using single-sum present worth or future worth factors. The best approach is usually to calculate the present worth of all of the cashflow streams with the following formula:

$$\text{NPW} = \sum_{j=0}^{j=N} A_j(1 + i)^{-j} \tag{7.1}$$

There is, of course, nothing mysterious about this formula. Take any set of cash flows $(A_0, A_1, \ldots, A_j, A_{j+1}, \ldots, A_{N-1}, A_N)$—some positive, some negative. Discount them using the P/F factor $(1 + i)^{-j}$ and add up the discounted present values. Once the NPW is obtained, the annual worth and future worth, if needed, are easily computed.

This concludes our discussion of the three worths, except for two important topics—capitalized cost and capital recovery. For these, we turn to Chapter 8.

7.6 SUMMARY

We remind you, once more, as we did in the summary of Chapter 6, that any single or continuous cash flow or any pattern or combination of single and continuous cash flows can be replaced by (1) an equivalent single sum, the present worth, at EOP 0, (2) an equivalent single sum, the future worth, at EOP N, and (3) an annual worth (an ordinary annuity) for which the first cash flow is at EOP 1 and the last at EOP N.

In developing these equivalence relationships, we found that the three worths—present, future, and annual—are so interrelated that by computing any one we can quickly obtain the other two. Thus, if the present worth has been computed, multiplying it by the proper A/P factor gives the annual worth and, by the proper F/P factor, the future worth.

However, in comparing the "worths" of alternative investment opportunities, the capital project selection process requires that all alternatives share a common planning horizon. This may require coterminating the life cycles.

Two approaches to cotermination were discussed—the LCM approach and the early-sale approach. Both apply to finite life spans. Annual worths are particularly helpful in cotermination, since the annual worth for one life cycle is identical with that of any number of cycles. However, in converting annual worths to their present worth equivalents, the P/A factor for the entire planning horizon must be used.

SUGGESTED READING

1. Janine Warsaw, "Elements of a $12 Million Personal Injury Case." *American Bar Association* 72 (Jan. 1, 1986): 82. This article discusses another application of the time value of money, namely, to compute the present worth of wrongful deaths and permanent disabilities in traffic and other accidents.

PROBLEMS

Cash Flow Equations

COMMENT: Our objective in Problems 7-1 to 7-10 is to drive home the concept of "equivalence." In each problem, you are given a cash flow or a set of cash flows and are asked to write out cash flow equations containing the factors for the present, future, and annual worths, that is $(P/F,i,N)$, $(F/P,i,N)$, $(P/A,i,N)$, and others. The rate of return is i, and the planning horizon is EOP 0 to EOP N. Assume discrete end-of-period cash flows.

7-1 Write the cash flow equations for the present, future, and annual worths of a cash flow P at EOP 0. *Answers:* $P = P$; $F = P(F/P,i,N)$; $A = P(A/P,i,N)$.

7-2 Write the cash flow equations for the present, future, and annual worths of a cash flow F at EOP N.

7-3 Write the cash flow equations for the present, future, and annual worths of a cash flow A at EOP 3.

7-4 Write the cash flow equations for the present, future, and annual worths of a cash flow A at EOP -2.

7-5 Write the cash flow equation for the annual worth of an annuity due for which the periodic payments are A. Draw a diagram illustrating your answer.

7-6 Write the cash flow equation for the annual worth of a uniform series A for which the first cash flow is at EOP -2 and the last at EOP 10.

7-7 Write the cash flow equation for the annual worth of a periodic lease payment A for which the first and last payments are paid up front. Draw cash flow diagrams for the lease payments and for the answer.

7-8 Write the cash flow equation for the annual worth of a gradient series G for which the first cash flow G is at EOP 1. Draw cash flow diagrams for the gradient series and your answer.

7-9 Write the cash flow equation for the annual worth of a geometric series with gradient g, for which the first cash flow is at EOP 0. Draw cash flow diagrams for the series and for your answer.

7-10 Write the cash flow equation for the future worth of a geometric series with gradient g, for which the first cash flow is at EOP -1.

The Three Worths

7-11 Consider the following cash flow pattern:

EOY	Cash Flow
1	$300
2	350
3	400
5	400
6	400
7	400

For an MARR of 20%, calculate (a) the NPW, (b) the AW without using the NPW, (c) the FW without using the NPW, (d) the AW and FW using the NPW.

7-12 A project being evaluated has the following cash flow pattern:

EOY	Cash Flow
0	$-$15,000
1	2,000
2	2,000
3	2,000
4	2,000
5	2,000
5	7,000

For an MARR of 15%, follow the instructions given in Problem 7-11.

7-13   Costs associated with a new process are projected to be $5,000 in the first year, $6,000 in the second year, $8,000 in the third year, and $10,000 in each of the next two years. If the funds are worth 8% annually, what is the future worth of these costs? What is the EUAC?

7-14   The cash flow patterns for two different alternatives are shown below:

	Alternatives	
	A	B
First cost	$60,000	$55,000
Annual expenses	$9,000	$5,500
Annual revenues	$16,000	$14,000
Salvage value	$7,000	$3,000
Life	10 years	10 years

a) Calculate the NPV for each alternative, using an MARR of 20%.

b) Which alternative is preferred?

c) Show that the incremental cash flow for the preferred alternative has a positive PW.

LCM Cotermination

7-15   The Red Dog Distillery is opening up a new facility at Sourwater Springs. Two types of still are being considered, and the following cost estimates have been received:

	Alternatives	
	A	B
First cost	$20,000	$30,000
Useful life	4 years	6 years
Salvage value	$0	$2,000
Maintenance costs		
First year	$1,000	$1,200
Increase each year	$200	$400

The MARR is 20%.

a) Draw the cash flow diagrams for both alternatives.

b) Calculate the AW for each alternative.

c) Calculate the PW for each alternative.

d) Which alternative would you choose?

7-16   A contractor is evaluating two different building insulation materials—urethane foam and fiberglass. The initial cost of the foam will be $70,000 with no salvage value, maintenance costs are estimated at $5,000 every three years, and savings in utility bills are estimated at $15,000 per year. The fiberglass may be installed for $25,000 and has no salvage value. There will be no maintenance costs for the fiberglass insulation, but the savings in energy costs are expected to be only $5,000 annually. The foam is expected to last 12 years, whereas the fiberglass will have to be replaced in 6 years. Calculate the EUAC of the two alternatives if the building owner's MARR is 15%.

7-17 Two machines are being evaluated for purchase. Machine A has a first cost of $15,000, annual costs of $3,000, and an expected life of five years. Machine B has a first cost of $12,000, annual costs of $2,500, and an expected life of three years.

a) Calculate the EUAC and the NPV of the two alternatives if the company's MARR is 20%.

b) Which of the two machines should be purchased?

Early-Sale Cotermination

7-18 Upon further investigation of the machines in Problem 7-17, a manager found that the estimated salvage value for machine A at the end of the third year is $6,000.

a) Using the early-sale cotermination approach, calculate the present value and the EUAC.

b) Does the decision in Problem 7-17 change with this additional information?

Loans

7-19 You are considering refinancing your house with a fixed-rate 15-year mortgage of 8%. The mortgage amount is $120,000.

a) Calculate the monthly payments.

b) Determine the split in monthly payments between the principal amount and the interest amount for the first and second months.

7-20 Deuce Transports is considering the purchase of a new van. To finance the purchase, its bank is offering a loan of $50,000 at 10% per year to be paid in equal monthly installments over a period of six years.

a) What will the monthly payments amount to?

b) How much of the principal will be repaid in the first six months?

7-21 You are considering the purchase of a new car worth $23,000. The dealer is offering you a financing package at 4% for 36 months with 10% down. Alternatively, your bank is offering to finance the full purchase at 5% for 48 months.

a) What are the respective monthly payments?

b) Which of the two financing deals is preferable if your monthly budget is tight?

APPENDIX 7A
AMORTIZATION FORMULAS FOR LOANS

Let P_0 be the amount of the loan. Then, for any i and N, the periodic payments A are

$$A = P_0(A/P,i,N)$$

At the end of the first period, after the payment A has been made, the outstanding principal P_1 is

$$P_1 = P_0(1 + i) - A$$

At the end of the second period, the outstanding principal is

$$P_2 = P_0(1 + i)^2 - A(1 + i) - A$$

and, at the end of any period j,

$$P_j = P_0(1 + i)^j - A[(1 + i)^{j-1} + \ldots + (1 + i)^2 + (1 + i) + 1]$$

The term in brackets equals $(F/A,i,j)$. Therefore,

$$P_j = P_0(F/P,i,j) - A(F/A,i,j)$$

Substituting $P_0(A/P,i,N)$ for A gives

$$P_j = P_0[(F/P,i,j) - (A/P,i,N)(F/A,i,j)]$$

There's an easy way to check this formula. Substitute N for j. P_N will equal zero, since $(A/P,i,N)(F/A,i,N)$ equals $(F/P,i,N)$. This is what the outstanding principal will be after the last A is paid.

To test the formula, we use it below for the outstanding principal at EOY 3 for the bank loan in Example 7.4.

$$P_j = P_0[(F/P,12,3) - (A/P,12,5)(F/A,12,3)]$$

$$= \$100,000(1.405 - 0.2774 \times 3.374)$$

$$= \$100,000 \times 0.46905$$

$$= \$46,905$$

The outstanding principal at the end of three years in Example 7.4 is $46,887. The difference of $18 between $46,887 and $46,905 is due to rounding errors

____8
CAPITALIZED COST AND CAPITAL RECOVERY

8.1 INTRODUCTION

In the preceding chapter, we introduced figures of merit for choosing among alternatives with relatively short-term planning horizons. In this chapter, we introduce a class of problems involving relatively long-term horizons—so long term, in fact, that we can often assume infinite horizons without introducing any appreciable errors in the capital selection process.

Three important topics are covered.

- Cotermination with infinite planning horizons
- Capitalized cost (CC), a present worth
- Capital recovery (CR), an annual worth

One way to coterminate capital investment opportunities is to assume an infinite planning horizon. For long-lived investments such as dams, tunnels, bridges, and highways, the use of infinite rather than finite planning horizons of 25 to 100 years introduces negligible errors into rate-of-return computations. In addition, as we shall see, there are occasions for which infinite planning horizons provide convenient shortcuts for cost studies involving short-lived investments.

The concept of an infinite planning horizon leads to the concept of capitalized cost (CC). This is the equivalent present worth of a uniform series of cash disbursements extending to infinity.

The last topic, capital recovery (CR), covers the cost of capital recovery with a return and its application to pricing and costing in the public sector.

8.2 INFINITE PLANNING HORIZONS

The assumption that a long-lived investment has an infinite rather than a finite life often simplifies rate-of-return calculations due to the behavior of the A/P and P/A factors as N approaches infinity.

You will recall from Chapter 6 that the A/P factors for any interest rate, i, approach i as N gets larger and larger. P/A factors, the reciprocal of A/P factors, therefore approach $1/i$. The proof, if you need one, is in Appendix 6A.

It follows that the equivalent present worth, P, of a perpetual uniform series, A, is

$$P = A(P/A,i,\infty) = A/i \qquad (8.1)$$

and the equivalent perpetual uniform series, A, of an investment, P, is

$$A = P(A/P,i,\infty) = Pi \qquad (8.2)$$

Equations (8.1) and (8.2) are convenient for investments that can be considered perpetual. If you were to invest $100,000 at some rate of return, say 5%, which could continue "forever," the annual income would be $5,000, as given by equation (8.2).

$$A = Pi = \$100,000 \times 0.05 = \$5,000$$

Similarly, if you wanted to endow a chair at your university with a sum to provide an annual income of $50,000 "forever," that sum, at 5%, would be $1,000,000, as given by equation (8.1).

$$P = A/i = \$50,000/0.05 = \$1,000,000$$

In Table 8.1 below, P/A factors are shown for rates of return of 10%, 15%, 20%, and 30%, and for life cycles of 25, 50, 100, and infinite years.

As expected, the higher the rate of return is, the smaller is the number of years for which the P/A factor does not differ appreciably from $1/i$. For 10%, there is a difference of less than 1% between the factors for 50 years and

TABLE 8.1   P/A Factors

Rate, %	25 Years	50 Years	100 Years	Infinity, $1/i$
10	9.047	9.915	9.999	10.000
15	6.464	6.661	6.667	6.667
20	4.948	4.999	5.000	5.000
30	3.329	3.333	3.333	3.333

infinity. At 20%, the difference between 25 years and infinity is less than 1%. For 30%, this difference is approximately 0.1%.

In Example 8.1, two long-lived investments are compared, using both finite and infinite life cycles.

Example 8.1 Tunnel or Bridge The Port Authority of one of our major cities is considering two options to ease the traffic congestion across the river, which divides the city in two. These are a toll tunnel and a toll bridge. The cash flow estimates in millions of dollars for the two alternatives are given below.

Alternative	First Cost	Annual Net Cash Flow	Life Span
Tunnel	− $100	$20	75 years
Bridge	− 50	12	50 years

The annual net cash flow is positive, since the revenue from toll collections is expected to exceed the operating and maintenance costs. The tunnel is estimated to cost twice as much as the bridge but, because of its more favorable location, is expected to produce substantially greater net cash flows. The MARR is 15%. The cash flow diagram is Figure 8.1.

The LCM of the two investments is 150 years. However, it makes little sense to coterminate using three replications for the bridge and two for the tunnel. Rather,

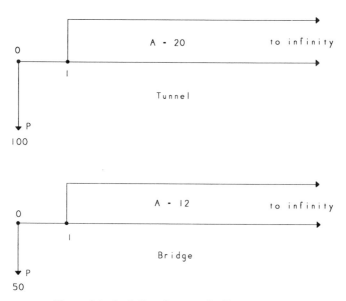

Figure 8.1. Cash flow diagrams for Example 8.1.

the cost study should be carried out for either a finite planning horizon of 50 years or an infinite planning horizon. For the tunnel, the AW is as follows:

For 50-Year Life
$$AW = -P(A/P,i,N) + A$$
$$= -\$100(A/P,15,50) + \$20$$
$$= -\$100 \times 0.1501 + \$20$$
$$= \$4.99 \text{ million}$$

For Infinite Life
$$AW = -\$100(A/P,15,\infty) + \$20$$
$$= -\$100 \times 0.1500 + \$20$$
$$= \$5.00 \text{ million}$$

You are probably asking, "How can we use a 50-year life for an investment that will last 75 years?" The reason is that at 15% the present value of the cash flows for years 51 to 75 is not significant. To see this, convert the uniform series for this time span to its present worth.

$$PW = \$20(P/A,15,25)(P/F,15,50)$$
$$= \$20 \times 6.464 \times 0.0009$$
$$= \$0.1 \text{ million}$$

We see that $20,000,000 per year for 25 years, starting 50 years from now, has a present worth of only $100,000.

For the bridge, the AW is as follows:

For 50-Year Life
$$AW = -\$50(A/P,15,50) + \$12$$
$$= -\$50 \times 0.1501 + \$12$$
$$= \$4.50 \text{ million}$$

For Infinite Life
$$AW = -\$50(A/P,15,\infty) + \$12$$
$$= -\$50 \times 0.1500 + \$12$$
$$= \$4.50 \text{ million}$$

Obviously, there is no significant difference between using the finite life of the shorter-lived (50-year) investment or an infinite life span.

The P/A factor for 50 years is 6.661. For infinity it is $1/i$ (1/0.15), which equals 6.667. These values are again so close that whether or not we use one or the other is immaterial. For the tunnel, the present value is $33 million (5.0/0.15) and for the bridge, $30 million (4.5/0.15).

The discounted cash flow computations favor the tunnel. Whether the Port

Authority decides to expend an additional $50 million for this alternative is one of the many factors, including a host of irreducibles, that impact on a final decision.

Does the assumption of end-of-year cash flows, as in Example 8.1, so distort our results that the conclusions reached cannot be taken too seriously? That this is not the case is illustrated by reworking Example 8.1 with more realistic cash flow assumptions.

Example 8.2   Tunnel and Bridge Revisited   A tunnel or a bridge will not spring up complete at the end of year zero. Neither will the annual cash flows all gush in at the end of years 1 to 50. A more reasonable assumption for the first cost is a 3-year construction period. For the annual cash flows, the continuous cash flow convention will give equivalent present or annual worths that closely approximate those for daily, weekly, or monthly cash flows.

A revised cash flow diagram for these assumptions is given in Figure 8.2. The EOY 0 has arbitrarily been set at the end of the construction period. The cash flow table, in millions of dollars, follows.

EOY	Tunnel	Bridge
−2	$−30	$−15
−1	−40	−20
0	−30	−15
1−50	20	12

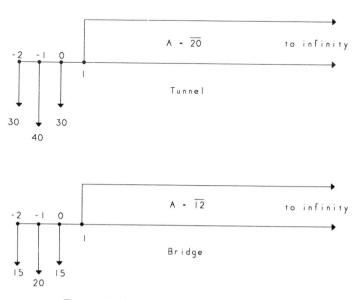

Figure 8.2. Cash flow diagrams for Example 8.2.

The equivalent present value of the first cost of the tunnel at EOY 0 is

$$PW = -[\$30(F/P,15,2) + \$40(F/P,15,1) + \$30]$$
$$= -[(\$30 \times 1.323) + (\$40 \times 1.150) + \$30]$$
$$= -\$116 \text{ million}$$

and for the first cost of the bridge

$$PW = -[\$15(F/P,15,2) + \$20(F/P,15,1) + \$15]$$
$$= -\$58 \text{ million}$$

For the uniform series, the equivalent present value is obtained by substituting $P/\overline{A}$ for P/A. But we know from Chapter 6 (refer to Table 6.4 and Appendix 6A) that

$$P/\overline{A} = P/A[i/ln(1 + i)]$$

Therefore, the equivalent present values of the annual cash flows equal those obtained in Example 8.1 multiplied by the continuous cash flow factor $i/ln(1 + i)$, which, for 15%, is 1.073 (0.150/0.1398). Values of these factors are given in Appendix D.

Summing up, we have

	Present Worths (in millions)	
	Tunnel	Bridge
First cost	$ - 116	$ - 58
Annual cash flows	143	81
Total	$27	$23

Our computations still favor the tunnel. In fact, the tunnel now looks somewhat better in comparison with the bridge. For the end-of-year assumption, its present worth was 10% higher than that for the bridge [($33 − $30)/$30]. For the more realistic assumptions, its present worth is 17% higher [($27 − $23)/$23)].

Does this comparison indicate that the preliminary analysis was worth doing? The answer is yes, since it clearly pointed us in the right direction. Should we proceed with a more refined analysis? Possibly, but especially if the comparisons based on end-of-year assumptions are close.

COMMENT: An end-of-year analysis should not be applied when one alternative actually has end-of-year cash flows and the other does not. Suppose a corporation has a choice between buying an existing facility or constructing a new one. The end-of-year assumption would apply to the first alternative, assuming, as is often the case, a one-time payment, but not to the second alternative, since funds would be expended over a period of time that might consist of several years.

The assumption of infinite life can also simplify rate-of-return calculations for short-lived investments, as illustrated by Example 8.3.

Example 8.3 Short-lived Investments Consider two relatively short-lived investments, A and B, for which the following data are available:

	A	B
Life cycle, years	7	9
Annual worth, thousands	$50	$55

What are the present worths of investments A and B?

The planning horizon is the LCM of 7 and 9, which is 63. We know from Chapter 7 (see Example 7.5) that the annual worths for life cycles of 7 and 9 years are identical with annual worths for a planning horizon of 63 years (the LCM of 7 and 9) or, for that matter, for any planning horizon, including infinity.

For an MARR of 10%, the P/A factor for 63 years is 9.975; for infinity, it is 10.0 ($1/i$ equals $1/0.10$). The difference is again negligible. For a P/A value of 10.0, the present worths of investments A and B are $500,000 and $550,000 respectively.

By this time, you have probably asked yourself, "Why do we call investments for which the planning horizon is 63 years short-term?" Are we really going to replicate alternative A nine times (63/7) and alternative B seven times (63/9) if we choose one or the other? The answer was given to you in Chapter 7: "Of course not."

There will be new and improved designs, new market forces, new competitors, new management teams among the old competitors. At the end of seven or nine years, when the first life cycle of one or the other alternative is near completion, we will conduct the same type of study to compare the alternatives then available. We can make a direct comparison using annual worths without worrying about replication. But for those decision makers who prefer present worths (and there are some), we have to coterminate to obtain the proper P/A factor for converting annual to present worths.

An alternate approach and a sound one for equipment for which second-hand markets exist is to use early-sale cotermination, but this, too, involves certain assumptions, none of which, such as an early sale, may actually occur.

The point we are making is that whether the assumed events on which LCM cotermination or early-sale cotermination are based ever happen is immaterial. The assumptions serve as a useful tool for comparing and selecting alternatives now.

8.3 CAPITALIZED COST

Capitalized cost is by definition the sum of the first cost, P, of an investment plus the present worth of perpetual periodic cash disbursements.

Consider the cash flow diagram in Figure 8.3. The capitalized cost (CC) of this set of cash flows is

$$CC = P + A/i \qquad\qquad (8.3)$$

You can picture CC as the amount of money you would have to have in hand in order to cover the first cost, P, with enough left over, namely the sum A/i, to enable you, if you invested it at i, to disburse A dollars annually forever.

> *COMMENT:* If A is a perpetual net cash inflow or receipt rather than a disbursement (i.e., a negative cash outflow) and A/i exceeds P, CC is, of course, negative. It then becomes, by changing its sign, a positive capitalized worth. However, this term is used infrequently.

Suppose, as is often the case, that there are not only annual cash disbursements but also other cash disbursements, such as major overhauls, which recur every few years and also go on forever. What then is the capitalized cost? Example 8.4 covers this problem.

Example 8.4   Capitalized Cost for a Highway Project   Consider a highway project with an initial cost of $100 million, annual maintenance expenses of $3 million, and major overhaul expenditures every five years of $5 million. What is the capitalized cost of this investment for an MARR of 10%?
    The cash flow diagram is given in Figure 8.4. The initial investment, P, is $100 million. In addition, there are two sets of perpetual cash disbursements. The first set is an annual uniform series, A, amounting to $3 million. The second is the overhaul expenditures, F, of $5 million that occur every five years.
    The cash flow table for this investment is given below. All figures are in millions of dollars.

End of Year	Symbol	First Cost	O&M Costs	Major Overhaul Costs
0	P	$100	—	—
1 to ∞	A	—	$3	—
5,10,15 . . . ∞	F	—	—	$5

Figure 8.3. Cash flow diagram for capitalized cost.

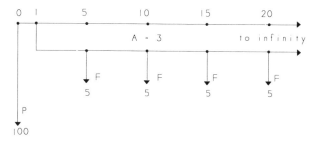

Figure 8.4. Cash flow diagram for Example 8.4.

The capitalized cost consists of three terms: the first cost, P; the capitalized cost of A, which we now know is A/i; and the capitalized cost of the major overhauls, F, which occur every five years. For the latter, we first have to find the equivalent perpetual uniform series. This series has an annual cost of

$$\text{AC of major overhauls} = F(A/F,i,p)$$

where p equals the interval between the major overhauls, which in this case is five years.

To see this more clearly, consider Figure 8.5. Diagram A is a uniform series in which a sum, F, recurs every p years. Diagram B is an equivalent cash flow diagram in which each F has been replaced by its equivalent uniform series, $F(A/F,i,p)$. Diagram C is obviously equivalent to diagram B and therefore to diagram A.

It follows that the perpetual annual uniform series $F(A/F,i,p)$ is equivalent to

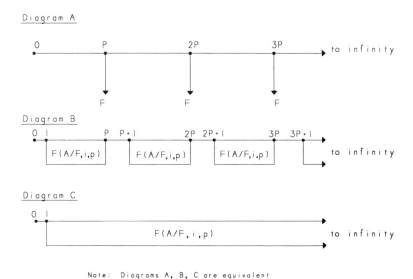

Figure 8.5. Equivalent cash flow diagrams for Example 8.4.

a perpetual series of cash flows, F, recurring every p years forever. The capitalized cost of this series is therefore $F(A/F,i,p)/i$.

The computations based on this discussion follow.

$$CC = P + A(P/A,i,\infty) + F(A/F,i,p)/i$$
$$= \$100 + \$3(P/A,10,\infty) + \$5(A/F,10,5)/0.1$$
$$= \$100 + \$3 \times 10 + \$5 \times 0.1638 \times 10$$
$$= \$100 + \$30 + \$8$$
$$= \$138 \text{ million}$$

There are, of course, many long-lived investments, such as toll bridges, highways, and tunnels, for which the perpetual uniform annual series is a net cash inflow. Suppose that in Example 8.4 the annuity A had been a cash inflow rather than an outflow of $3 million. Its present worth would have been plus $30 million, and the capitalized cost of the proposed facility would have been $78 million $(100 - 30 + 8)$.

Suppose we had used a life span of 50 years for the highway project in Example 8.4 and calculated the present worth and the EUAC for this life span. How close would these values be to those for an infinite life span? We already know the answer: very close. However, the more problems of this type you do, the more proficient you become in time-value-of-money computations and, we hope, the more convinced you become that infinite planning horizons make sense.

The calculations for a 50-year life span are given in Example 8.5. The cash flow diagram is Figure 8.6. We assume that net salvage value, which plays no part in infinite planning horizons, is negligible. (For a 50-year life cycle and an MARR of 10%, the P/F factor for salvage recovery, if there were any, is only 0.0085.)

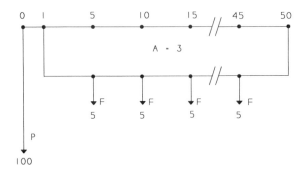

Figure 8.6. Cash flow diagram for Example 8.5.

Example 8.5 Finite Life Cycle for Highway Project For 50 years, the EUAC of the highway investment in Example 8.4 is

$$\text{EUAC} = \$3 + \$5[(P/F,10,5) + (P/F,10,10) + (P/F,10,15) \ldots$$
$$+ (P/F,10,45)](A/P,10,50) + \$100(A/P,10,50)$$

The first term is the annual O&M cost of $3 million. The second converts each of the nine major overhaul costs (there are only nine, since no major overhaul would be expended at the termination of the life cycle) to their present worths (the factors in brackets) and then multiplies the resultant sum by the A/P factor for 50 years to give the equivalent annual cost. The third term is the equivalent annual cost of the initial investment. Substituting in this equation gives

$$\text{EUAC} = \$3 + \$5[0.6209 + 0.3855 + 0.2394 + 0.1486$$
$$+ 0.0923 + 0.0573 + 0.0356 + 0.0221 + 0.0137] \times 0.1009$$
$$+ \$100 \times 0.1009$$
$$= \$3 + \$5 \times 1.6154 \times 0.1009 + \$100 \times 0.1009$$
$$= \$3 + \$0.8 + \$10.1$$
$$= \$13.9 \text{ million}$$

The difference between this value and the EUAC of $13.8 million obtained with an infinite life span is less than 1%.

You should convince yourself that the sum of the nine P/F factors is 1.6154 by checking the value of these factors in the rate tables of Appendix B. You should also make sure you understand how the above factor equation was derived.

There is one other question that you may have asked yourself: "Can we avoid discounting each of the nine major overhaul costs separately?" We can by recognizing that these overhauls represent a uniform series for which the period M is five years, the nominal interest rate, r, is 50% (5 times 10%), and the periodic interest rate from equation (5.3) in Chapter 5 is

$$i = (1 + 0.10)^5 - 1 = 1.6105 - 1 = 0.6105 \text{ or } 61.05\%$$

The P/A factor for this rate and for N equals 9 (there are 9 annuity payments, as shown in Figure 8.6) is therefore

$$P/A = \frac{(1 + i)^N - 1}{i(1 + i)^N} = \frac{(1.6105)^9 - 1}{0.6105(1.6105)^9}$$
$$= \frac{72.88 - 1}{0.6105 \times 72.88} = 1.6155$$

This is an excellent check against the sum of the P/F factors in Example 8.4, which equaled 1.6154.

8.4 CAPITAL RECOVERY

We don't need to remind you that investors expect to recover the capital they have invested in a project as early as possible but not later than its demise. In fact, they want to recover not only their capital but also a return.

Among the rate-of-return factors derived in Chapter 6 you will find one factor—the *A/P* factor—that is dubbed the "capital recovery" factor. A more descriptive name would be the "capital-recovery-with-a-return factor," but this is a little clumsy, so the shorter version is always used. However, the longer version emphasizes that, as investors or creditors, we have two objectives in mind—to recover our capital and to receive a return for investing or lending it.

The capital recovery of an investment is a uniform series representing the difference between the equivalent annual cost of the first cost and the equivalent annual worth of the salvage value. The cash flow diagram is shown in Figure 8.7. Figure 8.7A gives the two cash flows *P* and *S*. Figure 8.7B gives the two uniform series equivalent to *P* and *S*, and Figure 8.7C shows the capital recovery.

The equation for the capital recovery is

$$CR = P(A/P,i,N) - S(A/F,i,N) \qquad (8.4)$$

Since the *A/F* factor equals the *A/P* factor minus *i*, equation (8.4) can be

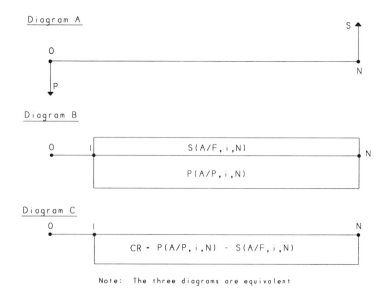

Note: The three diagrams are equivalent

Figure 8.7. Capital recovery with salvage.

written

$$CR = (P - S)(A/P,i,N) + iS \qquad (8.5)$$

or

$$CR = (P - S)(A/F,i,n) + iP \qquad (8.6)$$

These two equations are easier to apply in that we need to look up only one rate-of-return factor.

Because capital recovery (CR) finds so many applications in asset replacement studies and in the pricing of goods and services—particularly in the public sector—we examine the A/P factor more fully in the following subsections for its application to both finite and infinite planning horizons.

8.4.1 Capital Recovery and Finite Horizons

A new venture is under review, the cash flow diagram for which is shown in Figure 8.8A. Its first cost is P. The salvage value is S. The projected revenues have been converted into an equivalent annual series. Call this series A_R. Similarly, the estimated cash disbursements for expenses are represented by a uniform series A_C. The difference—$(A_R - A_C)$—is the equivalent net cash flow from operations that we first brought to your attention in our discussion of statements of income in Chapter 2.

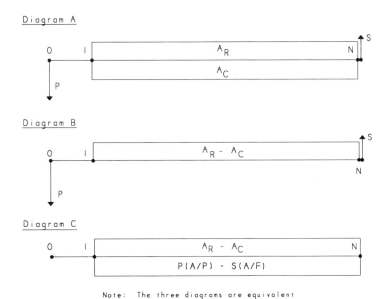

Note: The three diagrams are equivalent

Figure 8.8. Equivalent cash flow diagrams.

The annual worth of the cash flow pattern of Figure 8.8A is

$$AW = -P(A/P,i,N) + A_R - A_C + S(A/F,i,N)$$

The capital recovery cost is

$$CR = P(A/P,i,N) - S(A/F,i,N)$$

Therefore,

$$AW = -CR + (A_R - A_C)$$

As mentioned, Figure 8.8A is the cash flow diagram. Figure 8.8B combines A_R and A_C into one uniform series. Figure 8.8C does the same for P and S.

Three situations are possible, depending on whether $(A_R - A_C)$ is equal to, greater than, or less than CR:

- If equal, the proposed investment will just produce the return (the MARR) on which the time-value computations for CR, A_R, and A_C are based.
- If greater, the proposed investment will produce a return greater than the MARR.
- If less, the proposed investment will not satisfy the MARR.

8.4.2 Capital Recovery and Infinite Horizons

For perpetual life, the A/P factor equals i and the A/F factor equals zero. This means that we can forget S in equation (8.4), since an ultimate sale or dismantling will never occur or rather, when it does, its annual worth will be infinitesimal. The capital recovery cost then becomes

$$CR = Pi \qquad (8.7)$$

The three situations just mentioned can occur again; that is, CR can be equal to, greater than, or less than $(A_R - A_C)$

8.5 PRICING AND COSTING

An example of the application of capital recovery costs to pricing and costing a utility service in the public sector will bring much of the preceding discussion to life.

Example 8.6 Quebec Hydroelectric Project This project is located in western Quebec. It harnesses several rivers flowing into James Bay, which is an extension of Hudson Bay. The project was planned for several phases, of which phase 1 was completed in 1985 at a cost of 14 billion Canadian dollars, including transmission lines to such major consumption centers as Montreal.

The capacity of the first phase is 62.2×10^9 kilowatt hours annually. The transmission losses to consumers were estimated at 6%. The output for estimating the cost of electricity when operating at full capacity is therefore 58.5×10^9 kwh.

Operating and maintenance materials and labor are substantially independent of output for hydroelectric projects. These costs were estimated at 150 million Canadian dollars annually, or approximately 0.25 Canadian cents per kwh ($150 \times 10^8/58.5 \times 10^9$) for the output.

Capital recovery costs were based on a rate of return of 11.5% and a life cycle of 50 years, for which the CR factor $(A/P,11.5,50)$ equals 0.1155. (You will note that this is, for all practical purposes, identical to the A/P factor for infinite life, which equals 0.1150.) The annual capital recovery cost, neglecting salvage value, is therefore

$$CR = P(A/P,11.5,50)$$
$$= (\$14 \times 10^9)(0.1155)$$
$$= \$1.61 \times 10^9$$

The estimated minimum unit price at which electricity will have to be sold when operating at full capacity is then 3 Canadian cents per kwh, as shown below.

	$/year	Cents/kwh
O&M costs	\$ 150,000,000	0.25
Capital recovery costs	1,610,000,000	2.75
Total	\$1,760,000,000	3.00

COMMENT: You are wondering perhaps how an MARR of 11.5% was arrived at for this study. In this case, it was an estimate of the rate of return the Province would have to offer in order to issue bonds for financing the project.

This completes our discussion of the three worths and the related concepts of capitalized cost and capital recovery. We now proceed to the fourth figure of merit listed in the introduction to Chapter 7, the internal rate of return, or IRR.

8.6 SUMMARY

For capital investment studies involving long-lived alternatives—alternatives with life cycles greater than 20–25 years—two approaches are possible. One is to use an infinite planning horizon. The other is to assume a finite planning horizon for which the shortest life among the long-lived options will usually do. The first approach is the simpler and usually produces answers that do not deviate appreciably from the second.

Capitalized cost is defined as the present worth of the first cost of a perpetual investment plus the present worth of its cash disbursements forever and aye. The latter is obtained by converting the disbursements into a perpetual annual uniform series and then dividing this series by the rate of return. Capitalized cost is not as popular a figure of merit for comparing alternatives as it once was, but it is still a concept with which you should be familiar.

Capital recovery costs are the costs of recovering the first cost of investments, including a return thereon. They are negative annual worths, or better said, equivalent uniform annual costs. The concept applies to both finite and infinite planning horizons and finds important applications in asset replacement studies.

PROBLEMS

Infinite Planning Horizons

8-1   A company with limited resources is evaluating two new products, of which only one will be launched. Product A has a first cost of $140,000 in plant tooling and expected net annual receipts of $27,000 for seven years. Product B has a first cost of $160,000 and expected net annual receipts of $38,000 for nine years. The company uses an MARR of 20%.

    a) Use the annual worth method to decide which project should be launched.

    b) Now calculate the NPW.

    c) What would be the NPW for an infinite planning horizon?

8-2   The manager of a bowling alley can choose between two alternatives for a bowling pin polishing machine.

	Plan A	Plan B
Life cycle	16 yrs.	24 yrs.
First cost	$8,000	$10,000
Annual cost	$3,200	$1,500

    a) Draw cash flow diagrams for the two alternatives.

    b) Compute the annual worths of the two alternatives, using a before-tax interest rate of 7%.

    c) What is the NPW of the two alternatives?

    d) Would your answer change if you were to assume infinite life cycles?

Capitalized Cost

8-3   Two alternative designs are being considered for a new college gymnasium. The estimated cash flows for the two alternatives are as follows:

	Alternatives	
	Structure 1	Structure 2
First cost	$10,000,000	$25,000,000
Annual O&M costs	200,000	100,000

Calculate the capitalized cost of each alternative using an MARR of 5%.

8-4 A new highway is expected to have initial costs of $75 million. The highway must be resurfaced every five years at a cost of $10 million. Annual operating costs for snow removal and inspection are expected to be $1 million. Determine the capitalized cost of the highway, using an interest rate of 12% compounded annually.

8-5 A firm is planning to endow an advanced telecommunications research laboratory at a university. The endowment will be used to fund the laboratory start-up costs of $100,000, annual operating costs of $45,000, and $25,000 every five years for new equipment. What is the capitalized cost at a rate of 8% compounded annually?

8-6 A city is considering a new water main that will cost $20 million and will need to be replaced every 40 years. As far as the city planners can foresee, the need for the water main is permanent. If the city requires a return of 7% per year, what is the capitalized cost of the water main?

Capital Recovery

8-7 A high-precision lathe costs $20,000 and has a salvage value equal to 10% of the original cost after ten years. Determine the capital recovery at a rate of 8%, compounded annually.

8-8 A machine costs $25,000 and has annual operating costs of $6,000. The machine has a ten-year life and a salvage value of 5% of the original price. Assume an MARR of 10%.
a) What is the capital recovery cost?
b) What is the EUAC, including CR costs?
c) What would the EUAC be if the operating costs were continuous?

8-9 A new process has an expected first cost of $20,000 and a salvage value of $2,000 after five years. When implemented, the process is expected to generate net annual receipts of $5,000. What is the capital recovery cost and the annual worth of the process at an MARR of 15%?

8-10 Consider two projects with the following cash flows:

	Alternatives	
	Project A	Project B
First cost	$22,000	$40,000
Annual expenses	$4,000	$1,000
Salvage value	0	$10,000

The life of both projects is ten years.
a) Calculate the EUACs at 15%, compounded annually.
b) Calculate the capital recovery cost of both projects.

8-11 Compare projects A and B in Problem 8-10, assuming project B has a life span of 15 years.

Pricing and Costing

8-12 Sym's Locks have just purchased a new key-cutting machine for $15,000. Maintenance for the machine is estimated at $1,500 per year. The useful life of the machine is 20 years, and the expected average number of keys cut in a day is 40. If Sym's Locks wants a rate of return of 10%, what should be the minimum price charged to cut a key?

8-13 Metro Transit is considering building an additional bridge to relieve traffic on an extremely congested river crossing. The costs of construction of the bridge have been bid at $50 million. Operating and maintenance costs have been estimated at $4 million per year. Traffic conditions on the bridge are expected to average 13,000 cars per day. If the desired rate of return is 12%, what should be the amount of the toll per crossing? (Assume infinite life.)

8-14 Paradise Lines is considering running a new cruise ship to the Caribbean Islands. Buying and outfitting a new ship is estimated to cost $18.6 million. Operating and maintenance costs for running 26 two-week long cruises per year (including food and entertainment) have been estimated at $13 million per year. If the ship's capacity is 250 passengers and average expected occupancy is 85%, what should be the minimum fare? Assume an MARR of 20%.

8-15 Apex Consultants has just invested in a computer system costing $50,000. Maintenance for the system has been contracted for $5,000 annually for the useful life of the computer, which is estimated at five years. The system will be used for record keeping and preparation of reports. Computer usage has been estimated at 80 hours per job and at five jobs per month. If the company desires a 20% return on its investment, how much computer overhead should be applied to a current job that requires 100 hours of computer usage?

____9
THE INTERNAL RATE OF RETURN

9.1 INTRODUCTION

In the introduction to Chapter 7, we mentioned five figures of merit commonly used in assessing capital investment opportunities. Three of these—the three worths with their offshoots, capitalized cost and capital recovery—were covered in Chapters 7 and 8. Of the remaining two, the internal rate of return (IRR) is discussed here and the benefit-cost ratio (BCR) is discussed in Chapter 11.

You have already been introduced to the IRR, at least subliminally, in one of the examples in Chapter 6 (*see* Example 6.2), in which the present values of the cash inflows were set equal to the present values of the cash outflows in order to obtain the rate of return that made these two PV aggregates equal. This rate of return was defined as the internal rate of return, or IRR, that is, the rate for which the algebraic sum of the present or future or annual worths of all of the cash flows—positive and negative—is zero.

Another glimpse at the IRR occurred in Chapter 8, in which we equated the annual worth of the net cash flow differential between cash receipts and cash disbursements with the capital recovery cost (*see* Section 8.4.1). The rate of return that satisfied this equality was the IRR. Our objective now is to take a closer look at this figure of merit.

9.2 MARRs AND IRRs

You have by now had enough experience with rate-of-return calculations to recognize that the discount factors for computing present worth become smaller and smaller as the interest rate increases. It follows that

- If the present worth for a set of cash inflows and outflows is positive, the rate of return that makes the present worth zero—the IRR—will be greater than the rate of return—the MARR—for which the present worth of the set was calculated.
- If the present worth is negative, the IRR will be less than the MARR.
- If the present worth is zero, the IRR will equal the MARR.

What applies to present worth applies equally to annual worth and future worth.

> *COMMENT:* We have not yet described how an investor selects an MARR, except to point out that the selection is a personal one influenced by the attitude of the investor toward risk and by the opportunities that the investor will forgo if he or she invests here rather than there. A fuller discussion of this topic is given in Chapter 14.

As a figure of merit, the IRR is easily understood by investors. The financial pages of the leading daily newspapers all provide information on past, current, and expected future rates of return from a wide variety of credit instruments, including commercial loans, mortgages, U.S. government securities, tax-free municipal bonds, and corporate bonds. Earnings and yields on corporate stocks are also reported. Although these are not directly comparable with rates of return on loan instruments, they nevertheless do provide an additional parameter against which to compare particular capital investment opportunities.

The higher the risk of not recovering one's capital is, the higher is the desired rate of return or MARR. (If the cost studies still show an IRR higher than the MARR, so much the better.) The lowest rates of return commonly reported are the prime rate—the rate at which banks lend money to major corporations—and the rates on U.S. government securities, such as 30-year Treasury bonds. These rates serve as a bellwether for other rates, including those applied to project selection studies. Like most quoted rates, except municipals and other tax-exempt securities, they are before-tax rates. An investor, in comparing rates of return on high-risk capital investments with quoted returns on low-risk investments such as most credit instruments, must, of course, distinguish between before-tax and after-tax rates. Thus, for income taxes in the 30–40% range, a coupon rate of 10% on a low-risk corporate bond is roughly equivalent to a 6–7% after-tax return. The return on less secure investments is therefore a multiple (usually at least 1.5) of this return.

The MARRs used for the selection of public-sector projects often approach the rates at which the sponsoring agency can borrow. Since profit is not a motive and since risk is usually not a factor, the discounted cash flow methodology simply serves as the preferred way of allocating funds to those projects, among the many crying for attention, that appear to be the most feasible, considering monetary consequences alone. (We deal with the philosophy behind using MARRs for the public sector in Chapter 14.) Similar arguments apply to asset replacement studies, in which risks are low and discounted cash flow calculations are used to determine whether higher first costs justify lower operating and maintenance costs.

To sum up, the MARR is the minimum rate that investors want for the risks they expect, and the IRR is the return that they will get if the cash flow estimates in the cost studies prove to be true. If such studies are favorable, investors in corporate businesses will provide infusions of capital via equity financing (shares of stock) and creditor financing (bonds), and will anticipate returns via dividends and capital appreciation on shares and interest income on bonds. The expected return on share ownership will usually be substantially higher than that on creditor financing, excluding so-called junk bonds.

9.3 INTERNAL RATE OF RETURN

The IRR bears many names—the discounted cash flow rate of return (DCF-ROR), the hurdle rate, the target rate, the cutoff rate, and the profitability index (PI), to name a few.

There is no need to spend much time on the mathematics of finance for calculating IRRs. The fundamentals were covered in Chapter 6. The "given" in IRR calculations is that the present worth equals zero. The unknown is the rate of return (the IRR). This contrasts with present worth (or annual and future worth) calculations, for which the "given" is the rate of return (the MARR) and the unknown is the present worth.

For a present worth of zero, the following relationship holds [see equation (7.1)]:

$$0 = \sum_{j=0}^{j=N} A_j (1 + i)^{-j} \tag{9.1}$$

If the NPW is zero, then the present value of all of the positive cash flows will equal the present value of all of the negative cash flows; that is,

$$PW_{in} = PW_{out} \tag{9.2}$$

Equation (9.2) obviously says the same thing as equation (9.1) but in not quite as sophisticated a manner.

If all of the cash flows are in one direction or the other, we don't have an IRR. What do we do then? We use any of the three worths and select the option with the highest worth. However, this does not necessarily rule out applications of the IRR. We use it, as we did in Chapter 7, to check the rate of return on incremental investments. This topic is developed more fully in Part II.

9.4   IRR APPLICATIONS

In many cost studies, the present worth of each alternative is first calculated using the MARR. If the present worth is positive, the IRR is then routinely determined. There is a good reason for this. If you are not sufficiently interested in an investment to determine what rate of return the cash flow estimates might produce, you should not be investing at all. We proceed in this way, in the examples that follow.

Example 9.1   A Simple IRR Problem   The Gatehouse Company, an A/E firm (architects and engineers), needs to update its computer hardware and software for computer-aided drafting and design. The choice has been narrowed down to two alternatives, Alpha and Beta. The estimates on the basis of which a replacement of the existing equipment is to be made are summarized below.

	Alpha	Beta
Capital cost	$100,000	$230,000
Yearly savings	$30,000	$65,000
Service life	5 yrs.	5 yrs.

The yearly savings are estimates of the cost reductions that can be expected with a new installation as compared to the existing installation. The cash flow diagrams for the two alternatives are given in Figure 9.1. The factor formulas for calculating the present worths for an MARR of 10% before taxes follow.
   For Alpha,

$$PW = \$30,000(P/A,10,5) - \$100,000$$
$$= \$30,000 \times 3.791 - \$100,000$$
$$= \$13,700$$

and for Beta,

$$PW = \$65,000(P/A,10,5) - \$230,000$$
$$= \$65,000 \times 3.791 - \$230,000$$
$$= \$16,400$$

   Both alternatives show positive present worths. Therefore, the IRR for both is greater than the MARR of 10%. Beta has the higher present worth and is favored. However, before a decision on whether to go with Beta is made, the IRRs should be calculated.
   Setting the PW for Alpha to zero,

$$0 = \$30,000(P/A,i,5) - \$100,000$$
$$(P/A,i,5) = \$100,000/\$30,000$$
$$= 3.333$$

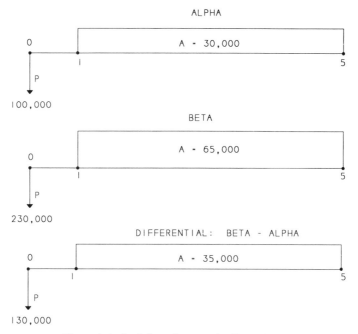

Figure 9.1. Cash flow diagrams for Example 9.1.

For Beta,

$$0 = \$65,000(P/A,i,5) - \$230,000$$

$$(P/A,i,5) = \$230,000/\$65,000$$

$$= 3.538$$

As we know, there are several ways to obtain the IRR in the preceding equations. The simplest way by far is to use a hand calculator that has been programmed to solve financial and business problems. The knowns are tabulated below. The letters within parentheses are the symbols usually used on hand calculators. For Alpha, any two numbers whose ratio is 3.333 can be punched in for P and A, respectively. This also applies to Beta but for the ratio 3.538.

	Alpha	Beta
P (PV)	3.333 or 100,000	3.538 or 230,000
A (PMT)	1 or 30,000	1 or 65,000
N (N or n)	5	5

The value of the unknown i is 15.2% for Alpha and 12.7% for Beta, indicating that ranking the two alternatives by their IRRs favors Alpha, although the ranking with PWs favors Beta. What we do about this anomaly will be discussed later.

If a hand calculator is not available, the interest rate tables in Appendix B can be used. For Beta, for example, the P/A values that bound the P/A ratio of 3.538 are 3.605 for 12% and 3.352 for 15%. The value of the IRR using straight-line interpolation is calculated below.

Rate	P/A	Differences
12%	3.605	
		0.066
IRR	3.539	
		0.187
15%	3.352	

Interpolating, we get

$$\text{IRR} = 12 + (15 - 12) \, \frac{0.066}{0.066 + 0.187}$$

$$= 12 + 3(0.066/0.253) = 12 + 3 \times 0.261$$

$$= 12.8\%$$

This answer differs from that obtained using a hand calculator by 0.1%, which is insignificant. However, the answer obtained from the hand calculator is the more accurate one, since it is not based on linear interpolation between variables that do not have a linear relationship.

With the present worths favoring Beta and the IRRs favoring Alpha, which figure of merit do we use for ranking, that is, for selecting one or the other of the two alternatives? Chapter 12 provides a full answer to this question, but the preview that follows will ease your misgivings on the value of what we have been doing so far.

The incremental investment in Beta is $130,000 ($230,000 − $100,000). The incremental savings are $35,000 ($65,000 − $30,000) per year for five years. What return is there on an investment of $130,000 that results in savings of this magnitude, or, to ask the question in another way, what rate of return makes the present worth of $35,000 for five years equal $130,000? The IRR for the differential investment is calculated below. The cash flow diagram is given in Figure 9.1.

$$0 = \$35,000(P/A,i,5) - \$130,000$$

$$(P/A,i,5) = \$130,000/\$35,000$$

$$= 3.714$$

The value of i is 10.8%, which is lower than that of Alpha or Beta but still higher than the MARR of 10%.

If the Gatehouse Company is serious about investing in replacements that meet its MARR investment policy, it will opt for Beta. However, before making a final decision, it will probably take a second look at Beta to convince itself that the added capacity and the added features offered are worth an additional $130,000. The question of whether it can afford the higher first cost for Beta should not be an issue, since, if this were the case, it should not have been included as a feasible alternative for comparison with Alpha.

By this time, you may have asked yourself, "Of what value is the IRR for problems that involve substantially all negative cash flows, as in some of the problems in earlier chapters?" You already know that you examine the incremental cash flows to see if they will produce a return. This is done once again in Example 9.2.

Example 9.2   A More Difficult IRR Problem   We label this problem a more difficult one than Example 9.1 with tongue in cheek. Most of the problem was worked out in Example 7.7, in which we looked at the cash flow differential between two trucking options. We now carry on from there. For convenience, the differential cash flow tabulation prepared for that example is reproduced below.

The present worth equation in factor form for the differential cash flows in the last column of Table 9.1 also comes from Example 7.7 and is reproduced below.

$$PW = [\$5(P/A,20,12) + \$36(P/F,20,4) + \$36(P/F,20,8)]$$
$$- [\$45(P/F,20,6) - \$1(P/F,20,12) + \$10]$$
$$= \$22,970$$

This result indicates that the rate of return on the incremental cash investment of $10,000 ($50,000 − $40,000) for the more expensive truck is much higher than the MARR of 10%. But what is this rate? Without a computer or a calculator, it is going to take work to find it by trial and error. However, our judgment tells us to start high. We try 60%. The calculations are worked out in detail, as follows:

$$PW = [\$5(P/A,60,12) + \$36(P/F,60,4) + \$36(P/F,60,8) + \$1(P/F,60,12)]$$
$$- [\$45(P/F,60,6) + \$10]$$
$$= (\$5 \times 1.661 + \$36 \times 0.1526 + \$36 \times 0.0233 + \$0.0036)$$
$$- (\$45 \times 0.0596 + \$10)$$
$$= \$14.7 - \$12.7$$
$$= \$2.0 \text{ k}$$

TABLE 9.1   (Duplicates Table 7.2)   Cash Flows, Dollars per year (in thousands)

End of Year	Option 2	Option 1	Option 2 Less Option 1
0	$ − 50	$ − 40	$ − 10
1–4	− 30	− 35	5
4	—	− 36	36
5–6	− 30	− 35	5
6	− 45	—	− 45
7–8	− 30	− 35	5
8	—	− 36	36
9–12	− 30	− 35	5
12	5	4	1

The present worth is still plus. On our next attempt, we try 70%.

$$PW = [\$5(P/A,70,12) + \$36(P/F,70,4) + \$36(P/F,70,8) + \$1(P/F,70\%,12)]$$
$$\quad - [\$45(P/F,70\%,6) + \$10]$$
$$= (\$5 \times 1.426 + \$36 \times 0.120 + \$36 \times 0.014 + \$0.002)$$
$$\quad - (\$45 \times 0.414 + \$10)$$
$$= \$12.0 - \$11.9$$
$$= \$0.1 \text{ k}$$

We are so close to zero that there is not much point in going further with trial-and-error calculations. However, if we did, we would find that the IRR would be 70.5%.

A rate of return of 70% has to be taken seriously, even if it is before taxes. It will be difficult to find an alternative opportunity (an opportunity forgone) for investing $10,000 that will improve on this return.

Example 9.2 illustrates why many investors want to see the IRR. A present worth is difficult to visualize and relate to other investment opportunities. A rate of return is not. We know the return will be substantially higher than the MARR, assuming the estimates on which the study is based are sound. However, we could not have known that it would go as high as 70% without computing the IRR.

Once you have the fundamentals in hand and have an understanding of what calculators and computers can do, you no longer need to go through tiresome trial-and-error solutions, as we just did. For computers, there are specific economic evaluation packages and spreadsheet programs, such as Lotus 1-2-3. These include algorithms for calculating present worths for any rate of return and for calculating the IRR. Graphical features are also available to graph PWs versus rates of return (i's). Example 9.3 illustrates such a curve for the problem discussed in Example 9.2.

Example 9.3   Graphical Solution of IRR   The present worths for various rates of return for the truck problem in Example 9.2 are tabulated as follows:

Rate of Return, %	Present Worth (000)	
20	23.0	(23.0)
30	13.7	
40	8.1	
50	4.5	
60	2.0	(2.0)
70	0.1	(0.1)
80	-1.3	
90	-2.4	
100	-3.3	

We (or, rather, our hand calculator) have calculated the points in the present worth column in the table. The numbers in parentheses are those from our trial-and-error calculations. The differences are due to rounding. A graph of i versus PW is given in Figure 9.2.

As expected, the present worth decreases as the rate of return increases, and the IRR is the rate at which the PW crosses the x-axis.

Such calculations are so simple with the proper tools that, if you ever become seriously involved with time-value computations, you should at least invest in a hand calculator or, if the mood seizes you, in a software program that will not only do the calculations but also draw graphs like those in Figure 9.2. Appendix 9A is a sample of what can be done with the hand calculator used in solving the preceding problem.

9.5 LOANS AND THE IRR

What is the IRR of a loan? The answer is so obvious that we wondered whether we would be accused of talking down to you if we asked this question. We decided to take the chance.

Consider the loan first discussed in Example 5.6. A creditor lends $1,000 at 12%, repayable with interest at the end of five years. The sum F to be repaid is $1,762. The PW for the transaction is given by

$$PW = \$1,762(P/F,12,5) - \$1,000$$
$$= \$1,762 \times 0.5674 - \$1,000$$
$$= \$0$$

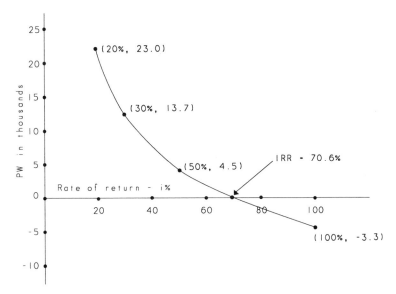

Figure 9.2. Graphical solution for IRR.

The IRR, therefore, equals the MARR.

If you need more convincing, go to Example 7.4, in which $100,000 was borrowed from a bank at 12%. The repayment schedule called for five end-of-year payments of $27,740. The IRR for this transaction also equals 12%, since

$$PW = \$27,740(P/A,12,5) - \$100,000$$
$$= \$27,740 \times 3.605 - \$100,000$$
$$= \$0$$

No matter what the repayment scheme, the IRR of a loan's cash flow pattern will always equal the interest rate on which the lender and the borrower had a meeting of the minds.

We now have one figure of merit to go—the benefit-cost ratio. However, before leaving the IRR, we need to look at some odd behavior patterns of both the IRR and the three worths. This is the major topic of Chapter 10.

9.6 SUMMARY

The IRR is the rate of return that makes the net present worth (and therefore the other two worths) of a set of cash flow streams equal to zero. In many cost studies for the selection of capital projects, the present or annual worth is first calculated for a given MARR. If it is positive, the IRR is then determined to see what the estimated rate of return on the investment could be if the estimates on which the study was based prove correct.

Many investors relate more easily to the IRR than to the present worth because of the ease of comparing it with market rates of return and other investment opportunities.

Several methods of computing the IRR were discussed, of which by far the simplest is the use of hand calculators programmed for financial and business applications. A second method relies on trial and error, using the interest rate tables in Appendix B. Still a third method is to apply one of the more sophisticated computer programs now available in which present worths are plotted against rates of return.

The IRR methodology is also applied to incremental cash flow patterns to determine the return on incremental investments due to lower expenses or higher revenues, or both. In short, do the incremental investments meet the MARR criteria? As mentioned, this topic is more fully developed in Part II.

PROBLEMS

Capital Budgeting and the IRR

9-1   As an amateur investor, you are presented with six independent investment alternatives.

Alternative	Initial Investment	IRR
A	$15,000	10%
B	20,000	25%
C	35,000	20%
D	10,000	12%
E	50,000	40%
F	30,000	35%

a) Which alternatives would you choose if your MARR were 22%? What would be the total funds required?

b) Which alternatives would you choose if your available funds totaled $60,000?

9-2 Lisa Green needs a refrigerator, cooking range, and microwave for her apartment. The local appliance store offers both purchase and lease packages on all three items. Lisa can either buy what she needs for $1,400 or lease the same items with semiannual payments of $300 as long as she remains in the apartment (assume four years). Determine the interest rate for which leasing and purchasing costs would be equal if the lease payments were due at the beginning of each period.

9-3 For Problem 9-2, determine what the effective interest rate would be if lease payments were $50, payable at the beginning of each month.

9-4 The Advanced Product Engineering Group has developed a list of potential, mutually exclusive project proposals as possible new investments. All have a ten-year life and no salvage value. Using IRR calculations and the data given in the following table, determine which project, if any, should be accepted. Use an MARR of 10%.

Project	First Cost	Annual Cash Flow
A	$100,000	$16,980
B	65,000	13,000
C	20,000	2,710
D	40,000	6,232
E	85,000	16,320
F	10,000	1,770

9-5 In 1985, Sam Smart purchased a small apartment building for $110,000. Receipts from rent have averaged $20,000 per year. Taxes, maintenance, and repair costs have totaled $6,000 per year. Sam intends to hold the property until he retires in 1995. At that time, he plans on selling it and estimates that he will at least get his investment of $110,000 back.

a) Draw the cash flow diagram for Sam's investment.

b) What is the internal rate of return on the investment?

c) Do you think that Sam's investment was a wise one? Why?

9-6 Corey Laboratories is evaluating two proposals for new research studies. Proposal 1 has an estimated initial cost of $1,500 and a positive cash flow that returns $200 the first year and increases by $200 each of the following years until the end of the five-year study period. Proposal 2 also has a five-year life and an initial cost of $1,600. Its positive cash flow is expected to remain constant at $500 per year for all five years.

a) Draw the cash flow diagram for each proposal.

b) What is the rate of return on proposal 1?

c) What is the rate of return on proposal 2?

d) Which proposal is preferred for an MARR of 15%?

9-7 Two alternative investment proposals are under consideration for a vacant lot owned by Spade Contracting. Plan A would require an immediate investment of $150,000 and first year expenses for property taxes, maintenance, and insurance totaling $5,000. These expenses are expected to increase at a rate of $1,000 per year. Plan B would have an initial cost of $200,000 and total first-year expenses of $10,000, which would also increase by $1,000 per year. The economic life of each project is ten years. The facilities from plan A will have no salvage value, and those from plan B will have a salvage value of $60,000. Plan A is expected to generate $35,000 annually and plan B, $45,000.

a) Draw the cash flow diagrams for the two alternatives.

b) Determine the IRR of each plan.

c) Draw a cash flow diagram for the incremental investment. Determine the IRR for this increment.

d) Which plan should Spade Contracting use for an MARR of 10%?

9-8 SHPE Fuel, Inc., is considering two alternatives for obtaining a new fuel delivery truck. SHPE's MARR is 10%.

	Alternatives	
	A	B
Initial cost	$85,000	$105,000
Annual cash receipts	$37,000	$49,000
First year disbursements	$12,000	$17,000
Increase in annual disbursements	$1,000	$2,000
Life (years)	10	15

a) Calculate the AW and the NPV for each alternative.

b) Determine the IRR for each alternative.

c) Perform an incremental analysis on the cash flows and calculate the IRR.

d) Which truck should SHPE Fuel purchase?

9-9 You are contemplating an investment of $145,000 that will return the following amounts: $25,000 in the first year, $30,000 in the second year, $50,000 in the third year, and $60,000 in the fifth year. If your MARR is 10%, does this investment attract you?

9-10 Three different methods can be used for recovering heavy metals from a waste stream. The investment cost and the income associated with each method are tabulated below. Assuming that all methods have a five-year horizon and the company's MARR is 10%, which of the methods, if any, should not be considered for further evaluation?

	Alternatives		
Method	A	B	C
First cost	$15,000	$18,000	$24,000
Salvage value	$5,000	$200	$3,000
Annual net cash flow	$5,000	$5,000	$4,300

9-11 Metals Manufacturing is planning to pay $19,600 for a production machine that should save the company $5,000 per year for the next ten years. Metals Manufacturing requires a rate of return on investments of 20%. Does the return on the machine meet Metals' requirements?

9-12 The A&E Engineering Group must choose between three exclusive projects as possible new investments. All have a ten-year life with no salvage value. Using IRR calculations and the data shown below, determine which alternative should be chosen, if any, using an MARR of 10%.

Project	Initial Investment	Annual Net Cash Flow
A	$110,000	$32,000
B	85,000	23,000
C	25,000	4,710

9-13 The management of a large corporation is considering constructing a parking garage on a company-owned plot of land. The project must pay for itself over 12 years. An MARR of 15% is to be used for the evaluation. Calculate the IRRs for the four alternatives given below to determine how many levels the garage should have.

Number of Levels	Construction Cost	Annual O&M Costs	Annual Income
1	$ 500,000	$ 40,000	$110,000
2	1,800,000	70,000	250,000
3	3,000,000	90,000	400,000
4	4,000,000	115,000	500,000

APPENDIX 9A
SOLUTION TO EXAMPLE 9.3

HEWLETT-PACKARD 12C HAND CALCULATOR

For the following solution, review Examples 9.2 and 9.3. For end-of-year (EOY) cash flows, refer to Figure 7.8.

Keystrokes	Display	Comment
f REG	0.00	Clears registers
10 CHS g CF0	−10.00	EOY 0 cash flow[a]
5 g CFj	5.00	EOY 1 cash flow
3 g Nj	3.00[b]	EOY 2 and 3 cash flow
41 g CFj	41.00	EOY 4 cash flow
5 g CFj	5.00	EOY 5 cash flow
40 CHS g CFj	−40.00	EOY 6 cash flow
5 g CFj	5.00	EOY 7 cash flow
41 g CFj	41.00	EOY 8 cash flow
5 g CFj	5.00	EOY 9 cash flow
3 g Nj	3.00[b]	EOY 10 and 11 cash flow
6 g CFj	6.00	EOY 12 cash flow

[a]For negative cash flows, press CHS before entering cash flow.
[b]Indicates that there are three successive cash flows of $5,000.

Once the data have been punched in, proceed as follows for the IRR or the net present value for any i.
    For IRR,

| f IRR | 70.5 | This is the IRR. |

For present worths,

20 i	20.00	20% rate of return
f NPV	22.97	PW (000) for 20%
30 i	30.00	30% rate of return
f NPV	13.69	PW (000) for 30%

Continue as above for other interest rates.

___10
THE EXTERNAL RATE
OF RETURN

10.1 INTRODUCTION

The IRR methodology described in Chapter 9 can produce some peculiar results. Whenever a set of cash flows has more than one sign reversal, more than one IRR can show up. All of them may be meaningless and/or incomprehensible.

Many cost studies for capital project selection begin with negative cash flows for the first part of the life cycle, followed by positive cash flows during the remainder of the life cycle. Cost studies for asset replacements often show negative cash flow streams for their useful lives, followed by a cash receipt for the salvage value. For such common cash flow patterns, there is only one reversal in sign and therefore only one IRR.

There are, however, many situations in which cash flows reverse more than once. Two that immediately come to mind are

- *Reinvestment or replacement capital.* For certain projects, it is necessary to invest substantial funds several times during their life cycles to replace equipment and often entire production lines in order to keep them in operation. Typical examples are mining, smelter, and similar operations in which erosion and corrosion cause excessive wear.
- *Large disposal or abandonment costs.* Such costs are becoming increasingly important. Two common examples are the decommissioning of

nuclear power plants and the reclamation of mining sites after strip mining operations.

In this chapter, we introduce a new figure of merit—the external rate of return (ERR)—which serves as a surrogate for the IRR when we are unable to get a reasonable answer for this figure of merit.

10.2 MULTIPLE IRRs

For discussing multiple IRRs, the relationship developed in Chapter 9 [equation (9.1)] is particularly useful, since it applies to any discrete cash flow pattern and is easily adapted to continuous cash flows as well. For convenience, this relationship is reproduced below.

$$\text{NPV} = 0 = \sum_{j=0}^{j=N} A_j (1 + i)^{-j}$$

You will recall that A_j is the cash flow at the end of any period j, N is the number of periods in the life cycle, and i is the rate of return. Any of the A's can be positive or negative or zero. As always, the IRR is the i that makes NPV zero.

Substituting x for $(1 + i)$, we get

$$0 = \sum_{j=0}^{i=N} A_j x^{-j} \tag{10.1}$$

Expanding the summation gives

$$0 = A_0 + A_1 x^{-1} + A_2 x^{-2} \ldots A_j x^{-j} \ldots A_N x^{-N} \tag{10.2}$$

and multiplying through by x^N gives

$$0 = A_0 x^N + A_1 x^{N-1} \ldots A_j x^{N-j} \ldots A_{N-1} x + A_N \tag{10.3}$$

which produces a polynomial of the Nth degree with real coefficients, that is, with values of $A_0, A_1, \ldots A_j \ldots A_N$ that are not complex numbers or imaginary numbers but ordinary positive or negative numbers, including zero. Such equations will have N roots—real or complex, or both. The real roots may be positive or negative. All those that are not real and not positive are discarded. Among those that are left there may be some that cannot be used, since the roots are values of $(1 + i)$, not i, and $(1 + i)$ can be positive even though i is negative.

Descartes's rule states that, for polynomials with real coefficients, the number of real positive roots is either equal to the number of changes in sign or is less than this by a positive even integer. Therefore,

Number of Changes in Sign	Number of Positive Real Roots
0	0
1	1
2	2 or 0
3	3 or 1
4	4 or 2 or 0
5	5 or 3 or 1
and so on	

Another rule with which you should be familiar is Norstrom's rule. It deals with changes in sign to the cumulative cash flow series, illustrated below.

EOY	Cash Flow	Cumulative Cash Flow Series
0	A_0	A_0
1	A_1	$A_0 + A_1$
2	A_2	$A_0 + A_1 + A_2$
.	.	.
.	.	.
N	A_N	$A_0 + A_1 + A_2 \ldots A_{N-1} + A_N$

If A_0 is negative, if the cumulative cash flow at EOY N is positive, and if the cumulative cash flow series from A_0 to A_N shows only one change in sign, then there is only one positive value of the IRR.

Example 10.1 illustrates an application of Descartes's and Norstrom's rules.

Example 10.1 Multiple IRRs A major customer of your company forecasts a short-lived surge in the demand of one of their product lines, followed by a sharp drop in sales for the next few years. In order to meet the demand, an order beyond your present production capacity has been placed with your company. To fulfill the order, you estimate that $100,000 has to be invested to expand capacity. The incremental net cash flow generated will be $400,000 during the following year. However, after that, a significant amount of plant capacity is expected to lie idle and, by the end of the second year, will have to be mothballed. The net cash flow for the second year is estimated at a negative $300,000. Is the first cost of $100,000 a good investment?

Before we answer this question, what do Descartes's and Norstrom's rules tell us for this cash flow pattern in thousands of dollars?

EOY	Cash Flow	Cumulative Cash Flow
0	$ − 100	$ − 100
1	400	300
2	− 300	0

By Descartes's rule, there could be two positive values of the IRR. By Norstrom's rule, since the cumulative cash flow at EOY 2 is not greater than zero, there will be more than one IRR.

Back to the question: "Is the first cost of $100,000 a good investment?" A quick look indicates that it isn't too bad. You invest $100,000 and get back $400,000 at EOY 1. You then invest this sum at a conservative 10% and have $440,000 at EOY 2. Of this, you need $300,000 to cover the negative cash flow of $300,000 at EOY 2. This leaves you with $140,000—a return of 40% in two years, or about 20% per year.

Let us now look at this investment a little closer. The cash flow diagram is given in Figure 10.1. All cash flows are assumed to be end-of-year cash flows. There are two changes in sign—one from the negative cash flow, P, to the positive cash flow, F_1, and the other from F_1 to the negative cash flow, F_2.

The factor formula for the net present value with an MARR of 15% is

$$NPV = -P + F_1(P/F,15,1) - F_2(P/F,15,2)$$

This gives an NPV of $21,100, as shown in the following equation:

$$NPV = -\$100,000 + \$400,000 \times 0.8696 - \$300,000 \times 0.7561$$
$$= -\$100,000 + \$347,900 - \$226,800$$
$$= \$21,100$$

The investment appears sound, but what is the IRR? To calculate it, you set the NPV at zero and solve for i:

$$0 = -\$100,000 + \$400,000(P/F,i,1) - \$300,000(P/F,i,2)$$

Since the NPV for 15% is positive, you start with an i of 25% to see if this will give you a negative NPV and thus help to define the range within which the IRR

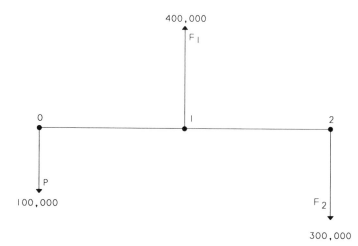

Figure 10.1. Cash flow diagram with two reversals in sign.

will lie. However, 25% produces an NPV of $28,000, which is greater than the NPV for 15%. Repeated trials with other interest rates don't seem to adhere to any known pattern. You then go back to the preceding equation and write it out algebraically:

$$0 = -\$100,000 + \$400,000(1 + i)^{-1} - \$300,000(1 + i)^{-2}$$

Next, you substitute x for $(1 + i)$, divide through by $100,000, and multiply through by $-x^2$. The result is

$$0 = x^2 - 4x + 3 = (x - 3)(x - 1)$$

The roots of x are plus 3 and 1. Therefore,

$$x = (1 + i) = 3 \text{ and } i = 2, \text{ or } 200\%$$
$$x = (1 + i) = 1 \text{ and } i = 0, \text{ or } 0\%$$

These results satisfy Descartes's rule. There are two sign changes and two real positive roots—1 and 3—for which the rates of return are 0% and 200%. Either rate will give you an NPV of zero. Neither rate looks reasonable. The results also satisfy Norstrom's rule which predicted more than one IRR.

We gain a better perspective of what is happening to the IRR by examining the behavior of the NPV. This is done in the next section.

10.3   PRESENT WORTH

With two values of the IRR, we would expect the NPV to approach zero from two directions. In Example 10.1, the present worth is zero for both 0% and 200% and $21,100 for the MARR of 15%. Does the present worth reach a maximum somewhere between 0% and 200%? Since we are not quite sure how the present worth behaves, we turn to a graphical solution, as shown in Example 10.2.

Example 10.2   Graphical Solution for IRR   We already have three points for sketching a graph—0%, 15%, and 200%. These and a few more derived from equation (10.1) are tabulated as follows:

i, %	PW
0	0
15	$21,100
25	28,000
50	33,300
100	25,000
150	12,000
200	0

The present worth is plotted against i in Figure 10.2. We note that

- The present worth gets larger as the discount rate increases from 0% to 50%. In the problems we have dealt with so far, present worths decreased as the discount rate was increased.
- The present worth behaves normally as the discount rate goes from 50% to 200%; that is, it gets smaller.
- The present worth reaches a maximum at an i of 50%. (You can easily verify that this is a true maximum with the help of a little calculus.)

COMMENT: If you worked Examples 10.1 and 10.2 using the program for hand calculators described in Appendix 9A, you could easily and quickly get all of the points you needed for drawing a graph such as the one in Figure 10.2. However, if you tried to obtain the IRR, the calculator would blink ERROR and you would either have to find more sophisticated hardware and software or go through a graphical solution as we just did.

In Examples 10.1 and 10.2, we presented a rather simple illustration of the "abnormal" behavior of both IRRs and PWs for a set of cash flows with two reversals in sign. Real-life problems can be much more complex. We have to find a better way to proceed, and we do so in the next section, first by enlarging on the example already discussed and then by going to one that is somewhat more sophisticated.

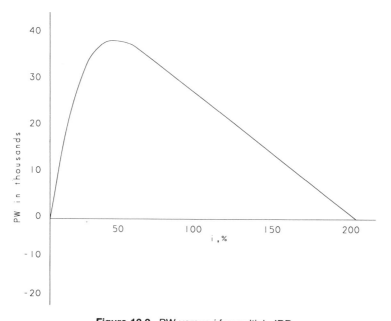

Figure 10.2. PW versus i for multiple IRRs.

10.4   **EXTERNAL RATE OF RETURN**

Our strategy is to restructure cash flow patterns to eliminate all but one reversal in sign. One way to do this is to move cash flows from one position to another on the time axis using an auxiliary rate of return that is usually, but not necessarily, the MARR. The IRR for the revised cash flow diagram, which now has only one sign reversal, is known as the external rate of return (ERR) because we needed an auxiliary or external input to help get it. The ERR serves as a surrogate for the IRR.

Before generalizing this methodology, we illustrate it in Example 10.3.

Example 10.3   External Rate of Return   Consider once again the situation in Example 10.1, for which a cash flow diagram was given in Figure 10.1. If you assume that the $400,000 received at EOY 1 can be reinvested at an auxiliary rate of 15% (the MARR), you would have $460,000 at EOY 2. The net cash flow for the end of that year would then be $160,000 ($460,000 − $300,000). The revised cash flow diagram is that of Figure 10.3.

All we need do now is find the interest rate that produces $160,000 in two years from an investment of $100,000:

$$0 = -\$100,000 + \$160,000(P/F,i,2)$$

$$(P/F,i,2) = \$100,000/\$160,000 = 0.625$$

From Appendix B, i lies between 25%, for which $(P/F,i,2)$ equals 0.6400, and 30%, for which this factor equals 0.5917. A more exact value is 26.5%, and this is the ERR. Since it lies above the MARR of 15%, the investment is economically justified.

The auxiliary rate need not necessarily be the MARR. The assumption that the $400,000 cash inflow, if invested one year from now, will earn 15% may appear unrealistic to some investors. For a 10% auxiliary rate, we already know from the

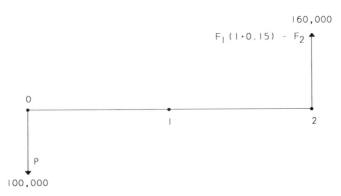

Figure 10.3. Restructuring Figure 10.1 to obtain the ERR.

quick assessment we made at the beginning of Example 10.1 that the return is $40,000 in two years. This produces an ERR of 18.3%, which is still higher than the MARR of 15%.

We can generalize the preceding approach for any number of reversals in sign by moving as many positive cash flow streams as necessary (but no more) to the right along the time-value line until there is only one sign reversal. This is done in Example 10.4.

Example 10.4 More ERR For this example, we use the cash flow pattern of Examples 9.2 and 9.3, which, for convenience, is reproduced in diagram A of Figure 10.4, with every net cash flow stream separately identified. The life cycle is 12 years, and the MARR is 20%.

The cash flow streams change signs three times. By Descartes's rule, there could be three positive IRRs, which is two more than what we want. Moving the cash flows for EOY 1 through EOY 5 inclusive to EOY 6 with an auxiliary rate of 20% (the MARR) produces the cash flow pattern of diagram B in Figure 10.4 in which there is only one change in sign. The computations are shown in the following table. All cash flows are in thousands.

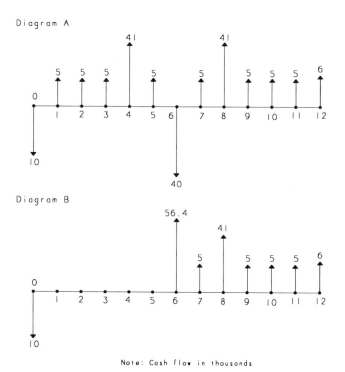

Note: Cash flow in thousands

Figure 10.4. Cash flow diagrams for Example 10.4.

EOY	Cash Flow	Rate-of-Return Factor	Value of Factor	Future Value of Cash Flow
1	$5	$(F/P,20,5)$	2.488	$12.4
2	5	$(F/P,20,4)$	2.074	10.4
3	5	$(F/P,20,3)$	1.728	8.6
4	41	$(F/P,20,2)$	1.440	59.0
5	5	$(F/P,20,1)$	1.200	6.0
6	− 40	$(F/P,20,0)$	1.000	− 40.0
			Total	56.4

The equivalent cash flow at EOY 6 is then a net inflow of $56,400, as shown in diagram B. For an NPV of zero, the factor formula for diagram B is

$$0 = -\$10 + \$56.4(P/F,i,6) + \$5(P/F,i,7) + \$41(P/F,i,8)$$
$$+ \$5(P/F,i,9) + \$5(P/F,i,10) + \$5(P/F,i,11)$$
$$+ \$6(P/F,i,12)$$

Solving for the ERR by trial and error indicates that it will lie between 40% and 45% (which you should confirm). The exact value is 42.7%.

10.5 WHEN TO USE AN ERR

In the introduction to this chapter, we mentioned that our objective is to find a surrogate for the IRR whenever a meaningful value for this figure of merit is unobtainable. We were not able to obtain one in Examples 10.1 and 10.2, for which the IRRs were 0% and 200%. However, by restructuring the cash flow diagram, we did get an ERR that made sense in Example 10.3, namely, 26.5%. For the more complicated problem in Example 10.4, in which there are three reversals in sign, we had no difficulty in finding an IRR. Norstrom's rule would have told us there would not be.

This brings us to, when to use an ERR. You already know the answer.

- Use Descartes's and Norstrom's rules to find out if there could be more than one IRR.
- If so, graph the behavior of present worth versus i, as we did in Example 9.3.
- If more than one i shows up, restructure the cash flow pattern to give only one reversal in sign, as we did in Example 10.4.

The use of an auxiliary interest rate to obtain an ERR may appear to you as an artificial device to come up with some kind of answer when all else fails. It emphatically is not. To assume that the cash inflows received from an ongoing project will be reinvested at a rate equal to, or even somewhat less than, the MARR is not unreasonable. In fact, it leads directly to an assumption that is inherent in computing equivalent present, future, and annual worths and that often has been criticized. This assumption is called the "reinvestment fallacy," but we will use a less strident term and refer to it simply as the "reinvestment assumption."

10.6   THE REINVESTMENT ASSUMPTION

To understand this assumption (and to remind you that we have been using it all along), go back to Example 6.1. For convenience, the cash flow pattern for that example is reproduced in Figure 10.5.

We know that the present worth, the annual worth, and the future worth are all zero for the IRR. This means that we arbitrarily assume that the sums received during the life of a project are reinvested at the IRR up to the end of the planning horizon.

For the cash flow pattern of Figure 10.5, for example, the IRR is 23.4% (*see* Figure 6.1). The equivalent present worth of the three cash flow streams of $5,000 at EOY 1, EOY 2, and EOY 3 must therefore be equal to $10,000 to make PW_{in} equal to PW_{out}. Similarly, the future worth of the three cash flow streams must also have a present value of $10,000, and this can only occur if these streams are reinvested at 23.4% from the time of receipt up to EOY N. The calculations follow:

$$FW = \$5,000[(F/P,23.4,2) + (F/P,23.4,1) + 1.000]$$
$$= \$5,000(1.523 + 1.234 + 1.000) = \$5,000 \times 3.757$$
$$= \$18,785$$

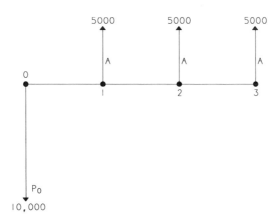

Figure 10.5. Cash flow pattern for section 10.6.

This future worth has a present value of $10,000:

$$PW_{in} = FW(P/F,23.4,3) = \$18,785 \times 0.5322$$

$$= \$10,000$$

We again have PW_{in} equal to PW_{out} as it must for the IRR.

The argument of those favoring an ERR rather than an IRR approach is that it is not reasonable to assume that future cash flow streams can be reinvested at the IRR. Rather, it makes more sense to assume that they can be reinvested at the MARR, because the MARR was selected by the decision maker on the basis of an opportunity forgone. For 15%, the future worth of the three cash flow streams of $5,000 in Figure 10.5 is $17,363, as follows:

$$FW = \$5,000[(F/P,15,2) + (F/P,15,1) + 1.000]$$

$$= \$5,000(1.3225 + 1.150 + 1.000) = \$5,000 \times 3.4725$$

$$= \$17,363$$

The rate of return that makes this future worth equivalent to the present worth of the capital investment of $10,000 in Figure 10.5 is 20.2%. The computations are as follows:

$$PW_{out} = PW_{in}$$

$$\$10,000 = \$17,363(P/F,i,3)$$

$$i = 0.202$$

The ERR of 20.2% is, according to the critics of the reinvestment assumption, a more realistic expectation of the rate of return that an investor will obtain than the IRR of 23.4%.

We will continue to do what we have been doing; that is, we will continue to use the IRR rather than the ERR in comparing investment opportunities. However, you should be aware of the criticism mentioned and accept the fact that someday the ERR may find a place next to the IRR as an investment criterion.

10.7 SUMMARY

In this chapter, you were introduced to a class of problems with cash flows that have more than one reversal in sign. This can result in multiple IRRs and in present worths that do not decrease as rates of return increase.

Such problems are first tested by examining the sign changes for both the cash flows and the cumulative cash flows. If it appears that more than one rate of return could show up, a graph of PW versus i is drawn to determine whether a solution for the IRR can be obtained and whether the solution makes sense. If it does not, an auxiliary rate—usually but not necessarily the MARR—can be applied to restructure a cash flow diagram so that there is only one reversal in sign. The restructuring is usually done by compounding cash flow streams using the auxiliary rate until the cash flow pattern has only one sign reversal. The rate of return that makes the present worth of the restructured cash flow pattern equal to zero is the ERR.

The ERR has also found favor when one is avoiding the reinvestment assumption. With this approach, all cash flow streams except the initial investment are compounded to the end of the planning horizon by using the MARR. The rate of return (the ERR) that makes the present worth of the resulting future worth equivalent to the initial investment is then calculated. This ERR is a more conservative rate of return than the IRR.

SUGGESTED READINGS

1. G. A. Fleischer, *Engineering Economy, Capital Allocation Theory*. (Belmont, CA: Wadsworth, 1984.) Pp. 70–74 will give you further insight into multiple IRRs. The following excerpt from page 74 is particularly pertinent: "If there is any question about the interpretation of IRR results, the analyst should prepare a graph of PW as a function of the interest rate. Graphing provides meaningful insight, because the relationship between PW and the rate(s) of return, if any, will be clearly indicated."
2. R. E. Terry, J. N. Harb, D. L. Whitman, and R. A. Branting, "ERR: An Alternate Method for DCFROR for Plant Economic Analysis." *Cost Engineering*, 33 (10) (October 1991): 11–13. This article states that the ERR possesses all of the advantages of the IRR, that it is a more correct measure of rate of return, and that it should replace the IRR at least for chemical engineering economic analysis.
3. Carl J Norstrom, "A Sufficient Condition for a Uniform Nonnegative Internal Rate of Return." *Journal of Financial and Quantitative Analysis* VII (June 1972): 1835–1839.
4. Donald G. Newnan, *Engineering Economic Analysis*, 4th ed. (San Jose, CA: 1988 Engineering Press. You will find an extensive discussion of the ERR and many worked examples in Chapters 7A and 18.

PROBLEMS

Multiple Rates of Return

10-1 Go to the cash flow pattern of diagram A in Figure 10.4. Check for multiple IRRs, using the cash flow and cumulative cash flow criteria. How do you reconcile the two answers?

10-2   How many positive rates of return will the cash flow pattern shown have?

EOY	Net Cash Flow
1	−$100,000
2	50,000
3	50,000
4	0
5	−100,000
6	50,000
7	50,000
8	−2,000
9	100,000

10-3   Consider an investment of $50,000 in a facility that will produce a net cash flow of $215,000 during year 1. The net cash flow during year 2 is −$78,000 including the cost of shutting the facility down.

a) Check the cash flow rule for multiple IRRs.

b) Check the cumulative cash flow rule for multiple IRRs.

c) Solve for the IRR or IRRs by setting up the cash flow equation for future worth as a quadratic equation, as we did in Example 10.1. (*Hint*: The equation can be factored.)

d) What would you do if the equation couldn't be factored?

10-4   Consider the following cash flow pattern:

EOY	Net Cash Flow
0	$−400
1	600
2	200
3	−400

a) Check for multiple IRRs, using the cash flow and cumulative cash flow tests.

b) Graph PW versus *i*, as we did in Figure 10.2.

c) What is the ERR for a discount rate (MARR) of 10%?

10-5   The cash flow pattern for a proposed short-term investment is tabulated below.

EOY	Cash Flow (000)
0	$−100
1	60
2	−2
3	60

  a) Check for multiple IRRs using the cash flow and cumulative cash flow criteria.
  b) What is the IRR?
  c) What is the ERR for a discount rate of 8%?
  d) Why are the IRR and ERR so close?

10-6 Consider the following cash flow pattern.

EOY	Net Cash Flow
0	824
10	$ – 10,000
11 to ∞	2,000

  a) Draw the cash flow diagram.
  b) Restructure the diagram so that there is only one sign change.
  c) Calculate the ERR using a discount rate of 15%.

The Reinvestment Assumption

10-7 A petroleum company is evaluating a site for a new refinery. The site and the construction of the refinery are expected to cost $200 million. Net cash flows are estimated at $50 million annually. The refinery is expected to be in operation for 15 years, at which time cleanup costs estimated at $50 million will be incurred. The MARR is 15%.
  a) How many sign changes are there?
  b) What is the IRR?
  c) What is the ERR if the net cash flow streams for year 1 to year 15 were reinvested at the MARR?

10-8 You have recently purchased a bond for $1,000. The semiannual interest payments are $50. Three years later there are rumors of bankruptcy. You sell the bond for $750.
  a) What was your IRR?
  b) If you had invested the interest payments at your MARR of 6%, what was your ERR?
  c) What would your reinvestment rate have to be to at least break even?

10-9 A company is contemplating the purchase of a new milling machine. The purchase price is $30,000. The useful life of the machine is estimated as five years. The machine is expected to generate $6,250 in net cash flow annually. The MARR is 8%.
  a) Calculate the IRR.
  b) What is the ERR, assuming the funds generated can be invested at the MARR?

10-10   Consider the following short-term investment, which has, as you will see, a very attractive return.

EOY	Net Cash Flow
0	$ – 6,000
1	10,000
2	10,000
3	10,000

a) What is the IRR?

b) Your MARR is 20%. What is the ERR for this investment, assuming the net cash flows will be reinvested at this rate?

c) Due to unexpected developments, you lower your MARR to 10%? What is the ERR for this discount rate?

d) Suppose your reinvestment rate is 0%. Is the investment still attractive?

10-11   We stated in this chapter that some analysts claim that the ERR is a better financial criterion than the IRR. Based on the results that you obtained in Problem 10-10, how do you feel about this claim? Answer the same question based on the results that you obtained in Problem 10-9. Why don't we substitute the ERR for the IRR when we are judging investments?

___11
BENEFIT-COST ANALYSIS

11.1 INTRODUCTION

The last major figure of merit that we need to discuss is the benefit-cost ratio (BCR). This ratio is the measure of "worthwhileness" now generally used by governmental entities at the federal, state, and local levels to justify their selection of projects among the many vying for attention.

The notion of estimating the dollar value of benefits to the public from government projects and comparing them with the estimated costs of producing such benefits dates back to the U.S. Flood Control Act of 1936, a relevant excerpt of which is reproduced:

> . . . the Federal Government should improve or participate in the improvement of navigable waters and their tributaries, including watersheds thereof, for flood control purposes if the benefits to whomsoever they may accrue are in excess of the estimated costs, and if the lives and social security of people are otherwise adversely affected.

During much of the 1930s, the federal government was committed to spending large sums of money to "prime the pump" and to bring the U.S. economy out of the Great Depression. A figure of merit was needed to help select the projects that should be implemented. Discounted cash flow methodology and such terms as present and annual worth were gaining popularity in the business sector for culling and selecting capital investment opportunities. However, the figures of merit derived therefrom, such as the internal rate of return, did not seem appropriate for the public sector. A new figure of merit was needed.

11.2   THE BCR RATIO

The excerpt from the Flood Control Act just quoted does not define a benefit-cost ratio. It simply says that benefits (B) "to whomsoever they may accrue" should exceed estimated costs (C); that is,

$$B > C \tag{11.1}$$

This interpretation matches that for private-sector business projects in which benefits (cash receipts or revenues) are expected to exceed costs (cash disbursements).

The concept of a ratio came later and was derived by dividing both sides of the inequality in equation (11.1) by C.

$$B/C > C/C \quad \text{or} \quad B/C > 1 \tag{11.2}$$

Thus, if the equivalent worth of benefits are estimated at \$50,000 and that of costs at \$25,000, the benefit-cost ratio (BCR) is 2.0 (\$50,000/\$25,000). The net equivalent worth (usually the annual worth, although the present worth is often used) is, of course, $(B - C)$, or \$25,000 (\$50,000 − \$25,000).

This act also says nothing about discounting the cash flows representing benefits and costs. However, this is now universal practice, except for present economy studies, such as those discussed in Chapter 3, and generally for any study involving short time spans (one or two years or less).

The MARR to be used for discounting has been and still is the subject of much philosophical discourse. At one extreme, there are proponents for zero return, which, as we know, is equivalent to using undiscounted cash flow estimates. At the other extreme, there are those who recommend MARRs as high as relatively risky business investments. We discuss this topic in further detail in Chapter 17.

Why didn't engineers, economists, and systems analysts simply use the excess of B over C rather than a ratio such as the BCR for comparing capital investment opportunities? This would have had the advantage of making the selection process for public projects similar to that for private projects, since the difference between discounted values of B and C is a net worth. There are several reasons they didn't:

- Equivalent worths are a difficult concept for the public and for many government officials. This is not intended to denigrate either group. However, some education and training in the material covered in this text is needed to make equivalent worths comprehensible. They lack "convincibility," "visibility," and "salability," or whatever it takes to convince the public that a project is worthwhile.
- IRRs are not as difficult a concept for the public to grasp as equivalent worths. The term "rate of return" is well known and understood from

familiarity with prime rates, bond rates, stock dividends, the rate of capital appreciation on stock ownership and the like. However, the term "rate of return" is associated in the public mind with profit and, therefore, as mentioned earlier, did not seem appropriate as a criterion for selecting government projects.

• This brings us to the BCR. It is easy to understand. If the ratio is greater than 1, the benefits exceed the costs, which is good. If the ratio is less than 1, the costs exceed the benefits, which is bad.

We shall see that the simplicity of the benefit-cost ratio is illusory. First of all, the BCR is a marginal or incremental concept, which means that we cannot compare the BCRs of one alternative directly with those of another unless we also analyze incremental cash flows. Second, the interpretation of what are benefits and what are costs is often blurred. We illustrate the first difficulty in Example 11.1 and the second in later sections of this chapter.

Example 11.1   Equivalent Worths and the BCR   Consider a proposed flood control project. From records that go back many years, the equivalent uniform annual cost (EUAC) for repairs and replacements due to flood damage is $1 million, based on a rate of return of 10% and a life of 50 years. Three alternatives to reduce this damage—X, Y, and Z—are under review. The annual worth of the expected benefits (the resulting savings from lower repair, replacement, and insurance expenses) and the annual costs of producing these benefits have been calculated and are tabulated below. The annual costs include the capital recovery of $1 million and operation and maintenance costs. The net annual worths $(B - C)$ and the BCRs are also given. All dollar figures are in thousands.

		X	Y	Z
Benefits	B	$500	$625	$680
Costs	C	200	275	350
Difference	$(B - C)$	300	350	330
BCR	B/C	2.5	2.3	1.9

Since we do not have to, and may not, proceed with this venture, we need to compare the do-nothing or null alternative with X, Y, and Z. For the do-nothing alternative, the BCR is 1. Any one of the three other alternatives is better than doing nothing, since, for each of them, the equivalent annual worth $(B - C)$ is positive and the BCR is greater than 1.

COMMENT: Why do we say that the do-nothing alternative has a BCR of 1? Go back for a moment to the concept of opportunity cost. When an investor selects an MARR, we assume that the selection is based on an opportunity forgone that could have earned the MARR. If it had, its IRR would be equal to the MARR, PW_{in} would be equal to PW_{out}, and the ratio PW_{in}/PW_{out}, which is a BCR, would be equal to 1.

The next step in our analysis is to set Z aside for the moment and compare X with Y. The net annual worth $(B - C)$ for Y is $50,000($350,000 - $300,000) higher than that for X. This makes Y the preferred choice. However, the BCR of 2.5 for X is higher than that of 2.3 for Y, making X the preferred choice. On what figure of merit—the annual worth or the BCR—do we base our recommendation?

The answer, which will be gone into more fully in Chapter 12 on ranking, is the net annual worth. If the annual worth of Y is higher than that of X, Y is the correct choice. The BCR does not allow such a simple comparison. Instead, we have to see if the BCR for the incremental discounted cash flows for Y minus X are greater or less than 1. This is done in the following equation:

$$B/C = \frac{B_Y - B_X}{C_Y - C_X} = \frac{(\$625 - \$500)}{(\$275 - \$200)} = \frac{\$125}{\$75} = 1.7$$

Since the ratio is greater than 1.0, Y is preferred to X, a result that is consistent with the higher net annual worth of Y.

Now that X is eliminated from the competition, we compare Z with Y. Both the net annual worth and the BCR for Y are higher than for Z, so Y is the clear winner. We note, too, that the BCR for the incremental cash flows is actually less than 1, as shown in the following equation:

$$B/C = \frac{B_Z - B_Y}{C_Z - C_Y} \frac{(\$680 - \$625)}{(\$350 - \$275)} = \frac{\$55}{\$75} = 0.7$$

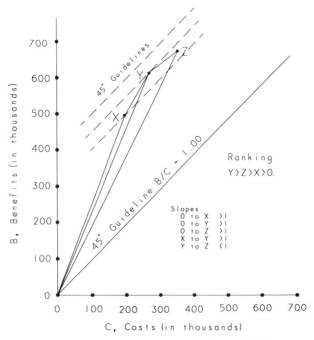

Figure 11.1. Graphical solution for Example 11.1.

You should have no trouble in showing that Z is better than X, and we recommend you do so following the above methodology.

The results are graphed in Figure 11.1. Note the 45-degree guidelines. All three alternatives show BCRs greater than 1, as indicated by the slopes of the lines connecting each alternative with (0,0). For the incremental cash flows, the slope of the line from X to Y is also greater than 1 but that from Y to Z is not.

The ranking from the most to the least attractive alternative in Example 11.1 was Y, Z, X for net annual worth and X, Y, Z for the BCR. In order to reconcile the two rankings, we had to calculate BCRs for incremental cash flows. When this was done, the ranking for both figures of merit was consistent, that is, Y, Z, X.

COMMENT: As mentioned, incremental analyses will be covered fully in Chapter 12. In the meantime, Example 11.1 provides a good introduction to this important topic and will help explain some of the other anomalies of BCRs discussed in the next section.

11.3 BENEFITS AND COSTS

Benefits and costs are both "netted" quantities. This is evident from the following definitions of the five groups of cash flows that participate in the analysis of public projects.

Symbol

B	Positive benefits that are favorable monetary consequences to the public.
D	Disbenefits (negative benefits) that are unfavorable monetary consequences to the public.
I	The initial cost of the project under review.
C	Cash disbursements for operation and maintenance.
R	Negative costs representing cash receipts user fees (tolls, parking fees, etc.)

With these terms, the conventional BCR is defined as follows:

$$\text{BCR} = \frac{(B - D)}{I + (C - R)} \tag{11.3}$$

As shown, net benefits are in the numerator and net costs are in the denominator. When we apply this equation, the five terms must, of course, be commensurable; that is, they must all be converted to one of the three worths, of which the present and the annual worths are the most frequently used.

11.3.1   Benefits and Disbenefits

Benefits are savings, that is, reduced expenditures by the public for transportation, education, health care, safety, protection of lives and property, and recreation. For the most part, they are the differences between what the public is now paying, or would have to pay, for such services and what it will be paying if the capital projects sponsored by government agencies are built. Examples are highway improvements, flood control projects, community colleges, public universities, hospitals, and parks. In economic studies for public projects—and not-for-profit private projects—identifying benefits and disbenefits, seeking a consensus on which benefits and disbenefits to include and not to include, and then estimating their cash flows often involves many practical difficulties, which are described more fully in Chapter 17 on public projects and regulated industries.

Benefits are often coupled with disbenefits. A dam may put agricultural land upstream under water while protecting valuable business and residential properties downstream. A highway relocation may reduce the cash flow out of the public's pocket for gas, oil, and car maintenance, but these savings may be offset—at least in part—by losses in net revenues for the highway businesses along the old route.

Benefits and disbenefits are usually treated as discrete cash flows, although they could just as easily be treated as continuous cash flows. They may vary from year to year, and in some years the disbenefits may outweigh the benefits.

Net benefits $(B - D)$ are usually positive, since otherwise a project could not be justified economically. For negative net benefits, the justification, if any, would have to proceed on the basis of nonmonetary attributes.

11.3.2   Positive and Negative Costs

As mentioned, positive costs (or simply costs) are estimated cash disbursements flowing out of a projected public facility for its initial cost (I) and for operating and maintaining it (C). Negative costs are cash receipts (R). Examples of negative costs include user fees for highway, bridge, and tunnel tolls; port, airport, and navigation fees; hospital and medical fees; receipts from the sale of power and water often in competition with the private sector; tuition at all levels of learning; recreation fees at public facilities; and all other cash inflows for direct sales of goods and services to the public by public and not-for-profit private organizations.

Net costs $(C - R)$ are also usually positive, since for many government ventures there are no cash receipts (negative costs) and for many more disbursements exceed receipts. However, there are exceptions, and these, as we shall see, require special handling.

> *COMMENT:* The discussion that follows will focus on public, that is, government projects. Most of what is said applies to not-for-profit organizations in the private sector as well.

An example illustrating what we have discussed follows.

Example 11.2 Highway Improvement Consider a new bridge and a highway, which will shorten the route between two population centers by 20 miles. The existing route will not be abandoned, since it will continue to serve a few localities. However, most of the current and projected future traffic is expected to use the new route. For an average of $0.15 per mile per vehicle for operating and maintenance costs, the new route will benefit the average user $3.00 per crossing (20 miles × $0.15) if toll free. For an estimated 1 million crossings per year, the total benefit B is then $3,000,000 annually.

The estimated capital cost of the proposed improvement is $15,000,000. The capital recovery (CR) cost for a 50-year life and a 10% rate of return is $1,500,000, that is, $15,000,000 times 0.10, since, by assuming infinite life, no appreciable errors are introduced, as you can confirm by looking at Appendix B. The annual maintenance costs are $500,000.

With the following substitutions,

Benefits	B	$3,000,000
Disbenefits	D	0
Initial cost	I	$1,500,000
O&M costs	C	$500,000
User fees	R	0

the conventional BCR is 1.5, as shown in the following equation:

$$B/C = \frac{B}{I + C} = \frac{\$3,000,000}{\$1,500,000 + \$500,000} = 1.5$$

If the highway authority decides on a $1.00 toll, this is not expected to affect the number of users, since they would still benefit by $2.00 per trip ($3.00 − $1.00) compared to the old route. For 1 million crossings per year, the benefits to the public are now $2,000,000 annually.

The costs are reduced by the user fees collected from the public, which amount to $1,000,000. The conventional BCR is now

$$B/C = \frac{B}{I + (C - R)} = \frac{\$2,000,000}{\$1,500,000 + \$500,000 - \$1,000,000}$$
$$= 2.0$$

If the toll were raised to $2.00 per crossing and the number of crossings remained the same, as it probably would, the BCR would be

$$B/C = \frac{\$1,000,000}{\$1,500,000 + \$500,000 - \$2,000,000} = \infty$$

This is a meaningless result. However, the difference between benefits and costs provides a useful answer.

$$B - C = \$1,000,000 - 0 = \$1,000,000$$

If the user fee for the new highway and bridge are set at \$3.00, the benefits to the public are zero under our assumptions. However, 1 million crossings per year may still be realistic, because the new route is quicker and more comfortable than the old route. The BCR is now

$$B/C = \frac{0}{\$1,500,000 + \$500,000 - \$3,000,000} = 0$$

This is, again, a meaningless result; however, B less C is not.

$$B - C = 0 - (\$-1,000,000) = \$1,000,000$$

Example 11.2 illustrates the difficulties we have with the BCR when we obtain results such as infinity or zero. Fortunately, these are easily resolved by switching to an equivalent worth. They are also resolved by using the modified benefit-cost ratio, which we will discuss later.

11.4 "TO WHOMSOEVER THEY MAY ACCRUE. . . ."

The members of the public who will be benefited or disbenefited from a proposed project include both users and nonusers. The Flood Control Act of 1936 does not distinguish between the two, as indicated by the famous phrase "if the benefits to whomsoever they may accrue. . . ." This is a broad mandate—so broad, in fact, that it is meaningless.

To clarify this point, consider once again the highway improvement project in Example 11.2.

Example 11.3 Users and Nonusers Look first at the users, and ask yourself whether or not the following benefits and disbenefits should be included in an economic study:

- For commercial traffic, the saving in time in using the new route may reduce payroll expenses. Is this a benefit that should be included?
- The reduction in payroll expenses, although a benefit to business, is a disbenefit to employees who are paid an hourly wage. Should this disbenefit be included?
- What about the value of time to noncommercial users, including commuters? Shall we attempt to put a value on it?
- What about reduced repair, medical, and hospital expenses for traffic accidents because the new highway is safer than the old?
- Fatalities due to highway accidents will also be reduced. Do we include "value-of-life" estimates in our study?

Consider next some nonusers.

- The businesses—gas stations, restaurants, shops—located along the old route will suffer. Should their reduction in net cash flows be included as disbenefits?
- New businesses will crop up along the new route. Should their net cash flows be included as benefits?
- What about property values? The owners of property along the old route may suffer, while those along the new route may prosper?
- The shorter route will reduce the income of oil companies from oil and gas sales. Should this be included as a disbenefit?
- The fees to repair shops, hospitals, and doctors will be reduced by the lower accident rate. Should this disbenefit be included?

We've said enough for now to show you that decisions on what benefits and disbenefits to include in an economic analysis can arouse considerable comment and often controversy. Proponents of a capital project will argue for maximizing benefits and minimizing disbenefits. Opponents will do the reverse. If we carried the chain of benefits and disbenefits to its logical conclusion, their sum total would be zero. There is, however, a consensus on how far we should go in many typical situations. We leave this to Chapter 17, which discusses public projects.

11.5 MODIFIED BENEFIT-COST RATIO

We have not yet mentioned one further problem with the BCR, which is sometimes referred to as the "numerator-denominator issue." This issue has resulted in a modified benefit-cost ratio that places all cash flows in the numerator except the initial cost. The formula for the modified ratio is

$$B/C = \frac{(B - D) - (C - R)}{I} \tag{11.4}$$

Figure 11.2, in which all cash flows have been converted to their equivalent annual worths, illustrates the difference between the two ratios. The upper diagram is for the conventional ratio, and the lower diagram is for the modified ratio.

Example 11.4, which is an extension of Example 11.2, shows that the modified ratio works better than the conventional ratio.

Example 11.4 Modified BCR The computations for the modified ratio and a comparison between the conventional and modified approaches are given in Table 11.1 for user fees ranging from $0 to $3.00 per crossing. The number of crossings annually is constant at 1 million.

A Conventional ratio

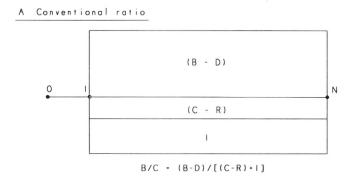

B/C = (B-D)/[(C-R)+I]

B Modified ratio

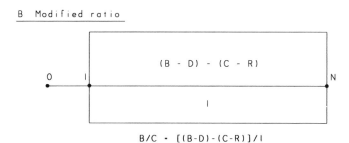

B/C = [(B-D)-(C-R)]/I

Figure 11.2. Equivalent uniform series diagrams for BCRs.

The modified ratio makes sense over the entire range of user fees, whereas the conventional ratio does not. The fact that the modified ratio remains the same, however, is specific to this particular problem. If we had varied the number of users as fees increased, this would not have occurred, as indicated in Example 11.5.

TABLE 11.1 Modified and Conventional BCRs

	Fee Per Use (in dollars)			
Symbols	0	1	2	3
B	$3,000	$2,000	$1,000	0
D	0	0	0	0
$(B - D)$	3,000	2,000	1,000	0
I	1,500	1,500	1,500	$1,500
C	500	500	500	500
R	0	1,000	2,000	3,000
$(C - R)$	500	−500	−1,500	−2,500
Numerator $(B - D) - (C - R)$	2,500	2,500	2,500	2,500
Denominator, I	1,500	1,500	1,500	1,500
Modified B/C	1.6	1.6	1.6	1.6
Conventional B/C from Example 11.2	1.6	2.0	∞	0

Example 11.5 User Fees and Disbenefits If user fees were raised to $4.00 per crossing, there would be a disbenefit of $1.00 per crossing, since the old route has not been abandoned. A survey indicates that the number of crossings would be reduced from 1 million to 800,000 annually. The pertinent equivalent annual worths are

			(In thousands)
Benefits	B		0
Disbenefits	D	($1 × $800,000)	$800
Initial cost	I		1,500
O&M costs	C		500
Receipts	R	($4 × $800,000)	3,200
Net benefits	$(B - D)$		−800
Net costs excluding I	$(C - R)$		−2,700

The modified BCR is then

$$B/C = \frac{(B - D) - (C - R)}{I} = \frac{\$-800 + \$2,700}{\$1,500} = \frac{\$1,900}{\$1,500} = 1.3$$

Example 11.5 illustrates the difficulties in some situations of defining benefits, disbenefits, and costs. For those who will continue to use the new crossing, the user fee of $4.00 is evidently not seen as a disbenefit of $1.00 compared to the old route or, if it is, as compensation for such irreducibles as less congestion, less commuter time, and better scenery. Without the disbenefits of $800,000 in the above BCR, the ratio would increase from 1.3 to 1.8 ($2,700/$1,500).

The numerator-denominator issue goes beyond simply defining a new ratio with only the initial costs in the denominator. This is best illustrated with another example that simulates some real-life situations.

Example 11.6 Costs or Disbenefits A study group has assembled the estimated equivalent annual worths given in the first column of the following table (original study) for a project that an influential senator, whom we shall call Senator Quagmire, is sponsoring for a particular government agency. All figures are in millions of dollars.

		Original Study	First Revision
Benefits	B	$100	$100
Disbenefits	D	0	20
Initial cost	I	50	50
O&M costs	C	35	15
User fees	R	5	5

The policy directive of the sponsoring agency specifies the conventional ratio as the figure of merit for the project selection process. This gives

$$B/C = \frac{(B - D)}{I + (C - R)} = \frac{\$100 - \$0}{\$50 + (\$35 - \$5)} = \frac{\$100}{\$80} = 1.25$$

Senator Quagmire is unhappy because a rival project for the same objective sponsored by a rival agency over which he exerts little influence shows a BCR of 1.30. He asks the study group to look at their data once again. This group, which is no stranger to such events, now decides that, of the $35,000,000 in costs, possibly $20,000,000 could qualify as disbenefits. This raises the BCR above 1.3:

$$B/C = \frac{(B - D)}{I + (C - R)} = \frac{\$100 - \$20}{\$50 + (\$15 - \$5)} = \frac{\$80}{\$60} = 1.33$$

The group may be as right in its revised assessment as it was in its original assessment. There are often no right and wrong answers as to what belongs in the numerator and what belongs in the denominator. If the group can be faulted at all, it is in not making the disbenefits—and therefore the BCR—as high as possible in the first place.

We don't need Senator Quagmire to point out that disagreement as to whether a particular cash flow belongs in the numerator or the denominator of the BCR is often legitimate. However, the major lesson to be learned from Example 11.6 is that, where there is some doubt as to whether a cash flow is a disbenefit or a cost, the BCR based on the conventional ratio can be varied by calling it one or the other.

If the sponsor had allowed the modified ratio, the BCR would be 1.4 for both the original study and the first revision. This approach is therefore a less subjective and fairer way of comparing one proposal with another.

COMMENT: By this time, you have probably wondered whether switching cash flows from the denominator to the numerator, or vice versa, will ever give a ratio greater than 1 for, say, the conventional BCR and a ratio less than 1 for the modified BCR. The answer is no. If the conventional ratio is greater than 1, the modified ratio will be, and, if the conventional ratio is less than 1, the modified ratio will be. This is easily proved algebraically, but we'll leave the proof to you.

11.6 SUMMARY PROBLEM FOR REVIEW

Example 11.7 wraps up many of the issues raised in this chapter and also introduces the BCR to problems involving cotermination.

Example 11.7 Wrap-up Problem   Consider two alternatives for building a scenic railway in a state park. Since the railway does not have to be built, we must also consider the null alternative.

The estimated undiscounted cash flows (not converted into equivalent annual worths, as in the previous examples) and the economic lives for the two alternatives are tabulated as follows (dollar figures are in millions).

		Alternatives	
		I	II
Economic life	N	20 yrs.	40 yrs.
Initial cost	I	$20.0	$37.5
Residual value	S	$1.5	$2.0
Annual receipts	R	$3.2	$4.0
Annual O&M costs	C	$0.8	$0.6

The cash flow diagrams for alternatives I and II and for the differential cash flow (II-I) are given in Figure 11.3.

We first compare the lesser initial cost alternative (alternative I) with the null alternative. For this comparison, we do not need to coterminate. (Why not?) The BCRs are calculated below for a rate of return of 10%, using the present rather than the annual worth.

The modified ratio treating the residual value as a receipt is

$$B/C = \frac{(\$3.2 - \$0.8)(P/A,10\%,20) + \$1.5(P/F,10\%,20)}{\$20.0}$$

$$= \frac{\$2.4 \times 8.514 + \$1.5 \times 0.1486}{\$20.0} = \frac{\$20.9}{\$20.0}$$

$$= 1.05$$

Since the ratio is greater than 1, alternative I bests the null alternative. This would obviously be the case for any number of repetitions, which is why we carried the analysis out for just one cycle.

In order to compare alternatives I and II, we must coterminate, for the reasons discussed in Chapter 7. We could begin by calculating and comparing the BCRs for each alternative. However, as we found out from Example 11.1, we might as well go directly to the BCR for the incremental cash flow. The differential cash flow diagram is given in Figure 11.3. In the computations that follow, we again use the modified ratio.

$$\frac{\Delta B}{\Delta C} = \frac{\$1.0(P/A,10,40) + \$18.5(P/F,10,20) + \$0.5(P/F,10,40)}{\$17.5}$$

$$= \frac{\$1.0 \times 9.779 + \$18.5 \times 0.1486 + \$0.5 \times 0.0221}{\$17.5} = \frac{\$12.6}{\$17.5}$$

$$= 0.72$$

What have we learned? The extra initial cost of $17,500,000, which provides (1) savings of $1,000,000 per year for 40 years, (2) a single-sum saving of $18,500,000 at EOY 20 for not having to reinvest in another cycle of alternative I, and (3) a single-sum saving of $500,000 at EOY 40 representing the difference in residual values, cannot be economically justified.

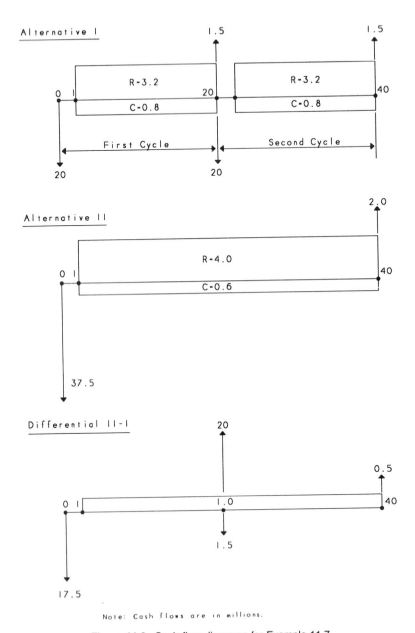

Note: Cash flows are in millions.

Figure 11.3. Cash flow diagrams for Example 11.7.

11.7 SUMMARY

You have seen that the BCR lacks the simplicity of the equivalent worths. Why, then, have we spent so much time on it? The answer, of course, is that the public sector uses this figure and that this sector is a major source of funding for capital expenditures.

You have also been introduced to the shortcomings of the conventional BCR, all of which can be overcome by using the excess of benefits over costs $(B - C)$ or the modified rather than the conventional BCR formula.

If you were asked to review and critique an economy study in which the BCR was the selected figure of merit, you would therefore have to find out whether the conventional or the modified ratio was used. If the conventional ratio was used, you would then have to make your own assessment about how to sort the cash flow streams into benefits, disbenefits, costs, and receipts. Next, you would have to find out how the estimates for the cash flow streams were prepared. Estimating costs is relatively easy, although the data gathering can be tedious. But estimating benefits and disbenefits for a public project is an entirely different ballgame, in which we often have to rely on opinion polls and surveys plus a heady influx of common sense and unbiased judgment to come up with any meaningful numbers.

SUGGESTED READINGS

1. George Malcolm Steiner, *Basic Engineering Economy*, rev. ed. (Glen Echo, MD: Books Associates, 1989). If you are still concerned about whether switching from the conventional to the modified ratio, and vice versa, will turn a BCR less than 1 into a BCR greater than 1, read page 150 of this text.

2. G. A. Fleischer, *Engineering Economy: Capital Allocation Theory* (Belmont, CA: Wadsworth, 1984). Chapter 5 of this text on incorrect and/or approximate methods discusses several modifications of the BCR. These include several so-called profitability indices (PIs), such as the net benefits-cost ratio $\{(B - C)/C\}$, the premium worth percentage (benefits less all costs, including initial cost divided by the initial cost), and SIR (savings/investment ratio). None of these offers any new insights into comparing the ratio of benefits to costs not offered by the BCR.

PROBLEMS

Start-up Exercises

11-1 For private-sector projects, revenues are often referred to as benefits and costs (other than the capital investment) are often referred to as disbenefits. In fact, we have done so ourselves. In this chapter, however, we have consistently distinguished between benefits and disbenefits, on the one hand, and revenues and costs, on the other hand.

a) How does the first set of cash flows differ from the second?

b) Which set of cash flows are the more difficult to estimate, and why?

c) What happens to benefits and disbenefits that cannot be monetized (estimated)?

11-2 Equation 11.4 for the modified BCR can be rearranged as follows:

$$\frac{(B + R) - (C + D)}{I}$$

What advantages does this format have over the one presented in the body of this chapter?

11-3 A solar-energy system costs $50,000 and produces savings of $3,000 per year. How many years are needed to obtain a benefit-cost ratio of 1.0 for a discount rate of 10%? What would the discount rate have to be to achieve a BCR of unity?

11-4 A town is considering building an athletic field for $200,000. It will be used approximately 200 days per year and is expected to attract an average of 200 players and spectators per day. What is the "benefit" to each user of the facility for a BCR of unity? What, if anything, have we left out in computing this "benefit"?

11-5 A project is estimated to cost $100,000. The benefits are expected to be $20,000 at the end of the first year and increase at a rate of 15% per year over an eight-year period. What is the BCR for a discount rate of 10%? (*Hint*: Use Appendix C.)

Conventional and Modified Benefit-Cost Ratios

11-6 The U.S. Bureau of Reclamation is considering a project that would extend irrigation canals into a desert area. The initial cost of the project is expected to be $1.5 million, with annual maintenance costs of $25,000 per year. The net cash flow from agricultural production is expected to be $175,000 per year. The interest rate is 6%, and the project's life is 20 years.

a) Draw a cash flow diagram of this project.

b) Perform a conventional B/C analysis to determine whether the project should be undertaken.

c) Rework the problem using the modified BCR.

11-7 A proposed public project has benefits with a PW of $75 million and costs with a PW of $55 million. Some members of the planning council suggest that, of the $55 million, $15 million should really be charged as disbenefits. What was the original BCR, and what is the BCR for the suggested change? If one of the two ratios is greater (or less) than unity, will the other ratio also be greater (or less)? Can you prove your point with a simple algebraic example?

11-8 Suppose that the project in Problem 11-7 was in competition with another project, for which the benefit-cost ratio is 1.45. What additional information does the planning commission need to know about this ratio in order to make a selection?

11-9 A state is planning on building a recreation and camping facility. Land acquisition and construction costs are estimated at $50 million. This cost will be spread equally over a 4-year period. Revenues from the park are expected to start at $5 million at the end of the third year and grow by $2 million each year for 7 years, at which time they are expected to level out. The planning horizon is 50 years and can therefore be assumed as infinite. Funds can be borrowed on the market at an annual rate of 7%.

a) Draw the cash flow diagram for this project.

b) Using present worths, calculate the BCR, using the modified method.

c) Should this investment be made?

11-10 Due to complaints of inefficiency from supervisors, top management decided to invest in a comprehensive training program for new and current employees. The program costs $2,000 per employee and lasts four weeks. The training period will cover one year and affect 500 employees. Experience with a pilot program indicates that a benefit-cost ratio of 1.75 could be attained, based on a planning horizon of five years. What annual cost savings can be expected from the program due to productivity gains and quality improvement? In answering this question, treat the investment in training as a continuous cash flow over a one-year period and assume that the cost savings are also continuous and will last five years after the program has been completed. The MARR is 25%. (*Hint*: Use Appendix D.)

11-11 A state highway department is considering the construction of a new highway through a scenic rural area. The road is estimated to cost $6 million, with annual maintenance costs of $120,000. The improved accessibility is expected to generate $650,000 in annual net cash flows from tourists. The road is projected to have a useful life of 25 years. Funds can be obtained at 8%. Determine the BCR, using the conventional and the modified methods.

Incremental Analysis with Two Alternatives

11-12 You have been asked to use the BCR method to compare two processes for removing sulfur from flue gases. Your analysis is to be based on an MARR of 20%. The following data apply:

	X	Y
Initial cost	$1,500,000	$2,000,000
Annual O&M costs	$190,000	$90,000
Useful life, years	10	10
Salvage value	$0	$0

a) Where are the benefits?

b) Which process do you recommend and why?

11-13   In Problem 11-12, which process would you recommend if the salvage values of alternatives X and Y were $150,000 and $300,000, respectively. (*Hint*: Use the capital recovery for the denominator.)

11-14   Two routes are under review for a new interstate highway. Route A would be 44 miles long, with an initial cost of $42 million. Route B would be 20 miles long, with an initial cost of $60 million which includes a tunnel. Maintenance costs are estimated at $80,000 per year for route A and $130,000 for route B. The volume of traffic is expected to be 800,000 vehicles per year, with operating expenses for each vehicle at $0.24 per mile. The study comparing the two routes is to be based on a 40-year life and an MARR of 12%. There will be no toll for the use of the tunnel.

a) What is the benefit to the consumer for each use of route B as compared to route A?

b) Which route should be selected based on the conventional BCR?

c) Which route should be selected based on the modified BCR?

11-15   Recompute Problem 11-14, using an infinite planning horizon. Does this change the result?

11-16   Suppose the highway authorities in Problem 11-14 decided to charge a toll of $2.00 for the use of the tunnel.

a) What are the benefits to the consumer for each use of route B?

b) What are the conventional and modified benefit-cost ratios of the investment?

11-17   Refer to Problem 11-16. What is the break-even toll, and what are the conventional and modified benefit-cost ratios for that toll, assuming the number of users does not change?

11-18   A salesperson must choose between two different cars to make her deliveries and pickups. One car has advantages in mileage and annual maintenance costs but is somewhat more expensive. The costs are summarized in the following table. The planning horizon is five years.

CAR	Alternatives	
	A	B
First cost	$25,000	$27,500
Annual costs	2,000	1,600
Salvage value	1,000	1,500

a) Draw a cash flow diagram for each alternative.

b) Using the incremental benefit-cost ratio and an MARR of 5%, which car should she purchase?

11-19 The U.S. Forest Service is considering two locations for a new national park. Location **E** will require an initial investment of $3 million and $50,000 in annual maintenance. Location **W** would require an initial investment of $7 million. Operating costs for location **W** will be $65,000 per year, but the Forest Service will also receive $25,000 in annual usage fees. The annual revenue from park concessionaires will be $500,000 at location **E** and $700,000 at location **W**.

a) Calculate the modified BCR for both locations, assuming infinite life and a discount rate of 10%.

b) Which alternative would you choose?

11-20 The Port Authority of New York and New Jersey is considering building a tunnel or starting a ferry service. Preliminary estimates for these alternatives are given in the following table. Dollar amounts are in millions. The MARR is 10%.

	Tunnel	Ferries
Investment	$1,500	$500
Annual O&M costs	$10	$40
Annual user fees	$200	$150
Life of asset, years	∞	20

a) Using the modified BCR ratio, which alternative would you choose?

b) Would the incremental investment in the tunnel be justified?

11-21 Two plans are under review in a study based on an infinite planning horizon. Both show net benefits (the numerator of the modified BCR) of $1,500,000 annually. The capital recovery cost of plan A is $1,000,000. The modified BCR is therefore 1.5.

Plan B requires an initial investment of $8,000,000 and an additional investment of $4,000,000 at a still indeterminate time in the future. In order to compete with plan A, plan B must show a BCR of at least 1.5. What is the earliest the additional expenditure of $4,000,000 can be made in order for plan B to be competitive with plan A?

Incremental Analysis with More Than Two Alternatives

11-22 Turn to Example 11.1. Show that Z bests X using the incremental approach that was used to show that Y bests X.

11-23 Your firm is considering three alternatives to bolster production and improve quality. They are as follows:

	X	Y	Z
First cost	$100,000	$200,000	$150,000
Annual benefits	$17,500	$40,000	$26,000
Useful life, years	10	20	30

The discount rate is 15%.

a) Which alternative do you recommend?

b) What assumptions (if any) did you have to make to provide an answer?

11-24 Select the best alternative from the following proposals, using the modified BCR. The MARR is 10% per year, and all projects have a useful life of 15 years. Assume that the cost of the land will be recovered when the project is terminated.

	Alternatives		
Item	1	2	3
Land cost	$50,000	$40,000	$80,000
Construction cost	200,000	150,000	185,000
Annual O&M costs	15,000	16,000	17,000
Annual income	52,000	49,000	50,000

SUMMARY OF PART I

Chapter 11 concludes Part I of this text on the basics of engineering economy. These basics are applied in Parts II, III, and IV. A summary of Part I follows. If you stumble over any part of it, we suggest that you go back to Part I before you proceed with Part II.

1. The selection process for capital projects is based on cash flow estimates and on the notion that money has a time value.

2. A given sum of money in "now" or "present" dollars is equivalent to a larger sum of money in "then" or "future" dollars. Conversely, a given sum of money in future dollars is equivalent to a smaller sum in present dollars.

3. Present and future cash flows cannot be compared without first making them equivalent.

4. The equivalence of present and future cash flow streams is expressed numerically through rates of return. These rates are used to discount or to compound cash flows in order to bring them to the same point in time or, for equivalent uniform series, the same planning horizon or time span.

5. For equivalence computations, effective, not nominal, rates of return are used.

6. The rate of return for the time-value-of-money computations is the investor's minimum attractive rate of return (MARR) based on his or her assessment of the opportunity forgone by not investing elsewhere.

7. Discounting and compounding computations are carried out with the aid of rate-of-return formulas that have been derived for a wide variety of cash flow patterns representing many typical investment situations. The formulas cover both discrete and continuous compounding and discounting, and both discrete and continuous cash flows.

8. All of the formulas are derived from two simple relationships—one for compounding single present sums to obtain equivalent future sums, namely, $F = P(1 + i)^N$, and the other for discounting single future sums to obtain equivalent present sums, namely, $P = F(1 + i)^{-N}$.

9. Five figures of merit based on equivalent cash flows are commonly used for comparing alternatives: the present worth, the annual worth, the future worth (these worths are referred to collectively as "the three worths"), the internal rate of return (IRR), and the benefit-cost ratio (BCR).

10. In an economy study, each alternative is distinguished from other alternatives by a unique cash flow pattern.

   a. The present worth of each pattern is the algebraic sum of all of the cash flow streams converted to their equivalent value at an arbitrary present time, referred to as EOP 0 (end-of-period zero).

   b. The future worth of each pattern is the algebraic sum of all of the cash flow streams converted to their equivalent value at a future point N in time, that is, at EOP N.

   c. The annual worth of each pattern is its equivalent uniform series over the time span EOP 0 to EOP N, with the first cash flow at EOP 1. N can be finite or infinite.

11. In any comparison of alternatives in which only economic consequences are considered, the alternative with the highest equivalent worth is favored.

12. The internal rate of return is the rate that makes the equivalent worth of a set of cash flows zero. It is the figure of merit preferred by investors because it can be compared directly to other current investment opportunities, to the current market for corporate and government se-

curities, and to the rate at which banks and other financial institutions are lending money.

13. However, IRRs, unlike equivalent worths, cannot be compared directly. Each increment of initial cost must justify itself. Furthermore, there may be problems in evaluating the IRR, which may require the introduction of an auxiliary rate of return (usually the MARR) with which a surrogate for the IRR, called the external rate of return (ERR), is computed.

14. The benefit-cost ratio is the figure of merit favored by decision makers responsible for selecting capital projects for the public sector and not-for-profit projects for the private sector. As its name implies, it is the ratio of benefits to costs.

15. The conventional BCR puts the net benefits flowing to the public in the numerator and the net costs of the owner in the denominator. The modified ratio puts the net benefits and the net costs, excluding the initial cost, in the numerator. The initial cost becomes the denominator.

16. Direct comparisons cannot be made with the BCR. As with the IRR, each increment of investment must stand on its own.

17. Alternatives cannot be compared unless their time frames are identical. The problem of selecting a common planning horizon is called "cotermination." Planning horizons can be finite or infinite.

18. The two most common techniques for cotermination are the early-sale approach and the LCM (lowest common multiple) approach. For the LCM approach, the annual worth is the recommended figure of merit because its value is independent of the number of repetitive cycles.

PART II
THE SELECTION PROCESS: ECONOMIC ANALYSIS

___12

RANKING FOR TECHNOLOGICAL EXCLUSIVITY

12.1 INTRODUCTION

The selection process for capital projects consists of two distinct exercises or steps. The first step deals with technological exclusivity. The second step deals with financial exclusivity. For both steps, we need to structure the alternatives that we wish to include in an economy study into a set of mutually exclusive alternatives (MEAs). Such sets are the fundamental building blocks of the capital selection process.

To what does technological exclusivity refer? It refers to a set of MEAs, consisting of competing alternatives, from which one alternative will be selected.

To what does financial exclusivity refer? It refers to sets of MEAs that are competing for the limited funding available and from which one set will be selected.

The second step always follows the first step, since the alternatives to be included in the second step are derived from the first step. This is illustrated in Figure 12.1

The ranking procedures for the two steps differ. For the first step, we need to coterminate if the life cycles of the members of the set differ; for the second step, we do not. For the first step, incremental analysis may be required; for the second, it is not.

The first step, which deals with technological exclusivity, is covered in this chapter. The second step, which deals with financial exclusivity, is covered in Chapter 13.

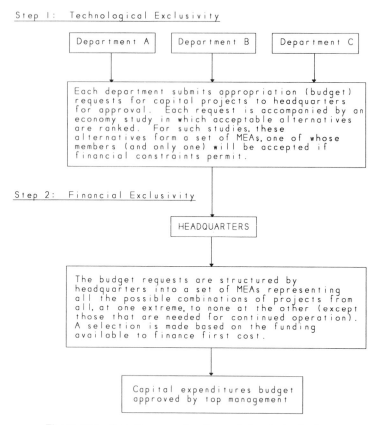

Figure 12.1. Two-step procedure for capital project selection.

The major questions asked and answered in Chapter 12 are

1. How far do we go with selecting competing alternatives for sets of MEAs whose members are technologically exclusive?
2. How do (a) mutually exclusive, (b) dependent, and (c) independent alternatives differ from each other?
3. How do we structure a set of MEAs for technological exclusivity if dependencies are present?
4. How do we rank order the members of a set of competing alternatives?

We begin with the selection of alternatives, but not before reminding you that this chapter deals only with technological exclusivity.

12.2 SELECTION OF ALTERNATIVES

Once an economic study for a capital investment opportunity has been approved, the study group must select the alternatives that should be included as members of a set of mutually exclusive alternatives competing with each other. If this initial step in the selection process is not done properly, the entire study is tainted and may well prove worthless; that is, the quality of the final decision may not be an optimum. There exist many "war stories" of how "pet" projects were approved because they were compared to weaker alternatives while stronger alternatives were suppressed or ignored. "Give me an opportunity to structure the alternatives, and I can justify anything" is a common sentiment, not only in the private sector, but also in the public sector.

The selection of competing alternatives is based on three characteristics—feasibility, exhaustiveness, and exclusivity. Once selected, they form a set that is usually referred to as a set of mutually exclusive alternatives, or MEAs for short.

> *COMMENT:* We could have mentioned one more characteristic, namely, risk, but we will leave this to Part III. In the meantime, you should assume that all of the alternatives in a given set of MEAs share approximately the same risk profile. If they did not, we would have difficulty in selecting an MARR, as you will find out in Chapter 14.

The tests for feasibility are technical and financial. We take technical feasibility as a given; that is, we presume that there are no technical limitations, that is, no legal, political, administrative, or physical hindrances that disqualify any of the alternatives under review. If there were, the alternative should have been deleted from the study.

Financial feasibility depends on available funding. Its place in the selection process is illustrated in Figure 12.1 and will be covered in considerable detail in Chapter 13.

A set of alternatives should also be exhaustive. Many a cost study has been presented to a decision maker with a recommended selection only to have that person ask, "Why didn't you consider this possibility?" However, exhaustiveness can be carried to unreasonable limits and has been in many studies.

Lastly, the set of alternatives should be mutually exclusive on technological grounds. This type of exclusivity is discussed in the next section.

12.3 SETS OF COMPETING ALTERNATIVES

As mentioned, engineering economy studies for a particular investment opportunity are grounded on selecting and examining sets of mutually exclusive alternatives. Each member of the set has its own distinctive cash flow pattern. One of the members may or may not be the do-nothing alternative, that is, leave well enough alone.

Technological exclusivity—the only type we are currently concerned with—means "one or the other," not "one and the other" and not "one and/or the other." It means that only one member of a set containing any number of members will be selected. Both a tunnel and a bridge for crossing a river are not going to be built at the same location. Either a low dam or a high dam or a dam somewhere in between, but not all three or any two, will be recommended for a flood control project. A firm is not going to select software that is incompatible with its computer hardware. A highway from points A to B will be constructed along this route or that. Machine A is not going to be replaced with machines B and C but with one or the other.

There are, however, situations in which one or more alternatives are dependent or contingent on the selection of other alternatives. How this situation is handled in order to derive a set of mutually exclusive alternatives is the topic of the next subsection.

12.3.1   Dependent Alternatives

The alternatives initially selected may not form a set of competing alternatives, because some of the members in the initial set are dependent on other members of the set. A crude pipeline to a proposed refinery is dependent on whether the refinery is built. The refinery, however, may have other supply sources, for example, a nearby port with tanker access. A proposed roadway and parking area to a scenic outlook will depend on whether at least one of the highway relocations under review will pass nearby. New and more modern testing equipment for an instrument maintenance facility may depend on whether new and more sophisticated instruments requested by the operating department are approved. In short, if B can only be done if A is done but A can stand alone, the options are not A or B or A plus B but simply A or A plus B. If the dependence is mutual, then there is only one opportunity— A plus B. To regroup a set of opportunities into a set of MEAs in which dependencies exist is usually not difficult, as Example 12.1 will show.

Example 12.1   Dependent Alternatives   You are asked to evaluate various CAD/CAM software packages for your employer. After completing the survey of vendors and after discussions with the design engineers in your company, you list the recommended alternatives as follows:

Alternative	Description
A	Do nothing, that is, continue with the software package now in use.
B	Buy a software package from Beta Company.
C	Buy a maintenance contract from Beta Company. The contract would provide for software updates and training in using the software package.
D	Develop your own software improvements and training.

Alternatives C and D are contingent on whether a software package is purchased from Beta under alternative B. Rearranging the four alternatives produces a set of MEAs containing three members. These are as follows:

Alternative	Description
A	Do nothing.
B	Buy the software package with maintenance contract from Beta Company.
C	Buy the software package from Beta Company, but generate improvements in house.

In Example 12.1, we limited the choices to one vendor. If we had considered three software purchase alternatives instead of one, the set of MEAs would have been substantially larger. Furthermore, we introduced the do-nothing alternative. This is not always one of the alternatives in a set of MEAs but depends on whether it is possible to get by with what is now in use.

A special form of dependency that sometimes crops up in economy studies is referred to as "reinvestment-dependency." We describe it in the following subsection.

12.3.2 Reinvestment-Dependency

There are situations in which an investment made today makes it possible to follow up with a special investment opportunity in the future that otherwise could not have been made. Without the first investment, the second could not take place, and without the second, the first may not be attractive. If so, the first investment is reinvestment-dependent. How to handle such situations is covered in Example 12.2.

Example 12.2   Reinvestment-Dependency   Alternative A has a first cost of $10,000 and will produce a net cash flow of $4,000 for four years. There is no foreseeable opportunity at this time for reinvesting the annual cash flows of $4,000 at more than the MARR of 10%. The salvage value at EOY 4 is zero.

Alternative B also has a first cost of $10,000 and will produce a net cash flow of $6,000 but for only two years. However, with this investment, one can realistically foresee an opportunity to reinvest the two annual cash flow streams in order to earn an estimated 20% up to EOY 5, at which time the salvage value will be zero.

How do the two alternatives compare? The cash flow diagrams before reinvesting are shown in Figure 12.2 for a study period of five years, since this is the life of the longest investment. In addition, an equivalent cash flow diagram for alternative B after reinvesting the two annual cash flows of $6,000 at EOY 1 and EOY 2 is given.

For alternative A, assuming no salvage value,

$$PW_A = -\$10,000 + \$4,000(P/A,10,4) = \$2,680$$

The present worth from reinvesting the annual cash flow streams of $4,000 at an MARR of 10% has, as we know, no effect on the present worth of alternative A. Why not?

For the present worth of alternative B after reinvestment, it is easier to calculate first the future worth. As shown in Figure 12.2, the cash flow streams at EOY 1 and EOY 2 are immediately reinvested so that the net cash flow at the end of these

Alternative A

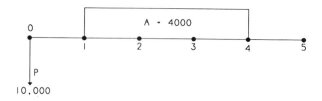

Alternative B   Before reinvestment

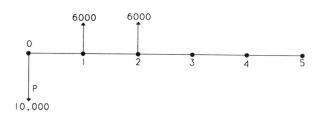

Alternative C   After reinvestment

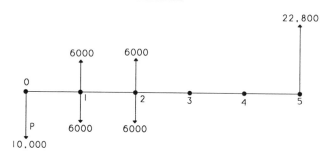

Figure 12.2. Reinvestment-dependency.

two years is zero. The equivalent future worth of the two streams is

$$FW = \$6{,}000(F/P,20,4) + \$6{,}000(F/P,20,3) = \$22{,}800$$

The present worth of alternative B is therefore

$$PW_B = -\$10{,}000 + \$22{,}800(P/F,10,5) = \$4{,}160$$

If the predictions on reinvestment are reasonable, alternative B is the better choice.

12.4 INDEPENDENT ALTERNATIVES

We introduce independent alternatives here only to tell you what they are and then set them aside until we reach Chapter 13. Independent investment opportunities are not technologically exclusive but, rather, as their name implies, independent. They are competing with each other only because the funding available to finance first costs is limited. Our objective, therefore, is not to select A or B or C or D but to find the best combination of A and/or B and/or C and/or D within an organization's funding constraints.

> *COMMENT:* Consider investment opportunity A. Three of the technologically exclusive members of its set of MEAs had positive NPWs. A_1 ranked the highest, A_2 was next, and A_3 was last. Investment opportunity B, which is independent of A, had two technologically exclusive members in its set of MEAs, B_1 and B_2, with positive NPWs. In Chapter 13 on financial exclusivity, you will learn that all five alternatives—A_1, A_2, A_3, B_1, B_2—have to be considered in structuring a set of MEAs to find the optimum combination within the constraint of a limited budget.

We have already mentioned that independent alternatives do not have to be coterminated and that incremental analyses play no part in their selection. Furthermore, the annual worth is not a good figure of merit with which to compare them. In Chapter 7, you learned that the annual worth is the ideal figure of merit for comparing alternatives whose life cycles differ. We only had to be careful in converting annual worths to present or future worths to use the proper (P/F) or (F/P) factor, that is, the factor for the length of the finite or infinite planning horizon rather than factors for the life cycle of each alternative. This feature of annual worths makes them misleading for comparing sets of alternatives for which our only objective is to determine how best to distribute the funds at hand.

With these brief comments on what is in store for you in Chapter 13, we swing back to technological exclusivity and to the key topic of this chapter—rank ordering, or simply ranking.

12.5 RANK ORDERING

Ranking a set of technologically exclusive alternatives is much like juggling balls. Most of us can learn to juggle two balls at a time, some of us can learn to juggle three, but juggling four or more is for the professional jugglers. In previous chapters, you learned how to rank two alternatives using equivalent worths, IRRs, and BCRs. In this chapter, you will learn how to rank many more, although for practical reasons we limit ourselves to five. We begin with a brief introduction to the ranking process.

1. Ranking can be carried out with any of the five figures of merit derived in Part I. With three of these—the three worths—ranking is straightforward, since it is only necessary to array them from the highest to the lowest worth.

2. With the remaining two—the IRR and the BCR—results consistent with those obtained for the three worths may require an incremental analysis, that is, an analysis of the differential cash flows between pairs of alternatives. If this is properly done, all five figures of merit produce the same ranking.

3. Without incremental analyses, ranking with the IRR or BCR is subject to two ranking errors:
   a. Selecting the option with the highest IRR or BCR.
   b. Selecting the option with the largest investment (first cost) that satisfies the MARR.

12.5.1   Ranking with Equivalent Worths

The direct ranking of alternatives using any one of the three worths is demonstrated in Example 12.3. Since all of the worths are related through rate-of-return factors, ranking by one is the same as ranking by any other.

Example 12.3   Ranking with Equivalent Worths   Your company is considering purchasing a computer integrated manufacturing (CIM) system that will be used to interconnect various robots and automated equipment in the production line.

A set of four MEAs have been identified, not including the do-nothing alternative. These are referred to as alternatives A, B, C, and D. The do-nothing alternative is represented by the symbol 0.

Cash flows are tabulated below. These are in thousands and are assumed to occur at the end of each year. Furthermore, the yearly savings for each alternative are uniform for the entire ten-year period.

		Alternatives			
	Year	A	B	C	D
First cost, P	0	$-2,000	$-3,000	$-5,000	$-6,000
Net yearly cash flows, A	1–10	+380	+645	+1,000	+1,020
Net cash flow for 10 years	—	+1,800	+3,450	+5,000	+4,200

The cash flow for the do-nothing alternative is not shown. Its present worth is zero, its IRR equals the MARR, and its BCR equals 1. In Chapter 11, we pointed out that, presumably, your selection of an MARR was made with another opportunity in mind—an opportunity forgone—which, for a comparable risk profile, would have earned an estimated return exactly equal to the MARR you selected. If so, this opportunity forgone or do-nothing alternative would, like a loan, have a present worth of zero and therefore an IRR equal to the MARR and a BCR of 1.

COMMENT: The preceding simplification of using uniform cash flows does not in any way detract from the conclusions we will reach. For most economic studies, periodic net cash flows or savings will not be uniform, and calculations must therefore be done on a period-to-period basis. Given the spreadsheets and specialized programs for engineering economic analysis that are now available, such cash flow patterns are almost as easily handled as uniform series but contribute nothing to a better understanding of such problems as this one.

A ranking based on net cash flow is, as we know, identical with a ranking based on a zero rate of return. It is good practice to check this ranking first, in order to cull those alternatives for which the net cash flow is zero or less. In this instance, there are none. All four alternatives show a positive cash flow balance and will therefore earn a return. The ranking by decreasing net cash flow or zero return is

$$C > D > B > A$$

The symbol $>$ stands for "is preferred to" or "is better than." Thus $C > D$ tells us that C is better than D.

Your company decides to compare the alternatives for an MARR of 12%, using the present worth as the figure of merit. The residual or salvage value is assumed to be zero. The rate-of-return equation for all four alternatives is

$$PW = -P + A(P/A,i,N)$$

For alternative A,

$$PW_A = -\$2,000 + \$380(P/A,12,10)$$

$$= -\$2,000 + \$380 \times 5.650 = -\$2,000 + \$2,147$$

$$= \$+147$$

The results of similar calculations for the remaining alternatives are tabulated as follows:

	Years	A	B	C	D
		\multicolumn{4}{c}{Alternatives}			
First cost	0	\$−2,000	\$−3,000	\$−5,000	\$−6,000
Net yearly cash flow	1–10	+380	+645	+1,000	+1,020
PW of savings	0	+2,147	+3,644	+5,650	+5,763
NPW	0	+147	+644	+650	−237

Since the net present worth of the do-nothing alternative is zero, it is a better choice than alternative D, for which the NPW is negative. The ranking in decreasing order of NPW is therefore the following: C is preferable to B, B to A, A to 0, and

0 to D, or more succinctly,

$$C > B > A > 0 > D$$

You should have expected that the ranking using discounted cash flow techniques would not necessarily be identical with that for a zero rate of return.

For annual worth, the rate-of-return formula for all four alternatives is

$$AW = A - P(A/P,i,N)$$

which, for alternative A, gives

$$AW_A = \$380 - \$2,000 \times 0.1770 = \$380 - \$354$$
$$= \$26$$

We could, of course, have obtained this figure directly from PW_A by multiplying the latter by the A/P factor; thus

$$AW_A = PW_A(A/P,i,N)$$
$$= \$147 \times 0.1770$$
$$= \$26$$

Similar arguments apply to the future worth, which can either be calculated directly from the following formula or obtained by multiplying the present worth by the F/P factor.

$$FW = A(F/A,i,N) - P(F/P,i,N)$$

or

$$FW = PW(F/P,i,N)$$

The table that follows sums up the calculations for the four alternatives and the do-nothing alternative. All worths are in thousands of dollars.

		Alternative			
	0	A	B	C	D
PW	0	$147	$644	$650	$ − 237
AW	0	$26	$114	$115	$ − 42
FW	0	$456	$2,000	$2,019	$ − 736
Rank	4	3	2	1	5

Our choice then is alternative C and, if this proves unacceptable for some reason of which we are not now aware, for example, an unacceptable non-monetary attribute, then our choice is alternative B.

COMMENT: In Chapter 13, you will find that alternative C may have to be replaced by alternative A or B because of its high first cost. In other words, as mentioned earlier, for a step 2 analysis on financial exclusivity, we need all of the acceptable results of the step 1 analysis.

Looking at the preceding table once again may have made you wonder if alternative C is really the best choice. Compare, for example, the following numbers (in thousands) for alternatives B and C.

	Alternative	
	B	C
First cost	$3,000	$5,000
Net present worth	644	650

Is an extra expenditure of $2,000,000 worth an increase in net present worth of only $6,000? The answer to this question is "yes," provided the additional $2,000,000 produces a rate of return equal to, or better than, the MARR of 12%. That it does so is obvious, since the net present worth for this incremental investment is $6,000($650,000 − $644,000), indicating a return slightly greater than 12%. The following calculations confirm this statement and also illustrate why equivalent worths can be ranked directly, that is, without proceeding with an incremental analysis. Cash flows are in thousands of dollars.

	Alternatives		
	B	C	C − B
First cost	$ − 3,000	$ − 5,000	$ − 2,000
Net yearly savings	645	1,000	355
PW of savings	3,644	5,650	2,006
NPW	644	650	6

As the last column indicates, the extra investment of $2,000,000 will bring in a net cash flow of $355,000 per year for ten years, which is equivalent to a rate of return slightly better than 12% (12.1%).

There is no point in arguing that there may be another way to spend the extra $2,000,000 and earn a much higher return than 12%. We set 12% as the objective we were seeking, and we meet this objective with alternative C. If we want to change this objective, we have a different problem and not the one with which we started. We come back to this argument after ranking the previous alternatives with the IRR.

12.5.2 Ranking with the IRR

From an engineering economics viewpoint, ranking using any of the three worths is usually preferred. Nevertheless, ranking by IRR is expected, and often demanded by decision makers and is therefore a technique that has to be mastered, since it gives many businesspeople a figure of merit they can easily compare with prime rates, Treasury bonds, corporate bonds, and other investment opportunities. Similarly, decision makers in the public sector may require ranking using the BCR.

Example 12.4 Ranking with the IRR In this example, we use the same data as Example 12.3. The pertinent cash flows and the computations for the IRR are given in the following tabulation.

		Alternatives			
	Year	A	B	C	D
First cost	0	$-2,000	$-3,000	$-5,000	$-6,000
Net yearly cash savings	1–10	$+380	$+645	$+1,000	$+1,020
P/A factor	—		5.26	4.65	5.00	5.88
IRR, %	—		14	17	15	11

As mentioned, the IRR for the do-nothing alternative for an MARR of 12% is 12%, since this is the opportunity cost (the opportunity forgone) of investing in any one of the other four alternatives.

The ranking by decreasing IRRs puts B ahead of C, which is contrary to the ranking based on the three worths. The complete sequence is

$$B > C > A > 0 > D$$

Alternative D does not meet the MARR criterion of 12%, just as it did not meet the requirement for an NPW equal to, or greater than, zero. This leaves us with the problem of reconciling the two preferential sequences:

$$\text{Net present worth sequence} = C > B > A$$

$$\text{IRR sequence} = B > C > A$$

To do so, we look at the IRRs for the differential cash flows between pairs of alternatives. Actually, we need to do so for only one pair—C and B—since A is at the bottom of the list for both figures of merit. However, you will become better acquainted with ranking by IRRs by examining several incremental analyses in series.

The calculations for the differential IRRs follow a step-by-step procedure. First, the alternatives to be compared are arranged in ascending order of first costs. This has already been done. Alternative A has the lowest first cost, and alternative C has the highest. Next, the first pair of alternatives—in this case, A and B—is analyzed. A is the defender and B the challenger. Whichever comes out ahead becomes the defender against the next challenger, in this case, alternative C.

The pertinent cash flows in thousands of dollars for alternatives A and B follow:

	First Cost	Net Annual Cash Flow
Alternative A	$-2,000	$+380
Alternative B	-3,000	+645
B less A	-1,000	+265

The differential investment of $1,000,000 produces a net cash flow of $265,000 every year for ten years. The P/A factor is 3.77 ($1,000/$265). The IRR is approximately 23%, which is well above the required MARR. Therefore, B dominates A and is now challenged by C.

The cash flows in thousands of dollars for comparing B with C are

	First Cost	Net Annual Cash Flow
Alternative B	$-3,000	$+645
Alternative C	-5,000	+1,000
C less B	-2,000	+355

We have already demonstrated that the differential investment of $2,000,000, which produces a net annual cash flow for ten years of $355,000, gives a rate of return slightly greater than the MARR. Therefore, C dominates B and the preference ranking using the IRR becomes identical with that for the net present worth; that is,

$$C > B > A$$

Since C dominates B and B dominates A, C will dominate A. It is therefore not necessary to compare C with A, although you may want to do so in order to make certain that you understand the preceding procedure. If you do, you will find that the differential investment of $3,000,000 produces a return of about 17%.

The following table compares the IRR rankings with the NPW rankings.

Comparison of IRR and NPW Rankings

Alternatives	Ranking by		
	IRR Only	Incremental IRR	NPW
0	4	4	4
A	3	3	3
B	1	2	2
C	2	1	1
D	5	5	5

Let us look at alternatives B and C again for an answer to the question we posed at the conclusion of Example 12.3. The pertinent figures are

	Alternatives		
	B	C	C − B
First cost	$3,000,000	$5,000,000	$2,000,000
IRR	17%	15%	12.1%

Why should we accept alternative C if alternative B will give a higher rate of return? The answer is the same as before. We specified an MARR of 12%. The differential investment satisfies this criterion. We could have discussed several other problems for which alternative B would clearly be the winner. If the MARR we had set as our objective were 16%, alternative B would be ranked ahead of alternative C. If we felt that we could find another opportunity for investing $2,000,000 that would earn 17% or better, we would again accept alternative B. However, that was not the problem we set up. For that problem, alternative C is preferable to alternative B.

12.5.3   Ranking with the BCR

Since the BCR is, like the IRR, a ratio (dimensionless number) rather than a number expressed in dollars, ranking with the BCR follows a procedure that is similar to that for ranking with the IRR. This is illustrated in Example 12.5.

Example 12.5   Ranking Using the BCR   We again use the data from Examples 12.3 and 12.4 for which the MARR equals 12%, the time horizon is ten years, and the calculations are based on end-of-year discount factors. The modified BCR is used. The numerator is the present worth of the net annual cash savings for ten years, and the denominator is the first cost. The calculations follow.

		Alternatives			
	Years	A	B	C	D
First cost (C)	0	$−2,000	$−3,000	$−5,000	$−6,000
Net yearly cash savings	1–10	$+380	$+645	$+1,000	$+1,020
PW of savings (B)[a]	—	$+2,147	$+3,644	$+5,650	$+5,763
BCR (B/C)	1.00	1.073	1.215	1.130	0.961

[a]For these figures, see Example 12.3.

The BCR for the do-nothing alternative is, by definition, 1.000. The ranking is identical with that for the IRR, namely

$$B > C > A > 0 > D$$

We can again eliminate alternative D, since its BCR is less than 1, and we need not consider the do-nothing alternative further. This leaves us with the following comparison between the present worth and BCR rankings:

$$\text{Net present worth sequence} = C > B > A$$

$$\text{BCR sequence} = B > C > A$$

We begin our analysis as we did with the IRR, by comparing the two alternatives with the lowest first cost. A is the defender, and B is the challenger. The differential investment of $1,000,000 has a BCR ratio of 1.497, as shown:

$$\text{BCR of B} - \text{A} = \frac{\$3,644 - \$2,147}{\$3,000 - \$2,000} = 1.497 \quad B > A$$

B clearly dominates A. Similar calculations for C as the challenger and B as the defender follow.

$$\text{BCR of C} - \text{B} = \frac{\$5,650 - \$3,644}{\$5,000 - \$3,000} = 1.003 \quad C > B$$

The differential BCR, like the differential IRR for C and B, is slightly greater than our objective. Therefore, C dominates B, and the preference ratings using the BCR are the same as those for the net present worth and the IRR. You should have no trouble in showing that the differential investment of $3,000,000 for (C − A) has a BCR of 1.168.

We have already noted that the rankings by the BCR and the IRR before incremental analysis agree with each other. This is usually, but not necessarily, the case. You cannot arbitrarily assume that they will agree, but you need to check them independently if rankings by both figures of merit are required.

12.6 ANNUAL COST ECONOMY STUDIES

We learned many chapters ago that only differences between alternatives are relevant. In economy studies for replacements, we assume that the cash flows from revenues and from costs other than those involved in replacements are the same for each alternative. We therefore work with only those cash flows associated with the proposed replacement. This produces cash flow patterns in which the major cash flows are all negative and for which the annual cost (AC or EUAC) is a convenient figure of merit. Our objective is to select the alternative with the lowest EUAC, which is, of course, the same as basing the selection on the highest annual or present worth. Consider Example 12.6.

Example 12.6 Annual Cost Economy Studies Three alternatives for an equipment replacement problem are under review. The life cycle of each is five years,
and the salvage value is zero. The MARR is 10%.

| | | Alternatives | | |
Line	Description	A	B	C
1	First cost	$40,000	$50,000	$60,000
2	Annual costs	35,000	30,000	25,000
3	PW of annual costs	− 133,000	− 113,000	− 95,000
4	NPW	− 173,000	− 163,000	− 145,000
5	EUAC	63,000	43,000	38,000

Notes:
1. Line 3 equals line 2 times $(P/A,10,5)$, or 3.791.
2. Line 4 equals line 1 plus line 3.
3. Line 5 equals line 4 times $(A/P,10,5)$, or 0.264.

The selection based on present worth is alternative C, since it has the highest NPW. The selection based on EUAC is also Alternative C, because it has the lowest annual cost.

For such studies, ranking is done using the present worth or annual worth. None of the alternatives has an IRR or a BCR, since all of the cash flows are negative. We can only get meaningful values for these two figures of merit by looking at the differential cash flows between pairs of alternatives. You already know how to do this, and we suggest that you do so. However, the answer is clear. Any time you can, with little or no risk, invest $10,000 and earn a return of $5,000 for five years, you have a good investment, provided, of course, you have the cash resources to cover it.

Example 12.6 serves as a brief introduction to Chapter 15, in which we will discuss replacement problems in considerable detail.

12.7   METHODOLOGY FOR RANKING

You may initially find the concept of ranking using incremental analyses difficult. The following outline of the procedure to be followed should be of help.

1. Make sure that the alternatives chosen are feasible, exhaustive, and mutually exclusive technologically. Coterminate the time horizons if necessary. Choose an MARR.
2. Calculate the present worth (or any worth) of each alternative, and eliminate those for which the present worth is less than zero.
3. Rank the remaining alternatives by their present worths in increasing order. This will be the correct ranking, regardless of the ranking obtained with the IRR or BCR before incremental analyses are carried out.
4. Calculate the IRRs or BCRs, or both, for each alternative. Compare the rankings for those obtained using present worths. If the rankings differ, proceed with an incremental analysis.

5. Begin the incremental analysis by letting the alternative with the lowest first cost be the defender. The remaining alternatives are the successive challengers.

6. Compare the defender with the alternative which has the next lowest first cost (the challenger) by calculating the IRR or BCR, or both, for the differential cash flow. If this IRR is equal to or greater than the MARR and if the BCR is equal to or greater than 1, the challenger is the preferred choice and becomes the defender against the next challenger in line; otherwise, the original defender meets a new challenger.

7. Continue with steps 5 and 6 until the last alternative has been compared with the last defender.

If this procedure is followed, the ranking by IRR and BCR will be identical with that for any of the equivalent worths.

12.8 SUMMARY

The major topic of this chapter is ranking the members of sets of competing alternatives that are feasible, exhaustive, and technologically exclusive. For such sets

- The present worth (or any of the other worths) can be used directly for ranking. This means that we need not look at incremental cash flow patterns.
- The IRR and the BCR can also be used for ranking. However, the rankings may differ from those for any of the worths. This discrepancy can be corrected by computing IRRs and BCRs for incremental cash flow patterns.
- Ranking by present and future worth gives results in dollars and by annual worth, in dollars per period. However, dollar values are not very helpful in judging the relative strength of an investment as compared with other investment opportunities.
- For this reason, projects for the private sector usually show rankings for both present worths and IRRs. The IRR gives results in ratios, that is, in nondimensional form. It enables investors to judge the relative strengths of a particular MEA and the relative strength of increments of investment against prime rates and other rates of return.
- Comparisons using the BCR find their major application in the public sector, in which a ratio of benefits to costs greater than 1 has, or should have, voter appeal.

The results of the ranking procedure described in this chapter become input for the ranking procedure described in Chapter 13. You already know that the input must consist not only of the optimum selection for each investment opportunity but also, because of financial constraints, the rank ordering of all acceptable selections.

SUGGESTED READING

1. James L. Riggs and Thomas M. West, *Engineering Economy*, 3rd ed. (New York: McGraw-Hill, 1986). For more on reinvestment-dependency, including some good examples, read pages 177–179 of this text.

PROBLEMS

Technological Exclusivity

12-1 For technological exclusivity, we select the best member of a set of mutually exclusive alternatives. However, we may not be able to exclude the other acceptable alternatives, that is, those that also meet or surpass the figure of merit, from the selection process. Explain in your own words why this may be so.

12-2 Name some (a) legal, (b) political, (c) administrative, and (d) physical hindrances that might disqualify alternatives for inclusion as members in a set of MEAs.

Dependency

12-3 The ABC Company proposes to buy truck A or truck B. Each truck may or may not be equipped with a hydraulic hoist from manufacturer Y or Z. Structure the set of MEAs.

12-4 Alternatives A_1 and A_2 are mutually exclusive. Alternatives B_1 and B_2 are independent. Alternative C depends on the selection of B_1. List the members of the set of MEAs.

12-5 Plans for a new private road from a mine to the port at which the ore is currently loaded are under review. The economic analysis indicates substantial savings in haulage costs for the mine owners. Concurrently, the state is considering deepening and extending the harbor to allow larger ships of all types to be berthed. The plans for the harbor improvement were initiated independently of the road study. In fact, the state was not aware of what the mine owners intended to do. Are new studies needed? If so, by whom and why?

12-6 An ice cream vendor has three wagons, each of which costs $2,800 per week to operate. The cost of keeping a truck idle can be disregarded. The vendor's franchise covers two routes, each of which must be serviced with at least one wagon. The estimated revenues that can be generated are given in the following table:

Number of Trucks in Service	Revenue Generated	
	Route 1	Route 2
1	$5,000	$3,800
2	8,200	7,000
3	9,000	8,000

a) Identify the feasible members of the set of MEAs.

b) How should the vendor's trucks be allocated?

c) If additional trucks can be leased and operated at a cost of $3,500 per week, how should they be assigned?

Reinvestment-Dependency

12-7 Two mutually exclusive investment opportunities have the cash flows shown in the following table:

EOY	Net Cash Flow	
	Project A	Project B
0	$ – 100,000	$ – 100,000
1	20,000	10,000
2	20,000	120,000
3	60,000	20,000
4	60,000	0
5	60,000	0

A third project, project C, is to begin two years down the road. It will require an investment of $100,000 at EOY 2 and will produce an estimated net cash flow of $75,000 for the next three years. If project B is selected, it is planned to obtain the investment funds for project C from the net cash flow from project B at EOY 2. The MARR is 10%.

a) What is the NPW of projects A and B?

b) What is the NPW of projects B and C, assuming that $100,000 of the cash flow at EOY 2 from project B is reinvested in project C? Draw the cash flow diagram for this situation, and then develop the cash flow equation.

c) Suppose there is a fourth project, project D, which also requires an initial investment of $100,000 at EOY 0. What uniform annual cash flow would make this proposal as attractive as projects B and C together over the same planning horizon?

12-8 You are in the business of lending money and have $50,000 to loan. You could invest this safely in corporate bonds and earn 10%. If needed, you could borrow funds from your local bank up to an additional $50,000 for 15%. Three opportunities present themselves, all of which are with borrowers who represent reasonably good credit risks based on your previous experience with them. Borrower A wants $25,000 and is willing to pay 15%. Borrower B wants $25,000 and is willing to pay 18%, and borrower C wants $25,000 and is willing to pay 20%.

a) Identify the members of the set of MEAs.

b) What should you do?

c) What would you do if you could borrow at 13%?

Ranking with the Three Worths

12-9 Refer to Example 12.3 and confirm the computations for each of the three worths for alternatives B, C, and D.

12-10 The cash flow patterns for three investment opportunities are given in the following table:

EOY	Option 1	Option 2	Option 3
0	$-2,500	$-3,000	$-7,000
1	500	250	2,250
2	500	500	2,000
3	1,000	750	1,750
4	1,000	1,000	1,500
5	1,000	1,250	1,250

a) Calculate the NPW for a rate of return of zero, and rank the options, including the do-nothing alternative.

b) Calculate the NPW for an MARR equal to 10%, and rank the options.

c) Do the same for the AW, but do not use the results from (b), except as a check on your work.

d) Do the same for the FW without using the results from (b), except as a check on your work.

e) At what rate of return would options 1 and 3 have the same NPW?

12-11 Perry Physics is relocating its manufacturing facility to one of four sites. The cash flow estimates for this relocation are given in the following table:

Site	Initial Investment	Annual Savings in Net Cash Flow
1	$3,300,000	$800,000
2	3,600,000	900,000
3	4,400,000	1,100,000
4	5,600,000	1,275,000

The new facility is expected to last 25 years and have no salvage value at that time. The before-tax MARR is 20%.

a) As a first approximation, use an infinite planning horizon to compute the annual worth of the four alternatives.

b) Redo the annual worth computations for a planning horizon of 25 years.

c) What do the results of (a) and (b) tell you?

12-12 A small manufacturing facility intends to reduce its heating costs. These are currently averaging $50,000 per year. Three options are under review. These vary by the thickness of the insulation to be applied. The planning horizon is 20 years, and the discount rate is 20%.

	Option 1	Option 2	Option 3
Thickness, inches	3½	6½	9½
Installation cost	$100,000	$140,000	$180,000
Estimated annual heating costs	$20,000	$12,000	$10,000

Which option do you recommend? Use the AW for your analysis.

12-13 The Hyco Company currently has three proposals under review, for each of which the cash flow pattern is given in the following table:

EOY	A	B	C
0	− $100,000	− $150,000	− $200,000
1–4	30,000	60,000	70,000

Although the three proposals are independent, Hyco Company does not have the resources to invest in more than one.

a) Which proposals are acceptable for an MARR of 25%? Use the PW for your analysis.

b) Which proposals are acceptable for an MARR of 15%?

12-14 Consider the five mutually exclusive alternatives that follow:

Alternative	Annual Net Cash Flow	Initial Cost
A	$10,000	$100,000
B	50,000	200,000
C	72,000	400,000
D	90,000	440,000
E	100,000	600,000

All of the alternatives are long-lived, and an analysis based on infinite life is therefore appropriate for a first approximation. The discount rate is 15%.

a) Rank the alternatives using the present worth.

b) Do the same using the annual worth.

Ranking with the IRR

12-15 Refer to Example 12.4, in which the IRRs are given for alternatives A through D.

   a) Confirm the values of the IRRs for the four alternatives.

   b) Sketch the cash flow diagrams, and confirm the values of the IRRs for the differential cash flow patterns for $(B - A)$, $(C - B)$, and $(C - A)$.

   c) Compare the ranking of alternatives A through D using the NPW computations from Problem 12-9, with the ranking based on the IRR from (a) and (b).

12-16 Calculate the IRRs for the three options in Problem 12-10, and compare the ranking (including the do-nothing alternative) with that for the present worth from that problem. Is an incremental analysis needed for the IRR? Justify your answer.

12-17 Compute the IRRs for the four sites in Problem 12-11, assuming an infinite planning horizon. Compare the ranking (including the do-nothing alternative) for the annual worth with that for the IRR both before and after incremental analysis.

12-18 Redo Problem 12-17 using a 25-year planning horizon, and compare the IRR ranking with the ranking obtained in that problem.

12-19 Compare the IRRs for the five alternatives in Problem 12-14, and then compare the ranking for the annual worth or present worth from that problem with that for the IRR.

12-20 Three proposals are being considered by your company. The planning horizon is seven years. The following estimates have been prepared for a project selection study:

Proposal	Initial Cost	Annual Revenue	Annual Costs	Salvage Value
1	$80,000	$36,000	$22,000	$20,000
2	60,000	30,000	22,000	12,000
3	140,000	49,000	29,000	40,000

Compare the rates of return for these proposals, and make a recommendation as to which proposal should be accepted if the MARR is 6%.

12-21 Beechies is considering buying a new machine for one of its processing lines. Three machines are under study, for which the following estimates have been assembled.

Machine	Initial Cost	Annual Net Cash Flow	Useful Life, in Years
1	$10,000	$2,500	5
2	30,000	3,250	10
3	40,000	4,500	10

The MARR is 5%, the salvage value of all three machines is zero, the planning horizon is ten years, and the study is based on replacing machine 1 with an identical machine at the end of five years. Sketch the cash flow diagrams for the three proposals, and compare them using the IRR.

Ranking with the BCR

12-22 Three mutually exclusive alternatives are being reviewed. Each alternative has a ten-year life. The salvage value is zero, and the discount rate is 10%. The following data are available for project selection.

Alternatives	Present Worth of Costs	Annual Benefits
1	$80,000	12,800
2	40,000	8,200
3	120,000	22,000

a) Calculate the present or annual worths.

b) Calculate the IRRs, using incremental analysis, if necessary.

c) Calculate the BCRs, using incremental analysis, if necessary.

d) Compare the rankings for the three methods.

12-23 The following data apply to four mutually exclusive alternatives. The planning horizon is 20 years, and the discount rate is 10%.

Alternative	Initial Cost	Net Annual Benefits
Slam	$ 0	$ 0
Boom	100,000	30,000
Whack	150,000	38,000
Thud	200,000	40,000

a) Calculate and rank the annual worths.

b) Calculate the BCRs of the four alternatives, and rank them without making an incremental analysis.

c) Rank the BCRs using incremental analysis.

d) Compare the three rankings.

12-24 Four training programs are under review. The initial cost of each program and the expected benefits over a planning horizon of five years are given in the following table:

Alternative	Initial Cost	Net Annual Benefits
1	$15,000	$4,500
2	50,000	13,900
3	75,000	18,880
4	90,000	23,800

If the MARR is 10%, which is the best alternative based on BCR analysis?

12-25 Refer to Example 12.5, in which the BCRs are given for alternatives A through D and the do-nothing alternative.

a) Confirm the values of the BCRs.

b) Check the BCRs of the differential cash flows (B − A), (C − B), and (C − A).

c) Compare the BCR ranking with the present worth ranking in Problem 12-9 and the IRR ranking in Problem 12-15.

12-26 Calculate the BCRs of the three options in Problem 12-10, and compare the ranking with the present worth of that exercise and with the IRR ranking in Problem 12-16.

12-27 Compute the BCRs for the four sites in Problem 12-11, assuming an infinite planning horizon. Compare the ranking for the annual worth with that for the BCR both before and after incremental analysis.

12-28 Compare the BCRs for the five alternatives in Problem 12-14, and then compare the ranking for the annual worth or present worth with those for the BCR and those for the IRR in Problem 12-19.

12-29 Go back to Problem 12-20 and make your recommendation on which proposal should be selected using the BCR method.

Annual Cost Economy Studies

12-30 What assumption is inherent in comparing alternatives based on their equivalent uniform annual costs?

12-31 The three alternatives in the following table all have a useful life of five years and no salvage value. The MARR for the selection process is 10%.

Alternative	Initial Cost	Annual O&M Costs
1	$60,000	$22,500
2	75,000	15,000
3	90,000	10,000

a) Calculate the annual worths, and make a selection on that basis.

b) Compute the return on the extra investment in alternative 2 over alternative 1.

c) Compute the return on the extra investment in alternative 3 over alternative 2.

d) What is your recommendation?

12-32 Consider the following three alternatives for which the data needed for the selection process are given. The MARR is 6%.

	Alternative		
	A	B	C
Service life, in years	5	10	20
Initial cost, in $1,000s	20	40	50
Annual O&M costs, in $1000s	4	3	2
Salvage value, in $1000s	2	6	10

Assume "repeatability"; that is, assume that, for a planning horizon of 20 years, each alternative will be replaced with an identical unit at the end of its service life.

a) Calculate the EUAC of alternative A for a 5-year cycle, of alternative B for a 10-year cycle, and of alternative C for a 20-year cycle.

b) Sketch the cash flow diagrams of the three alternatives for the common 20-year planning horizon.

c) Calculate the EUAC of each alternative for the common 20-year planning horizon.

d) Can the higher initial cost of alternative B over alternative A and of alternative C over alternative B be justified based on rate-of-return calculations?

___13
RANKING FOR FINANCIAL EXCLUSIVITY

13.1 INTRODUCTION

In the introduction to Chapter 12, we mentioned a two-step procedure for the capital allocation process. The first step, which was covered in that chapter, dealt with ranking the members of sets of technologically exclusive, that is, competing, alternatives. The second step, which is covered in this chapter, takes the results of the first step to find an optimum solution (or, if not an optimum, then at least a reasonable or heuristic solution) on which of the capital projects under review to expend the limited capital funding available. The relationship between the two steps was illustrated in Figure 12.1.

The subject matter of Chapter 13 breaks down as follows:

- Master planning, or master budgeting
- Capital budgeting and its role in master planning
- Structuring and ranking sets of MEAs for financial exclusivity

We begin with master planning.

13.2 MASTER PLANNING

To plan is not the only function of management, but without plans all other management functions cannot be performed effectively or efficiently.

The planning or budgeting process begins with a master plan or budget prepared toward the end of the current fiscal year in preparation for the next fiscal year. It is usually an annual plan, broken down by months, which covers the year ahead in considerable detail. A long-term plan that looks ahead two to four years but on a quarterly or annual rather than a monthly basis usually accompanies the annual plan.

Master plans consist of two parts—the operating budget and the financial budget. Each of these consist of several sections, as shown in the following list:

Operations budget

Sales or revenue budget
Purchases budget
Cost-of-goods and services sold budget
Operating-expense budget
Other income and expense budget
Pro forma income statement

Financial plan

Capital expenditures budget
Pro forma cash flow statement
Pro forma balance sheet

For a manufacturing entity, the purchases budget is replaced by a manufacturing budget, which breaks down into a production budget and direct materials, direct labor, and factory overhead budgets. Similarly, the cost-of-sales budget is replaced by budgets for the cost of goods manufactured and the cost of goods sold.

The operations plan or budget (the words *plan* and *budget* are used synonymously) starts with revenues. The sales department prepares a preliminary sales plan. The production and staff departments then prepare cost budgets. The sales and cost budgets are the input for the monthly and annual pro forma income statements in which the net income to be earned next year and two to four years after are presented.

The financial plan or budget begins with the capital expenditures budget, which is prepared by first reviewing the appropriation or budget requests for capital projects submitted by the various departments and divisions. The level of expenditure finally approved depends on the funding available from both internal and external sources.

The pro forma cash flow statements are prepared from the pro forma income statements and the capital expenditures budget, and include the cash flow from expected borrowings to help finance capital expenditures.

The last items in the master plan are the pro forma balance sheets. These are prepared from the income statements and the statements of cash flow.

The detailed budgets that make up the master budget feed back to each other, and master budgeting usually goes through several major revisions before a final budget is approved by top management. It then becomes the standard against which overall, divisional, and departmental performance is measured and judged.

In the section that follows, we examine the capital expenditures or capital budget more fully.

13.3 CAPITAL BUDGETING

For any organization of any size, capital budgets are culled from numerous capital expenditure requests (budget requests) submitted by divisions and departments to headquarters. The budget requests fall into two categories: the necessary or must-do and the optional or would-like-to-do.

The *necessary* are those that have to be done now, that is, this year in order to keep production lines in operation and roofs from leaking. For these there is no viable do-nothing alternative.

The *optional* are those that do not have to be done this year or at all. For these there is a viable do-nothing alternative.

In more sophisticated organizations, the budget requests are buttressed with studies based on the time value of money using MARRs set by policy directives. This applies to both of the preceding categories, since there is always (or nearly so) more than one way to proceed.

Far more budget requests for capital expenditures are usually submitted than can be implemented with available funds. It therefore becomes necessary for management to structure the requests received into a set of mutually exclusive alternatives. How this is done is introduced in Example 13.1.

Example 13.1   Structuring Sets of MEAs for Financial Exclusivity   As a plant manager, you are evaluating budget requests for new equipment from three of your departments. Each department has analyzed its operations, submitted appropriate economy studies, and forwarded you the following requests:

Department	Description
A	New gear cutter
B	New conveyor system
C	New product-testing facilities

These are independent alternatives; that is, the costs and benefits of each are not dependent on the other two, and neither does any one alternative exclude any other. The life cycles of the three alternatives are not identical and do not have to be coterminated. Furthermore, each of them has presumably satisfied your company's policy on the MARR. The only restraint is your company's capital funding.

Three independent alternatives can be grouped into a set of MEAs containing eight members. These are identified in the following table:

Member	Departmental Requests Approved	Description
1	None	Do nothing, assuming this is a viable alternative
2	A	Approve department A request
3	B	Approve department B request
4	C	Approve department C request
5	A & B	Approve department A and B requests
6	A & C	Approve department A and C requests
7	B & C	Approve department B and C requests
8	A, B, & C	Approve all three departmental requests

Once the members of the set have been identified, those for which first costs exceed the budget constraint are culled. The present worth of the remaining members is computed and compared with their first cost, and an appropriate selection is made.

The results of Example 13.1 can be generalized as follows:

A set of n independent alternatives can be regrouped into a set of 2^n mutually exclusive alternatives, including the do-nothing alternative.

In Example 13.1, three independent alternatives produced 8 MEAs. Four would have produced 16 (2^4), and 5 would have produced 32 (2^5). As the number of alternatives increases, the set of MEAs often becomes large enough to make the selection of a "good" or "heuristic" (rule-of-thumb) solution more practical or realistic than the selection of an "optimum" solution, unless a computer is brought into the selection process.

We mentioned the present worth in Example 13.1 as the figure of merit for comparing independent alternatives. This is usually the case. For reasons stated in Chapter 12, it should not be the annual worth, although it could be the future worth. The IRR or BCR, or both, will also be of interest to many investors. If so, these are also computed, but incremental analyses are not made. For independent alternatives, such analyses are meaningless.

13.4 STRUCTURING INDEPENDENT SETS OF MEAs

The situation we usually find ourselves in when we are structuring independent alternatives is a little more complicated than we have described. We mentioned in Chapter 12 that budget requests submitted for review and approval must show the ranking of the competing alternatives. Example 13.2 illustrates how a set of MEAs is structured from independent sets of MEAs submitted by several departments.

Example 13.2   Independent Sets of MEAs   Toward the end of the current fiscal year, the following requests for capital expenditures from departments A, B, C, and D are sent to headquarters for review and approval. The proposals from each department are not dependent on those of any other department.

Department A	$\{A_1, A_2, A_3\}$
Department B	$\{B_1, B_2\}$
Department C	$\{C_1, C_2, C_3, C_4\}$
Department D	$\{D_1\}$

Department A submitted one budget request, consisting of a set of MEAs with three members that are technologically exclusive. Each of the other departments also submitted one set of MEAs that are technologically exclusive, consisting of 2, 4, and 1 members, respectively.

COMMENT: You will recall that braces { } are often used to enclose and define the members of a set.

Since there are four departments, each of which is submitting one set of MEAs (competing alternatives), your first impulse may be to say that there are 2^4 or 16 members in the set for selecting the best combination of projects within the limits of available funding. This is an understatement. The correct number is 120, as derived from the following equation:

$$n = \prod_{j=1}^{s} (m_j + 1) = (m_1 + 1)(m_2 + 1) \ldots (m_s + 1) \qquad (13.1)$$

s is the number of sets of MEAs, in this case 4, and m is the number of technologically exclusive members in each set. This gives

$$n = (3 + 1)(2 + 1)(4 + 1)(1 + 1) = 120$$

120 is, of course, still a formidable number of members but far less than what it would be, namely 2^{10} or 2048, if we had ten independent alternatives rather than four independent sets containing a total of ten alternatives.

If department A had presented two sets of MEAs, say $\{A_1, A_2\}$ for one and $\{A_3, A_4\}$ for the other, the number of members would have been 270, as you should verify using equation (13.1). Lastly, if department A had submitted one set of MEAs with two members—A_1 and A_2—and, in addition, two independent alternatives—A_3 and A_4—the number of members would have been 360.

COMMENT: You can test your algebra again by deriving the previous equation. In lieu of this, you can try it out on two departments, say A and B, each of which submits a set of MEAs with two members. The total number of MEAs by equation (13.1) is nine. That this is so is easy to see by lining up the following possibilities:

$$A_1 \qquad A_1, B_1$$
$$A_2 \qquad A_1, B_2$$
$$B_1 \qquad A_2, B_1$$
$$B_2 \qquad A_2, B_2$$

This gives eight. The null alternative makes nine.

You may have noticed that equation (13.1) reduces to 2^s if all of the members are independent.

How do managements handle such sets as those in Example 13.2? The answer is, with the help of a computer or manually. With a computer, an integer program is usually used (see Appendix 13A). If a solution is sought manually, which it often is, shortcuts are used. These may not produce the optimum answer but will at least produce a good or reasonable one. Such shortcuts are discussed later.

13.5 CAPITAL BUDGETING REVISITED

Before we proceed, we need to complete our discussion on preparing a capital expenditures budget. In section 13.2, we divided budget requests into two categories: the necessary or must-do and the optional or would-like-to-do.

Management's first task is to determine how much capital funding is needed for the must-do requests. Only then will management know how much is available for the would-like-to-do requests.

Consider the following example, in which all of the budget requests are must-do. Management has no choice but to select an option containing one member from each set.

Example 13.3   Must-do Budget Requests   Assume that departments A, B, and C each submitted one set of MEAs for necessary replacements or enhancements, or both, as shown:

$$\text{Department A} \qquad \{A_1, A_2, A_3\}$$
$$\text{Department B} \qquad \{B_1, B_2\}$$
$$\text{Department C} \qquad \{C_1, C_2\}$$

Equation (13.1) gives us 36 members ($4 \times 3 \times 3$), but we can only use those that have one member from each department. This gives just 12—as you can easily verify—from which the best selection considering both first cost and present worth is made.

Once management knows how much funding is needed for the must-do-or-else requests, a similar analysis has to be made for those that are optional, that is, those that will pay their way or more than pay their way but do not have to be done. Consider Example 13.4.

Example 13.4   Good Versus Optimum Selections   You are the financial officer of your firm. The budget for the projects that have to be implemented has been finalized. You now know how much funding remains for those projects that could wait or perhaps need never be done at all. It is $2,800,000. Budget requests for eight such projects have been submitted. They are shown in the following tabulation. All dollar amounts are in thousands.

Department	Project	NPW	First Cost
A	A_1	$600	$600
	A_2	640	800
B	B_1	300	300
	B_2	320	400
C	C_1	1,200	1,200
	C_2	1,280	1,600
D	D_1	700	700
	D_2	740	900

Each of the four departments has presented two requests, for which the net present worths have been calculated using MARRs specified by your financial division.

Assume first that the two requests from each department are independent, that is, that A_1 and A_2 are not competitive projects (i.e., are not technologically exclusive) and that the same applies to B_1 and B_2, C_1 and C_2, and D_1 and D_2. If there were no financial constraints, you would approve all eight requests. However, if there are such constraints, you structure the eight independent alternatives into a set of MEAs, as we did in Example 13.1. This set will contain 2^8 (256) members, as we found in Chapter 12. Your chore is to locate that member or those members of the set that produce the highest net present worth for the available funding. However, it would be a little tiresome for you (and us) to go through 256 alternatives, even though most of them could be culled quickly either because they did not begin to use up the available funding or because they exceeded it. Fortunately, computer programs for solving such problems and giving us the viable options are available. The rather straightforward mathematics on which these programs are based is discussed in Appendix 13A. With the help of such a program, the answer we obtain for the optimum solution is the set $\{A_1,B_1,C_1,D_1\}$ for which the total NPW is $2,800,000 and the total first cost is $2,800,000.

Suppose now that the two requests for project approval from each department are not independent but mutually exclusive. You now have four projects to contend with—A, B, C, and D—for each of which two mutually exclusive alternatives have been presented in the budget requests. By equation (13.1), the number of members is 3^4 (81). This is still too large a number for you (and us) to work with, so again we refer you to Appendix 13A. The optimum solution is again the set

$\{A_1,B_1,C_1,D_1\}$ for which the total NPW is $2,800,000 and the total first cost is $2,800,000.

Assume next that your firm, like many firms, handles the selection procedure you now face, not with a sophisticated computer program, but heuristically, that is, using rules of thumb or shortcuts. One shortcut is to pick the better of the two mutually exclusive requests from each department and to structure a set of MEAs from these requests. The members with the highest present worths are A_2, B_2, C_2, and D_2. The set will then contain 2^4 (16) members, consisting of combinations of these four alternatives. The members of this set are compared in Table 13.1. The do-nothing alternative is not shown, although it is a viable option. As mentioned, the financial constraint is $2,800,000.

Member 11 with a first cost of $2,800,000 and a present worth of $2,240,000 looks like the best selection. This makes departments A, B, and C happy but leaves D with nothing.

The head of department D asks for permission to review your analysis. His findings differ from yours. They are based on another common "approximate method," in which the ratio of NPW over first cost is used to cull projects for the selection procedure. The ratios are given in the following tabulation. The dollar figures are in thousands.

Department	Project	NPW	First Cost	Ratio
(1)	(2)	(3)	(4)	(5) = (3)/(4)
A	A_1	$600	$600	1.00
	A_2	640	800	0.80
B	B_1	300	300	1.00
	B_2	320	400	0.80
C	C_1	1,200	1,200	1.00
	C_2	1,280	1,600	0.80
D	D_1	700	700	1.00
	D_2	740	900	0.82

The four alternatives with the highest ratio—A_1, B_1, C_1, and D_1—have a first cost equal to $2,800,000. Their total NPW is also $2,800,000, which is $560,000 higher than member 11 in Table 13.1. If funding were available to accommodate more requests, D_2 would be next in line, since its ratio of 0.82 is higher than those of A_2, B_2, and C_2.

The answers that we obtained for the preceding mixture of independent and mutually exclusive alternatives are compared below:

Integer program (Appendix 13A)	$\{A_1,B_1,C_1,D_1\}$
Approximate solution using highest NPW from each department	$\{A_2,B_2,C_2\}$
Approximate solution based on the ratio of NPW to first cost	$\{A_1,B_1,C_1,D_1\}$

The optimum solution is the integer program solution that examined all 81 combinations. The approximate method based on the ratio of NPW to first cost just happened, in this instance, to give us the same answer. Even if it had not done

TABLE 13.1 Analysis of Set of MEAs with 15 Members (all figures in thousands)

Member	Alternatives	NPW	First Cost	Comment
1	A_2	$640	$800	Feasible
2	B_2	320	400	Feasible
3	C_2	1,280	1,600	Feasible
4	D_2	740	900	Feasible
5	A_2, B_2	960	1,200	Feasible
6	A_2, C_2	1,920	2,400	Feasible
7	A_2, D_2	1,380	1,700	Feasible
8	B_2, C_2	1,600	2,000	Feasible
9	B_2, D_2	1,060	1,300	Feasible
10	C_2, D_2	2,020	2,500	Feasible
11	A_2, B_2, C_2	2,240	2,800	Feasible
12	A_2, B_2, D_2	1,700	2,100	Feasible
13	A_2, C_2, D_2	2,600	3,300	Infeasible
14	B_2, C_2, D_2	2,340	2,900	Infeasible
15	A_2, B_2, C_2, D_2	2,780	3,900	Infeasible

so, this does not necessarily make the two approximate methods "wrong." They are "good" methods in the sense that either method may more nearly distribute the available funding available in ways that better serve management's objectives than totally haphazard or off-the-cuff approaches.

> *COMMENT:* Frequently, the selected alternative does not quite use up the available funding. We then assume that the difference between what is available and what will be spent is invested at the MARR. Since the present worth of this difference is zero, it adds nothing to the present worth of the selection. The logic behind this assumption is similar to that for the do-nothing alternative.

Example 13.4 demonstrates why budget requests are not submitted that show only the best of the competing alternatives but show all those that are technologically acceptable. These should be ranked, not only by present worth, but also by first cost.

Each department or division usually submits more than one budget request. The best option could be one that includes projects from only one or two departments. In such situations, management may decide to spread the available funding among most of the departments and often among all departments to help sustain departmental morale.

Management must also consider the nonmonetary attributes that often play a dominant part in the selection process. Employee morale is an example of such an attribute.

13.6 SUMMARY

So, where are we? What have we learned about ranking when we are faced with a financial constraint?

1. In structuring sets of MEAs for financial constraint, neither cotermination nor incremental analysis plays a part in the selection process.
2. The funding available for capital expenditures is defined by the capital expenditures budget.
3. The budget is prepared by first classifying budget requests for capital expenditures into those that have to be done and those that can wait.
4. The budget requests that must be implemented are structured into a set of MEAs that are ranked not only for present worth but also for first cost.
5. The remaining budget requests are then analyzed, and the set of MEAs structured from these requests is also ranked for both present worth and first cost.
6. Preselection, that is, heuristic or rule-of-thumb solutions, may produce a good selection but not necessarily the optimum one.
7. Study groups may not be familiar with computer software for handling sets of MEAs containing numerous members. (This statement does not apply to organizations handling sophisticated aerospace, nuclear, defense, and similar projects, but it still applies to the capital budget procedure in use by many organizations.) Therefore, the sheer weight of numbers may make finding a good answer (satisficing) a more practical approach than finding the optimum answer (optimizing).
8. Top management may dictate spreading the available funds among all or at least several departments, even though this solution is not "optimum" or at least as "good" as it might otherwise be.
9. On the other hand, top management may accept solutions that focus on very few departments in an effort to restructure and downsize the organization.
10. Annual worths should not be used when comparing independent alternatives.
11. IRRs and BCRs can also be used to compare options but should not be used for ranking.

SUGGESTED READINGS

1. G. A. Fleischer, *Engineering Economy, Cost Allocation Theory* (Boston: PWS Publishers, 1984). Example 13.4 took its inspiration from the examples on the preselection error covered in pages 112–114 in Chapter 4 of this text.

2. Henry Malcolm Steiner, *Basic Engineering Economy*, rev. ed. (Glen Echo, MD: Books Associates, 1989). Integer programming, for which examples of the mathematics behind this procedure are given in Appendix 13A, is covered in Chapter 14, not only for independent alternatives and mixtures of independent alternatives and sets of MEAs, but also for interdependent alternatives. This chapter is well worth your time and effort if you would like to know more about computer programs for capital allocation problems.

PROBLEMS

Warm-up Problems

13-1   Why don't we have to coterminate for financial exclusivity? Why don't we have to use incremental analysis?

13-2   Master planning follows the sequence given in section 13.2; that is, it starts with the sales budget and ends with the balance sheet. Explain in your own words why it proceeds in this way. With what parts of the master plan is the selection process for capital projects involved? Where might present economy studies be applied?

13-3   Convince yourself that, with two independent alternatives, say A and B, the set of MEAs for financial exclusivity has four members; with three independent alternatives, say A, B, and C, the set of MEAs has eight members.

13-4   You are the head of a department that has just submitted a budget request to corporate headquarters. The request is for a new machine. The study on which the request is based shows the following results:

Alternative	NPW	First Cost
A	-500	$40,000
B	5,000	50,000
C	10,000	60,000
D	14,000	70,000

Which of these alternatives would appear in your budget request? Explain.

13-5   Four departments have submitted budget requests, as shown in the following table:

Department	Requests
A	W_1
B	X_1, X_2, X_3
C	Y_1
D	Z_1, Z_2

a) If the requests are all for independent alternatives, how many members does the set of MEAs have for financial exclusivity?

b) If the requests from each department are mutually exclusive, how many members are there?

c) If X_1 is independent but X_2 and X_3 are mutually exclusive, how many members are there?

13-6 Show that equation (13.1) reduces to 2^s if all of the options are independent.

Selection Based on the IRR

13-7 The following proposals are under consideration:

Proposal	First Cost (in thousands of dollars)	IRR, %
A	$400	21%
B	200	20
C	100	19
D	200	18
E	100	15
F	100	10

a) If the MARR is 18%, which proposals should be selected?

b) Which proposals should be selected if the MARR must be no less than 15% and the capital expenditure budget is $800,000?

13-8 The following proposals are being considered by a company that leases construction equipment to contractors:

Option	Description	Initial Cost, $	Incremental IRR, %	On Investment Over
A—Repair old trailer		$10,000	30%	0
B—Buy new trailer				
1—Model A		30,000	18	0
2—Model B		35,000	11	B_1
C—Buy new truck				
1—Model X		40,000	20	0
2—Model Y		45,000	15	C_1
D—Upgrade office				
1—Plan V		10,000	12	0
2—Plan W		15,000	10	D_1

a) $100,000 is available for investment. Which options should be chosen?

b) If the company could borrow additional funds for 10%, which alternatives should be selected?

13-9 You are considering the following investment proposals from Marketing (M), Engineering (E), and Production (P):

Proposal	Initial Cost	Annual Saving
M_1	$40,000	$6,500
M_2	80,000	15,400
E_1	80,000	21,500
E_2	160,000	35,000
P_1	80,000	22,000

Assume that all of the proposals are independent and that each has an expected life of seven years. Salvage values are zero. The MARR is 10%.

a) Calculate the internal rates of return.

b) If the capital expenditures budget is $240,000, which proposals should be accepted?

Selection Based on Equivalent Worth

13-10 The initial costs and net present worths of five proposals are given in the following tabulation. All dollar figures are in thousands. The MARR is 10%.

Proposals	Initial Cost	NPW
X_1	$40	$30
X_2	50	15
Y_1	42	-2
Y_2	44	2
Z	60	20

X_1 and X_2 are mutually exclusive. So are Y_1 and Y_2, but these two proposals are also contingent (dependent) on whether X_2 is accepted. Z is contingent on the acceptance of Y_1.

a) Identify the members of the set of MEAs.

b) Which member of this set is optimal?

c) If the budget constraint for capital expenditures is $100,000, which member of the set is optimal?

13-11 Go back to the proposals in Problem 13-9, for which the expected life is seven years and the salvage value is zero. The MARR is 10%. Assume that alternatives M_1 and M_2 are mutually exclusive, as are E_1 and E_2.

a) How many members are there in the set of MEAs?

b) Prepare a tabulation listing each member with its initial cost and net present worth.

c) Which member of the set is optimal?

d) If you had unlimited funds, which alternative would you select?

e) If your budget for investment was $240,000, which alternative would you choose?

f) Would your answer to (c), (d), and (e) be the same if you had used the ratio method (see Example 13.4 in the chapter) as your investment criterion?

13-12 The city of Smithtown can borrow money for 10%. The planning department has ten independent projects under review, for which the estimated first costs and the present worths of the net benefits are presented in the following table. The computations for present worth are based on an MARR of 10%.

Proposals	1	2	3	4	5	6	7	8	9	10
First cost, $1000s	75	50	60	80	90	40	70	90	40	35
PW of net benefits, $1000s	100	60	90	88	120	50	80	105	60	45

The city uses the ratio method as its investment criterion. Which proposals should be selected for a budget of $300,000? Would you get the same answer if the NPW were used as the investment criterion?

13-13 As the manufacturing manager of an aerospace machine shop, you have to choose the projects that will be approved for the next year. Your capital budget is $500,000. Budget requests for eight projects have been received, for which the initial costs, annual savings, and expected lives are tabulated as follows:

Projects	Initial Cost, $	Annual Savings, $	Life, Years
Tooling Department			
A—EDM machine	$100,000	$40,000	6
B—6-axis milling machine	120,000	30,000	8
Forging Department			
C—High-capacity forge press	200,000	50,000	7
D—Side-action forge press	130,000	50,000	6
E—Automatic slug-cut- ting saw	50,000	30,000	5
CNC Department			
F—Two 5-axis CNC ma- chines	200,000	45,000	6
G—Hardwiring of com- puter system	100,000	40,000	5
H—Off-machine setup tool	30,000	25,000	5

a) If all of the projects are independent, how many financially exclusive members are in the set of MEAs?

b) Assume that the two tooling department requests are technologically exclusive, because both machines essentially do the same job, that is, make forging dies. Additionally, the two forge press requests from the forging department are technologically exclusive, since it now appears that there is not enough room for both presses. How many financially exclusive members are now in the set of MEAs?

c) Assume further that the automatic slug-cutting saw is a must-do budget request. How does this change the answers to (a) and (b)?

13-14 Rank order the eight projects in Problem 13-13 based on their first cost. The MARR is 10%.

13-15 The owner of the machine shop does not have a computer integer program and does not intend to get one. She decides to reduce the number of financially exclusive members by picking the optimal option from those machines that are technologically exclusive, that is, from options A and B in the tooling department and from options C and D in the forging department. The automatic slug-cutting machine is not included, since it is a must-do alternative.

a) Is what the owner is doing correct? Justify your answer and explain why, if it is not correct, it is often done.

b) What is the optimal selection for A versus B and for C versus D?

c) What projects are left for a selection based on financial exclusivity, and how many members will there be in such a set?

13-16 Prepare a table that lists the members of the set of MEAs identified in Problem 13-15 (c). Show the first costs and NPWs, and then answer the following questions.

a) What is the optimal solution (the highest NPW), assuming no budget constraints?

b) If all investments earning 10% or better are acceptable and funds are unlimited, what is the optimal solution?

c) If all investments earning 10% or better are acceptable but funds are limited to $240,000 for should-do requests, what is the optimal solution?

13-17 Redo Problem 13-16, but use the ratio of NPW to first cost instead of NPW as the investment criterion.

Integer Program

13-18 Set up the equations for an integer program for Problem 13-16, using a financial constraint of $240,000 (see Appendix 13A). Solve the problem if a suitable commercial program is available to you, and compare your results with the answers to Problem 13-16.

13-19 Do the same, assuming all eight machine projects are technologically independent and with a financial constraint of $750,000.

APPENDIX 13A INTEGER PROGRAM FOR CAPITAL BUDGETING

13A.1 INTRODUCTION

In this appendix, we look at integer programming for situations in which (1) all alternatives are independent and (2) there is a mixture of independent and mutually exclusive alternatives. For dependent alternatives, you should see Suggested Readings.

13A.2 INDEPENDENT ALTERNATIVES

The objective of capital budgeting is to maximize a function Z for which

$$\text{Max } Z = \sum_{1}^{m} p_j x_j \qquad (13A.1)$$

In this expression, m is the number of projects, p_j is a profitability measure, such as the NPW for any project j, and x_j is a decision variable whose value is either 0 or 1, depending on whether project j is or is not in the combinations structured by the number of independent alternatives at hand.

The function Z is subject to a constraint. The total first cost of the projects cannot exceed the funding F; that is,

$$F \geq \sum_{1}^{m} c_j x_j \qquad (13.A2)$$

where c_j is the first cost of project j and x_j is again zero or 1.

For the eight projects in Example 13.4, assuming independence and a financial constraint F of $2,800,000,

$$\text{Max } Z = 600x_1 + 640x_2 + 300x_3 + 320x_4 + 1{,}200x_5$$
$$+ 1{,}280x_6 + 700x_7 + 740x_8$$
$$2{,}800 \geq 600x_1 + 800x_2 + 300x_3 + 400x_4 + 1{,}200x_5$$
$$+ 1{,}600x_6 + 700x_7 + 900x_8$$

For the first member of the set, the do-nothing alternative, all of the values of x are zero. For the second member, x_1 is 1 and all of the other x's are zero, and so on up to the last member, the do-it-all alternative, for which all of the values of x are 1.

The computer program will rank the 256 alternatives by first cost and by figure of merit and toss out the ones that are not feasible. For this particular problem, the optimum solution is the set $\{A_1, B_1, C_1, D_1\}$.

13A.3 INDEPENDENT AND MUTUALLY EXCLUSIVE ALTERNATIVES

If the mix of projects includes independent and mutually exclusive projects, the preceding equations take the following form:

$$\text{Max } Z = \sum_1^m \sum_1^n p_{ij} x_{ij} \tag{13A.3}$$

and

$$F \geq \sum_1^m \sum_1^n p_{ij} x_{ij} \tag{13A.4}$$

These equations are not quite as formidable as they look. The letter i identifies the project, that is, A, B, C, or D. A is project 1, B is project 2, and so on. The letter j identifies the mutually exclusive alternatives for each project. For any project i, for which there are j mutually exclusive alternatives, either none of the j alternatives is selected for the optimum solution or at the most 1.

The matrices for the four projects in Example 13.4 are given in the following table:

Project	Decision Variable		Net Present Worth		First Cost	
	Alt. 1	Alt. 2	Alt. 1	Alt. 2	Alt. 1	Alt. 2
A	x_{11}	x_{12}	$600	$640	$600	$800
B	x_{21}	x_{22}	300	320	300	400
C	x_{31}	x_{32}	1,200	1,280	1,200	1,600
D	x_{41}	x_{42}	700	740	700	900

The equations for Z, F, and x are as follows:

$$\text{Max} = 600x_{11} + 640x_{12} + 300x_{21} + 320x_{22} + 1200x_{31}$$
$$+ 1{,}280x_{32} + 700x_{41} + 740x_{44}$$

$$2,800 \geq 600x_{11} + 800x_{12} + 300x_{21} + 400x_{22} + 1,200x_{31}$$
$$+ 1,600x_{32} + 700x_{41} + 900x_{42}$$

$$x_{11} + x_{12} = 0 \text{ or } 1, \qquad x_{21} + x_{22} = 0 \text{ or } 1$$
$$x_{31} + x_{32} = 0 \text{ or } 1, \qquad x_{41} + x_{42} = 0 \text{ or } 1$$

The computer solution is the set $\{A_1, B_1, C_1, D_1\}$.

It is obviously not necessary for each project to have the same number of mutually exclusive alternatives. Thus, if there were three projects—the first with three MEAs, the second with two, and the third with only one—the decision variables would be

Project 1 $x_{11} + x_{12} + x_{13} = 0 \text{ or } 1$

Project 2 $x_{21} + x_{22} = 0 \text{ or } 1$

Project 3 $x_{31} = 0 \text{ or } 1$

____14

CAPITAL FUNDING AND THE MARR

14.1 INTRODUCTION

In Chapter 13, we introduced you to master planning and the role that capital expenditures play in master plans. Such expenditures must be funded, and the figures of merit with which they are justified must be based on the selection of a rate of return that is attractive and acceptable to investors. Both funding and the MARR are discussed in this chapter. The major topics covered are

- The sources of funding and funding plans
- The effect of leverage on the return to owner
- The selection of the MARR
- The weighted average cost of capital
- Leasing as a surrogate for borrowing

Under sources of capital, we discuss both ownership and creditor financing, and introduce the important topic of leverage, that is, how owners can improve their returns on proposed ventures by borrowing.

For capital project selection studies—preliminary, definitive, and all shades in between—an MARR has to be selected. So far this variable has been treated as a given. It is now time to discuss how investors go about choosing it. One element in its selection is the "weighted average cost of capital."

For leasing we cover both ordinary leases, which are treated as expenses, and capital leases, which are treated as capital expenditures. Developing cash flow patterns for the latter will introduce you to a new wrinkle in noncash expenses.

14.2 SOURCES OF FUNDING

The sources for funding are owners and creditors, including, for the latter, lessors. Funding by owners depends on the availability of cash from operations and on the willingness of owners to provide additional paid-in capital, if needed. Funding by creditors is in the form of notes and bonds.

The pro forma statement of cash flows (see Chapter 2 for a discussion of this statement) in the master budget for the year ahead covers estimates of the net cash flows from operations, from financing, and from investing. Financing, you will recall from Chapter 2, refers to owners adding to paid-in capital and to creditors accepting notes and bonds. Investing, on the other hand, refers to the capital expenditures budgeted for the coming year and to cash receipts from the disposal of assets.

Master budgets also include long-term plans that forecast cash flows to and from the sources just mentioned for at least an additional three to five years. Management decides, on the basis of this information, how much cash can currently and in the future be made available for capital expenditures.

There is usually no dearth of investors and creditors for attractive (and often not so attractive) investment opportunities. For major funding by corporations, the creditors are usually bondholders and the owners purchasers of shares of preferred and common stock. For sole proprietorships and partnerships, the major sources of external funding are bank loans (notes) and capital contributions by owners. Our emphasis in this chapter is on corporations.

14.3 LEVERAGE

We've said many times that it is customary to conduct preliminary economic studies for the selection of capital projects as if there will be no recourse to borrowing. This means that the funding needed to cover the first cost and the initial working capital will be supplied debt-free by owners. If the results from such studies look promising and if alternative sources of funding will be or might be needed, for reasons discussed further later on, such sources are then investigated in more definitive studies. These comments lead us to leverage.

Leverage is an important topic and one that has been much in the news in connection with the sale of so-called junk bonds. The best way to illustrate this phenomenon is with an example.

Example 14.1 Leverage You are in charge of deciding how best to finance a $1,000,000 investment by your firm. The investment is expected to produce an annual net cash flow of $165,000 after taxes for ten years. The salvage value is negligible. The MARR after taxes is 10%.

The cash flow pattern for the preliminary economic study, which was based entirely on owner financing, is shown in Figure 14.1A. All dollar figures are in thousands. The net present value is about $14,000, as shown in the following equation.

14.1A All-owner financing

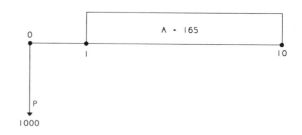

14.1B Loan cash flows

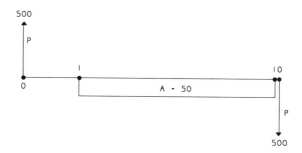

14.1C Part-creditor financing

Note: All cash flows are in thousands

Figure 14.1. Leverage.

$$NPV = -\$1,000 + \$165(P/A,10,10)$$
$$= -\$1,000 + \$165 \times 6.145$$
$$= +\$13.9 \text{ k}$$

The NPV is so close to zero that you know the estimated IRR is only a little better than 10%. (It is actually 10.3%, as you should confirm.)

You next look at funding one-half of the investment with a 10% loan. The cash flow diagram for the loan is shown in Figure 14.1B. The principal is repayable at the end of ten years. Interest payments are $50,000 per year for each of ten years.

Your firm's income tax rate is 40%. Therefore, the loan will only cost 6% rather than 10%, and the annual net cash outflow covering the interest payments less the tax savings is only $30,000. The cash flow pattern for this situation is given in Figure 14.1C for which A is $135,000, that is, $165,000 less the net cash outflow of $30,000 for interest payments.

> *COMMENT:* For a composite income tax rate of 40%, every $100 your firm pays out in interest reduces its tax bill by $40. The interest cost to your firm is therefore only $60. Bonds usually come in denominations of $1,000. A bondholder receiving 10% interest ($100 annually on each bond) costs your firm only 6% ($60 annually).

The cash flow at EOY 0 is your investment of $500,000. (If it is not clear to you why we show only $500,000 here, go back to Chapter 3 and read what we said there about Figure 3.10B.) The net cash flow each year for ten years is $135,000. At EOY 10, there is a principal repayment of $500,000.

The return on your investment of $500,000 is 18.8%, as you can confirm from the following equation:

$$\text{NPV} = 0 = -\$500 + \$135(P/A,i,10) - \$500(P/F,i,10)$$

> *COMMENT:* Before you accept this value, think back on Chapter 10, which deals with the external rate of return. The cash flow diagram of Figure 14.1C has two reversals in sign. However, Norstrom's rule (see Chapter 10) indicates there will be only one IRR.

You now know what leverage is. The term refers to debt-equity ratios. For all-owner financing in Example 14.1, the ratio was 0 (0/$1,000,000). For part-creditor financing, it was 1/1 ($500,000/$500,000). For all-creditor financing, it would be infinity.

The greater the debt-equity ratio that is associated with an investment, the greater is the return on the equity, provided the rate of borrowing after taxes (in Example 14.1, this was 6%) is less than the IRR on all-owner financing (this was slightly more than 10% in Example 14.1).

If leverage is such a boon to increasing the IRR on an investment, why not always use it? The difference between 10% and 19% should not dazzle you. The first was for an investment of $1,000,000, which brought in $165,000 annually for ten years, and the second was for an investment of $500,000, which brought in $135,000 for ten years but saddled you with a debt of $500,000 to be repaid at the end of ten years. The deciding factor on what to do is, or should be, the most judicious use of your company's resources. If an IRR of 10% is attractive, why burden yourself with a debt? If your cash resources are ample, where else could you go to earn 10% or more after taxes?

In Example 14.1, we used a very simple loan repayment scheme (Figure 14.1B) to permit us to work with a uniform series. This is only one of the repayment schemes shown in Figure 3.10 in Chapter 3. More complicated schemes would not have added anything to our illustration of leverage but will be applied in later chapters.

14.4 THE SELECTION OF THE MARR

There was a time when lenders needed to show little concern for inflation. Traditionally, they would lend money to prime debtors at rates of 3–4% before taxes. However, with anticipated rates of inflation of, say 5%, they require returns of 8–10% before taxes to give them both a real rate of return of 3–5% and a purchasing power adjustment of approximately 5%.

Investors, as contrasted with lenders, behave in the same way. If the purchasing power of money declines due to inflation, they must consider this for arriving at their MARR.

In Table 14.1, we list the components that go into the selection of a before-tax MARR. The final selection for a particular study is by the responsible party who reviews, accepts, and approves the results of the capital project selection process.

> *COMMENT:* The MARR is, with rare exceptions, expressed as an effective annual rate. For using it with cash flow patterns involving continuous, monthly, quarterly, or semiannual cash flows, the rate must be converted to an equivalent nominal rate for continuous cash flows and to an equivalent periodic rate for discrete cash flows.

The percentages in Table 14.1 are typical of current (1992) conditions. Comments on several of the components follow. Inflation has averaged about 5% during the past ten years. Will it continue at this rate or not? No one really knows. Therefore, cost studies with inflation of about 5% are probably as realistic as we can make them. Furthermore, if inflation does rise, it is reasonable to assume that both revenues and expenses will increase in about

TABLE 14.1 Components of the MARR

Item	Component	Typical Before-Tax Value
1	The traditional inflation-free rate for sound loans	3–5%
2	The expected rate of inflation	5%
3	The anticipated change in the rate of inflation, if any, over the life of the investment	Usually taken at 0%
4	The risk of defaulting on a loan	0–5%
5	The risk profile of a particular venture	0–50% and higher

the same proportion, although individual commodities and services may show wide deviations from the norm.

The risk of defaults on loans vary from debtor to debtor but are generally small. For particular cases, the risk can be evaluated from credit ratings of borrowers.

The sum of items 1–4 in Table 14.1 is the before-tax MARR expected by creditors. For the prime rate (the rate offered to financially sound, large corporate borrowers), returns are in the range of 8–10%, since the risk of default is low. When the risk of default is high, as in "junk-bond" situations, creditors require MARRs of 12–15% or higher.

Stockholders and other investors expect higher rates of return than do creditors. For creditors, there is always the risk of default, but this is usually slight compared to the risks of no-return faced by investors. In Example 14.5 on page 268, an established multibillion dollar firm for which a history of stock performance was available offers new common stockholders the expectation of a 15% return. In many instances, however, economic analyses are concerned with relatively small and risky new ventures for which no background of financial performance exists except the knowledge that many such ventures go bust. For these, entrepreneurs may have to rely on venture capitalists who expect (or hope for) returns as high as 50% before taxes from the few ventures that manage to survive. Thus, for owners of shares in new ventures, the MARR is the sum of items 1, 2, 3, and 5.

14.4.1 Private-sector MARRs

For the private sector, MARRs run the gamut from before-tax rates near prime at one extreme to after-tax rates of 50% for very high risk ventures at the other extreme. For the risk profiles common to most of the opportunities in the private sector, MARRs fall nearer the lower than the higher extreme. Most after-tax MARR selections by businesses are in the range of 12–15%. Such rates are usually associated with so-called normal risks. For higher risks, higher MARRs are used, and, for lower risks, such as in replacement studies, lower MARRs are used.

14.4.2 Public-sector MARRs

In recent years, interest rates for government borrowing have varied from 5–12%, depending on the level of government—that is, federal, state, or local—on tax exemption privileges, on the length of the loan, and on current economic conditions. There is a strong consensus that project selection studies for government projects should be based on returns that are at least equal to the cost of borrowing money.

The U.S. Office of Management and Budget established the following discount rate policy in 1972 (2).

The discount rates to be used for evaluations of programs and projects . . . are as follows:

a. A rate of 10 percent and, where relevant,
b. Any other rate prescribed by or pursuant to law, Executive Order, or other relevant Circulars

The prescribed discount rate of 10% represents an estimate of the average rate of return on private investment, before taxes, and after inflation.

This policy was still in effect as of 1992. It was based on the average return before rather than after taxes to balance the taxes that governments can lose when publicly funded projects displace privately funded projects. It has remained in effect since 1972, because, very wisely, it established a criterion based on a true or real rate, that is, a rate before losses in purchasing power due to inflation. If one had to pick a range that most nearly represented the rates that governments currently specify for cost-benefit studies, it would be 8–10% before taxes.

14.5 WEIGHTED AVERAGE COST OF CAPITAL (WACC)

Many firms in the private sector use the weighted average cost of capital (WACC) as a first approximation to an appropriate discount rate or MARR for selecting capital projects. A corporation sees the returns to its sources of capital—creditors and investors—as "costs" and the weighted cost of capital as the return that it must earn to cover these "costs." Example 14.2 illustrates how a weighted average cost of capital is computed.

Example 14.2 Weighted Average Cost of Capital You are the chief financial officer (CFO) of a very large corporation. Your CEO (chief executive officer) has asked you to raise $100 million from external sources in order to finance a major acquisition. You begin by computing your current average cost of capital. To do this, you need the current market value of your firm's debt and equity.

- Your firm has bonds outstanding with a face value of $400,000,000. They are selling at 101. The current market value of the debt is then $404,000,000 ($400,000,000 × 1.01).
- 1,000,000 shares of preferred stock are outstanding and are currently selling for $99 per share. Their market value is $99,000,000.
- 250,000,000 shares of common stock are outstanding and are currently selling at $21 per share. The market value of the common stock is $525,000,000 (250,000,000 × $21).

The total current market value of your firm's debt and equity and the proportionate share of each is then as follows:

	Market Value, $	Share, %
Debt	$404,000,000	39.3%
Preferred stock	99,000,000	9.6
Common stock	525,000,000	51.1
Total	$1,028,000,000	100.0%

Next, you must find out from your bank and your investment banker the interest rate that you would currently pay on borrowed funds and the rates of return that would attract preferred and common stockholders to firms of your size, reputation, and future prospects. Assume that your investment bankers tell you that these rates are 10%, 12%, and 15% respectively.

The weighted average cost of capital for your firm is now computed from the following formula:

$$i = r_b i_b (1 - t) + r_p i_p + r_c i_c \qquad (14.1)$$

where

$r_b, r_p, r_c =$ Ratio share of capital funding provided by borrowers, preferred stockholders, and common stockholders, respectively

$i_b, i_p, i_c =$ Rate of return expected by borrowers, preferred stockholders, and common stockholders, respectively

$t =$ Combined income tax rate for federal, state, and local (if any) income taxes

$i =$ Weighted average rate of return, also called weighted average cost of capital

The weighted average cost of capital in equation (14.1) is after tax. Interest is a deductible expense, and the true cost of interest to a borrower is therefore the rate of interest on debt instruments i_b multiplied by the difference between 1 and the tax rate, that is, $(1 - t)$.

For a corporation, the return on preferred stock i_p and that on common stock i_c are after tax. The return on preferred stock is the preferred stock dividend. The return on common stock includes (1) the common stock dividend and (2) the earnings retained in the business after dividends are distributed to preferred and common stockholders. In short, all that is left out of a corporation's NIAT (net income after taxes) after preferred stock dividends are paid accrues to the common stockholders.

The data given earlier for calculating your firm's current weighted average cost of capital are summarized in the following tabulation:

Source	Market Value, $ (in Millions)	Share, %	Rate, %
Debt	$404	39.3%	10%
Preferred stock	99	9.6	12
Common stock	525	51.1	15

For a combined income tax rate of 40%, the weighted cost of capital is then

$$i = r_b i_b (1 - t) + r_p i_p + r_c i_c$$
$$= (0.393 \times 0.10)(1 - 0.40) + (0.096 \times 0.12)$$
$$+ (0.511 \times 0.15)$$
$$= 0.113 \text{ or } 11.3\%$$

This concludes Example 14.2. You have computed the current weighted average cost of capital for your firm. It equals 11.3%. You apply this rate to the cash flow estimates for the proposed acquisition and find that the results are favorable. The present worth for 11.3% is positive, and the IRR is close to 18%. You now go back to your banking group to discuss funding.

14.6 FUNDING PLAN

You and your bankers could obviously make any number of suggestions on how the $100 million that your firm wants to borrow can be raised—all creditor financing or all common stock financing, or any number of combinations, including some preferred stock. The combinations could vary from low to high debt-equity ratios, that is, higher or lower than the current ratio of approximately 4/6 ($404,000,000/$624,000,000). The decision on the amount of creditor financing will depend very much on you, the CFO, since you are in a better position than anyone to judge the impact of additional debt on future cash flows. The experience of your bankers, on the other hand, will be helpful in deciding how additional issues of common stock will affect the current market for your firm's outstanding shares. After much discussion, it was decided to take a closer look at the following funding plan:

Source	Proportion, %	Funding, $ (in millions)	Estimated Rate, %
Bonds, 10%, 20-year	25	25	10
Preferred stock,			
12%, $100 par	5	5	12
Common stock, no par	70	70	15

In Examples 14.3, 14.4, and 14.5, for bonds, preferred stock, and common stock, respectively, we examine this plan more fully. Our objective is to demonstrate how rate-of-return and equivalence calculations are applied to the funding packages with which major capital projects are financed.

Example 14.3 Bonds In their initial analysis, your bankers suggest that 25% of the funding come from 10%, 20-year bonds. Further studies indicate that, under current and near-term market conditions, the bonds will have to be sold below par. The bankers' recommended offering price is 97½, that is, $975 for a $1,000 bond (bond prices are usually quoted in whole numbers and fractions rather than percentages, as any sensible human being would do). In addition, there is a flotation charge of 1.5%—the cost of floating the bonds, that is, getting them into the hands of the public. For each bond sold, your firm will therefore receive only $960 ($975 − $15). Although the nominal interest rate of the bonds is 10%, your firm obviously will be paying somewhat more. You or your bankers now will have to calculate how much more.

Bond interest is usually paid semiannually. The 10% quoted rate is a nominal rate. The periodic (semiannual) rate is 5%, and the effective annual rate is

$$i = (1 + r/M)^M - 1$$
$$= (1 + 0.10/2)^2 - 1$$
$$= 0.1025 \ (10.25\%)$$

The cash flow diagram for computing the true cost of the bonds is given in Figure 14.2. The return to your firm is $960, the semiannual interest payments are $50 ($1,000 × 0.05) per bond for 40 successive semi-annual payments, and the retirement payment at maturity is $1,000. The unknown is the IRR, which makes the present worth zero. The equation for solving for the IRR follows.

$$PW = 0 = \$960 - \$50(P/A,i,40) - \$1,000(P/F,i,40)$$

A trial-and-error solution or the use of a hand calculator gives 5.24%. The effective annual rate is then 10.8%, as you can easily verify. For a tax rate of 40%, your firm will incur a cost of 6.5% after taxes (10.8% × 0.6).

Example 14.4 Preferred Stock   In the preliminary plan, your bankers suggest that 5% of the funding come from 12%, $100 par preferred stock. Although preferred stock dividends, unlike bond interest, do not have to be paid, you have to assume that they will be. Flotation costs are estimated at 2.5% of the par value. Interest on preferred stock is usually paid quarterly, thus obligating your firm to a $3 dividend every quarter. There is no maturity date, on the assumption that your venture will be a going concern with, for all practical purposes, an infinite life span.

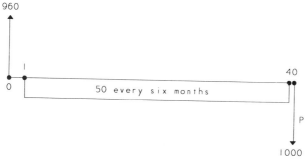

Figure 14.2. Cash flow diagram for bonds.

Your bankers estimate that the stock can be sold at $105 per share. The flotation costs will reduce your firm's take to $102.5 ($105.0 − $2.5).

The correct equivalent annual rate is calculated below with the help of Figure 14.3. The cash inflow is $102.50 per share. The cash outflow for each share is $3 per quarter, presumably forever. The cost of this portion of the capital is therefore

$$0 = 102.5 - 3/i$$

so that

$$i = 3/102.5 = 0.0293$$

The value of i is 2.93% per quarter, which yields a nominal annual rate of 11.7% and an effective annual rate of 12.3%.

Example 14.5   Common Stock   Your bankers have suggested that you fund 70% of your venture with common stock. Their estimate of the return expected by common stockholders is 15%. One of the methods they used in arriving at this rate was the CAPM (capital asset pricing model), in which the rate of return on common stocks, i_c, consists of two portions—a risk-free portion, i_{crf}, and a risk portion, i_{cr}. Then

$$i_c = i_{crf} + i_{cr} \tag{14.2}$$

For the risk-free portion, the yields on Treasury bills or bonds are often used. A stock has to do at least as well as these securities; otherwise, the venture should be dropped. Your bankers take 9% for this portion. For the risk portion, the following formula is applied:

$$i_{cr} = b(i_m - i_{crf}) \tag{14.3}$$

In equation (14.3), b is the estimated future beta value of the stock and i_m is the estimated market rate of return on a composite stock, as measured, for example, by the weighted average returns on the stocks included in a stock index, such as that in the *New York Times*. For a beta of 1.2 (we'll come back to beta in a moment) and market expectations of 14%, i_c is 15%, as shown in equation (14.4).

Figure 14.3. Cash flow diagram for preferred stock.

$$i_c = i_{crf} + b(i_m - i_{crf})$$
$$= 9.0 + 1.2(14.0 - 9.0) \tag{14.4}$$
$$= 15\%$$

COMMENT: Beta is a measure of the volatility of a given stock relative to the volatility of a stock index such as that of the *New York Times* or Value Line. A beta of 1.0 indicates that the stock is expected to be no more volatile than the stock index. If the stock index moves up or down 10%, so will the stock. For a beta of 2.0, if the stock index goes up or down 10%, the stock goes up or down 20%. Similarly, for a beta of 0.5, if the stock index goes up or down 10%, the stock will only go up or down 5%.

The preceding data, which are summarized in the following table are now used to compute the weighted average cost of capital.

Source	Proportion, %	Funding, $ (in millions)	Cost, %
Bonds, 10%, 20-year	25	25	10.8
Preferred stock, 12%, $100 par	5	5	12.3
Common stock, no par	70	70	15.0

Applying equation (14.1), we get

$$i = r_b i_b(1 - t) + r_p i_p + r_c i_c$$
$$= (0.25 \times 0.108)(1 - 0.4) + (0.05 \times 0.123)$$
$$+ (0.70 \times 0.150)$$
$$= 0.1274$$

You now know that the very least the proposed acquisition should earn is 12.7% and that there should be enough room in your estimates and forecasts to assume that this return can be obtained.

14.7 LEASING AS A SURROGATE FOR BORROWING

Leasing may be an attractive option to borrowing. When external or internal sources of funding are scarce, it may be the only option, whether it is attractive or not. In discussing leasing, we need to distinguish between ordinary leases and capital leases.

An *ordinary lease* is one for which the lease payments are treated as expenses. A *capital lease* is one in which the lease payments have to be converted to their equivalent present worth, which is then treated as a depreciable lump sum.

We consider two examples (Examples 14.6 and 14.7). Example 14.6 compares an outright purchase with an ordinary lease, and Example 14.7, an outright purchase with a capital lease.

Example 14.6   Ordinary Lease   You are asked to compare the purchase of a large mobile crane for $100,000 with leasing for a five-year period at $30,000 per year. The data you need for the analysis are as follows:

Purchase:	Price	$100,000
	Salvage value	$12,500
	Annual repair and property taxes	$5,000
	Service life, years	5
Lease:	Annual rental	$30,000

Under an ordinary lease, the lessor is the owner of the property, which reverts to his or her use at the termination of the lease. Leases come with a wide variety of conditions. In this particular lease, repairs and property taxes are paid by the lessor. Operating costs (operators, gasoline, lubricants, routine maintenance) are paid by the lessee but apply to both alternatives and therefore need not be considered, that is, are not relevant to the comparison of the two options. Cash flow diagrams for the two alternatives are given in Figure 14.4. Cash flow tabulations follow. Those for the purchase option are based on straight-line depreciation of the full purchase price of $100,000 over a five-year period. The tax rate for income and for gain on disposal of assets is 40%.

EOY (1)	Cash Flow Before Taxes (2)	Depreciation (3)	Taxable Income (4) = (2) − (3)	Tax Saving (5) = 0.4(4)	Cash Flow After Taxes (6) = (2) + (5)
			Purchase		
0	$ − 100,000	—	—	—	$ − 100,000
1–5	− 5,000	$20,000	$ − 25,000	$10,000	5,000
5	12,500	—	12,500[a]	− 5,000	7,500
			Lease		
0	$ − 30,000	—	—	—	$ − 30,000
1–4	$ − 30,000	—	$ − 30,000	$12,000	− 18,000
5	—	—	− 30,000	12,000	12,000

[a]Since the book value of the crane at EOY 5 is zero ($100,000 − 5 × $20,000), there is an estimated taxable gain of $12,500 from its disposal at the end of five years.

What rate of return makes the present value of the two options the same? The following tabulation for differential cash flow helps answer this question.

A   Purchase option

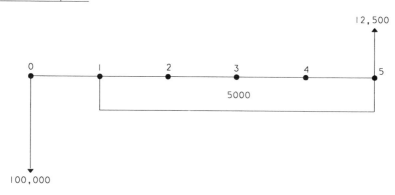

B   Lease option

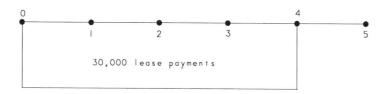

Note: Cash flows are before taxes.

Figure 14.4. Ordinary lease.

Differential Cash Flow

EOY	Purchase	Lease	Purchase Less Lease
0	$-100,000	$-30,000	$-70,000
1-4	5,000	-18,000	23,000
5	12,500	12,000	500

Setting the present value of the differential cash flows to zero gives

$$0 = -\$70,000 + \$23,000(P/A,i,4) + \$500(P/F,i,5)$$

You should have no trouble in showing that the value of i (the IRR) is just over 12%; that is, leasing is equivalent to borrowing $70,000 at a rate of 12%. For this situation, you may find leasing attractive or you may not. As mentioned, if a cash shortage looms, you may find it necessary to lease.

In Example 14.6, we treated the lease as an ordinary lease rather than as a capital lease. A lease qualifies as a capital lease if it meets any *one* of the following three criteria:

1. The title is transferred to the lessee at the end of the lease.
2. The term of the lease is at least 75% of its estimated useful life.
3. The present value of the lease payments is at least 90% of the market value of the leased property.

The second qualification indicates that we do have a capital lease. We will soon see that this also pertains to the third qualification. In short, we have to treat the lease as a capital lease, whether we want to or not. Example 14.7 shows you how to proceed.

Example 14.7 Capital Lease Your first step is to calculate the present value of the lease payments for some reasonable rate of return acceptable to the Internal Revenue Service (IRS), say 10%. "Reasonable" is the rate you might have paid if you had borrowed the money to purchase the equipment. For the lease payments in Example 14.6,

$$PV = \$30,000 + \$30,000(P/A,10,4)$$
$$= \$30,000 + \$30,000 \times 3.170$$
$$= \$30,000 + \$95,100 = \$125,100$$

Since this value represents more than 75% of the cost of the equipment, we have further proof that the IRS will require us to treat this lease as a capital lease.

For the next step, the present value of $125,100 is treated as a depreciable asset over the life of the lease. For straight-line depreciation, the annual depreciation expense over the five-year service life is $25,020 ($125,100/5). For a 40% tax rate, the annual saving in taxes due to depreciation expense is therefore $10,008 ($25,020 × 0.4).

The third step is to amortize the four future lease payments, of which the present value was $95,100. The computations are similar to those for borrowed funds, as shown:

Year (1)	Outstanding Balance at Beginning of Year (2)	Interest Expense (3) = 0.1(2)	Lease Payment (4)	Outstanding Balance at End of Year (5) = (2) + (3) − (4)
1	$95,100	$9,510	$30,000	$74,610
2	74,610	7,461	30,000	52,071
3	52,071	5,207	30,000	27,278
4	27,278	2,728	30,000	6[a]

[a]This is a rounding error, which we will neglect.

The interest expense in this instance is not a cash outflow, but it does impact on income taxes. Tax savings due to this expense are 40% of the figures in column 3. With these figures, you now have all of the numbers you need for the last step, that is, the cash flow table for the capital lease. The cash flow diagram is given in Figure 14.5.

The cash outflows are the lease payments. The cash inflows are the tax savings due to depreciation and interest expense. Depreciation is, as we know, not a cash outflow, and, in this instance, neither is interest expense.

EOY (1)	Lease Payment (2)	Tax Saving Due to Depreciation (3)	Tax Saving Due to Interest (4)	Net Cash Flow (5) = (2) + (3) + (4)
0	$ – 30,000	---	—	$ – 30,000
1	– 30,000	$10,008	$3,804	– 16,188
2	– 30,000	10,008	2,984	– 17,008
3	– 30,000	10,008	2,083	– 17,909
4	– 30,000	10,008	1,091	– 18,901
5	—	10,008	—	10,008

The differential cash flow between the outright purchase option and the capital lease option is

EOY	Purchase	Lease	Purchase Less Lease
0	$ – 100,000	$ – 30,000	$ – 70,000
1	5,000	– 16,188	21,188
2	5,000	– 17,008	22,008
3	5,000	– 17,909	22,909
4	5,000	– 18,901	23,901
5	12,500	10,008	2,492

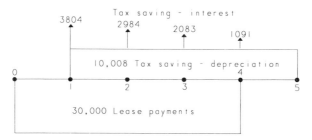

Figure 14.5. Capital lease.

We can see at a glance that the IRR of the differential cash flow pattern is about the same IRR—12%—as in Example 14.6. The correct value obtained with the aid of a hand calculator is 11.6%.

This concludes our discussion of leases. We went further than is usually done to show you another application of the time value of money and to give you another example of an expense that is not a cash flow.

14.8 SUMMARY

Funding for capital expenditures is provided by owners and creditors. Taking on debts requires scheduled cash outflows for interest and principal. Taking on new owners requires neither, since dividends do not have to be paid and stocks do not have to be repurchased.

Preliminary economic studies are usually based on all-owner financing and followed up if necessary by part-creditor/part-owner financing. Part-creditor financing produces leverage by which the rate of return on the owner financing is increased over what it would be if there were no creditor financing. However, the higher rate of return is on a smaller amount of equity capital and incurs a debt obligation.

The MARR selected by investors is an effective annual rate assembled from estimates of the "true" or "real" inflation-free rate, the rate of inflation, the risk of default for creditors, and the risk of a proposed venture performing as expected for both owners and creditors.

The weighted average cost of capital (WACC) ("capital" here refers to both long-term debt and equity) is a measure of what it currently could cost a corporation to attract investors and creditors. The WACC often serves as a surrogate for the MARR, that is, as the minimum value of the MARR for the funding required for a capital investment.

Leasing is an alternative to borrowing and is often a very attractive one. Leases are classified as ordinary or capital. Ordinary lease payments are treated as expenses. Capital leases are treated like depreciable assets and introduce an interest expense (so-called) which is not a cash flow.

REFERENCE

1. U. S. Office of Management and Budget, *Discount Rates to Be Used in Evaluating Time-Distributed Costs and Benefits*, Circular No. a-94 (rev.), March 27, 1972.

SUGGESTED READING

1. Charles T. Horngren and Walter T. Harrison, Jr., *Accounting*, 2nd ed. (Englewood Cliffs, NJ: Prentice-Hall, 1992). In Example 14.2, the bonds were sold at a discount,

that is, for less than their face value. Bonds are also sold at a premium, that is, for more than their face value. In both instances, the differences between the face value and the actual receipts are spread over the life of the bonds, using time-value-of-money calculations. Chapter 16 in this suggested reading has a good introduction on how bond discounts and premiums are handled.

PROBLEMS

Leverage

14-1 Compare your decision to borrow money on a house by obtaining a mortgage with a corporation's decision to raise external capital through a bond issue. How are these decisions similar? How are they different?

14-2 From a bank's viewpoint, how is your decision to secure a mortgage on your house the same as a corporation's decision to mortgage its property? How is it different?

14-3 In Example 14.1, the rate of return on the owner's investment was 10.3% with all-owner financing and 18.8% with 50% owner and 50% creditor financing, that is, with a debt-equity ratio of 1:1. Redo this problem with a debt-equity ratio of 3:2. Assume the same tax rate and loan conditions as in Example 14.1.

14-4 In Problem 14.3, is the rate of return on the owner's investment a before-tax or an after-tax return? Explain your answer.

14-5 The cash flow pattern for Problem 14.3 shows two sign changes. Did you check the possibility of obtaining more than one rate of return with Norstrom's criteria (see Chapter 10)? If not, you should do so now and comment on the result.

14-6 Redo Example 14.1 with a loan rate of 20% and all other conditions the same, including the tax rate of 40%. What conclusions can you make about the impact of the tax rate on the rate of return on the owner's investment? (*Hint*: Explain what happens to the IRR as the loan rate increases from a rate below that of the MARR to a rate above it.)

14-7 A regional commuter airline is considering the purchase of three new aircraft at $3 million each. This purchase is expected to increase the airline's annual net cash flow from operations by $2.4 million for the next 12 years. The salvage value of the planes at that time is taken as zero.

   The purchase can be financed internally, that is, by issuing stock, or externally, that is, by borrowing. For external financing, loans are available at 10% for a term of 10 years. The annual payments are one-tenth of the principal plus the interest on the outstanding prin-

14-24 The voters of your state approved a bond issue of $500 million at a rate of 8%. Interest was paid annually. The bonds bore serial numbers that were used to redeem the bonds so as to make the sum of the interest and principal payments the same each year for 15 years. Par value of bonds is $1,000.

a) What were the annual payments?

b) How many bonds were redeemed in the first year?

c) How many bonds were redeemed in the tenth year?

14-25 Example 14.5 on common stock introduced you to the beta value and to equation (14.4) for estimating the return that investors expect on this type of security. Go to the financial section of your newspaper for current values of i_{cf} and i_m, and compute the value of i_c for betas of 0.8, 1.0, and 1.2.

Ordinary Leases

14-26 In Example 14.6, take the annual rental fee as $35,000 instead of $30,000 and proceed as follows.

a) Calculate the NPWs of the purchase option and of the lease option.

b) Sketch a differential cash flow diagram, prepare a cash flow table, and calculate the IRR of the cash flow pattern.

c) What does the IRR represent?

14-27 The owner of an apartment building decides to establish laundry facilities on her premises. She has two options. The first is to buy four washers and four dryers for a total cost of $3,200, with an annual maintenance contract of $400. The second is to rent the eight machines for an annual fee of $480 plus an installation charge of $100 per machine. Compare the two options for an MARR of 20%, a useful life of five years, and no salvage value. Assume straight-line depreciation for the machines and a tax rate of 40%.

14-28 A highway department is considering buying or leasing a machine, for which the expected useful life is five years. The purchase price is $96,000. The salvage value at EOY 5 is $16,000. The lease payments at EOY 0, 1, 2, 3, and 4 are $34,000, $30,000, $26,000, $22,000, and $18,000, respectively. The net cash flow from operations at the end of each of the five years is $26,000. Should the department buy or lease if an MARR of 10% is used to compare options?

14-29 Highway departments are often faced with a choice between leasing and renting trucks, cranes, and other construction equipment. Consider the following two options. The first option is to lease a piece of equipment for an entire year at a cost of $15,000 per year, not including operating costs, which will run $400 for each day of use. The second

Stocks and Bonds

Note: Financial analysts apply the discounted cash flow methodology to the selection of investment opportunities in securities. The similarity between the methodologies for selecting capital projects, on the one hand, and securities, on the other, is obvious from the following examples.

14-16 Suppose in Example 14.3 that the bankers' recommended offering price was 102, that is, $1,020 for a $1,000 bond. Given that all other factors are the same, what would be the effective annual rate of the bonds?

14-17 A $1,000 face value bond matures in five years. It is currently selling for $950. Interest payments amount to $60 every six months. What is its yield to maturity; that is, what is the annual rate of return this investment would earn if it were bought now and held to maturity?

14-18 Treasury bonds and notes are quoted in 32nds of a percent. Thus, a quotation of 93.5 actually means 93 and 5/32%. If you bought a $10,000 Treasury bond with an 8% coupon (the annual nominal rate) which was quoted at 93.5, what would be the semiannual interest payment and how much would you pay for the bond?

14-19 Zero-coupon bonds are bonds for which the only return is due to appreciation. What would you pay for a zero-coupon bond with a par value of $1,000 (the par value is what you receive when the bond is redeemed at its maturity) that matures three years from now? (*Hint*: What is your opportunity forgone if you invest in such a bond?)

14-20 Axis Corporation is in trouble. It decides to issue bonds paying 16% for a term of 25 years. In spite of this attractive return, the bonds sell for 92.5. The flotation charge is 1%. Calculate the rate of return earned by an investor who holds the bonds until maturity. (*Hint*: Assume that Axis Corporation does not go bankrupt.)

14-21 You bought 1,000 shares of Trendy stock for $12 per share seven years ago. You have received dividends of $150 each quarter during these seven years. The stock is now selling for $19 per share. If you sold your holdings today, what would be your before-tax rate of return? Neglect flotation charges and brokerage fees.

14-22 What would be the return on the stock in Problem 14-21 if your tax rate were 30% both on the dividends you received and on the capital gain?

14-23 You bought an 8%, $1,000 bond for $1,020 ten years ago. Interest payments are semiannual. You sold the bond recently for a price that gave you a nominal return of 9%. What was the price? Neglect flotation charges and brokerage fees.

14-24 The voters of your state approved a bond issue of $500 million at a rate of 8%. Interest was paid annually. The bonds bore serial numbers that were used to redeem the bonds so as to make the sum of the interest and principal payments the same each year for 15 years.

a) What were the annual payments?

b) How many bonds were redeemed in the first year?

c) How many bonds were redeemed in the tenth year?

14-25 Example 14.5 on common stock introduced you to the beta value and to equation (14.4) for estimating the return that investors expect on this type of security. Go to the financial section of your newspaper for current values of i_{cfr} and i_m, and compute the value of i_c for betas of 0.8, 1.0, and 1.2.

Ordinary Leases

14-26 In Example 14.6, take the annual rental fee as $35,000 instead of $30,000 and proceed as follows.

a) Calculate the NPWs of the purchase option and of the lease option.

b) Sketch a differential cash flow diagram, prepare a cash flow table, and calculate the IRR of the cash flow pattern.

c) What does the IRR represent?

14-27 The owner of an apartment building decides to establish laundry facilities on her premises. She has two options. The first is to buy four washers and four dryers for a total cost of $3,200, with an annual maintenance contract of $400. The second is to rent the eight machines for an annual fee of $480 plus an installation charge of $100 per machine. Compare the two options for an MARR of 20%, a useful life of five years, and no salvage value. Assume straight-line depreciation for the machines and a tax rate of 40%.

14-28 A highway department is considering buying or leasing a machine, for which the expected useful life is five years. The purchase price is $96,000. The salvage value at EOY 5 is $16,000. The lease payments at EOY 0, 1, 2, 3, and 4 are $34,000, $30,000, $26,000, $22,000, and $18,000, respectively. The net cash flow from operations at the end of each of the five years is $26,000. Should the department buy or lease if an MARR of 10% is used to compare options?

14-29 Highway departments are often faced with a choice between leasing and renting trucks, cranes, and other construction equipment. Consider the following two options. The first option is to lease a piece of equipment for an entire year at a cost of $15,000 per year, not including operating costs, which will run $400 for each day of use. The second is to rent the equipment for $700 per day, which includes the operating costs.

a) For how many days of use will the cost of leasing equal that of renting?

b) Is this an example of a present economy study (see Chapter 3)?

Capital Leases

14-30 Your manufacturing firm has two options for acquiring an item of equipment. The first option is a capital lease that requires six annual payments of $10,000 each. The first payment is due at the beginning of the lease. The interest rate on the lease is 16%.

The second option is to buy the equipment for $36,000. Annual repair and property taxes are estimated at $2,000 per year. Depreciation expense is taken as $6,000 per year for six years and the salvage value at that time as zero.

The study is based on a combined income tax rate made up of a federal rate of 30% and a state rate of 6%.

a) What will this equipment cost your firm under the lease; that is, what is the present value of the lease payments?

b) What is the annual depreciation expense for amortizing the lease?

c) Compute the imputed interest payments that help to reduce the tax burden under a capital lease.

d) Prepare the cash flow tables, and compute the NPWs of the purchase and lease options.

e) Prepare the table for the differential cash flow of the purchase minus the lease option, and calculate the IRR.

f) What is your recommendation?

____15
RETIREMENTS AND REPLACEMENTS

15.1 INTRODUCTION

In Chapter 1, we described the capital stock of national economies. An accountant, using the nomenclature of Chapter 2, would call this accumulation of wealth, "a stock of fixed assets"—assets that are always in the process of wearing out and becoming technologically obsolete and uneconomical to operate. The business and nonbusiness entities that own this stock are therefore continuously evaluating whether and when to retire and/or replace their share. Probably 90% or more of all cost studies for capital investment decisions are concerned with such evaluations.

Much research has dealt, and is dealing, with physical testing, preventive maintenance, reliability, and quality control to help management reach decisions on physical limits and replacement times for plant and equipment. In addition, such techniques as technical limits analysis (TLA) and product life cycle analysis are used to forecast when a product or a process may become technologically obsolete (1).

These techniques are complemented by a well-established methodology within engineering economics that deals with replacements. This methodology is the major topic of this chapter.

15.2 CHARACTERISTICS OF REPLACEMENT STUDIES

Replacement studies are distinguished by six features, which apply to all members of this class of problems.

First, replacement problems are usually handled as least-cost problems, that is, problems in which decision makers are interested in minimizing costs. It is generally assumed that revenues are not affected by replacement decisions and that cost reductions therefore result in additions to net income. Because of the emphasis on cost, equivalent uniform annual costs (EUACs, or simply ACs) are almost always used as the figure of merit. With EUACs, we can avoid cotermination, although, as we found out in Chapter 7, we have to be careful to use a coterminated planning horizon to convert annual costs to present worths.

Second, these problems, and particularly those relating to equipment and machinery replacements, are usually concerned with short life cycles—ten years or less and often five years or less. Studies dealing with the replacement of manufacturing processes, however, may cover much longer periods and, since the rebuilding of entire facilities may be involved, are handled as major new investments rather than as simple replacements.

Third, retirements and replacements are a form of investment that usually involves little risk. Therefore, the minimum acceptable rate of return (MARR) used in cost studies is usually no higher, and often somewhat less, than that used in comparing relatively safe, risk-free investments.

Fourth, replacement studies are often carried out on a before-tax basis. However, software programs are now available with built-in depreciation options (to be covered in Chapter 16) and income tax rates with which one can go directly to after-tax analyses.

Fifth, the effects of inflation are seldom considered in replacement studies. There is no reason why they could not be, but their presence would, in most circumstances, not affect the conclusions reached.

Sixth, the irreducibles or nonmonetary factors are usually not significant. This is not to say that they are unimportant. Rather, most replacement decisions relating to existing products, processes, and equipment are relatively straightforward problems in which the economics dominate. However, cost engineers and analysts cannot be oblivious to new equipment and processes that could introduce environmental and health hazards that have not yet been fully evaluated and must therefore be treated as nonmonetary attributes.

15.3 TERMINOLOGY

Code Z94.5 of the American National Standards Institute (ANSI) has standardized much of the terminology used for replacement studies. The following definitions are based on this code:

Replacement policy. A set of decision rules for the replacement of facilities that wear out, deteriorate, become obsolete, or fail over a period of time. Replacement studies generally are concerned with comparing increased costs associated with aging equipment against the costs of alternative new (or used) equipment.

Defender. In replacement analysis, the defender is the existing asset that is being considered for retirement or for replacement by a challenger.

Challenger. This is the asset which is being considered as a replacement for the defender. (You will recall that we also used this terminology in Chapter 12 for ranking the members of a set of MEAs.)

Economic life (N^*). This is the period of time over which a prudent owner will retain an existing facility to minimize costs.

EUAC*. The equivalent uniform annual cost for an asset's economic life, N^*. All EUACs for keeping an asset in use for shorter or longer time periods are greater than the EUAC*.

Physical life. The period of time after which an asset can no longer be repaired or refurbished so that it can perform a useful function.

Service life. The period of time after which an asset cannot perform its intended function without a major overhaul. Such an overhaul is an investment for which a new economic life has to be determined.

Project life. The time period over which the cost study for a replacement is conducted. The service life or physical life sets the upper limit for this period, but shorter periods, for example, early disposal options, are also common.

Opportunity cost. The opportunity forgone by not selling an existing asset. In replacement studies, it is the sum that could currently be obtained by disposing of the defender. This sum becomes the current investment in the defender for comparison with the initial cost of a challenger.

Sunk cost. A cost that, since it occurred in the past, has no relevance with respect to estimates of future receipts or disbursements but unfortunately often crops up where it should not.

The two most common errors in retirement and replacement problems involve the proper use of sunk costs and opportunity costs.

Sunk costs are not relevant to an economic choice. If an existing piece of equipment on which a major overhaul was made two months ago is compared with a challenger that has just come on the market, the cost of the major overhaul is irrelevant. What was paid for a defender when it was purchased is also irrelevant. What it can be disposed for today or in the future is, however, relevant.

For after-tax studies, the rate at which a defender is being depreciated is relevant for determining depreciation expenses for tax purposes. Furthermore, current book values are also relevant to determine whether there would be a gain or loss on disposal. These topics were covered in Chapter 2 and will be examined again in Chapter 16.

Opportunity costs are often more easily visualized as opportunities forgone rather than costs. If you are comparing your current car with a new one and are preparing cash flow analyses for both, your car's current resale value is the cost of keeping it. It is the opportunity forgone in not selling it and using the proceeds otherwise.

15.4 COST ELEMENTS

The two major cost elements in replacement studies are (1) capital recovery costs and (2) operating and maintenance (O&M) costs.

15.4.1 Capital Recovery Costs

The annual costs of capital recovery (CR) were discussed in Chapter 8. There we found that the CR of an investment, P, with an expected salvage value, S, at EOY N is given by equation (8.4), derived in Chapter 8.

$$CR = P(A/P,i,N) - S(A/F,i,N)$$

In that chapter, we also derived an alternate formula for CR based on the following identity:

$$(A/F,i,N) = (A/P,i,N) - i$$

which gives us equation (8.5):

$$CR = (P - S)(A/P,i,N) + iS$$

Lastly, we pointed out that the advantage of using equation (8.5) is that we need look up only one rate-of-return factor. Its disadvantage is that, unlike equation (8.4), it does not properly represent the cash flows actually present in replacement studies. Both equations reduce to CR equal to $P(A/P,i,N)$ for S equals zero.

The annualized return on the salvage value of an asset usually declines with time, for two reasons: the resale value declines, and the return is spread over a longer period of time. There are, however, exceptions, of which the most common are artwork and land. For these, the disposal value can be much larger than the original purchase price, and the capital recovery cost can therefore be negative, indicating a capital return. Such cases are easily handled when they arise.

Example 15.1 illustrates the behavior of capital recovery costs as the period under study is extended.

15.1 Capital Recovery Costs The New York Cab Company is analyzing the costs of keeping its taxis for one, two, three, or four years. The set of MEAs in this problem, therefore, consists of four alternatives, that is, replacement every year, every two years, every three years, or every four years. These alternatives are mutually exclusive. They are also exhaustive, since the estimated service life of the taxis is four years.

The first step in the analysis is to estimate the annual capital recovery costs. Estimates of the salvage value at the end of each period are given in the following table. The MARR before taxes is 7%.

End of Year, j	Initial Cost, P	Salvage Value, S_j
0	$20,000	—
1	—	$14,000
2	—	10,000
3	—	5,000
4	—	0

The CRs of the initial cost, P, for periods covering one, two, three, and four years are shown in the following tabulation.

End of Year, j (1)	First Cost, P (2)	Factor, $(A/P,7,j)$ (3)	Annualized First Cost (4) (2) × (3)
0	$20,000	—	—
1	—	1.0700	$21,400
2	—	0.5531	11,062
3	—	0.3811	7,622
4	—	0.2952	5,904

The calculations for the annualized return from the salvage value follow a similar pattern.

End of Year, j (1)	Salvage Value, S_j (2)	Factor $(A/F,7,j)$ (3)	Annualized Return (4) (2) × (3)
1	$14,000	1.0000	$14,000
2	10,000	0.4831	4,831
3	5,000	0.3111	1,556
4	0	0.2252	0

The CR for each of the periods under review, as given by equation (8.4), is shown in the following tabulation.

Period, Years (1)	Annualized Cost of P (2)	Annualized Return From S (3)	Capital Recovery Cost, CR (4) (2) − (3)
1	$21,400	$14,000	$7,400
2	11,062	4,831	6,231
3	7,622	1,556	6,066
4	5,904	0	5,904

You, the manager of the New York Cab Company, must of course interpret these figures correctly. If you keep the cab one year and the estimated salvage value proves to be correct, the capital recovery cost of keeping the cab, including a return of 7% on the capital invested, is $7,400. If you keep the cab four years, the cost of keeping it is equivalent to an annual cost of $5,904 for each of four years. It is not the annual cost for the fourth year only.

As mentioned, the results of Example 15.1 are typical for facilities for which the resale value declines, as it usually does, the longer the facility is kept in service.

15.4.2 Operating and Maintenance Costs

Operating and maintenance (O&M) costs behave differently than capital recovery costs. They generally increase during the service life of a facility. Breakdowns and overhauls become more frequent and expensive. Fuel and utility consumption increases. The combined effect is a steady rise in O&M costs, although, for the first two or three years, they may show little change.

In calculating the EUAC of these costs, either discrete or continuous factors can be used. Continuous factors are generally more realistic, because most of the cash flow for operation and maintenance expenses is spread over one year.

The methodology used to calculate the EUAC of the O&M costs involves three steps:

1. The present value of the estimated O&M costs for each year are calculated by using continuous or discrete cash flow factors.
2. The cumulative present value of the O&M costs for each alternative is then obtained by adding the present values for each year.
3. These cumulative totals are converted into equivalent uniform discrete cash flow series, that is, EUACs, using an appropriate discrete (not continuous) A/P factor.

In formula form, the EUAC of a set of periodic O&M costs, assuming continuous cash flows, is given by

$$\text{EUAC} = (A/P,i,N) \sum_{j=1}^{N} A_j(P/\overline{F},i,j) \tag{15.1}$$

Note that, in this equation, A_j is the O&M cost for any year j and that the bar over F in the factor $(P/\overline{F},i,j)$ is the continuous cash flow factor that converts the A_j's to their present values.

Example 15.2 illustrates the methodology just described.

Example 15.2 Operating and Maintenance Costs The estimated O&M costs for the taxis in Example 15.1 and the calculations for the EUACs are presented in the following tabulation.

Year j	O&M Costs $/yr.	Present Worth Factor $(P/\bar{F},7,j)$	Net Present Value $/yr.	Cumulative NPV $	Uniform Series Factor $(A/P,7,j)$	EUAC $/yr.
(1)	(2)	(3)	(4) $(2) \times (3)$	(5)	(6)	(7) $(5) \times (6)$
1	$7,000	0.9669	$6,768	$6,768	1.0700	$7,242
2	9,000	0.9037	8,133	14,901	0.5531	8,242
3	14,000	0.8445	11,823	26,724	0.3811	10,184
4	19,000	0.7893	14,996	41,721	0.2952	12,316

Since O&M costs usually increase and capital recovery costs usually decrease with time, total costs may reach a minimum at some time during the service life under review. This time defines the economic life of the asset N^* as illustrated in Example 15.3.

Example 15.3 Economic Life The EUACs of the capital recovery costs and the O&M costs are combined in the following table.

Year	CR Costs	O&M Costs	Total EUAC
(1)	(2)	(3)	(4) = (2) + (3)
1	$7,400	$7,242	$14,642
2	6,231	8,242	14,473
3	6,066	10,184	16,250
4	5,904	12,316	18,220

The economic life, N^*, of the taxis is therefore two years, since this is the alternative for which the EUAC* is a minimum.

The EUACs for capital recovery costs, O&M costs, and total costs for Examples 15.1, 15.2, and 15.3 are plotted in Figure 15.1. This figure is not typical. Many replacement studies show total costs as rather flat curves throughout much of their range. For such curves, the EUACs on either side of the minimum do not differ substantially from the minimum. The economic life is therefore often looked upon as a range covering the time span from the year before to the year after the minimum.

If present worths rather than annual worths are called for, this is best done by first computing EUACs and then converting these to their present worths with appropriate P/A values. The procedure is shown in Example 15.4.

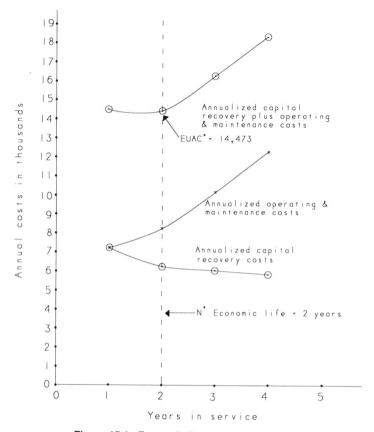

Figure 15.1. Economic life and minimum EUACs.

Example 15.4   Present Worths in Replacement Studies   Consider the set of EUACs for the taxis in Example 15.3. For convenience, these are posted below.

Alternative	Description	EUAC
1	Replacement every year	$14,642
2	Replacement every two years	14,473
3	Replacement every three years	16,250
4	Replacement every four years	18,220

You already know from Chapter 7 that it is not proper to compare the present worths of a set of MEAs without coterminating them. This means extending the study period to 12 years—the lowest common multiple of 1, 2, 3, and 4—which gives 12 replications for alternative 1, 6 for alternative 2, 4 for alternative 3, and 3 for alternative 4.

You also know that the EUAC for one cycle is the same as the EUAC for any number of cycles. (This topic was dealt with extensively in Chapter 7.)

The EUACs are easily converted to present worths or capitalized costs (the present worth for infinite life). For present worths, we multiply by the P/A factor for 12 years, which is 7.943 for 7%. The results follow.

Alternative	Description	Present Worth
1	Replacement every year	$ – 116,300
2	Replacement every two years	– 115,000
3	Replacement every three years	– 129,100
4	Replacement every four years	– 144,700

If we were dealing with a set of MEAs covering replacements for years 1 through 7, the lowest common multiple (LCM) would be 210. For that number of years, the difference between the present worth and the capitalized cost, which we get by simply dividing by i, is immaterial.

15.5   TYPES OF REPLACEMENT PROBLEMS

Retirement and replacement problems are commonly grouped into four types.

Type 1—Problems in which the defender will not be replaced but will be retired unless it can continue to pay its way.

Type 2—Problems in which the defender is compared with a current challenger that is identical, or nearly so, to the defender.

Type 3—Problems in which the defender is compared with a current nonidentical challenger.

Type 4—Problems in which the defender is compared not only with a challenger currently available, whether identical or nonidentical, but also with challengers that will most likely be available in the not-too-distant future.

15.6   RETIREMENT—TYPE 1

This type of problem is similar to many of those in Part I of this text. The figure of merit usually used is the present worth (PW). The net cash flows over the remaining life are discounted by the MARR and then are compared to the opportunity cost of not selling the asset today. If the resulting PW is less than zero, the asset should be retired. If the PW is greater than zero, it should be kept for at least one more year. Example 15.5 illustrates this procedure.

Example 15.5   Simple Retirement   Your company has been operating an old but still serviceable box machine for a number of years. The machine produces special boxes for a small number of clients whose requirements go beyond the standard product lines now manufactured in a modern processing facility.

The remaining life of the machine is conservatively estimated at four years. The selected MARR before taxes is 15%. If the machine were sold now, the company would net $20,000, which just happens to be its book value.

Based on forecasts from the few customers for whom the boxes are still being produced and on estimates of manufacturing costs, the net cash flows for the next four years are forecasted as follows:

Year	Net Cash Flow
1	$15,000
2	10,000
3	10,000
4	5,000

You should have no trouble showing that the present value of these cash flows is $30,039. The opportunity cost of keeping the machine is $20,000, since this is what you give up by not selling it. The net present value of $10,039 ($30,039 − $20,000) favors keeping it for at least one more year.

Suppose now that the current disposal value and therefore the opportunity forgone is $40,000 rather than $20,000. If it were sold for $40,000 although its book value is only $20,000, there would be a tax on the gain of $20,000. For a 40% tax rate, the tax would be $8,000, which makes the opportunity cost $32,000 rather than $40,000. The NPV would then be $−1,961. Should the box machine be sold? The economics say yes, but the sales manager may say no. He has too many customers who not only buy the special boxes but are also major buyers of the current product lines.

15.7 REPLACEMENT WITH AN IDENTICAL CHALLENGER— TYPE 2

Retirement of machines, equipment, and other assets often leads to their replacement with identical (or nearly so) assets. This is true if the technology and/or cost of the replacement has not changed appreciably over time or if the changes are relatively insignificant and cost and efficiency parameters are not greatly affected. The taxi problem discussed in Examples 15.1, 15.2, and 15.3 is typical of such replacement studies.

A more general approach to this type of replacement problem follows. Consider an asset that has been in service for N_0 years. Its estimated remaining service life is N_r years, indicating a total service life of $N_0 + N_r$ years. The economic life of the defender is N^* years, and, since the challenger is identical to the defender, N^* is also the economic life of the challenger. Therefore,

If $N_0 < N^*$, keep the defender

If $N_0 = N^*$, replace the defender

If $N_0 > N^*$, replace the defender

Example 15.6 illustrates these relationships.

Example 15.6   Replacement with an Identical Challenger   The taxis in Examples 15.1, 15.2, and 15.3 have been in service one year (N_0) and are estimated to have a remaining service life before abandonment of three years (N_r). Their economic life was computed as two years (N^*). Since N_0 is less than N^*, the taxis should be kept another year. If their service life was two years or more, they should be replaced.

15.8   REPLACEMENT WITH NONIDENTICAL CHALLENGERS— TYPE 3

Challengers with first costs, O&M costs, and service lives differing from those of the defender may present an opportunity for cost savings that need to be reviewed. The economic life of a nonidentical challenger may be, and usually is, different from that of the defender. The methodology for such cost studies is outlined in four steps:

Step 1:   Identify the set of MEAs. These depend on the remaining service life of the defender. If the defender is estimated to have N more years of service, the set of MEAs consists of N alternatives, of which the first is replacement in one year, the second is replacement in two years, and so on up to the last alternative, which assumes the defender will be kept in service N more years.

Step 2:   Calculate the EUACs of the defender for each of the N alternatives. For this step, we follow the procedure illustrated in Examples 15.1, 15.2, and 15.3. Our objective is a set of EUACs that we can compare directly with the EUAC* of the challenger at its economic life.

Step 3:   Calculate the EUAC* for the challenger's economic life, N^*. Here, we also proceed as we did in Examples 15.1, 15.2, and 15.3.

Step 4:   Compare the challenger's EUAC* with the EUACs for operating the defender $1, 2 \ldots N - 1$, and N years.

The comparison mentioned in step 4 and the decision rules attached to it are explored further below. Three cases are possible:

Case 1:   Replace the defender when, as its EUACs rise, they become larger than the EUAC* of the challenger.

Case 2:   If none of the defender's EUACs fall below the EUAC* of the challenger, the defender should be replaced immediately.

Case 3:   If all of the defender's EUACs are less than the EUAC* of the challenger, the defender should be kept.

All three cases are illustrated in Figure 15.2. The EUAC* of the challenger for Case 1 is the solid horizontal line identified as such. The solid curve of the set of EUACs of the defender decreases as the length of the operating

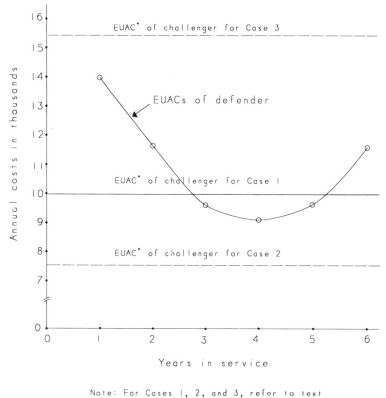

Figure 15.2. Replacement with nonidentical challenger.

period increases and finally falls below the minimum EUAC of the challenger. In Figure 15.2, this occurs between years 2 and 3. The curve then passes through a minimum and rises to cross the EUAC* of the challenger again between years 5 and 6. The defender should therefore be replaced at the end of year 6 or shortly after this second crossing, when the EUAC is on the rise.

Cases 2 and 3 are easily visualized with the help of the horizontal dashes in Figure 15.2. For Case 2, the dashes representing the EUAC* of the challenger are below the EUAC curve of the defender. The defender should obviously be replaced as soon as possible. For Case 3, the horizontal dashes representing the EUAC* of the challenger are entirely above the EUAC curve of the defender. The defender should therefore be kept at least until a more suitable challenger is found or until it must be replaced. Example 15.7 follows.

Example 15.7   Replacement with Nonidentical Challenger   Suppose that a defender with an estimated remaining service life of six years is being examined for replacement. The estimated EUACs for each of the six operating periods have been computed and are tabulated as follows:

Length of Operating Period, yrs.	EUAC
1	$14,000
2	11,500
3	9,600
4	9,000
5	9,600
6	11,500

Its service life is longer, or at least as long as the remaining service life of the defender. The EUAC* of the nonidentical challenger is $9,500. By comparing the sum of $9500 with the above tabulation, we see that the defender should be kept four more years. During each of the four years, the EUAC is $9,000, and, assuming no other challenger is found, the defender should then be replaced by the challenger for which the EUAC is $9,500.

> *COMMENT:* Actually, you should interpret the previous finding as follows. The defender should be kept at least one more year, at which time the estimates on which the study was based should be reexamined.

15.9   GENERALIZED REPLACEMENT MODELS—TYPE 4

The replacement problems that we have looked at so far are based on the assumption that future challengers differ in no substantial way from current challengers. However, in a competitive society, future challengers are often superior in first cost, or operating and maintenance expenses, or service life, or any combination of these features to challengers that are currently available. This leads to the following scenario:

> Cost studies indicate that the defender should be replaced now by an identical or nonidentical challenger. However, an improved challenger will most likely be available a year from now, and, based on past experience, additional improvements can probably be expected for several years thereafter. Under these circumstances, should we continue with the defender for another year and review the market again at that time?

This problem is a very real one for all of us who have held up buying a new car or appliance because we heard something better would soon be available. Many equipment and machinery items show small but steady improvements from year to year. Others—computers are an excellent example—show substantial gains in capacity and reliability, accompanied by cost reductions. Example 15.8 shows how such a replacement scenario can be handled to decide whether any action should be taken now.

Example 15.8 Future Challengers   Assume that an existing challenger has an economic life of six years and an EUAC* of $5,000. The defender has been in service several years. Its remaining useful life is estimated at three years. Computations on the EUACs for retaining one, two, or three more years gave the following results.

Retainage Period, yrs.	EUAC
1	$6,000
2	7,000
3	8,000

Since the EUAC* of the current challenger is only $5,000, the figures in the table indicate that the defender should be replaced now. However, experience with equipment of this type and hearsay from the marketplace indicate that the challenger available next year will most likely have the same economic life but that its EUAC* will be $250 less. Similar improvements can be expected in the second and third years, at which time the defender will have to be replaced. There are thus four members of the set of MEAs.

1. Replace the defender with the current challenger now.
2. Keep the defender one more year and replace it with the challenger, which is expected to be available at that time.
3. Keep the defender two more years and then replace it.
4. Keep the defender three more years, at which time it must be replaced with the then current challenger.

You should now go to Figure 15.3, in which D is the defender, C_0 is the current challenger, and C_1, C_2, and C_3 are the challengers expected to be available one,

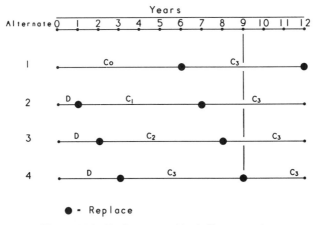

Figure 15.3. Replacement with challengers-to-be.

two, and three years from now. We assume no further price reductions after C_3. The planning horizon is nine years since beyond that time, by our assumptions, there are no relevant differences among the four alternatives.

For alternative 1, the defender, D, is replaced immediately with C_0, the current challenger.

$$EUAC_1 = [\$5,000(P/A,10,6) + \$4,250(P/A,10.3)(P/F,10,6)](A/P,10,9)$$

$$= \$4,816$$

For alternative 2, the defender is replaced at EOY 1 with C_1 and at EOY 7 with C_3 which, by our assumptions, is the challenger at that time.

$$EUAC_2 = [\$6,000(P/A,10,1) + \$4,750(P/A,10,6)(P/F,10,1)$$

$$+ \$4,250(P/A,10,2)(P/F,10,7)](A/P,10,9)$$

$$= \$4,878$$

You should have no trouble in proving that the EUACs for alternative 3 and 4 are $5,234 and $6,667 respectively. This indicates that the defender should be replaced either immediately or one year from now, since the EUACs for these two options are close.

> *COMMENT*: Dynamic programming is an optimization technique that has been used for the generalized replacement problem. We do not include a discussion of the technique in this text because we feel it is a little far-fetched to do so. In other words, we don't think it is practical to look ahead to more than two or, at the most, three replacements because of the uncertainty of what will be available in the future. However, dynamic programming is a fascinating technique that has many practical applications in fields related to our main topic—the capital project selection process. For this reason, we have provided several references for those of you who have no acquaintance with this technique but would like to know more about it (2,3,4).

15.9.1   MAPI Replacement Models

Anyone involved with replacement studies should be aware of the work done by the Machinery and Allied Products Institute (MAPI) under the direction of George Terborgh.*

To those of us who have been trained in engineering economy (which should now include you), the formula approach used by MAPI is too confining, unless the assumptions made therein happen to coincide with the study

---

*There are three versions of MAPI, all of which are published by the Machinery and Allied Products Institute, Washington, D.C. The first covers replacements only and was described in *Dynamic Equipment Policy* (1949) and in the *MAPI Replacement Manual* (1950). The second version appears in *Business Investment Policy* (1958), and the third version appears in *Business Investment Management* (1967).

at hand. However, like many formula approaches, it has an excellent checklist and is relatively easy to use. If, as mentioned earlier, you become seriously involved in replacement studies, you should become familiar with MAPI to see if it suits the type of problems with which you are dealing.

15.10 SUMMARY

Retirement and replacement problems are the largest single class of cost studies performed by business and nonbusiness entities. Generally, such problems are least-cost problems, and the decision criterion is to minimize EUACs.

> *COMMENT:* If revenues stay the same for a replacement problem— a logical assumption—minimizing costs maximizes profits. There is, therefore, no conceptual difference between these two objectives.

Four types of problems were identified. Of these, the simplest type is retirement without replacement. The proposed retirement has to continue paying its way or is scrapped unless "irreducible constraints" (such as the sales manager in our example) intervene.

The second type assumes that replacements are identical to the defender, which means that the challenger and the defender have the same economic life. The defender is considered for replacement when its economic life—the period during which its EUAC reaches a minimum—is exceeded.

The third type assumes a nonidentical challenger. The methodology used here is to compare the set of EUACs for the remaining service life of the defender with the EUAC* of the challenger. The defender should be considered for replacement when its annual costs are rising and exceed those of the challenger at the latter's economic life.

Lastly, more generalized replacement models were discussed, in which a defender is compared not only with a challenger currently available but also with challengers not yet on the market. The question posed by these problems is, "Shall we delay replacement because a better model will be along shortly?"

One concern you should keep in mind has been mentioned several times during the course of this chapter. The objective of replacement analysis is to decide whether a defender should be kept for one year or, at the most, two or three more years, or replaced now. The objective is not to finalize a replacement schedule for an indefinite number of years ahead.

REFERENCES

1. Merino, Donald N., *Developing Economic and Non-Economic Incentives to Select Among Technical Alternatives. The Engineering Economist* 34:4 (Summer 1989): 275–290.

2. S. E. Drayfus, *A Generalized Equipment Replacement Study. Journal of the Society of Industrial and Applied Mathematics* 8:3 (September 1960): 425–435. An early article with a numerical example that will introduce you to dynamic programming.

3. F. C. Jelen (ed.), *Project and Cost Engineers' Handbook*. (American Association of Cost Engineers, 1979), Chaps. 1 and 8. This and reference 4 are an excellent introduction to dynamic programming for those of you who have no background in this technique.

4. Frederic C. Jelen and James H. Black (eds.), *Cost and Optimization Engineering*, 2nd ed. (New York: McGraw-Hill, 1983), pp. 288–293. See reference 3.

PROBLEMS

In the following problems, assume discrete cash flows unless otherwise noted.

Opportunity Cost

15-1 Including an opportunity cost in retirement and replacement problems may at first be a little difficult to see, since this cost is not a visible cash outflow for the "keep" option. To help you understand why such costs are included in economy studies, consider the following exercise.

a) An asset can be sold now for P dollars. Draw the cash flow diagram, and label it alternative X.

b) The above asset can produce net cash flows of A dollars for the next N years. Draw the cash flow diagram, and label it alternative Y.

c) Prepare a differential cash flow table, and draw a differential cash flow diagram for alternative Y minus alternative X. Do you see the opportunity cost P and why it must be included, even if we decide to keep the asset?

15-2 Refer to Problem 15-1, and carry out steps a, b, and c using the following data. An asset can be sold for $22,500 now. The net cash flow for the next five years is tabulated below.

EOY	Net Cash Flow
1	$7,500
2	6,500
3	5,400
4	4,100
5	2,500

Based on a pretax MARR of 10%, should the asset be kept?

Note: In the problems that follow, there is no need to go through parts a, b, and c, as we did with Problems 15-1 and 15-2. You should go directly to the differential analysis, as we did in the body of the chapter, by treating the asset considered for retirement or replacement as an opportunity cost or an opportunity forgone.

15-3 A local newspaper is considering the retirement of an old typesetter. The machine can be sold to a smaller newspaper for $10,000. Its estimated useful life is three years. The projected net cash flows for the next three years are as follows:

EOY	Net Cash Flow
1	$7,000
2	5,000
3	3,500

a) Sketch the cash flow diagram, and calculate the annual worth for a pretax discount rate of 15%.

b) What should be done with the machine and why?

15-4 A company is considering the retirement of an existing machine. The following estimates apply.

EOY	Cash Flow In	Cash Flow Out	Salvage Value
0	0	0	$10,000
1	$8,000	$4,000	4,000
2	9,000	5,000	3,000
3	10,000	6,000	2,000
4	11,500	7,000	1,100
5	11,500	9,000	700
6	11,500	11,000	0

Should the machine be retired if the before-tax discount rate is 20%?

15-5 Superior Limousine Service is considering retiring one of its stretch limousines. The projected service life is four years, and the current market value (a firm offer is in hand) is $30,000. The estimated net cash flows for the next four years are as follows:

Year	Net Cash Flow
1	$9,000
2	8,500
3	8,000
4	7,500

a) Sketch the cash flow diagram for continuous cash flow, and compute its present worth for a pretax MARR of 15%.

b) Should the car be kept and, if so, why?

c) Could you have gotten the same answer by inspection? How?

15-6 The Farmer Jones Rental Company has a tractor with a projected service life of five years for which it has been offered $14,000. The estimated net cash flows from rentals for the next four years are as follows:

EOY	Net Cash Flow
1	$5,500
2	5,200
3	4,500
4	4,000

Set up the cash flow diagram, and find its annual worth for a pretax discount rate of 15%.

Replacement with an Identical Challenger

15-7 Nelson's Dairy Farm has purchased new cheese processing facilities for $250,000. The estimated annual operating costs and salvage values for the next five years are given below.

EOY	Operating Cost	Salvage Value
1	$148,000	$220,000
2	156,000	196,000
3	176,000	162,000
4	198,000	124,000
5	240,000	90,000

a) Identify the members of the set of MEAs.

b) For a pretax MARR of 10%, when should the replacement occur?

15-8 A photocopy machine with an initial cost of $15,000 has the following operating costs and salvage values.

EOY	Operating Cost	Salvage Value
1	$7,400	$12,200
2	7,800	9,800
3	8,800	8,100
4	9,900	6,200
5	12,000	4,500

When should the replacement occur for a before-tax discount rate of 10%?

15-9 Smitty's Trucking Company is considering the purchase of several large refrigerated trucks. Each truck will cost $105,000. The estimated service life is six years. Operating expenses are expected to start at $35,000 for the first year and increase by $5,000 annually. The salvage values in thousands of dollars are estimated as follows:

EOY	1	2	3	4	5	6
Salvage value	80	50	45	35	20	10

When should the replacement occur for an MARR of 15%?

15-10 A special water pump has an initial cost of $15,000 and first year O&M costs of $3,000. The O&M costs will increase by $600 annually for the expected four-year life. The current salvage value is $9,000 and will decrease by $2,000 annually. For a before-tax MARR of 10%, how long should the water pump be kept?

15-11 The city of Hoboken's Department of Public Works is considering replacing an old street cleaner. Compute the economic life of the new cleaner based on the data supplied. Assume an MARR of 10%, and treat the estimated disbursements as continuous cash flows.

EOY	Market Value	Disbursements
0	$70,000	0
1	56,000	$15,000
2	44,000	18,000
3	34,000	21,000
4	26,000	24,000

15-12 The Electro Company is considering the purchase of a test machine. The following data have been gathered for a cost evaluation:

The useful life is estimated as six years.

The purchase price is $90,000, not including installation costs of $10,000.

Operating expenses are estimated at $40,000 for the first year, with an increase of $8,000 each year for six years.

The residual (salvage) values are estimated as $60,000, $40,000, $30,000, $22,000, $16,000, and $12,000 at the end of years 1–6.

Determine the economic life based on a pretax MARR of 20%.

Replacement with a Nonidentical Challenger

15-13 Sunset Construction is considering the replacement of an item of construction equipment. Estimates of market value and operating costs are given below for both the defender and the challenger. The MARR is 20%.

	Defender		Challenger	
EOY	Market Value	Operating Costs	Market Value	Operating Costs
1989	$90,000	$30,000	—	—
1990	65,000	32,000	—	—
1991	50,000	34,000	—	—
1992	40,000	36,000	$80,000	$38,000
1993	32,000	38,000	68,000	38,000
1994	26,000	40,000	59,000	38,000
1995	22,000	42,000	59,000	38,000
1996	—	—	59,000	40,000
1997	—	—	55,000	40,000
1998	—	—	50,000	40,000

It is now the end of 1992. The planning horizon begins with the first day of 1993. The defender will probably last until the end of 1995, at which time the entire operation is expected to be phased out. Should the defender be replaced now? Justify your answer.

15-14 You have decided to replace an existing facility with a new facility costing $100,000 or a new facility costing $160,000. The quality of the production is the same for both facilities, and replacement studies show the same economic life and the same equivalent uniform annual cost for both alternatives. What additional information, if any, do you need to make a selection?

15-15 A semiautomatic system bought four years ago for $100,000 is expected to last another five years, at which time its salvage value is estimated to be zero. Its estimated annual operating and maintenance costs are $40,000. If sold today, it would bring no more than $8,000 because of state-of-the-art advances. A new system with more automatic features can be purchased for $200,000. Its useful life is estimated at ten years, its annual O&M costs at $5,000, and its salvage value at EOY 10 as zero. Assuming a pretax discount rate of 20%, what does the salvage value of the new system have to be at EOY 5 in order to justify replacing the old system?

15-16 A power plant bought a heat exchanger six or seven years ago for $50,000. The maintenance costs on this unit have shown a steady increase from year to year. They are expected to be $5,000 next year and increase $1,000 annually for four or five more years. The plant manager is considering a replacement, for which the EUAC is estimated at $4,000 for its economic life. She estimates that the cost of removing the old exchanger will be $10,000 over and above any possible recovery for scrap metal. The discounted pretax rate of return is 15%.

a) Should the replacement be made now?

b) When should it be made, assuming that all of the estimates hold?

15-17 You have bought and installed a new machine for inspecting electronic components for $100,000. Operating and maintenance costs are estimated at $5,000 annually throughout its expected eight-year life. Due to rapid advancements in the design of this equipment and the high cost of removing it, it is realistic to assume that the salvage value is zero from the time of purchase. What is the economic life of the machine based on these assumptions?

15-18 A diesel-generating station in a remote location needs more capacity. The choice is between replacing the existing diesel unit with a larger unit or supplementing its capacity with a smaller unit. An economic study is under way to help with this decision. The estimates on which the study is based follow.

The existing unit was purchased four years ago for $225,000. Operation and maintenance costs have averaged $42,500 annually and are expected to remain at this level for five years.

The existing unit has a trade-in value of $50,000 for the purchase of a new generator that has a market value of $325,000 and an estimated five-year life, at which time the unit will probably be abandoned. The estimated annual O&M costs are $40.000, and the estimated salvage value is $100,000 at the end of five years.

A smaller diesel unit to supplement the existing unit would cost $150,000 and have an expected salvage value of $25,000 at the end of five years. Its annual operating and maintenance costs are estimated at $27,500.

Should the current generator be replaced if the study is based on a before-tax MARR of 20%?

15-19 Consider the following situation faced by a company that has a choice of buying a new office building or refurbishing an old one. The new building would cost $120,000. This includes a plot of land in a very favorable location.

The old building could be sold for $15,000 or refurbished for $35,000. It would probably last no more than 10 years and have no salvage value at that time.

The annual operating and maintenance costs of the two buildings are estimated to be approximately the same.

Due to its favorable location, it is estimated that the new building could be sold for $200,000 at the end of 20 years. This estimated increase in value of $80,000 ($200,000 − $120,000) is not due to inflation but to realistic estimates based on growth forecasts for the area in which the building is located. The MARR is 10%.

a) What are the EUACs of the two alternatives?

b) What should the company do?

c) What assumptions did you make in order to solve this problem, and how did you handle cotermination?

15-20 You have just purchased a new car for $18,000. Its useful life is estimated at ten years. One week after you purchase it, a nuclear-powered unit—the Nuke—comes on the market. It sells for $30,000, has no operating costs except tire replacement, and will run perfectly for exactly ten years, at which time it must be abandoned due to excessive radioactive contamination. The disposal costs are included in the first cost of the unit. Its resale value decreases linearly by $3,000 per year. Assume an MARR of 10%.

The resale value of your car is now zero. Its O&M expenses for the first year are $2,700 and increase by $600 for each additional year. These costs do not include tire replacement.

a) Should you keep your car for at least one more year?

b) Should you keep it for ten years?

c) When should it be replaced?

Future Challengers

15-21 The useful life of a machine is expected to be three years, with EUACs estimated as follows:

Year	EUAC
1	$20,000
2	23,000
3	25,000

The machine could be replaced with a newer model that has an EUAC of $18,000 for an economic life of seven years. However, advances in technology are expected to lower the EUAC by $2,000 per year for the next three years. The MARR is 10%.

a) Identify the members of the set of MEAs.

b) Calculate the EUACs of each member.

c) What do you recommend and why?

15-22 Rob Guy currently owns an automobile with an expected useful life of three years. The MARR is 15%. The EUACs for these years are estimated as follows:

EOY	EUAC
1	$3,200
2	3,700
3	4,200

An economic study for a new model indicates an economic life of three years with an EUAC of $4,000. However, still newer models are expected to show a further reduction in the EUAC of $400 per year for each of the next two years. What should Rob do?

15-23 A hospital is currently operating with an old X-ray machine. Its useful life is estimated at four years. The EUACs over this period are expected to be as follows:

EOY	EUAC
1	$7,500
2	7,750
3	8,600
4	9,500

A challenger is now available, for which the economic life is nine years, with an EUAC of $6,500. Improvements over the next two years will reduce the annual costs by an estimated $500 per year for each of the next two years and by $200 per year for the two years after that. The current machine probably will have to be replaced in four years.

a) Define the members of the set of MEAs.

b) Compute the EUACs of the alternatives for a pretax MARR of 10%.

c) What do you recommend and why?

____16

DEPRECIATION AND AFTER-TAX ANALYSIS

16.1 INTRODUCTION

The figure of merit that investors look at most closely is not the before-tax IRR but the after-tax IRR. We've been through many examples on before-tax analysis. Why, you may ask, has it taken so long to get to after-tax analysis? There are several reasons.

1. After-tax analysis brings nothing new to the fundamentals on which engineering economy is based, that is, on the time value of money and the equivalence of cash flows at different points and periods of time.

2. For after-tax analysis, we need to introduce depreciation and other noncash expenses, such as amortization and depletion, in order to compute cash outflows for tax payments. In our opinion, the best time to introduce this complication is after one has had a thorough grounding in the basics. This you now have.

3. Public-sector and not-for-profit, private-sector projects do not pay income taxes. This means that the techniques we have learned to date apply directly to this large class of capital expenditures.

4. For many projects, particularly those with significant capital expenditures that need to be broken down into property classes (as discussed later) in order to arrive at realistic estimates for depreciation expenses, preliminary economic studies are often based on before-tax analyses.

5. A good approximation of the after-tax IRR can often be obtained by multiplying the before-tax IRR by $(1 - t)$, where t is the combined income tax rate.

In what follows, we illustrate in some detail the application of engineering economics to after-tax cost studies. However, federal, state, and local income tax laws frequently change, and tax treatments vary from industry to industry. Therefore, if you become involved in such studies, you will have to bring current tax laws and treatments to your particular situation.

COMMENT: This is a good time to review Chapter 2, in which the effect of noncash expenses, such as depreciation on income taxes and cash flow, is illustrated. Furthermore, Chapter 2 will remind you once again that the "bottom line" (net income after taxes) is not a cash inflow and is not to be confused with "making money" (which only the mint can do).

16.2 INCOME TAXES

Income taxes are major tax outflows levied on taxable income by foreign, federal, state, and local governments. Your first objective is to determine which taxes apply against the investment opportunity under review. Federal and state income taxes will almost certainly have to be included. However, some local jurisdictions also levy income taxes (New York City and San Francisco are two of many examples). For an international project, you will have to consider foreign jurisdictions and how tax payments to such jurisdictions impact on taxes paid in this country. In addition, you may have to deal with special income taxes, such as the windfall profit tax that was levied in the energy crisis of the mid-1970s on domestic oil producers.

Next, you need to determine the appropriate tax rate for each jurisdiction. For the federal government, the tax rates for corporations are given in Table 16.1. Since proprietorships and partnerships are not separate legal entities, proprietors and partners pay personal income taxes on their taxable income from these sources. Individual income tax rates for unmarried taxpayers are also given in Table 16.1. For married proprietors and partners and for heads of households, you will have to turn to IRS publications. However, if you do use the rates in Table 16.1, you will at least be conservative, which, as we've pointed out several times, is all to the good in economy studies.

Similar rate tables are, of course, available for state and local jurisdictions, although the rates are much lower. A common characteristic of all such tables is that they are bracketed. It is therefore necessary for you to select the tax bracket that applies to your study. This is usually but by no means always the bracket with the highest rate.

Many industrial corporations have very wisely established effective tax rates to be applied to capital selection studies. The jurisdictions to which they apply are usually specified, since tax rates differ from state to state and from locality to locality.

If there are no corporate guidelines to help you, you should have a tax accountant nearby or on call, not only to advise you on current tax laws, but

TABLE 16.1 Federal Income Tax Rates—1992

Individual Income Tax Rates[a]

If taxable income is	The tax is
Not over $20,350	15% of income
Over $20,350 but not over $49,300	$3,053 + 28% of the excess over $20,350
Over $49,300	$11,159 + 31% of the excess over $49,300

Corporate Income Tax Rates

If taxable income is	The tax is
Not over $50,000	15% of taxable income
Over $50,000 but not over $75,000	$7,500 + 25% of the excess over $50,000
Over $75,000 but not over $100,000	$13,750 + 34% of the excess over $75,000
Over $100,000 but not over $335,000	$22,250 + 39% of the excess over $100,000
Over $335,000	34% of taxable income

[a]The rates shown are conservative, since they apply to unmarried proprietors and partners, for whom rates are considerably higher than for married owners.

also to give you some informed guesses on the direction that taxes might take.

However, there is one thing you can easily do for yourself, namely, compute a combined income tax rate. If t_f, t_s, and t_l are the tax rates for federal, state and local jurisdictions, respectively, the combined tax rate is

$$\text{Combined tax rate} = 1 - (1 - t_f)(1 - t_s)(1 - t_l) \qquad (16.1)$$

That this is so is clear from the following illustration for a taxable income of $100:

Taxable income	$100.00
Local income taxes at 5%	5.00
Taxable income for state taxes	95.00
State income taxes at 10%	9.50
Taxable income for federal taxes	85.50
Federal income taxes at 30%	25.65
Net income after taxes	59.85

The total income taxes paid were $40.15 ($5.00 + $9.50 + $25.65). The combined tax rate is therefore 40.15% and not the sum of the three rates, which is 45%. Equation (16.1) gives the same result.

You should also remember that the cash flow estimates with which you are working are seldom better than two and never (or almost never) better than three significant figures. Therefore, a tax rate good to two figures is usually all you need. Sensitivity analysis, the major topic of Chapter 21, will show what happens to figures of merit if the tax rate is above or below that used in your study.

16.3 DEPRECIATION

The cost of a long-lived asset must be included in the cost of the goods and services that it helps produce. It would not be reasonable to charge its entire cost to the period in which it was bought. Therefore, we allocate or spread its cost over all or part of its estimated useful life.

The terms "depreciation," "amortization," and "depletion" all refer to accounting procedures with which the costs of long-lived assets are allocated. The term "depreciation" is used for tangible property, that is, physical assets such as buildings and equipment; the term "depletion" is used for natural resources, such as timber and mineral wealth; and the term "amortization" is used for intangible property, that is, nonphysical assets, such as patents, copyrights, and franchises. For such assets, "depreciation" is often used as a synonym for "amortization."

In Chapter 2, we gave you a brief introduction to depreciation. You will recall that it is not a cash flow expense, but, since it impacts on income taxes, it must be brought into cash flow analyses to compute the cash outflow for taxes. Except for depletion and amortization, it is usually the only noncash expense that needs to be considered in an evaluation of capital projects.

> *COMMENT:* This is a good time for a comment on goodwill, which is often an important factor in merger and acquisition studies. Goodwill is the difference between what is paid for net assets (the assets purchased less the liabilities assumed as part of the purchase) and their market and/or book value on the date of purchase. This difference, if positive, shows up as a long-lived nonphysical asset—goodwill—on balance sheets and as an expense spread over 5–40 years (take your pick) on income statements. However, the IRS does not allow goodwill to be depreciated for tax purposes, because it does not have a determinable useful life. This is another instance in which financial performance statements differ from income tax statements.

The methods used for depreciating tangible property include straight-line (SL), unit-of-production (UOP), and accelerated depreciation. Under the straight-line method, the cost of a fixed asset less its estimated salvage value (which is often assumed to be zero) is spread uniformly over its depreciable life. Under UOP depreciation, a fixed asset is expensed at so much per unit of production. Under accelerated depreciation, the early years of an asset's depreciable life bear more of this expense than later years.

There are three accelerated cost recovery systems with which you should be familiar:

1. Modified Accelerated Cost Recovery System (MACRS), including its alternate methods
2. Declining balance (DB), of which two important varieties are double declining balance (DDB or 200% DB) and 150% DB
3. Sum-of-years-digits (SYD)

MACRS replaced the Accelerated Cost Recovery System (ACRS) under the Tax Reform Act of 1986 and is now mandatory for federal tax returns. A brief description of the system is given in the subsection that follows. A fuller description, as well as descriptions of UOP and the other two accelerated depreciation methods named, are given in Appendix 16A.

COMMENT: You will now ask, "Why must I become familiar with three systems if only the first is mandatory?" There are at least two good reasons. The first is that not all state and local jurisdictions have accepted MACRS, but they still accept declining balance or sum-of-years-digits. A second reason is that financial performance statements, unlike tax statements, are not based on MACRS but on one of the other systems, of which straight-line is the most common.

16.3.1 MACRS

Tangible property consists of real property and personal property. "Real property" or "real estate" (the distinction is important to lawyers but not to us) is defined as the earth's surface (land) and anything permanently attached to it by nature or by people, such as buildings, roads, railroad tracks, trees, fences, retaining walls, and generally all site improvements. Personal property is everything else.

MACRS defines eight property classes—six for personal property and two for real property. These classes identify the number of years over which the cost of any item in a class can be recovered. The eight classes and their recovery periods are shown in Table 16.2.

Land is not shown in Table 16.2, because land is not depreciable.

Each property class covers property with a range of useful or service lives, which the IRS refers to as "class lives." The ranges for the six classes of personal property are given in Table 16.3.

You will notice that assets with class lives of 5–16 years fall into just two property classes—5-year and 7-year.

The class lives of specific assets are given in IRS Publication 534 (2) and are shown for certain selected items in Table 16A.3 of Appendix 16A.

TABLE 16.2 MACRS Classes

Property Class	Typical Assets	Depreciation Method
	Personal Property Classes	
3 years	Special tools and devices	DDB
5 years	Automobiles, light trucks, computer equipment	DDB
7 years	Office furniture and fixtures, most equipment and machinery	DDB
10 years	Other equipment and machinery	DDB
15 years	Site improvements	150% DB
20 years	Power plant equipment	150% DB
	Real Property Classes	
27½ years	Residential rental property, such as apartment buildings	SL
31½ years	Nonresidential real property, such as stores, warehouses, office buildings, hotels, manufacturing buildings	SL

For MACRS, depreciation rates for personal property are based on zero salvage value, on declining balances, and on certain conventions, such as the half-year and midquarter conventions, of which we will use only the half-year. The rate tables for the six classes based on the half-year convention can be found in Table 16A.1 of Appendix 16A. For real property, straight-line depreciation with zero salvage value is used, although the rates are again subject to certain conventions, such as the midmonth convention.

There are several options under MACRS with which you should be familiar but which we will not apply in this text. They are briefly described in Appendix 16A.

TABLE 16.3 Class Lives

Property Class	Range of Lives, Yrs.
3-year	≤ 4
5-year	5–10
7-year	11–16
10-year	16–20
15-year	21–25
20-year	> 25

16.3.2 Application to Economy Studies

How are we going to proceed? Will we break estimates of first cost down into their property classes to get a good fix on depreciation expenses? Where states or localities have not accepted MACRS but have accepted declining balance or sum-of-years-digits, will we apply two separate depreciation methodologies to obtain cash outflows for income taxes? What about the conventions tied to the rate tables? Are we going to apply all of these to our income tax computations? The answer to all of these questions is no; rather, we plan to proceed as follows.

- Use composite depreciable lives and composite depreciation rates wherever an investment consists of more than one property class.
- Use straight-line depreciation for illustrating concepts.
- For personal property, use MACRS with the half-year but not the midpoint and other conventions in illustrative examples.
- For real property, use MACRS without the midmonth and other conventions.
- Use a combined tax rate for federal, state, and local income taxes.
- Forget other accelerated depreciation methodologies. Appendix 16A covers these if you need them for a real-life study.

COMMENT: None of these simplifications will interfere with the presentation of the concepts and methodologies that you need to know in order to handle after-tax analyses. What they do is get rid of much burdensome detail in which you may have to get involved in handling a real-life problem but which would only get in our way now.

For a preliminary study, it is common to use straight-line depreciation over the estimated useful life of the study project. The figures of merit obtained in this way are neither right nor wrong. They are preliminary in the same sense that estimates of first costs, revenues, and operating costs range from preliminary estimates at one extreme to definitive estimates at the other.

One point in favor of initiating a study with straight-line depreciation is that the figures of merit obtained will be conservative, since this method understates cash flows in the early years of life cycles. Therefore, if the investment criteria are satisfied, we can say with some assurance that it is worthwhile to proceed with a more definitive study. If the figures of merit fall short but are close to meeting a company's investment criteria, accelerated depreciation may achieve this goal.

Refining our studies by breaking estimates down into property classes and computing a composite depreciation rate will not be done in this text but may be necessary in a real-life study. This can also be done to various levels of detail. As a first approximation, the initial investment for a project (excluding land, which is not depreciable) could be divided into (1) real property, for which straight-line depreciation is used, and (2) personal property, using the seven-year class into which most equipment and machinery falls.

For short-lived projects—ten years and under, and particularly those with depreciable property in the three-year, five-year, and seven-year property classes—the rates for the property class that dominates the study could be used as a first approximation and might indicate that no further refinements are needed.

16.4 AMORTIZATION

We have already used the term "amortization" for loan repayment schedules for which the amount repaid is constant for each payment period, although the proportions representing principal and interest change with each successive payment. However, as mentioned, the term is also used for depreciating the cost of nonphysical assets to which a definite future life can be assigned. Straight-line depreciation based on future life is specified by the IRS.

16.5 DEPLETION

Owners of mineral properties, of oil, gas, and geothermal wells, of standing timber, and of all other assets that are classified as natural resources may take a deduction for depletion in addition to the deduction for depreciation on the physical facilities. There are two ways of figuring this deduction. One is cost depletion, and the other is percentage depletion. The latter is not allowed for timber and for most oil and gas wells.

Cost depletion is computed by dividing the adjusted basis (for the definition of "adjusted basis," see Appendix 16A) of a mineral property and of oil, gas, and geothermal wells by the estimated total number of recoverable units (ounces of gold, tons of coal, etc.) in the deposit to obtain a cost per unit. The depletion deduction for tax purposes is the number of units sold during the tax year multiplied by this unit cost.

Percentage depletion is a percentage of the gross revenue earned during the tax year. The deduction cannot be more than 50% of the taxable income computed without the deduction for depletion. Depletion percentages currently vary from 5% for sand, stone, and gravel to 22% for lead, zinc, nickel, sulphur, and uranium. The percentage allowed for coal is 10% and for gold, silver, copper, and small oil and gas producers, 15%.

Depletion allowances should be figured for both the cost and percentage completion methods—where both methods are allowed—and the greater of the two amounts used in tax returns. Example 16.1 illustrates both methods.

Example 16.1 Depletion Consider a property for which revenues from the sale of coal are $1,000,000 during the tax year and mining expenses other than depletion are $850,000 (these expenses will include depreciation on buildings, equipment, and other depreciable property).

Then, by the percentage method, the allowable depletion expense is as follows:

Revenue for the year	$1,000,000
Depletion percentage for coal	10%
Allowable depletion expense	$100,000

However, this allowance cannot exceed 50% of the taxable income computed without depletion.

Revenue for the year	$1,000,000
Expenses for the year	850,000
Taxable income excluding depletion	$150,000

Fifty percent of the taxable income is $75,000, which would be the depletion expense under the percentage method.

For the cost method, assume that the estimated coal reserves of this particular owner totaled 500,000 tons at the time the property was purchased and were bought for $5,000,000, not including the land and the mining facilities, if any. This is equivalent to $10 per ton. If 10,000 tons were mined during the current year, the allowance for depletion would be $100,000 (10,000 tons times $10). Since this exceeds the allowance by the percentage method, the cost method would be used.

Depletion is not a topic for amateurs. (Neither, for that matter, is depreciation or amortization.) If you become involved in a cost study for a depletable resource, you may need to consult your company's tax department or a tax consultant to advise you once you go beyond a preliminary assessment.

16.6   TAX CREDITS

Federal, state, and local governments grant tax credits to stimulate investment. Only the investment tax credit (ITC) of the federal government is discussed below. At present, the current tax laws exclude this credit for almost all investments. However, the ITC comes and goes with some regularity and is therefore a credit with which you should become familiar. If the past is a proper guide, the return of the ITC (if and when it comes) will involve the government in efforts to move the economy out of a recession. In addition, governments use tax credits to favor projects with certain specific objectives, such as reducing pollutants, conserving energy, and the like.

The ITC is usually expressed as a percentage applied to that part of the first cost that meets government requirements for such credits. The sum obtained is deducted, not from taxable income, but directly from the tax payments otherwise due. An application of the credit is given in Example 16.6 near the end of this chapter.

16.7 CAPITAL GAINS AND LOSSES

Capital gains and losses result from the disposal of property that the IRS labels as a capital asset. Such property receives special treatment in tax computations, which do not apply to gains and losses from the disposal of plant assets (another name for long-lived assets) used in business.

Common examples of capital assets include investments in stocks, bonds, and land. Gains and losses on disposal are netted. A net capital gain is currently taxed at the same rate as ordinary income, that is, operating income. However, net capital losses are handled differently.

Businesses operating as proprietorships or partnerships cannot deduct more than $3,000 of net capital losses from ordinary income in any one year. The excess can be used to reduce taxable income in future years. Corporations may not offset net capital losses against ordinary income but can carry such losses back three years or forward five years to be offset against capital gains in these carry-back/carry-forward years. The above limitations on offsetting losses do not apply to net losses from the disposal of plant assets.

Except for the disposal of land, capital gains and losses have very little to do with the selection process for capital projects.

16.8 OTHER TAXES

As we know, income taxes are not the only taxes that impact on business entities. Two important taxes, which, unlike income taxes, have to be paid whether or not a business is operating profitably, are sales taxes and property taxes.

Sales taxes are levied by federal, state, and local governments. Estimates of revenue should be presented net of these taxes. This is an assumption we have made throughout this text.

Property taxes are levied by local governments. They are an operating expense and are included in the estimated cash outflows for these expenses.

16.9 AFTER-TAX APPLICATIONS

The after-tax cost studies in this section cover the following topics:

Example 16.2 Equity Financing
Example 16.3 Creditor Financing
Example 16.4 Replacement
Example 16.5 Replacement with Cotermination
Example 16.6 The Investment Tax Credit

In these examples, we generally use short lives and small investments so as not to clutter the presentation although the methodologies illustrated apply to investments of any size and any time span. We also assume discrete end-of-year cash flows for first costs, revenues, cost of sales, operating costs, and all other cash flows. However, you now have the know-how to substitute continuous cash flows; quarterly, monthly and other periodic cash flows; first costs that are spread over more than one time period, either discretely or continuously. And you know how to make other modifications that, in your opinion, better fit the study at hand.

16.9.1   Equity Financing—Example 16.2

Your employer has asked you to look at a capital investment opportunity involving the purchase of construction equipment and a small parcel of land for its outdoor storage. The estimated first cost is $120,000, and the useful life of the equipment is six years. The pertinent assumptions and estimates on which the study is to be based are itemized below. Some of the numbers were prepared under your guidance and some were not. However, for this preliminary analysis, you decide to take what was given to you and discuss possible modifications later.

First cost of investment	
Depreciable portion	$100,000
Nondepreciable portion (land)	20,000
Total	$120,000
Working capital	$20,000
Residual (salvage) value at EOY 4	
Depreciable portion	0
Nondepreciable portion (land)	20,000
Total	$20,000
Annual cash flow from sales	$150,000
Less annual cash expenses	100,000
Net cash flow before taxes from operations	$50,000
Composite income tax rate	40%
MARR after taxes	15%

We begin with a quick check on the net cash flow before taxes and the before-tax IRR before we compute the after-tax IRR.

The cash flow diagram for the before-tax cash flows is given in Figure 16.1. As shown, you have assumed that the working capital of $20,000 will be completely recovered at the end of four years and that the nondepreciable portion of the first cost (land), which also amounts to $20,000, could be disposed of at its original cost. Both of these assumptions are often made in economy studies.

One assumption you did not make but which was given to you as a basis for the study was that the salvage value of the depreciable portion of the first cost at EOY 4 was zero. As mentioned, you accept this for the time being.

The computations for the IRR before taxes follow. For the source of the figures, see the previous tabulation and Figure 16.1.

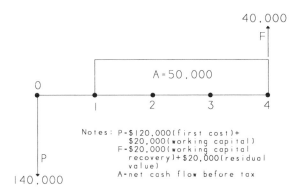

Figure 16.1. Before-tax cash flow diagram for Example 16.2.

$$NPV = 0 = \$-140,000 + \$50,000(P/A,i,4) + \$40,000(P/F,i,4)$$

Trial and error or a hand calculator will give you 23.0% for the IRR. You now estimate that the IRR after taxes will be about 14%, that is, about 60% of 23% (100% minus the tax rate of 40%), which is lower than the MARR of 15%. However, this does not mean that you can avoid an after-tax analysis.

Two convenient formats for computing after-tax cash flows were presented in Chapter 2. One format was in the form of a pro forma income statement (see Table 2.1). The other was an amputated version of this table rotated 90° (see Table 2.2). We use the latter format here.

EOY	Net Cash Flow Before Taxes	Depreciation Expenses	Taxable Income	Income Taxes, 40%	Net Cash Flow After Taxes
(1)	(2)	(3)	(4) = (2) − (3)	(5)	(6) = (2) − (5)
0	$-140,000	—	—	—	$-140,000
1–4	50,000	$25,000	$25,000	$10,000	40,000
4	40,000	—	—	—	40,000

In column (2), the net cash flow before taxes at EOY 0 is the sum of the first cost and the working capital, the net cash flow before taxes from operating activities for EOY 1 to EOY 4 is $50,000, and the additional cash flow at EOY 4 is the $20,000 recovery from working capital plus the sale of the nondepreciable portion of the first cost for $20,000. With straight-line depreciation, the annual depreciation expense is $25,000, as shown in the following equation.

$$\frac{\text{Depreciable value} - \text{salvage value}}{\text{Estimated useful life in years}} = \frac{\$100,000 - 0}{4}$$

You now complete the above tabulation as shown. The depreciation expense for years 1–4 is in column (3). This expense is subtracted from the net cash flow before taxes to obtain the net income before taxes, that is, the taxable income, in column (4). The income tax in column (5) is obtained by multiplying the taxable income by the tax rate of 40%. The net cash flow after taxes in column (6) is simply the cash flow before taxes less the tax.

The computations for the present worth for an MARR of 15% are shown in the following equation. The cash flow diagram is given in Figure 16.2. All dollar figures are in thousands.

$$NPV = -\$140 + \$40(P/A,15,4) + \$40(P/F,15,4)$$
$$= -\$140 + \$40 \times 2.855 + \$40 \times 0.5718$$
$$= -\$2.9 \text{ k}$$

This computation did not come out the way you wanted, but it did come out the way you expected. The NPV is $-2,900, indicating that the investment will not quite satisfy the MARR. The IRR, as you can easily confirm, is 14.1%, which is close to your estimate based on the IRR of 23.0% before taxes.

However, your study is far from complete. Your next task is to carry out a more definitive study that begins with a review of all of the preliminary cash flow estimates. This review indicates that two estimates should be changed:

1. The working capital estimate of $20,000 was furnished by the Accounting Department, which now agrees that this sum was too conservative and can be reduced to $15,000. (Don't be surprised. This often happens to working capital and other expenses on a second go-around.)
2. The residual value of the depreciable portion of the first cost was taken as zero. Based on a market survey, initiated by you, you conclude that a more realistic value is a net recovery of $10,000 at EOY 4.

Furthermore, your enhanced study will be based on MACRS, since the IRS will ultimately determine how the cash outflow for income taxes will be

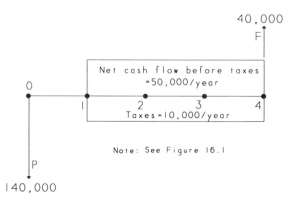

Figure 16.2. After-tax cash flow diagram for Example 16.2.

computed. You assume the investment qualifies for the three-year property class. Due to the half-year convention, the depreciation expenses are spread over four years at the rates shown in the following table. (See Table 16A.1 in Appendix 16A.)

	Rate Applied to Depreciable Cost of $100,000	Depreciation, $
First year	0.3333	$33,330
Second year	0.4444	44,440
Third year	0.1481	14,810
Fourth year	0.0742	7,420
	1.0000	$100,000

The revised depreciation expenses and the previous modifications in cash flows are summarized in Table 16.4.

For an MARR of 15%, the NPV for this cash flow pattern is given by the following equation:

$$NPV = \$-135{,}000 + \$43{,}332(P/F,15,1) + \$47{,}776(P/F,15,2)$$
$$+ \ \$35{,}924(P/F,15,3)$$
$$+ \ (\$32{,}968 + \$6{,}000 + \$15{,}000 + \$20{,}000)(P/F,15,4)$$

TABLE 16.4   After-Tax Cash Flows

EOY	Net Cash Flow Before Taxes	Depreciation Expense	Taxable Income	Income Taxes, 40%	Net Cash Flow After Taxes
(1)	(2)	(3)	(4) = (2) − (3)	(5)	(6) = (2) − (5)
0	$− 135,000	—	—	—	$− 135,000
1	50,000	$33,330	$16,670	$6,668	43,332
2	50,000	44,440	5,560	2,224	47,776
3	50,000	14,810	35,190	14,076	35,924
4	50,000	7,420	42,580	17,032	32,968
4 (a)	10,000	—	10,000	4,000	6,000
4 (b)	15,000	—	—	—	15,000
4 (c)	20,000	—	—	—	20,000

Notes:

(a) The $10,000 cash inflow in column (2) is from the sale of the equipment at EOY 4. Since the cost was completely written off, the sale represents a gain, which is subject to a 40% tax.

(b) This is the recovery of the working capital.

(c) This is a conservative estimate of what could be recovered from the sale of the land.

If you insert the proper values for the *P/F* factors, you will get a positive NPV of $4,719. You should also confirm that the IRR after taxes is 16.4%.

This concludes at least the first phase of your study. You take it to management with a "go" recommendation or for their approval to proceed with a more definitive study.

> *COMMENT:* Purely as an aside, the cash flows before taxes in column (2) in Table 16.4 would show an IRR before taxes of 25.6%. Sixty percent of this rate comes to an after tax rate of 15.3%, which, for a first approximation, is reasonably close to the more accurate figure of 16.4% obtained above.

16.9.2 Creditor Financing—Example 16.3

Management now asks you to redo the same study on the basis that the investment will be partially financed with $70,000 of borrowed capital. (We worked on a similar example in Chapter 14, but our objective here is to go step by step from a preliminary study to a more and more refined study.) The remaining funds required for the first cost and the working capital—$65,000—will be supplied with equity financing. The interest rate on the loan is 10%, and it is to be repaid in four equal annual installments; otherwise, the estimates and the assumptions of Example 16.2 still hold. Your first task is to break up the four annual loan payments into principal and interest, since interest is a deductible expense for arriving at taxable income. If you did not do so, you would not be able to calculate the cash outflows for income taxes. Each of the four annual payments amount to $22,083 as shown in the following equation:

$$A = P(A/P,i,N) = \$70,000(A/P,10,4)$$
$$= \$70,000 \times 0.3155$$
$$= \$22,083$$

In Chapter 7, you learned how to break down these payments into interest and principal. This is done again in the following table:

Year	Beginning-of-Year Balance	Annual Payment	Interest	Principal	End-of-Year Balance
(1)	(2)	(3)	(4) 10% of (2)	(5) (3) − (4)	(6) (2) − (5)
1	$70,000	$22,083	$7,000	$15,083	$54,917
2	54,917	22,083	5,492	16,591	38,326
3	38,326	22,083	3,833	18,250	20,076
4	20,076	22,083	2,007	20,076	0
			Total	$70,000	

You begin, as you did in Example 16.2, with a before-tax cash flow analysis. The cash flows are shown in the following tabulation and in Figure 16.3.

EOY	Net Cash Flow Without Debt Repayment	Annual Debt Payment	Net Cash Flow With Debt Repayment
(1)	(2)	(3)	(4) = (2) + (3)
0	$ – 65,000	—	$ – 65,000
1–4	50,000	$22,083	27,917
4	45,000	—	45,000

The cash outflow at EOY 0 is the first cost ($120,000) plus the working capital ($15,000) less the amount to be borrowed ($70,000). The cash inflows for years 1–4 are self-explanatory. The cash inflow for EOY 4 comes from the sale of the depreciable portion of the investment for $10,000, the recovery of $15,000 from the investment in working capital, and the value of the nondepreciable portion of the first cost of $20,000.

The IRR before taxes is 38.5% on the equity investment of $65,000 by the owners. You therefore expect the after-tax IRR to be somewhere near 60% of that figure, or approximately 25%.

Before you can compute the after-tax cash flow, the format used in Example 16.2 has to be expanded to bring interest expense into the taxable income calculations and the repayment of principal into the cash flows. This is done in Table 16.5.

You should have no difficulty in confirming the figures in this table. The figures in column (2) are the basic before-tax cash flows on which Examples 16.2 and 16.3 are based. The figures in columns (3) and (10) are the split between the interest and principal on the loan payments. The figures in column (5) are the depreciation expenses for MACRS that were given in Example 16.2. Table 16.5 shows how to move from one column to the next in order to come up with the final results in Column (11).

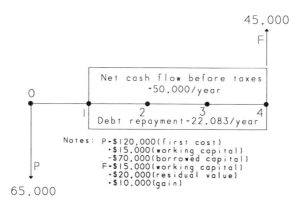

Figure 16.3. Before-tax cash flow diagram for Example 16.3.

TABLE 16.5 After-tax Cash Flow with Loan Repayment—Example 16.3

(1) Year	(2) Net Cash Flow Before Interest and Taxes	(3) Interest Expense	(4) Net Cash Flow Before Taxes (2) – (3)	(5) Depreciation Expense	(6) Taxable Income (4) – (5)	(7) Income Tax, 40% 0.4 (6)	(8) Net Income After Taxes (6) – (7)	(9) Add Back Depreciation (5) + (8)	(10) Principal Portion of Debt Payment	(11) Net Cash Flow (9) – (10)
0	$ – 65,000	—	—	—	—	—	—	—	—	$ – 65,000
1	50,000	$7,000	$43,000	$33,330	$9,670	$3,868	$5,802	$39,132	$15,083	24,049
2	50,000	5,492	44,508	44,440	68	27	41	44,481	16,591	27,890
3	50,000	3,833	46,167	14,810	31,357	12,543	18,814	33,624	18,250	15,374
4	50,000	2,007	47,993	7,420	40,573	16,227	24,344	31,764	20,076	11,688
4 (a)	10,000	—	—	—	10,000	4,000	6,000	6,000	—	6,000
4 (b)	15,000	—	—	—	—	—	—	—	—	15,000
4 (c)	20,000	—	—	—	—	—	—	—	—	20,000

Notes:
(a) Cash flows due to sale of equipment at a gain. See Table 16.3.
(b) Recovery of working capital.
(c) Assumption of sale or transfer of land at its first cost at end of life cycle.

The net present value for the cash flow pattern of Table 16.5 for an MARR of 15% is given by the following equation:

$$NPV = \$-65,000 + \$24,049(P/F,15,1) + \$27,890(P/F,15,2)$$
$$+ \$15,374(P/F,15,3)$$
$$+ (\$11,688 + \$6,000 + \$15,000 + \$20,000)(P/F,15,4)$$
$$= \$17,234$$

The IRR after taxes is 26.2%.

A comparison of the results for equity and creditor financing are given below.

	All-Equity Financing	Part Creditor Financing
Total investment		
Equity	$135,000	$65,000
Borrowed funds	0	70,000
Total	$135,000	$135,000
IRR on equity financing		
Before taxes	25.6%	38.5%
After taxes	16.4%	26.2%

For all-equity financing, the return to the owners after taxes is an estimated 16% after taxes. For partial funding by outsiders, the return to the owners is substantially higher—in this case, 26%. As mentioned in Chapter 14, if, for any proposed investment, funds can be borrowed at an after-tax rate lower than the IRR at full equity financing, the return on the funds furnished by owners is higher than if the owners furnished all of the financing.

Our next example involves a replacement problem for which the significant cash flows are negative. We also look at this problem both before and after taxes.

16.9.3 Replacement Problems

As mentioned in Chapter 15, the great bulk of economy studies is concerned with replacements. For these, the computer programs available today will easily produce IRRs after taxes for the appropriate MACRS property class. However, we have again chosen first to calculate the IRR before taxes for no other reason than to provide an easy transition from before-tax to after-tax computations.

Replacement problems are usually handled as minimum-cost rather than maximum-revenue problems. This means that we assume revenues are not affected by the choice of the replacement and that they therefore need not be included in the analysis, since they are irrelevant. If the choice of a replacement did affect revenue (if, for example, it increased sales), we could not proceed in this way.

Example 16.4 Replacements Suppose your company has to replace an item of personal property. The do-nothing alternative is no longer a viable option. You've found two candidates for replacement. The pertinent data are given in the following table:

	A	B	B − A
Useful life, years	5	5	5
First cost	$10,000	$12,500	$2,500
Annual O&M costs (savings)	$4,000	$3,000	($1,000)

The incremental investment of $2,500 gives a return of $1,000 per year for five years, indicating an IRR of about 30% before taxes. You therefore estimate an IRR of 18% (60% of 30%) after taxes. To get a more accurate figure, you calculate the IRR after taxes for the differential tax cash flows, using the format applied in Examples 16.2 and 16.3.

EOY	Net Cash Flow Before Taxes	Depreciation Expense	Taxable Income	Income Taxes, 40%	Net Cash Flow After Taxes
(1)	(2)	(3)	(4) = (2) − (3)	(5)	(6) = (2) − (5)
0	$−2,500	—	—	—	$−2,500
1–5	1,000	$500	$500	$200	$800

For this cash flow pattern, the IRR is given by

$$0 = -\$2,500 + \$800(P/A,i,5)$$

$$(P/A,i,5) = \$2,500/\$800 = 3.13$$

$$i = 18\%$$

The IRR of 18% checks the above approximation.

Example 16.4 was a rather simple one. In Example 16.5, we consider a more complicated problem, which involves cotermination.

Example 16.5 Replacement with Cotermination The basic data for this problem are as follows:

	A	B
Useful life, years	4	6
First cost	$10,000	$15,000
Annual O&M costs	$4,000	$3,500

Since the useful lives are not the same, we first calculate the EUACs for each alternative.

For A,

$$EUAC = \$10,000(A/P,10,4) + \$4,000$$
$$= \$10,000 \times 0.3155 + \$4,000$$
$$= \$7,155$$

For B,

$$EUAC = \$15,000(A/P,10,6) + \$3,500$$
$$= \$15,000 \times 0.2296 + \$3,500$$
$$= \$6,944$$

COMMENT: You will recall from Chapter 7 that we can compare EUACs directly for alternatives whose lives differ. However, to convert these EUACs to NPVs, you have to use a *P/A* factor for which *N* is the LCM (lowest common multiple), which in this case is 12.

Alternative B wins; that is, it costs less to replace it every six years than to replace A every four years. However, the difference is only 3%. What would happen to this difference on an after-tax basis? This is examined next using straight-line depreciation. The depreciation expense for A is $2,500 annually for four years ($10,000/4) and $2,500 annually for six years for B ($15,000/6). The after-tax computations are in the following table.

EOY	Net Cash Flow Before Taxes	Depreciation Expense	Taxable Income	Income Tax Savings (40%)	Net Cash Flow After Taxes
(1)	(2)	(3)	(4) = (2) − (3)	(5) 0.4(4)	(6) = (2) + (5)
For Alternative A					
0	$ − 10,000	—	—	—	$ − 10,000
1–4	− 4,000	$2,500	$ − 6,500	$2,600	− 1,400
For Alternative B					
0	$ − 15,000	—	—	—	$ − 15,000
1–6	− 3,500	$2,500	$ − 6,000	$2,400	− 1,100

The respective calculations for the EUACs follow.

For A,

$$EUAC = \$1,400 + \$10,000(A/P,10,4)$$
$$= \$1,400 + \$10,000 \times 0.3155$$
$$= \$4,555$$

For B,

$$EUAC = \$1,100 + \$15,000(A/P,10,6)$$
$$= \$1,100 + \$15,000 \times 0.2296$$
$$= \$4,544$$

The heading in column (5) has been changed to "Income Tax Savings," and, as shown, column (5) is added to, not subtracted from, column (2). Losses reduce taxes that would otherwise be paid, and the taxes thus amount to a cash inflow rather than an outflow. This assumes that there are other sources of income that are taxable.

The difference in the EUACs between the two alternatives is now so small ($11) as to be irrelevant; that is, alternative B is as good a selection as alternative A. A decision between one or the other should be based on whether the difference between the first costs could better be applied elsewhere.

The last problem we discuss in this chapter deals with the investment tax credit (ITC), which, as mentioned, comes and goes, depending on whether Congress decides it is needed, or not needed, to stimulate capital investment.

16.9.4   Effect of ITC—Example 16.6

Suppose in Example 16.4 that alternative B has a higher first cost because, among other reasons, it incorporates certain energy-saving features for which tax credits can be obtained.

In applying these credits, it is necessary to do two things:

Determine how much of the investment is subject to a tax credit. We assume that this is $5,000 of the first cost of $15,000 for B.

Determine the percentage deduction that applies. It has varied from 6–10%. We use 10%.

Under these assumptions, there is a tax credit of $500 (10% of $5,000) if B is selected rather than A. The calculations for the effect on the EUAC of B follows.

EOY	Net Cash Flow Before Taxes	Depreciation Expense	Taxable Income	Income Tax Savings (40%)	Net Cash Flow After Taxes
(1)	(2)	(3)	(4) = (2) − (3)	(5)	(6) = (2) + (5)
				0.4(4)	
0	$ − 15,000	—	—	$500	$ − 14,500
1–6	− 3,500	$2,500	$ − 6,000	2,400	− 1,100

For B now, the

$$EUAC = \$1,100 + \$14,500(A/P,10,6)$$
$$= \$1,100 + \$14,500 \times 0.2296$$
$$= \$4,429$$

The figure of \$4,429 compares with the \$4,544 that we obtained without the tax credit and puts alternative B more solidly in front of A as the preferred candidate.

16.10 SUMMARY

Depreciation, amortization, and depletion are three noncash expenses with which economy studies on project selection must deal because they affect cash outflows for income taxes.

Depreciation spreads the depreciable cost of tangible property over its depreciable life. This is done either on a straight-line basis or on an accelerated basis, or on a unit-of-production basis. The IRS has mandated the use of MACRS or one of its options for tax returns and has classified all depreciable property into eight recovery periods, of which six apply to personal property and two to real property. Salvage value is always taken as zero.

Many states and localities have accepted MACRS for their tax returns; some have not. These allow the declining-balance method and the sum-of-years-digits method for accelerated depreciation.

Amortization is akin to depreciation but applies to such intangible property as patents, copyrights, and franchises. For amortization expenses, straight-line depreciation is used.

Depletion refers to spreading the first cost of natural resources over their expected recovery period. Depletion expense is calculated using cost or percentage depletion. If both apply, the method that produces the lowest tax return is used.

The investment tax credit (ITC), when available, serves as an inducement to invest. The credit is a deduction from income taxes, not from taxable income.

REFERENCE

1. Gerald A. Fleischer, *Engineering Economy: Capital Allocation Theory*. (Boston, MA: PWS Publishers, 1984). You will find a rather complete treatment of the IRS as it was in 1983 on pages 225–230. It may not come back in this form but will probably come close to it.

SUGGESTED READING

1. U.S. Department of the Treasury, *Depreciation*, IRS Publication 534 for 1990 Tax Returns, Catalog Number 150640, U.S. Government Printing Office. This is where to go for class lives, property classes, recovery periods, and other information on MACRS and its options.

PROBLEMS

COMMENT: Problems 16-1 to 16-12 are intended to familiarize you with Appendix 16A, which covers various depreciation methods for spreading the depreciable costs of long-term assets over their depreciable life.

16-1 Explain in your own words how the selection of (a) the estimated residual (salvage) value and (b) the estimated depreciable life affect the "bottom line" on financial performance statements. What effect do these selections have on income statements for tax purposes?

16-2 Prepare a table comparing SL, SYD, and DDB depreciation for the truck in Appendix 16A, assuming a residual value of $3,000 and a six-year life. For DDB, use the straight-line convention.

16-3 Repeat Problem 16-2 for MACRS. Table 16A.3 indicates that trucks fall into the five-year personal-property class.

16-4 An automated car-washing machine has an estimated useful life of 300,000 cars. The installed cost of the machine is $450,000. In the first year, 25,000 cars are washed, and, in the second year, 35,000 cars are washed. Using UOP depreciation, what is the depreciation expense for each of these years?

16-5 Go to Table 16A.1, and show how the rates for the first two years of the 15-year and 20-year personal-property classes were computed.

16-6 Table 16A.2 gives the rate structure and the book value for each dollar of an asset that falls into the MACRS five-year property class. Prepare a similar table for the three-year property class.

16-7 See Problem 16-6. Do the same for the seven-year property class.

16-8 What part does book value play in preparing cash flow patterns for the project selection process?

16-9 Rate structures for various depreciation methods are given in Table 16A.4 for a property with a depreciable life of five years that qualifies for the MACRS five-year recovery period. Prepare a similar table for a three-year property.

16-10 See Problem 16-9. Do the same for MACRS seven-year property.

16-11 Compare depreciation expenses for a property with a cost basis of $100,000 and a residual value of $10,000, using straight-line depreciation and the MACRS straight-line option. Use a 3-year life.

16-12 Table 16A.3 shows that for office equipment the recovery period is seven years for regular MACRS and ten years for the 150% DB option. Compare the rate structures for the two depreciation methods. Which would you use if cash flow was your prime concern? Why? Which one would you use if net income was more important to you?

Income Taxes

16-13 In Table 16.1, where do the following numbers come from?
   a) $3,053
   b) $11,159
   c) $7,500
   d) $13,750
   e) $22,250.

16-14 If the federal, state, and local tax rates are 25%, 8%, and 3%, respectively, what is the combined tax rate? What is the net income after taxes if the taxable income is $1 million?

16-15 Your business is subject to federal and state income taxes. If the combined tax rate for both jurisdictions is 40% and the federal tax rate is 35%, what is the state tax rate?

Depreciation Methods

16-16 The text says that SL depreciation understates net cash flows in the early years of an asset's life and therefore serves as a more conservative approach for preliminary studies than accelerated cost depreciation. Explain in your own words why this is so.

16-17 In the text, goodwill is mentioned as one instance of how income statements for financial performance differ from those prepared for tax purposes. Name one other instance that directly affects the selection process. Why is it important to be aware of such differences?

16-18 An asset cost $4,000. Its scrap value is estimated as $500 at the end of an expected useful life of seven years. It qualifies as a five-year property under MACRS. Prepare a table in which the depreciation expense and the book value of the asset are compared for straight-line depreciation and MACRS.

16-19 In 1988, Adventure Airlines purchased several baggage-handling conveyors for $200,000 each. The purchase qualifies as a five-year MACRS property. Prepare a table in which the depreciation expense and the book value are compared for the appropriate MACRS schedule and for the MACRS alternative straight-line method.

16-20 A materials-testing machine was purchased for $40,000. Its useful life is estimated as five years and its salvage value, as $5,000. It qualifies as a five-year property under MACRS.

    a) Prepare a table in which the depreciation expense and the book value are compared for SL, DDB, and MACRS depreciation methods.

    b) Prepare a graph with the book value as ordinate and the depreciable life as abscissa for SL, DDB, and MACRS depreciation.

16-21 Explain why keeping track of depreciation expense is one of the major tasks with which accounting departments are faced.

16-22 Assume that your firm has only two depreciable assets. One is an industrial building that was two years old at the beginning of this fiscal year. The other is equipment and machinery that falls into the seven-year property class and was three years old at the beginning of the year. What will be the depreciation expense of your firm for this fiscal year?

Amortization

16-23 You have just been issued a patent, for which the Good Hope Company offers you $1,700,000. You accept the offer. Five years later, Good Hope Company sells its rights to the patent to the Good Luck Corporation for $4,000,000. What is Good Hope's annual amortization expense under MACRS? What is Good Luck's? (*Hint*: Patent protection is for 17 years from the time of issue.)

Depletion

16-24 A small lumber company bought a tract of land containing timber. The price was $550,000, of which $50,000 was the appraised value of the land. The remainder was the estimated value of 10 million board-feet of standing timber. In the first year, 500,000 board-feet were cut, and, in the second year, 450,000 board-feet were cut. What was the depletion allowance for each of the two years? (*Note*: For standing timber and for most oil and gas wells, only cost depletion is permissible.)

16-25 Your firm has purchased an oil property for $500,000. The estimated recoverable reserves are 150,000 barrels. During the first year, 10,000 barrels were produced for a cost of $30,000, not including depletion expense. The selling price was $10 per barrel. What was the depletion expense for the year for the cost and percentage methods? (*Note*: Small oil and gas producers can use either the cost or percentage methods for computing depletion expense. The depletion allowance is 20% for the percentage method.)

16-26 A coal mining company purchased a mine five years ago for $3.5 million. The estimated recoverable reserves of coal at that time were 2 million tons. The following table sums up the performance of the company during the past five years.

Year	Tons Recovered	Revenue, $ Unit	Revenue, $ Total	Expenses Not Including Depletion, $
19X1	40,000	$15	$600,000	$500,000
19X2	52,000	20	1,040,000	700,000
19X3	58,000	18	1,044,000	650,000
19X4	60,000	18	1,080,000	800,000
19X5	56,000	25	1,400,000	900,000

Calculate the depletion expense by the percentage and cost methods for each of the five years, and select the appropriate method for each year. The depletion allowance for coal is 10%.

After-tax Analysis—Owner Financing

16-27 A proposed investment is expected to produce an annual net cash flow of $20,000 for the next eight years. The asset has a first cost of $60,000 and qualifies as a seven-year MACRS property. The combined income tax rate is 40%, and the after-tax MARR is 12%. The salvage value is zero.

a) Compute the after-tax present worth for SL depreciation.

b) Compute the after-tax present worth for MACRS.

c) Compute the after-tax IRR for MACRS.

16-28 An aircraft assembly fixture has a purchase price of $60,000 and qualifies as a three-year MACRS property. However, the fixture is expected to last five years and produce savings of $33,000 each year. Its salvage value at that time is zero.

a) Compute the before-tax NPW of the investment, using an MARR of 20%.

b) Compute the after-tax NPW for a tax rate of 40% and an after-tax MARR of 12%.

c) Compute the before- and after-tax IRRs.

d) How does the after-tax IRR compare with an approximate value obtained by multiplying the before-tax IRR by $(1 - t)$ where t is the tax rate?

16-29 The Barnes Bus Company has assembled the following data for a new bus to be used for runs to Atlantic City. The bus qualifies as a five-year MACRS property.

EOY	Before-tax Cash Flow
0	$ – 70,000
1	42,000
2	44,000
3	28,000
4	23,000
5	20,000

The combined income tax rate is 34%, and the after-tax MARR is 20%. The sale of the bus at EOY 5 is expected to bring in $20,000. What is the after-tax NPW of the investment for the MACRS straight-line option? (*Hint*: Don't forget the gain or loss on disposal, if any. Assume that the income tax rate applies.)

After-tax Analysis—Creditor Financing

16-30 The Allied Corporation intends to buy a 12-seat plane for its executives. The price is $2,500,000. The plane qualifies as a five-year MACRS property. The operating and maintenance expenses are estimated at $250,000 for the first year and are expected to increase by $15,000 every year for five years. The salvage value at that time is $250,000. The tax rate is 30% and applies to both income and gains and losses on disposal.

a) Prepare a cash flow table, assuming all-equity financing. (Round all of the figures to the nearest dollar.)

b) Compute the EUAC for a five-year planning horizon based on an after-tax MARR of 9%.

16-31 The CFO of the Allied Corporation (see Problem 16-30) finds it expedient to borrow all the funds required for the purchase of the airplane from a cash-rich subsidiary of Allied. The terms of the loan are four equal end-of-year payments covering the principal plus interest at 6%.

a) Prepare a cash flow table for this situation.

b) Compute the EUAC as specified in (b) of Problem 16-30.

16-32 Repeat Problem 16-31 for part-owner and part-creditor financing. The loan will be for $2 million and will be repaid in four installments.

Each installment will cover one-fourth of the principal plus the interest on the outstanding balance.

16-33 The Mega Corporation is considering the purchase of a processing line for one of its food products. The cost of the unit is $1,000,000, and it is expected to produce savings of $300,000 annually for five years. For study purposes, the salvage value at that time is taken as zero. The equipment can be purchased with a down payment of $200,000. The principal of the loan ($800,000) will be paid off at the rate of $200,000 per year plus 7% on the outstanding principal. The equipment falls into the five-year MACRS property class. The effective income tax rate is 40%.

a) What is the after-tax present worth of this investment, based on an MARR of 15%?

b) What is the after-tax IRR on the original investment of $200,000, using the MACRS straight-line option?

After-tax Analysis—Replacement

16-34 An automatic milling machine was purchased three years ago for $50,000. It has been depreciated with the SL method, using a nine-year period and an estimated salvage value of $5,000 at the end of the ninth year. Operating and maintenance expenses average $3,000 per year and are expected to remain at this level. The machine can be sold now for $30,000 or for an estimated $7,500 six years from now. The effective tax rate is 50%, and the MARR after taxes is 10%. What is the EUAC after taxes if the machine is kept an additional six years?

16-35 What would the EUAC after taxes be for the machine in Problem 16-34 if it had been treated as a seven-year property under MACRS?

16-36 A toy manufacturer is considering the purchase of equipment for $34,000 to produce a new toy that may or may not be a smashing success but that, even if it is, will probably phase out in four years. The manufacturer asks you to make a replacement analysis based on disposing of it in one, two, three, or four years. The combined tax rate is 50%, and the after-tax MARR is 10%. The new equipment qualifies as a three-year property under MACRS. With the manufacturer's help, you gather the following data:

EOY	Residual Value	Estimated O&M Costs
1	$32,000	$3,200
2	26,000	3,400
3	14,000	3,600
4	12,000	3,700

Compute the equivalent uniform annual cost after taxes for keeping the equipment one, two, three, or four years.

Investment Tax Credit

Note: In the problems that follow, assume the ITC was recovered at EOY 1.

16-37 Your company wants to invest $100,000 in a new laser and, if it does so, will receive a 10% investment tax credit. The before-tax cash flows are $20,000 for the first year, increasing by $10,000 for each of three years. At EOY 3, the sale of the laser is expected to yield $60,000. The combined income tax rate is 50%. The gain on disposal, if any, is also taxed at this rate. The MARR is 12%. The laser falls into the three-year MACRS property class.

a) Calculate the after-tax NPW.

b) Calculate the after-tax IRR.

16-38 Jacks, Inc., has acquired a machine for $90,000, which falls into the five-year MACRS property class. The operating and maintenance costs start at $2,000 and increase by $200 per year for five years. The revenue generated is $20,400 per year for five years. An inducement to buy the machine is a 10% investment tax credit. The combined tax rate is 40%, and the after-tax MARR is 10%. The salvage is zero.

a) What is the after-tax NPW of this investment?

b) What is its after-tax IRR?

16-39 Mary Lou's Catering Service is looking at new equipment, which would cost $10,000 and have an estimated salvage value of $2,000 after its seven-year life. The net cash flows before income taxes are given in the following table:

EOY	Net Cash Flow
1	$1,000
2	1,900
3	2,900
4	4,200
5	4,600
6	5,000
7	5,400

The combined tax bracket is 45%, and the MARR is 10%. There is also an investment tax credit of 5%. Compute the NPW, using the MACRS straight-line option for five-year property.

APPENDIX 16A
DEPRECIATION METHODOLOGIES

16A.1 INTRODUCTION

Five depreciation methods were mentioned in the body of this chapter, namely

Straight-line (SL)
Units-of-production (UOP)
Double-declining balance (DDB)
Sum-of-years-digits (SYD)
Modified Accelerated Cost Recovery System (MACRS)

Each of these methods allocates the depreciable cost of a long-term asset over its depreciable life.

16A.2 DEPRECIATION

The three quantities needed to compute the depreciation expense of a long-term asset are

Cost of asset (adjusted basis)
Estimated residual value
Estimated depreciable life

The depreciable cost of an asset is its adjusted basis less its estimated residual value, which may or may not be zero.

16.A.2.1 Cost of Asset

The adjusted basis or cost of a physical or nonphysical asset includes the purchase price, applicable taxes, purchase commissions, and all other amounts that are paid to acquire the asset and to get it ready for its intended use. Some comments on specific groups of physical assets follow:

- The cost of land includes expenditures for grading and clearing, and for demolishing and removing any unwanted structures. However, it does not include site improvements, such as fencing, paving, lighting, sprinkler systems, and landscaping. The cost of land is not depreciable; the cost of site improvements is.
- The cost of a new building includes the cost of constructing it plus fees and permits. For an existing building, cost includes expenditures for repairing and renovating for the intended use.

- The cost of equipment and machinery includes its purchase price (less discounts), transportation charges, insurance while in transit, sales and other taxes, installation costs, and expenditures for testing before it is put into service.

16.A.2.2 Residual Value

The residual value (also known as "salvage value" or "scrap value") is a user estimate of how much an asset could be sold for at the end of its useful life. Such estimates are based on forecasts (usually guesses) of future market value less the cost of preparing for sale. For MACRS, residual values are, by IRS rules, zero. For the other depreciation methods, there is nothing to prevent users from estimating zero for residual values. In fact, this is often the most sensible thing to do. However, it is not done as often as it might be because it increases the depreciation expense and thus reduces the net income (the bottom line) shown on financial performance statements.

16.A.2.3 Depreciable Life

For MACRS and its options, the depreciable life of physical assets is defined by the IRS. For the remaining methods, the depreciable life is a user estimate. These estimates can be conservative, realistic, or optimistic, depending on the user and the effect on net income.

The description of the depreciation methods that follow include examples based on the purchase of a new truck. The pertinent data are as follows:

Cost of truck	$45,000
Estimated residual value	5,000
Depreciable cost	$40,000
Estimated useful life, in years	5
Estimated useful life, in units of production—miles	200,000

We could, for ease of computation, have made the residual value zero, which it has to be for MACRS. However, this would oversimplify the computations for some of the other methods of computing depreciation expense.

16A.3 STRAIGHT-LINE (SL) DEPRECIATION

This method of depreciation was described in this chapter and was applied in several examples. Annual SL depreciation is simply the depreciable cost divided by the number of years of depreciable life. For the truck, the annual depreciation expense is $8,000, as shown in the following equation:

$$\text{Annual SL depreciation} = \frac{\text{Depreciable cost}}{\text{Depreciable life}} \qquad (16\text{A}.1)$$

$$= \$40,000/5$$

$$= \$8,000$$

16A.4 UNITS OF PRODUCTION (UOP)

The unit of production in our example is miles, and the depreciation expense is $0.20 per mile ($40,000/200,000). If the mileage for the first year of ownership is 35,000, the depreciation expense for that year is $7,000 ($0.20 × 35,000) and the book value at EOY 1 is $38,000 ($45,000 − $7,000).

If the truck is sold before 200,000 miles of usage, say at 180,000 miles, the book value is the residual value plus the depreciation for the unused mileage, that is, $9,000 ($5,000 + $0.20 × 20,000 miles). If it is operated for more than 200,000 miles, the miles over this amount cannot be charged with depreciation, since the book value remains at $5,000 until disposal.

16A.5 SUM-OF-YEARS-DIGITS (SYD)

SYD depreciation is computed by multiplying the depreciable cost by a fraction, for which the denominator is the sum-of-years-digits and the numerator is the depreciable life for the first year, one year less than that for the second year, and so on. The sum of the years' digits is easily obtained from the following formula:

$$\text{Sum-of-years-digits} = N(N + 1)/2 \qquad (16\text{A}.2)$$

Thus, for three years, the sum is 6; for four years, 10; for five years, 15; for ten years, 55; and so on. The formula for SYD depreciation is

$$\text{SYD depreciation} = \text{Depreciable cost} \times \frac{\text{Years digit*}}{\text{Sum-of-years-digit}} \qquad (16\text{A}.3)$$

For the truck, the fraction for the first year is 5/15, for the second year, 4/15, and so on. Thus, the first year's depreciation is

$$\text{SYD depreciation, first year} = \text{Depreciable cost} \times \frac{5}{15}$$

$$= \$40,000/3$$

$$= \$13,333$$

*Largest digit first.

16A.6   DOUBLE DECLINING BALANCE (DDB)

The double-declining-balance method is based on a geometric progression for which the gradient is twice the SL depreciation rate. For a five-year property, the SL rate is 1/5, or 20%; for a seven-year property, it is 1/7, or 14.3%; and for a ten-year property, it is 1/10, or 10%. The corresponding geometric gradients for DDB are therefore 40% (2 × 20%) for a five-year property, 28.6% (2 × 14.3%) for a seven-year property, and 20% (2 × 10%) for a ten-year property. The gradient is applied, not to the depreciable cost, but to the book value of the asset at the beginning of each year of depreciable life. Since a geometric gradient will never completely eat up the depreciable cost, this introduces some adjustments for the last part of an asset's life. The following computations for the truck illustrate these adjustments.

Year	Beginning Book Value, $	DDB Rate	Depreciation Expense, $	Accumulated Depreciation, $	Ending Book Value, $
(1)	(2)	(3)	(4) = (2) × (3)	(5)	(6) $45,000 − (5)
1	$45,000	0.40	$18,000	$18,000	$27,000
2	27,000	0.40	10,800	28,800	16,200
3	16,200	0.40	6,480	35,280	9,720
4	9,720	0.40	3,888	39,168	5,832
5	5,832	—	832	40,000	5,000

When the asset was placed in service, its book value was its cost (not its depreciable cost). This is then the book value at the beginning of the first year of use, and, as noted, the book value at the end of one year is the book value at the beginning of the next year. Since the depreciable cost of the truck is only $40,000, the depreciation in the fifth year is just enough to bring the asset to its residual value, at which time it is carried until sold or otherwise disposed of.

An alternate approach is to switch to straight-line depreciation near the end of the depreciable life. At the beginning of the fourth year, the book value is $9,720 and the depreciable value is $5,000 less, or $4,720. For the straight-line convention, the depreciation for the fourth and fifth years of life is therefore one-half of $4,720, or $2,360. For these two years, the previous tabulation would appear as follows:

Year	Beginning Book Value, $	DDB Rate	Depreciation Expense, $	Accumulated Depreciation, $	Ending Book Value, $
(1)	(2)	(3)	(4) = (2) × (3)	(5)	(6) $45,000 − (5)
4	$9,720	—	$2,360	$37,640	$7,360
5	7,360	—	2,360	40,000	5,000

There are more declining-balance depreciation methods than the DDB or 200% DB method. Another common method is the 150% DB method, in which the geometric ratio for computing the depreciation expense is 50% greater than the SL depreciation rate. Thus, for a depreciable life of five years, the gradient would be 30% (1.5 × 20%); for ten years, it would be 15% (1.5 × 10%), and so on.

16A.6 MODIFIED ACCELERATED COST RECOVERY SYSTEM (MACRS)

Since MACRS and its options are mandated by the IRS, MACRS is ultimately the system we have to use to compute the cash flow for income taxes as our studies become more and more refined and definitive.

MACRS rates are based on a residual value of zero, on the declining-balance method, and on certain conventions. Of these, we will use only the mid-year convention. The rates for the six classes of personal property named in Table 16.2 in the body of the chapter are given in Table 16A.1. They apply to the midyear convention.

TABLE 16A.1 Rate Tables for Personal-Property Classes

Year	3-Year	5-Year	7-Year	10-Year	15-Year	20-Year
1	0.3333	0.2000	0.1429	0.1000	0.0500	0.03750
2	0.4444	0.3200	0.2449	0.1800	0.0950	0.07219
3	0.1481	0.1920	0.1749	0.1440	0.0855	0.06677
4	0.0741	0.1152	0.1249	0.1152	0.0770	0.06177
5		0.1152	0.0892	0.0922	0.0693	0.05713
6		0.0576	0.0892	0.0737	0.0623	0.05285
7			0.0892	0.0655	0.0590	0.04888
8			0.0446	0.0655	0.0590	0.04522
9				0.0655	0.0590	0.04462
10				0.0655	0.0590	0.04461
11				0.0328	0.0590	0.04462
12					0.0590	0.04461
13					0.0590	0.04462
14					0.0590	0.04461
15					0.0590	0.04462
16					0.0295	0.04461
17						0.04462
18						0.04461
19						0.04462
20						0.04461
21						0.02231

Note: You will find similar tables for the midquarter convention (one for each quarter) in IRS Publication 537.

TABLE 16A.2 Rates for 5-Year Property Class

Year	Beginning Book Value, $	DDB Rate	Depreciation Expense, $	Accumulated Depreciation, $	Ending Book Value, $
(1)	(2)	(3)	(4)	(5)	(6)
1	$1.0000	0.2000	$0.2000	$0.2000	$0.8000
2	0.8000	0.4000	0.3200	0.5200	0.4800
3	0.4800	0.4000	0.1920	0.7120	0.2880
4	0.2880	0.4000	0.1152	0.8272	0.1728
5	0.1728	—	0.1152	0.9424	0.0576
6	0.0576	—	0.0576	1.0000	0

How were these rates obtained? As mentioned, MACRS is based on the declining-balance method. In Table 16A.1, the declining-balance gradient is DDB (200% DB) for the 3-year to 10-year property classes and 150% DB for the 15-year and 20-year property classes. For the 5-year property class, every dollar would be depreciated as shown in Table 16A.2.

The expenses in column (4) match the rates for 5-year property in Table 16A.1. They are based on DDB, except for years 5 and 6. At the beginning of year 5, there are 3 one-half year periods left—two in year 5 and one in year 6. For straight-line depreciation, each half-year gets one-third of the beginning book balance at year 5, or $0.0576 ($0.1728/3).

16A.8 OPTIONS UNDER MACRS

Under MACRS, there are four ways in which you can recover the cost of your property:

1. Regular MACRS, which was described earlier
2. Straight-line MACRS
3. 150% DB MACRS
4. Alternate MACRS method

For the straight-line option, the eight property classes are the same as for regular MACRS, the residual value is also zero, and the same conventions apply, including the midyear convention.

For 150% DB MACRS, an alternate recovery period is used, which comes closer to the service life than the eight recovery periods for regular MACRS. Residual value is also zero, and the same conventions apply as for regular MACRS.

Alternate MACRS is a straight-line method for assets used in the farming business, for assets used predominantly outside the United States during any tax year, and for other special assets for which you will have to turn to IRS

Publication 534 but which we are not going to pursue further. Throughout this text, we will use only regular MACRS.

16A.9 IRS PUBLICATION 534

The current edition of IRS Publication 534 is handy to have around. All you have to do is send for it. A selection from "Table of Class Lives and Recovery Periods" in the 1990 edition is given in Table 16A.3.

16A.10 COMPARISON OF SYSTEMS

Rates for the various depreciation methods just discussed are compared in Table 16A.4 for five-year property.

16A.11 AMORTIZATION

Intangible property is amortized, that is, depreciated, using the straight-line method over its determinable useful life. Patents and copyrights have useful

TABLE 16A.3 Class Lives and Recovery Periods for Selected Assets

| | | Recovery Period, Yrs. | |
Asset	Class Life, Yrs.	Regular MACRS	150% DB Option
Airplanes	6	5	6
Automobiles	3[a]	5	5
Buses	9	5	9
Computers	6	5	5
Construction equipment	6	5	6
Equipment and machinery for food manufacture[b]	12	7	12
Land (site) improvements	20	15	20
Office furniture and equipment	10	7	10
Trucks, light	4[a]	5	5
Trucks, heavy	6	5	6
Personal property with no class life	—	7	12
Real property with no class life	—	7	40

[a]The recovery period for the 150% DB option is usually the class life. However, there are exceptions for which the class life is actually less than both the regular and the optional recovery period. Why this is so only the IRS can tell you.
[b]There are recovery periods for the assets required to manufacture a wide variety of products. Many, but by no means all, fall into the five-year and seven-year classes.

TABLE 16A.4 Comparison of Depreciation Rates

Year	SL	SYD	DDB	MACRS	MACRS SL Option
1	0.20	5/15	0.400	0.2000	0.10
2	0.20	4/15	0.240	0.3200	0.20
3	0.20	3/15	0.144	0.1920	0.20
4	0.20	2/15	0.108	0.1152	0.20
5	0.20	1/15	0.108	0.1152	0.20
6	—	—	—	0.0576	0.10
Total	1.00	1.00	1.000	1.0000	1.00

lives set by the federal government. For other nonphysical assets, such as franchises, a determinable life must be shown. The amortization expense for spreading the cost of goodwill is not allowed for tax purposes, because a useful life cannot be assigned.

____17
PUBLIC PROJECTS AND REGULATED INDUSTRIES

17.1 INTRODUCTION

You were introduced to public projects in Chapter 11, where we defined and discussed the benefit-cost ratio as the figure of merit most commonly used for evaluating and ranking capital expenditures for public purposes. In this chapter, we take a broader view of projects in the public sector and how these differ from projects in the private sector. In addition, we introduce you to multipurpose projects, which are not unique to, but many of which are found in the public sector, and to regulated public utilities. The latter provide electricity, gas, water, telephone, and other utility services, and are found in both the public and the private sectors. They are subject to regulation by state utility commissions because they enjoy monopoly privileges within the areas they serve and are therefore not subject to the market forces faced by most private-sector entities.

We begin with a discussion of the differences between public and private projects and to the rationale for discounting cash flows rather than using undiscounted cash flow estimates, even though public projects are nonprofit entities.

17.2 DIFFERENCES BETWEEN PRIVATE AND PUBLIC PROJECTS

The major difference between private and public projects was discussed in Chapter 11. For a private entity, only one set of cash flow streams has to be identified, namely, the set consisting of the streams that flow into and out of the entity itself. For a public entity, we are involved with two sets. The first consists of the cash flows into and out of the entity, and the second consists of the cash flow streams that bypass the entity and flow directly into and out of the pockets of the public.

Other significant differences between private- and public-sector projects are commented on below.

Public projects do not pay income taxes. However, this does not mean we can neglect such taxes entirely. If a public project is to replace a private project, the loss in taxes from the private project should be included in the analysis. If a public project is to be in competition with a private project, the fact that the latter pays taxes cannot be neglected if the analysis is to be carried out properly.

> *COMMENT:* The preceding situations are by no means uncommon. Publicly owned power companies compete with privately owned companies in many areas, although each serves specific locales within those areas. The rates charged for power are usually comparable. This often enables the public entity to show a substantial surplus (surplus is to public entities what profit is to private entities), which serves as a relatively painless surrogate for taxes.

Rates of return for discounting cash flows for public entities were discussed in Chapter 14. The rates are generally lower than for private projects due to the absence of risk. Answering to taxpayers for the success of a public project is not quite the same as answering to private investors for the success of a private project. What, for example, is the risk of building a recreation facility? Those who use it will be glad it's there, even if their numbers are far less than the projections on which the project was launched. Those who don't use it will most likely be unaware that attendance is not up to expectations.

Multiattribute analysis plays a larger part in public projects than in private projects. We will meet such analyses in Part IV of this text.

Public projects, like private projects, vary in size from small (a new firehouse) to large (TVA). However, there are more "gigaprojects" (multibillion dollar projects) in the public sector than in the private sector. Consider, for example, such projects as the supercollider; our space launchings; our multibillion dollar defense projects, including the SDI (Strategic Defense Initiative); the gas from coal plant in Beulah, North Dakota, which was to be a prototype for many similar plants for reducing our dependence on imported oil; our interstate highway system; and the Quebec hydroelectric project, which supplies electricity to some of our northeast states.

17.3 DISCOUNTING CASH FLOWS FOR PUBLIC PROJECTS

Why discount? Well, why not? Taxpayers must ultimately pay for public projects. The opportunities forgone by paying taxes include investments on which a rate of return could have been earned. For most taxpayers, such investments would most likely have been new automobiles or new homes and/or home improvements, or corporate and government securities earning modest returns. It therefore seems not only reasonable but also eminently fair to have public projects justify their selection by discounting the estimated cash flow streams that impact on them. If you accept this, you'll probably agree that the discount rate should be close to what most of us would or could earn if we invested funds not needed for taxes. Currently (1992), this is in the range of 8–10% before taxes.

Another rationale often cited was mentioned in Chapter 14. The cash flows identified for projected public projects ought to be discounted at a rate equal to the cost of borrowed funds or, better said, at the rate at which funds could be borrowed if it were decided to do so. Discount rates under this assumption would not differ much from those cited earlier.

In reviewing MARRs for both the public and private sectors in Chapter 14, we saw that federal, state, and local jurisdictions often specify the MARR to be used in economic analyses. Such specifications may also include a range of rates for carrying out sensitivity analyses.

17.4 IDENTIFICATION OF CASH FLOW STREAMS

This is probably the thorniest topic in the analysis of public-sector projects. In the discussion that follows, we distinguish between the two sets of cash flow streams first identified in Chapter 11.

The cash flow streams that flow directly into and out of a proposed project are easily identified. The cash outflows—first costs and operating and maintenance costs—can usually be estimated without difficulty. The cash inflows from user fees depend on estimates of the number of users, which in turn depends on the amount of the fee. Surveys on how the number of users will vary with the magnitude of the fee are often conducted to provide "some realism" for estimates of cash inflows from this source. We say "some realism" with tongue in cheek, since such surveys are notorious for their errors. What people say they will do is often not what they actually do.

For the second set of cash flow streams—those that impact on members of the public, providing favorable monetary consequences for some and unfavorable monetary consequences for others—we have to decide how far to go. If we go the whole way (an impossible task), the monetary benefits to some members of the public would exactly balance the monetary disbenefits to other members of the public.

COMMENT: In Chapter 11 on the benefit-cost ratio, Examples 11.2 and 11.3 cited the benefits and disbenefits to users and nonusers of a proposed highway and bridge improvement but mentioned that a discussion of which benefits and disbenefits should be included in economic analyses for public projects would be left to Chapter 17.

A good place to begin is with a classification into primary, secondary, tertiary, and even more remote effects. Consider first the users of the proposed highway improvement project discussed in Example 11.3. The primary effects are

- Lower gas, oil, maintenance, and repair costs for commuters and other users due to a shorter, safer route.
- Lower medicine, doctor, and hospital bills for commuters and other users due to a safer route.
- Lower payroll expenses for employers paying overtime to employees delayed by frequent traffic snarls and tie-ups.

COMMENT: This brings us to a controversial point. Is the reduction in payroll expenses a disbenefit to the employees? If so, it cancels out the benefit to the employers.

For nonusers, there is a whole host of secondary, tertiary, and more remote effects:

- Gas stations will sell less product, which reduces their cash flow. This secondary effect can be tracked further to wholesalers, refiners, and, ultimately, to crude oil producers, suppliers to the oil producers, and so on, ad infinitum.
- The cash flow to doctors, nurses, and hospitals will be reduced as the number of traffic accidents and fatalities decrease. This secondary effect can also be tracked further to pharmacists, pharmaceutical companies, medical equipment suppliers and producers, and so on.
- An improved highway may require less maintenance than the highway it replaces. This impacts on highway crews and the highway commissions that employ them. This, in turn, may reduce taxes or at least not make them increase as much as they otherwise would.

We could subject almost any public project to an analysis such as the one above and find endless ramifications. A new park will benefit the users, but its first cost and upkeep will also impact on nonusers. Depending on the location of the park, some tax payers may be benefited by an increase in property values, offset in part by an increase in property taxes. On the other hand, again depending on location, some may be disbenefited by a decrease in property values without a corresponding decrease in property taxes.

Similarly, a theater supported in part by state and local government funds will benefit the users, will benefit some nonusers (e.g., adjacent restaurants), and will disbenefit other nonusers who must necessarily share the tax burden.

As you can see, identifying benefits and disbenefits is a murky topic in which common sense and fair and impartial judgment (if there is such a thing in analyzing public projects) must prevail. Some guidelines that make sense are the following:

1. First, identify the primary effects. These are heavily oriented toward users.
2. Next, identify at least the major secondary effects. These will be heavily oriented toward the nonusers.
3. Include the primary effects in the analysis and at least those secondary effects that you and your study group decide should be included. The restaurant owners mentioned earlier might fall into place here.
4. Neglect tertiary, quaternary, and other remote effects.

Once the cash flow streams that directly impact on the public are identified, they must be estimated. This is often as murky a topic as the identification of the cash flow streams themselves. Examples and guidelines on this topic are left to Chapter 20 on estimation.

17.5 SPECIAL CONSIDERATIONS

Other topics that impinge on public projects more so than on private ones include the following:

- Point of view
- Forgotten taxes
- Overcounting
- Shadow pricing

17.5.1 Point of View

A private-sector project focuses on one point of view—that of the investors—although, in today's regulatory environment, other points of view cannot be overlooked. A public-sector project may have many points of view. As individuals, we may feel one way about a proposed public project, but, as participants and members of governmental bodies—villages, towns, cities, counties, states, the nation, and the international community—we may feel differently. Recreational facilities are desirable, but taxes to pay for them are not. Acid rain damages the environment (an example of where an international viewpoint is important), but reducing its effects raises the cost of power. The poor should be helped but not if helping brings them too close physically to the well-to-do. What is best for the nation may not be best for the state or for the local government or for you.

An informed electorate and a power elite less concerned with staying in power than in doing what is best could do much to bring disparate viewpoints together. Are the ultimate costs of living with a contaminated atmosphere greater than the cost of alleviating air pollution now? Answers to this and similar questions are now so mired in studies and restudies and more restudies that points of view that are free from immediate gratification and self-interest have little chance to emerge.

17.5.2   Forgotten Taxes

Forgotten taxes were commented on earlier. The example most often cited in this context is that of the benefits received by state governments for highway improvements. Up to 90% of such costs will, under certain circumstances, be paid by the U.S. government. If only the 10% paid by state and local governments is included in the initial cost, the proposed improvement may show a very favorable BCR. If the remaining 90%, which is a burden on the national population, is included, it may not.

17.5.3   Overcounting

Overcounting is another prevalent error that appears constantly in two forms. The first is double counting. The second is using total costs when incremental costs should be used.

In public-health and accident prevention studies, the hours lost are used to estimate lost revenues from lost production. However, the loss to industry is not the loss in revenues but the loss in net earnings (profits), which is, of course, much less.

A similar situation relates to removing people from the welfare rolls by providing employment in the production of useful goods and services. Assume that the cost of welfare payments is currently $1,000,000 annually. Assume further that meaningful work can be made available, for which the contribution to the production process (payroll costs) will be 50% greater than the welfare payments. The total benefits are not $2,500,000, that is, the reduction in the welfare payments of $1,000,000 plus the contribution to the production process of $1,500,000. They are the latter only, that is, $1,500,000. You either pay $1,000,000 in taxes for welfare, or you buy goods whose price includes the above wages of $1,500,000.

Using total costs rather than incremental costs is probably more prevalent than the preceding error. Total costs are frequently used by the private sector to berate governments for the increased costs of inspections, accident prevention, and environmental cleanup. The incremental costs, as many critics have pointed out, are usually much less and sometimes even negligible.

17.5.4   Shadow Prices

The topic of shadow prices is an important one for projects in developing countries and one at which we can only hint in this text. Such countries have limited resources of materials, skilled labor, management, and foreign exchange. A new venture, which would scarcely impact on an economy like ours or those of Western Europe and Japan, might not be able to attract indigenous resources or foreign exchange unless the prices paid were substantially higher than current market prices.

Skilled labor in developing countries is usually scarce. So is skilled management. A new venture requiring skilled labor and/or skilled management may have to pay higher prices for these factors of production than current market rates. The higher prices might include training costs, the costs of importing and housing foreign skilled labor, the necessity of paying for some costs in scarce foreign exchange, and any combination of the above. The estimated price arrived at is a shadow price. The United Nations (UN) is one of the best sources of information and know-how on shadow prices. If you become involved with cost studies for Third World projects, you should visit the UN for current publications on feasibility studies and project evaluations (2).

17.6 EVALUATING MULTIPURPOSE PROJECTS

The main concern of this section is how to justify each use of multipurpose or multiple-use facilities. The most common examples involve dam projects for which flood control, power generation irrigation, navigation, and recreation, may all play a part. In theory, each purpose must stand on its own; that is, must justify the benefits it produces.

There are two accepted ways of proceeding with such studies. They are referred to in this text as the add-on approach and the cost allocation approach.

The *add-on approach* estimates the cash flow streams for the primary purpose or purposes of a proposed multipurpose project and then prepares an economic analysis for justifying those purposes. If the analysis is favorable, incremental cash benefits and costs are estimated for each secondary purpose to see if it can meet the specified investment criteria. Example 17.1 uses this approach.

The *cost allocation approach* makes each purpose justify itself without reliance on a primary purpose to make it appear cost-effective. If one of the purposes of building a dam is to produce power, the power generation facilities have to be justified by a comparison with facilities producing power by burning fuel oil or coal. This approach is more sophisticated than the add-on approach, as you will see from Example 17.2.

Example 17.1 Add-on Approach Consider a project that has six purposes: (1) flood control, (2) irrigation, (3) power generation, (4) domestic and industrial water supply, (5) fisheries, and (6) navigation. The estimated first cost of the total project is $400,000,000. The present worth of the annual operating and maintenance costs is $80,000,000, and the present worth of the benefits from all six purposes is

$1,000,000,000. (You don't have to know the planning horizon or the MARR, since the present worths have been given to you.)

The conventional BCR is then 2.1, as shown in the following equation.

$$\text{BCR} = \frac{\text{PW of benefits}}{\text{First cost plus PW of O\&M costs}} = \frac{\$1,000,000,000}{\$480,000,000}$$

The present worth of the benefits was obtained by adding up the contribution from each purpose. These were estimated as shown in Table 17.1.

It is estimated that if flood control were deleted as one of the objectives, the first cost plus the present worth of the operating and maintenance costs of what is now a five-purpose facility would be reduced to $398 million from $480 million. This makes the add-on cost of flood control $82 million ($480 million–$398 million). The present worth of the flood control benefits is, from Table 17.1, $110 million. Therefore, the add-on BCR for flood control is 1.3 ($110/$82), indicating that this purpose can be justified.

Table 17.2 gives the present worth calculations and the BCRs for all six purposes. All dollar figures are in millions.

Before you proceed, make sure you understand Table 17.2. The first column of figures is the present worth of the first cost plus the O&M costs without the special purpose; for example, without flood control, the project would cost $398 million, without irrigation, $384 million, and so on. The second column is simply the difference between the total cost of the six-purpose project—$480 million—and the figures in the first column. The third column of figures comes from Table 17.1. As indicated, all six purposes are cost-effective, since all have a BCR greater than 1.

A more sophisticated approach—at least one that some analysts accept as more sophisticated—is the "separable cost-remaining benefits" method of cost allocation, which we refer to as the "cost allocation approach."

Example 17.2 Cost Allocation Approach For this approach, we estimate what a single-purpose facility would cost for each of the six purposes. The results are given in the first column of figures in Table 17.3. These include both the first cost and the present worth of the operating and maintenance costs. The cost of the

TABLE 17.1 Present Worth of Benefits

Purpose	PW of Benefits, in Millions of Dollars
Flood control	$110
Irrigation	550
Power generation	130
Water supply	170
Fisheries	20
Navigation	20
	$1,000

TABLE 17.2 Benefit-Cost Ratios of Each Purpose

Special Purpose	First Cost Plus PW of O&M Costs Without Special Purpose	PW of Add-on Costs for Special Purpose	PW of Benefits of Special Purpose	BCR
	(1)	(2) $480 - (1)$	(3)	(4) (3)/(2)
Flood control	$398	$82	$110	1.3
Irrigation	384	96	550	5.7
Power generation	378	102	130	1.3
Water supply	460	20	170	8.5
Fisheries	470	10	20	2.0
Navigation	470	10	20	2.0
		$320	$1,000	

power plant was based on a coal-burning facility of the same kilowatt capacity as the hydroelectric facility. The cost of the water supply was based on a source independent of a new dam.

The second column of figures comes from Table 17.1. The third column is simply the lower of columns (1) or (2) and tells us how much we can afford to invest in order to obtain a BCR of unity for each purpose. Since there is no way that fisheries and navigation can be structured as single facilities, the justifiable expenditures for these two purposes were arbitrarily taken as identical to the estimated benefits. All dollar figures in Table 17.3 are in millions.

You will recall from Example 17.1 that the total present worth of the costs of this project were $480 million. Of these, $320 million were add-on or separable costs [see column (2) in Table 17.2]. This leaves $160 million for the present worth of the so-called joint costs. The joint costs are prorated to each of the six purposes on the basis of the differences between the justified expenditures of each purpose and its separable costs. The calculations are shown in Table 17.4. All dollar figures are in millions and represent present worths.

TABLE 17.3 Justified Expenditures for Each Purpose

Purpose	PW of Cost of Single-Purpose Facility	PW of Benefits of Single-Purpose Facility	Justified Expenditure for a BCR of Unity
	(1)	(2)	(3)
Flood control	$200	$110	$110
Irrigation	300	550	300
Power generation	130	130	130
Water supply	160	170	160
Fisheries	—	20	20
Navigation	—	20	20
		$1,000	$740

TABLE 17.4 Allocation of Joint Costs

Purpose	Justified Expenditures for BCR = 1	Separable Costs	Difference	Allocation, %
	(1)	(2)	(3)	(4)
			(1) − (2)	(3)/420
Flood control	$110	$82	$28	6.7
Irrigation	300	96	204	48.5
Power generation	130	102	28	6.7
Water supply	160	20	140	33.3
Fisheries	20	10	10	2.4
Navigation	20	10	10	2.4
Total	$740	$320	$420	100.0%

Note: The figures in column (1) come from column (3) of Table 17.3, and those in column (2) come from column (2) of Table 17.2.

The present worth of the joint costs of $160 million is now prorated to each of the six purposes. The results are shown in Table 17.5.

The BCR ratios for the two methods differ substantially, with the add-on approach giving higher BCRs than the allocation approach. However, for the latter approach, the BCRs are still equal to or better than 1. This is not necessarily typical.

You will now ask, "Which of the two approaches should I use?" This depends on the nature of the problem. If the decision to proceed with a project that has one or two main purposes has been made, the add-on approach can be used to justify any additional purposes. If, however, you are

TABLE 17.5 Benefit-Cost Ratio of Each Purpose

Purpose	PW of Separable Costs	PW of Joint Costs	PW of Total Costs	PW of Benefits	BCR
	(1)	(2)	(3)	(4)	(5)
			(1) + (2)		(4)/(3)
Flood control	$82	$10	$92	$110	1.1
Irrigation	96	78	174	550	3.2
Power generation	102	10	112	130	1.2
Water supply	20	54	74	170	2.3
Fisheries	10	4	14	20	1.4
Navigation	10	4	14	20	1.4
	$320	$160	$480	$1,000	2.1

Note: You should have no trouble in tracing these figures, except for column (2). These figures are the product of the allocation percentages in Table 17.4 and the total separable costs of $160 million.

starting from scratch and are in the process of identifying all of the purposes that the project should have, you should use the cost allocation approach.

17.7 REGULATED INDUSTRIES

Today, all business entities are subject to regulation by federal, state, and local governments. The federal agencies that immediately come to mind are the EPA (Environmental Protection Agency), OHSA (Occupational Health and Safety Administration), EEO (Equal Employment Opportunity), and IRS (Internal Revenue Service), whose functions are to set standards and to establish guidelines for pollution, safety, employment policies and practices, and income reporting, respectively. Similar concerns are monitored by state and local governments, sometimes in conflict with federal standards but more often extensions of them. With local governments, zoning provisions can be particularly restrictive on what businesses can and cannot do.

In this chapter, we are not concerned with the general regulations that apply to all business entities but with the special regulations that pertain to public utilities. These are, for the most part, privately owned businesses that furnish the public with telephone, telegraph, gas, water, and power services. They are subject to special regulation because they operate as monopolies— a privilege given them by government because it would be inefficient, that is, an unwise use of resources, to build duplicate (or triplicate, quadruplicate, etc.) facilities to serve a given area with its utility needs.

Public utilities in interstate commerce are regulated by federal and state commissions. Such commissions have the authority to set "fair rates" that limit what public utilities can charge for their services and thereby limit the return they can earn on their investments. The time value of money is very much a part of the "rate-setting" procedure, which is why we devote space to it in this text.

Fair rates are based on a rate structure that allows a public utility to recover its costs and earn a fair return for bondholders and shareholders; that is,

$$\text{Permitted revenue} = \text{Costs} + \text{Fair return} \tag{17.1}$$

Costs include cash disbursements for the cost of the services produced, for operating expenses, and for income taxes. In addition, costs include such noncash expenses as depreciation. Interest on borrowed funds are not treated as a cost, except for evaluating income taxes, but are handled as one component of fair return, in this case, fair return to the suppliers of borrowed funds. The fair return to stockholders is the net income after taxes, including both the earnings retained by the utility and what is distributed as dividends.

Fair return and the rate base (capital investment) on which it is based are discussed in the two subsections that follow.

17.7.1 Fair Return

Chapter 14 on funding defined two sources of funds—creditor financing and equity financing. Equity financing, in turn, was broken down into funds from preferred stockholders and funds from common stockholders. All three sources play a part in the financing of public utilities. The definition of "a fair return," therefore, begins with the dollar magnitude of the cash flows to bondholders, preferred stockholders, and common stockholders. In what follows let

I = The interest payments on bonded debt. This is the fair return to lenders.

P = The dividends to preferred stockholders.

E = The return to common stockholders.

The dollar magnitude of the fair return is then

$$\text{Fair return} = I + P + E \tag{17.2}$$

As mentioned, in this formula, E is the earnings retained in the business plus the dividends to common stockholders.

In Chapter 14, we derived equation (14.1) for the weighted average cost of capital, which is pertinent here, namely

$$i = r_b i_b (1 - t) + r_p i_p + r_e i_e$$

However, for regulated industries, we use the weighted average return before income taxes to creditors and investors, not the weighted average cost of capital to the public utility. The equations for the two concepts are identical except for the term $(1 - t)$; that is

$$i = r_b i_b + r_p i_p + r_e i_e \tag{17.3}$$

Example 17.3 applies this equation to a typical public-utility investment.

Example 17.3   Fair Rates of Return   The estimated initial rate base for a proposed power-generating facility rated at 1,000 megawatts (1 million kilowatts) is $500 million. Forty percent of the funding is to come from bondholders, 10% from preferred shareholders, and 50% from common shareholders. Fair rates of return (feasible rates acceptable to the financial community) are estimated to be 10% on bonds, 12% on preferred stock, and 15% on common stock. The weighted average rate of return, i, is then

$$
\begin{aligned}
i &= r_b i_b + r_p i_p + r_e i_e \\
&= 0.40 \times 0.10 + 0.10 \times 0.12 + 0.50 \times 0.15 \\
&= 0.127 \ (12.7\%)
\end{aligned}
$$

Assuming pending or future approval by the regulatory body, this weighted average and the individual rates of which it is composed serve as the fair rates of return for a study on the economics of the proposed venture.

17.7.2 Rate Base

Many of the utility commissions in the United States define the rate base for any given period of time as the depreciated book value of the assets used in providing services. Working capital, as well as fixed assets (property, plant, and equipment), is usually included in the rate base. Thus, for the first year of a utility's life, the rate base is the initial capital investment (the book value at the beginning of year 1), for the second year, it is the book value of this investment at the beginning of year 2, and so on for the third and remaining years of the utility's life.

Let the initial rate base be B and the depreciation expense for year j be D_j. Then the rate base for the first and subsequent years of operation is

Year	Rate base
First	$B_1 = B$
Second	$B_2 = B - D_1$
Third	$B_3 = B - (D_1 + D_2)$
.	
.	
.	
jth	$B_j = B - \sum_{j=1}^{j=(j-1)} $

To simplify our presentation without doing harm to the concepts behind rate regulation, we use straight-line depreciation in what follows. If the depreciation expense, D, is the same for each year of the utility's life, then

$$B_j = B - (j - 1)D \qquad (17.4)$$

Thus, the rate base for the first year of operation is B, for the second year $(B - D)$, for the third year $(B - 2D)$, and so on.

The dollar magnitude of the fair return for any given year—say year j—and the dollar magnitudes for the three components of this return are given by

$$\text{Fair return} = iB_j = r_b i_b B_j + r_p i_p B_j + r_e i_e B_j \qquad (17.5)$$

As shown, the dollar magnitude of the fair return differs from year to year, because the rate base is not based on the initial investment but on the depreciated value of that investment for each year.

Example 17.4   Fair Returns   For a $500 million investment and the rates used in Example 17.3, the fair return to creditor and equity investors for the first year of operation is as follows:

$$\text{\$, Millions}$$

$$I = r_b i_b B_1 = 0.40 \times 0.10 \times 500 = \$20.0$$

$$P = r_p i_p B_1 = 0.10 \times 0.12 \times 500 = \quad 6.0$$

$$E = r_e i_e B_1 = 0.50 \times 0.15 \times 500 = \quad \underline{37.5}$$

$$\$63.5$$

The fair return of $63.5 million will decline during the life of the utility as the rate base shrinks due to deductions for depreciation. For the sake of simplicity, assume that the entire sum of $500 million is depreciable over a 25-year period. The annual depreciation expense is then $20 million, indicating that the rate base, B_j, shrinks $20 million per year. For the first year, it is $500 million; for the second, $480 million; and so on. In formula form, using the third year as an example, we get

$$B_j = B - (j - 1)D$$

$$= \$500 - (3 - 1)(20)$$

$$= \$460 \text{ million}$$

17.7.3   Permitted Revenue

The permitted revenue was defined in equation (17.1) as the sum of costs plus a fair return for any given operating period. In symbols, this is

$$R_j = C_j + D_j + T_j + I_j + P_j + E_j \tag{17.6}$$

where, for any year j,

R_j = Permitted revenue

C_j = Cash disbursements, that is, cash costs

D_j = Depreciation expense

T_j = Income taxes

I_j = Interest on borrowed debt

P_j = Return to preferred stockholders

E_j = Return to common stockholders

The sum of C_j, D_j, and T_j is the costs, and the sum of I_j, P_j, and E_j is the fair return. The subscript j refers to a specific period or year, since, as we found out, the rate base changes each year and with it the dollar magnitude of at least the following streams—R, T, I, P, and E. D also varies with each year if depreciation expense is not computed on a straight-line basis.

Utility rates are not reduced each year as the rate base for earning a fair return declines. If they did, we, the consumers, would be paying much more during the first year of a utility's life than during its last year. Rather, rates are based on levelized cash flows, that is, on cash flows that have been smoothed by converting them to a uniform annual series. How this is done is covered in the next subsection.

17.7.4 Levelized Income Taxes

Our objective now is to derive a formula for the uniform series T for income taxes equivalent to the variable income tax cash flows throughout the life cycle. The derivation, which is straightforward, is given in Appendix 17A. The result is reproduced in equation (17.7) for straight-line depreciation.

$$T = a[B - D(A/G,i,N)] \tag{17.7}$$

In this formula, a is a constant equal to

$$a = \frac{t}{(1 - t)} (i - r_b i_b) \tag{17.8}$$

where t is the income tax rate.

COMMENT: You should have no problem in following the derivations in Appendix 17A for the levelized income tax, T, and we suggest that you take the time to do so. One reason is that the equations are easily adaptable to a wide variety of situations, including depreciation methodologies other than straight-line and inflationary increases in cash costs.

Example 17.5 Levelized Income Taxes We first calculate the constant a for a tax rate of 0.45 using equation (17.8). The other quantities needed for the computation are found in Examples 17.3 and 17.4.

$$a = \frac{0.45}{(1 - 0.45)} (0.127 - 0.40 \times 0.10)$$

$$= 0.07118$$

The annualized income tax rate, T, for the weighted average rate of return of 12.7% is computed below with the help of equation (17.7). Dollar figures are in millions.

$$T = a[B - D(A/G,12.7,25)]$$

$$= 0.07118[500 - 20(6.548)]$$

$$= \$26.3 \text{ (million)}$$

In words, the uniform series for income taxes, T, of $26.3 million covering a time span of 25 years is equivalent to the set of variable cash flows T_j from j equals 1 to j equals N.

The levelized income tax, T, is often expressed in terms of $1.00 of capital investment, B. The corresponding equation is derived by dividing equation (17.7) by B and simplifying, as shown in equation (17.9).

$$\tau = \frac{T}{B} = a\left[1 - \frac{D}{B}(A/G,i,N)\right] \qquad (17.9)$$

With straight-line depreciation over N years and no salvage value, D/B equals $1/N$. Therefore,

$$\tau = a\left[1 - \frac{1}{N}(A/G,i,N)\right] \qquad (17.10)$$

This is one of several formulations of the levelized tax rate used for regulated industries.

17.7.5 Levelized Permitted Revenue

We are now nearing home base; that is, we are ready for the levelized permitted revenue on which the rate structure for charging users depends. Example 17.6 illustrates how we arrive at its value.

Example 17.6   Levelized Permitted Revenue   The costs of generating power for a public utility can be broken down into the fixed charges, which are estimated as a percentage of the investment, and the operating costs, which vary with output. The fixed charges include the levelized income tax, the capital recovery cost based on the weighted average cost of capital, property taxes, and maintenance costs. The income tax per unit of investment is, by equation (17.10) and by the value of a computed in Example 17.5, equal to

$$\tau = 0.07118\left[1 - \frac{1}{25}(A/G,12.7,25)\right]$$

$$= 0.07118(1 - 0.04 \times 6.548)$$

$$= 0.0525$$

The capital recovery cost for zero salvage value is given by

$$CR = P(A/P,i,N)$$
$$= \$500(A/P,12.7,25) = \$500 \times 0.1337$$
$$= \$66.9 \text{ (million)}$$

This equals 0.1337 per unit of investment (66.9/500). Property taxes are estimated at 1% of the investment, and annual maintenance costs are estimated at 2%. The total annual fixed charge per unit of investment is then 21.62%, as shown below:

Taxes	0.0525
Capital recovery	0.1337
Property taxes	0.0100
Maintenance	0.0200
	0.2162

The operating costs, which vary directly with output, are estimated at $0.02 per kilowatt-hour, or $175.20 per kilowatt-year.

The estimated first cost of $500 million was for a plant rated at 1 million kilowatts. The investment cost per kilowatt is then $500, and the annual cost (including capital recovery) of a kilowatt-year of production is the sum of the annual fixed charges and operating costs; that is,

$$AC = \$500 \times 0.2162 + \$175.2 = \$283$$

Since this annual cost includes capital recovery, it is the permitted revenue. $283 per kilowatt-year is equivalent to $0.032 cents per kilowatt-hour when the plant is operating at full capacity. If this is a lot less than you have been paying don't forget that it covers power generation only (i.e., it does not include transmission and distribution costs) and that no plant runs at full capacity the year round.

This brings us to the end of our discussion on regulated utilities. Computing rate structures for such facilities is an interesting and intricate topic, which we have only skimmed (1). However, we have shown you how this topic relates to the time value of money and encompasses several of the key concepts that we introduced in earlier chapters, such as uniform, i.e., levelized, cash flows and capital recovery costs.

17.8 SUMMARY

This chapter covered three major topics:

1. Differences between private- and public-sector projects
2. Multipurpose projects
3. Public utilities

Public entities do not pay income taxes. There is, therefore, no need to cope with depreciation. Public entities are involved with two sets of cash flows—one set for revenues and costs and the other for benefits and disbenefits. Discount rates for analyzing public entities are lower than for private entities due to lower (or nonexistent) risk levels.

The philosophy behind discounting cash flows for public capital expenditures is sound. The discount rate should at least be what run-of-the-mill taxpayers like you and we could obtain by investing the funds we would have if our taxes did not include the cost of public ventures. As a practical matter, the discount rate should at least equal or approximate the cost of borrowing.

Selecting the cash flows that do not flow directly into or out of public entities should be limited primarily to the users of such entities. Theoretically, the benefits and disbenefits could be tracked ad infinitum, but, if this were done (or could be done), the net benefits would be zero.

Special considerations that impinge on public projects more than on private projects include points of view, forgotten taxes, overcounting, incorrectly touting total benefits or costs rather than incremental benefits or costs, and shadow pricing.

For multipurpose projects, there are two ways of justifying each purpose. The add-on approach looks at the major purpose and then estimates the additional costs and benefits of each secondary purpose. The cost allocation approach looks at each purpose separately. The two approaches produce results that often differ widely. The latter approach is considered the more sophisticated by most analysts, but each one has its place.

Rates for regulated industries, such as public utilities, are set by utility commissions and other regulatory bodies on the basis of a fair return to creditors (interest) and equity investors (dividends and capital appreciation). Fair return is a percentage of book value, which, due to depreciation, decreases year by year. Therefore, the time value of money is used to levelize, that is, to compute uniform series for, income taxes and revenues for setting rate schedules.

REFERENCES

1. Gerald A. Fleischer, *Engineering Economy: Capital Allocation Theory.* (Boston: PWS Publishers, 1984). Chapter 9 has much more on the revenue requirement method for public utilities. However, to become an expert on this topic, you will have to go to the specialized literature on how rates for public utilities are set.

2. *The Initiation and Implementation of Industrial Projects in Developing Countries.* (New York: United Nations, 1975).

PROBLEMS

Identifying benefits and disbenefits

17-1 Why is the benefit cost ratio usually selected as the figure of merit for comparing capital investment options in the public sector? (*Note:* You may have to go back to Chapter 11 to answer this question.)

17-2 Every now and then a suggestion crops up to convert a toll highway to a freeway. A recent example is the Garden State Parkway in New Jersey. Identify the primary and the more significant secondary effects of such a change on users and non-users and discuss its implications with questions such as the following in mind. What are the benefits and disbenefits and to whom do they accrue? Which entities and groups would be benefited and which would be disbenefited? Which of the benefits and disbenefits can be monetized and what data are needed to carry out such estimates? Are those which cannot be monetized, if any, as significant as those that can?

17-3 Suggestions opposite to that in Problem 17-2 are also common. Should the bridges crossing the East River which connect Manhattan with Queens and Brooklyn be converted to toll bridges? Handle this problem as you did Problem 17-2.

17-4 The current toll for a bridge crossing is $2.00. The annual usage is 2,000,000 vehicle crossings and is expected to stay at about this level. However, surveys indicate that if no toll were charged, the usage could increase to 5,000,000 crossings annually. Assuming a straight line relationship (a common assumption but not necessarily the only assumption) between tolls and usage, what would be the estimated annual usage if the toll were reduced from $2.00 to $1.00? Under the same straight line assumption, what would be the estimated total annual dollar benefit to 5,000,000 users if no tolls were charged? What would be the total annual benefit to users if a $1.00 toll were charged?

17-5 Can such projects as the supercollider, the space launchings including trips to the planets, the gas from coal plant in Beulah, North Dakota, and others which are not defense-oriented be justified on monetary or cost-effective grounds? Identify some of the grounds on which they are justified.

17-6 One of the examples in the text mentions that one benefit of shorter less congested highways is lower operating expenses for commercial users, for example, savings in overtime wages paid drivers of commercial vehicles. The text then points out that this benefit, which accrues to employers, is a disbenefit to the employees. How do you reconcile the two viewpoints and which viewpoint, if any, should prevail? Can you generalize the answer to this question so as to cover not only this example but related situations which pose the same dilemma?

17-7 Many corporations are downsizing. Identify the primary effects as seen by the corporations, the employees that have been discharged, the communities most immediately effected, the state and federal governments, and any other entities that, in your opinion, should be considered in assessing the impact of sizable, permanent reductions in the number of employees by major industries.

17-8 Corporation A has announced it will downsize its forces by 10,000 people in the coming year. The total saving is estimated at $300,000,000. The Labor Department of the state in which Corporation A is located estimates that on the average it will take one year for the downsized employees to find new employment and that the costs to local, state, and federal governments in unemployment compensation, food stamps, and other sources of aid will amount to $100,000,000. For Corporation A, is this sum an offset against the expected savings due to downsizing? On whom will these costs fall? Could the $300,000,000 savings reduce prices by a like amount or at least sufficiently to compensate purchasers for higher taxes due to higher unemployment?

17-9 Country A's efforts to reduce air and water pollution could benefit Countries B, C, and so on. Similarly, Country A's refusal to do anything at all, or to do very little, could disbenefit Countries B, C, and so on. The example in the text on acid rain is one such situation. Can you think of any others? Should Countries B, C, and others be asked to contribute to projects which would reduce air and water pollution in Country A and in other countries as well? Should the benefits to other countries be incorporated in economy studies for selecting environmental projects? Discuss your answers.

Special considerations

17-10 A new highway is under review by local and state authorities. There is a possibility of incorporating the highway into the interstate highway system but no efforts in this regard have yet been made. The estimated annual benefits of the project are $4 million and the estimated annual costs (including capital recovery) are $10 million. If the proposed extension were incorporated into the interstate highway system, the federal government would pay 90% of the costs.

    a) What is the benefit cost ratio if the proposed highway extension becomes part of the state highway system?

    b) What is the benefit cost ratio if the extension becomes part of the interstate highway system?

    c) How does the difference in sponsorship effect the dispersion of the benefits and disbenefits?

17-11 The benefits of flood protection projects are (a) savings due to reducing or possibly eliminating the expected damage from floods and (b) increased values of properties previously subject to flooding. Are the savings and the increase in property values additive? Explain your answer.

17-12 A strike shut down the ABC Corporation's manufacturing operation for two months during which ABC reduced its office and other nonmanufacturing staff to a minimum. The loss in sales over the two month period was estimated as $10,000,000. Is this a true measure of what the strike cost ABC? How would you arrive at a more satisfactory estimate?

17-13 You have a choice of going to jail for one weekend on a speeding charge or paying a fine of $100. You decide on jail with the expectation of selling your experience there. You are in luck. A magazine buys your article for $150. One friend says that you made $50 by going to jail, the $150 for the article less the $100 fine. Another says that you made $150 since you did not pay the fine. Who is right?

17-14 You sell goods on commission. Your expenses are not reimbursed. You have spent about $150 promoting the sale of equipment which will bring you a commission of $500. How much more than the $150 you have already spent should you be willing to spend to get the sale?

17-15 Explain the need for shadow pricing to arrive at realistic cost estimates for proposed capital investments in developing countries.

17-16 The official exchange rate for the currency of a West African country is two francs to the dollar. However, to sell some of the goods it produces for export and to buy some of the goods it needs to import the country must resort to barter agreements and to subsidizing local producers. These practices, in effect, circumvent the official rate. A realistic assessment of the "market" or "shadow" rate of exchange is approximately four francs to the dollar. What exchange rate should be used in evaluating a capital project for which foreign goods will have to be imported. Is this a "shadow rate".

17-17 Agricultural production is subsidized in many countries including the USA. In evaluating projects which would increase production (for example, water projects) should the increased output be evaluated at cost, including the subsidies, or at the market price?

Multipurpose projects

17-18 A project has two purposes—Purpose A and Purpose B. The capitalized benefits of Purpose A are estimated at $25 million and those of Purpose B at $15 million. The cost of the entire project is $25 million. This includes both the first cost and the capitalized cost of all annual cash expenses. A project built for Purpose A alone would cost $18 million and one for Purpose B alone, $16 million.

a) Compute the benefit cost ratio of the project.

b) Compute the benefit cost ratios of each of the two purposes using the add-on approach.

c) Compute the benefit cost ratios of each of the two purposes using the cost allocation approach.

17-19 A further look at the project of Problem 17-18 indicates a possible third purpose—Purpose C—which would add $2 million to the costs and the same amount to the benefits. However, Purpose C could not stand alone but would depend on whether one or both of the other two purposes are built. Redo Problem 17-18 incorporating Purpose C.

17-20 A proposed project has two purposes—flood control and irrigation. The first cost of the project plus the capitalized annual cash expenses total $35 million. The capitalized benefits are $40 million of which $25 million is contributed by flood control. A project for flood control only would cost $18 million and one for irrigation alone would cost $24 million.

a) What is the benefit cost ratio of the total project?

b) What are the benefit cost ratios of each of the two purposes using the add-on approach?

c) What are the benefit cost ratios of each of the two purposes using the cost allocation approach?

d) What is your recommendation?

17-21 The Happiness Amusement Park intends to add six new rides to its roster. The total cost of the project is estimated at $9.6 million which includes $8.0 million for the first cost and $1.6 million for the capitalized costs of the annual cash expenses. The pertinent data on which the economy study was based are tabulated below.

Name of ride	Capitalized benefits ($000)	Capitalized cost without ride ($000)	Cost of single purpose facility ($000)
Happy	$4000	$8300	$2300
Giggly	3000	8700	1900
Smiley	3000	8100	2400
Joyous	2000	8400	1800
Glad	4500	8850	3000
Lucky	3500	7600	2100

a) Compute the benefit cost ratio for the project as a whole.

b) What are the benefit cost ratios of each ride using the add-on approach?

c) What are the benefit cost ratios of each ride using the cost allocation approach?

17-22 Suppose the Happiness Amusement Park had budget constraints under which the sum of the first costs and the capitalized costs of the annual cash expenses could not exceed $8 million.

a) Which ride or rides would be eliminated?

b) What would be the benefit cost ratio of the remaining rides using the cost allocation approach?

17-23   A large lake near important urban centers is being contaminated with toxic wastes. The state is now monitoring stringent controls on industrial effluent discharges and other sources of contamination. In addition, it plans to spend an estimated $20 million with four benefits in mind—safer drinking water, wildlife and fish preservation, added recreational facilities, and a science center devoted to research on water pollution. Discuss how the benefits associated with each of these purposes could be estimated.

Regulated industry

17-24   Refer to Equation 17.3 in the text for the fair return on a public utility investment. Why is the return to creditors before tax rather than after even though the interest paid by the utility is deductible for tax purposes? Why is the return to common stockholders before dividends rather than after?

17-25   Wall Electric is building a 500 megawatt steam generating facility. 45% of the funding is to come from bondholders, 25% from preferred stockholders, and the remainder from common stockholders. Fair rates of return are estimated to be 7%, 13%, and 18% on bonds, preferred stock, and common stock, respectively. What is the overall cost of capital, that is, the fair rate of return.

17-26   A public utility has the following bond issues outstanding.

Date of issue	Outstanding amount	Maturity date	Interest rate payable, %
8/1/1972	$10,000,000	1992	6.5
8/1/1985	20,000,000	2005	10.0
6/1/1990	25,000,000	2010	9.0

a) What was the imbedded cost of debt capital (that is, the interest rate on the total outstanding debt) before the issue of 8/1/1972 was redeemed?

b) What is the imbedded cost of debt capital after borrowing $10,000,000 to redeem the 8/1/1972 issue and an additional $10,000,000 to modernize services. The new bonds carry an interest rate of 7.8%.

c) If the utility maintains a debt/equity ratio of 60/40 and if a fair return on equity capital is 12%, what fair return on debt plus equity capital would be allowed?

17-27   A new steam generating plant has just started up. The initial investment consists of the following components.

Land	$20,000,000
Buildings and land improvements	100,000,000
Steam generating equipment	170,000,000
Working capital	10,000,000

  a) What is the rate base for the first year of the utility's life?

  b) Assuming straight line depreciation of 40 years on buildings and land improvements, 20 years on stean generating equipment, and zero salvage value what is the rate base for the second year?

  c) What is the rate base for the tenth year?

17-28   What is the value of "a" in Equation 17.8 for (a) all equity financing, and (b) all creditor financing?

17-29   Suppose a public utility has invested P dollars of equity capital in land for a future power plant site. What is the value of τ, that is, the ratio of the levelized income tax per one dollar of P? What is the value of T, the levelized income tax?

17-30   The fair return allowed by the Public Utilities Commission is 12%. The income tax rate is 40%. Assuming all equity financing and 100% salvage value.

  a) What is the value of "a" (*see* Equation 17.8)?

  b) What is the ratio of the levelized income tax to the initial investment?

  c) What is the levelized income tax payment resulting from adding an initial investment of $20 million to the rate base in a nondepreciable asset such as land?

17-31   The allowable fair return is 11%. Half of the financing is borrowed at 8%. The income tax rate is 35%.

  a) What is the value of "a"?

  b) What is the τ for 100% salvage value?

  c) What is the levelized income tax payment for an initial investment of $20 million?

17-32   A public utility buys a maintenance truck for $50,000 which becomes part of the rate base. Its service life is estimated at 5 years at the end of which it will be sold for an estimated $5000. The fair return is 12%, the debt/equity ratio is 50/50, the cost of debt is 8%, and the income tax rate is 40%.

  a) How much revenue is required to cover the tax payment T assuming straight line depreciation?

  b) How much revenue is required to cover capital recovery?

17-33 Explain in your own words how we compute permitted revenue once the levelized revenues to cover income taxes and capital recovery are computed?

17-34 Redo Part (a) Problem 17-32 assuming MACRS depreciation for a five-year property. The depreciation rates are given in Appendix 16A. (*Note*: Calculate T_j for each of six years using the formulas in Appendix 17A and levelize the tax payments.)

17-35 The fair rate of return is 12%, the income tax rate is 45%, the debt/equity ratio is 55/45, and the cost of borrowed capital is 7%.

    a) What is the ratio τ to cover an investment in a public utility with a life of 25 years and zero salvage value? Use straight line depreciation.

    b) What is the capital recovery cost per dollar of investment?

    c) What is the fixed charge rate (FCR) if maintenance and other costs which are usually estimated as a percentage of the investment amount to 4%.

17-36 Redo Part (a) of Problem 17-35 assuming 20-year property under MACRS. The service life remains at 25 years.

17-37 The FCR (*see* Problem 17-35) of a steam generating plant rated at 500 megawatts and owned by a public utility is 20%. Operating costs other than fixed charges are $20 per kilowatt per year. The investment cost per kilowatt is $500.

    a) How much revenue is needed to cover the annual fixed charges.

    b) What is the total EUAC per kilowatt?

    c) What is the total EUAC for the plant?

    d) What is the levelized permitted annual revenue?

APPENDIX 17A   SOME RATE FORMULAS FOR REGULATED INDUSTRIES

We begin with equation (17.6), for which the meaning of the symbols was given in the body of this chapter.

$$R_j = C_j + D_j + T_j + I_j + P_j + E_j$$

The income tax, T_j, equals the difference between revenues and costs multiplied by the tax rate, t.

$$T_j = t[R_j - (C_j + D_j + I_j)] \tag{17.1A}$$

Substituting the value of R_j from equation (17.6) and simplifying gives

$$T_j(1 - t) = t(P_j + E_j)$$

and

$$T_j = \frac{t}{(1 - t)}(P_j + E_j) \qquad (17.2\text{A})$$

But

$$P_j = r_p i_p B_j \quad \text{and} \quad E_j = r_e i_e B_j$$

It follows from equation (17.5) in the body of this chapter that

$$(P_j + E_j) = (i - r_b i_b)B_j$$

Substituting in equation (17.2A) gives

$$T_j = \frac{t}{(1 - t)}(i - r_b i_b)B_j \qquad (17.3\text{A})$$

or T_j equals aB_j where a equals the constant:

$$a = \frac{t}{(1 - t)}(i - r_b i_b) \qquad (17.4\text{A})$$

For straight-line depreciation,

$$B_j = B - (j - 1)D \qquad (17.5\text{A})$$

so that

$$T_j = a[B - D(j - 1)] \qquad (17.6\text{A})$$

Equation (17.6A) represents a cash flow pattern consisting of a uniform annual series, aB, and an arithmetic gradient series with a gradient of aD. The cash flow pattern is given in Figure 17.1A. The equivalent uniform series is

$$T = a[B - D(A/G,i,N)] \qquad (17.7\text{A})$$

This equation is often expressed in terms of $\$1.00$ of B. Let $T/B = \tau$. Then

$$\tau = a[1 - (D/B)(A/G,i,N)] \qquad (17.8\text{A})$$

Cash flow diagrams for tax payments before levelizing

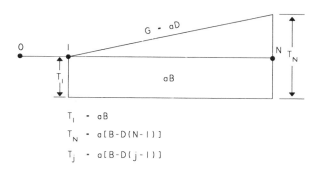

$$T_I = aB$$
$$T_N = a[B - D(N - I)]$$
$$T_j = a[B - D(j - I)]$$

Equivalent levelized cash flow diagrams for tax payments

$$T = a[B - D(A/G, i, N)]$$

Figure 17.1A. Levelized income taxes.

Now let v equal the residual salvage value, S, divided by the constant B; that is, $v = S/B$. For straight-line depreciation

$$D = (B - S)/N \qquad \text{and} \qquad D/B = (1 - v)/N$$

Therefore,

$$\tau = a\left[1 - \frac{(1 - v)}{N}(A/G, i, N)\right] \tag{17.9A}$$

For no salvage value, $v = $ zero and equation (17.9A) reduces to

$$\tau = a[1 - (1/N)(A/G, i, N)] \tag{17.10A}$$

____18
EQUIVALENT RATES OF RETURN AND INFLATION

18.1 INTRODUCTION

So far we haven't had much to do with cash flow patterns involving geometric gradients. We introduced such patterns in Chapter 3 (*see* Figure 3.7) and developed a formula for calculating their present worth in Chapter 6 (*see* Appendix 6A and Table 6.2). However, that's about as far as we've gotten, except for a brief mention of such gradients here and there.

The assumption that in many situations cash flow patterns can be represented as geometric gradients is a common one. The best-known example is, of course, inflation, that is, the effect on cash flow forecasts of rising prices. Other examples include cost reductions due to productivity gains and technological innovations and growth or declines in sales volume and related costs irrespective of price level effects.

We shall see that in these situations it is often more convenient to use an equivalent rate of return rather than the MARR to compute figures of merit. Why and how this is done is the major topic of this chapter.

18.2 EQUIVALENT RATES OF RETURN

Consider once again the cash flow pattern of Figure 3.7, which for convenience is reproduced in the upper half of Figure 18.1. In this figure, the ratio of any end-of-period cash flow, say A_j, to the preceding end-of-period cash flow, A_{j-1}, is $(1 + g)$. The factor $(1 + g)$ is the geometric gradient of the cash flow series. The symbol g, standing by itself, is usually expressed as a percentage representing a compounded annual or periodic change due to any of

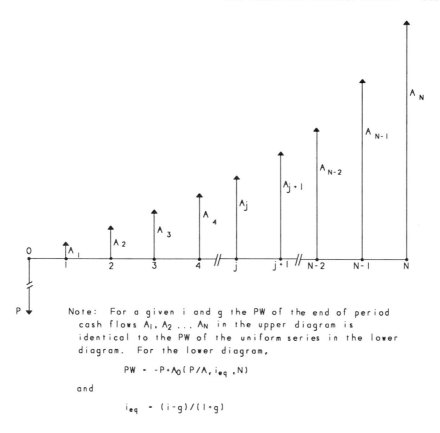

Note: For a given i and g the PW of the end of period cash flows A_1, A_2 ... A_N in the upper diagram is identical to the PW of the uniform series in the lower diagram. For the lower diagram,

$$PW = -P + A_0 (P/A, i_{eq}, N)$$

and

$$i_{eq} = (i-g)/(1+g)$$

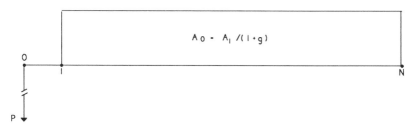

Figure 18.1. Equivalent cash flow diagrams.

the situations mentioned in the introduction. However, like rates of return, it becomes a ratio rather than a percentage in mathematical expressions.

The factor $(1 + g)$ can be greater than 1 or less than 1 depending on whether g is positive or negative. For estimated increases in revenues and costs due to rising prices (inflation) and for estimated increases in sales volume and production costs independent of inflation, the gradient factor $(1 + g)$ is greater than 1. For decreases in sales volume and production costs and for gains in productivity and technological innovations, it is less than 1. However, since economy studies and cash flow estimates may be affected not only by price level effects but also by some or all of the other factors mentioned, the factor $(1 + g)$ often stands for a composite of several geometric gradients.

The equivalent rate of return, i_{eq}, which can be substituted for the MARR, i, in rate-of-return computations for geometric cash flow patterns, is derived below.

Let A_1 in Figure 18.1 equal $A_0(1 + g)$. Then A_2 equals $A_0(1 + g)^2$, A_3 equals $A_0(1 + g)^3$, and so on up to A_N equals $A_0(1 + g)^N$.

COMMENT: In estimating the first cash flow in the geometric series of Figure 18.1, that is, the cash flow A_1 at EOP 1, an estimator necessarily uses quantities, costs, and prices at EOP 0. In other words, he or she first estimates a cash flow A_0 in "today" or "now" or "constant" dollars and then uses the gradient factors that apply to the particular study in hand (inflation, productivity, etc.) to obtain A_1 at EOP 1 (the first cash flow in the series) and all of the remaining cash flows up to A_N.

For the MARR i, the present worth, P, is then

$$P = A_0[(1 + g)/(1 + i) + (1 + g)^2/(1 + i)^2 \\ + \ldots (1 + g)^N/(1 + i)^N] \tag{18.1}$$

Let the equivalent rate of return i_{eq} be defined by

$$(1 + i_{eq}) = (1 + i)/(1 + g) \tag{18.2A}$$

or

$$(1 + i_{eq})^{-1} = (1 + g)/(1 + i) \tag{18.2B}$$

These expressions can be rearranged to give

$$i_{eq} = (i - g)/(1 + g) \tag{18.3}$$

Substituting $(1 + i_{eq})^{-1}$ for $(1 + g)/(1 + i)$ in equation (18.1), we get

$$P = A_0[(1 + i_{eq})^{-1} + (1 + i_{eq})^{-2} + \ldots (1 + i_{eq})^{-N}] \tag{18.4}$$

which can be written

$$P = A_0 \sum_{j=1}^{j=N} (1 + i_{eq})^{-j} = A_0(P/A, i_{eq}, N) \tag{18.5}$$

You can easily verify that the two expressions for the present worth P in equation (18.5) are one and the same by turning to Appendix 6A. It follows that a uniform series A_0 such as that shown in the lower half of Figure 18.1 will, with an equivalent rate of return i_{eq}, produce the same present worth as the cash flow pattern in the upper half of Figure 18.1 with a rate of return i. To obtain the present worth of a geometric series, we can therefore proceed in one of two ways.

1. Substitute A_1, g, and i (the MARR) in the formula given in Table 6.2; that is,

$$P = A_1 \frac{[1 - (1 + g)^N (1 + i)^{-N}]}{(i - g)}$$

In using this formula, don't forget that A_1 equals $A_0(1 + g)$.
2. Substitute A_0 and i_{eq} in the conventional formula for the P/A factor; that is,

$$P = A_0 \frac{(1 + i_{eq})^N - 1}{i_{eq}(1 + i_{eq})^N} = A_0(P/A, i_{eq}, N) \tag{18.6}$$

Using the second approach is simpler than using the first, since it permits us to apply the P/A factors from the interest rate tables in Appendix B to obtain the present worth of a geometric series or to use a hand calculator programmed for financial analyses. Such calculators can handle uniform periodic series but not geometric gradient series.

As mentioned, the gradient $(1 + g)$ can be a composite of several geometric gradients. Suppose, for example, that in an economy study we expect sales prices to inflate by 5% annually and the sales volume, by 3% annually. Letting f stand for the compounded percentage change in prices and q for the compounded change in volume, the inflation factor $(1 + f)$ equals 1.05 and the volume factor $(1 + q)$ equals 1.03. The value of $(1 + g)$ for computing i_{eq} and for estimating the present value of the cash flow from sales is then

$$(1 + g) = (1 + f)(1 + q) = (1.05)(1.03) = 1.08150$$

that is, g equals slightly more than 8%.

COMMENT: It is usually sufficiently accurate to add or subtract percentages directly, that is, for an f of 5% and a q of 3%, to take g as 8%. The reason this works is that estimates of f, q, and other factors that impact on g are seldom more accurate than two, and often no better than one, significant figure. However, it is up to you to decide whether the estimates you have at hand warrant this simplification.

The corresponding value of i_{eq} for an MARR of 12% and a gradient g of 8% is 3.7%, as shown in the following equation:

$$i_{eq} = (i - g)/(1 + g) = (0.12 - 0.08)/(1 + 0.08)$$
$$= 0.04/1.08$$
$$= 0.037 \ (3.7\%)$$

Similarly, if unit costs are expected to increase by 4% due to inflation and by 3% due to increased sales volume with no improvements in productivity, then the gradient is given by

$$(1 + g) = (1 + f)(1 + q) = (1.04)(1.03) = 1.071$$

This gives a value of g that is just over 7%. If, however, we expect a productivity gain, p, to reduce cash flows by 1%, then the gradient becomes

$$(1 + g) = (1 + f)(1 + q)(1 + p)$$
$$= (1.04)(1.03)(0.99)$$
$$= 1.060 \ (6\%)$$

For a value of g of 6% and an MARR of 12%, the equivalent rate of return is 5.7%.

$$i_{eq} = (i - g)/(1 + g)$$
$$= (0.12 - 0.06)/(1.06)$$
$$= 0.0566 \ (5.7\%)$$

There are occasions when the gradient factor $(1 + g)$ equals or even exceeds the MARR factor $(1 + i)$. Substantial geometric increases in estimated sales prices due not only to inflation but also to expected demand plus increases in sales volume to meet demand can trigger such an occurrence. If i equals g, the corresponding i_{eq} is zero, the value of $(1 + i_{eq})$ is 1, and the present value of the geometric cash flow series is

$$P = NA_0 = NA_1/(1 + g)$$

Convenient tables for obtaining the present value of geometric cash flow series for limited ranges of rates of return and geometric gradients are given in Appendix C. The P/A factor in these tables is defined as $(P/A,i,g,N)$, where i is the MARR and g is the percentage from which the gradient factor $(1 + g)$ is derived. The cash flow for these tables is A_0, which, as we know from the previous discussion, is not the estimated value of the first cash flow but the hypothetical cash flow from which all of the cash flows, including that at EOP 1, are derived. An example on the use of Appendix C follows.

Example 18.1   Present Value of Geometric Gradients   An economy study produced the following estimates of annual percentage increases for various sets of cash flows.

Cash inflow from sales	8%
Cash outflow for the cost of goods sold	6%
Cash outflow for operating costs	4%
Cash outflow for interest payments	0%

Sales are impacted by inflation and volume effects. These also impact on the cost of goods sold and on operating costs but, as you will see in later examples, not necessarily in the same proportion. Interest expenses are fixed, and for these the value of g is therefore zero.

For an MARR of 15%, the corresponding $(P/A,i,g,N)$ factors for a life of five years can be obtained directly from Appendix C and are tabulated as follows:

Sales	$(P/A,15,8,5)$	3.8498
Cost of goods sold	$(P/A,15,6,5)$	3.7185
Operating costs	$(P/A,15,4,5)$	3.5919
Interest	$(P/A,15,5)$	3.352

The preceding discussion has shown you how to apply the rate-of-return equations for uniform series to geometric series by substituting i_{eq} for the MARR. Our derivations have only covered the present worth, but we know that the annual worth and the future worth are easily calculated once the present worth is known. To obtain the equivalent uniform series A, make sure that you use $(A/P,i,N)$ and not $(A/P,i_{eq},N)$. Similarly, for the future worth, use $(F/P,i,N)$, not $(F/P,i_{eq},N)$.

The IRR is also no problem. IRR_{eq} is the rate that produces a present worth of zero. Once i_{eq} is known, the IRR is found from equation (18.2A). The benefit-cost ratio, if needed, can be obtained by calculating the equivalent uniform series for the benefits and then by dividing this number by the equivalent uniform series of the costs.

Of all the situations that impact on cash flows and that are usually modeled as geometric series, the most common are those due to price level effects. These are the main topic of the remainder of this chapter.

18.3   PRICE LEVEL EFFECTS

During the 1984 presidential campaign, the Republicans claimed that they had reduced interest rates. The Democrats countered by claiming that interest rates were higher than they had been at the end of 1980. Both parties were right. The Republicans were talking about market rates, which did go down. The Democrats were talking about "real" or "true" rates (inflation-free rates), which did go up.

In Chapter 14, we gave you the components that make up the selection of an MARR. These included a traditional inflation-free rate of 3–5% for sound (low-risk) investments. For rates of inflation estimated at 5%, the corresponding market rates—MARRs before taxes for low-risk investments such as Treasury certificates and premium corporate bonds—are on the order of 8–10%. In the late 1970s and early 1980s, market rates for such investments reached 20%.

> *COMMENT:* You have probably noticed that market rates on low-risk investments come close to obeying the "law of zero return." For before-tax rates of return of 8–10%, after-tax returns are on the order of 5–7%. This doesn't leave investors much to compensate them for losses on the order of 4–6% in purchasing power due to inflation; thus, the law

$$\text{Before-tax rate of return} - \text{Tax rate} - \text{Rate of inflation}$$

$$= \text{approximately zero}$$

Price indices for measuring price level effects are dimensionless ratios that compare the prices of a specified set or combination of goods and services in a selected base period (usually a year) to the prices of the same or a functionally equivalent set at any other period. The index for the base period is usually set at 100. Any year or range of years can be selected as a base. Price indices that go up indicate rising prices and signal inflation for the goods and services represented. Price indices that go down signal disinflation or deflation. In this text, we use the word *inflation* algebraically to cover any price level change, whether up or down.

You may well ask, "Do prices ever go down?" The answer is, certainly. Fuel prices are particularly volatile, but there are many other examples. In the early 1980s, when construction of process and industrial plants fell far below the level of the 1970s, such capital goods as pressure vessels, heat exchangers, compressors, and pumps, as well as engineering and design services for such plants, could be bought at out-of-pockets costs, that is, with little or nothing to cover operating costs. The theory was that a slow demise is better than a quick one, because the patient might still be alive and curable when the market improves.

Price level indices fall into two broad classifications—general indices and specific indices. General price indices are based on weighted averages of hundreds of goods and services. Specific indices are based on one good or service or on a set of closely related goods and services, such as those employed by the construction industry. We briefly look at examples of both types in the next two subsections.

18.3.1 General Price Indices

The two best-known price indices are the Consumer Price Index (CPI) and the Producers Price Index (PPI). Both are compiled and issued by the U.S. government. There are now two CPIs. One is the CPI-W for the "market basket" of goods and services bought by wage earners and clerical workers. It represents about 40% of the population. The other is the CPI-U for all urban dwellers and represents about 75% of the population. The difference between the two is, for our purposes, immaterial. The Producer Price Index (PPI) for capital goods was formerly called the Wholesale Price Index. It measures the level of prices for goods at the wholesale or producer stage.

Values of the two indices are compared in the following tabulation for the base period 1982–1984 equal to 100.

	CPI-U	PPI
1980	82	97
1983	100	100
1989	124	119
1990	131	123
1991	136	127
1992	139	131
Ratio -1992/1980	1.7	1.35
Compounded annual increase, %	4.5	2.5

The smaller increases in the indices for the PPI as compared with the CPI demonstrate the effect of the slowdown in the construction of industrial facilities mentioned earlier on the demand for capital goods.

Estimates of the CPI going back to 1800 are summarized in the following tabulation. The base year is 1967.

CPI (1967 = 100)

Period	Beginning	End	Ratio	Annual Growth, %
1800–1900	51	25	0.49	−0.7
1900–1910	25	28	1.12	+1.1
1910–1920	28	60	2.14	+7.9
1920–1930	60	50	0.83	−1.8
1930–1940	50	42	0.84	−1.7
1940–1950	42	72	1.71	+5.5
1950–1960	72	89	1.24	+2.2
1960–1970	89	116	1.30	+2.7
1970–1980	116	248	2.14	+7.9
1980–1990	248	399	1.61	+5.0
1950–1990	72	399	5.54	+4.4

Obviously, the set of goods and services—the market basket—used in the preparation of the CPI has changed and will continue to change. However, the intent of the index has not. Its purpose is to give us a single figure that best measures the change in the price level of the "basket" of goods and services bought and consumed by our urban population.

The nineteenth century ended with the CPI at half of its value at the beginning of that century. However, there were very substantial and rapid upswings during the War of 1812 and the Civil War, and as substantial although not as rapid downswings after these wars.

The price level changes from 1900 onward are grouped by decades. For two of the decades—1920–1930 and 1930–1940—prices were lower at the end of the decade than at the beginning of the decade. The value of the CPI in 1933 was 39 compared with over 300 today.

For the remaining decades, the price level increased. The decade 1970–1980 showed a rate of inflation averaging 7.9%. The decade 1980–1990 showed a lower rate, namely, 5.0%. However, even rates of 4–5%, which is as good a guess as any on what we might expect in the future, will double the price level in 14–18 years; at 2%, it takes 35 years.

Although the CPI and the PPI are often used for preliminary economic analyses in which it is assumed that all unit prices and unit costs will behave in the same way, specific price indices are used for more detailed and refined studies. Some comments on such indices follow.

18.3.2 Specific Price Indices

There are literally dozens, if not hundreds, of indices that are concerned, not with changes in the general price level, but with specific commodities such as steel and cement, with groups of commodities such as food, clothing, and agricultural products, with wage and salary levels of blue- and white-collar workers, and with commodity and labor aggregates, such as construction cost indices.

One of the most important cash flows for the capital project selection process is, of course, the first cost. If first costs on recently completed projects are available, construction cost indices are used for preliminary estimates of similar facilities. This procedure is illustrated in Appendix 18A, which goes into some detail on how these indices are used in economy studies.

For equipment replacement studies, specific indices for the type of equipment to be replaced, or, if such indices are not available, the PPI can be used for a first approximation of first cost. However, for such studies, it is usually convenient to ask manufacturers for budget prices.

The cash flows covering revenues and costs are, as we know, not only subject to price level effects but also to productivity gains (if any) and technological innovations. Furthermore, sales prices and sales volume and the costs associated with increases in sales volume may show expected increases or decreases due to demand and supply factors, which are independent of price level effects and the other influences mentioned earlier.

For this reason, the expected cash inflows from each major sales product and the expected cash outflows for each major cash cost should be looked at individually. Forecasts of long-term sales trends require careful study to determine what the future may bring with regard to consumer demand and foreign and domestic competition. In all such forecasts, price level effects are an important but not necessarily the only component in estimating cash flows.

There are many sources of price level data to which those who are responsible for economic studies can go—government agencies, industry trade associations, banks and other lending institutions, and private firms that specialize in econometric data, such as Standard & Poor's and Data Resources. Furthermore, most large firms monitor not only the prices of what they sell but also the prices of what they buy. Such data are often the most useful sources of information for cash flow projections.

18.4 EQUIVALENT RATES OF RETURN FOR INFLATION

In the remainder of this chapter, we use the terms "market" and "real" to distinguish between rates that are not adjusted for inflation, that is, for changes in the purchasing power of the dollar (market rates) and those that are (true rates). Market rates are the actual rates with which corporate and other borrowers must deal and which investors must consider in selecting their MARRs. Real, also called "true," rates are estimates of how much more or less a dollar will buy than it did a year ago. Although we—and other authors—refer to these rates as real or true, they are, of course, fictitious but serve as useful approaches to what market rates might be if there were no inflation.

We will also find it convenient to introduce the terms "constant dollars" and "current dollars." Cash flow estimates over a life cycle based on constant dollars (also called "today" or "now" dollars) are not adjusted for price level effects. Cash flow estimates that are adjusted for such effects are in current dollars (also called "then" dollars).

The rate of return equivalent to the real or true rate is often defined as the market rate less the rate of inflation. This is almost, but not quite true. The correct relationship is given in the discussion that follows.

Let i be the MARR, f the rate of inflation, and i_{eq} the equivalent rate of return, that is, the real or true rate.

$$(1 + i_{eq}) = (1 + i)/(1 + f) \tag{18.7}$$

and i_{eq} equals

$$i_{eq} = (i - f)/(1 + f) \tag{18.8}$$

Solving equation (18.7) for i gives

$$i = (1 + i_{eq})(1 + f) - 1$$
$$= i_{eq} + f + i_{eq}f \tag{18.9}$$

If we neglect the term $i_{eq}f$, which is much smaller than the other two, then as a first approximation—and usually a close one—we obtain the following expressions:

$$i = i_{eq} + f \quad \text{and} \quad i_{eq} = i - f \qquad (18.10)$$

Many cost studies are based on "constant" dollars, that is, on dollars whose purchasing power is assumed to remain constant at today's value (or the value at EOP 0) throughout the lives of the capital projects under review. In the past, this simplification was often justified on the basis that any estimate of what the rates of inflation might be over the lives of long-lived projects is at best a guess and would not be significant.

However, for the rates of inflation in effect today—in fact, in effect since the 1970s—and likely to remain with us long into the future, the above simplification and its defense are no longer as serviceable as they once were. Therefore, cost studies are now frequently carried out in current dollars, using market rates, or in constant dollars, using true rates. We use both approaches in Example 18.2.

18.5 PURCHASING POWER

All of us know from experience that positive rates of inflation decrease the purchasing power of the dollar and that negative rates increase it. Those of us who remember the Great Depression will recall how well we did, provided, of course, that we kept our jobs and maintained our salaries, as prices came down.

The purchasing power of $1.00 at the end of N years for various rates of inflation is given by equation (18.11).

$$\text{Purchasing power factor} = \frac{1}{(1 + f)^N} \qquad (18.11)$$

The following tabulation is based on this equation.

Rate of Inflation, f	Purchasing Power of $1.00 in N Years						
	$N = 1$	$N = 5$	$N = 10$	$N = 15$	$N = 20$	$N = 25$	$N = 30$
−5.0	1.05	1.29	1.67	2.16	2.79	3.61	4.66
−2.5	1.03	1.14	1.29	1.46	1.66	1.88	2.14
0.0	1.00	1.00	1.00	1.00	1.00	1.00	1.00
+2.5	0.98	0.88	0.78	0.69	0.61	0.54	0.48
+5.0	0.95	0.78	0.61	0.48	0.38	0.30	0.23
+7.5	0.93	0.70	0.49	0.34	0.24	0.16	0.11
+10.0	0.91	0.62	0.39	0.24	0.15	0.09	0.06

An example on purchasing power follows.

Example 18.2   Purchasing Power   You lend someone $1.00 to be returned in one year with 15% interest. At the time of the loan, $1.00 would buy two of your favorite candy bars. When the loan is paid off, the CPI is 10% higher than it was one year ago. Candy bars have followed the general price trend and are now selling for $0.55 each. Instead of being able to buy 2.3 candy bars ($1.15/$0.50), you can only buy 2.09 bars ($1.15/$0.55). Your net gain in terms of purchasing power is 0.09 candy bars, representing a rate of return of 4.5% This is far below the return of 15% that you felt was due you, both for the risk you took and for forgoing your immediate craving for more candy bars.

In order to have gained the same purchasing power plus the additional 15% you wanted, you would have had to find a borrower willing to pay 26.5% interest.

$$i = (1 + i_{eq})(1 + f) - 1 = (1.15 \times 1.10) - 1$$
$$= 0.265 \ (26.5\%)$$

At the end of the year, you get back $1.265, which will buy 2.3 candy bars ($1.265/$0.55), or exactly the 15% return you wanted for the risk you took and for forgoing current consumption.

With 10% inflation, the purchasing power of $1.00 one year from now is, by equation (18-11), only $0.91. It will only buy 1.82 candy bars ($1.00/$0.55) instead of two.

As indicated in Example 18.1 we need not use the same value of i_{eq} for estimating the present worth of all of the cash flows in an economy study. Furthermore, we need not use the same rate of inflation throughout the life cycle of a capital project. We could select a rate for the first few years of the cycle for which projections based on current rates of inflation might be realistic, and another rate, perhaps a lower one, for the remainder of the cycle. However, for preliminary studies, which are generally deterministic, such refinements are only warranted under more or less extreme conditions, such as the inflationary rates of 18–20% that we saw in the early 1980s.

18.6   APPLICATIONS

Three examples on the application of equivalent interest rates to cost studies follow. The first applies to a retirement fund; the second looks at variable rate mortgages; and the third covers a life cycle cost analysis on a capital project.

If you follow these exercises step by step, you should have no trouble in handling any geometric gradients that come your way.

Example 18.3   Retirement Funds   You are considering investing in a retirement fund into which you will have to pay $2,000 annually until you reach age 65. You are now 35 years old. The fund is expected to earn 10%. If so, at retirement you will receive $329,000.

$$F = A(F/A,10,30) = \$2,000 \times 164.50 = \$329,000$$

The cash flow diagram for this fund is shown in the upper half of Figure 18.2. Its present value is $18,870.

$$P = A(P/A,10,30) = \$2,000 \times 9.437 = \$18,870$$

The rate of inflation is estimated at 5%, compounded annually. (You will recall that the rate for the period 1950–1990 was about this value.) For this rate, the estimated purchasing power of the future value of $329,000 in constant (end-of-year-zero) dollars is $76,120.

$$\frac{F}{(1 + f)^{30}} = \frac{\$329,000}{(1.05)^{30}} = \$76,120$$

Offhand, it doesn't look like a particularly attractive retirement fund. You will pay out $60,000 (30 times $2,000) and get back $76,120 in equivalent purchasing power. However, this way of looking at your return is totally incorrect. The annual payments of $2,000 differ in purchasing power. The last payment of $2,000, for example, has a purchasing power in end-of-year-zero dollars of only $463.

$$\frac{A}{(1 + f)^{N}} = \frac{\$2,000}{(1.05)^{30}} = \$463$$

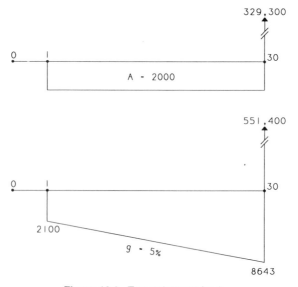

Figure 18.2. Two retirement funds.

For anyone whose income level has at least kept up with inflation, the annual payments become easier and easier to maintain.

You therefore ask yourself what the annual payments would be for the retirement fund shown in the lower half of Figure 18.2, in which the payments increase geometrically with time to keep up with an estimated 5% rate of inflation. If we let A_0 equal $2,000, then the first end-of-year payment is

$$A_1 = A_0(1 + f) = \$2,000(1.05) = \$2,100$$

and the last end-of-year payment is

$$A_{30} = A_0(1 + f)^{30} = \$2,000(1.05)^{30} = \$8,643$$

Both of these payments are in current dollars. Each of them—and all of the payments in between—have a purchasing power of $2,000 measured in constant dollars, that is, in the purchasing power of dollars at the end-of-period zero.

The i_{eq} for computing the present value of this retirement plan is 4.762%, as shown in the following equation.

$$i_{eq} = (i - f)/(1 + f) = (0.10 - 0.05/1.05) = 0.04762$$

The present worth is $31,600.

$$P = A_0(P/A, i_{eq}, N) = \$2,000(P/A, 4.762, 30)$$

$$= \$2,000 \times 15.79$$

$$= \$31,600$$

At the end of 30 years, you would receive the sum of $551,400 in current (end-of-year 30) dollars.

$$F = P(F/P, i, N) = \$31,600(F/P, 10\%, 30)$$

$$= \$31,600 \times 17.489$$

$$= \$551,400$$

In constant dollars, this sum is worth $127,600.

$$\frac{F}{(1 + f)^N} = \frac{\$551,400}{(1.05)^{30}} = \$127,600$$

What was your real or true rate of return on your 30 payments? If our calculations were carried out correctly, it was 4.762%. That they were is shown by the fact that a present sum, P, of $31,600 would grow to a future sum, F, of $127,600 if invested for 30 years at 4.762%.

$$\frac{F}{P} = (1 + i)^N = \frac{\$127,600}{\$31,600} = 4.038 = (1 + i)^{30}$$

Solving for i gives 4.762%.

The next example applies to mortgage payments and shows how these could be structured to accommodate your pocketbook by adopting a payment plan that incorporates a geometric series.

Example 18.4 Mortgages You buy a house for $140,000, paying $40,000 down. The remainder is covered by a mortgage for $100,000. Two payment options are offered to you. The first is a conventional 12% mortgage. The term is 30 years. Payments are monthly for 360 months. The nominal interest rate is 12% annually or 1% per month, which means that you are actually paying 12.7% annually [$(1.01)^{12}$]. For a straight mortgage, the monthly payments are $1,029. This figure comes from the formula for P/A.

$$A = P(A/P,i,N) = \$100,000(A/P,1,360)$$

$$= \$100,000 \times 0.01029 = \$1,029$$

The second option is a 12% mortgage, for which the initial monthly payment is set at about $800 because you cannot or do not want to pay any more but the payments increase geometrically over the life of the mortgage. For A_0 equal to $800, the i_{eq} is 0.745% per month. This value is derived from the following equation:

$$\frac{P}{A_0} = (P/A,i_{eq},360) = \frac{\$100,000}{\$800} = 125$$

If your calculator won't handle this equation, that is, won't give you a value for the i_{eq} because of too many periods (360), don't take our word for the value of i_{eq} of 0.745% but check it as follows.

$$(P/A,i_{eq},N) = \frac{(1 + i)^N - 1}{i(1 + i)^N}$$

$$= \frac{(1.00745)^{360} - 1}{(0.00745)(1.00745)^{360}}$$

$$= 125$$

For an i of 1% per month and an i_{eq} of 0.745% per month, the value of g is 0.253% per month.

$$(1 + g) = \frac{(1 + i)}{(1 + i_{eq})} = \frac{1.010}{1.00745} = 1.00253$$

The first payment at EOM 1 is therefore $802 ($800 × 1.00253), and the last payment at EOM 360 is $1,986 ($800 × $(1.00253)^{360}$). If your earnings keep up with inflation, you should have no difficulty in paying this sum.

The next example covers many of the situations that can arise in a real-life study: revenues for which the geometric gradient differs from that for costs, costs that move with the general price level, costs that do not move with the general price level, accelerated depreciation rates, and income taxes. For ease of presentation, the study covers only three years, but the approach used can be expanded to any number of years and any mix of situations. Other simplifying assumptions, such as no salvage value and no working capital, should not concern you, since you already know how to incorporate these end-of-period cash flows into economic studies. Furthermore, you also know how to scrap the end-of-year convention and to substitute monthly or continuous cash flows wherever you think this is necessary.

Example 18.5   A Capital Project   Consider an investment opportunity with a first cost of $150,000 and a salvage value of 0. The revenues for its three-year life are estimated to increase 7% annually due both to inflation and to an increase in sales prices and volume that are not subject to inflation. The costs other than depreciation and income taxes fall into two groups. One group, the cost of goods sold (*see* Chapter 2 if you've forgotten where this cost is found on an income statement), is estimated to increase 8% annually due both to inflation and to increased demand. The other group of costs, operating expenses, is expected to show no greater increase than the general price level, that is, 5%. The depreciation rate is the MACRS (modified accelerated cost recovery system) for three-year property for which the depreciation rates are 0.3333, 0.4444, 0.1481, and 0.0742 for years 1, 2, 3, and 4, respectively (we will round these rates out to 33%, 44%, 15%, and 8% in the computations that follow). The fourth year comes into the analysis because of the half-year convention (*see* Appendix 16A).

The base estimates for revenues and costs in EOY 0 or "now" dollars are in the first column of Table 18.1. The remaining columns show the estimated cash flows for each of the four years of the life cycle. All cash flows are in thousands of dollars.

The combined income tax rate is 40%, and the MARR is 30% before tax. For the MARR after tax, we multiply 30% by $(1 - t)$, where t is 40%. This gives 18%.

TABLE 18.1   Pro Forma Income and Cash Flow Statement

Description	Base Estimate	Estimated Cash Flows			
		Year 1	Year 2	Year 3	Year 4
Revenues (7%)	$1,000	$1,070	$1,145	$1,225	—
Cost of goods sold (8%)	700	756	816	882	—
Operating expenses (5%)	200	210	221	232	—
Income before depreciation and income taxes	100	104	108	111	—
Depreciation	—	33	44	15	$8
Net income before taxes	—	71	64	96	−8
Income taxes	—	−28	−26	−38	+3
Net income after taxes	—	43	38	58	−5
Plus depreciation	—	33	44	15	8
Net cash flow	—	76	82	73	3

The diagram for the cash flows before taxes is given in Figure 18.3. The equation for the NPV is as follows.

$$\text{NPV} = \$104(P/F,30,1) + \$108(P/F,30,2) + \$111(P/F,30,3) - \$150$$
$$= \$46$$

The IRR can be obtained by trial and error or by directly using a hand calculator. Its value is 50%.

An alternative approach for calculating the NPV is to use the base estimate and equivalent rates of return. These rates are computed in the following equations for each set of before-tax cash flow streams.

$$i_{eq}, \text{ revenues } = (i - g)/(1 + g) = 0.23/1.07 = 21.5\%$$
$$i_{eq}, 8\% \text{ costs } = (i - g)/(1 + g) = 0.22/1.08 = 20.4\%$$
$$i_{eq}, 5\% \text{ costs } = (i - g)/(1 + g) = 0.25/1.05 = 23.8\%$$

The NPV is then

$$\text{NPV} = \$1,000(P/A,21.5,3) - \$700(P/A,20.4,3)$$
$$- \$200(P/A,23.8,3) - \$150$$
$$= \$2,058 - \$1,465 - \$397 - \$150 = \$46$$

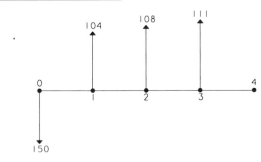

Before-tax cash flow

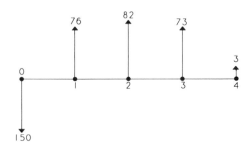

After-tax cash flow

Figure 18.3. Cash flow diagrams for Example 18.5.

What, you may ask, is the advantage of using equivalent rates? It was just as much work, if not more, to compute the NPV using such rates as to do it directly. We are not going to dwell on this point, except to say that you should know how to handle equivalent rates and that, when you are dealing in studies with life cycles of 20–25 years or more, equivalent rates often provide a convenient shortcut, particularly, as you will see, for before-tax calculations.

Our next task is to compute the after-tax NPV for an MARR of 18%. The cash flow diagram is given in Figure 18.3, and the NPV is given by

$$NPV = \$76(P/F,18,1) + \$82(P/F,18,2) + \$73(P/F,18,3) + \$3(P/F,18,4) - \$150$$
$$= \$18$$

The equivalent rates of return for the alternate approach are computed as follows:

$$i_{eq}, \text{ revenues} = (i - g)/(1 + g) = 0.11/1.07 = 10.3\%$$
$$i_{eq}, 8\% \text{ costs} = (i - g)/(1 + g) = 0.10/1.08 = 9.3\%$$
$$i_{eq}, 5\% \text{ costs} = (i - g)/(1 + g) = 0.13/1.05 = 12.4\%$$

The corresponding present values are

$$PV, \text{ revenues} = \$1,000(P/A,10.3,3) = \$2,473$$
$$PV, 8\% \text{ costs} = -\$700(P/A,9.3,3) = -\$1,765$$
$$PV, 5\% \text{ costs} = -\$200(P/A,12.4,3) = -\$477$$

Because we are using MACRS for depreciation, the income tax flows do not form a geometric series. The PV of these cash flow streams must therefore be computed as shown:

$$PV, \text{ taxes} = -\$28(P/F,18,1) - \$26(P/F,18,2) - \$38(P/F,18,3)$$
$$+ \$3(P/F,18,4)$$
$$= -\$63$$

This gives us all of the present worths that we need for computing the NPV.

$$NPV = \$2,473 - \$1,765 - \$477 - \$63 - \$150 = \$18$$

You again have reason for complaint. It was easier to get the NPV the first way. What fouled things up was the fact that income taxes with MACRS do not fall into a convenient geometric or uniform series, as they would with straight-line depreciation. All we can do is to remind you again that equivalent rates of return are one of the tools that you should have in your repertoire and that they often come in handy for projects with long life cycles, involving not only inflation but also other factors that can best be expressed as geometric series.

The IRR after taxes is 26%, as you should confirm. This comes within hailing distance of the IRR before taxes multiplied by $(1 - t)$, where t is the tax rate.

$$\text{IRR after tax} = \text{IRR before tax } (1 - t)$$
$$= 50 \ (1 - 0.4) = 30\% \ \text{(approximately)}$$

This concludes our presentation of equivalent rates of return and, except for one chapter on the criticisms that have been leveled against the discounted cash flow method, completes Part II of our text.

18.7 SUMMARY

The emphasis in this chapter is on equivalent rates of return and their application to geometric gradient series. Such series are convenient models for estimating the effect on cash flows of inflation, productivity gains, technological innovation, and sales volume and price changes independent of price level effects.

Equivalent rates of return allow us to convert a set of cash flows that increase or decrease geometrically into an equivalent uniform series for which the cash flow is based on current estimates, that is, estimates at EOP 0. In short, we can replace the following formula for present worth,

$$P = A_1 \frac{[1 - (1 + g)^N (1 + i)^{-N}]}{(i - g)}$$

with a much simpler formula, namely

$$P = A_0(P/A, i_{eq}, N)$$

in which $(1 + i_{eq})$ equals $(1 + i)/(1 + g)$.

Cash flow estimates are often subject to more than one situation, which can best be approximated as a geometric gradient. If so, the gradients are combined into one for substitution in the preceding formulas.

One of the more common applications of geometric gradients is for inflation, that is, for price level effects. With inflation, a dollar today can buy more than a dollar tomorrow and less than a dollar yesterday.

Changes in purchasing power are measured by price indices that fall into two broad classifications—general indices and specific indices. The best known of the general indices are the Consumer Price Index (CPI) and the Producers Price Index (PPI). There are numerous specific indices that track prices and that are used to estimate particular cash flows.

For preliminary studies, the CPI is often applied to all cash flow forecasts. However, as studies are refined, this simplification is replaced with more sophisticated estimates on which direction each major cash flow might take.

SUGGESTED READING

1. G. A. Fleischer, *Engineering Economy, Capital Allocation Theory* (Belmont, CA: Wadsworth, 1984). Chapter 10, Appendix A on index numbers is an excellent dissertation on types of index numbers and the methods used for computing them.

PROBLEMS

18-1 Test your algebraic skills once again by showing that the equation for the present worth of a geometric series in Table 6.2 becomes $P = NA_0$ for g equal to i.

18-2 Get familiar with the factors in Appendix C by considering the following questions.

a) Do we multiply A_0 or A_1 by these factors to get the present worth of a geometric series?

b) Why is the first line (the line for $N = 1$) in each of the tables of Appendix C the same for all values of g?

c) Why is the column for which g equals i in all of the tables an arithmetic progression. What is the value of G for this progression?

18-3 At Montclair Marbles, the cost of goods sold is expected to rise 3% due to inflation and 5% due to increased sales volume.

a) What is the gradient g?

b) What is the i_{eq} for this cash flow stream for an MARR of 10%?

18-4 For Kim Cosmetics, sales prices are expected to increase by 7% annually and sales volume by 5% annually.

a) What is the gradient g?

b) If the MARR is 15%, what is the i_{eq} for the cash inflow due to sales?

18-5 Norton's Neckties is expecting cost increases of 5% due to inflation and 9% due to increased sales volume. However, they are also predicting a productivity gain of 2% due to new quality control procedures.

a) What is the gradient g?

b) What is the i_{eq} of this cash flow stream if the MARR is 10%?

c) Calculate the P/A factor for this i_{eq} for a planning horizon of 10 years.

18-6 TCP Inc. commanded a price of $500 per day for its management consulting services in 1970 when the CPI was 37. What would be the charge for the same service in 1990 if TCP's pricing had kept current with the CPI? (Use Table 18.1A.)

18-7 Mr. Johnson was hired by Leaf Inc. in 1975 at a salary of $1,000 per month. At that time the CPI was 51.

a) If his salary had "kept up with inflation", what would his monthly salary be in 1988 at which time the CPI was 118?

b) Johnson's actual salary in 1988 was $4,000 per month. What is the gradient *g* for this increase?

18-8 If you are now fully employed and have been for some time, compare the ratio of your current and your old salary with what has happened to the CPI. How much better have you done than the "law of zero return"?

18-9 Has the growth rate of the per capita GDP (Gross Domestic Product) over the past ten years kept pace with the CPI? Answer the same question for the last five years. (NOTE: You will have to do a little research to answer these questions.)

18-10 There are four construction cost indices in Table 18.1A. In addition, the CPI is also shown. Would it be unreasonable to use the CPI as a measure of what has happened to construction costs over the period shown in the above table? Justify your answer.

18-11 Why do we call the inflation-free rate of return the real or true rate? To what do the words "true" or "real" relate?

18-12 The MARR currently used by a firm is 17%. The general rate of inflation is 7%. What is the firm's real or true rate of return using

a) The exact formula developed in the text?

b) The approximate formula?

18-13 You expect the CPI to increase an average of 5% each year for the next few years. Your investment aim is a true rate of return of 5%. What do you expect this true rate to do for you? What would be your MARR?

18-14 You invest $34,000 at EOY 0. Your "real" MARR is 10%. The rate of inflation is estimated at 8% annually for the next 4 years.

a) What is the future worth of your investment at EOY 4 based on the "real" MARR.

b) What is its future worth for the "market" MARR?

c) How many goods and services expressed in today's dollars will the future worth you obtained in (b) buy?

18-15 The cash flow table shown below is an estimate of cash flows not adjusted for inflation. The MARR not including an estimate for inflation is 10%. The estimated rate of inflation is 5%.

EOY	Cash flow
0	$ – 5,000
1	3,000
2	3,000
3	3,000
4	3,000

a) Calculate the present worth using the "true" MARR.

b) Adjust the cash flows for inflation and calculate the present worth using the "market" MARR. Treat each cash flow separately applying the proper P/F factor.

c) Calculate the present worth using the formula for the geometric series in Table 6.2.

d) Check your answer with Appendix C using 15% for the MARR.

18-16   What sum of money at EOY 30 will have the same purchasing power as $60,000 today if inflation averages 5% annually over the next 30 years? How much would a couple have to set aside at the end of each year for 30 years to reach this sum if they could invest their funds at 10% before taxes? The income tax rate is 30%.

18-17   Suppose the income of the couple in Problem 18-16 keeps pace with inflation, that is, increases 5% per year for 30 years. Suppose, further, that the couple wants to pay the same proportionate share of their income each year to accumulate the sum arrived at in Problem 18-16. Compute the following payments.

a) The first payment at EOY 1.

b) The payment at EOY 15.

c) The last payment at EOY 30.

18-18   A proposal has an initial cost of $4000. Net cash flows before taxes are estimated at $1,700 per year for three years in today's dollars. An MARR of 20% before taxes has been selected in anticipation of a 10% annual rise in inflation for at least the next three years. Use the present worth to determine whether or not the proposal should be accepted.

18-19   You are given two proposals of which you have to select one. Proposal A is in constant dollars, that is, the annual operating costs do not include an allowance for inflation. For Proposal B, the net operating costs include an adjustment for inflation which, by happenstance, just balances the annual cost reductions if these costs were expressed in constant dollars. If the "market" MARR is 20% and inflation is expected to run 8% per year which proposal should you select? Use annual worth analysis.

	Proposal A	Proposal B
Initial cost	$75,000	$100,000
Annual operating cost	$40,000	$25,000
Life, years	7	5

What is the present worth of the two proposals?

18-20   Two configurations—A and B—for a metal processing by-product recovery system are being evaluated.

	EOY	A	B
Investment ($000)	0	−75	−90
Annual savings ($000)	1 to 5	25	27
Salvage value ($000)	5	0	20

Inflation is estimated at 4% annually for all future cash flows including the salvage value. The income tax rate is 40% on operating income and 30% on gains due to disposal of assets. The MARRs, which include an allowance for inflation, are 15% before taxes and 9% after taxes.

a) Compare the present worths before taxes of the two proposals.

b) Compare the IRRs before taxes of the two proposals.

c) What are the after-tax present worths? Assume that both investments are depreciated over a five year period using straight line depreciation.

d) What are the after-tax IRRs?

18-21   If you did Problem 18-20 correctly you would have found that the present worths of the two options are fairly close but favor Proposal A. Are there any reasons why, based on monetary considerations alone, you might favor Proposal B?

18-22   Two projects—A and B—are being considered for investment. The cash flow data in today's dollars are as follows.

	EOY	A	B
Investment ($000)	0	−100	−165
Annual savings ($000)	1 to 4	30	60
Salvage value ($000)	4	40	50

Which project should be selected given an after-tax MARR of 11% including inflation? Base your analysis on each investment qualifying as 3-year MACRS property. The tax rate is 40% for both operating income and gains on disposal of assets. The annual rate of inflation is expected to be 5% on all future cash flows including salvage value. Use present worth analysis.

18-23 TCP Inc. is considering buying one of two machines. Data on cash flow in today's dollars and on service lives are given below.

	Machine A	Machine B
Investment	$100,000	$150,000
Annual operating costs	$30,000	$15,000
Salvage value	$10,000	$12,000
Service life, years	5	7

Although the estimated service lives differ both machines qualify as five-year MACRS property and both qualify for an investment tax credit of 3% on the total investment. The average annual rate of inflation is estimated at 6%. The tax rate for both income and gains on disposal of assets is 40%. The selected after-tax MARR is 15% including inflation. Use annual worth analysis to recommend a selection.

18-24 Your firm is convinced of the desirability of a new piece of equipment which would help reduce annual costs. It requires an immediate investment of $150,000 and would provide annual net savings of $35,000 in the first year, rising by $5,000 per year, at today's prices. The service life is estimated at six years and the equipment qualifies as a five-year MACRS property. It is anticipated that at EOY 6 the equipment would be worth $15,000 at today's prices.

As an alternative to buying your firm could rent the equipment for six years at $30,000 per year. The lease payments would be made at the beginning of each annual period and are not subject to inflation. The tax rate is 50%.

Compare the two options on an after-tax basis. Assume all future cash flows, except lease payments, are subject to inflation at an estimated annual rate of 6%. The tax rate is 50% and the after-tax MARR not adjusted for inflation is 10%.

APPENDIX 18A CONSTRUCTION COST INDICES

18A.1 INTRODUCTION

The more familiar construction cost indices are compared in Table 18A.1, not only with each other, but also with the CPI. All are based on pricing certain selected market baskets made up of goods and services that enter into construction projects.

TABLE 18A.1   Construction Cost Indices

Index	Department of Commerce Composite	ENR Construction	ENR Building	Chemical Engineering Plant Cost	CPI
Where found	Survey of Current Business	ENR McGraw-Hill	ENR McGraw-Hill	Chemical Engineering McGraw-Hill	—
Applications	Composite	Civil projects	Buildings	Chemical plants	—
Base	1985	1985	1985	1985	1985
Indices					
1970	34	32	35	39	37
1975	53	53	54	56	51
1980	85	79	81	80	77
1985	100	100	100	100	100
1986	102	103	102	98	104
1987	104	105	105	99	112
1988	110	108	107	115	118
1989	112	110	108	119	117
1990	115	113	112	120	124
1991	116	115	113	122	128
1992	117	119	115	121	131
Ratios					
1980/1970	2.51	2.37	2.33	2.07	2.14
1990/1970	3.38	3.53	3.45	3.08	3.35
1992/1970	3.44	3.72	3.29	3.10	3.54
Annual Rate, %					
1970–1980	9.6	9.0	8.8	7.5	7.9
1980–1990	3.0	3.6	3.3	4.1	4.9
1970–1992	5.8	6.2	5.6	5.3	5.9
Adjustments					
Productivity	No	No	No	Yes	—
Technology	No	No	No	No	—

18A.2   TYPES OF CONSTRUCTION COST INDICES

Some construction cost indices contain many items, and some contain few. The former include weighted averages of process and industrial equipment, construction materials, labor, and supervision. The latter consist of weighted averages of a few typical construction materials (steel, cement, lumber) and construction labor. There is considerable evidence that an index based on a few selected items is as good as one based on many items. One example is an index with just two components—labor and steel—in which the cost of labor is weighted at 70% and steel at 30%. It finds its widest applications in country-to-country comparisons of construction cost indices and works reasonably well for preliminary estimates.

Table 18A.1 shows a rather close correspondence, not only among the various construction cost indices, but also between these indices and the CPI.

The construction cost index that shows the smallest change is the Chemical Engineering Plant Cost Index, which, for the period 1970–1992, increased 5.7% annually as compared with approximately 7% for the other indices. However, this index includes a labor productivity improvement factor of about 2–2.5%, compounded annually. If we assume as a rough approximation that labor is about one-third of construction costs, then an increase in labor productivity of 2.5% eases the effect of inflation by about 1%. Adding 1% to the Chemical Engineering Plant Cost Index brings it in line with the other indices.

18A.3 USING CONSTRUCTION COST INDICES

There are many cautions to keep in mind when you are using construction cost indices. A brief review of these follows.

18A.3.1 Using the Proper Index

Construction cost indices for major civil projects should not be used for process and industrial plant facilities. The converse is, of course, also true.

Civil projects include roads, highways, tunnels, bridges, sewer systems, water systems, and the like. Process plants are facilities that convert materials into saleable products through chemical processing. Typical examples are refinery and chemical units for which most of the processing equipment is located outdoors. Industrial plants convert materials into saleable products through mechanical processing. Typical examples are power plants, automobile assembly plants, and food processing plants. Usually, a substantial part of these facilities is housed.

The above differences and distinctions have many exceptions (food processing, for example, involves both chemical and mechanical processing) but are nevertheless valid when you are selecting a cost index from among those in Table 18A.1 and others that are available.

18A.3.2 Extrapolation

Most experts agree that construction cost indices should not be used for extended projections backward or forward. Four to five years is generally considered the limit. Two to three years is better yet.

18A.3.3   Limitations

There are many limitations. A construction cost index generally does not correct or adjust for any of the following:

Process changes
Technological advances
Learning effects
Labor productivity
Effect of supply and demand

Technological changes are of two types, often referred to as "process changes" and "technological advances." Process changes include the many improvements and the more economical designs that result from operating and maintenance experience.

Technological advances are major breakthroughs in how to produce a given product. It is not unusual for an old and well-known process to be replaced by a new one that requires less capital investment for producing the same quality and quantity of an end product. In addition, it may show lower operating and maintenance costs. If the old process cannot be upgraded to show similar cost improvements, it is no longer a viable candidate for consideration in cost studies.

Learning effects refers to repetitive design and construction projects for which the mere fact of having built a particular facility once makes it easier and cheaper to build a duplicate (or near duplicate), and cheaper yet to build a triplicate. However, such cost reductions flatten out as the number of duplicate units increases.

Learning effects and process changes are often difficult to differentiate. This is also true to a lesser extent for process changes and technological advances. In Chapter 18, we lump these three items together and refer to them as "technology improvements."

Labor productivity has already been mentioned, and the adjustment made in one of the indices in Table 18A.1 has been described.

The last item listed—the effect of supply and demand—is often neglected but is particularly important in the short term. From 1981 to 1984, the prices of many equipment and material items declined due to lack of demand. As mentioned, some capital goods were sold for out-of-pocket costs and so were engineering services, particularly by firms engaged in designing process and industrial plants.

We wrap up this subsection on limitations by looking at one of the oldest construction cost indices—the ENR Construction Cost Index. This index consists of four items, weighted as follows:

Structural steel	2.5	tons
Cement	1.128	tons
Lumber	1088	board feet
Common (unskilled) labor	200	manhours

If the total price of these items changes from $5,000 at the end of one year to $5,200 at the end of the next year, the index will have gone up proportionately, that is, by the ratio of 1.04 (5,200/5,000).

The index does not correct for the fact that the relationship (the weighting) among the four items has changed over the years. Nevertheless, the index works. This is indicated by comparing it with other indices in Table 18A.1. One of these, the Chemical Engineering Plant Cost Index, is made up of over 100 items. Nevertheless, the two indices are close when we allow for the fact that the latter has an adjustment for gains in productivity.

18A.3.4 Location Indices

An inflation index should not be confused with a location index. At any given time, material and labor costs differ from one location to another. This applies not only to differences in prices between one country and another but also to changes within a country, particularly one as large and diversified as the United States. (See the list of references in Chapter 20 for where to go for location indices.)

18A.3.5 Foreign Indices

All industrial nations now publish construction cost indices. These must be consulted for studies on capital projects outside the United States. (You will also find references of where to find foreign indices in Chapter 20.)

COMMENT: There was a story going around in the early 1980s— probably apocryphal—that one of our major engineering contractors bid a fixed price on a multiunit, billion dollar petrochemical plant in the Middle East by tripling the cost of a similar plant in the United States and then adding an additional 25% to cover overhead and profit. We have no information on the results, but the contractor is still in business.

18A.4 AN EXAMPLE

An example of the application of construction cost indices follows.

Example 18A.1 First-Cost-Estimates It's 1984. Your company has a cost study underway for a new industrial facility that is similar in all significant respects to one built two years ago. (We selected 1984 rather than a more recent year because it provides a good example of how much inflation rates can vary in a two- to three-year period.) As a first approximation, the study team decides to use location and construction cost indices to obtain a preliminary estimate of what the first cost might be one year from now.

The location index of the old plant two years ago (1982) was 102. (The reference base of 100 for location indices for process plants is usually the U.S. Gulf Coast.)

For the new location, this index two years ago was 98. If the plant had been built there, it would have cost an estimated $9,610,000.

$$\text{Revised location price} = \$10,000,000 \times \frac{98}{102} = \$9,610,000$$

The proposed plant will take about one year to build. This means that the above estimate should be escalated for three years of rising costs.

The study group decided to use the Chemical Engineering Plant Cost Index. The value of the index for each of the years 1980–1984 is given in the following table.

Year	Index	Annual Change, %
1980	238	—
1981	271	+13.9
1982	283	+4.4
1983	286	+1.1
1984	292	+2.1

For the five-year period, the average increase was 5.2%. The increase of about 15% from 1980 to 1981 reflects the high rate of inflation experienced at that time. The drop to about 1% in 1983 and 2% in 1984 reflects the depressed state of petroleum refining and chemical production.

The study group decided that, for the three-year period between the expected completion of the new plant and the actual completion of the old plant, an average inflation rate of 2.5% would be used. This gives the following projection for the first cost of the new plant:

$$\text{Preliminary first cost} = \$9,610,000 \times (1.025)^3 = \$10,350,000$$

In making this decision, the group was influenced by the following factors:

- The productivity gain included in the index would continue at 2.5%.
- Technological improvements might ease inflationary expectations somewhat, but this effect would be marginal at best.
- Capital equipment prices, which had actually deflated in the period 1981–1984, would increase somewhat and therefore raise the rate of inflation above the 1983 and 1984 levels.

____19
CRITICISMS OF ECONOMIC ANALYSIS*

19.1 INTRODUCTION

Criticisms of economic analysis fall into two broad categories. The first category deals with using, or rather misusing, discounted cash flow (DCF) methodology for capital project selection in both the private and the public sectors. The second category deals with the shortcomings of benefit-cost analysis and is therefore primarily, but by no means exclusively, concerned with the public sector.

Both groups of criticisms are discussed in this chapter. We begin with the time value of money, on which all of the work we have done to date is based.

19.2 DISCOUNTED CASH FLOW METHODOLOGY

The discounted cash flow methodology for the selection of capital projects has been attacked by economists, cost analysts, corporate planners, government planners, management consultants, business school faculties, and all others who are genuinely concerned about the need for adding to our stock of wealth—and particularly our infrastructure—through worthwhile capital investments. Rates of return are now so high that the MARRs used in cost studies have made the present worth of cash flows during the later years of a project's life cycle of little significance compared to the cash flows for the earlier years. Much long-range planning by production managers has proved to be fruitless because it could not satisfy the rates of return demanded by

*See reference 2 under "References" at the end of this chapter.

corporate managements. The result has been "a failure of American managers to keep their companies technologically competitive over the long run" (1).

The failure to replace and upgrade aging facilities is often cited as the major cause of our inability to compete successfully with Western European and Far Eastern manufacturers in many product areas. According to informed observers, too many of our corporate management teams share two unfortunate characteristics: (1) an aversion to risk taking, and (2) a tendency to focus on the wrong objectives.

Discounted cash flow methodology is accused of reinforcing these characteristics by making a "numbers game" out of the selection process for capital expenditures at the expense of common sense, sound judgment, and a willingness to take risks.

We agree that the preceding comments still have validity, although less so than just a few years ago. It is not, however, DCF methodology that is at fault; rather, the fault lies in its application.

19.3   MISUSE OF DCF METHODOLOGY

Is it true that the misuse of DCF has, in the words of one critic, "contributed to America's decline in that managers using DCF have systematically rejected investments critical to the livelihood of many U.S. industries"? (1)

To answer this question, we have to ask ourselves if there is something inherently wrong with discounting cash flows.

We believe we have shown you that there would be something inherently wrong in *not* discounting cash flows. No one sees a future cash flow as commensurate with a present cash flow. All of us know that a dollar now is more likely to buy more goods than a dollar a year from now. For this reason, most critics accept the DCF methodology but look at two frequent misapplications:

- The rates of return used in economic studies are not realistic for long-term investments.
- The cost of doing nothing is not evaluated properly.

COMMENT: A current dollar has not always bought more than a future dollar. You could buy more with the dollars that circulated during the Great Depression of the 1930s than the dollars that circulated during the Roaring Twenties. However, since World War II, and as far as we can see into the future, the industrial economies have had to, and will have to, control inflation, not deflation.

19.3.1   MARR for Long-term Investments

As we mentioned in Chapter 18, the DCF methodology first gained acceptance 30 or 40 years ago when 3% after taxes was considered a reasonable rate. At

3%, a cash flow of $1,000 due in 20 years had a present value of $554. An investor, who in today's market can earn 5% after taxes on a high-grade corporate bond, often looks for a return of 15–20% after taxes on relatively low-risk capital investments. At 20%, $1,000 twenty years from now is worth only $26 today. Many capital projects—and certainly many of those that require major capital expenditures—have life expectancies of 20 years or more.

Several questions come to mind.

1. Are we applying rates based on the market, that is, rates that include an inflation factor, without inflating the cash flow streams themselves?
2. Are we assuming too often that high prime rates and high rates of inflation will last throughout the life cycles of long-term capital projects?
3. Are the risk factors included in the selection of MARRs too high?

The first question brings up a common mistake. If we use an MARR based on market rates that include inflation, we must also include inflation in the cash flow streams affected by inflation. With inflation at 5%, the equivalent MARR (the i_{eq}) will be substantially lower than the market rate MARR (the i), and it is the equivalent rate that should be used if we are not inflating cash flows. This problem was covered in Chapter 18, and there is no need for us to go into it again here.

With regard to the second question, consider the situation faced by decision makers during 1980–1981 when the prime interest rate exceeded 20% and the rate of inflation was close to 15%. For these rates, an investor might require 40% or 50% before taxes, even for relatively low-risk capital investments. For 40%, the inflation-free rate for 15% inflation is a little over 20%, which is still high but might have brought in some projects that 40% would kill. Cost studies based on the assumption that the conditions existing in 1980 would last 20 or 30 years would have eliminated many good capital projects and would certainly not have been in the best interests of our economy.

There is no easy answer to the third question except to say that, if the private sector is so risk averse that many things that should be done do not get done, the public sector will have to take over.

19.3.2 Do-nothing Alternative

The do-nothing alternative is the opportunity forgone if the project under study is implemented. In theory, this opportunity earns a return that equals the MARR for which the proposed project was appraised. For this reason, as we have pointed out several times, the do-nothing alternative has an NPW of zero, an IRR equal to the MARR, and a BCR of 1.

The do-nothing alternative is too often treated as an abstraction for which the figures of merit mentioned above hold. However, these figures cannot be taken for granted. The do-nothing alternative must be examined seriously if it is to serve as the alternative against which do-something alternatives are to be tested.

This testing process works well under certain circumstances but, as the critics of the DCF method point out,

> . . . is completely out of place in others. Too often, they say, managers, planners and cost analysts fail to analyze the costs and the losses in revenue associated with doing nothing. These can be substantial. What will be a firm's short, medium, and long term position if it does not improve quality, reduce operating costs, expand capacity, and enlarge its domestic and foreign markets? What are its competitors doing? What must it do to at least stay even? If nothing is done will prices have to be reduced because competitors are offering better quality or will sales volume have to be reduced to maintain current prices, or both? These are difficult questions to answer. However, they must be answered and dollar values must be attached to the contingencies that may occur. This goes far beyond straightforward cost estimation and brings management face to face with sponsoring realistic forecasts of what might and could happen (2).

The forecasts referred to in this quotation are obviously subject to personal bias. If we are optimists, we look at the future one way, and, if we are pessimists, we look at the future in another way. Some of us argue that we need more realists who can evaluate the cost of doing nothing objectively and bring this evaluation into the selection process properly.

19.4   FOCUSING ON THE WRONG OBJECTIVES

Undue pessimism and focusing on the wrong objectives often go hand in hand. The last three decades have seen Japan and Western Europe outwit and outsell us, not only throughout the rest of the world, but also in our own country. Korea, Taiwan, and others have also become formidable competitors. Anyone interested in how and why this happened must read, if they have not done so already, "Managing Our Way to Economic Decline" by R. H. Hayes and W. J. Abernathy, which was quoted several times in the previous section and which appeared in the *Harvard Business Review* during July-August 1980 (1). This article and many others put the blame directly on management shortcomings, of which overemphasis on short-term profits and a lack of commitment to growth and quality lead the rest.

Management shortcomings have been the subject matter of hundreds of articles and numerous books. They obviously do not apply across the board (does anything ever?) but critics contend with a great deal of justification that they apply to far too many companies, including those that have the biggest impact on our growth and well-being (3). Even companies that have been innovative see their markets invaded by foreign competitors producing not only cheaper but higher quality products. You need only look at an issue of *Consumer Reports* (4) to see how foreign corporations are rated against domestic corporations for product quality and customer satisfaction on many goods.

19.5 BENEFIT-COST ANALYSIS AND THE BCR

Of all the figures of merit, none has been as soundly berated as the benefit-cost ratio (BCR). Its critics include the federal government, which originally legislated that the BCR should be applied to flood control projects and has since required it for all projects of any significance sponsored by its agencies. A quotation from a 1981 House Subcommittee Report is pertinent: ". . . [BCA is] simply too primitive a tool to make it a decisive factor in rule-making." (5)

Does this mean we should stop using it? Certainly not. Even a primitive tool is better than none, and it serves as a somewhat easier concept for a taxpayer to grasp than the present worth or the internal rate of return. What it does mean is, as one critic puts it, ". . . that it is at best a blunt tool to help shape, though not control [decisions]." (6)

19.5.1 Benefit-Cost Analysis Methodology

Since the cash flow estimates for benefits and costs are discounted in the application of benefit-cost analysis, the criticisms of the DCF methodology obviously apply to this technique and to its figure of merit, the BCR. High MARRs do not give positive net cash flows that occur later in the life cycle their proper due, and, as mentioned, the do-nothing alternative may not be evaluated at all but simply assumed to be one.

However, the criticisms of benefit-cost analysis go much deeper than the methodology of DCF. The major concern is the identification and estimation of the cash flows for benefits and disbenefits. Lack of objectivity is a common failing in cost studies but never more so than for these imputed cash flows.

Most public projects have their proponents and their opponents. The former will often seek out every benefit and trivialize every disbenefit; the latter will do the reverse. For either side, a passionate commitment (including greed) frequently will bring innocent mistakes and devious inaccuracies into the estimation process. Examples of innocence and deviousness are brought out in the following quotation.

Among the fairly innocent [mistakes] are

- A tendency of analysts to concentrate on the items that are easiest to handle and with which they have some familiarity.
- Lack of experience in identifying and costing imputed cash flows (the benefits and disbenefits to the public).

Among the more devious ones are

- A tendency to overplay those items which will twist the analysis in the direction in which analysts and/or their superiors wish to go.
- Downright misrepresentation and fraud in identifying or not identifying benefits and costs and in over or under estimating cash flows to make a study come out with a preordained result (2).

For an example of "deviousness," consider the following. One of the authors had the opportunity to review the financial analysis of a proposed multibillion dollar venture that had been prepared by a reputable financial investment firm. The study was based on DCF methodology. The base estimates for first cost and for revenues and expenses were well prepared. The figures of merit were the present worth and the IRR. A sensitivity analysis was also included. (You will learn in Chapter 21 of Part III that a sensitivity analysis looks at every key estimate to see what would happen to the figures of merit if the cash flows proved better or worse than their base estimates.) This analysis examined every key cash flow except revenue, which was taken as invariant, even though the product (an international commodity) was subject to competitive pressures from many sides.

None of us can quarrel with the aim of benefit-cost analysis to help find and select opportunities for capital investment for which benefits exceed costs and for which the benefit-cost ratio is therefore greater than 1 (or at least equal to 1). However, even if we forget the difficulty of estimating benefits and disbenefits and assume that this can be done, there are two other matters that often distort the results of a study. We quote again:

First, the members of the public benefited are often different from the members of the public disbenefited. The example most often cited is the construction of a dam for flood control. Those below the dam will be benefited by less frequent and less severe flooding. Those above it may lose their land. Acid rain provides a more recent example. The public disbenefited by the acidification of lakes and the loss of forests in the Northeastern States and Canada is hundreds of miles from the public which reside in the Midwest and benefit from lower utility costs.

Second, BCA is mute on the subject of equity, that is, on whether the redistribution of wealth which a public project may cause is equitable. The disbenefit of flooding a $5,000,000 estate carries the same weight as the benefit of saving one hundred homes each worth $50,000 from inundation (2).

This quotation raises the question of equity. Equity is a nonmonetary attribute or factor that enters into multiattribute analysis. We therefore leave this topic for now and resurrect it in Part IV.

19.5.2. Misuses of BCA

One misuse of the BCA has already been mentioned—unrealistic estimates. Revenues and benefits are exaggerated and costs and disbenefits are down-sided by the proponents of a venture. The reverse is done by its opponents. Two other misuses often mentioned are (1) substituting gross costs for incremental costs and (2) attempting to cost the uncostable.

Private industry doesn't like governmental regulation. This is understandable. What is difficult to understand is its tendency to fight all regulations, including, at one extreme, those that private industry sees as bureaucratic meddling and, at the other, those that are badly needed. Examples of the latter are given in the following quotation.

> A prominent European car manufacturer has claimed that most of the arguments presented by American car manufacturers on the cost of meeting federal regulations [on fuel efficiency] are not aimed at the substance of the regulations but "purely at resisting" them.
>
> The Rubber Manufacturers Association argued before Congress that the industry did not know how to comply with a proposed standard for controlling benzene emissions. At the same time, one of the rubber companies was telling its shareholders that "it is expected that such standards will have no material adverse effect" on operations, that is, on profit.
>
> By now we are all aware of the depletion of the ozone layer by fluorocarbons, the compounds used in aerosol cans and as refrigerants. When the ban on these compounds was under review the corporations producing them never acknowledged that replacements were available for little or no higher cost (2).

Other examples include the American Medical Association's fight against Medicare and the American Tobacco Institute's fight against health warnings on smoking. Since Medicare and Medicaid, in their current format, have proven to be a windfall for the medical profession, can we expect the same effort at misrepresentation to keep the system as private and as profitable as it now is?

When fighting regulation, industry uses gross income and gross costs rather than incremental income and incremental costs in presenting its objections to government and to the public. The net loss from sales—the difference between gross income and the cost of goods sold—is not mentioned unless asked for. When a "beleagured" industry cites the costs of regulation, gross costs are touted. If the cost of a proposed regulation is x dollars per unit and the cost of the regulation currently in effect is y dollars per unit, we see the x but not the difference between x and y, which may be quite small.

When it comes to costing the uncostables, there has been, and will continue to be, progress in estimating cash flows for benefits and disbenefits that have in the past been treated as nonmonetary attributes. However, in many instances, it is often more realistic and honest to continue treating them as nonmonetary and incorporating them into multiattribute analyses in this form. Attempts to do otherwise have often failed because the data base covered too small a population, because the data were obtained from questionnaires that were often difficult to answer, and because experience has shown that the answers given to surveys often differ substantially from actual behavior later on.

Two areas in which there has been some success in monetizing benefits and disbenefits are recreational facilities and employee morale. For the former, prospective users are asked to indicate what they would be willing to pay for visits to a particular facility, say a campsite, for specified periods of time and how often they would use this facility. From such data, a range of present values is derived that, for a BCR of 1, sets an upper limit on what should be spent.

For employee morale, the benefits to both employers and employees of a "satisficed" work force are low absenteeism and quality output. Both of these effects can be evaluated in money terms if sufficient data are available and if comparisons with other companies having similar problems, or rather lacking such problems, can be made.

A common problem in many benefit-cost analyses is how to put a price tag on human life. We know that human life cannot be valued in terms of dollars, but we also know that there are many situations in which the available funding sets a limit on how much can be spent, not only to save lives, but also to improve the quality of life.

19.5.3   The Value of a Human Life

How do we value human life when we are comparing one alternative with another? There are many approaches to this problem. These were summed up by one author:

> The DCF value of what a deceased person would have earned for the remainder of his or her life.
>
> The average value of jury awards in court cases involving accidental death.
>
> The results of questionnaires in which respondents are asked what salary cuts they would accept for a less hazardous job, or conversely, what additional pay they would require for more hazardous employment.
>
> The reduction in the probability of death due to a capital improvement (2).

DCF methodology can compute the present worth of projected earnings based on life expectancy data and on the history of earnings to date. But, is a dead low-wage earner therefore worth less than a dead high-wage earner? Is a retired person worth no more than the present value of his social security payments if he or she has no other income? These questions suggest that there may be no satisfactory way to measure the present worth of a human life with the discounted cash flow approach and that other approaches need to be considered.

For the second approach, we turn to jury awards. These vary from relatively small to relatively large sums. An average means nothing, because no one knows what a jury will do. Usually, however, a jury will award more for the present worth of future medical expenses than for a death. This may seem harsh, but it is understandable. One of the references at the end of the chapter gives you the facts on one such case (7).

The third approach simply tells us what we already know. People take riskier jobs for higher pay because they want current satisfaction. The attitude is, "Somebody else, but not me, will be hurt." The results of this approach often indicate that we value our lives at insignificant sums because we find it difficult to equate higher pay with a higher probability of death or injury.

The attitude of the federal government is inconsistent on the value of human life. This is illustrated in the following quotation.

> Under an executive order, Congress forbids regulatory actions "unless potential benefits to society from the regulation outweigh the potential costs to society." This order obviously falls into the pattern of the legislation mentioned in Chapter [11] under which the benefit cost criterion was to be applied to flood control projects.
>
> To stay with this regulation, government agencies must put a value on human life. In 1985 the Federal Aviation Administration used a value of $650,000. At the same time the Environmental Protection Agency used a range of $400,000 to $7 million, with an average range of $1 million to $2 million, and the Occupational Safety and Health Administration used a range of $2 million to $5 million. For both the EPA and OSHA the choice of what figure to use within these wide ranges was arbitrary and illustrates how [a cost analysis] can be fudged depending on what the decision maker wants (2).

These comments bring us to the fourth approach. This is examined in Example 19.1 and more fully in Chapter 26, which is the first chapter in Part IV on multiattribute analysis.

Example 19.1   To-belt or Not-to-belt   Safety belts save lives. They also cost money. Can we use their cost as a rough measure of the value of human life?

During the 30-year period, 1960–1990, motor vehicle registrations increased from about 70 million to about 190 million, or about 2.7 times. During the same period, motor vehicle fatalities increased from an average of about 40,000 per year to about 50,000 per year, or only 1.25 times.

At least a part of the slower growth in fatalities compared to registrations is due to the use of seat belts. In what follows, we arbitrarily assume that about 25,000 lives per year were saved because state governments insisted that safety belts be installed and used.

For an average cost of $250 and for an average life of five years, the EUAC per vehicle for a seat belt installation is $50 ($250/5). If we further assume that all 190 million vehicles have seat belts, the EUAC is $9.5 billion. For 25,000 lives saved, the value of a human life, as measured by this criterion, is therefore about $400,000

As mentioned, we leave this topic now to resurrect it in Chapter 26. In that chapter, we will apply a technique known as cost effective analysis to compare capital improvements for reducing traffic injuries and fatalities.

19.6 SUMMARY

The three most serious criticisms leveled against the discounted cash flow methodology in its application to the capital project selection process are that

1. High MARRs eliminate worthwhile projects
2. The do-nothing alternative is improperly evaluated
3. Estimates of cash flows lack objectivity

High MARRs are symptomatic of risk aversion, that is, of an aversion to accepting risks by requiring rates of return that eliminate projects that would make our industries more competitive at home and in world markets.

This misuse is exacerbated by not treating the do-nothing alternative properly. In theory, this alternative is the opportunity forgone by implementing a do-something alternative. In practice, a realistic appraisal of doing nothing would often indicate that the do-nothing alternative should either have been omitted as a member of a set of MEAs because something has to be done or, if included, should have been impaled on its shortcomings.

The lack of objectivity in estimating cash flows works in two ways. Proponents of a venture will overestimate revenues and benefits and will underestimate costs and disbenefits. Many of the projects on which the now defunct savings and loan institutions provided funding never had the objective review by these institutions that they should have had. The result is excessive capacity in noncompetitive facilities and a waste of resources that could have been used more profitably and more equitably elsewhere.

Opponents, on the other hand, will overplay costs and disbenefits and will underplay revenues and benefits. This is often evident in the hue and cry raised over losses in property values if social service facilities are located here rather than there and in minimizing the disbenefits due to insults to the environment, such as acid rain.

The value of a human life is an important consideration in capital projects dealing with efforts to reduce fatalities. Since we cannot put a monetary value on human life, we must rely on what we can afford to spend. We refer you to the Suggested Reading at the end of this chapter, which carries the provocative title, "Value of One Life? From $8.37 to $10 million."

What is the cure for misuses? A simple answer for the selection of public-sector projects is an informed electorate and informed officials—officials who understand the time value of money and an electorate that recognizes that capital expenditure decisions should not be made on monetary considerations alone.

For the selection of private-sector projects, there is no easy answer. Honest mistakes will always be made, since the future can only be guessed at. But aversion to risk (a euphemism for "laziness" in many situations) and the opportunity to make a "quick buck" will always be with us.

REFERENCES

1. R. H. Hayes and W. J. Abernathy, "Managing Our Way to Economic Decline." Harvard Business Review (July-August 1980): 67. This article gives you the full flavor of what many observers have concluded is wrong with U.S. management philosophy.
2. Hans J. Lang, *Cost Analysis for Capital Investment Decisions* (New York: Marcel Dekker, 1989). Chapter 19 in our text is a condensation of the material covered in Chapters 15, 16, and 17 of this reference.
3. David Halberstam, *The Reckoning* (New York: William Morrow, 1986). A fascinating book on the automobile industry, which bears out much of what you will find in reference 1.
4. *Consumer Reports*, a publication of Consumers Union, Mount Vernon, New York. Most of you are familiar with these monthly reports. Time and again, foreign goods are listed as outperforming ours.
5. Baruch Fischhoff, *The Art of Cost Benefit Analysis*, U.S. Department of Commerce, National Technical Information Service, Publication AD/A 041526. An excellent report on the pitfalls of BCA.
6. Mark Green and Norman Waitzman, Cost Analysis Needs Analysis. The New York Times, February 8, 1981. A rather searing indictment of benefit-cost analysis.
7. Janine Warsaw, "Elements of a $12 Million Personal Injury Case," American Bar Association Journal 72 (January 1, 1986): 82. Here is where to go if you want to know more about the case discussed under the section on the value of human life and on the application of DCF methodology in settling lawsuits.

SUGGESTED READING

1. William R. Greer, "Value of One Life? From $8.37 to $10 Million," *The New York Times*, June 26, 1985. All you need to know about the value of your life.

PROBLEMS

19-1 When Donald Trump built the Trump Palace resort in the early 1980s in Atlantic City, New Jersey, he foresaw a highly profitable casino and hotel. Less than a decade later, however, not only has the casino/hotel not been a success, but also Donald Trump has lost much of his empire. What went wrong?

19-2 In 1990, a Japanese conglomerate purchased the golf course at Pebble Beach in California. A year later, Pebble Beach golf course was back on the market at a vastly reduced selling price. The Japanese investors lost a fortune on the resale. What prompted the Japanese to sell the golf course at such a huge loss after only one year of ownership?

19-3 In the late 1980s, Olympia & York, the world's largest real estate development firm, began the development of a major office complex called Canary Wharf in the old docklands of London. The project was expected to draw tenants who would relocate from the old financial district of London into new technologically superior office buildings. Soon after the first new occupants arrived, Olympia & York was forced to file for court protection from its creditors in Britain, the United States and Canada. What could have gone so wrong?

19-4 United States Lines was the world's largest shipping company when it ordered 12 of the largest container ships ever built in order to expand its capacity. The vessels were designed to favor fuel efficiency over speed during a time of rapid increases in the price of oil. Within a year of the delivery of the vessels in 1985, United States Lines had gone out of business and the 12 ships had been sold to its rival Sea-Land for approximately one-tenth of their cost. What factors should United States Lines have included in a sensitivity analysis?

19-5 Volkswagen of America built a production facility near Pittsburgh in order to accommodate anticipated demand in North America for Volkswagen automobiles. By 1992, Volkswagen had abandoned this facility, while BMW announced that they would build an automobile factory of their own in South Carolina. Is BMW destined for the same failure? Aside from factors specific to the automobile industry, what issues could account for the difference between success and failure for these two German companies?

19-6 The New York Daily News was faced with bankruptcy unless a "White Knight" could infuse enough cash to meet the paper's financial obligations. British financier Robert Maxwell agreed to assume control over the *Daily News* in exchange for certain wage concessions. What other considerations should Maxwell have taken into account before he made his decision to invest?

19-7 Your friend has just been killed in an automobile accident. You are the beneficiary of his insurance policy. The insurance company wants to pay you $500,000 in today's dollars. Your friend was 25 years old, with a degree in engineering. Using your engineering economics skills, determine if this is a just offer?

   Hint: Assume a starting salary of $30,000, a working life of 50 years, and an inflation rate of 4% per year.

19-8 The federal government is contemplating building a new dam that would flood a wilderness area. After doing a benefit-cost analysis, it has determined to build the dam because of the huge recreational benefits that could be realized. Is this a misuse of the BCA?

19-9 American automobile manufacturers of the late 1970s and the 1980s stood by and watched foreign competition upgrade manufacturing facilities to produce high-quality, low-cost vehicles. Discuss this in terms of the do-nothing alternative.

19-10 In Part III of this text on risk analysis, you will learn that capital expenditures are a form of lottery or random experiment in which no one really knows the outcome. Do the preceding examples indicate that this is so?

19-11 At what dollar figure do you value your life? To answer this question, consider the following scenario. You know where a fortune of X dollars is hidden. The location is a difficult and dangerous one. Your chance of getting there and returning safely is $Y\%$. What is your value of X for Y equal to 50%, 75%, and 99%?

SUMMARY OF PART II

Part II is built on the basics of Part I. Before reviewing the summary of Part II, you should review the summary of Part I to make sure that everything said there still has meaning and relevance for you. If it doesn't, take the time to catch up. Every sound bite below (reader bite would be more appropriate) should mean something to you. If it doesn't, refresh yourself by going back to the text.

1. The process of ranking alternatives consists of two distinct steps. The first deals with technological exclusivity, and the second deals with financial exclusivity.

2. Alternatives that are ranked for technological exclusivity are competing with each other. Only one will be selected.

3. Ranking for technological exclusivity can be done with any of the three worths and with the IRR and the BCR. For consistent results, incremental cash flow analyses may be required for the IRR and the BCR.

4. For technological exclusivity, all of the alternatives in a set of MEAs must be coterminated.

5. Ranking for financial exclusivity is one step in the preparation of annual master plans by for-profit and not-for-profit organizations.

6. A master plan includes a capital expenditure budget prepared from departmental budget requests. These requests are ranked for financial exclusivity in order to identify that set of projects (budget requests) that produces the highest figure of merit for the limited funds available for investment.

7. In ranking for financial exclusivity, not only the alternative with the highest figure of merit for each budget request but also all of the

acceptable alternatives submitted with such requests take part in the ranking procedure.

8. Ranking for financial exclusivity does not require cotermination or incremental cash flow analysis.

9. Capital funding for capital expenditures is provided by creditors and owners. Corporations look at interest paid to creditors and dividends paid to shareholders as their weighted average cost of capital and use this cost as a step in selecting MARRs.

10. MARRs for discounting cash flows are composites made up of the estimated true (inflation-free) rate of return plus the estimated rate of inflation plus an estimate of risk.

11. Part-creditor and part-owner financing can produce higher rates of return for owners, but on a smaller base, then all-owner financing. This phenomenon is known as leverage.

12. Leasing is an alternative to raising cash from creditors or owners. Ordinary leases are handled as expenses. Capital leases are treated as a form of creditor financing.

13. Replacement problems are a special breed of capital investment project in which the economic lives of defenders and challengers are compared. For each participant in the selection process, the number of members in the set of MEAs depends on the number of years of service. The year of service that produces the least annual cost defines the economic life.

14. There are four types of replacement problems, namely, (1) retirement only, (2) replacement with an identical (or near identical) unit, (3) replacement with an unidentical unit, and (4) generalized replacement models. These models often look too far into the future to have much practical application for replacement studies.

15. For after-tax analyses, it is necessary to consider noncash expenses, since these impact on income taxes. The major noncash expense is depreciation.

16. The federal income tax laws mandate the use of the Modified Accelerated Cost Recovery System (MACRS) for tax returns, that is, for federal income statements prepared specifically to compute the tax burden.

17. However, income statements for financial performance often use straight-line depreciation. This method is also commonly used for preliminary project selection studies.

18. Public-sector projects differ from private-sector projects in several respects. The most important are that public projects do not pay income taxes and that cash flow analysis must cope with two sets of cash flows—one covering costs and fees (revenues) and the other, benefits and disbenefits flowing into and out of the public's pocket.

19. Multipurpose projects are found in both the public and the private sectors but more often in the public sector. Two approaches are used for justifying each purpose—the add-on approach and the cost allocation approach.

20. The add-on approach identifies a primary purpose. Each secondary purpose then has to justify itself with its add-on revenues and costs.

21. The cost allocation approach has each purpose justify itself as if it were the only purpose for which a multipurpose facility were being built.

22. Regulated industries are allowed a fair return on the depreciable value of their investment by their government sponsors. Since this value decreases from year to year due to depreciation, revenues and taxes are levelized (converted into equivalent uniform series) to set rate schedules.

23. Geometric gradients serve as convenient models for estimating cash flows that change from year to year due to price level effects (inflation), gains in productivity, technological changes, and sales volume and price increases and decreases independent of inflation.

24. An equivalent rate of return is a surrogate rate that permits handling a geometric cash flow pattern as a uniform series.

25. The critics of the DCF methodology claim, with some justification, that managers have substituted a "numbers game" (discounted cash flow methodology), played with loaded dice (high MARRs, biased estimates, and improper appraisal of the do-nothing alternative), for making decisions on the selection of capital projects.

PART III
THE SELECTION PROCESS: RISK ANALYSIS

_____20
ESTIMATION

20.1 INTRODUCTION

With Chapter 20 we leave behind Part II, for which the estimates of cash flows on which our studies were based were deterministic or "errorless," and enter Part III, for which these estimates are probabilistic. However, before we touch on the concept of probability and its many ramifications for the capital project selection process, we need to describe a common form of risk analysis that does not depend on probability but serves as a useful introduction to it. This is sensitivity analysis. We cover it in Chapter 21 but lay the groundwork for it in this chapter.

Sensitivity analysis takes the ranges within which the base estimate for each cash flow stream may fall (the base estimate is the estimate used for deterministic studies) and uses these to obtain the ranges of accuracy within which the figures of merit may fall. Sensitivity analysis is thus essentially a "what-if" analysis. A computer can relieve us of much drudgery and save us much time in such analyses.

Where then does this chapter fit in? In this chapter, we take the view that you are, or may sooner or later be, in responsible charge of an economy study on capital project selection and that you are working for or with a large corporation. As such, what should your study group and you know about how estimates are put together, about types of estimates and estimating methods, and, in particular, about the ranges of accuracy with which you will have to deal in carrying out a sensitivity analysis?

We cannot make an estimator or a cost engineer out of you in this chapter, but, if you have never had any experience in these disciplines, we can at least give you some background on the topics raised in the preceding question.

20.2 ESTIMATION AND ECONOMY STUDIES

The most time-consuming effort in carrying out economy studies is usually gathering data for, and preparing, cash flow estimates. So far these estimates have been handed to you as "givens" and will often continue to be handed to you in this way. Unless you have some background in estimation and have spent some time as a cost engineer or an estimator, there are details of which you should be made aware and which, if the responsibility for performing an economic study falls on you, will help you focus on the questions you should be asking yourself and others on cash flow estimates. These questions include the following:

1. What cash flow streams should be considered for the particular study at hand?
2. Who is involved, or should be, or should have been in preparing the cash flow estimates for these cash flow streams?
3. What types of estimates are needed at any particular stage of a study— rough and ready or fine and detailed, or something in between?
4. What ranges of accuracy can be expected for the various types of estimates?
5. Are estimates of probability distributions available from which expected values can be computed?

Questions 1 and 2 are discussed in the two subsections that follow. Questions 3 and 4 will be discussed in later sections of this chapter. Question 5 is deferred to Chapter 22.

20.2.1 Cash Flow Streams

You already know the cash flow streams that impact on economic analyses for capital project selection. For convenience, we list them below to help structure the remainder of the chapter.

- First cost, also known as initial cost, investment cost, capital cost, fixed capital cost, fixed investment, and capital expenditure
- Revenues, also known as sales and gross income
- Cash expenses
  - Cost of goods and services sold, also called cost of sales
  - Operating expenses, also called (unfortunately) overhead
  - Interest expense on borrowed funds
- Income taxes (including the noncash expenses needed to estimate these)
- Benefits and disbenefits
- Repayment of principal on borrowed funds
- Working capital
- Disposal and termination costs

We did not include nonoperating revenues and expenses in this list, because they usually play a small part, if any, in project selection studies. The major exception is interest expense on borrowed funds, which is the reason we listed it.

Of the cash flow streams listed, the most difficult items to forecast are sales volumes and prices for revenue estimates, and the most difficult items to estimate are the imputed cash flows for benefits and disbenefits. Estimates for benefits and disbenefits are, by their nature, often guesstimates rather than estimates. However, that does not make them less important; it just makes them more controversial.

Estimates for cash expenses follow estimates for revenue. Estimates for non-cash expenses (principally depreciation) which are needed for estimating income taxes are derived from first-cost estimates. Estimating first costs is usually straightforward unless there is no background of experience on the product or the process or the materials of construction or the location, or any combination of these and other factors for which previous experience is lacking.

20.2.2 Responsibility for Estimates

Who should be involved in preparing estimates for those cash flow streams listed? To answer this question, assume that an economic study for a major physical facility—a bridge or a tunnel, an office building or a hotel, a steel plant or a petrochemical unit—has begun.

The first cost is usually prepared by cost engineers or estimators who are familiar with the type of facility to be built. Revenue estimates come from volume projections and prices furnished by the marketing, sales, or planning departments. Estimates for the cost of sales come from the production department or are prepared from quantity input furnished by it. Estimates of operating expenses (overhead) and working capital or the input for preparing these are furnished by the financial department with support from other staff departments as needed. Estimates of benefits and disbenefits, if the project is within the public sector, are more difficult to pinpoint. Often it is left to the study group to ferret out the imputed cash flows and then to seek help for estimating their magnitude within the organization or externally.

The preceding description is typical for a definitive estimate, but much of it also applies to order-of-magnitude (OOM) and other shortcut estimating methods. You and your study group may have enough experience and background to put OOM estimates together quickly, and on your own, but the results should always be seen and approved by the responsible departments involved.

Obviously, many departments and many people will participate in the estimation of cash flows. What then do you do? If you are in charge, as we have assumed, you have to (1) bully everyone to get their estimates in on time; (2) review and critique the estimates and, in particular, know the level of detail on which they are based; (3) check the estimates, or have them checked, for consistency against previous estimates for similar installations;

(4) ask for and get estimates on the ranges of accuracy for carrying out sensitivity analyses, and use the background and experience of yourself and your study group to revise these ranges if necessary; and (5) do anything else that has to be done to manage the estimating function for your assignment.

20.3   FIRST-COST ESTIMATES

We saw in Chapter 13 on ranking for financial exclusivity that first costs are as important in the capital selection process—and often more so—as the figures of merit themselves. Furthermore, estimates of first costs are used in the preparation of many other estimates. Depreciation expenses, as we know, are based on capital investment and property taxes, insurance, and maintenance expenses are often estimated as a fixed charge on investment (refer to Example 17.6).

In the following subsection, we discuss types of first-cost estimates, and in subsection 20.3.2, we discuss some estimating methods commonly used for each type.

20.3.1   Types of First-Cost Estimates

First-cost estimates basically fall into three types: (1) order-of-magnitude (OOM), (2) factor, and (3) definitive. There are no sharp divisions between one type and another. Rather, as OOM estimating becomes more refined, it merges into factor estimating, and, as factor estimating becomes more sophisticated, it merges into definitive estimating.

OOM estimates are estimates based on unit capacity cost data or turnover ratios derived from existing facilities. Examples are given under estimating methods.

Factor estimates are estimates in which one or more components of the first cost are estimated in some detail and factors, expressed as ratios or percentages, are then used to arrive at the total cost. One of the best known is the Lang factor.

Definitive estimates are estimates in which substantially all of the components of the first cost are clearly defined and estimated in detail. The input for such estimates is whatever is needed to define the project, for example, flowsheets, plot plans, equipment and material specifications, equipment lists, bills of material, work specifications, and construction drawings.

In discussing the types of estimates mentioned and the ranges of accuracy associated with them, we find it convenient to classify capital projects as we did in Appendix 18A in our comments on construction cost indices. Additional detail on what we said there is given below.

- Civil projects
  - Residential and nonresidential buildings—apartments, hotels, office buildings

- Heavy civil, also called heavy construction projects—highways, bridges, tunnels
- Mechanical projects
  - Process plants—fluid processing plants, such as petroleum refining, petrochemical, and chemical units
  - Manufacturing plants—solid and solid/fluid processing plants, such as steel mills (solid), automobile assembly plants (solid), alumina plants (solid/fluid)

Civil Projects   For building construction, the previous classification of types of estimates, although valid, goes by somewhat different names.

Type of Estimate	Range of Accuracy, %
Order of magnitude	+/− 20
Square or cubic foot	+/− 15
System estimate (factor)	+/− 10
Unit price estimate	+/− 5
Definitive estimate	+/− 5

OOM estimates are based on unit capacity cost ratios, such as the cost per bed for hospitals, the cost per room for hotels, the cost per parking stall for garages, and the like.

Unit costs per square foot and per cubic foot estimates are really OOM estimates but are identified as a separate category because of the vast amount of data available on them. The data comprise almost any conceivable type of building. They are classified by low class, average class, and good class construction and in ranges of lower quartile, median, and upper quartile. Their ranges of accuracy are narrow, as compared, for example, with OOM estimates for mechanical projects (plus or minus 20% versus 50%).

The system estimate breaks a building down into its components and applies separate unit costs to each component, for example, sitework, masonry, plumbing, heating, and so on. A wealth of data—more than for any other type of capital investment—is also available for such estimates. The calculated costs arrived at are checked against percentages or factors for buildings of comparable function, size, and construction. Mechanical and electrical work for apartment buildings of a certain size and type, for example, averages about 20%. For hospitals, this figure is 40%. Unit price estimates (the word *cost* would serve as well here, but *price* is commonly used) are definitive estimates based on firm bills of materials prepared from finished specifications and drawings. Such estimates are used to bid firm unit prices for labor only or for labor plus material and often include overhead and profit.

Definitive estimates have been defined. They are the basis for firm price (lump-sum) bids for complete facilities, including materials, labor, overhead, and profit.

The preceding classification of types of estimates does not apply to other civil projects, since these are too diverse in function, size, location, type of construction, and other variables. First-cost estimates for such facilities are usually defined as OOM, preliminary, and definitive. The following ranges of accuracy are typical.

	Range, %
Order-of-magnitude	+/− 30 to 40
Budget (factor)	+/− 15 to 25
Definitive	+/− 5 to 10

Mechanical Projects Process plants are outdoor installations that process fluids, such as natural gas and crude oil and intermediates from natural gas and crude oil, in order to produce more refined products. The building component of such plants is small. It usually consists of no more than a control house and a small building for housing auxiliary electrical equipment, such as motor starters.

Manufacturing plants differ from process plants in that they usually have a substantial building component and process solids or solids and fluids (solids in part of the process and fluids or solid suspensions in the remainder) instead of just fluids.

First-cost estimates for mechanical plants are usually classified into five types. These, with the ranges of accuracy commonly associated with them, are tabulated below.

Type of Estimate	Range of Accuracy, %
Order-of-magnitude (OOM)	+/− 50
Study (factor)	+/− 30
Budget (refined factor)	+/− 20
Definitive (project control)	+/− 10
Detailed (firm)	+/− 5

The first type—OOM—has already been discussed. The next two types are factor estimates. For study estimates, relatively simple and straightforward factor methods are used. For budget authorization estimates, more refined and sophisticated factor methods are applied. Definitive and detailed methods differ in the amount of data made available for estimation. With definitive estimates, many of the relatively low-cost components of first cost are obtained with factors (e.g., piping insulation cost as a percentage of piping cost). With detailed estimates, all, or almost all, of the components are estimated from hard input.

Before we leave this section, a few comments on ranges are in order.

- Ranges are usually specified as "plus or minus $x\%$." They should be specified as "between plus $x\%$ and minus $y\%$." For costs, x should be a larger percentage than y. In the real world, costs (any cost) are under-estimated far more frequently than they are overestimated. For revenues, on the other hand, x should be a smaller percentage than y in order to counterbalance our tendency to be optimistic on how well we can do.

- The accuracies mentioned apply to an entire estimate. Many first-cost estimates are made up of hundreds of items grouped into 15–20 major cost categories (site improvements, buildings, process equipment, etc.), for some of which the ranges of accuracy are lower than for others. In this case, the range of accuracy for an entire estimate is a weighted average.

- The more accurate the estimate, the narrower is the range of accuracy but the higher is the cost of the estimate. Studies usually begin with OOM and factored estimates, and develop into definitive and detail estimates if the results look promising.

20.3.2 Methods of Estimating First-Cost Estimates

The more common methods of estimating first costs are listed below.

- Order-of-magnitude estimates
  - Unit capacity cost ratios
  - Turnover ratios
  - Capacity exponent method (sometimes called the six-tenth rule)
- Factor estimates
  - Lang factor method
  - Refined factor methods
- Definitive and detail estimates

Unit Capacity Costs Unit capacity costs from past installations are available for most capital projects. Examples are dollars per square foot or cubic foot for residential and nonresidential buildings, dollars per ton or pound or volume of capacity per day or month or year for process and manufacturing plants, dollars per linear foot for highways of a given width and construction, and so on. The Suggested Readings at the end of this chapter tell you where to go for such information.

Many unit capacity costs are not current, and many do not necessarily apply to the location in which a proposed facility is to be built. Where unit costs need updating, construction cost indices, such as those given in Appendix 18A, are used. However, extrapolation from more than five years in the past (and, at the outside, ten years) is not recommended. Location indices are handled in the same way. This was illustrated in the example in Appendix 18A.

A real-life illustration of how useful the unit cost approach can be is given below. One of the companies that one of the authors worked for was asked to develop an order-of-magnitude estimate for a stadium to be built in Seoul,

Korea, for the 1988 Olympics. We were given two days for this assignment. Half a day was spent in searching through old issues of architectural, engineering, and construction magazines to find out who had designed and constructed other large arenas. This search was followed up with telephone calls, by which we confirmed construction costs, seating capacities, and other important variables, such as type of construction. In addition, we asked for, and usually got, guesstimates on what such facilities would cost today and the impact of location on cost. We soon discovered that the unit cost per seat, after adjustments for inflation and location indices (for these, see Appendix 18A), fell within relatively narrow limits. This unit cost became the basis for our OOM estimate. Based on the information we were given and our own assessment, we estimated that its range of accuracy was $+30\%$ and -0%.

Turnover Ratio Method   Not as much data are available on the turnover ratio method as on unit capacity costs, but the data are nevertheless helpful at times. The turnover ratio is the estimated annual revenue from sales divided by the first cost. To apply it, we first obtain or prepare an estimate of revenue and then apply the turnover ratio, either one found in the available literature or one based on in-house data. Ratios range from 0.2 for power plants to 8.0 for certain specialty chemical plants.

The ratio can also be used to obtain very preliminary estimates of revenue from estimates of first cost.

Six-tenth Rule or Capacity Exponent Method   The six-tenth rule, which is sometimes called the two-thirds rule, equates the ratio of the total costs of two similar plants of different capacities to the ratio of the capacities raised to a power, which varies typically between 0.6 and 0.9. In formula form, it is

$$C_2/C_1 = (V_2/V_1)^n$$

where C_2 and C_1 are the two costs and V_2 and V_1 are the two capacities; n is the capacity exponent. This rule has some theoretical foundation. It works because capacities are measures of volume (linear dimension cubed), but many costs tend to vary more with surface area (linear dimension squared) than with volume. This, as you can easily verify, gives an exponent of $\frac{2}{3}$. Example 20.1 gives an application of this rule.

Example 20.1   Capacity Exponent Rule   A 1,000-ton-per-day (V_1) ammonia plant was completed in 1988 in the Baton Rouge, Louisiana, area at a total cost of $300 million. The Chemical Engineering Cost Index (see Appendix 18A) at that time was 115. It is currently (June 1992) 121. The estimated first cost, C_1, of a 1,000-ton-per-day plant at current (1992) prices is then $316 million, as shown in the following equation:

$$C_1 = 300(121/115) = \$316 \text{ million}$$

Correlations relating first costs and capacities for ammonia plants give an exponent of 0.7. An OOM estimate (C_2) for a proposed 1,500-ton-per-day (V_2) plant at a location for which the location index is the same as the one in Baton Rouge is then

$$C_2/C_1 = (V_2/V_1)^n$$

$$C_2/316 = (1,500/1,000)^{0.7} = 1.328$$

$$C_2 = 316 \times 1.328 = \$420 \text{ million}$$

The capacity exponent rule is used not only for extrapolating total plant costs but also for equipment costs. For more information on this feature, turn to the Suggested Readings at the end of this chapter.

Lang Factor Method The Lang factor method was developed for process plants for which the civil component is small. It can, with discretion, be applied to the noncivil component of manufacturing plants.

The factor is the ratio of the total cost of a plant to the delivered cost (delivered on-site) of the process equipment—the pumps, compressors, heat exchangers, pressure vessels, heaters, dryers, tanks, filters, conveyors, and other equipment in which raw materials and intermediate products are physically handled and chemically altered to produce final products.

The Lang factors are intended to be all-inclusive, that is, to deliver the estimated cost of a complete facility, including commissioning. However, the owner's costs for monitoring a contractor's performance are not included. These are usually no more than a few percentage points of the total plant cost. In order to use the factor, flowsheets of the process and the size of the process equipment are needed. The process engineering departments of all major engineering contractors who design and construct process and manufacturing plants can turn this information out quickly. Budget estimates for each item of equipment are usually obtained from manufacturers or estimated from in-house data. The appropriate Lang factor is then applied in order to obtain the total cost of the plant. There are three of these factors.

Fluid-handling plants	4.7
Solid- and fluid-handling plants	3.6
Solid-handling plants	3.1

Further work on this factor since the original studies were published indicate an average overall factor for chemical plants of 3.9.

Refined Factor Methods There are many such methods. Some are more refined than others (i.e., some break an estimate down into more cost components than others), but all are based on using separate factors for each cost component. Example 20.2 describes one such method.

Example 20.2   Refined Factor Method   Let the cost of process equipment delivered to the site be represented by 100. Factors for other components of plant cost obtained from published or in-house data are listed in the following tabulation.

	Factor		
	Low	Median	High
Cost of process equipment	100	100	100
Cost of bulk materials	76	95	152
Field labor	72	90	144
Construction supervision and overhead	24	30	48
Home office engineering and design	28	35	56
Total	300	350	500

You will find much more detailed breakdowns in the literature than those just listed. These have the advantage of allowing an experienced estimator to fit an estimate to a particular project. If, for example, one chemical plant is instrumented more heavily than another because the owners of the first plant want it that way, the factor for instrumentation is selected accordingly.

Definitive and Detailed Estimates   The equipment and material component for these estimates comes from equipment lists and specifications and from bills of material. Labor costs come from unit man-hour data, of which there is an ample amount in the literature. Construction supervision and indirects (temporary construction, construction equipment, small tools, etc.) are estimated from input furnished by the construction department. Similarly, home office services for engineering, design, and procurement are estimated from input furnished by the engineering and procurement departments.

COMMENT: We have not yet mentioned that the approximate methods described all apply to inside battery limit (IBL) facilities and not to the outside battery limit (OBL) or off-site facilities that may accompany them. Thus, a new petroleum-refining unit may require feed and product tankage and pumps in a tank farm some distance from the unit. These tanks and the facilities and installations that go with them are OBL facilities. Similarly, the square foot cost of a building and its systems does not include site improvements, such as landscaping, roadways, parking areas, and utility and sewer lines up to a point or points near the building. OBL work will usually range from 15–25% of IBL, but this percentage can be as low as 5% or less and as high as 100% or more.

We conclude this section by reminding you once again that estimating first costs is not for the amateur. This applies to OOM, factor, and definitive estimates. It should be done by cost engineers and estimators who are familiar with how the facilities under study are designed, built, and operated.

20.4 REVENUE AND EXPENSE CASH FLOW ESTIMATES

The difference between revenues and cash expenses for each period of the life cycle of a capital project gives the net cash flow from which the first cost of a new facility is to be recovered with a return.

Revenue estimates depend on forecasts of sales volume and prices. As mentioned, the input data for these variables should be provided by the sales, marketing, or planning departments. The ranges of accuracy vary from relatively narrow to very wide. The relatively narrow belong to established products for which firm markets already exist but for which existing plant capacity may be inadequate. The very wide apply to new products for which markets will have to be developed and for which a new plant or a new process line or the complete renovation of an old plant may be required.

> *COMMENT:* Procter & Gamble may be able to foresee quite accurately where its sales of toothpaste and soap will head. This also applies to such established products as Campbell's tomato soup and Johnson & Johnson's Tylenol. But what will be the revenue from new drugs that Johnson & Johnson and such competitors as Merck and Bristol are now developing, and what new competitive threats can the U. S. automobile and other industries expect in 1993 from the European Community?

Cash flow estimates for the cost of goods and services sold depend on quantities and costs. Quantities are a function of sales volume. They should, if necessary, be provided by the production department. Costs are another matter. Production may not have the expertise to forecasts costs. Neither may the purchasing department, although it should. If so, extrapolating past and current costs may fall into the collective lap of your study group by using trending techniques briefly referred to later.

Operating expenses (also called general, sales, and administrative expenses) include payroll and nonpayroll expenses of the executive staff and of the sales, legal, human resources, financial, and other administrative departments or, to put it simply, include any cost that cannot be charged directly to a unit of sales or to nonoperating costs such as interest. A new facility or any major capital expenditure may increase or decrease the expenses of some or all of the above departments. One of the important functions of a study group is to make certain that these departments understand the impact a new venture may have on their functions and to obtain the input from them (or help them) to prepare estimates of the changes to their operating expenses. Estimates of operating expenses, if done properly, usually fall into relatively narrow ranges.

Interest expense was also listed in the breakdown at the beginning of section 20.2. It can be estimated accurately (down to the last penny) as soon as the terms of the loan on which your study is based are known. So can the repayment of principal.

Such noncash expenses as depreciation depend on first cost and on whatever depreciation methodology you select. For preliminary studies, this is usually the straight-line method. For more definitive studies, it is the one that the IRS and state and local governments allow you to use.

For revenue and expense estimates, there is no accepted terminology for types of estimates differing in their ranges of accuracy. Such terms as "pessimistic," "most likely" (or "base"), and "optimistic" (or, more euphemistically, "minimum anticipated value," "most likely value," and "maximum anticipated value") are frequently used. Accountants use the term "relevant range" when they are preparing master plans (*see* Chapter 13), which is of some help in setting limits. We discuss this term in section 20.7 on break-even analysis.

For preliminary economic studies, the assumption is often made that revenues and expenses will remain the same throughout the life cycle or will show a geometric increase due to inflation only. For more definitive studies, considerable planning time is spent in estimating annual sales volumes and prices for a new facility for the next three to five years. After that, annual sales volume (but not prices) is often assumed to remain constant for the remainder of the life cycle, although it is not unusual to show a decline in volume toward the end of the cycle. This is where the application of equivalent rates of return (Chapter 18), first in the early time zone and then in later time zones with different rates, is useful (*see* Example 6.5).

Trending is a common technique for forecasting revenues and expenses where past and current data are available. Trending plots revenue and expense items, including volumes and prices and their product over the past five to ten years and extrapolates the results some years into the future. The plotting can be as simple as drawing a curve by hand and extrapolating it by eye or as sophisticated as having a software program draw a curve based on a regression analysis. Often the simple methods give as good results as the sophisticated.

Revenue and expense cash flow estimates rely on judgment and common sense (and luck) much more than first-cost estimates. For them, we can repeat with even more emphasis, *they are not for amateurs*. This is doubly true when we remind you that you may have to bring productivity gains and technological innovations into the cash flow patterns, as we did in Chapter 18.

20.5   CASH FLOW ESTIMATES FOR BENEFITS AND DISBENEFITS

What are you going to do about cash flow estimates for benefits and disbenefits? When a new public project (e.g., a highway extension or rerouting, a bridge or tunnel, a recreation facility, a new school building, a town swimming pool, water resource projects, reclamation projects, land development projects, waste recovery projects, an incinerator, solar energy projects, to name a few) is first announced, there is a clamor both from those who want it and from those who don't. Some of the arguments for and against will be trivial. Those that are not fall into two classes—those for which cash flow estimates can be prepared and those (the irreducibles) for which they cannot. The latter we leave to our discussion of multiattribute analysis in Part IV. The others are commented on below.

We have already told you that the burden of estimating cash flows for benefits and disbenefits may fall on your study group. If so, one of the first things for you to do is to obtain copies of studies for similar facilities. State highway and park commissions will furnish copies of such studies if you are sufficiently persuasive and persistent, since such studies are, after all, public property. This also applies to water and sewer districts, to counties, cities, and towns, and, in fact, to most public entities, including the federal government (e.g., the Departments of Energy and Transportation), international monetary institutions, and, in particular, the United Nations. In addition, there is an extensive literature on costing benefits and disbenefits, which you may have to research for examples of how such estimates were prepared for facilities similar to those of your current assignment.

In this text, we can do no more than give you a few general guidelines on how to proceed.

1. Estimate how many people would use the proposed facility, how often they would use it, and what they would be prepared to spend in user fees. You may have to recommend and insist on a survey in order to obtain this information.

2. Obtain similar information for existing facilities, if any, that are now being used by the population center or centers to be served by the new facility.

3. Estimate the benefits to users for using the proposed facility as against using the existing facilities.

4. If there are no existing facilities, use what potential users say they would expend for fees for using the new facilities as a measure of potential benefits.

This approach is not too difficult for a highway relocation or a new bridge or a tunnel that shortens an existing route now in use. You saw this in Chapter 11. However, assembling such data for a new recreation facility and interpreting the data properly are more difficult. Consider Example 20.3.

Example 20.3 A New Park Facility A new park is proposed, which is much nearer to a substantial population center than existing facilities. A survey indicates that 20,000 families would use the new facility two or three times per year. This indicates 50,000 user days per year where the user unit is the family.

About 90% of the families who say they would use the new facility are not using existing facilities because, they say, a round trip by car would consume too much of the day and the cost of $30 for gas, tolls, and parking fees is more than they can afford. However, they say (these "they says" are important) that they would gladly spend $10 per day to get to the new facility and back. The findings are summed up as follows:

User days per year	50,000
User day cost—new facility	$10
User day cost—nearest existing facilities	$30

These figures indicate that the new facility will, as shown below, produce a benefit of $1,000,000 per year.

$$\text{Benefit} = \$50,000(\$30 - \$10) = \$1,000,000$$

The cost of operating the new facility is estimated at $400,000 annually and its first cost at $3,000,000. The park commission has a policy of using 8% for time-value-of-money computations. Based on a 25-year life, the annual worth of the first cost is $281,000 ($3,000,000 × 0.0937). The modified BCR is then

$$\text{BCR} = \$1,000,000 - \$400,000)/\$281,000 = 2.1$$

Property owners adjacent to the new facility may voice objections to it. If so, they will probably challenge your data, that is, your "they says." They may, for example, argue that the benefits are not calculated properly and should have been based on those people who are now using the existing facilities. Since less than 10% of those surveyed said they were, the benefits would not cover operating costs.

Opponents may also argue—this time quite correctly—that user surveys are notoriously incorrect and that many of the people who say they will use the new facilities will not do so. However, if only one-half of them do, the BCR will still be greater than 1.

20.6   OTHER CASH FLOW ESTIMATES

We are left with two other cash flow estimates—working capital and disposal and termination costs.

20.6.1   Working Capital

You were given the accountant's definition of "working capital" in Chapter 2: the difference between current assets and current liabilities. This definition gives us the basis for evaluating the required investment in working capital.

Working capital is the investment in current assets, such as cash, accounts receivable, and inventory, required to operate a new facility less the extent to which creditors will accept current liabilities, such as accounts payable and short-term notes, before cash flows in from sales.

Working capital, like land, is not depreciable. Neither is it tax deductible as an expense. It is usually assumed that the original investment in working capital is recovered at the end of the life cycle.

For preliminary estimates, a common assumption is that working capital requirements will be from three to five weeks (6–10%) of the revenue projected for the first year of operation. For definitive estimates, each of the components that make up working capital is estimated separately, usually with the help of the financial department.

20.6.2 Disposal and Termination Costs

Net cash flow for asset disposal at the end of the life cycle is, for extended life cycles, at best an intelligent guess. For long-lived capital investments (over 20 years) other than land, it is often taken as zero, even for definitive estimates, because, at today's rates of return, cash flows 20–25 years from now contribute very little to present value.

As for land, a conservative estimate is that it can be sold for, or is worth as much, as its original price or, alternatively, that its market value will keep pace with inflation.

Restoration costs, such as the reclamation of landfill after strip mining and decommissioning nuclear power plants can be sufficiently high to require inclusion, even though they may be many years away. Restoration costs for land reclamation are fairly easy to estimate. Others, such as decommissioning nuclear power plants, are more difficult due to lack of know-how and experience.

Any disposal and termination costs that are not included among the cash flows because they cannot be estimated must at least be mentioned as possible future cash burdens.

20.7 BREAK-EVEN ANALYSIS

Problems in break-even analysis appear in many situations. Wherever there is a break-even point, it makes no difference whether we go with one alternative or the other. If we find ourselves on one side of the break-even point, we go one way, and if on the other side, we go the other way.

For short time frames, such problems are usually handled as present economy studies (see Chapter 3). Consider a situation in which you have a choice between leasing machine A or B. Machine A can be leased for a fixed cost of $12,000 annually plus a variable cost of $70 per hour of operation. For machine B, the fixed cost is $16,000 annually and the variable cost is $65 per hour. The break-even point X in hours of operation is

$$\$12,000 + \$70X = \$16,000 + \$65X$$
$$\$5X = \$4,000$$
$$X = 800 \text{ hours}$$

If you expect to operate less than 800 hours per year, you would lease machine A, and if more, you would lease machine B.

Leasing versus buying options often have a break-even point. This, for example, might be the number of months at which it makes no difference whether you lease or buy. Above that number, one alternative, usually buying, is better, and below that number, the other alternative, usually leasing, is better.

The MARR is itself a break-even point. To see this, we remind you that the MARR is the minimum return that an investor wants, because an opportunity forgone could provide the same return. For a PV of zero for which the IRR equals the MARR, it is therefore immaterial, on a purely monetary basis, whether an investor proceeds one way or the other. However, if the estimated return is greater than the MARR, the opportunity under review looks better than the opportunity forgone. If the estimated return is less than the MARR, the reverse is true.

One of the most common applications of break-even analysis is to determine the estimated sales revenue below which there will be a loss and above which there will be a profit. Accountants call this type of analysis a "cost-volume-profit," or CVP analysis, and we discuss it here because it is useful in defining relevant ranges for revenue and cost forecasts.

As you saw in Chapter 2, expenses or costs in statements of income fall into three categories—the cost of goods and services, operating expenses, and other expenses, such as interest expense. This classification is not convenient for break-even analysis, for which accountants classify costs into variable, fixed, and mixed.

- Variable costs are directly proportional to output, that is, to sales volume, as shown in Figure 20.1A.
- Fixed costs are fixed within relevant ranges of output, as shown in Figure 20.1B.
- Mixed costs are part variable and part fixed, as shown in Figure 20.1C.

Examples of variable costs include many of the items in the cost of goods sold—direct labor, direct materials, direct supervision, spoilage, and delivery expense.

Examples of fixed costs include rent, depreciation, executive salaries, research and development expenses, advertising budgets, and generally most of the payroll and nonpayroll costs of staff departments, such as legal and human resources.

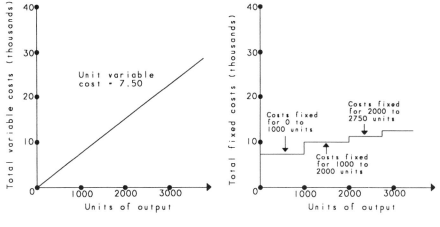

Figure 20.1A Variable costs

Figure 20.1B Fixed costs

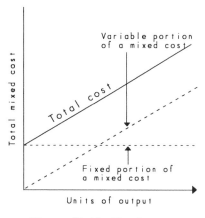

Figure 20.1C Mixed costs

Figure 20.1. Variable, fixed, and mixed costs.

Examples of mixed costs include salespersons' compensation, part of which is fixed and part of which comes from commissions, and utility expenses for some of which there is a fixed charge per month plus a variable charge for usage.

Since mixed costs can be separated into a variable and a fixed component, we are left with just two cost categories, namely, variable costs (VC) and fixed costs (FC).

The net income before taxes (NIBT) of a business is its revenue (R) less its variable and fixed costs. Therefore, for any given level of output,

$$R = VC + FC + NIBT \qquad (20.1)$$

The net income after taxes (NIAT) equals

$$NIAT = NIBT(1 - t) \qquad (20.2)$$

where t is the tax rate.

It follows that

$$R = VC + FC + [NIAT/(1 - t)] \qquad (20.3)$$

At the break-even point, revenue just covers the variable and fixed costs.

$$R \text{ at break-even} = VC + FC \qquad (20.4)$$

Suppose now that, in preparing a master plan, the marketing department projects a lower limit forecast, a most likely forecast, and an upper limit forecast for revenue for the coming year. The relevant range for sensitivity analysis is the difference between the upper and the lower limits. This range will vary from one year to the next.

A cost-volume-profit graph is helpful in seeing the above relationships. Go back for a moment to equation (20.1). The components of this equation are plotted in Figure 20.2. The most likely revenue and sales volume for the coming year is shown as a point on the graph. A straight line is then drawn from this point to the origin. Next, the fixed cost lines are added, as shown. Lastly, the variable costs are superimposed on the fixed costs to give the total cost line. The break-even point is where the revenue and total cost lines cross. To the left of this point, there are losses, and, to the right of this point, there are profits.

In Figure 20.2, we have also shown the expected upper and lower limits for the forecasts of revenue. These bound the most likely forecast and define the relevant range for which a sensitivity analysis should be conducted. In Figure 20.2, all three forecasts are to the right of the break-even point. However, this is not necessarily always so.

In the preceding discussion, we assumed that revenue and variable costs vary directly with sales volume, that is, the relationships are linear. This is often a reasonable assumption, since within the relative range the revenue and cost lines, even though nonlinear, may closely approximate straight lines.

20.8 THE DELPHI METHOD

We close this chapter with a brief comment on the Delphi method. This method asks a group of experts who are working independently of each other to forecast a specific issue relating to the future, for example future sales, future technological breakthroughs, and future energy needs and sources. Here is how the method works.

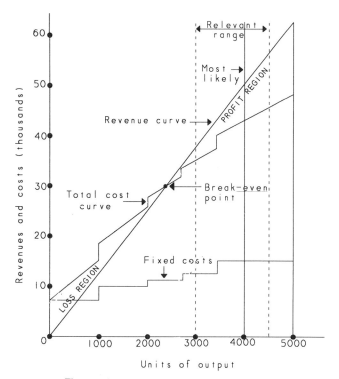

Figure 20.2. Linear cost-volume-profit graph.

1. A panel of experts is selected.
2. Each member of the panel is asked for his or her advice on the issue in question. This is done anonymously and through an intermediary.
3. The ranges of the answers are fed back to the panel members by the intermediary. Each panel member is free to change his or her original response but should also state why he or she has done so.
4. The responses (still anonymous) are again gathered by the intermediary. The range of the responses on the second round is usually narrower than on the first round.
5. The procedure may or may not be repeated for a third time (seldom more), at which time the response of each panel member is usually fixed and a range of forecasts or judgments has been obtained that serve as input for the study being conducted.

The Alaska Department of Commerce and Economic Development used the Delphi method to help prepare a plan on how to develop its energy resources. For the capital project selection process, for-profit and not-for-profit organizations have applied the Delphi method to sales forecasting and to probability distributions or profiles from which expected values can be computed. We come back to this application in Chapter 24 on simulation.

20.9 SUMMARY

Our concern in this chapter is with the estimation of cash flows. Since no estimate is perfect, each estimate has to be associated with a range of accuracy. These ranges provide the input for the technique known as "sensitivity analysis," which is the leading topic of the next chapter.

First-cost and revenue estimates are particularly important for the project selection process, since estimates for so many of the other cash flows—cost of sales, operating expenses, working capital, depreciation, and termination costs—depend on sales and on capital investment.

For first costs, estimates fall into three types—OOM, factor, and definitive.

OOM estimates have ranges of accuracy as high as $+/-50\%$. Unit capacity cost data, turnover ratios, and the capacity exponent method are used to obtain, as the name implies, an order-of-magnitude estimate of the first cost.

Factor estimates rely on detailed estimates for one or several of the key elements that make up the first cost. The remaining elements are then obtained by applying factors to the key element or elements. The ranges of accuracy are $+/-20\%$ or better.

For definitive estimates, all but a small number of the minor elements that enter into first costs are estimated in detail, using equipment and material specifications, bills of material, construction drawings, unit man-hour estimates, and whatever else is available to define, both quantitatively and qualitatively, the scope of the project. Ranges of accuracy are $+/-10\%$ or better.

OOM and factor estimates are used for estimating first costs for preliminary studies. If the project appears favorable, more rigorous estimates are then prepared.

For revenue estimates, there are few guidelines on ranges of accuracy. The ranges depend on whether the sales volume and price forecasts on which revenues are based are for an established product in an established market or for a new product in a new market. For the latter, estimates have been wildly pessimistic and wildly optimistic, which is one reason why organizations that can afford it sometimes use the Delphi method to obtain a consensus from a group of experts on what the future may bring.

Benefits and disbenefits play an important role in the capital selection process for not-for-profit organizations, including, in particular, those in the public sector. Estimates of the cash flows associated with these items are often the most difficult to prepare. Surveys of potential users and what they would be willing to pay for the proposed services are often used but have to be properly interpreted, since the public has a knack for behaving differently than it says it will.

The last topic covered in the chapter is break-even analysis. Such analyses appear in a wide variety of settings. They define a point of indifference between going one way or another. One of the best-known applications is cost-volume-profit analysis, which determines the point at which sales revenues just cover costs. Above this point, there is a profit, and below it, there is a loss. The MARR is itself a break-even point on which go/no-go decisions for implementing capital projects depend.

It is sometimes said that economic analysts and cost engineers are fortune⁺ellers and that accountants are historians. This is a canard. Everyone who deals with the future, as accountants must do when they are preparing master plans, are fortunetellers, and some of us are better at it than others. One of the major points that you should therefore take with you from this chapter is that estimation deals with an uncertain future and that the preparation of the cash flow estimates on which project selection depends is often the most demanding and the most frustrating of all of the tasks with which you will have to deal as the leader of a project selection study.

In closing, we urge you to at least scan the Suggested Readings that follow in order to become familiar with where you can find some of the data needed for cost estimation.

SUGGESTED READINGS

The Suggested Readings are organized as follows:

Cost/Price Indices
Civil Projects
Mechanical Projects
Benefit-cost Analysis
Other

COST/PRICE INDICES

1. *Cost Engineer's Notebook*, American Association of Cost Engineers, Morgantown, WV. Every cost engineer and estimator should be familiar with the publications of the AACE. Three useful publications on price/cost indices are the *International Cost/Price Indexes*, issued 11/89; the *U.S./Canadian Cost/Price Indexes*, issued 11/89; and the *Worldwide Location Cost Factors for Capital Cost Estimation*, issued 11/89.

CIVIL PROJECTS

For estimating first costs on civil projects, you should turn to manuals such as those of Dodge, Means, and others. A partial list of such publications follows.

2. *Dodge Manual for Building Construction Pricing and Scheduling*, annual edition, McGraw-Hill Information Systems Company, Princeton, NJ.

3. *Dodge Guide to Public Works and Heavy Construction*, see reference 2.

4. *Means Building Construction Cost Data*, annual edition, R. S. Means Company, Kingston, MA.

5. *Means Man-Hour Standards*, see reference 4.

6. *Means Square Foot Costs*, see reference 4.

7. *Valuation Quarterly*, Marshall & Swift, Los Angeles, CA. Marshall & Swift call themselves "The Building Cost People." Their *Valuation Quarterly* is very helpful for quickly putting together a building estimate.

8. *McMahon Heavy Construction Cost Guide*, annual edition, Leonard McMahon, Quincy, MA.

MECHANICAL PROJECTS

Some of the publications listed below go back ten or more years. No current updates are planned. They are, nevertheless, valuable references on types of estimates, estimating methods, and factors, ratios, and exponents for OOM estimates.

9. O. P. Kharbanda, *Process Plant and Equipment Cost Estimation* (Carlsbad, CA: Craftsman Book Company, 1979). This book has a wealth of information on process plants and process equipment that is particularly useful for preparing OOM and factored estimates for process plants. See, in particular, Chapters 6 and 7 on types of estimates and estimating methods and Chapters 14–18 on production, equipment, and plant costs. There are many nomograms for both equipment and plant costs that are based on the capacity exponential method.

10. K. M. Guthrie, *Process Plant Estimating Evaluation and Control* (Carlsbad, CA: Craftsman Book Company, 1974). See the comments for reference 9, which also apply to this text.

11. *Gulf Publishing Company Project Management and Estimating Library*, including a seven-volume set on estimation by John S. Page. One of the volumes is on conceptual (a euphemism for OOM and factor) estimating. The other six are for preparing definitive estimates.

12. R. H. Perry and C. H. Chilton, (eds.), *Chemical Engineers Handbook*, latest edition, McGraw-Hill Book Company, New York. Section 25 (in the 5th ed.) by James B. Weaver and H. Carl Bauman on cost and profitability estimation is an excellent reference for process plant economic analyses.

13. A. E. Kerridge, "Evaluate Project Cost Factors." *Hydrocarbon Processing* (July 1982): 203–216.

14. D. S. Remer and L. H. Chai, "Design Cost Factors for Scaling-up Engineering Equipment." *Chemical Engineering Progress* (August 1990): 77–82.

15. M. S. Peters and K. D. Timmerhaus, *Plant Design and Economics for Chemical Engineers* (New York, McGraw-Hill, 1980).

16. John Cran, "Improved Factored Method Gives Better Preliminary Cost Estimates." *Chemical Engineering* (April 6, 1981).

17. S. G. Kirkham, *Preparation and Application of Refined Lang Factor Costing Technique. AACE Bulletin* (October 1972).

BENEFIT-COST ANALYSIS

18. R. Lanyard, (ed.), *Cost Benefit Analysis* (Baltimore, MD: Penguin Books, 1976). A difficult book in parts but possibly the best single text on this subject.

19. C. A. Collier and W. B. Ledbetter, *Engineering Economics and Cost Analysis*, 2nd ed. (New York: Harper & Row, 1988). Chapter 14 on benefit-cost analysis is an excellent discussion on some of the difficulties that occur in estimating cash flows for benefits and disbenefits.

20. J. L. Riggs and T. M. West, *Engineering Economics*, 3rd ed. (New York, McGraw-Hill, 1986). Extension 10C on page 262 discusses the quantification of benefits. Chapter 15 offers a thorough discussion of cost-volume-profit analysis that covers both linear and nonlinear and both single and multiproduct applications.

OTHER

21. J. Price Gittinger, *Economic Analysis of Agricultural Projects* (Baltimore, MD: Johns Hopkins University Press, 1972). This book was sponsored by the International Bank for Reconstruction and Development.

22. Hans A. Adler, *Economic Appraisal of Transport Projects, a Manual with Case Studies* (Bloomington, IN: University of Indiana Press, 1971). This book does for transportation projects what reference 21 does for agricultural projects.

23. United Nations Publications. There are a wealth of these. A few that were published by the United Nations Industrial Development Organization (UNIDO) in Vienna are listed below:

Guidelines for Project Evaluation, 1972

Manual for the Preparation of Industrial Feasibility Studies, 1978

The Initiation and Implementation of Industrial Projects in Developing Countries, 1975

Guide to Practical Project Appraisal, 1978

Unfortunately, there are no plans to update these publications, but they remain valuable for approaching and appraising projects in developing countries.

PROBLEMS

Note: For construction and other costs and for price indices referred to in the problems that follow, see Table 18.1A.

20-1 In the introductory section of this chapter, we say that sensitivity analysis is essentially a what-if analysis. Explain this statement in your own words.

20-2 Do estimates of first costs depend on estimates of revenues or the other way round, or both ways?

20-3   Why are estimates of first costs and revenues so important for preparing estimates of other pertinent cash flows?

20-4   Why are the ranges of accuracy for first-cost estimates of buildings narrower than those of other civil projects and of mechanical projects.

20-5   Chapter 20 has been concerned entirely with cash flow estimates. What other variables are needed for a project selection study? Why weren't these covered in this chapter?

20-6   What is a factor estimate? What does it mean when we say that factor estimates gradually merge into definitive estimates?

20-7   What, in your opinion, is the difference between a forecast and an estimate? Does the statement "Good forecasts make good estimates!" have any meaning for you?

20-8   Order-of-magnitude estimates for first costs are generally based on unit capacity correlations, for example, costs per square foot, costs per 1,000 barrels of refinery capacity, costs per ton of sugar production, and so on. How would you expect unit capacity estimates to correlate with the size of the facilities under consideration? Why do size and unit costs correlate in this way?

20-9   The cost of estimating first costs depends on the type of estimate.
a) Explain why this is so.
b) How do you decide what type of first-cost estimate you need?

20-10   The first-cost estimate of a proposed capital investment totals $10 million. The estimated annual cash costs for the first year of operation are $12 million. The total available funding, including borrowed capital, is $11 million. Comment on the sufficiency of the funding.

First-cost Estimates

20-11   Data on four construction cost indices and on the Consumer Price Index (CPI) are given in Table 18A.1. Is there some justification for saying that the CPI is an adequate forecasting and estimating tool for first costs, even though it covers a much wider range of goods and services than those found in the construction industry?

20-12   Compare the Chemical Engineering Cost Index in Table 18.1A for 1985, 1986, and 1987 with the three other construction cost indices. What could explain the difference in the behavior of these indices?

20-13   The year is 1991. Your company has a cost study underway for a new industrial facility that is similar to one built in 1989. Your study team decides to use location indices and construction cost indices to obtain a preliminary estimate of what the first cost might be for a facility of the same size to be built in 1991. The first cost of the old plant was

$15 million, and its location index was 102 in 1989. The location index of the proposed plant was 98 at that time.

a) What would the cost of the old plant have been in 1989 if it had been built at the new location?

b) What is the estimated cost of the new plant, using the ENR Construction Cost Index for forecasting where construction costs may go?

20-14 A chemical plant with an output of 2,500 tons per day was completed in 1989 for a total cost of $70 million. The Department of Commerce Construction Cost Index at that time was 112. It is 117 today (1992). What is an order-of-magnitude estimate for the first cost of a 3,500-ton-per-day plant to be built in a similar location in 1994? The capacity exponent for this type of plant is 0.65.

20-15 Equipment for a new process facility in an existing oil refinery is estimated to cost $12,300,000. What is the OOM estimate for the complete facility, using the Lang factor?

20-16 Equipment for a proposed coal liquefaction plant is estimated to cost $110 million. What is the OOM estimate for the complete facility, using the Lang factor?

20-17 A plant producing 1,000 units per day of a given product cost $1 million. A similar plant producing 1,500 units per day in the same location cost $1.3 million. What is the capacity exponent factor?

20-18 You need to estimate the cost of a conveyor to carry 10,000 bushels of wheat per hour. The following data are available from company records on previous purchases of conveyors for this service:

a) A 5,000-bushel-per-hour conveyor cost $100,000 in 1988, at which time the CPI was 118.

b) A 7,500-bushel-per-hour conveyor cost $140,000 in 1990, when the index was 124.

You estimate that the index will be 127 when the conveyor is purchased and installed. Estimate the cost of the new conveyor.

Revenues and Expenses

20-19 Why are future revenues difficult to forecast? How do we attempt to get around this difficulty?

20-20 For which of the following revenue and expense estimates for the coming year would you use a relatively narrow range and for which a relatively wide range? Justify your answers.

a) Sales estimates of a new cologne to be produced by Calvin Klein

b) Sales estimates by Mercedes-Benz for U.S. car sales.

c) Worldwide sales of airplanes by Boeing.

d) Macy's operating expenses for the coming year.

20-21   Contrast the difficulty of forecasting the cash inflow from revenue with that of estimating the cash outflow for the cost of goods and/or services sold.

20-22   Contrast the data-gathering function for estimates of cash outflows for the cost of goods and services sold with that for estimates of operating expenses.

Break-even Analysis

20-23   The break-even point is the "go" or "no go" point, the "yes" or "no" point, the "this way" or "that way" point. What is the break-even point for the IRR? For the BCR? For any of the three worths?

20-24   Graph each of the following relationships over a relevant range from 0 to 10,000 units:
a) Variable expenses of $10 per unit
b) Fixed expenses of $50,000
c) Mixed expenses made up of $20,000 of fixed costs and $6 per unit of variable costs.

20-25   Mack's Auto Supply has fixed monthly expenses of $7,200 and a contribution margin ratio (the ratio of sales less variable costs divided by sales) of 30%.
a) What must monthly sales be to break even?
b) To earn $6,000 before taxes?
c) To earn $4,000 after taxes for a tax rate of 40%?

20-26   The ABC Paint Company has fixed expenses of $80,000 and variable expenses of $3 per unit. The sales price of its products is $6 per unit.
a) What is the break-even point in units?
b) What is the break-even point in dollars?

20-27   The Pensy Chemical Company has two major product lines. The dollar sales of each product are about the same each month. The first product has a contribution margin ratio (*see* Problem 20-25) of 40%, and the second, of 50%. Fixed costs average $100,000 per month.
a) What must monthly sales be to break even?
b) To earn $50,000 before taxes?

20-28   The sales price is $100 per unit. The variable costs are $30 per unit, and the fixed costs are $350,000 annually.
a) What is the break-even point in number of units sold annually?

b) What is the break-even point in annual sales dollars?

c) What will be the net profit before taxes if the number of units sold is 2,000 above the break-even point?

d) What will be the total cost per unit if the number of units sold is 2,000 above the break-even point?

e) Suppose that 3,000 units could be sold in a foreign market for $45 per unit. What is the incremental gain or loss, if any, assuming the incremental cost of sales for this transaction will be $15,000.

20-29 Sketch the following graphs, using the data and computations of Problem 20-28:

a) Total unit cost versus output

b) A cost-volume-profit graph similar to Figure 20.2, assuming no sales abroad

c) A cost-volume-profit graph showing the effect of selling 3,000 units abroad.

20-30 Using the data in Problem 20-28, assume that the master plan for next year projects a net income after taxes of $125,000. The tax rate is 50%.

a) How many units have to be produced, assuming no sales abroad?

b) How many units have to be produced, assuming 3,000 units are sold abroad?

20-31 A large firm has a manufacturing division with a normal capacity of 1 million units, which sell for $60 each. The price is built up from $30 for variable costs, $20 for fixed costs, and a markup of 20% to cover profit before taxes. Suppose a severe recession in which only 200,000 units can be sold and then only if the price is reduced to $50 per unit. Fixed costs can be cut 15% if the plant stays open to produce 200,000 units only and 30% if the plant is shut down until the situation improves.

a) Should the plant stay open or be shut down?

b) At what price for the reduced production level should the plant be shut down?

20-32 A firm has two plants to produce a given product. Each plant has a capacity of 10,000 units per year. Plant A has fixed costs of $100,000, and Plant B of $80,000. Plant A has two processing lines, one of which can produce 4,000 units at a variable cost of $10 per unit, and the other of which, a much older and less automated line, can produce 6,000 units at a variable cost of $12 per unit. Plant B has two modern processing lines, one of which can produce 5,000 units at a variable cost of $9 per unit, and the other of which can produce 5,000 units at a variable cost of $8 per unit. What load should be assigned to each unit if production varies between 1 and 20,000 units?

Miscellaneous Problems

20-33 Agricultural production in many countries, including ours, is subsidized. A new water project is under review for increasing agricultural production. Should the increased output be estimated at market prices or higher?

20-34 A new project gives an unemployed worker a job. Should the unemployment benefits that he or she does not receive be included as a cost saving in evaluating the project?

20-35 Contrast the Delphi method with brainstorming. How can the two methods be combined?

20-36 Get a group together (no less than four and no more than six people), and attempt to run a Delphi study in order to reach a consensus on some topic of mutual concern; for example, what kind of economic system will prevail in the former Soviet Union two years from now, what will be the rate of inflation in the United States three years from now, and so on?

____21
SENSITIVITY ANALYSIS

21.1 INTRODUCTION

In the introduction to Chapter 20, we mentioned that sensitivity analysis differs from the more sophisticated analyses to be presented in Chapters 22 and 23 in that probabilities are not assigned to base estimates or to the upper and lower limits of their ranges of accuracy or to any values in between. Rather, we take the ranges of accuracy that were examined in Chapter 20 for all the cash flow streams usually encountered in economy studies, and from these we calculate the ranges within which the figures of merit will fall.

You will see that sensitivity analysis allows us to determine which parameters (both cash flow and noncash flow variables, such as planning horizons) are the most sensitive to a project's economic feasibility. Highlighting these gives us the opportunity to examine them more closely and possibly to improve the pertinent cash flow estimates (e.g., narrowing the ranges of accuracy by gathering additional data) in order to give us greater confidence in our conclusions and recommendations.

21.2 SENSITIVITY ANALYSIS—EXAMPLES

With the background you now have, the best way to begin the study of sensitivity analysis is with examples illustrating the behavior of figures of merit as cash flow and other parameters are varied. This is done in the examples that follow.

Example 21.1   A Parking Structure   You are employed by an A/E (architect/engineer) firm that has just received a contract to perform a feasibility study for an indoor parking structure. Your firm expects this study ultimately to lead to a contract to design the structure and supervise its construction. You have been selected to handle the study.

Your client, a nearby university, is a not-for-profit entity. The initial investment is not to exceed $5 million, of which $1 million is the cost of a property on which the university has a purchase option. An OOM estimate indicates that an indoor multilevel parking structure costing approximately $4 million can provide 500 parking spaces. Of these, the university plans to reserve 125 spaces for members of its staff at an annual fee of $200. Parking facilities are currently so scarce in the neighborhood surrounding the university that it sees no problem in renting the remaining 375 spaces for $1,500 annually. This assumption is subsequently confirmed by your study. In fact, there are some indications that it could go higher but need not go lower.

The remaining cash flow estimates for the study are prepared by your study group. These include the operating and maintenance costs, which are estimated at $100,000 annually, the salvage value, and the working capital.

For the salvage value, you recommend $1 million, the purchase price of the land. This assumption is a common one and is obviously conservative. It assumes that the land will not appreciate in value and that the building will be worth little or nothing at the end of the planning horizon, which is taken as 30 years.

For working capital, you and your client agree that this will be negligible. Rental fees are received in advance, and there is no investment in inventory other than maintenance and cleaning equipment and supplies.

The preceding parameters, which represent the base case on which the study is to proceed, are summarized in Table 21.1.

At a meeting with your client, it was agreed that a preliminary study would first be carried out under the following simplifying assumptions:

- All cash flows would be treated as end-of-year discrete cash flows.
- No replacement capital would be required over the life of the investment.

TABLE 21.1   Base Case Estimates

First cost	
Land	$1,000,000
Buildings	$4,000,000
Working capital	0
Annual revenue	
Staff (125 × $200)	$25,000
Area residents (375 × $1,500)	$562,500
Annual operating costs	$100,000
Net cash flow from operations	
($25,000 + $562,500 − $100,000)	$487,500
Salvage value	$1,000,000
Planning horizon, yrs.	30

- External funding, that is, loans or mortgages, would not be considered at this time.
- The IRR will be the dominant figure of merit.
- Inflation will be ignored.
- An MARR of 8% would be used for discounting cash flows.

It was further assumed that the university would not be required to pay income taxes. Therefore, depreciation need not be considered. The fact that the university has been chartered as a not-for-profit entity makes this assumption reasonable, even though most of the facility would be leased to outsiders.

The cash flow diagram for this example is given in Figure 21.1. The cash flow table is given below.

EOY	Cash Flow Stream	Symbol	Cash Flow, $
0	Initial investment	P	$5,000,000
1–30	Net cash flow from operations	A	487,500
30	Salvage	S	1,000,000

The factor equation for this set of cash flows is

$$PW = -P + A(P/A,i,N) + S(P/F,i,N) \qquad (21.1)$$

The present worth for the base conditions and an MARR of 8% is then

$$PW = -P + A(P/A,8,30) + S(P/F,8,30)$$
$$= -\$5,000,000 + \$487,500 \times 11.26 + \$1,000,000 \times 0.10$$
$$= +\$589,250$$

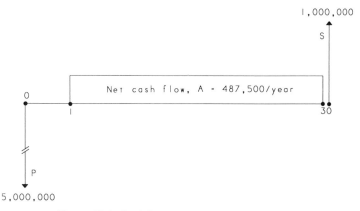

Figure 21.1. Cash flow diagram for Example 21.1.

TABLE 21.2 Limits of Accuracy

First cost	
Land	0%
Buildings	$-10\%, +20\%$
Revenue	
University staff	0%
Area residents	$0\%, +16\frac{2}{3}\%$
Operating costs	$-10\%, +10\%$
Salvage value	0%

Setting the PW equal to zero gives an IRR of 9.2%. You obtained this value with the help of a hand calculator or by interpolating from the interest rate tables for 9% and 10% in Appendix B or by accessing your firm's computer program for handling time-value-of-money computations.

After completing your calculations, you meet with your client to discuss ranges of accuracy. The results of this discussion are given in Table 21.2.

As mentioned, the university has an option to purchase the property on which the garage is to be built for $1 million. Therefore, this cash flow is fixed. The cost of the building was derived from a square foot estimate (*see* Chapter 20). Its range of accuracy was taken as 20% on the upside and 10% on the downside.

For the revenue from its staff, the university has committed itself to annual fees of $200 per space and 125 spaces, so this cash flow is also fixed, at least for this preliminary study. However, for the area residents, the market survey indicates that the $1,500 annual fee per space is conservative. Due to the prime location of the parking facility, fees as high as $1,750 ($16\frac{2}{3}\%$ larger than the base estimate) could be charged and might still maintain full occupancy.

The operating costs are fairly easy to estimate. It was assumed that the range of accuracy would be plus or minus 10%. The salvage value is fixed by the assumption that it will equal the original cost of the land.

The preceding information is summed up in the following tabulation, which shows the cash flows for the base case and for the upper and lower limits of each cash flow stream.

	Cash Flow Estimates (000)		
Stream	Lower Limit	Base	Upper Limit
Land	$1,000	$1,000	$1,000
Building	3,600	4,000	4,800
Total first cost	$4,600	$5,000	$5,800
Staff revenue	$25	$25	$25
Area resident revenue	562	562	656
Total revenue	$587	$587	$681
Operating costs	$90	$100	$110
Salvage value	$1,000	$1,000	$1,000

To carry out the sensitivity analysis, you take one cash flow at a time and, holding all of the others at their base value, you calculate the present worths and the IRRs at the lower and upper limits of its range. For the first cost, for example, you substitute first the lower limit of $4,600,000 and then the upper limit of $5,800,000 for P in equation (21.1). The results are given in the following tabulation. The present worth is based on an MARR of 8%.

First Cost	Estimated Cash Flow, $	Present Worth, $	IRR, %
Lower limit	$4,600,000	$989,000	10.1%
Base	5,000,000	589,000	9.2
Upper limit	5,800,000	−211,000	7.6

The present worth and the IRR are plotted against the first cost in the sensitivity graph of Figure 21.2. At an IRR equal to the MARR (8%), the first cost is $5,580,000. This is then the break-even point (the go/no-go point) for this parameter, with all other parameters at their base value.

Each of the other cash flow streams is examined in the same way, that is, by holding all other cash flow streams at their base estimates. The IRR resulting from one of these computations is given in the following equation. It applies to the upper limit of the revenue from area residents, which is $656,250. The net cash flow from operations is therefore $571,250 ($656,250 + $25,000 − $110,000), and the equation for calculating the IRR is

$$0 = -\$5,000,000 + \$571,250(P/A,i,30) + \$1,000,000(P/F,i,30)$$

The IRR is 11% or approximately 20% higher than for the base case revenue from area residents.

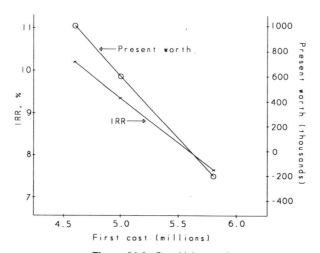

Figure 21.2. Sensitivity graph.

In Table 21.3 that follows, the values of the IRR for the base case and for the upper and lower limits of each parameter are given. In addition, the absolute value of the difference between the lower and the upper limits is given.

COMMENT: You will recall from high school algebra that the absolute value of $-x$ is $+x$, or simply x, and that this is written

$$|-x| = x$$

Thus, for the area residential value in Table 21.3,

$$|(1) - (3)| = |9.2 - 11.0| = |-1.8| = 1.8$$

The two most sensitive parameters are the first cost of the building and the area resident revenue. We could have foretold this by the magnitude of the cash flows and the wider ranges of accuracy as compared to the other cash flows. However, we could not have foretold that the figure of merit would vary from a minimum of 7.6% to a maximum of 11.0%.

In Example 21.1, we conducted a sensitivity analysis only for the cash flow parameters. We can, of course, go further by including variations in parameters other than cash flows, for example, the planning horizon and rate of inflation. Consider first the planning horizon.

For the base case, the horizon was 30 years. You recommend looking at shorter time periods, namely 20 and 25 years, but not at longer time periods, since, in your opinion, 30 years is already on the high side for an investment of this type (*see* reading 2 in the Suggested Readings at the end of this chapter). For the base case cash flows, a planning horizon of 25 years reduces the IRR from 9.2% to 8.8% and for 20 years, to 8.0%, indicating that this parameter is a sensitive one. (You should have no trouble in confirming these figures.)

TABLE 21.3 Range of Values for IRR

	IRR, %			
Cash Flow Stream	Lower Limit	Base Case	Upper Limit	Absolute Value of Difference
	(1)	(2)	(3)	$|(1) - (3)|$
First cost—land	9.2	9.2	9.2	0
First cost—building	10.1	9.2	7.6	2.5
Staff revenue	9.2	9.2	9.2	0
Area resident revenue	9.2	9.2	11.0	1.8
Operating costs	9.4	9.2	9.0	0.4
Salvage value	9.2	9.2	9.2	0

For the rate of inflation, which was ignored, that is, taken as zero for the preliminary study, we go to Example 21.2.

Example 21.2 Inflation   You and your client agree to redo the preceding study without the assumption that inflation is zero. You suggest an annual rate of inflation, f, of 4% over the 30-year period, and your client accepts this suggestion. This means that the revenue from staff and area residents and the operating costs will rise 4% annually, and that the salvage value at the end of 30 years will be $3,240,000 [$1,000,000 \times (1.04)^{30}$].

The new MARR is now about 12%, that is, (8% + 4%). The exact value from equation (18.9) is 12.3%, as shown below:

$$\text{MARR} = (1 + i_{eq})(1 + f) - 1$$

$$= (1.08)(1.04) - 1 = 0.123 \text{ or } 12.3\%$$

The easiest way to solve this problem is to use the equivalent rate of return, i_{eq}, which is 8%. The computations performed in Example 21.1 for this value of i remain as is, except that the values of IRR in Table 21.3 are now IRR_{eq}'s, that is, equivalent internal rates of return rather than IRRs. However, these are easily converted to IRRs through the relationship

$$\text{IRR} = (1 + \text{IRR}_{eq})(1 + f) - 1$$

This is done in the following tabulation for the first cost only.

First Cost	Estimated Cash Flow, $	IRR_{eq}, %	IRR, %
Lower limit	$4,600,000	10.1%	14.5%
Base	5,000,000	9.2	13.6
Upper limit	5,800,000	7.6	11.9

The IRR is, as expected, about 4% higher with inflation than without inflation, indicating that the rate of inflation is more sensitive than any of the other parameters. However, this is misleading. The present worth for an MARR of 12.3%, including 4% inflation for all cash flow streams, is identical to the present worth for an MARR of 8% with no inflation. For this reason, the rate of inflation is not included as a parameter in the graphical and tabular presentations in the next two sections of this chapter.

COMMENT: This example illustrates why the present worth is a simpler and better figure of merit than the IRR, not only for ranking, but also for sensitivity analyses. Economic analysts generally prefer the PW to the IRR, but, as mentioned several times, many investors feel more at home with the IRR. If, by the way, you do not recall that you will get the same present worth for uninflated cash flows using i_{eq} as for inflated cash flows (assuming they are all inflated by the same compound amount factor) using i, you had better refresh your memory by rereading Chapter 18.

Suppose now that, due to some unforeseen (and possibly unforeseeable) soil condition, at least part of the structure will require piling and that its estimated cost, based on preliminary sketches and designs, is now $5,000,000 plus or minus 10%. For the upper limit of this range ($5,500,000), what parking fees would have to be charged area residents in order to recover a return of 8%? This question is covered in Example 21.3.

Example 21.3   Revised First-Cost Estimate   The unknown in this example is the revenue from area residents. Call this X. It follows that

	Annual Cash Flow (000)
Area resident revenue	X
Revenue from staff	$25
Operating costs	$100
Net cash flow	$(X - 75)$

Substituting in equation (21.1) with i equal to the MARR of 8%, PW set at zero, and cash flows in thousands gives

$$0 = -\$6,500 + \$(X - 75)(P/A,8,30) + \$1,000(P/F,8,30)$$
$$= -\$6,500 + \$(X - 75) \times 11.26 + \$1,000 \times 0.10$$
$$\$(X - 75) = \$6,400/11.26 = \$568$$
$$X = \$643$$

The fee per space for 375 spaces would therefore have to be $1,715 ($643,000/375), which means that the parking structure is still a viable project, for an MARR of 8% since the market survey indicated fees as high as $1,750 should assure full occupancy.

21.3   GRAPHICAL PRESENTATION OF SENSITIVITY ANALYSIS

The graphical presentation discussed in this section is called a "relative sensitivity graph." It is one of the most common and useful diagrams for displaying the result of a sensitivity analysis in which more than one parameter is examined. In such graphs, the horizontal axis is the percent change in the parameters from their base values, and the vertical axis is the figure of merit. This is usually the present worth or the IRR. Often two figures are prepared—one for each of these profitability criteria.

The relative sensitivity graph for the parking structure in Example 21.1 is plotted in Figure 21.3. The figure of merit is the IRR.

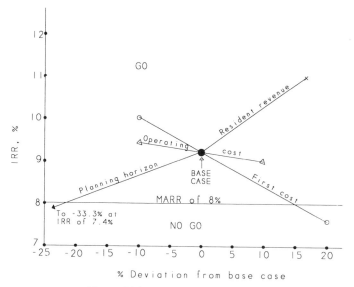

Figure 21.3. Relative sensitivity graph.

In Figure 21.3, four parameters are plotted: (1) First cost, (2) area resident revenue, (3) operating cost, and (4) planning horizon.

The sensitivity line for each parameter extends from the lower limit of its range to its upper limit. The limits are expressed as percentages of the base value. Thus, for the first cost, the limits are -10% and $+20\%$ and for the area residents, 0% and $+16\frac{2}{3}\%$. The steeper the slope of a parameter's sensitivity line is, the more sensitive is the parameter and the more pronounced is the change in the figure of merit.

Figure 21.3 shows that the area resident revenue has the steepest slope and is therefore the most sensitive parameter. The first cost comes next, followed by the planning horizon. The least sensitive parameter is the operating cost, due not only to its small size but also to the fact that the estimated range of accuracy for such costs is relatively small. Three of the parameters—the staff revenue, the cost of land, and the salvage value—have zero sensitivity and are therefore not shown.

When you are preparing sensitivity graphs, keep the following in mind.

- Don't extend sensitivity lines beyond the percentages that define their upper and lower limits. In other words, don't extrapolate.
- If you have too many parameters on a single graph, some of the lines may be so close together that the graph will be difficult to read. If so, use two graphs or limit a single graph to the most sensitive parameters.
- The three points for each line—the base case and the upper and lower limits—are often connected with a pair of straight lines. Remember,

however, that this is equivalent to linear interpolation and that the lines are really curved.

- If, for any parameter, the two straight lines connecting the base case with its limits differ substantialy in slope, figures of merit for points between the lower limit and the base case and between the base case and the upper limit should be calculated so that a proper curve can be sketched.

21.4 TABULAR PRESENTATION OF SENSITIVITY ANALYSIS

Tabular presentations are often used to supplement or even replace graphical presentations, particularly when there are so many variables that placing them all on one graph produces a jumble of lines that are difficult to read. Table 21.4 is typical of the format used to present the results of the computations from Example 21.1 and to provide comparative data as well.

Table 21.4 is broken down into two parts. The first part gives the percentage range of each parameter and its estimates for the base case and for the upper

TABLE 21.4 Results of Sensitivity Analysis

Parameter	Range of Parameter		Figure of Merit (FOM), IRR, %	Deviations from Base Value	
	%	Value		Numerical	Percent
	A	B	C	D	E
				(C − 9.2)	(D/9.2)
Cost of land, $	0	$1,000,000	9.2	0	0
Cost of building, $					
Upper limit	+20	$4,800,000	7.6	−1.6	−17.4
Base case	0	4,000,000	9.2	—	—
Lower limit	−10	3,600,000	10.1	+0.9	+9.8
Resident revenue, $/yr.					
Upper limit	+16⅔	$656,000	11.0	+1.8	+19.6
Base case	0	562,500	9.2	—	—
Lower limit	0	562,500	9.2	0	0
Staff revenue, $/yr.	0	$25,000	9.2	0	0
Operating costs, $/yr.					
Upper limit	+10	$110,000	9.0	−0.2	−2.2
Base case	0	100,000	9.2	—	—
Lower limit	−10	90,000	9.4	+0.2	+2.2
Salvage value, $	0	$1,000,000	9.2	0	0
Planning horizon, yrs.					
Upper limit	0	30	9.2	0	0
Base case	0	30	9.2	—	0
Lower limit	−33⅓	20	7.4	−1.8	−19.6

TABLE 21.5 Ranking Parameters by Their Impact on Figures of Merit

Parameter	Percent Change in Parameter	Percent Change in FOM	Sensitivity Ratio
	A	B	|B/A|
Resident Revenue			
Upper limit	+ 16⅔	+19.6	1.18
Cost of Building			
Lower limit	− 10	+9.8	0.98
Upper limit	+ 20	−17.4	0.87
Planning Horizon			
Lower limit	− 33⅓	− 19.6	0.58
Operating Costs			
Upper limit	+ 10	−2.2	0.22
Lower limit	− 10	+2.2	0.22

Note: Columns A and B come from columns A and E in Table 21.4. The sensitivity ratio in column C is the absolute value of B/A.

and lower limits. The second part gives the figure of merit and its numerical and percentage deviation from its base case value.

The data from Table 21.4 are often used to rank order the parameters by their impact on the figure of merit (FOM), in this case, the IRR. This is done in Table 21.5.

From Table 21.5 we see that the two most sensitive parameters are the resident revenue and the building cost and that the lower limit of the building cost is more sensitive than the upper limit. A 16⅔% change in resident income produces a 19.6% change in the IRR, or, on a relative basis, a 1% change in resident income produces a 1.18% change in the IRR.

Rank ordering the sensitive parameters, as we did in Table 21.5, allows us to concentrate our efforts on the most important variables and to decide for which variables, if any, more data should be gathered to improve the quality of the study and ultimately the quality of the decision.

21.5 COMBINATION SENSITIVITY ANALYSIS

So far we have matched the variation or range of the figure of merit with the range of accuracy of individual parameters. The next question is, "What about variations in combinations of parameters?" With more than a few parameters, the number of combinations is endless (or seems so), which is why we usually create scenarios that appear reasonable or, if not reasonable, at least set the limits within which the figures of merit could fall.

> *COMMENT:* You will recall that we had a similar situation in Chapter 13 when we were determining the number of members in sets of MEAs to be considered for budgeting capital expenditures.

One scenario is to look at what happens if everything that could go wrong does go wrong. Although this is not a likely case (you will see in Chapter 22 how unlikely it is), it does establish a maximum downside risk. Conversely, we can also look at what happens if everything goes right. This is also an unlikely event but will establish a maximum upside benefit.

For situations that, like the parking structure, have long planning horizons, scenarios could include the impact of a few years of recession or prosperity during which revenues and costs are lower or higher than their base case estimates. For capital expenditures with short planning horizons—five years or less—such scenarios could cover much or all of the life cycle. Some interesting results sometimes crop up. A recession that is expected to reduce the cash flow for revenues and operating costs may also reduce the first cost and produce a figure of merit that is still attractive.

One of the best ways to handle combinations is to use the Monte Carlo simulation technique that will be described in Chapter 24. This and a good computer will do more for you than attempting to create scenarios.

21.6   ISO-QUANT GRAPHS

Iso-quant curves are another important addition to techniques for presenting the results of a sensitivity analysis. "Iso-quant" means "the same quantity." As applied to sensitivity graphs, it means a set of lines, for each of which the figure of merit is a constant.

In Example 21.1, we found that the two key variables in deciding to build a parking structure were the area resident revenue and the building cost. We use these two parameters in Example 21.4 to construct iso-quants.

> *Example 21.4 Iso-quant Graphs* In the iso-quant graph of Figure 21.4, the *x*-axis is the first cost of the parking structure and the *y*-axis is the area resident revenue. The iso-quant lines are lines for each of which the figure of merit—in this case the IRR—is constant. To see how these lines were obtained, go back to equation (21.1) in Example 21.1, which, for convenience, is reproduced below:
>
> $$PW = -P + A(P/A,i,N) + S(P/F,i,N)$$
>
> Now set PW equal to zero, since the iso-quants are IRRs. Substitute the base case values of the parameters that do not change in equation (21.1). These are *N* at 30 years, the value of the land at \$1,000,000, and *S* at \$1,000,000. The net cash

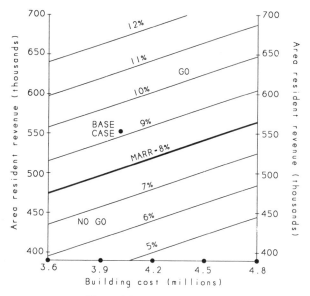

Figure 21.4. IRR Iso-quants

flow, A, is made up of one parameter that changes—the resident revenue, X—and two that do not, namely, the staff revenue at \$25,000 and the operating costs at \$100,000. The values of A is then

$$A = X + \$25,000 - \$100,000 = X - \$75,000$$

P is made up of the cost of the building B plus the cost of the land and therefore equals $(B + \$1,000,000)$.

We first calculate the iso-quant for IRR equals 8%. Substituting 8% and the previous values in equation (21.1) and expressing the cash flow in thousands gives

$$0 = -\$(B + 1,000) + \$(X - 75)(P/A,8,30) + \$1,000(P/F,8,30)$$

We now set B equal to its lower limit of \$3,600,000 and solve for X. We do the same for B at its base value of \$4,000,000 and for its upper limit of \$4,800,000. For the lower limit,

$$0 = -\$4,600 + \$(X - 75)(P/A,8,30) + \$1,000(P/F,i,30)$$
$$= -\$4,600 + \$(X - 75)(11.26) + \$1,000 \times 0.10$$

Solving for $(X - 75)$ and then for X, we get

$$\$(X - 75) = \$4,500/11.26 = \$400$$
$$X = \$475$$

The resident revenue for the base case building cost and for the upper limit building cost are $510,000 and $581,000, respectively, and should be checked by you. The following tabulation sums up the computations.

Building Cost, $	Resident Revenue, $
3,600,000	475,000
4,000,000	510,000
4,800,000	581,000

We proceed as above for other values of the IRR to produce the family of curves in Figure 21.4. The base case for a building cost of $4,000,000 and resident revenue of $562,500 shows an IRR of 9.2%, which is what we obtained in Example 21.1.

In Figure 21.4, the curve for 8% appears in boldface. Since the MARR is 8%, this rate of return separates the figure into two parts. The part above the curve is "go," the part below the curve is "no-go," and the curve itself is an indifference line for which an investor is indifferent between the situation under review and the opportunity forgone.

COMMENT: In this chapter, you were given simple examples on the application of sensitivity analysis. In real life, the problems are generally more complex; that is, there are more variables and often wider ranges of accuracy. For many of these, the use of computer programs is almost mandatory.

There are at least two basic types of computer programs. The first type is specifically designed to do economic analyses for project selection. Many large companies have developed in-house programs for this purpose, and, if these are available to you, you should learn how to use them. A number of vendors have produced similar programs, for most of which adequate instruction manuals are available.

The second type includes general-purpose spreadsheets, such as Lotus 1-2-3, Multiplan, and others. These can be used to do economic analyses, but they require that you set up a program to carry out the calculations.

For more information on computer programs for project selection, turn to the Suggested Readings (3,4,5,6,7) at the end of this chapter.

21.7   SUMMARY

Sensitivity analysis takes the ranges within which cash flow estimates and other parameters fall to compute the range within which the selected figure of merits will fall.

Initially, such analyses vary only one parameter at a time so that its effect on the figure of merit can be gauged. In this way, the sensitivity of each parameter is determined and the more sensitive parameters are identified. Further analyses may then be conducted in which more than one parameter at a time is varied. Due to the many possible combinations, such analyses are often limited to pairs of parameters, with emphasis on those that are the most sensitive.

The two most common graphical representations of the results of a sensitivity analysis are relative sensitivity graphs and iso-quants. A relative sensitivity graph plots the selected figure of merit against the percentage deviation of the parameters from their base values.

An iso-quant graph is a family of curves, each member of which has a constant value for the selected figure of merit. The two most sensitive parameters usually serve as the input for such graphs. If there are more than two such parameters, more than one iso-quant is drawn.

Tabular presentations are also common for summing up the results of a sensitivity analysis. The results are ranked using a sensitivity ratio that measures changes in the figure of merit resulting from the ranges of accuracy in the estimated value of each parameter.

SUGGESTED READINGS

1. Ted Eschenbach, *Cases on Engineering Economy* (New York: John Wiley & Sons, 1989). A first of its kind. This is a text with which every engineering economist should be familiar. The three chapters preceding the cases include an excellent example of sensitivity analysis, complete with relative sensitivity graphs, iso-quants, and histograms in which the sensitivity of eight parameters are compared.

2. *Life Cycle Cost Analysis, a Guide for Architects* (Washington, DC: The American Institute of Architects, 1977). This is an excellent guide and has numerous examples of life cycle cost analysis for buildings and site improvements. The following statement is found on page 13:

   Even when the owner plans to maintain the project for an indefinite time, uncertainty about costs far into the future suggests that analyses which extend significantly beyond 20 or 30 years begin to lose their validity.

3. Donald G. Newnan, *Engineering Economic Analysis*, 4th ed. (San Jose, CA: Engineering Press, 1991). Chapter 19 covers minicomputer programs for solving problems concerned with the time value of money.

4. Henry Malcolm Steiner, *Basic Engineering Economy*, rev. ed. (Glen Echo, MD: Books Associates, 1989). See Appendix A on using a personal computer with Lotus 1-2-3 for financial analyses.

5. *Business Management I: Financial Decisions*, Century Software Systems, 2601 Ocean Park Blvd., Suite 204, Santa Monica, CA. A series of modules for the analysis of financial problems on IBM personal computers and compatibles.

6. John T. Canada and George L. Hodge, "Microcomputer Software Costing Less Than $1,000 for Economic and Multiattribute Decision Analysis," *The Engineering Economist* 33:2 (Winter 1988): 130–144.

7. "Review of Three Financial Software Packages," *Info World* 28 (January 9, 1990): 51–56.

PROBLEMS

21-1 Confirm a few of the computations in Table 21.3, for example, the IRRs for the lower and upper limits of the building cost.

21-2 In the discussion following Example 21.1, the IRRs for planning horizons of 20 and 25 years were given as 8.0% and 8.8%, respectively. Confirm these computations.

21-3 Redo Example 21.2, using an inflation rate of 5%. Assume, as we did in that example, that the MARR of 8% does not include inflation.

21-4 In Example 21.3, what would be the rental fee per space that would earn an 8% return for a building cost of $4.5 million? To answer this question, hold all other parameters at their base value.

21-5 Refer to Example 21.4 and Figure 21.4. Do the computations for the 10% iso-quant and compare your results with Figure 21.4.

21-6 An international hotel chain is considering the building of a 400-room hotel. A planning horizon of 20 years and an MARR of 12% before taxes are being used for the economic analysis. The initial cost of the hotel is estimated at $40 million. The cost of the land is $10 million. The total salvage value of the hotel at EOY 20 is estimated at $1.5 million. For the land, the estimated value at EOY 20 is conservatively estimated at its current value. The furnishings of the hotel will cost an estimated $2 million and, for study purposes, are assumed to last five years and to have no salvage value. The annual operating and maintenance expenses are estimated at $2 million. Estimates of revenue are based on an average rate per room of $100 per day and a 70% occupancy rate for year-round operation.

a) Compute the PW and the IRR for the baseline case of 70% occupancy.

b) Evaluate the economic feasibility of the project based on occupancy rates varying from 60% to 90%. Use both the PW and the IRR as the figures of merit.

c) For the baseline case of 70% occupancy, calculate the PWs and the IRRs for average room rates varying from −15% to +5% from the baseline.

21-7 Use the data in Problem 21-6 to draw a relative sensitivity graph, such as Figure 21.3, for variations in occupancy rates and room rates. Use the IRR as the figure of merit.

21-8 Use the IRRs computed in Problem 21-6 to do the following:

a) Make a tabular presentation of the percentage variations for the average daily occupancy rates and the average room rate per day. Use Table 21.4 as a guide.

b) Rank order the input variables by their impact on the present worth. Use Table 21.5 as a guide.

21-9 Draw a set of iso-quants similar to Figure 21.4, using the occupancy percentage as ordinate and the room rate as abscissa for the hotel in Problem 21-6.

21-10 The State Engineering Institute—a not-for-profit entity—is planning to modernize its telecommunications laboratory. The plan currently under review requires an investment estimated at $3.5 million. The planning horizon is 15 years, and the estimated residual value at the end of this period is $300,000. Modernization should result in annual savings of $700,000 for operating and maintenance expenses. An MARR of 15% is used by the Institute.

a) Determine the PW for the baseline case defined above.

b) Calculate the PWs for the range −12% to 15% for the equipment costs. All other variables remain at their base value.

c) Calculate the PWs for a range of +/−33⅓% for the planning horizon.

d) Calculate the PWs for a range of −10% to +8% in operating and maintenance costs.

21-11 Use the data from Problem 21-10 to draw a relative sensitivity graph for this study. Use Figure 21.3 as a guide.

21-12 Use the data from Problem 21-10 to do the following:

a) Prepare a tabular presentation similar to Table 21.4 in the text.

b) Rank order the input variables for their impact on the PW, as we did in Table 21.5

21-13 A major department store intends to modernize the warehouse operation at one of its outlets. The modernization involves adding a new building and automatic storage and retrieval equipment. The building has a projected life of 20 years and the equipment, of 10 years. For study purposes, it is assumed that identical equipment will be replaced at that time and for the same cost. An MARR of 12% before taxes is to be used in the economic analysis. Presently, 100 people are employed. The new facility would reduce the work force by 50%. Each employee costs $20,000 per year. The estimated cost of the building is $2 million and of the equipment, $1.5 million. Operation and maintenance costs, not including labor, are estimated at $460,000 annually. Salvage value is taken as zero for study purposes for both the building and the equipment.

a) Determine the PW for a 20-year planning horizon.

b) Calculate the PWs for building costs varying from −10% to +15% of the base estimate of $2,000,000, assuming the equipment cost remains the same.

c) Calculate the PWs for equipment costs varying from −15% to +12% of the base estimate of $1,500,000, assuming the building cost remains the same.

21-14 Use the data in Problem 21-13 to draw a relative sensitivity graph that is similar to Figure 21.3.

21-15 Use the data in Problem 21-13 to do the following:
a) Prepare a tabular presentation similar to Table 21.4.
b) Rank order the input variables by their impact on the present worth, as we did in Table 21.5.

21-16 Draw an iso-quant for the present worths in Problem 21-13. (*Hint*: Refer to Figure 21.4, but use the present worth as the iso-quant.)

21-17 A university nonprofit project is estimated to have a life of 15 years. it is being evaluated at a social discount rate of 7%. The initial cost is estimated at $1.5 million, and the expected annual costs at $600,000. The range of accuracy for the initial cost is −10% to +20% and for the annual costs, +/−5%. The most probable estimate of benefits is $800,000, with a range of +/−15%. The project is being evaluated with the modified B/C ratio.
a) Calculate the base case B/C ratio.
b) Calculate the worst case B/C ratio.
c) Calculate the best case B/C ratio.
d) What do the best and worst case ratios tell you?

21-18 Using the data in Problem 21-17, draw a set of iso-quants for the B/C ratio. Let the benefits be the ordinate and the initial cost, the abscissa. For the annual costs, use $600,000. The set should include iso-quants for at least the following B/C ratios: 0.5, 1.0, 1.5, and 2.0.

21-19 A petroleum company in Athabasca is considering building a new pipeline for transporting crude oil from an oil rig to a crude stabilization unit. The initial cost of the project is estimated at $5 million. The pipeline has a useful life of 30 years, with no salvage value. The company expects to transport 100 million barrels per year the first 4 years, 150 million barrels per year the next 20 years, and 75 million barrels per year the remaining years. The net revenue for transporting each 1 million barrels is $5,000. An MARR of 12% before taxes is to be used for the economic analysis. Plot a relative sensitivity chart for a revenue range of +/−10% and an initial cost range of −12% to +15% of the base case. Use PW as the figure of merit.

21-20 Use the data and computations in Problem 21-19 to do the following:
a) Prepare a tabular presentation similar to Table 21.4.
b) Rank order the input variables by their impact on the figure of merit, as in Table 21.5.

21-21 The management of a housing complex comprising 30 units is planning to construct a modern gymnasium. The first cost is estimated at $800,000, which includes $100,000 for the land and $700,000 for the building. The residents of the complex are to be charged an annual fee of $200 per year per complex. However, the managers of the complex have obtained permission from its residents to offer membership to outsiders living nearby for an annual fee of $1,000, with a limit of 200 members. The annual operating costs are estimated at $75,000, the useful life is set at 15 years, and the salvage value is taken as $100,000, the cost of the land. An MARR of 9% before taxes is to be used for the economic analysis.

    a) Determine the present worth and the IRR of the proposal for the baseline conditions.

    b) Compute the cost of the building for which the IRR would equal the MARR of 9%.

    c) Plot the relative sensitivity graphs of both the PW and the IRR on one graph, assuming that the cost of the building will vary between -5% to $+10\%$ of the base value.

21-22 In Problem 21-21, the annual revenue from members outside the housing complex was given as $1,000 per member, for a total of 200 members. Calculate the membership fee that would make the IRR of the proposed venture equal to the MARR of 9%, assuming 200 outsiders sign up.

21-23 Construct an iso-quant for the project described in Problem 21-21, using the IRR as the figure of merit and letting the set of curves range from 7% to 12% in steps of 1%. Use the building cost and the revenue from outside members as the input variables.

21-24 A real estate investor is considering the purchase of a rental property for which the following data have been gathered for a before-tax analysis:

Initial cost	$450,000
Annual rental income	$55,000
Annual maintenance costs	$12,000
Planning horizon, years	8
Estimated resale value	$650,000
Cost of capital (MARR), %	10

Negotiations currently underway indicate that the initial cost will be close to $450,000. For the remaining monetary variables, the ranges are estimated as follows:

	Optimistic	Pessimistic
Rental income	$+30\%$	-30%
Maintenance	-10%	$+10\%$
Resale value	$+30\%$	-30%

Given that the initial cost, the planning horizon, and the MARR are fixed, construct a relative sensitivity graph, showing the effects of changes in the above three variables.

21-25 Construct a relative sensitivity graph for the following proposal in which all of the variables listed below (including the planning horizon and the MARR) show deviations of $+/-33\frac{1}{3}$percent.

Initial investment	$45,000
Salvage value	0
Planning horizon, yrs.	6
Annual net cash flow	$21,000
MARR, %	15

21-26 The management of Double Duty Doggie Shampoos must decide whether to install a new Super Duper Doogie Shampooer. The initial cost of the shampooer is $180,000, and its economic life is estimated at four years. Savings due to reducing shampooing time and the quantity of shampoo per washing are estimated at $60,000 per year. There is no salvage value. The MARR is 12%.

a) There still exist doubts as to the effectiveness of the shampooer. Create a relative sensitivity chart to show how the PW would vary for MARRs between 5% and 25%.

b) Assume that there is as much as a 50% variability on both sides of the estimates of life, revenues, and costs, and develop a relative sensitivity graph that reflects the individual variations on the present worth.

c) Do you recommend that the new shampooer be installed? Why or why not?

21-27 A modernization plan requires an investment of $6 million. The planning horizon is ten years, and the salvage value at the end of that period is $1.2 million. The savings in operating and maintenance costs are anticipated at $2.8 million. The MARR before taxes is 20%.

a) Compute the ranges of accuracy for the initial cost and the annual savings that would abort this modernization plan.

b) Prepare a graph with the savings as the abscissa and the first cost as the ordinate, and draw the iso-quant for PW equals zero. Identify the "go" and "no-go" regions.

21-28 The best estimates for the data on which a proposed investment is based are tabulated below:

Initial cost	$30,000
Net annual cash flows	$5,000
Planning horizon, yrs.	10
Residual value	0
MARR, %	15

a) Compute the present worth of this proposal.

b) Consider each of the above four parameters separately, and determine what percentage change is needed to make the proposal attractive.

c) To which of the four parameters is the decision to proceed the most sensitive?

d) Select the two most sensitive parameters, and prepare a graph in which these parameters serve as abscissa and ordinate. Draw the iso-quant for the IRR equal to the MARR, and identify the "go" and "no-go" regions.

____22
PROBABILITY: PART 1

22.1 INTRODUCTION

Chapter 21 showed us that sensitivity analysis is a useful analytical tool. However, it has two serious shortcomings:

1. It does not give us probability distributions with which we can compare the risk profiles of alternative investment opportunities.
2. It works well for letting one or, at the most, two variables vary over their range while holding all other variables constant; beyond that, it becomes unwieldy.

The first shortcoming is covered in this chapter and in Chapter 23. The second is covered in Chapter 24.

We have mentioned risk many times throughout this text and first introduced you to a significant application in Chapter 14 on the selection of an MARR. An assessment of risk plays an important part in this selection. If we expect the rate of return on a portfolio of risky investments to average out at a return at least equal to that on a portfolio of relatively risk-free investments—U. S. Treasury bonds, bonds of major corporations, certificates of deposit—the MARR on the investments in the risky portfolio must be high enough to compensate for inevitable losses. If losses were not inevitable, the portfolio would not be a risky one.

Risk analysis depends on the sound application of probability theory. In this and the next chapter, we cover as much of this theory as we need for comparing the risk propensity of alternative investment opportunities. This chapter concentrates on discrete probability distributions, and Chapter 23 concentrates on continuous distributions. Much of the basics for both types of distributions are covered in this chapter.

We begin with two important rules that underlie probability theory—the addition rule and the multiplication rule.

22.2 RULES OF PROBABILITY

What is the probability of a fair coin falling heads or tails? The toss of a coin is a random experiment for which the random variable can take two, and only two, possible values—heads or tails. These values constitute the set of outcomes or events. The toss of a die is a random experiment for which the random variable can take six possible values—the integers 1, 2, 3, 4, 5, or 6. Building a new chemical facility, or hotel, or office building, or proceeding with any other capital expenditure is a random experiment (as many investors know), with random variables or possible events ranging from great success to dismal failure. Synonyms for a random experiment are "a situation," "an occurrence," "a trial," "an experience," "a controlled operation," and, as we shall see, "a lottery." A random variable is, as we saw, a possible event, happening, or outcome of a random experiment. In practice, we often use the term "event" before a trial occurs and the term "outcome" after the trial has occurred.

> *COMMENT:* Why do we use the term "random"? A coin toss, the roll of a pair of dice, picking a card from a deck, or investing in a capital project are all random experiments, because the outcome is not known. The term "random" or its synonym, "stochastic," can also be applied to capital investment projects that, as mentioned, may have outcomes other than the outcome on which the decision to proceed was made.

The events that can occur in any given random experiment form a set consisting of two subsets. The first subset contains the event or events that represent—at least from an investor's viewpoint—desirable or favorable outcomes, that is, outcomes of interest. The second subset contains the event or events that are unfavorable or of no interest. This distinction brings us to a definition of probability:

Probability is the ratio of the number of trials in which an event occurs, divided by the total number of trials during which it could have occurred.

This definition holds if the number of trials is large enough to show that a distinctive, that is, a limiting, ratio actually exists.

> *COMMENT:* In ten tosses of a fair coin, it may fall heads ten times or tails ten times or any combination in between. For a very large number

of trials (say, 10,000), heads will show up in very close to one-half the number of trials. As the number of trials approaches infinity, the probability of tossing heads approaches 0.5.

This definition applies specifically to objective probability, that is, to probabilities that can be estimated from observed data or for which past results are available, or when the underlying mechanism or physical characteristics of the situation gives us an answer, as it does with the toss of a fair coin or die. There is, as we shall see, no comparable definition for subjective probability, for which there is no opportunity for repeated trials. This applies particularly to capital investment opportunities, since each project is unique. Thus, subjective probability is essentially a guessing or judgmental game based on expert (hopefully) know-how of what the probability ratio would be if a large number of trials were conducted. Once the guesses or, more euphemistically, the estimates, are accepted, they are handled as if they were objective.

COMMENT: An important application of the Delphi method, which we described in the preceding chapter, is to have a panel of experts produce expert "guesses." These guesses substitute for our inability to repeat a large number of trials from which objective probabilities could be obtained.

The preceding definition of probability indicates that probabilities are expressed as dimensionless ratios ranging from 0 to 1. Complete certainty (e.g., the sun will rise tomorrow) has a probability of 1. Complete uncertainty (e.g., the sun will not rise tomorrow) has a probability of 0. Thus, negative probabilities do not exist. This leads us to the following truisms, which apply if all of the possible events for a given situation have been identified, that is, if the list of possible outcomes is exhaustive.

- The probability that one of the possible outcomes will occur is 1.
- The probability that none of the possible outcomes will occur is 0.

Our interest, however, is not with all of the outcomes, but with one or more specific outcomes.

22.2.1   The Addition Rule

The random experiment is the toss of a coin. The possible outcomes are heads and tails. The probability of heads—P(H)—is 0.5, and the probability of tails—P(T)—is also 0.5. By the addition rule, the probability that the coin will fall heads or tails is 1; that is,

$$P(H \text{ or } T) = P(H) + P(T) = 0.5 + 0.5 = 1$$

COMMENT: It is at least conceivable that a coin might fall on its edge. We correctly assume that this is a nonevent, that is, an event so close to an impossibility that we take its probability of occurrence as zero.

For a fair die with six faces, the probability of rolling any number, say 2, is ⅙. The probability of rolling any number between 1 and 6 is, by the addition rule, 1, that is, 6 times ⅙. By the same rule, the probability of rolling either a 2 or a 6 is

$$P(2 \text{ or } 6) = P(2) + P(6) = 1/6 + 1/6 = 1/3$$

Applying the addition rule to a proposed capital project works the same way. Suppose that our estimates on the possible returns from investing in a hotel or any other capital project give the following probability distribution.

Event	Probability	
	Symbol	Ratio
Less than adequate return	$P(1)$	0.10
Adequate return	$P(2)$	0.65
Better than adequate return	$P(3)$	0.25

The probability of an adequate return or better is then

$$P(2 \text{ or } 3) = P(2) + P(3) = 0.65 + 0.25 = 0.90$$

COMMENT: The hotel example should help you see why we included the word *lottery* as a synonym for "random experiment."

The addition rule follows.

For any two outcomes of a random experiment, say A and B, the probability that either A or B will occur is the sum of the probability of A and the probability of B.

In mathematical shorthand,

$$P(A \text{ or } B) = P(A) + P(B) \tag{22.1}$$

This rule is obviously expandable to any number of outcomes.

22.2.2 The Multiplication Rule

The multiplication rule says:

For any two outcomes of a random experiment, say A and B, the probability that outcome A will occur in the first trial and outcome B in the second trial is the probability of A multiplied by the probability of B.

In mathematical shorthand, this would be

$$P(A \text{ and } B) = P(A,B) = P(A) P(B) \tag{22.2}$$

A coin is tossed twice or two coins are tossed at the same time. The probabilities of two heads is, by the multiplication rule,

$$P(H,H) = 0.50 \times 0.50 = 0.25$$

This is also the probability of two tails, or first heads and then tails, or first tails and then heads. The probability of some one of these four exhaustive and exclusive events occurring is, by the addition rule, 1; that is,

$$P(H,H) + P(T,T) + P(H,T) + P(T,H) = 0.25 \times 4 = 1$$

For a fair die, the probability of rolling first a 1 and then a 2 is, by the multiplication rule,

$$P(1) \times P(2) = P(1,2) = 1/6 \times 1/6 = 1/36$$

This is also the probability of rolling first a 2 and then a 1. Thus, the probability of rolling 3 with a pair of fair dice is, by the addition rule,

$$P(1,2) + P(2,1) = 1/36 + 1/36 = 2/36 = 1/18$$

In the preceding examples, the random experiments were independent. One toss of a coin has no effect on subsequent tosses. Tossing a fair coin 10,000 times could produce 10,000 heads. However, by the multiplication rule, the probability of such an occurrence is $0.5^{10,000}$, which, you will have to agree, is a rather small number.

So far in the above examples, we have used "fair" coins and "fair" dice. Assume now that we cannot take "fairness" for granted.

Example 22.1   A Loaded Die   You suspect a die is unfair. For this reason, you can no longer rely on the underlying mechanics of the situation to tell you what to expect. For a fair die, there would be very nearly 1,666 or 1,667 appearances for each face out of every 10,000 tosses (10,000 × 1/6). For a loaded die, you cannot arrive at an objective probability without an extensive series of trials.

If the die is loaded, some number, say 3, will be favored and will show up a disproportionate number of times, say 1,690. You may have to run many more trials than 10,000 to determine the ratio that the probability P(3) approaches to an accuracy of four to five significant figures.

Our purpose in Example 22.1 is to point out that, if we can rely on "fairness," there are situations in which it is not necessary to run repeated trials in order to determine the probability of a particular event. The underlying symmetry or common sense of the situation will give us objective probabilities. Unfortunately, such situations do not occur very often in the application of probability theory to capital project selection. Thus, as mentioned, we have to rely on subjective probability to give us "guesstimates" of what the probability ratios would be if the opportunity for numerous trials were available.

22.3 PROBABILITY DISTRIBUTIONS

Probability distributions are discrete or continuous. For the roll of a die, the random variable can take on any one of, and no more than, six discrete values—the integers 1 to 6—for each of which the probability of occurrence is, as we know, ⅙. A bar chart for this discrete uniform distribution is given in Figure 22.1. If the heights of the bars are added together, the total is 1, as it would be for any discrete distribution.

For discrete distributions, the outcomes are countable, as for the roll of a die. For continuous distributions, the outcomes are not countable. There are an infinite number of outcomes, for each of which the possibility of occurrence is zero.

For capital project selection studies, continuous probability distributions are more common than discrete ones, since the random variables with which we deal—time, cash flows, cash ratios, such as rates of return—are all continuous.

The more common discrete and continuous distributions covered in texts on probability and statistics are as follows:

Discrete	Continuous
Uniform	Uniform
Binomial	Normal
Poisson	Triangular
	Beta

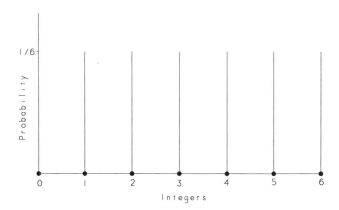

Figure 22.1. Discrete distribution for roll of a die.

Of these distributions, the discrete uniform distribution and the four continuous distributions are the most useful for our purpose. However, whether a set of data can be represented by one or the other of these distributions is not critical. If the data do fit a particular distribution, there is the advantage of applying the mathematical relations that define it; if not, we proceed otherwise as discussed later in this chapter and in the chapters that follow.

We can explain much of the basics of probability distributions—whether discrete or continuous—with the help of a well-known discrete distribution for the random experiment of rolling a pair of dice.

Example 22.2   Probability Mass Distribution   You should have no problem in confirming the distribution in Table 22.1 for repeated tosses of a pair of fair dice. It is called a "probability mass distribution." The possible events or outcomes, that is, the values that the random variable can take, are any integer from 2 to 12.

A bar chart for the mass distribution is given in Figure 22.2 and for the cumulative distribution, in Figure 22.3. The cumulative column in Table 22.1 quickly answers such questions as, "What is the probability of 5 or less (10/36), of 8 or more [(36 − 21)/(36 = 15/36)] and so on?"

Inspection of the two figures shows that the probability distribution is symmetrical; that is, it is not skewed to the right or left. The outcomes 2 and 12 have the same probability. So do the outcomes 3 and 11. The probability of rolling 1 or 13 or any number other than the integers 2 to 12 is zero. The probability of rolling the dice and coming up with some integer between 2 and 12 is 1.

In what follows, we denote the random experiment by X and the values of its random variable by x. Thus, if X is the roll of a pair of dice, the x's are a set of 11 integers, ranging from 2 to 12. If X is a coin toss, the x's are

TABLE 22.1   Probability Mass Distribution for a Pair of Dice

Outcome	Tosses Leading to Outcome (first die, second die)	Probability Each Outcome	Cumulative
2	(1,1)	1/36	1/36
3	(1,2),(2,1)	2/36	3/36
4	(1,3),(3,1),(2,2)	3/36	6/36
5	(1,4),(4,1),(2,3),(3,2)	4/36	10/36
6	(1,5),(5,1),(2,4),(4,2),(3,3)	5/36	15/36
7	(1,6),(6,1),(2,5),(5,2),(3,4),(4,3)	6/36	21/36
8	(2,6),(6,2),(3,5),(5,3),(4,4)	5/36	26/36
9	(3,6),(6,3),(4,5),(5,4)	4/36	30/36
10	(4,6),(6,4),(5,5)	3/36	33/36
11	(5,6),(6,5)	2/36	35/36
12	(6,6)	1/36	36/36

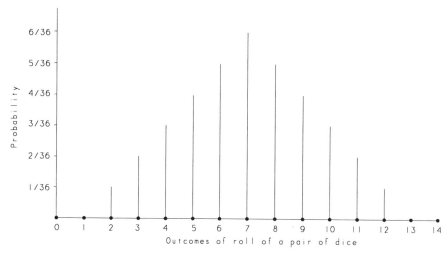

Figure 22.2. Bar chart for discrete distribution.

a head and a tail. If X is a proposed capital investment, the x's are cash flows that range from a minimum to a maximum anticipated value.

22.4 PROPERTIES OF PROBABILITY DISTRIBUTIONS

The properties or characteristics of probability distributions are defined by the following measures.

Measures of Central Tendency	Measures of Dispersion
Mode	Range
Median	Variance
Expected value (mean)	Standard deviation

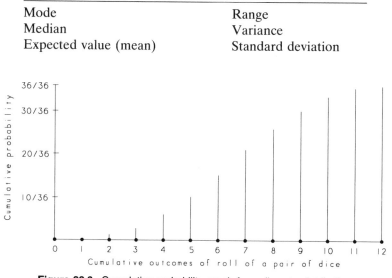

Figure 22.3. Cumulative probability graph for a discrete distribution.

The mode, median, and expected value (also called the "mean") are measures of central tendency or central location. Each is a single value whose magnitude acts as a surrogate or a representative for the entire distribution. The most important of the three is the mean.

The range, variance, and standard deviation are measures of dispersion. They show how far the random variable spreads out from its measure of central tendency and therefore serve as measures of risk. The bigger the dispersion, the bigger the risk.

We apply these measures to discrete distributions in this chapter and to continuous distributions in Chapter 23.

22.4.1 Measures of Central Tendency

The mode and median are easily disposed of. The expected value will occupy most of this subsection.

Mode.   The mode is that value of the random variable that occurs most often or, in other words, is most likely to occur. In Figure 22.2, the mode is clearly 7 with a probability of 6/36 or $\frac{1}{6}$. Don't confuse "most likely" with "majority." For a "majority," the mode would have to be greater than $\frac{1}{2}$. A probability distribution can have more than one mode. A distribution with two modes (bimodal) would resemble the back of a camel rather than the back of a dromedary.

Median.   The median is the value of the random variable that falls in the middle if the values that the variable can assume are arranged in order of magnitude. For discrete distributions, if there is an odd number of values, the median is the middle value, which for the roll of a pair of dice is 7. If there is an even number of values, the median is the average of the two middle values. For the toss of a single die, the median is 3.5 [(3 + 4)/2]. Thus, for a discrete distribution, the median need not be a member of the set of random variables.

Expected Value.   The expected value of a random experiment X, for which the random variables are a discrete set of x's, each with an associated probability $P(x)$, is given by equation (22.3).

$$E[X] = \sum x \, P(x) \tag{22.3}$$

Equation (22.3) has a simple interpretation. All we are doing is computing the weighted average of the random variable over its range, using probabilities as weights. This is no different from calculating any weighted average. If there are three people in a room, of which two are 5 feet tall and one is 6 feet tall, the weighted average height is not 5.5 feet but 5.33 feet. The big E stands for expected value, and the big X inside the brackets [ ] stands for the random experiment.

The expected value is also called the "expectation." However, the most common name is the mean value or simply the mean. It is usually represented by the Greek letter mu (μ).

If we apply equation (22.3) to tossing of a pair of fair dice and use the probability distribution given in Table 22.1 for computing the expected value, we find that $E[X]$ is 7. The computations are shown below.

$$\mu = \frac{1}{36}(2) + \frac{2}{36}(3) + \frac{3}{36}(4) + \cdots + \frac{1}{36}(12) = 252/36 = 7$$

For symmetrical distributions with only one mode, such as that for the roll of a pair of dice, the mode, the median, and the mean are identical. This will not be the case with the unsymmetrical distributions we will meet later in this chapter and in Chapters 23 and 24.

Laws of Expected Value. Expected values follow certain mathematical laws, which simplify their application to probability distributions. We state these laws without proof. However, several of the examples that follow and Appendix 22A give you the opportunity to verify them.

For any two random experiments X and Y,

$$E[X + Y] = E[X] + E[Y] \tag{22.4}$$

$$E[X - Y] = E[X] - E[Y] \tag{22.5}$$

These relationships hold whether the two random experiments are dependent or independent, that is, whether the values of y for experiment Y do not depend on (are not influenced by) the values of x for experiment X, and vice versa. However, the multiplication law, which follows, holds only for independent random experiments.

$$E[XY] = E[X]\,E[Y] \tag{22.6}$$

The laws expressed by equations (22.4), (22.5), and (22.6) can be generalized to include any number of variables. They also give rise to the following truisms, where c is a constant. For our purpose, these constants are generally time-value factors, such as P/F, P/A, and others for any given i and N.

$$E[c] = c \tag{22.7}$$

$$E[cX] = E[c]\,E[X] = c\,E[X] \tag{22.8}$$

$$E[X + c] = E[X] + E[c] = E[X] + c \tag{22.9}$$

22.4.2   Measures of Dispersion

Measures of dispersion included the range, the variance, and the standard deviation.

Range.   The simplest of the measures of dispersion is the range, since it can be applied whether we have a probability distribution or not. It is the maximum less the minimum anticipated value. The range for the roll of a pair of dice is 12 less 2, or 10.

Variance.   The more sophisticated measures of dispersion and the ones with which we will usually be embroiled are the variance and its square root, the standard deviation. For the standard deviation, we use the Greek symbol for sigma (σ) and for the variance "σ^2."
For discrete distributions, the variance, V, of the random experiment, X, is defined by equations (22.10) and (22.11).

$$V[X] = \sigma^2 = E[(x - \mu)^2] = \sum (x - \mu)^2 \, P(x) \qquad (22.10)$$

which can also be written

$$V[X] = \sigma^2 = E[X^2] - \mu^2 = \sum x^2 \, P(x) - \mu^2 \qquad (22.11)$$

With the first term of equation (22.11), we compute the weighted average of x^2, using the probability of x as the weighting factor. The second term is just the mean squared. That equations (22.10) and (22.11) give identical results will be obvious to many of you. If it is not, go to Appendix 22A.

Laws of Variance.   Like expectation, variance also follows certain laws, which simplify calculations for comparing the risks of alternative investment opportunities.

$$V[X + Y] = V[X] + V[Y] \qquad (22.12)$$

$$V[X - Y] = V[X] + V[Y] \qquad (22.13)$$

These identities apply only if X and Y are independent.
For any constant, c,

$$V[c] = 0 \qquad (22.14)$$

$$V[X + c] = V[X] \qquad (22.15)$$

$$V[cX] = c^2 \, V[X] \qquad (22.16)$$

TABLE 22.2 Variance for Rolling a pair of Dice

Outcome, x	x^2	Probability of x, $P(x)$	$x^2 P(x)$
2	4	1/36	0.1111
3	9	2/36	0.5000
4	16	3/36	1.3333
5	25	4/36	2.7778
6	36	5/36	5.0000
7	49	6/36	8.1667
8	64	5/36	8.8889
9	81	4/36	9.0000
10	100	3/36	8.3333
11	121	2/36	6.7222
12	144	1/36	4.0000
			54.8333

$$\Sigma\, x^2\, P(x) = 54.8333$$

We cannot multiply V[X] by V[Y] to get V[XY], even if X and Y are independent. If we want V[XY], it has to be calculated separately.

We again give no proof for these laws, but you have an opportunity to see that they work in Appendix 22A.

In Example 22.3, we use equation (22.11) to compute the variance and the standard deviation of the random variable X for tossing a pair of dice.

Example 22.3   Variance and the Standard Deviation   The first term in equation (22.11) is calculated in Table 22.2.

The second term is the square of the expected value. We computed this value and found it to equal 7 when we applied equation (22.3) to the roll of a pair of dice. The second term is therefore 7^2, or 49. The variance is the difference between 54.8333 and 49.

$$V[X] = 54.8333 - 49.0000 = 5.8333$$

The standard deviation is $(5.8333)^{0.5}$, or 2.42. Like the median for the roll of a die, the standard deviation need not be a member of the set of random variables.

Figure 22.4 is the bar chart of Figure 22.2, with a few additions. The mode, median, and mean are identified, as well as the abscissas, which are one and two standard deviations to the right and left of the mean, respectively. The total probability of the bars that fall within one standard deviation of the mean is 24/36, or 67%, as you can easily verify. For two standard deviations, this figure is 34/36, or 94%. Both of these values, as you will see in Chapter 23, approximate those of the normal (continuous) distribution.

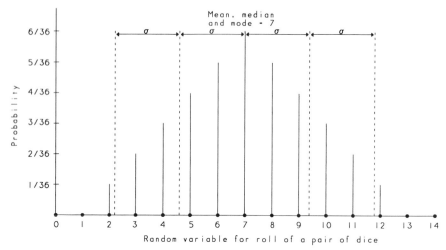

Figure 22.4. Standard deviation.

22.5 DECISION TREES

Decision trees are useful devices for illustrating what happens when the multiplication rule is applied to a succession of random experiments. Consider the roll of a pair of dice but with a difference. Rather than roll the dice together, we roll first one and then the other. Rolling the first die is the random experiment X, and rolling the second die is the random experiment Y. We then ask, "What is the probability distribution for (X,Y)?" We know the answer from Table 22.2. However, we can also arrive at the same result and learn something along the way by drawing a decision tree, such as the one in Figure 22.5.

Each branch of the tree is identified by two numbers. One is the value of the random variable, and the other is the probability P(x) associated with that value.

For random experiment X, the random variable x can take six values—the integers 1 to 6—for each of which the probability P(x) is ⅙. Each integer can be paired with the six random variables y from experiment Y, for each of which the probability P(y) is also ⅙. Hence, we get the tree of Figure 22.5.

The first column on the right of the tree shows the sum of the two faces x and y, and the second column shows the combined probability of x and y, which is 1/36 for every branch. If the number of times the integers 2, 3, 4, and so on show up are counted, the probability distribution is identical to that of Table 22.2. If column 1 is multiplied by column 2 and the resulting products are added together, the total is 252/36, or 7, which is the expected value.

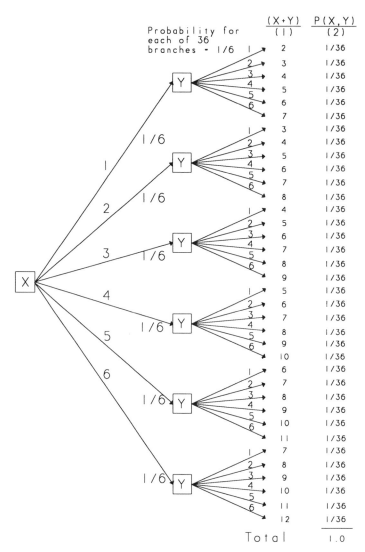

Figure 22.5. Decision tree for roll of a pair of dice.

22.6 SOME APPLICATIONS

We now introduce several examples, in which the preceding concepts are applied to the project selection process. We begin modestly and end up exhaustively.

Example 22.4 Floods There is no way to protect ourselves completely from floods. However, if adequate data are available on their frequency and magnitude and on the damage they wreak, an optimum level of protection can be determined. Consider the following data on crop damage, collected over the past 60 years and summarized in columns (1) and (2) in the following tabulation.

	Damage, $ (000)		
Probability	Alternative 0	Alternative A	Alternative B
(1)	(2)	(3)	(4)
0.01	1,600	1,450	1,350
0.04	800	725	650
0.15	600	500	450
0.40	200	150	100
0.40	0	0	0

Columns 1 and 2 tell us that, during any one year, there is a 1% probability under alternative 0 (the do-no-more alternative) that crop damage will reach $1,600,000, a 4% probability that it will reach $800,000, and so on. For this alternative, the expected value of the annual crop damage is therefore $218,000, as shown in the following equation.

$$E[\text{Alternate } 0] = 0.01 \times \$1,600 + 0.04 \times \$800 + 0.15 \times \$600$$

$$+ 0.40 \times \$200 + 0.40 \times \$0$$

$$\mu = \$218 \text{ (thousands)}$$

Any capital expenditure to reduce flooding must be judged against its capacity to reduce the expected damage below $218,000 annually.

Alternatives A and B are based on several studies for constructing dikes and small earth dams. It is estimated that floods of similar intensity to those experienced in the past would revise the damage due to flooding by the figures given in columns (3) and (4). The expected values of alternatives A and B and the savings compared to alternative 0 follow.

Alternative	E[Damage], $	E[Savings], $
A	178,500	39,500
B	147,000	71,000

The estimated capital expenditures are $350,000 for alternative A and $800,000 for alternative B. For a 50-year life and an MARR of 10%, the annual costs of these expenditures can be approximated using infinite life. Therefore, alternative A is justified, since the annual saving of $39,500 is greater than the annual cost of the capital expenditure of $35,000 (10% of $350,000). Alternative B, however, cannot be justified on monetary grounds alone, because its annual cost of $80,000 (10% of $800,000) is greater than the annual savings of $71,000.

Example 22.5 Telephone Pole Mortality In this example, we discuss three cases on telephone pole mortality based on objective probabilities computed from data on the lives and replacement costs of hundreds of poles.

Case 1 The mortality is probabilistic, but the cost of replacement is deterministic.
Case 2 The mortality is deterministic, but the cost of replacement is probabilistic.
Case 3 Both mortality and replacement costs are probabilistic.

The probability distributions for mortality and replacement costs are given in the following tabulation.

Mortality, yrs.		Replacement Cost, $	
N	$P(N)$	c	$P(c)$
5	0.01	350	0.01
10	0.10	375	0.06
15	0.16	400	0.08
20	0.17	425	0.09
25	0.20	450	0.15
30	0.22	475	0.20
35	0.07	500	0.12
40	0.04	525	0.10
45	0.03	550	0.09
Total	1.00	575	0.07
		600	0.03
		Total	1.00

For case 1, we assume that only the probability distributions for mortality are available. For the installation cost, we use a deterministic value obtained from accounting department records by dividing the total cost of replacing poles by the number of poles replaced. This figure is $500 per pole.

The expected annual cost (AC)$_1$ for case 1, using an MARR of 12%, is then

$$E[(AC)_1] = \$500 \sum (A/P,12,N) \, P(N)$$

$$= \$500[0.01(A/P,12,5) + 0.10(A/P,12,10)$$

$$+ 0.16(A/P,12,15) + \cdots + 0.03(A/P,12,45)]$$

$$= \$500[0.01 \times 0.2774 + 0.10 \times 0.1770$$

$$+ 0.16 \times 0.1468 + \cdots + 0.03 \times 0.1207]$$

$$= \$500 \times 0.1366 = \$68.30$$

You should note that the annual cost of each dollar expended for replacement is $0.1366 ($68.30/500). This figure is needed for computing case 3.

For case 2, we assume that the replacement cost is probabilistic and that the mortality is deterministic. The expected value of the replacement cost is $479, which you should confirm. For an average pole life of 25 years, the expected value of the equivalent annual cost is then

$$E[(AC)_2] = (A/P,12,25) \, E[\text{Cost}] = (A/P,12,25) \sum c \, P(c)$$

$$= 0.1275 \times \$479$$

$$= \$61.07$$

For case 3, in which probability distributions for both mortality and replacement cost are available,

$$E[(AC)_3] = \sum (A/P,12,N) \, P(N) \sum c \, P(c)$$

The value of the first summation from case 1 is 0.1366, and the value of the second summation from case 2 is $479. Therefore,

$$E[(AC)_3] = 0.1366 \times \$479 = \$65.40$$

We have three answers. Which answer is correct? They all are. The one you use depends on the data available and whether the data can be structured into probability distributions. You could still obtain a useful answer if your only information came from telephone crews who told you that, based on their experience, the average life of poles is about 25 years and the average replacement cost is about $500. For these data, the annual cost per pole is

$$AC = \$500(A/P,12,25)$$
$$= \$500 \times 0.1275$$
$$= \$63.75$$

Example 22.6   Drilling Wildcat Wells for Oil and Gas   A wildcatter doesn't drill anywhere. He searches for sites that, based on seismic and other data, give the "look and feel" of sites that have produced in the past and are producing now. The "look and feel" are made up of many factors, for which you will have to turn to a text on oil and gas exploration (1). In what follows, we combine these factors into three groups, which we refer to, without further elaboration, as structure, reservoir, and environment, respectively.

Based on their experience in drilling wells, a wildcatter and his crew might singly or together (singly if we use the Delphi approach described in Chapter 21) estimate the probability of a favorable result, using a form similar to the one illustrated.

Factor	Probability, %										
Structure	0	10	20	30	40	50	**60**	70	80	90	100
Reservoir	0	10	20	30	40	50	60	**70**	80	90	100
Environment	0	10	20	30	40	**50**	60	70	80	90	100

Each crew member marks his or her best guesstimate of the probability, and, after some discussion, a group consensus is reached. For the underlined probabilities shown, the overall probability of success is, by the multiplication rule,

$$\text{Probability} = 0.60 \times 0.70 \times 0.50 = 0.21 = 21\%$$

Probability distributions for the expected recovery of oil and gas and for the expected sales price are also made. From these estimates, the expected revenue is

TABLE 22.3 Cash Flow Parameters

	Dollars (000)		
	Base Estimate	Life Cycle Cash Flow	Type of Estimate[a]
	(1)	(2)	
Cost of land	$1,000	$ − 1,000	D
Cost of building	4,000	− 4,000	P
Revenue from staff	25	+ 750	D
Revenue from residents	562.5	+ 16,875	P
Operating costs	100	− 3,000	D
Salvage value	1,000	+ 1,000	D

[a]D = deterministic; P = probabilistic.

The next two examples illustrate most of the concepts discussed in this chapter, including the application of decision trees. They deserve a careful reading on your part. In studying them, do not let the simplicity of the probability distributions disturb you. This was done so that you could clearly see the laws of expectation and variance at work without being distracted by lengthy computations that, once you knew the principles involved, could be handled by computer.

In both examples, we use the parking structure of Chapter 21 as the model for assessing the risk of a capital investment opportunity. A decision tree is used in the first example, and the laws of expected value and variance, in the second.

Example 22.7 Decision Tree Analysis You will recall that the parking structure in Example 21.1 had six cash flow parameters. The base estimate and the total cash flow over the 30-year life of the project for each cash flow stream are given in Table 22.3.

The revenues and operating costs in column (1) are annual figures. In column (2) the revenues and costs are 30 times the annual figures, since the estimated life of the investment is 30 years.

If you reread Example 21.1, you will find that only three of the cash flow estimates are deterministic—the cost of land, the staff revenue, and the salvage value. However, in what follows, the operating costs are also treated in this way, since they have relatively little impact on the final result. This leaves us with two cash flows, which will be handled probabilistically (if you can say this word smoothly, you have mastered risk analysis)—the cost of the building and the area resident revenue. Their estimated probability distributions are tabulated as follows:

Random Variable x, Cost of Building		Random Variable y, Annual Resident Revenue	
x(000)	P(x)	y(000)	P(y)
$4,000	0.7	$562	0.6
4,800	0.3	656	0.4

Construction costs tend to overrun. For this reason, the possibility of the building costing less than $4,000,000 was taken as zero and of costing more than $4,000,000, that is, $4,800,000 was given a rather high probability. For the resident revenue, you will recall that there was every reason to believe that the parking structure would be fully occupied with an annual rental of $1,500 per space. Furthermore, the marketing survey indicated that these rates could go as high as $1,750 and full occupancy might still be maintained. For this reason, the probability of resident revenue reaching $656,000 was given as rather high.

The decision tree for the net cash flow over the life cycle is given in Figure 22.6. An explanation of this figure follows.

The deterministic cash flows, including the operating costs, total $-2,250,000 as you can readily see from Table 22.3 ($-1,000,000 + $750,000 - $3,000,000 + $1,000,000). They can be treated together, since their probability is by definition 1.0. The two values for the first random experiment—building costs—branch out from the end of the arrow representing the deterministic costs. The two values for the second random experiment—the resident revenue—branch out from each of the arrows of the first experiment.

The three columns to the right of the decision tree show, respectively, the total cash flow for each branch, the probability of each branch, and the product of the cash flow times the probability. For the top branch, for example, the net cash flow is $10,625,000, the algebraic sum of $-2,250,000, $-4,000,000, and $+16,875,000. The ratio 0.42 is obtained by applying the multiplication rule (1.0 × 0.70 × 0.60 = 0.42). The figure in the last column—$4,463,000—is then the product of $10,625,000 and 0.42. The expected net cash flow, that is, E[net cash flow] for the tree is the total at the bottom of the third column, namely, $11,508,000.

We could use a similar tree for calculating the expected value of the net present worth by substituting the present worth for the cash flow on each branch. (In fact, it would have made more sense to do this, but we decided to leave it to you. See Problem 22-36.) The present worth of the deterministic cash flows is $-1,746,000. This is shown by the following tabulation, for which $(P/A,8,30)$ equals 11.26 and $(P/F,8,30)$ equals 0.0994.

Stream	Factor	Cash Flow ($000)	Present Worth ($000)
Land	$(P/A,8,0)$	$-1,000	$-1,000
Annual staff revenue	$(P/A,8,30)$	+25	+281
Annual operating costs	$(P/A,8,30)$	-100	-1,126
Salvage value	$(P/F,8,30)$	+1,000	+99
		Total	$-1,746

The present worths for the two estimates for the building are, of course, the same as the first costs, that is $4,000,000 and $4,800,000. For the area resident revenue, the present worths are

60% probability $562,500 $(P/A,8,30)$ = $6,334,000

40% probability $656,000 $(P/A,8,30)$ = $7,387,000

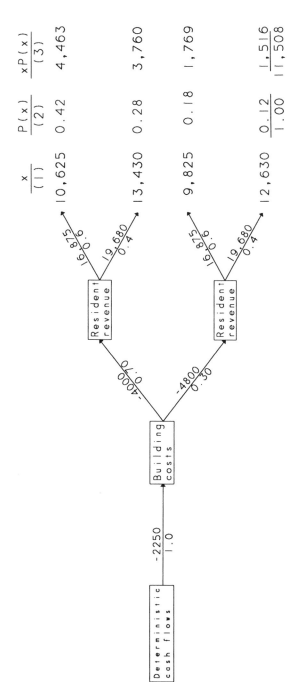

Figure 22.6. Cash flow tree for Example 22.7.

TABLE 22.4   Expected Values and Variances for Parking Structure

	Dollars (000)		
	Base Estimate	Expected Value	Standard Deviation
Cost of land	$1,000	$ – 1,000	0
Cost of building	4,000	– 4,240	$367
Revenue from staff	25	+ 25	0
Revenue from residents	562	+ 599	46
Operating costs	100	+ 100	0
Salvage value	1,000	– 1,000	0

If we place these present worths on a decision tree similar to that of Figure 22.6 (which you should do), we get the following results for the four branches.

Branch	Net Present Worth, $	Probability	Product, $
(1)	(2)	(3)	(4) = (2)(3)
1	$588,000	0.42	$247,000
2	1,641,000	0.28	460,000
3	– 212,000	0.18	– 38,000
4	841,000	0.12	101,000
		E[NPW] =	770,000

The effective value or mean of the NPW is $770,000.

Our next chore is to use the parking structure in order to demonstrate that the laws of expected value will give the same answers as those we get from a decision tree and, also, to apply the laws of variance.

Example 22.8   Application of Laws for μ and σ^2   The base estimates for each of the parking structure's cash flows are repeated in the first column of dollar figures in Table 22.4. The expected values and variances in the other two columns will be referred to as we work our way through the example.

For the four deterministic cash flow estimates, the expected values are the same as the base estimates and the variance and standard deviation are zero.

For the two probabilistic cash flows, the estimated probability distributions were given in Example 22.7. The calculations for the expected value and variance of the first of these—the building costs—are as follows:

x	$P(x)$	$xP(x)$	$x - \mu$	$(x - \mu)^2$	$(x - \mu)^2 P(x)$
$4,000	0.7	$2,800	$ – 240	57,600	40,320
4,800	0.3	1,440	+ 560	313,600	94,080
		μ = $4,240		σ^2 =	134,400
				σ =	$367

The mean ($4,240,000) is calculated using equation (22.3) and the variance (^{2} 134,400 × 10^6) using equation (22.10). The units of the mean are dollars and of the variance dollars squared (^{2}). The units of the standard deviation, the square root of the variance, are dollars, in this case, $367,000. Both the mean and the standard deviation have been posted in Table 22.4.

The calculations for the expected value and the variance of the resident revenue cash flow follow.

y	$P(y)$	$yP(y)$	$y - \mu$	$(y - \mu)^2$	$(y - \mu)^2 P(y)$
$562.5	0.6	$337	$-36.5	1,332	799
656.0	0.4	262	+57.0	3,249	1,300
		$\mu =$ $599		$\sigma^2 =$	2,099
				$\sigma =$	$46

The calculations show a mean of $599,000 per year for resident revenue with a standard deviation of $46,000.

For any given i and N, in our case 8% and 30 years, respectively, $(P/A,i,N)$ is a constant. It follows from equation (22.8) that the expected value of the present worth of the resident revenue is

$$E[\text{PW revenue}] = E[(P/A,i,N)(\text{cash flow})]$$

$$= (P/A,8,30)\ E[\text{cash flow}]$$

$$= 11.26 \times \$599$$

$$= \$6,745 \text{ (thousands)}$$

The expected value of the net present worth of the cash flow pattern for the parking structure is obtained by applying equations (22.4) and (22.5), that is, by adding (algebraically) the expected value of the present worths of the individual cash flow streams. The results are shown in Table 22.5, in which, for convenience, the expected values of both the cash flows and the present worths are given.

TABLE 22.5   Expected Value of Net Present Worth

Stream	E[cash flow]	E[NPW]
Land	$-1,000	$-1,000
Building	-4,240	-4,240
Staff revenue	+25	+282
Resident revenue	+599	+6,745
Operating costs	-100	-1,126
Salvage value	-1,000	+99
	Total	$+760

Note: For E[cash flow], see Table 22.4. For the annual cash flows, the mean of the present worth equals the mean of the cash flow times $(P/A,8,30)$, or 11.26. For the salvage value, the mean of the present worth equals the mean of the cash flow times $(P/F,8,30)$, or 0.0994.

The expected value for the present worth of the parking structure is $760,000, which, except for rounding errors (which tend to proliferate in an example such as this), is what we found in Example 22.7.

For the variance of the net present worth, we need to consider only two cash flows—the cost of the building and the resident revenue—since the variance of all of the deterministic variables is, by definition, zero.

The variance of the present worth of the building cost is the same as the variance of its cash flow, which was $134,400 \times 10^6$ dollars squared. For the resident revenue,

$$V[\text{Present worth}] = V[(P/A,i,N)(\text{cash flow})]$$

but, since $(P/A,i,N)$ is a constant, it follows from equation (22.16) that

$$V[\text{present worth}] = (P/A,i,N)^2 \, V[\text{cash flow}]$$

$$= (11.26)^2 \times 2,099 \times 10^6$$

$$\sigma^2 = 266,000 \times 10^6$$

We combine the two variances, using equation (22.13):

$$V[\text{NPW}] = V[\text{PW building}] + V[\text{PW revenue}]$$

$$\sigma^2 = (134,400 + 266,000) \times 10^6 = (400,400) \times 10^6$$

$$\sigma = \$633,000$$

What have we learned? We now have the mean and the standard deviation of the net present worth, based on an MARR of 8% and a planning horizon of 30 years. They are

Mean	$760,000
Standard deviation	$633,000

Both figures are useful in comparing this particular investment with others. However, we can learn much more from the decision tree analysis that was made earlier. If you go back to those results and calculate the IRR for each branch, you will get the results shown in Table 22.6.

TABLE 22.6   IRRs for Decision Tree Branches

Branch	Net Present Worth, $	IRR, %	Probability
(1)	(2)	(3)	(4)
1	$590,000	9.0	0.42
2	1,643,000	11.1	0.28
3	−210,000	7.4	0.18
4	843,000	9.3	0.12

Certainly, this information is worthwhile. By the addition rule, there is an 82% probability (0.42 + 0.28 + 0.12) that the IRR will equal or exceed 9.0%, that is, exceed the MARR by at least 1%. Furthermore, even the 18% probability of not earning the MARR doesn't look too bad. Many of us would be satisfied with a return of 7.4% on a low-risk, tax-free investment.

22.7 COMPARING INVESTMENT OPPORTUNITIES

Let us assume that we have carried out a risk analysis for two investment opportunities that are similar to the one carried out for the parking structure. Five cases present themselves when we compare the two options with one another. The conclusions reached are easily extended to any number of cases, since we usually proceed from one pair to the next, as we do in replacement and other studies.

	Mean	Standard Deviation	Selection
Case 1	$\mu_1 = \mu_2$	$\sigma_1 = \sigma_2$	Depends
Case 2	$\mu_1 = \mu_2$	$\sigma_1 < \sigma_2$	Option 1
Case 3	$\mu_1 > \mu_2$	$\sigma_1 = \sigma_2$	Option 1
Case 4	$\mu_1 > \mu_2$	$\sigma_1 < \sigma_2$	Option 1
Case 5	$\mu_1 > \mu_2$	$\sigma_1 > \sigma_2$	Depends

For case 1, the mean that measures value and the variance that measures risk are the same or, as a practical matter, so close that a decision on which option to proceed with should be made on nonmonetary considerations, that is, on the irreducibles. For case 2, since the two means are equal, or nearly so, the choice, based on monetary considerations alone, should be option 1, which has the lower risk profile.

For case 3, the two options have the same risk potential, but, since option 1 has the larger mean, it should be selected. For case 4, both the mean and the standard deviation favor option 1. For case 5, there is no clear-cut answer. Option 1 has the higher mean, but it also has the higher risk potential. The selection depends on the decision maker's approach to risk. Is he or she willing to accept more risk for a greater gain? This is a personal decision that can only be made by the investor.

If the investment alternatives are substantially different in size, a comparison based on the coefficient of variation is in order. This coefficient is simply the standard deviation divided by the expected value, that is,

$$\text{Coefficient of variation} = \sigma/\mu \qquad (22.17)$$

Consider the two alternatives below, for which the expected value and the standard deviation of the net present worth are given.

Alternative	Expected Value of NPW, $	Standard Deviation of NPW, $	Coefficient of Variation
1	$4,000,000	$450,000	0.11
2	1,000,000	150,000	0.15

Based on the coefficient of variation, alternative 1 is less risky than alternative 2. However, this can be misleading. You may have the cash resources to handle deviations of $150,000 but not $450,000.

This concludes Part 1 of our presentation on probability and its application to the project selection process. We now proceed to Part 2, in which we describe several well-known continuous probability distributions.

22.8 SUMMARY

In probability theory, the digit 1 represents absolute certainty and the digit 0, absolute uncertainty. The values between 0 and 1, often expressed as percentages, define the probability of a particular occurrence or outcome.

In order to apply the theory, all of the possible outcomes (the random variables) of a particular situation (the random experiment) have to be identified. The probability that none of these outcomes will occur is 0. The probability that at least one will occur is 1.

The two rules of probability theory that we use throughout this chapter and the remainder of this text are the addition rule and the multiplication rule. The addition rule says that the probability that either A or B will occur is the sum of the probability of A and the probability of B. The multiplication rule says that the probability that both A and B will occur is the probability of A multiplied by the probability of B, provided the values that A can take are not dependent on the values of B, and vice versa.

Probability distributions are discrete or continuous. A discrete distribution lists the possible outcomes and gives estimates of the probability of each outcome. The sum of the probabilities for all of the outcomes is, of course, 1.

Probability distributions, whether discrete or continuous, are characterized by measures of central tendency and measures of dispersion. The most useful measure of central tendency is the mean. The most useful measures of dispersion are the variance and the standard deviation.

For risk analysis, one or more of the cash flows and other parameters in a capital project selection study are treated as random experiments for which the means and variances have to be combined to obtain the mean and the variance of the project as a whole. This is done with the help of the laws of expected value and variance.

In comparing one project with another for risk analysis, we look not only at the mean or expected value of the figure of merit but also at its variance or standard deviation. If the mean of project A is higher than that of project

B and its variance is lower, the choice is an easy one. If both the mean and the variance of project A are higher than for project B, the decision depends on the willingness of the decision maker to trade risk for profit, or vice versa.

A measure of risk that is sometimes used to compare projects that differ in size is the coefficient of variation. This coefficient is the ratio of the standard deviation to the mean.

REFERENCE

1. R. E. Megill, *Introduction to Exploration Economics* (Tulsa, OK: Petroleum Publishing Company, 1971). Chapters 8 and 9 of this text demonstrate how risk analysis is applied to gas and oil exploration.

SUGGESTED READINGS

1. Gerald Keller, Brian Warrack, and Henry Bartel, *Statistics for Management and Economics*, 2nd ed. (Belmont, CA: Wadsworth Publishing Company, 1990). We recommend this text to anyone who has never taken a course in statistics or who has been away from this discipline for some time. You don't have to go much further than the first four chapters to cover the application of risk analysis to the project selection process.
2. Wilfred J. Dixon and Frank J. Massey, *Introduction to Statistical Analysis*, 4th ed. (New York: McGraw-Hill, 1983). Another fine text for you to refer to if you have any questions on the material covered in Chapters 22 and 23 of our text.
3. John A. White, Marvin H. Agee, and Kenneth E. Case, *Principles of Engineering Economics Analysis* (New York: John Wiley & Sons, 1989). Chapter 9 has excellent examples on the use of decision trees for sequential analysis.

PROBLEMS

Laws of Expected Value and Variance

COMMENT: Problems 22-1 to 22-7 are intended to familiarize you with Appendix 22A on the laws of expectation and variance.

22-1 For $E[X] = 3.8$ and $E[Y] = 1.0$, $E[X - Y] = 2.8$ if equation (22.5) holds. Show that it does, using the approach in Appendix 22A for $E[X + Y]$.

22-2 For $E[X] = 3.8$ and $E[Y] = 1.0$, $E[XY] = 3.8$ if equation (22.6) holds. Show that it does, but remember that we can only use this equation if random experiments X and Y are independent.

22-3 Show that equations (22.8) and (22.9) can be derived from equations (22.4), (22.6), and (22.7).

22-4 For V[X] = 1.96 and V[Y] = 0.40, show that equation (22.13) holds, that is, that V[X − Y] equals 2.36. Why does V[X − Y] equal V[X + Y]?

22-5 Show that V[cX] equals c^2 V[X].

22-6 In the text, we said that V[X] V[Y] is not equal to V[XY], even if X and Y are independent random experiments. Show that this is so, using the values of V[X] and V[Y] from Problem 22.4.

22-7 Suppose that we had a third random experiment, Z, which we decided to treat deterministically. Its value is 3. What is E[Z], V[Z], E[X + Y + Z], and V[X + Y + Z] for the values of X and Y in Appendix 22A?

Rules of Probability

22-8 A single die is tossed. What is the probability of tossing
  a) At least two points?
  b) At most three points?
  c) At most six points?

22-9 A fair coin has been tossed ten times and comes up heads each time.
  a) What is the probability of tossing heads ten times in succession?
  b) What is the probability of tossing heads on the eleventh roll?

22-10 A friend argues that there are only three possibilities in tossing a fair coin twice—two heads, two tails, or one of each. This makes the probability of tossing two heads equal to ⅓. What is wrong with this argument? How would you convince your friend of his error?

22-11 A pair of dice is rolled. What is the probability of getting
  a) A prime number?
  b) An even number?
  c) First a 7 and then another 7?
  d) First an even number and then an odd number?

22-12 How would you use the roll of a die to simulate a coin toss? How would you use the roll of a pair of dice to do the same thing?

22-13 A pack of playing cards is shuffled thoroughly. (Why is this important?) What is the probability of getting
  a) A diamond?
  b) A black card?
  c) A face card?

d) A pair without replacement (not put back into the deck) of the first card drawn?

e) A pair with replacement of the first card drawn? (Obtaining the same card on the second draw as on the first draw doesn't count.)

22-14 A zero-sum game is one for which the expected value is zero. Consider the following games.

    a) You are to pick a card from a pack of playing cards. If you pick a spade, you get $10. What do you pay if you lose?

    b) A die is tossed. If you win, you get $5. What do you pay if you lose?

    c) Someone offers to pay you $10 for every double 6 you role with a pair of dice. You are to pay $0.40 if you lose. Should you play?

    d) Why are zero-sum games?

    e) What kind of games do casinos play?

22-15 Two people are to be selected from a group of two men and two women by drawing straws. What is the probability that they will be of the same sex?

Expected Value (Means) and Variance

22-16 X, Y, and Z are three random experiments for which the random variables have the following distributions:

x	$P(x)$	y	$P(y)$	z	$P(z)$
2	$\frac{1}{4}$	2	$\frac{1}{8}$	1	$\frac{1}{4}$
4	$\frac{1}{4}$	4	$\frac{3}{8}$	4	$\frac{1}{4}$
6	$\frac{1}{4}$	6	$\frac{3}{8}$	6	$\frac{1}{4}$
8	$\frac{1}{4}$	8	$\frac{1}{8}$	9	$\frac{1}{4}$

    a) Determine the mean of each experiment by inspection.

    b) Confirm your answer to (a).

    c) By inspection, determine which experiment has the highest variance.

    d) Calculate the variances for the three experiments.

22-17 The random experiment is the repeated toss of a die. What are the mean value, the variance, and the standard deviation of the experiment? What are the values of the random variable within one standard deviation of the mean? What is the probability of falling within this range?

22-18 Go back to Example 22.4, and confirm that the expected values of alternatives A and B are $178,500 and $147,000, respectively. What capital expenditure could be justified for alternative B?

22-19 There is no way of protecting large metropolitan areas from hurricanes and other natural disasters. However, plans can be prepared for evacuating such areas, major evacuation routes can be identified and improved, buildings and other structures can be reinforced, power and telephone lines can be buried, and a host of other measures can be taken in order to reduce the potential damage resulting from such disasters. Two alternatives are under study with the above in mind. They are compared in the following table with the do-nothing alternative.

	Damage Estimates in Millions of Dollars		
Probability	Do-nothing	Alternative A	Alternative B
0.01	$950	$600	$500
0.10	500	300	200
0.19	250	100	70
0.20	100	75	30
0.20	75	50	10
0.30	50	5	1

Compute the expected value of the annual savings that are possible with alternatives A and B.

22-20 The estimated investment costs for plans A and B in Problem 22-19 are $600 million and $1,200 million, respectively. It will take five years to put the proposed changes for plan A into effect and eight years for plan B. The metropolitan area uses 10% and a 25-year life for capital investment studies on damage reduction expenditures due to natural disasters. It also assumes a continuous outflow of cash to cover these expenditures. Are plans A and B justified? Which plan would you select?

22-21 Calculate the expected life of a telephone pole from the data in Example 22.5, and use this to calculate the annual cost of a telephone pole for a replacement cost of $500. Why does this figure differ from the answer for case 1? Which is the correct way to do this problem and why?

22-22 Confirm that the annual cost of a telephone pole is $479 from the data given in Example 22.5.

22-23 Graph the results of case 1 in Example 22.5 as a mass function, in which the age is the abscissa and the percent retired is the ordinate.

22-24 Consider the following data for the life and replacement cost of creosoted piles for docks, jetties, bulkheads, and other marine installations. The replacement costs do not include the cost of the piles themselves.

Life		Unit Replacement Cost	
Years	Probability	Dollars	Probability
3	0.01	$200	0.08
12	0.10	300	0.09
15	0.16	500	0.15
18	0.17	600	0.24
21	0.20	700	0.15
24	0.22	800	0.10
27	0.07	900	0.09
30	0.04	1,000	0.07
33	0.03	1,200	0.03

If life is treated as a random variable and the cost as deterministic, what is the expected value of the annual cost of a pile? The cost from accounting records averages $625 per pile. The discount rate is 10%.

22-25 Refer to Problem 22-24. Redo this problem, assuming that cost is the random variable and that the life is deterministic. Use 20 years for the average life.

22-26 Compute the expected value of the annual cost of replacing piles if both life and cost are treated as random variables. Use the results you obtained in Problems 22-24 and 22-25.

22-27 In the course of a random experiment, the following probability distribution was obtained after numerous trials.

Outcome	Probability
2	0.05
3	0.10
5	0.15
8	0.20
12	0.25
17	0.15
23	0.10

a) Compute the expected value.
b) Compute the variance and the standard deviation

22-28 The optical department of a large communications company has, for one of its projects, prepared the following estimates of annual net cash flow and the probability of attaining them.

Net Cash Flow	Probability
$15,000	0.3
20,000	0.5
25,000	0.2

The planning horizon is eight years, the initial investment is $100,000, the estimated salvage value is $20,000, and the discount rate is 8%. These data are firm.

a) What is the expected value of the present worth?

b) What is the probability of the present worth being greater than zero?

22-29 In Example 22.9, we used Equation 22.10 for computing the variance of the cost of the building and of the resident revenue. Confirm these computations by computing the variances using equation (22.11).

22-30 Draw the cash flow diagrams for the four branches of the decision tree of Figure 22.6, and then confirm the IRRs given in Table 22.6 of Example 22.8.

22-31 Consider the following probability distributions for the recovery of natural gas and for the sales price of the gas.

Recovery in Billions of Cubic Feet		Sales Price per 1,000 Cubic Feet	
Recovery	Probability	Price	Probability
0.7	0.3	$2.00	0.5
1.0	0.6	2.50	0.4
1.5	0.1	3.00	0.1

a) Compute the expected values of the production, of the price, and of the revenue.

b) Can production and price be considered independent variables?

22-32 A major construction company has purchased an insurance policy for $1,000,000 per year to insure against four types of losses. The average cost associated with each loss and the probability of its occurrence are given below.

Cost, $	Probability
$200,000	0.15
1,600,000	0.10
3,000,000	0.08
5,000,000	0.04

Administrative expenses are 25% of the cost of the policy.

a) What is the expected profit to the insurance company?

b) What is the standard deviation of the profit?

Decision Trees

22-33 The random experiment is the roll of a pair of dice, each of which has the following faces—1, 1, 2, 3, 4, and 5.
a) Identify the random variables.
b) Sketch a tree diagram similar to that of Figure 22.5.
c) Compute the mean, variance, and standard deviation

22-34 In Example 22.7, make sure you understand the decision tree of Figure 22.6 and convince yourself that the figures at the end of each branch are correct. How would the addition of $1,000,000 to the deterministic costs affect the dollar values at the end of each branch?

22-35 Would we get the same result for each of the branches if the sequence of events was changed from that in Figure 22.6? Justify your answer by drawing a tree in which the resident revenue comes first, the first cost comes next, and the deterministic estimates come last.

22-36 Draw a decision tree for the present worths of the cash flow streams of Example 22.7. Use Figure 22.6 as a guide.

APPENDIX 22A   EXPECTATION AND VARIANCE

22A.1   INTRODUCTION

In the body of this chapter, we gave you two equations for the variance—equations (22.10) and (22.11)—which, for convenience, are reproduced below.

$$V[X] = \sum (x - \mu)^2 \, P(x) = \sum x^2 \, P(x) - \mu^2$$

In addition, we gave you six equations for the laws of expected value (expectation) and five for the laws of variance. These are also reproduced below. You will recall that, in these equations, X and Y are random experiments and c is a constant.

Equation	Expected Value	Equation	Variance
22.4	$E[X + Y] = E[X] + E[Y]$	22.12	$V[X + Y] = V[X] + V[Y]$
22.5	$E[X - Y] = E[X] - E[Y]$	22.13	$V[X - Y] = V[X] + V[Y]$
22.6	$E[XY] = E[X] \, E[Y]$	22.14	$V[c] = 0$
22.7	$E[c] = c$	22.15	$V[X + c] = V[X]$
22.8	$E[cX] = c \, E[x]$	22.16	$V[cX] = c^2 \, V[X]$
22.9	$E[X + c] = E[X] + c$		

22A.2   EQUATIONS FOR VARIANCE

The definition of the variance of a random variable is from equation (22.10):

$$V[X] = E[(x - \mu)^2] = \sum (x - \mu)^2 P(x)$$

Expanding $(x - \mu)^2$ gives

$$V[X] = \sum (x^2 - 2\mu x + \mu^2) P(x)$$
$$= \sum x^2 P(x) - 2\mu \sum x P(x) + \mu^2 \sum P(x)$$

The second term in this equation equals $-2\mu^2$, since $\Sigma x P(x)$ equals μ. The third term equals μ^2, since the summation $P(x)$ of the probabilities is 1. It follows, as in equation (22.11), that

$$V[X] = \sum x^2 P(x) - \mu^2$$

22A.3   LAWS OF EXPECTED VALUE

We don't intend to give you a formal, rigorous proof of the six laws of expected value. However, we will show you that the laws work. In addition, we ask you to do so yourself in some of the problems at the end of the chapter. Consider two random experiments X and Y with the probability distributions given as follows:

	Experiment X			Experiment Y	
x	$P(x)$	$x\,P(x)$	y	$P(y)$	$y\,P(y)$
2	0.3	0.6	0	0.2	0.0
4	0.5	2.0	1	0.6	0.6
6	0.2	1.2	2	0.2	0.4
	$\mu = E[X] =$	3.8		$\mu = E[Y] =$	1.0

The sum of the two means is 4.8 (3.8 + 1.0). Is this also the sum of E[X + Y]? We proceed as follows to show that it is.

x	y	$(x + y)$	$P(x + y) = P(x)P(y)$	$E[x + y]$
2	0	2	$(0.3)(0.2) = (0.06)$	0.12
	1	3	$(0.3)(0.6) = (0.18)$	0.54
	2	4	$(0.3)(0.2) = (0.06)$	0.24
4	0	4	$(0.5)(0.2) = (0.10)$	0.40
	1	5	$(0.5)(0.6) = (0.30)$	1.50
	2	6	$(0.5)(0.2) = (0.10)$	0.60
6	0	6	$(0.2)(0.2) = (0.04)$	0.24
	1	7	$(0.2)(0.6) = (0.12)$	0.84
	2	8	$(0.2)(0.2) = (0.04)$	0.32
			Totals 1.00	4.80

22A.4 LAWS OF VARIANCE

For the laws of variance, we use the above probability distributions for X and Y. To illustrate the addition rule—equation (22.12)—we proceed as follows.

	Experiment X				Experiment Y		
x	x^2	$P(x)$	$x^2P(x)$	y	y^2	$P(y)$	$y^2P(y)$
2	4	0.3	1.2	0	0	0.2	0.0
4	16	0.5	8.0	1	1	0.6	0.6
6	36	0.2	7.2	2	4	0.2	0.8
			16.4				1.4

The variances of X and Y by equation (22.11) are then

$$V[X] = \sum x^2\, P(x) - \mu^2 = 16.4 - (3.8)^2 = 1.96$$
$$V[Y] = \sum y^2\, P(y) - \mu^2 = 1.40 - 1.00 = 0.40$$

and the variances of their sum is 2.36. Does V[X + Y] equal V[X] + V[Y]? That it does is shown with the help of the following tabulation:

x	y	$(x + y)$	$(x + y)^2$	$P(x)P(y) = P(x,y)$	$(x + y)^2P(x,y)$
2	0	2	4	0.06	0.24
	1	3	9	0.18	1.62
	2	4	16	0.06	0.96
4	0	4	16	0.10	1.60
	1	5	25	0.30	7.50
	2	6	36	0.10	3.60
6	0	6	36	0.04	1.44
	1	7	49	0.12	5.88
	2	8	64	0.04	2.56
			Total	1.00	25.40

Applying equation (22.11) with E[X + Y] equal to 4.8 gives

$$V[X + Y] = 25.40 - (4.8)^2 = 2.36$$

23

PROBABILITY: PART 2

23.1 INTRODUCTION

In Chapter 22, we included investments in capital projects as examples of random experiments or lotteries. Some investments turn out as planned or nearly so. Some do worse, and some do better. It would be pure happenstance to have an investment turn out exactly as planned, that is, down to the crossing of the last tee.

The random variables in capital investment projects are cash flows, ratios such as rates of return, and time. All of these are continuous rather than discrete. Planning horizons can vary continuously from one date to another. Cash flows and rates of return can vary continuously between a lower and an upper limit. Why then, you ask, do we spend so much time on discrete distributions?

There are, in our opinion, three good reasons for doing so. First of all, as we mentioned in Chapter 22, the basics of probability theory apply to both discrete and continuous distributions. Second, these basics are more easily introduced with coins and dice than with time and cash flows. Third, we often treat continuous distributions as if they were discrete.

We begin this chapter with a comparison of discrete and continuous distributions. We then examine several continuous distributions that are widely used in cost studies of our type. Lastly, we present certain "principles of choice" for risk analysis, which complement the principles of choice that will be illustrated in Chapter 25 on uncertainty analysis.

23.2 CONTINUOUS DISTRIBUTIONS

A discrete distribution is one in which the values of the random variable are countable as they are with a coin toss, the roll of a die, and a draw from a pack of cards. A continuous distribution is one in which the values of the random variable cannot be counted. There are an infinite number of planning horizons between 10 years and 12 years, an infinite number of cash flows between *a* dollars and *b* dollars, and an infinite number of MARRs between one percentage and another.

You are no stranger to the concept of continuity. In Chapter 5, we developed equations for continuous compounding of rates of return, and, in Chapter 6, we developed equations for continuous cash flows from their discrete forebears. We intend to develop the concept of continuous probability distributions in the same way, that is, by showing how the discrete merges into the continuous.

Example 23.1 Continuous Probability Distributions Consider a random experiment on a sample of the height of 100 men. The minimum height is 64 inches, and the maximum is 78 inches. The random variable, the height x, can have an infinite number of values between these extremes, including the two extremes themselves. In order to prepare a continuous probability distribution for this variable—or any continuous random variable—we first have to organize the raw data, which are always finite, into a discrete number of classes. For the following tabulation, we select a class width or interval of 2 inches.

Class Width[a]	Number of Men in Interval	Proportion of Men in Interval
64–66	8	0.08
66–68	18	0.18
68–70	26	0.26
70–72	22	0.22
72–74	14	0.14
74–76	8	0.08
76–78	4	0.04
	100	Total 1.00

[a]Each class includes all of the values from the lower limit up to, but not including, the upper limit.

The results are plotted in Figure 23.1 as both a histogram and a polygon. The abscissa is the random variable, that is, the height x. The ordinate is the probability $P(x)$. The polygon is a series of straight lines connecting the midpoints of the tops of the bars or rectangles of the histogram. Such polygons are usually brought down to the abscissa by adding an additional class interval at each end with zero probability. The polygon gives us a general idea of what a continuous distribution looks like. The evidence indicates that it will be skewed to the right.

For Figure 23.1, the question "What is the frequency of being 69 inches tall?" has no meaning. The question "What is the probability of being between 68 and

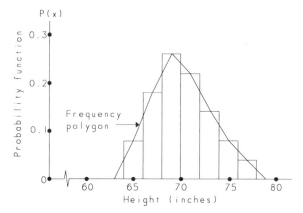

Figure 23.1. Frequency histogram and polygon.

70 inches tall?" does. For the first question, the answer is zero; for the second, it is the area of the rectangle bounded by 68 and 70 inches, divided by the total area of all of the rectangles. This, as shown below, equals 26%.

$$P(68 < x < 70) = \frac{2 \times 0.26}{2 \times 1.00} = 0.26 = 26\%$$

For this sample, the probability of a man having a height somewhere between 64 and 78 inches is 1. We therefore redraw Figure 23.1 so that the total area of all of the bars is also 1. In this way, we define a probability density function $f(x)$, which equals the probability function $P(x)$ divided by the class interval. Since the interval is 2 inches in width, $f(x)$ equals one-half of $P(x)$. A histogram of $f(x)$ versus height is given in Figure 23.2. This histogram is identical to that of Figure 23.1, except for one important difference; namely, the ordinate is now $f(x)$ rather

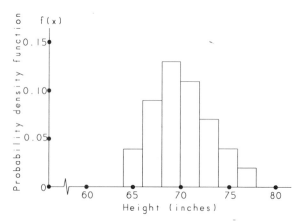

Figure 23.2. Probability density function.

than P(x). The total area of the rectangles under $f(x)$ is now unity, and the area of the rectangle between 68 and 70 inches is 0.26 (2 × 0.13). Therefore,

$$P(68 < x < 70) = \frac{2 \times 0.13}{1.00} = 0.26 = 26\%$$

If we enlarged the sample and reduced the size of the class width, the histogram of Figure 23.2 would approach nearer and nearer to a smooth curve and would eventually have an appearance similar to that of the continuous distribution in Figure 23.3. The two figures resemble each other in their general shape. Both are unimodal, and both are positively skewed, that is, skewed to the right. For both, the area under $f(x)$ is 1.

We conclude that, for a continuous distribution, the function with which we must deal is the probability density function $f(x)$ and that, for this function, the area under the curve of $f(x)$ versus x is unity. Therefore, the probability of the random variable x belonging to any given range of x is the area under $f(x)$ for that range. This is further illustrated in Example 23.2.

Example 23.2 Probability of a Continuous Variable How can we get the probability of the height of an adult male falling between any two limits—say 67 and 71 inches—from a smooth continuous probability distribution such as Figure 23.3? We can obtain the answer in several ways.

- Reproduce the histogram of Figure 23.2 or the smooth curve of Figure 23.3. on cross-section paper, count the number of squares below $f(x)$ that fall between 67 and 71 inches, and divide this number by the total number of squares under the curve.
- Use calculus to compute the area under the curve that falls between 67 and 71 inches. This, however, can only be done if we express the relation between $f(x)$ and x as an integrable equation.

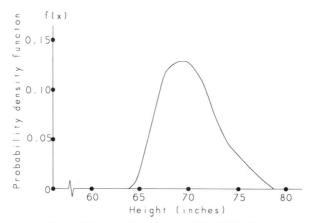

Figure 23.3. Continuous probability distribution.

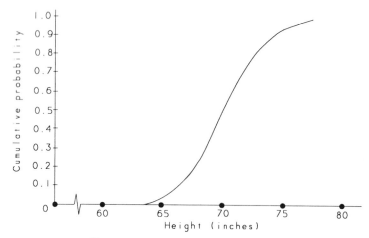

Figure 23.4. Cumulative probability graph.

- Draw a cumulative probability curve either by counting squares or by integration, and read the difference between the cumulative probabilities at 67 and 71 inches.

A cumulative probability curve for the distribution in Figure 23.3 is given in Figure 23.4. The cumulative probability of 67 inches is 0.15 and of 71 inches, 0.64. Therefore, the probability of falling within the range of 67 to 71 inches is the difference, or 0.49 (49%).

23.3   EXPECTED VALUE AND VARIANCE

You were introduced to expected values and variances in Chapter 22. However, the equations presented there were for discrete distributions. We now adapt them to continuous distributions.

The probability of a continuous random variable, x, falling between any two values of x, say x_1 and x_2, is given by the shaded area in Figure 23.5 and equals

$$P(x_1 < x < x_2) = \int_{x_1}^{x_2} f(x)\, dx \tag{23.1}$$

If this integration is carried out between a and b—the upper and lower limits of the range of x—then

$$P(a < x < b) = \int_{a}^{b} f(x)\, dx = 1$$

since the total area under the curve is 1.

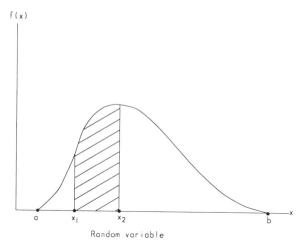

Figure 23.5. Interpreting continuous distributions.

The limits a and b, or both a and b, may extend to infinity. If they do, they will have to approach the abscissa asymptotically so that the area under $f(x)$ does not exceed unity.

The equations for the expected value and variance of continuous distributions resemble those for discrete distributions. To see this, compare equations (23.2) and (23.3) with equations (22.3) and (22.11). For any random experiment X, for which the random variable x is continuous between a and b (one or both of which could be infinity), the expected value is given by

$$E[X] = \mu = \int_a^b x\, f(x)\, dx \tag{23.2}$$

and the variance by

$$V[X] = \sigma^2 = \int_a^b x^2 f(x)\, dx - \mu^2 \tag{23.3}$$

Before we proceed to discuss several continuous distributions, a brief aside is in order to correct an impression that you might have gained on how discrete distributions merge into continuous ones.

Systems analysts and others who are responsible for gathering data and putting it into usable form have to begin with a limited sample such as the sample of 100 used for Figure 23.1. Do they then gather more and more data to obtain more and more refined histograms and frequency polygons in order to produce a curve that is as smooth (or nearly so) as that of Figure 23.3? The answer is no. The amount of data gathered depends on the cost of gathering it, on the judgment of the study group on how much data are needed, and on how much data are actually available. We are not tossing coins or dice, or reviewing weights, heights, crime statistics, life expectancies, fire risks, and other variables for which a host of data exists. Therefore, we often resort to sketching continuous curves from a limited amount of data. The reason we do so is to get a better view of an important variable that we know is continuous by using our judgment, common sense, and intuitive feel for how the variable would behave if an infinite amount of data were available.

23.4 CONTINUOUS UNIFORM DISTRIBUTION

Often the most sensible judgment or best guess that one can make is that there is an equal likelihood for all of the possible outcomes within a given range to occur. This brings us to the continuous uniform distribution.

Such a distribution is illustrated in Figure 23.6. The range is $(b - a)$. The function $f(x)$ is a constant with the value $[1/(b - a)]$. The probability of the random variable x falling between x_1 and x_2 is obtained by substituting $1/(b - a)$ for $f(x)$ in equation (23.1).

$$P(x_1 < x < x_2) = \frac{1}{b - a} \int_{x_1}^{x_2} dx = \frac{1}{b - a} (x_2 - x_1) \qquad (23.4)$$

COMMENT: It is our hope that you remember enough calculus to confirm the integration in this equation.

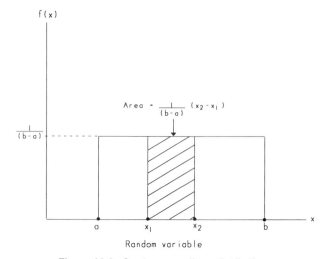

Figure 23.6. Continuous uniform distribution.

The expected value and variance of a uniform distribution are easily derived with the help of equations (23.2) and (23.3). (We will let you do the derivation in one of the problems at the end of this chapter.)

$$E[X] = \mu = (a + b)/2 \tag{23.5}$$

$$V[X] = \sigma^2 = (b - a)^2/12 \tag{23.6}$$

We will use these equations in Example 23.3.

Example 23.3   Uniform Continuous Distribution   You are the chief financial officer of a large corporation. You have asked your controller to come up with projections for the coming year for the net cash flow from sales (revenues minus cash expenses) for a new product that your corporation is launching and for which there is therefore no historical data. He tells you that this sum could vary from $0 to $6 million and that discussions with sales and other departments indicate that the likelihood of reaching any number between these limits is the same as the likelihood of reaching any other number. In short, with the help of subjective probability, he and the other members of top management have concluded that the distribution is uniform.

If we express the random variable—the net cash flow—in millions of dollars, the values of a and b are 0 and 6, respectively, and the value of $1/(b - a)$ is therefore $\frac{1}{6}$.

Applying equations (23.4), (23.5), and (23.6) gives

$$P(a < x < b) = 1$$
$$E[X] = 6/2 = 3 \quad (\$3,000,000)$$
$$V[X] = 36/12 = 3 \quad (\$3,000,000 \times 10^6 \text{ dollars}^2)$$
$$\sigma = 1.732 \ (\$1,732,000)$$

As shown, the units of $E[X]$ and σ are millions of dollars and of $V[X]$, millions of dollars squared. One standard deviation to the right and to the left of the mean covers a range of $3.464 million (2 × 1.732), or 58% of the total area.

23.5   STANDARD NORMAL DISTRIBUTION

The normal distribution, including its standard version, is the familiar bell-shaped curve of Figure 23.7. A comparison of Figures 22.2 and 23.7 shows that it looks like a curvaceous variation of the discrete distribution for the roll of a pair of dice.

Since the normal distribution is symmetrical and unimodal, the mode (the high point), the median, and the mean are identical. The distribution extends to infinity in both directions, and, as it must, the area under the curve equals 1. The mode is no longer the most likely value (it is just the high point),

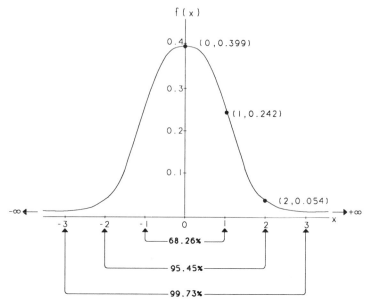

Figure 23.7. The normal density function.

because, like any value of x for a continuous distribution, its probability is zero. The median is the value of x that divides the area under $f(x)$ in half.

The standard normal distribution (the special version of the normal) has a mean of zero and a standard deviation of 1. The equation of its probability density function $f(x)$ is given in equation (23.7).

$$f(x) = \frac{1}{\sqrt{2\pi}} e^{-x^2/2} \quad \text{or} \quad \frac{1}{\sqrt{2\pi}} \{\exp[-x^2/2]\} \qquad (23.7)$$

It follows from equation (23.1) that the probability of the random variable x falling between any interval such as x_1 and x_2 is

$$P(x_1 < x < x_2) = \int_{x_1}^{x_2} f(x)\, dx$$

where $f(x)$ is given by equation (23.7). Furthermore,

$$P(-\infty < x < +\infty) = \int_{-\infty}^{+\infty} f(x)\, dx = 1$$

COMMENT: We think it is important at this time for you to spend a little time with equation (23.7). We do so in Appendix 23A, to which you should now turn.

The equations for the expected value and variance of a standard normal distribution are derived from equations (23.2), (23.3), and (23.7). They are reproduced below.

$$E[X] = \mu = \int_{-\infty}^{+\infty} x\, f(x)\, dx = \frac{1}{\sqrt{2\pi}} \int_{-\infty}^{+\infty} x\{\exp[-x^2/2]\}\, dx \qquad (23.8)$$

$$V[X] = \sigma^2 = \int_{-\infty}^{+\infty} x^2 f(x)\, dx - \mu^2$$

$$= \frac{1}{\sqrt{2\pi}} \int_{-\infty}^{+\infty} x^2\{\exp[-x^2/2]\}\, dx - \mu^2 \qquad (23.9)$$

Integrating these equations gives a value of zero for the mean and of 1 for the variance and the standard deviation (see Appendix 23A). That the mean is zero is obvious, since the probability density function $f(x)$ is symmetrical about zero.

The areas under $f(x)$ that are 1, 2, and 3 standard deviations to the right and to the left of the mean are shown in Figure 23.7, and for convenience are reproduced below.

Range in Standard Deviations	Area Under Density Distribution, %
−1 to +1	68.3
−2 to + 2	95.5
−3 to +3	99.7
−∞ to +∞	100.0

This is obviously valuable information. The probability of x falling within one deviation from the mean is 68.3%; within two deviations, 95.5%; and within three deviations, 99.7%. The area beyond three deviations represents only 0.3% of the total.

A cumulative graph for the standard normal distribution is given in Figure 23.8. You already know how to use such graphs from Example 23.2; however, you will find Table 23.1 handier.

COMMENT: If you feel that you need more than three significant figures in solving problems such as those we will be discussing, you can go to the tables in any of the many texts on probability and statistics. However, two significant figures is usually the best that one can hope to obtain with subjective probability estimates.

Table 23.1 gives the areas under the standard normal curve for any distance from the mean. For three standard deviations on either side of the mean, the

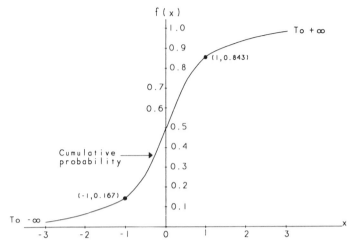

Figure 23.8. The cumulative normal density function.

area to two significant figures is 0.50 or, if you wish to be more precise, 0.499. To obtain the area between 1.25 standard deviations to the left of the mean and 1.75 standard deviations to the right of the mean, we simply interpolate between these two numbers. Thus, for 1.25, the area is 0.394 and for 1.75, 0.460. This gives about 85%, as shown in the following equation:

$$P(-1.25 < x < 1.75) = 0.394 + 0.460 = 0.854 = 85\%$$

TABLE 23.1   Areas Under the Standard Normal Curve

Distance from Mean[a]	Area	Distance from Mean[a]	Area
0.0	0.000	1.6	0.445
0.1	0.040	1.7	0.455
0.2	0.079	1.8	0.464
0.3	0.118	1.9	0.471
0.4	0.155	2.0	0.477
0.5	0.192	2.1	0.482
0.6	0.226	2.2	0.486
0.7	0.258	2.3	0.489
0.8	0.288	2.4	0.492
0.9	0.316	2.5	0.494
1.0	0.341	2.6	0.495
1.1	0.364	2.7	0.497
1.2	0.385	2.8	0.497
1.3	0.403	2.9	0.498
1.4	0.419	3.0	0.499
1.5	0.433	∞	0.500

[a]Distance is expressed in standard deviations.

Many of the situations that we run into in real life can be modeled with bell-shaped symmetrical, normal distributions, but very few will favor us with a mean of zero and a standard deviation of 1, that is, will qualify as a *standard* normal distribution. However, as you will see, Table 23.1 can be used to obtain probabilities for any normal distribution whether standard or not.

23.6 NORMAL DISTRIBUTION

A normal distribution or its skewed offspring can often be used to approximate the distribution of many of the random variables that play a part in capital investment decisions—revenues, expenses, first costs, salvage values, planning horizons, sales volumes, prices, and so on. The skewed offspring will be discussed later. The symmetric or normal distribution, which includes the standard normal distribution, is discussed next.

For many cost studies, we can reasonably assume from our observations, estimates, and judgments (the latter hopefully tempered by common sense) that several of the preceding parameters will cluster around a measure of central tendency and will disperse symmetrically to form a bell-shaped curve for which the correspondence between the random variable x and a function $f(x)$ is expressed by the following equation:

$$f(x) = \frac{1}{\sigma\sqrt{2\pi}} \left\{ \exp\left(-\frac{1}{2} \left[\frac{x - \mu}{\sigma} \right]^2 \right) \right\} \qquad (23.10)$$

If we substitute 0 for the mean and 1 for the standard deviation, we get the normal probability density function for the standard curve, that is, equation (23.7).

The shape of the bell depends on the value of the standard deviation. If the deviation is zero, the curve becomes a vertical line, as shown in Figure 23.9. As the deviation becomes larger and larger, the hump on the curve becomes less and less pronounced and the limit approaches the abscissa.

It is apparent from equation (23.10) that a normal distribution is completely defined by its mean and variance. In order to use the distribution, we first have to convince ourselves that the random variable is normally distributed. We do this from an analysis of the raw data available or from how this variable and similar variables have behaved in the past or from what our judgment on how such a variable will behave tells us. Once we have accepted a normal distribution as a reasonable fit, we have to estimate the mean and the variance. For the time being, we treat these two parameters as givens.

Assume now that we have the mean and the standard deviation for an important random variable. Do we then use equation (23.10) to draw a normal curve from which we can obtain the probability of the variable falling between any two values of x from the area under the curve? The answer is no; we can use the standard normal distribution with the help of a simple transformation. This is the topic of Example 23.4.

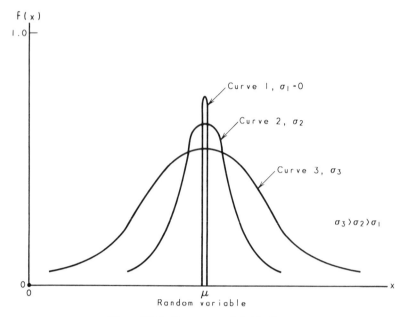

Figure 23.9. Some normal distributions.

Example 23.4   Transforming Normal Distributions   The random variable x is the net cash flow from operations for a proposed capital investment. You have studied the available data and have satisfied yourself that the probability density distribution for x can be approximated by a normal distribution. In addition, you have found the mean and the standard deviation, which are $600,000 and $80,000, respectively. What is the probability that the cash flow in the coming year will lie between $600,000 and $700,000?

$$P(\$600,000 < x < \$700,000) = ?$$

As mentioned, this area could be obtained by plotting the probability density function $f(x)$, using equation (23.1) and obtaining (by integration or by counting squares) the area under the curve between $600,000 and $700,000. To avoid this rather cumbersome procedure, we use the standard normal distribution for which these areas are given in Table 23.1. In what follows, the letter z refers to the standard normal distribution in order to distinguish it from the distribution for x.
    The relation between x and z is given by

$$z = (x - \mu)/\sigma \qquad (23.11)$$

For x equals $600,000, the corresponding z is then

$$z = (\$600,000 - \$600,000)/\$100,000 = 0$$

and for x equals $700,000,

$$z = (\$700{,}000 - \$600{,}000)/\$80{,}000 = 1.25$$

The probability of z lying between 0 and 1.25 on the standard curve will be the same as the probability of x lying between \$600,000 and \$700,000 on its curve; that is,

$$P(\$600{,}000 < x < \$700{,}000) = P(0 < z < 1.25)$$

Interpolating between 1.2 and 1.3 in Table 23.1 for z equal to 1.25 gives 0.394, which indicates about a 40% probability of the sales revenue falling between the above limits. Other samples of what we can glean from Table 23.1 are given in the following tabulation:

Values of x, Range of Cash Flow $/yr. (000)	Values of z, Matching Range for Standard Distribution	Area Factors Lower Limit	Upper Limit	Probability
400–800	−2.5 to +2.5	−0.49	+0.49	0.98
500–700	−1.25 to +1.25	−0.39	+0.39	0.78
600–800	0 to +2.5	0.00	+0.49	0.49
550–700	−0.625 to +1.25	−0.24	+0.39	0.63

You should have no trouble in checking this table with the help of equation (23.11) and Table 23.1, from which the area factors are obtained. The last column gives the probability of the cash flow stream for revenues being within the ranges shown. Thus, there is a 98% probability that revenues will fall between \$400,000 and \$800,000 (2.5 standard deviations equal \$200,000) and a 63% probability that revenues will fall between \$550,000 and \$700,000.

23.7 SKEWED CONTINUOUS DISTRIBUTIONS

In real life, continuous random variables do not conveniently fall into symmetrical bell-shaped curves, such as those for normal distributions. Among the most common deviates are unimodal curves, which resemble the bell-shaped normal distribution but show a bias toward the right (positively skewed) or a bias toward the left (negatively skewed). The curve in Figure 23.3 was skewed to the right.

Let us assume that we have gathered what we consider to be sufficient data for the topic of our choice—a continuous random variable—that we have organized the data into a histogram and a frequency polygon, and that we have then sketched a smooth curve that, in our opinion, best resembles the relationship between $f(x)$ and x. We could always approximate (or attempt to approximate) this relationship with an equation or a set of equations, but often it is much more practical to use the midpoints of the bars on a histogram as surrogates for the probabilities of the class intervals. When we do this, we can, of course, choose any class interval we like; that is, we can use the smooth curve to draw a histogram with smaller class intervals. The smaller we make the interval, the closer we approach the mean and variance for the smooth distribution. However, the result is not necessarily any better than the result we would have obtained from the original histogram.

We demonstrate this procedure in Example 23.5.

Example 23.5 From Continuous to Discrete Distributions We assume that we have satisfied ourselves that a continuous distribution, such as the one in Figure 23.3, best approximates the heights of a large group of men. To compute the mean and the variance of the distribution, we use Figure 23.1, for which the class interval is 2 inches. The computations are given in the following tabulation:

	Mean			Variance	
x	$P(x)$	$xP(x)$	$(x - \mu)$	$(x - \mu)^2$	$(x - \mu)^2P(x)$
65	0.08	5.2	−5.1	26.0	2.1
67	0.18	12.1	−3.1	9.6	1.7
69	0.26	17.9	−1.1	1.2	0.3
71	0.22	15.6	0.9	0.8	0.2
73	0.14	10.2	2.9	8.4	1.2
75	0.08	6.0	4.9	24.0	1.9
77	0.04	3.1	6.9	47.6	1.9
		$\mu = \overline{70.1}$		$V =$	9.3
				$\sigma =$	3.0

The x's are the midpoints of the rectangles on the histogram of Figure 23.1, and the probabilities are those of the class intervals to which the midpoints belong. The mean is 70.1 inches, and the standard deviation is 3 inches.

This procedure can be followed for any continuous function $f(x)$ for which sufficient data are available. In Chapter 24, we will show how means and variances can be approximated with just three points—a minimum anticipated value, a most likely value, and a maximum anticipated value.

As mentioned, bell-shaped continuous distributions often show a bias toward the right (positively skewed) or toward the left (negatively skewed). For these and other skewed curves, a coefficient of skewness (or just skewness) is defined by the following formula:

$$\text{Skewness} = E[(x - \mu)^3]/\sigma^3 \qquad (23.12)$$

We compute the skewness of Figure 23.1 in Example 23.6.

Example 23.6 Coefficient of Skewness We already have the mean and the variance for Figure 23.1 from Example 23.5. The computation of the coefficient of skewness, therefore, proceeds as follows.

x	$(x - \mu)$	$(x - \mu)^3$	$P(x)$	$(x - \mu)^3\,P(x)$
(1)	(2)	(3)	(4)	(5) = (3)(4)
65	−5.1	−132.7	0.08	−10.6
67	−3.1	−29.8	0.18	−5.4
69	−1.1	−1.3	0.26	−0.3
71	0.9	0.7	0.22	0.2
73	2.9	24.4	0.14	3.4
75	4.9	117.6	0.08	9.4
77	6.9	328.5	0.04	13.1
			Total =	9.8

The standard deviation is 3, and its cube is 27. Therefore,

$$\text{Skewness} = E[(x - \mu)^3]/\sigma^3 = (9.8/27) = 0.36$$

Since the coefficient is positive, the distribution is, as we knew it would be, skewed to the right.

The variables used in the capital selection process are generally unimodal and bell-shaped, and many of them show a bias to the right or the left. Consider the first cost of capital projects. It would be unusual for a $1 million project to underrun by $200,000, but it is not unusual for such a project to overrun by $500,000. First costs, in short, tend to be skewed to the right. Revenues, on the other hand, tend to be skewed to the left; that is, actual revenues will more often be less than estimated rather than more than estimated and by a greater percentage. Expenses, like first costs, tend to be skewed to the right. There may be a pattern here. The worst that can happen— higher first costs, lower revenues, higher expenses—proves in real life to show a greater bias than the best that can happen.

23.8 PRINCIPLES FOR MAKING DECISIONS UNDER RISK

There are certain principles of choice for comparing alternatives under risk that often serve as surrogates for the more complete analyses discussed previously and in Chapter 22. These are

- Range
- Principle of expectation
- Expectation variance principle
- Most probable future principle
- Aspiration level principle

Each principle will be discussed with the help of the following matrix, in which five alternatives are compared.

| | Possible Outcomes | | | | | |
Alternative	P_1 0.30	P_2 0.40	P_3 0.20	P_4 0.10	Maximum	Minimum
A_1	25	18	28	17	28	17
A_2	23	22	22	23	23	22
A_3	24	27	15	24	27	15
A_4	16	19	24	22	24	16
A_5	17	20	24	25	25	17

Assume that the numbers in the matrix are in millions of dollars and that the matrix serves as either a cost matrix, in which the figures stand for EUACs (negative annual worths), or a profit matrix, in which the figures are positive annual worths. By using annual worths, we avoid the problem of cotermination. However, in a comparison such as this one, the alternatives are often long-term and a life of 25 years or an infinite time span serves well as a common planning horizon.

Before we compare the five principles, we need to say something about dominance. For a cost matrix, A_4 dominates A_5, since every EUAC for A_4 is either less than, or no more than, the EUACs for A_5. For a profit matrix, the reverse is true. We could, therefore, eliminate A_4 or A_5, depending on whether we were comparing negative or positive annual worths. However, we are not going to do this, because we want to emphasize once again that the selection process does not depend on monetary factors alone. The non-monetary factors (the irreducibles) are often as important as the monetary factors—or more so—and it is therefore better to leave all of the candidates in the ring until the irreducibles have been examined.

We apply the five principles to the matrix. The results for all but the aspiration level principle are shown in Table 23.2.

23.8.1 Range

The range is simply the difference between the maximum and minimum values of any alternative. For A_1, it is the difference between 28 and 17, which equals 11. For this criterion, A_2 is the least risky alternative.

TABLE 23.2 Principles for Decisions Under Risk

Alternative	Range	Principle of Expectation	Expectation Variance Principle	Most Probable Future Principle
A_1	11	22.0	4.3	18
A_2	1	22.4	0.5	22
A_3	12	23.4	4.4	27
A_4	8	19.4	2.9	19
A_5	8	20.4	2.9	20

23.8.2 Principle of Expectation

The principle of expectation compares the expected value or mean of each alternative. For A_1, the mean is

$$E[A_1] = 0.30(25) + 0.40(18) + 0.20(28) + 0.10(17)$$
$$= 22.0$$

A_4 shows the lowest mean (19.4) and is the preferred choice if the matrix is a cost matrix. A_3 shows the highest mean (23.4) and is the preferred choice if the matrix is a profit matrix.

23.8.3 Expectation Variance Principle

The expectation variance principle measures the variance or standard deviation of each alternative. For A_1, using equation (22.11),

$$V[A_1] = [0.3(25)^2 + 0.4(18)^2 + 0.2(28)^2 + 0.1(17)^2]$$
$$- (22)^2$$
$$\sigma^2 = 18.8$$
$$\sigma = 4.3$$

The variance, as we know, is also a measure of dispersion and a more sophisticated one than the range. A_2 has the lowest dispersion (0.5), as it did for the range.

23.8.4 Most Probable Future Principle

The most probable future principle states that the alternative to select is the one with the highest probability of success. The numbers in Table 23.2 for this principle are identical to those in the matrix for a probability of 0.4. For a cost matrix, A_1 with a value of 18 would be the selection and, for a profit matrix, A_3 with a value of 27.

23.8.5 Aspiration Level Principle

The aspiration level principle sets a goal or level of aspiration. If, for example, we aspire to a level of annual costs no greater than 18, we eliminate the possible outcomes higher than 18. For A_1, there is a 50% chance ($P_2 + P_4$) of staying at 18 or under. For A_2, there is no possibility of doing so. For A_3, there is a 20% probability (P_3); for A_4, a 30% probability (P_1); and for A_5, a 30% probability (P_1). A_1 is therefore the preferred choice.

23.8.6 Comparison of Principles

For the sample matrix, the preferred outcomes for all of the principles of choice except the aspiration level principle are summarized as follows:

	Cost Matrix	Profit Matrix
Range	A_2	A_2
Principle of expectation	A_4	A_3
Expectation variance principle	A_2	A_2
Most probable future principle	A_1	A_3

For the aspiration level principle, the choice depends upon the goal.

Which of the preceding answers is the correct one? The answer depends on the decision maker. Is his or her interest, the size of the cash flow, the propensity for risk, or a trade-off between cash flow and risk expressed through an aspiration level?

23.9 SUMMARY

Continuous probability distributions differ from discrete distributions in that the random variable is not countable. It can take an infinite number of values between any two limits, no matter how close. The random variables with which we deal in the project selection process, such as cash flows, rates of return, and time, are all continuous.

For continuous distributions, the significant question is, "What is the probability of the random variable falling between any two of its values?" For the answer, we define a probability density function, $f(x)$, for which the integral, $f(x) \, dx$, is unity for the upper and lower limits of the range of x.

The continuous distributions described in this chapter are the uniform, the normal, and the skewed. The standard normal distribution is an important version of the normal distribution. Its mean is zero, and its standard deviation is unity. It can be used to obtain the probability between any two values of any normal distribution, whether standard or not.

The parameters for the project selection process can often be approximated with normal distributions or with bell-shaped distributions that resemble the normal distribution but are skewed to the right or to the left. For these, a coefficient of skewness can be calculated. If it is positive, the skewness is to the right, and if negative, to the left.

Five principles of choice were discussed. Two of these—the range and the expectation variance principle—are measures of dispersion. A third, the principle of expectation, is a measure of central tendency. The fourth is the most probable future principle. It simply selects the outcome for any alternative that has the highest probability of success. The fifth, the aspiration level principle, sets a goal to be obtained and then selects those outcomes with which that goal is most likely to be reached.

There is no best or worst among these principles. Which one to apply and under what circumstances are left to the decision maker.

SUGGESTED READINGS

The Suggested Readings at the end of Chapter 22 also apply to Chapter 23.

PROBLEMS

Continuous Distributions

23-1 The first cost of a major investment prospect currently under review could range between $20 million and $30 million, depending on certain assumptions about what might happen once it is decided to proceed. The best estimates by a panel of experts show the following probability distributions:

First Cost, $ (millions)	Probability, $P(x)$
Less than 20	0.00
20–21.9	0.07
22–23.9	0.15
24–25.9	0.27
26–27.9	0.34
28–30	0.17
More than 30	0.00
	1.00

a) Calculate the expected value of the distribution, using the midpoints of the class intervals.

b) Calculate the standard deviation.

23-2 Refer to Problem 23-1, and proceed as follows.

a) Draw a histogram of the distribution. Use Figure 23.1 as a guide.

b) Superimpose a frequency polygon on the histogram of (a).

c) Is the distribution skewed? If so, positively or negatively?

d) How would you expect a distribution of first cost to be skewed and why?

23-3 Sketch a graph (an intelligent approximation) of the continuous probability distribution of the first cost of the investment opportunity in Problem 23.1. How did you obtain the probability density function, $f(x)$? Have you checked your graph to make sure that the area under $f(x)$ equals 1? (*Note*: A rough check will do.)

23-4 Prepare a cumulative probability distribution for the first cost of Problem 23-1.

    a) What is the probability of the first cost exceeding $26.5 million?

    b) Of being less than $24.5 million?

    c) Of lying between $24.5 and $27.5 million?

    d) Of being equal to $28.0 million?

23-5 The net annual revenue from a project that is now in the planning stage could, according to the best estimates available, vary between $1.7 and $2.9 million. For a preliminary study, a probability distribution was estimated for a rather broad class interval, namely, $0.2 million. The results are given in the following tabulation. For a later and more definitive study, a more refined estimate of the probability distribution was made, using a smaller class interval, namely, $0.10 million. The results are also given.

Class Width of $0.2 Million		Class Width of $0.1 Million	
Sales (000s)	$P(x)$	Sales (000s)	$P(x)$
1,700–1,899	0.11	1,700–1,799	0.04
1,900–2,099	0.18	1,800–1,899	0.07
2,100–2,299	0.27	1,900–1,999	0.08
2,300–2,499	0.24	2,000–2,099	0.10
2,500–2,699	0.16	2,100–2,199	0.12
2,700–2,899	0.04	2,200–2,299	0.15
Total	1.00	2,300–2,399	0.13
		2,400–2,499	0.11
		2,500–2,599	0.09
		2,600–2,699	0.07
		2,700–2,799	0.03
		2,800–2,899	0.01
		Total	1.00

    a) Compute the expected values and the standard deviation for the class width of $0.2 million.

    b) Do the same for the class width of $0.1 million.

    c) Compare and comment on the results of (a) and (b).

23-6 Refer to Problem 23-5, and proceed as follows.

    a) Draw a histogram for each of the two frequency distributions, using Figure 23.1 as a guide.

    b) Superimpose frequency polygons on the histograms of (a).

    c) Compare and comment on how much more the refined estimate tells you than the original preliminary estimate.

23-7 The two histograms of Problem 23-6 have the probability function, $P(x)$, as the ordinate. Is the area of each histogram equal to unity? If not, add another ordinate to each of the histograms for the probability density function, $f(x)$. Check what you have done to make sure that for $f(x)$ the total area of the histograms is equal to unity.

23-8 Sketch a graph that approximates a continuous probability distribution for the annual revenue of Problem 23-5. Sketch another graph that gives the cumulative probability distribution for this cash flow.

Continuous Uniform Distributions

23-9 Integrate equations (23.2) and (23.3) for a continuous uniform distribution between the limits a and b. The result should be equations (23.5) and (23.6) for the mean and variance.

23-10 Confirm the results given in Example 23.3 for the mean, variance, and standard deviation.

23-11 Suppose there is an equal likelihood that a random variable can take any value between $-\$3$ million to $+\$3$ million. What is the expected value, the variance, and the standard deviation of this distribution? Do the same for $-\$2$ million and $+\$8$ million.

23-12 Based on the best information available and on the opinion of those who should know, there is an equal likelihood that the time span of a given project lies between 8 and 12 years. What is the expected value, the variance, and the standard deviation of this distribution? What value for the time span would a risk-prone, a risk-neutral, and a risk-averse investor use for a project selection study?

Normal Distribution

23-13 With the help of a table of integrals and a hand calculator programmed for powers of e, confirm the following probabilities for a standard normal distribution defined by the probability density function of equation (23.7).
  a) $P(0 < x < 1)$ $\qquad = 0.34$
  b) $P(0 < x < 2)$ $\qquad = 0.48$
  c) $P(-3 < x < +3)$ $\quad = 1.00$ (or nearly so)

23-14 Refer to Figure 23.8. The coordinates for two points on the curve are given. How were the ordinates of these coordinates obtained?

23-15 The mean and standard deviation of the probability distribution for a random variable x, which we can reasonably assume conforms to a normal bell-shaped distribution, are 75 and 15, respectively.

    a) What is the probability of x being greater than 75?

    b) Of x being less than 75?

    c) Of x being equal to 90 or less?

    d) Of x being equal to 105 or less?

    e) Of x being greater than 60?

    f) Of x lying between 50 and 90?

    g) Of x lying between 45 and 70?

23-16   In a normal distribution with a standard deviation of 6, the probability that an observation selected at random exceeds 6 is 0.15. What is the mean of the distribution?

23-17   Engineering contractors handle EPC projects (also called "turnkey projects"), for which they are responsible for the engineering, design, procurement, and construction of process units for the petroleum refining, petrochemical, and chemical industries. One important input for bidding is the estimated hours spent by home office personnel on these functions. Many correlations have been developed to help prepare hourly estimates. One of these is the home office hours per item of process equipment. The data represent a bell-shaped curve, for which the mean value is 350 hours per item. On 5% of the projects, the hours exceed 500. What is the standard deviation?

23-18   Find yourself a piece of cross-section paper, and reproduce Figure 23.3 on it. Superimpose a histogram with a class interval of 3 inches on top of the graph. Calculate the mean and the variance, and compare them with the results in the chapter for a class interval of 2 inches.

Skewness

23-19   What is the coefficient of skewness for the normal distribution? Justify your answer.

23-20   What is the coefficient of skewness for the probability distribution of Problem 23-1?

23-21   What is the coefficient of skewness for the probability distribution of Problem 23-5 for the larger class interval?

Principles of Choice Under Risk

23-22   Refer to Table 23.2. Confirm the principle of expectation for A_2 through A_5.

23-23   Do the same for the expectation variance principle.

23-24   What is the preferred alternative if the aspiration level for profit is 22 for the matrix in the chapter?

23-25   You are an investor comparing the principles of choice for A_2 and A_3. Which alternative would you select and why?

23-26 The following matrix represents the annual benefits in millions of dollars that could result from four possible, mutually exclusive situations.

	Situations			
Options	s_1	s_2	s_3	s_4
A_1	1	3	4	2
A_2	2	0	1	3
A_3	3	2	0	1
A_4	4	4	2	0

The probability that one of these situations will occur is unity. The probabilities of any particular situation occurring are $\frac{1}{5}$, $\frac{2}{5}$, $\frac{1}{5}$ and $\frac{1}{5}$ for situations 1 through 4, respectively. Check for dominance, and eliminate any option dominated by another option. Then, determine which option is best, using (a) range, (b) expectation, (c) expectation variance, and (d) the Laplace principle. Do you have sufficient information to make a recommendation? What is lacking?

23-27 A cost matrix with five options and five possible outcomes or states of nature is as follows:

	Possible Outcomes				
Options	s_1	s_2	s_3	s_4	s_5
A_1	26	20	14	16	10
A_2	20	14	16	16	18
A_3	5	4	12	16	26
A_4	14	18	24	16	16
A_5	24	23	18	16	14

The probabilities of occurrence are 0.2, 0.1, 0.25, 0.2, and 0.25 for s_1 through s_5, respectively. Check for dominance, and then use the following principles of choice for making a selection: (a) range, (b) expectation, (c) expectation variance, and (d) the aspiration level for maximizing costs at 12.

23-28 Consider the following revenue matrix. It has four states of nature, with the following probabilities of occurrence: 0.4, 0.2, 0.25, 0.15 for s_1 through s_4, respectively.

	States of Nature			
Options	s_1	s_2	s_3	s_4
A_1	17	12	13	19
A_2	16	18	12	12
A_3	9	15	6	13
A_4	2	23	11	12

Check for dominance, and then apply the following principles of choice: (a) range, (b) expectation, (c) expectation variance, (d) most probable future, and (e) aspiration level for minimum revenues of 14.

APPENDIX 23A   NORMAL DISTRIBUTIONS

The equation of the normal distribution is

$$f(x) = \frac{1}{\sigma\sqrt{2\pi}} \left\{ \exp\left[-\frac{1}{2}\left[\frac{x - \mu}{\sigma}\right]^2 \right] \right\} \tag{23.10}$$

For the standard normal distribution, μ is 0 and σ is 1. Therefore,

$$f(x) = \frac{1}{\sqrt{2\pi}} \left\{ \exp[-x^2/2] \right\} \tag{23.7}$$

You should have no trouble in confirming the following values of $f(x)$ for the standard normal distribution. However, you may recall that any number raised to the 0th power is 1.

x	$x^2/2$	$\exp - x^2/2$	$f(x)$[a]
(1)	(2)	(3)	(4)
0	0.0	1.0000	0.3989
$+1, -1$	0.5	0.6056	0.2420
$+2, -2$	2.0	0.1353	0.0534
$+3, -3$	4.5	0.0111	0.0044

[a]Column (4) equals column (3) times $1/\sqrt{2\pi}$ which equals 0.3989.

Several of the values of $f(x)$ can be spotted in Figure 23.7. You already know that these values are not probabilities but merely the height of the curve at x.

You can hone your integration skills by computing the area under the curve (which equals 1), the mean (which equals 0), and the standard deviation (which equals 1). All you need are the equations given in this chapter and a table of integrals. Good luck.

___24
SIMULATION

24.1 INTRODUCTION

We could have titled this chapter, "Probability: Part 3," but we felt that it was about time to introduce the word *simulation*. Actually, we should have done so long ago, since we started simulating in Part I and have been simulating ever since.

Simulation is the act of imitating real-life situations and occurrences with models. Our models have been cash flow patterns and mathematical equations representing the time value of money. The cash flow patterns to which the equations are applied are, as we know, idealized versions of actual cash flow patterns or, rather, of what the actual patterns would resemble if our assumptions and estimates were correct.

So far, our approach to risk analysis has been an analytical approach, in which we use the rules of probability and the laws of expected value and variance to compare alternative capital investment opportunities. We complete our presentation of that approach in this chapter with a discussion of two continuous probability distributions that we have not yet addressed, namely, the triangular and the beta distributions. We then proceed to another simulation technique, which differs radically from the analytical approach. This technique is the Monte Carlo method. With it, we use probability distributions to enter into random number tables for selecting values of random variables. The computer allows us to do this hundreds or thousands of times in order to produce risk profiles for the projects under review.

24.2 SIMULATING THE PROJECT SELECTION PROCESS

We began our study of the capital selection process with a simple deterministic model that contained no random variables. The inputs for such models—the cash flows, planning horizons, and MARRs—were single-valued. The outputs—the figures of merit—were therefore also single-valued. Our idealized simulations included end-of-period and continuous cash flows and the assumption that "reasonable" investors (the reasonable investor is to engineering economics what the reasonable person is to law) are governed by a minimum attractive rate of return (MARR) that represents opportunities forgone.

These simple deterministic simulations work, and so does the simulation technique—sensitivity analysis—that accompanies them.

A simple model is the best way to approach an economic study, and frequently it is the best way to finish it. Risk is often treated implicitly by selecting an MARR that is above the one required and by using conservative estimates for cash flows. To quote Gerald W. Smith, the author of a well-known textbook on engineering economics (1), "single-valued estimates ought to be used most of the time in most studies." He further implies that such studies are often all that is necessary because of the conservative assumptions named earlier.

However, "most studies" is, by no means, the same as "all studies." Risk analysis has found a place in engineering economics because there are situations in which we recognize that single-valued variables are too simplistic and should be treated as random variables. We therefore restructure our simple models into more complex models that now include estimated probability distributions.

Before starting a cost study, a study group should decide which parameters will be treated deterministically and which will be treated probabilistically. Such conclusions are obviously not cast in stone but can be modified as the study proceeds. Any number of scenarios suggest themselves.

We can, for example, create scenarios with combinations of random and deterministic variables that cover any conceivable situation, including the two extremes, that is, treating every variable as deterministic, which has been our practice to date and which often suffices, and treating every variable as probabilistic, which is seldom necessary.

The real world exists between these extremes but, for many studies, comes closer to the former than to the latter. Several scenarios that contrast deterministic and probabilistic approaches follow:

1. Consider an economic study for a new plant similar to an existing plant. The product is well established, and past sales forecasts have proved reliable. Compare this with a new plant that is producing a new product with a new process. The latter almost cries for a risk analysis; the former does not.

2. A corporation has the option of buying an existing facility or building a new facility. The first cost of the first option is more deterministic than the first cost of the second option.

3. Environmental laws and regulations have made it difficult for many industries, and particularly for the food and drug industries, to estimate when plans for investing in capital projects can be implemented. This has introduced a random variable—the planning horizon—which, in the past, was usually treated deterministically.

4. Retirement and replacement problems, which abound in the capital selection process, are usually treated deterministically. There is seldom any justification for treating them otherwise.

It is possible, of course, to be overly simplistic, even with probabilistic models. Occasionally, one sees a study in which the figures of merit for each alternative are calculated deterministically and a probability distribution for the possible outcomes is then estimated in order to compute an expected value and a variance for comparison with other alternatives. There is nothing wrong with this approach (in fact, we used it ourselves for the principles of choice under risk in Chapter 23) if the study group, with input from experienced managers and possibly outside consultants, feels competent to develop such distributions. Usually, however, more and better results can be obtained by estimating probability distributions individually for key random variables, and by using decision trees and the laws of expected value and variance to compare the risks associated with alternative investment opportunities.

These comments on when, and when not, to use risk analysis bring us first to the triangular and beta distributions and then to Monte Carlo simulation.

24.3 THE TRIANGULAR DISTRIBUTION

Assume that we have selected the key variables to be treated probabilistically and have divided them into two groups:

1. Those for which sufficient data are or can be made available to structure histograms and frequency polygons for estimating probability distributions with which expected values and variances can be calculated, as we did in Chapters 22 and 23.

2. Those for which only a limited amount of data are available and for which a way has to be found to approximate expected values and variances and, if need be, to also approximate a smooth probability density function.

For the second group, we may have no more data than the base estimate and its range. We use these data for both the triangular and beta distributions to define three quantities:

Minimum anticipated value	L
Most likely value	M
Maximum anticipated value	H

The two anticipated values are often referred to as the "pessimistic" and the "optimistic," although which is which depends, of course, upon the nature of the variable. For costs, the lower value is the optimistic value, and, for revenues, the higher value is the optimistic value. For the planning horizon and the MARR, it could be one or the other, depending on the situation.

The L estimate is the lower bound of the random variable. The probability of going below this value is zero or so close to zero (say less than 2–3%) that its occurrence can be considered a nonevent. The H estimate is the upper bound of the random variable. The probability of going above this value is also treated as a nonevent. The M estimate is the most likely value, that is, the highest point or mode, of the distribution.

For cash flows, the most likely value is usually based on normal contingencies, the optimistic value is usually based on the assumption that everything or almost everything will (within reason) go well (e.g., good weather, no late deliveries of critical materials, no computer breakdown, an adequate supply of skilled labor, trouble-free start-up), and the pessimistic value is usually based on the assumption that everything or almost everything will (within reason) go badly. It is not intended to embrace so-called acts of God, such as earthquakes, floods, and fire.

The probability density function, $f(x)$, for the triangular distribution is given in Figure 24.1. At the mode or most likely value M, $f(x)$ equals $2/(H - L)$. At L and H, $f(x)$ equals 0. You should have no trouble in showing that the area under the curve $f(x)$ equals 1.

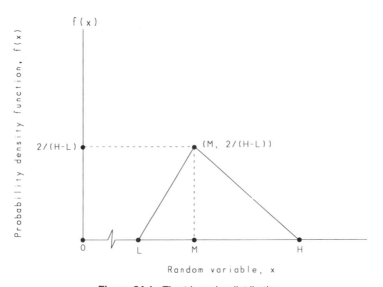

Figure 24.1. The triangular distribution.

The expected value and variance of a triangular distribution are given by the following equations:

$$E[X] = (L + M + H)/3 \qquad (24.1)$$

$$V[X] = (L^2 + M^2 + H^2 - LH - MH - ML)/18 \qquad (24.2)$$

The standard deviation is, as always, the square root of the variance.

In Example 24.1, we assume that the building cost of the parking structure that we examined in Chapters 21 and 22 can be represented by a triangular distribution.

Example 24.1 Triangular Distribution for Building Cost The base estimate of the building cost was $4,000,000, and the percentage range of this cost was -10 to $+20$. For these estimates, the values of L, M, and H are as follows:

$$L = \$3,600,000$$

$$M = \$4,000,000$$

$$H = \$4,800,000$$

The expected value, variance, and standard deviation from equations (24.1) and (24.2) are computed as follows, using millions of dollars as the dimensional unit.

$$E[X] = (3.6 + 4.0 + 4.8)/3 = 4.1 \ (\$4,100,000)$$

$$V[X] = (3.6^2 + 4.0^2 + 4.8^2 - 3.6 \times 4.8 - 4.0 \times 4.8$$

$$-4.0 \times 3.6)/18$$

$$= 0.0622 \qquad (6.22 \times 10^{10} \text{ dollars}^2)$$

$$\sigma = 0.25 \qquad (\$250,000)$$

We could treat any of the other random variables for the parking structure in the same way and then use the laws of expected value and variance to compute the mean and the variance of the present worth, as we did in Example 22.8. However, we will reserve this exercise for the beta distribution.

24.4 THE BETA DISTRIBUTION

For a random experiment X, for which we assume the random variable x can be represented by a beta distribution, the expected value, the variance, and the standard deviation are given by

$$E[X] = (L + 4M + H)/6 \qquad (24.3)$$

$$V[X] = [(H - L)/6]^2 \qquad (24.4)$$

$$\sigma = (H - L)/6 \qquad (24.5)$$

These equations include some simplifying assumptions that work well in many situations, including cost estimation and scheduling, not only when data are limited, but also for quick approximations. For scheduling, the application to network systems, such as PERT (Program Evaluation Review Technique), was developed by the U. S. Navy during its work on the Polaris Missile. Example 24.2 gives an application of the beta distribution to the parking structure of Chapters 21 and 22.

Example 24.2   Beta Distribution for Parking Structure   For convenience, the estimates and ranges that were used in Chapter 21 for a sensitivity analysis on this facility are reproduced in the following tabulation.

Parameter	Base Estimate, Dollars (000)	Ranges, %
Cost of land	$1,000	Deterministic
Cost of building	4,000	−10, +20
Annual staff revenue	25	Deterministic
Annual area resident revenue	562	−0, +16⅔
Annual operating expenses	100	−10, +10
Salvage value	1,000	Deterministic

In addition, we assumed that the MARR of 8% was deterministic and that the planning horizon was random. For the horizon, the base estimate was 30 years and the percentage range was −33⅓ to +0.

Four variables (three cash flows and the MARR) are deterministic, and four variables (three cash flows and the planning horizon) are random. The values of L, M, and H for the four random variables are given in the following tabulation (all dollar figures are in thousands).

	Building Cost	Annual Resident Revenue	Annual Operating Costs	Planning Horizon, yrs.
L	$3,600	$562	$90	20
M	4,000	562	100	30
H	4,800	656	110	30

The expected values, variances, and standard deviations are easily calculated with equations (24.3), (24.4), and (24.5). A sample calculation for the building cost is

$$\mu = (\$3,600 + (4 \times \$4,000) + \$4,800)/6 = \$4,067 \ (\$4,067,000)$$

$$V = [(\$4,800 - \$3,600)/6]^2 = 40,000 \ (40,000 \times 10^{6*})$$

$$\sigma = (\$4,800 - \$3,600)/6 = \$200 \ (\$200,000)$$

*The units are dollars squared.

Comparable figures for the triangular distribution were a mean of $4,100,000 and a standard deviation of $250,000.

A similar calculation using the beta distribution for the planning horizon gives

$$\mu = (20 + 4 \times 30 + 30)/6 = 28 \text{ years}$$

$$V = [(30 - 20)/6]^2 = 2.78 \text{ years}^2$$

$$\sigma = (30 - 20)/6 = 1.67 \text{ years}$$

The calculations for all four random variables are summarized in the following tabulation. For the cash flows, the mean and the standard deviation are in thousands of dollars and the variance is in millions of dollars squared.

	Building Cost	Annual Resident Revenue	Annual Operating Costs	Planning Horizon, yrs.
μ	$4,067	$578	$100	28
V	40,000	245	11	2.78
σ	$200	$16	$3.3	1.67

The factor equation for the parking structure was given by equation (21.1) (*see* Example 21.1) as

$$PW = -P + A(P/A,i,N) + S(P/F,i,N) \qquad (21.1)$$

For expected values, this equation can be rewritten as follows:

$$E[PW] = -E[P] + E[(P/A,i,N)]E[A] + E[(P/F,i,N)]E[S]$$

Applying the laws of expected value gives

$$E[P] = E[\text{Building cost}] + (\text{Cost of land})$$
$$= \$4,067 + \$1,000 = \$5,067$$

$$E[A] = E[\text{Resident revenue}] + \text{Staff revenue}$$
$$\quad - E[\text{Operating costs}]$$
$$= \$578 + \$25 - \$100 = \$503$$

$$E[S] = \$1,000$$

For the expected values of $(P/A,i,N)$ and $(P/F,i,N)$, we use 8% for i and 28 years for N. The expected value of the present worth of the parking structure is then

$$E[PW] = -\$5,067 + \$503(P/A,8,28) + \$1,000(P/F,8,1,000)$$
$$= -\$5,067 + \$503 \times 11.05 + \$1,000 \times 0.116$$
$$= \$607 \ (\$607,000)$$

For the variance, assuming the four variables are independent (a not unreasonable assumption for this situation) and treating P/A and P/F as constants, we get

$$
\begin{aligned}
V[\text{NPW}] &= V[\text{Building cost}] \\
&\quad + (P/A,8,28)^2\, V[\text{Resident revenue}] \\
&\quad + (P/A,8,28)^2\, V[\text{Operating costs}] \\
&= 40{,}000 + (11.05)^2\,(245 + 11) \\
&= 40{,}000 + 31{,}258 = 71{,}258\ (71{,}258 \times 10^6\ \text{dollars}^2) \\
\sigma &= \$267\ (\$267{,}000)
\end{aligned}
$$

These results for the present worth of the parking structure differ from those we obtained in Example 22.8, in which we assumed that only the building cost and the resident revenue were random.

	Chapter 22— Example 22.8	Chapter 24— Example 24.2
μ, dollars	760,000	607,000
V, (dollars)$^2 \times 10^6$	400,000	71,258
σ, dollars	633,000	267,000

Which set of solutions is correct? We answer this question as we have answered several similar questions throughout this text. The answers you get depend upon the assumptions you make on probability distributions. You can see at a glance that the answers for Example 24.2 would not have changed much if we had treated the planning horizon and the operating costs deterministically, as we did in Example 22.8. Therefore, the differences in the two sets of solutions are due primarily to the differences in the probability distributions of two key variables—the building cost and the area resident revenue. For Example 22.8, we used very simple probability distributions for computing the expected values and variances of these two variables so that we could more easily demonstrate how the laws of expectation and variance work without immersing ourselves and you in excessive clutter. The results we obtained in Examples 24.1 and 24.2 for the triangular and beta distributions are better approximations because they are based on more realistic estimates of how such random variables will probably be distributed.

24.5 CONSTRUCTING CONTINUOUS DISTRIBUTIONS

The triangular and beta distributions can be used to guesstimate probability density distributions for random variables for which our data bank does not consist of much more than L, M, and H estimates.

COMMENT: Risk analysis for capital project selection is an exercise in "guesstimating" rather than estimating, since we are dealing almost exclusively with subjective rather than objective probability.

Before we discuss "guesstimating" probability density distributions more fully, a few comments about the beta distribution are in order.

We stated earlier that the equations for the mean and variance of the beta distribution included some simplifying assumptions, but we did not go into any detail as to what these were. We do not intend to do so in this text, but, if this matter interests you, refer to reference 2 at the end of this chapter. We do, however, think that it is important to give you a better understanding of the beta distribution than we have done so far.

Just as there are "standard normal" and "normal" distributions, so there are "standard beta" and "beta" distributions. For the standard beta distribution, the values of L and H are 0 and 1. For the beta distributions that we run across in practice, L and H are whatever we estimate them to be for the study problem at hand.

The equation of the probability density function for the standard beta distribution is

$$f(x) = c\, x^a (1 - x)^b \qquad (24.6)$$

The function is defined by three constants. The constant c satisfies the condition that the area under $f(x)$ is equal to 1, and the constants a and b define the shape of $f(x)$.

The curves in Figure 24.2 are all derived from equation (24.6). If a and b are 0, the shape is the probability density function for the uniform distribution (curve 1 in Figure 24.2). If a and b are equal and greater than 0, the curve will be symmetric and bell-shaped with the mode at 0.5 (curves 2 and 3). If $a < b$, the distribution is skewed to the left (curve 4), and, if $b > a$, it is skewed to the right. If a or b are 0 and b or a are positive, the shape is that of the letter *J*. Such a curve is not shown.

These curves are typical of several of the unimodal continuous probability distributions that we have discussed—uniform, bell-shaped, and positively and negatively skewed. In other words, we can duplicate a wide variety of shapes with the beta distribution.

How, then, do we approximate the shape of $f(x)$? There are formulas for calculating the values of a, b, and c in equation (24.6) (2). With these, a graph of the probability density function $f(x)$ could be prepared. The area between any two values of the random variable under $f(x)$ would give us the probability of the variable falling between these ranges. The mean and variance could then be obtained by integration, using equations (23.2) and 23.3). This is again a cumbersome procedure, and we drop it in favor of the procedure discussed next.

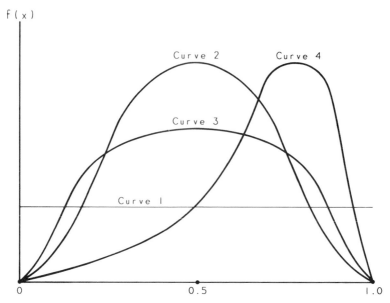

Figure 24.2. Some beta distributions.

Consider the three situations shown in Figure 24.3. In the top diagram, M is halfway between L and H; in the middle diagram, M is closer to L than to H; and, in the bottom diagram, M is closer to H than to L.

If we assume a triangular distribution for all of three diagrams, the value of $f(x)$ for the mode M would be $2/(H - L)$. This value can be used as a first approximation for drawing a symmetrical bell-shaped curve or curves skewed to the right or to the left. Where we go from there is illustrated in Example 24.3.

Example 24.3 Structuring a Probability Distribution Refer to Figure 24.4, in which the L, M, and H estimates of the building cost of the parking structure are shown on the abscissa of a graph, which should be drawn on a sheet of cross-section paper. Now proceed as follows.

1. Calculate the value of $f(x)$ for M as if we had a triangular distribution.

$$2/(H - L) = 2(4.8 - 3.6) = 1.667$$

2. Plot this value as the ordinate of M, and draw two light lines to define the triangular distribution. We already know that the area under this curve equals unity.

3. Sketch the curve that best represents the shape of the probability density distribution. If your curve is fuller than the triangular distribution, bring the $f(x)$ for M down a bit. (In our example, we arbitrarily brought it down to 1.5.) If

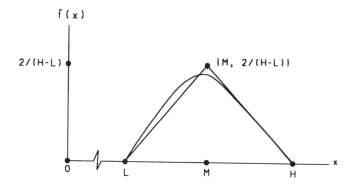

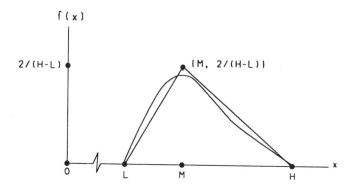

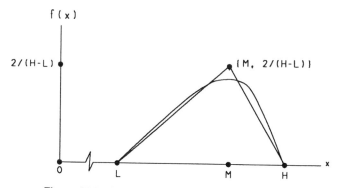

Figure 24.3. Constructing probability density functions.

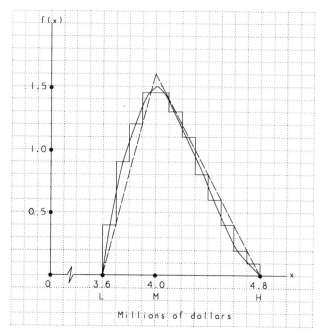

Figure 24.4. Probability density distributions for building costs.

your curve tends to fall inside the triangular distribution, bring the $f(x)$ for M up a bit.

COMMENT: In sketching an important random variable, ask questions such as, "Will the crown be narrow or broad?" "Does the variable approach the minimum and maximum anticipated values concavely or convexly?" For an important variable the answers to these and other questions should be based on a consensus of your study group, including any internal and/or external consultants.

4. Draw a histogram that follows the curve as closely as possible. In Figure 24.4, we used a class width of 0.1 ($100,000). For the ordinate scale shown, each square on the cross-section paper equals 0.01. The area under the histogram therefore has to be 100 squares ($0.01 \times 100 = 1$).

5. Prepare a probability distribution as we have done below.

Range	$f(x)$	Range	$f(x)$
3.6–3.7	0.04	4.2–4.3	0.11
3.7–3.8	0.09	4.3–4.4	0.08
3.8–3.9	0.12	4.4–4.5	0.06
3.9–4.0	0.145 (0.15)	4.5–4.6	0.04
4.0–4.1	0.145 (0.15)	4.6–4.7	0.02
4.1–4.2	0.13	4.7–4.8	0.01

6. The sum of the values of $f(x)$ should be close to unity. In the preceding tabulation, this sum equals 0.99. The difference of 0.01 (1.00 − 0.99) was arbitrarily added to two of the class widths, as indicated by the numbers within parentheses. If your first try shows a substantial difference, prorate it among the values of $f(x)$ or redraw the curve by raising or lowering the apex in order to keep the area under $f(x)$ at unity.

7. You already know how to calculate the mean and variance of this distribution by using the midpoints of the class intervals on the histogram. We leave this to you. The answers you should get are $4,070,000 for the mean and $250,000 (in round numbers) for the standard deviation.

We now have all the tools we need for applying the Monte Carlo method. This method depends on having a probability distribution for every variable that should be treated probabilistically. If ample data are available for approximating such distributions, fine. If the only estimates are the values of L, M, and H then we can proceed as described in Example 24.3.

24.6   THE MONTE CARLO METHOD

In the Monte Carlo method (also called "digital computer simulation"), we use tables of random numbers to select the values of the random variables with which we calculate figures of merit. We do this hundreds or thousands of times (or rather, our computer does) in order to obtain a risk profile for the variable.

You could easily prepare such a random number table yourself. One way to proceed is to put ten identical balls (identical except for being numbered from 0 to 9) into an opaque container that is then shaken thoroughly. You draw a ball from the container and record the number. The ball is put back, the container is shaken again, you draw another ball, and record its number. You do this, say 1,000,000 times, at the end of which you have a start on a table of random numbers. The digits in your effort will be scattered randomly throughout the table, but each digit will be represented by about 100,000 entries.

Random number tables are not prepared in this way. The computer takes over and gives us a table of pseudorandom numbers. They are called "pseudo" because computers can only perform if they are fed algorithms. The algorithms that have been developed are tested by checking the distribution of digits in millions of runs. A small portion (very small) of such a table is given in Appendix E.

Random number tables can be used to simulate a wide variety of situations, a few of which are illustrated in Example 24.4.

Example 24.4   Using a Random Number Table   A coin toss can be simulated by assigning the digits from 1 to 5 to heads and from 6 to 0 to tails. We open the text to Appendix E, close our eyes, and put our index finger down on any part of the table. Suppose that it comes down at the start of the third line, for which the digit is 8. We can now move in any direction—up, down, sideways, and diagonally. Assume that we move sideways across the third line, for which the numbers are reproduced below, together with an H or a T to tell us whether we have simulated the toss of heads or tails.

```
8 0 9 3 2   2 6 1 2 3   0 6 0 1 7   4 5 1 5 9   2 2 1 1 6
T T T H H   H T H H H   T H T H T   H H T H T   H H H H T
```

For 25 simulated tosses, we get 15 heads and 10 tails. As the number of tosses becomes larger and larger, the ratio of heads to tails will approach unity and the ratio of heads (or tails) to the total number of simulated tosses will approach 0.5.

For the toss of a single die, we assign random numbers from 0 to 9 as follows:

Face of Die, x	$P(x)$	Random Number, n
1	1/6	1
2	1/6	2
3	1/6	3
4	1/6	4
5	1/6	5
6	1/6	6
Nonevent	0	7,8,9,0

Since the random number assigned to a face of the die will show up an equal number of times, each face is equally represented.

To simulate the roll of a pair of dice, we need random numbers with at least two digits. These are assigned as follows:

Roll of Dice, x	$P(x)$	Random Number Pairs, n
2	1/36	01–02
3	2/36	03–06
4	3/36	07–12
5	4/36	13–20
6	5/36	21–30
7	6/36	31–42
8	5/36	43–52
9	4/36	53–60
10	3/36	61–66
11	2/36	67–70
12	1/36	71–72
Nonevent	0	73–00

The number pair in the upper-left-hand corner of Appendix E is 26. If we start there and move down, our simulated dice rolls give

```
n = 26   58   80   09   13   60   00   95   98   59   91   06   32
x =  6    9   —    4    5    9   —    —    —    9   —    3    7
```

A random number table can also be used to prepare a table of standard normal deviations (usually called "random normal deviates" or "RNDs"). This is just a random number table for use with variables that are normally distributed.

You could also prepare such a table yourself. You need both a coin and a box with numbered balls. The numbers on the balls correspond to the "distance from the mean" in Table 23.1. First, toss the coin. If you get heads, the deviate is on the right side of the mean, and, if you get tails, it is on the left side of the mean. Now pull a ball from the box. If you tossed heads and pulled number 0.60, the deviate is 0.60σ, that is, 0.60 standard deviations to the right of the mean. If you tossed tails and pulled number 1.3, the deviate is -1.3σ, that is, 1.3 standard deviations to the left of the mean. Do this several 100,000 times, and you have a small start on a random-number deviate table. We don't recommend this procedure. It is much easier to let the computer turn out pseudodeviates, as we did for Appendix F. The pluses are to the right of the mean, and the minuses are to the left. Example 24.5 shows how to use this appendix.

Example 24.5 Random Normal Deviates (RNDs) For this exercise, we assume that the building cost of the parking structure fits a normal distribution, with a mean of $4,200,000 and a standard deviation of $200,000.

If we start with the number in the sixth row and the third column of Appendix F (0.21) and move down the third column, the building cost (in thousands) would take the following values:

RND =	0.21	0.44	0.94	0.63	1.06	-0.64	0.77	-0.84
Cost =	4242	4288	4388	4326	4212	4072	4354	4032

A sample calculation for the first random value of $4,242,000 follows.

$$x = \mu + (RND)\sigma \qquad (24.6)$$
$$= \$4,200 + 0.21 \times \$200 = \$4,242 \ (\$4,240,000)$$

In what follows, we apply what we have learned to adapting the Monte Carlo method to the selection process for capital projects.

24.7 APPLICATION TO THE CAPITAL SELECTION PROCESS

Two examples—a simple one to get started and a more sophisticated one to close the chapter—are now developed.

Example 24.6 The Parking Structure and Monte Carlo Method For this example, we follow Examples 22.7 and 22.8, and treat only the building cost and the area resident revenue as random. The probability distributions we used for those examples are repeated here. The numbers in the n columns are the random number assignments.

Building Cost (000), x			Resident Revenue (000), y		
x	$P(x)$	n	y	$P(y)$	n
$4,000	0.7	1–7	$562	0.6	1–6
4,800	0.3	8–0	656	0.4	7–0

The first ten trials for the building cost and the resident revenue give the following results:

	Building Cost		Resident Revenue	
Trial	n	x	n	y
1	4	$4,000	7	$656
2	7	4,000	2	562
3	4	4,000	1	562
4	8	4,800	0	656
5	5	4,000	1	562
6	7	4,000	8	656
7	2	4,000	1	562
8	5	4,000	0	656
9	3	4,000	4	562
10	9	4,800	2	562
	Total	$41,600		$5,996
	Average	$4,160		$600

For 1,000 or more trials, the averages above would approach very closely to what we obtained in Example 22.8, namely, $4,240,000 for the mean of the building cost and $599,000 for the mean of the resident revenue. For these values, the net present worth would, of course, be $760,000, as it was in Example 22.8.

What was the point of Example 24.6? We came up with the answer that we got in Chapter 22 for Example 22.8, and took a lot more paper and time to do so.

The answer is that we can use the Monte Carlo method to give us a risk profile of the net present worth (or the IRR) by letting the computer insert random values for the building cost and area resident revenue directly into the factor equation for the net present worth. The computer can then sort the results by a class interval selected by us (an interval of $100,000 might do nicely) and present the results in a format resembling that of Figure 24.5. With this figure, an investor can read the probability of exceeding any particular present worth or IRR.

Example 24.7   The Parking Structure   In Example 24.7, we are going to take the exercise with the parking structure a little further than we did in Example 24.6 in order to cover the concepts that we introduced in section 24.6 more fully.

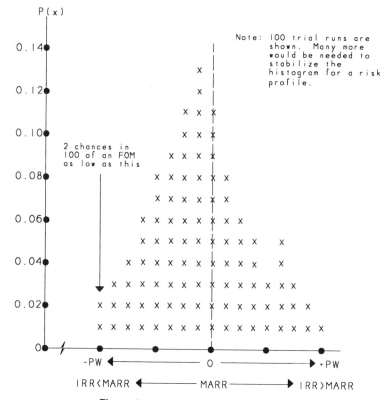

Figure 24.5. Risk profile of figure of merit.

The environment on which the preliminary study for the parking structure was originally based has changed (this often happens). You have heard and have confirmed that one and possibly two developers will build a garage not too far from your location. You no longer feel as confident as you did about the area resident revenue. Your latest estimates for the mean and the standard deviation are $540,000 and $60,000, respectively. You decide on a new study based on the following parameters:

Land cost	Fixed at $1,000,000
Building cost	Probabilistic with the distribution given in Example 24.3
Resident revenue	Probabilistic based on a normal distribution for the estimates given
Staff revenue	Fixed at $25,000 annually
Operating expenses	Fixed at $100,000 annually
Salvage value	Fixed at $1,000,000
MARR	Fixed at 8%
Planning horizon	Probabilistic based on the distribution discussed below

For the planning horizon, you base your study on the garage operating successfully for at least 20 years but no more than 30 years. For a probability distribution, you use the following tabulation:

Year	Span, yrs.	P(x)
20–21	2	0.08
22–25	4	0.32
26–30	5	0.60
		1.00

The input data for the building cost and the planning horizon, including the random numbers assigned to each class interval, are given in Table 24.1.

The random numbers and RNDs for ten simulated trials are given in Table 24.2.

In Table 24.2, the random numbers come from Appendix E and the random number deviates (RND), from Appendix F. The deviate for any trial is used to calculate the revenue for that trial, as in the example below.

$$\text{Revenue} = \mu + (\text{RND})\sigma \tag{24.6}$$
$$= 540 + (-0.79)60 = 493 \ (\$493{,}000)$$

The present worth for the first trial is calculated below. You should notice that the P/A and P/F factors are for the year shown in Table 24.2 for trial 1, that is, year 26.

$$\text{NPW} = -P + A(P/A,8,26) + S(P/F,8,26)$$
$$= -4{,}050 - 1{,}000 + (493 + 25 - 100)(10.81)$$
$$+ 1{,}000(0.135)$$
$$= -396 \ (-\$396{,}000)$$

TABLE 24.1 Input Data for Parking Structure

Building Cost ($ millions)			Planning Horizon, yrs.		
Cost, x	P(x)	n	Time, y	P(y)	n
3.6–3.7	0.04	01–04	20	0.04	01–04
3.7–3.8	0.09	05–13	21	0.04	05–08
3.8–3.9	0.12	14–25	22	0.08	09–16
3.9–4.0	0.15	26–40	23	0.08	17–24
4.0–4.1	0.15	41–55	24	0.08	25–32
4.1–4.2	0.13	56–68	25	0.08	33–40
4.2–4.3	0.11	69–79	26	0.12	41–52
4.3–4.4	0.08	80–87	27	0.12	53–64
4.4–4.5	0.06	88–93	28	0.12	65–76
4.5–4.6	0.04	94–97	29	0.12	77–88
4.6–4.7	0.02	98–99	30	0.12	89–00
4.7–4.8	0.01	00			
	1.00			1.00	

TABLE 24.2 Random Numerals for Parking Structure

	Building		Project Life		Revenue		
Trial	Number	Random Cost, $000	Random Number	Year	Normal Deviate	$/yr., $000	NPW, $000
1	42	$4,050	46	26	−0.79	$493	$−396
2	25	3,850	39	25	0.97	598	1,010
3	37	3,950	80	29	0.26	556	525
4	35	3,950	39	25	−1.93	424	−1,078
5	54	4,050	35	25	−1.60	444	−963
6	09	3,750	92	30	−0.04	538	562
7	44	4,050	33	25	0.06	544	105
8	41	4,050	73	28	0.86	592	779
9	83	4,350	34	25	1.13	608	488
10	21	3,850	17	23	−1.88	427	−1,029
						Total	$399
						Average	$40

Note: For the building cost, the midpoint of the range given in Table 24.1 was used.

The ten trials in Example 24.7 gave us an average NPW of $40,000, but this result is meaningless. For an average to mean anything at all, many more trials would have to be run. The results could then be added to a figure such as Figure 24.5 to show the probability of the NPW exceeding zero or, if we use the IRR, of that figure of merit exceeding the MARR.

24.8 WHICH APPROACH TO USE

We have used three approaches to risk analysis, namely,

- Decision trees
- Laws of expected value and variance
- Monte Carlo method

Each has its place, and often more than one approach is used.

Decision trees provide a picture of where the probable outcomes for any alternative might take us, but they are not particularly helpful if we are comparing one alternative with another. For this purpose, the laws of expected value and variance are more useful, since they give us two figures of merit— the mean and the variance—with which alternatives can be directly compared. The Monte Carlo method has the advantage of giving us a risk profile of the figure of merit for any alternative. A selection can then be made on the basis of the most attractive profile.

24.9 SUMMARY

A deterministic model coupled with a sensitivity analysis is often as far as we need to go in carrying out an economic analysis for the selection of a capital project. However, there are situations in which we need to go further and carry out a risk analysis as well.

In carrying out such an analysis, the study group must decide which parameters will be treated as random variables. Where only a limited amount of data are available, the mean and the variance for random variables are estimated from their most likely value and their minimum and maximum anticipated values. For constructing probability density functions for such distributions, the triangular distribution provides the approximate peak of the function and a rough outline of its shape.

In the Monte Carlo method, random number tables (or computer random number programs) are used to select the random variables with which figures of merit are computed.

The three approaches discussed in this and the preceding two chapters—decision trees, the laws of expected value and variance, and the Monte Carlo method—are all pertinent. Decision trees and the laws of expected value and variance share the same concepts. The Monte Carlo method is different. With it, we simulate the life cycle of a proposed investment hundreds or thousands of times to see what might or could happen in the real world.

However, when you are applying these methods, there is one caveat you cannot ignore. Our presentation on these approaches has been limited to the relations between independent variables, that is, to random variables that are not beholden to other random variables for the values they can take. For dependency, you will have to turn to a text on statistics (*see* Item 1, Suggested Reading). We believe, perhaps naively, that most problems on the selection of capital projects can be handled with the material that we have given you and will continue to give you in the remaining chapters of this text.

We close with a pertinent quotation:

> . . . the penalties of an overzealous search or model may be as great as those of an inadequate effort. (1)

In short, keep it simple but not too simple.

REFERENCES

1. Gerald W. Smith, *Engineering Economy, Analysis of Capital Expenditures*, 4th ed. (Ames, IA: Iowa State University Press, 1987). The quotations in section 24.2 and at the end of the summary come from pages 275 and 274, respectively.
2. Chan S. Park and Gunter P. Sharp-Bette, *Advanced Engineering Economics* (New York: John Wiley & Sons, 1990). See section 10.5.1, "Beta-Function Estimators

for Single Cash Flows," on page 425, for the standard and general beta distribution and for how to find the constants in equation (24.5) of our text.

3. Hans J. Lang, *Cost Analysis for Capital Investment Decisions* (New York: Marcel Dekker, 1989). See Chapter 22 on "Risk and Uncertainty" and a discussion of the Monte Carlo method, which starts on page 387.

SUGGESTED READING

1. For dependency, turn to the Reference and Suggested Readings at the end of Chapter 22. You will find this topic covered in such headings as covariance, regression analysis, and correlation analysis.

PROBLEMS

Triangular Distribution

24-1 Refer to Figure 24.1. How was the ordinate, $2/(H - L)$, obtained? Prove that the area under $f(x)$ equals unity.

24-2 The values of L, M, and N are \$1,000, \$1,800, and \$1,800, respectively. Draw the triangular distribution, and calculate the mean and the standard deviation. Show that the area under $f(x)$ equals 1. Can you think of any real-life situations in which M and H might have the same or close to the same value?

24-3 Reverse the values of L and H in Problem 24-3, and follow the instructions there. Can you think of any real-life situations in which L and M might have the same or close to the same value?

24-4 Go back to Problems 23-1 and 23-2 on the first cost of a major investment project, and proceed as follows:

a) Draw a triangular distribution, using the values of L, M, and H for the frequency polygon that you drew in Problem 23-2. (*Hint*: You should have gotten 19, 27, and 31 for L, M, and H, respectively.)

b) Compute the expected value and the variance of the distribution.

c) How do the above values compare with those in Problem 23-1?

d) Would you recommend using a triangular distribution to obtain preliminary estimates of the expected value and variance for bell-shaped normal and skewed distributions?

24-5 Proceed as you did in Problem 24-4, but this time use the frequency polygon that you drew for Problem 23-6 on revenue forecasts.

Beta Distribution

24-6 The beta distribution is a much more sophisticated distribution than the triangular distribution, but, as mentioned in the text, certain simplifying assumptions that work well in practice for scheduling and cost estimation give us equations for the mean, the variance, and the standard deviation, which are easy to work with [equations (24.3), (24.4), and (24.5)]. In what ways is the beta distribution, as applied in this text, similar to the triangular distribution? In what ways is it different?

24-7 Use the values of L, M, and H that you applied to the triangular distribution in Problem 24-4, but this time treat them as members of a beta distribution. Calculate the mean, the variance, and the standard deviation, and compare them with the values for the triangular distribution.

24-8 Do the same for the values of L, M, and H that you used for the triangular distribution in Problem 24-5.

24-9 Three estimates have been prepared for each of the input variables of a proposed investment. The results follow. Dollar figures are in thousands. The MARR is 10%.

	Pessimistic Value	Most Likely Value	Optimistic Value
First cost	$106	$100	$100
Net annual cash flow	$19	$20	$22
Salvage value	$0	$0	$10
Useful life, years	9	12	12

a) Calculate the present worth for the pessimistic, most likely, and optimistic scenarios.

b) Do the same for the IRRs.

c) Calculate the effective value of each of the input variables for the beta distribution.

d) Compute the present worth and the IRR, using the effective values from (c).

e) Compare and comment on the results of (a) and (b), on the one hand, and (d), on the other.

24-10 A manufacturer is considering introducing a new product. The initial cost is estimated at $110,000, the cost of each unit sold at $9, and the service life at 15 years. These values can reasonably be taken as deterministic. However, this is not the case for the units sold annually, the price per unit sold, and the salvage value. For these, the following estimates have been prepared:

	Minimum Anticipated Value	Most Likely Value	Maximum Anticipated Value
Units sold annually	6,000	7,500	8,000
Price per unit	$10	$13	$16
Salvage value	$15,000	$18,000	$20,000

a) Use the beta distribution to provide estimates of the expected value and standard deviation of each of the preceding parameters.

b) Use the effective values from (a) to compute the expected annual worth and its variance. The MARR is 20%.

24-11 In Example 24.2, were we correct in treating P/A and P/F as constants in order to compute the variance? If not, why did we do it?

Constructing Continuous Distributions

24-12 In Example 24.3, explain our instruction on moving $f(x)$ for M "up or down a bit" when converting the triangular distribution into a smooth bell-shaped distribution.

24-13 Go to Example 24.3, for which the mean and the standard deviation were given as $4,070,000 and $250,000, respectively. Confirm these figures for the probability distribution given in the example.

24-14 Go to Example 24.7. Draw a graph of $P(x)$ versus time and of $f(x)$ versus time for the planning horizon. Make sure that the area under $f(x)$ equals 1, and then compute the mean and variance of the distribution.

Monte Carlo Simulation

24-15 Why are the random numbers selected by your computer called pseudo-random numbers? How would sets of such numbers be tested to determine their "randomness"?

24-16 Look at the first two lines of the random number table in Appendix E. Each contains 50 digits. How "random" are the 100 digits in these two lines?

24-17 How could you use the roll of a pair of dice to construct a random number table? Test your answer with 100 rolls. How would you use a deck of 52 cards, which are well shuffled before each selection, to construct such a table?

24-18 Look at Appendix F. There are 250 deviates in this table. How many deviates greater than $+3$ or less than -3 can you find? How many would you expect to find?

24-19   The text suggested preparing a table of random normal deviates by first tossing a coin and then drawing a ball from a container. The ball would be labeled with one of the "distance" numbers in Table 23.1. How many balls would there be in the container, and how would they be marked?

24-20   Describe how you could use a deck of cards to create a random normal deviate table.

24-21   Suppose you want a finer breakdown than that given in Table 23.1, particularly for distances less than 1.5 standard deviations from the mean. How would you proceed? (*Note*: Remember, you have no computer. All you have are dice or cards or balls in a container, or a spinner, or whatever other tools your imagination comes up with. However, you do have lots of time.)

24-22   Refer to Table 24.2 in Example 24.7. Prepare a similar table for sets of random numbers and deviates selected by you from Appendices E and F. Compare the average value you obtained for the net present worth with that of Table 24.2.

24-23   The probability distribution for the parking structure building was given in Example 24.3. The expected value for this distribution is $4,070,000. The expected value of the area resident revenue was given as $540,000 in Example 24.7. In Problem 24-14, you were asked to compute the mean of the planning horizon for the probability distribution given in Example 24.7. You should have obtained 27 years. Calculate the net present worth of the investment in the parking structure, using the above expected values and assuming that all of the other parameters in the parking structure problem are deterministic. Compare your answer with the average of the 20 trial runs that you have available: 10 from Example 24.7 and 10 from Problem 24-22.

24-24   Assume that the net annual cash flows of Problem 23-5 apply to the capital investment for which first cost estimates were given in Problem 23-1. Calculate the net present worth of this investment opportunity, using the effective values for revenue and first cost that you computed in these problems. The MARR is 10%, and the planning horizon is 30 years. The salvage value at the end of that time can be taken as zero.

24-25   Refer to Problem 24-24. Assign random numbers to the probability distributions for the first cost and net annual cash flows (use the distribution with the $0.2 million class width). Assume that all other parameters are deterministic, and make 25 trial runs to obtain the net present worth. Compare the average of your result with that of Problem 24-24.

24-26 Suppose you have six probabilistic values for any given capital project selection study. Three of the parameters require the assignment of one-digit random numbers, two of two-digit random numbers, and one of three-digit random numbers. You are asked to assign random numbers to the six parameters. There are many ways in which this could be done. Name and comment on some of them.

24-27 An investment opportunity has four parameters, three of which are probabilistic—the net annual cash flow, the planning horizon, and the MARR. The first cost, P, is deterministic.

a) The MARR may vary between 8% and 13%, with a most likely value of 13%. If this parameter is beta distributed, what is its expected value and variance?

b) The planning horizon is a random variable with a mean of 10 years and a standard deviation of 2 years. Draw 25 samples of random normal deviates from Appendix F, and calculate the average of the samples.

c) The net annual cash flow is a linear function of time (t):

$$A = 200t - 400$$

Calculate the expected value of A, using the expected value of the planning horizon from (b).

d) Write the equation for the present worth, using the above effective values.

24-28 PW_{in}, the present worth of the cash flows in, and PW_{out}, the present worth of the cash flows out, have been calculated, and the probability distributions of each set of cash flows has been estimated. The results follow. The dollar figures are in thousands.

PW_{in}	Probability	PW_{out}	Probability
$190–$200	0.1	$190–$200	0.1
200–210	0.2	200–210	0.3
210–220	0.3	210–220	0.2
220–230	0.2	220–230	0.2
230–240	0.1	230–240	0.1
240–250	0.1	240–250	0.1

Each class includes all of the values from the lower limit up to, but not including, the upper limit. In answering the questions below, use the midpoint of the class interval.

a) What are the minimum and maximum possible values of the present worth?

b) What are the expected values, variances, and standard deviations of PW_{in}, PW_{out}, and the net present worth?

c) Assign random numbers, and draw 25 samples from Appendix E to compute the average value of the present worth.

Computer Applications

24-29 If a computer is available, solve two or three selected problems from the above set, using a minimum of 2,000 trial runs. Program the computer to produce a diagram such as Figure 24-5 or, at least, to present the results of the computations so that you can draw such a diagram.

____25
UNCERTAINTY

25.1 INTRODUCTION

Uncertainty exists when the likelihood of this outcome or that outcome cannot be estimated, that is, when there is no rational basis for even rough approximations of probability. We therefore fall back on "principles of choice," the selection from which can be, and often is, a highly personal matter. The risk-prone will go one way, the risk-averse another, and the risk-neutral somewhere within the wide gap that often exists between the two extremes.

25.2 STATES OF NATURE

We handle uncertainty by preparing scenarios about what could occur and then by preparing cost analyses for each scenario. Selecting the scenarios is called "selecting the states of nature" or "the state variables." Once selected, estimates are prepared for revenues, operating costs, first costs, planning horizons, and the other parameters from which figures of merit are computed. Some examples of states of nature follow.

- Some capital projects, for example, power plants, aluminum reduction plants, and others are very sensitive to energy costs. We cannot predict what will happen to such costs because we cannot control the oil-producing nations. The states of nature for cost analyses might consist of (1) the assumption that energy prices will increase at the same rate as general price indices, such as the CPI, and (2) the assumption that energy prices, in spite of the volatility they have shown, will increase, over the long run, at a substantially greater rate. The rate or rates are selected by the study group and become states of nature.

- Investors are now looking at joint ventures in Eastern Europe, the Baltic States, Russia, the Ukraine, and other members of the Commonwealth of Independent States. A whole host of scenarios could be written on what might or might not happen on privatization, management control by foreign interests, government regulations, definition of profit, and repatriation of hard-currency investments and profit. To none of these happenings could we realistically assign probability distributions. The study group assigned to such investment opportunities has the responsibility of preparing well-thought-out scenarios, each of which represents a possible state of nature.

- Tax reform is in the air. Will there or will there not be a reduction in the capital gains tax? If this could have a major effect on a particular cost study, the obvious states of nature are (1) no change in the tax, (2) a lower tax, and (3) a still lower tax. How much lower would be set by the study group by culling input from a wide variety of sources— members of Congress, economists, the White House staff, spokespersons for the Federal Reserve Board, financial reporters, and so on.

- Weather is an important factor in the first cost of capital projects. It does help to have data for the past 100 years available on how often severe winters or unusually heavy rains and snows occurred. However, not even the sophisticated techniques the weather bureau now has at its disposal can tell us if the winters are going to be mild, normal, or extreme during the next two years when the project under question will be built. The states of nature you might select would be (1) mild weather, which would give low construction costs; (2) average or normal weather, which would raise costs somewhat; and (3) extreme weather, which would severely impact on costs and schedule.

- Introducing a new product into the marketplace is always a hazard, since no one really knows what the sales volume might be. It is customary to select at least a minimum anticipated value, a most likely value, and a maximum anticipated value, and prepare cost analyses for these three states of nature. Assigning probabilities to such states is often meaningless, since no one knows what the public will do until the public acts. In fact, many practitioners of engineering economy believe that it often makes more sense to handle such problems with uncertainty rather than by means of dubious estimates of probability.

- Many proposed projects are, or rather will be, subject to environmental restraints for which legislation is currently under consideration and, in many instances, has been under consideration for several years or more. The states of nature selected depend on the best information that can be gathered on how far the restraints might go and how far they could go. Imagine, for example, what could happen to our domestic automobile industry's plans for the future if the government strengthened pollution emission standards beyond those now being considered.

We could continue with many more examples dealing with political and economic factors that push and pull international, national, state, and local economies this way and that and, in doing so, impact on decisions to proceed or not to proceed with capital investments.

Obviously, selecting states of nature for a capital selection process is the most important part of an economy study based on uncertainty and one on which the best, the most knowledgeable, and, above all, the most sensible minds available, whether or not they participate in the actual study, should be involved. In such selections, it is usually a mistake to create too many scenarios. One approach is to base one scenario on the worst situation that might *reasonably* occur, another on the best situation that might *reasonably* occur, and one or, at the most, two more scenarios that bridge these two extremes.

25.3 PRINCIPLES OF CHOICE

Certain principles of choice have been developed that can assist you in making a decision under uncertainty. These are

- Minimax and maximin principles
- Minimin and maximax principles
- Hurwicz principle
- Equal likelihood (Laplace) principle
- Minimax regret (Savage) principle

The principles are not consistent in the answers they give, nor should we expect them to be. This suggests the following two questions:

- Which principle or principles shall we apply?
- Which answer, if these differ, do we accept?

We leave the answers to these questions for the end of the chapter. For now, we will look at each principle with the help of the matrix that we used in Chapter 23, which is reproduced here.

Alternative	States of Nature				Minimum	Maximum
	s_1	s_2	s_3	s_4		
A_1	25	18	28	17	17	28
A_2	23	22	22	23	22	23
A_3	24	27	15	24	15	27
A_4	16	19	24	22	16	24
A_5	17	20	24	25	17	25

There are five alternatives and four states of nature. The numbers in the sample matrix are in millions of dollars. The two columns to the right of the matrix give the minimum and maximum values found in each row. As it did in Chapter 23, the matrix will again serve as either a cost matrix, in which the figures stand for EUACs (negative annual worths), or a profit matrix, in which the figures are positive annual worths. If it serves as a cost matrix, A_4 still dominates A_5, as in Chapter 23, and, if it serves as a revenue matrix, A_5 still dominates A_4. However, we again stress that neither alternative should be disposed of arbitrarily on purely economic grounds. There may be irreducibles that could swing a decision toward one alternative or the other (or, in fact, toward any alternative in the matrix), in spite of favorable monetary consequences.

25.3.1 Minimax and Maximin Principles

The minimax and maximin principles are conservative principles of choice. Minimax applies to cost matrices, and maximin applies to profit matrices.

For minimax, the maximum costs for each alternative are tabulated as follows:

Alternative	Maximum Costs
A_1	28
A_2	23
A_3	27
A_4	24
A_5	25

The minimum of these maximum values (hence, minimax) is $23 million for alternative A_2.

For maximin, we proceed in the same way, but, as shown in the following tabulation, we use the minimum profit for each alternative.

Alternative	Minimum Profit
A_1	17
A_2	22
A_3	15
A_4	16
A_5	17

The maximum of these minimum values (hence, maximin) is $22,000,000, which makes A_2 the preferred choice.

25.3.2 Minimin and Maximax Principles

These minimin and maximax principles are optimistic, gung-ho choices. Minimin applies to cost matrices and maximax, to profit matrices.

For minimin, we take the minimum of the estimated minimum costs and, for maximax, the maximum of the estimated maximum profits. Consider, for example, the following tabulation:

Alternative	Minimum Costs	Maximum Profits
A_1	17	28
A_2	22	23
A_3	15	27
A_4	16	24
A_5	17	25

For minimin, the choice is A_3, for which the cost of $15,000,000 is the lowest of the five alternatives. For maximax, the choice is A_1, because the profit of $28,000,000 is the highest.

The application of these four principles must be leveraged with common sense. Consider the following matrix, for which a selection is to be made using the maximin (profit) criterion.

Alternative	s_1	s_2	Minimum Value
A	2	1	1
B	0	100	0

The maximum of the minimum values is 1, which favors alternative A. However, because of the low returns for either state of nature with this alternative, many conservative investors would favor alternative B.

Another example of using these principles blindly is based on the following matrix:

Alternative	s_1	s_2	Maximum Value
A	75	70	75
B	0	100	100

If maximax is the principle of choice, even an optimistic investor would probably pick alternative A, although maximax selects alternative B.

Another possible shortcoming or, rather, "caution" is the lack of what is called "column linearity." This fancy term is illustrated by comparing the following two profit matrices by using the maximin principle of choice.

Alternative	s_1	s_2	Minimum	Alternative	s_1	s_2	Minimum
A	25	100	25	A	125	100	100
B	50	75	50	B	150	75	75

For the matrix on the left, the choice is the maximum of the minimum values, which makes alternative B the selection. Suppose now that the cash flow estimates on which the figures of merit were based left out an important cash inflow that should have been included for all alternatives under s_1. This inflow raises the annual worth of both alternatives by $100, as shown in the matrix on the right. The choice is now alternative A, even though the change had the same effect on both alternatives. There is, in other words, no column linearity.

25.3.3 Hurwicz Principle

The major problem with the four principles of choice described is, as we saw, that they are somewhat simplistic. The Hurwicz principle (also called the "partial-optimism principle" or "criterion") attempts to get around this problem by establishing a coefficient of optimism, alpha (α), which can vary from 0 to 1. An alpha of 0 represents complete pessimism, and an alpha of 1 represents complete optimism.

For costs, the Hurwicz criterion (H) is given by the following formula:

$$H = \alpha(\text{minimum cost}) + (1 - \alpha)(\text{maximum cost}) \qquad (25.1)$$

This formula is applied to each of the five alternatives for an α of 0.4:

$$H_1 = 0.4 \times 17 + (1 - 0.4) \times 28 = 23.6$$

$$H_2 = 0.4 \times 22 + (1 - 0.4) \times 23 = 22.6$$

$$H_3 = 0.4 \times 15 + (1 - 0.4) \times 27 = 22.2$$

$$H_4 = 0.4 \times 16 + (1 - 0.4) \times 24 = \mathbf{20.8}$$

$$H_5 = 0.4 \times 17 + (1 - 0.4) \times 25 = 23.8$$

The choice is then alternative 4, for which the Hurwicz criterion is at a minimum.

For revenues, the Hurwicz criterion is given by

$$H = \alpha(\text{maximum revenue}) + (1 - \alpha)(\text{minimum revenue}) \qquad (25.2)$$

For an alpha of 0.4,

$$H_1 = 0.4 \times 28 + (1 - 0.4) \times 17 = 21.4$$

$$H_2 = 0.4 \times 23 + (1 - 0.4) \times 22 = \mathbf{22.4}$$

$$H_3 = 0.4 \times 27 + (1 - 0.4) \times 15 = 19.8$$

$$H_4 = 0.4 \times 24 + (1 - 0.4) \times 16 = 19.2$$

$$H_5 = 0.4 \times 25 + (1 - 0.4) \times 17 = 20.4$$

The choice is alternative 2, which, at $22.4 million, has the highest value.

There is a close connection between the Hurwicz criterion and the four minimum/maximum criteria. This is illustrated by Figure 25.1, which is based on using the sample matrix as a profit matrix. The figure has a straight line for each alternative, running from alpha 0, the most pessimistic profit projection, to alpha 1.0, the most optimistic. The straight lines cross alpha equal to 0.4 at the H values just computed.

Figure 25.1 is instructive. It shows that alternative 2 is the choice from alpha 0 to about alpha 0.45. For higher levels of optimism, alternative 1 becomes the preferred choice. The Hurwicz values for alpha 1 are identical to those we obtained for maximax, and the values for 0 are identical to those we obtained for maximin.

We could have drawn Figure 25.1 for costs rather than profits. In such a diagram, the minimax principle would apply to alpha 0 and the minimin, to alpha 1. The straight lines would run downward from left to right, making the cost figure a mirror image of the profit figure. However, you can accomplish the same result by simply letting the abscissa read 0 to 1 from right to left rather than from left to right.

For applying the Hurwicz principle, the choice of alpha is all important. How is alpha chosen? Alpha should be a selective judgment made by the study group, which may be accepted or modified by the decision maker if he or she is not a member of the group. It should be more than a number picked out of the air or otherwise selected by chance, but it should at least have the imprint of an "educated guess" or "intuitive feel." Drawing a diagram such as Figure 25.1 often helps bring such a guess to life. A study group, after much discussion and reflection, might, for example, conclude that there is

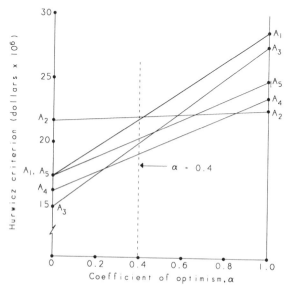

Figure 25.1. Hurwicz principle of choice.

no obvious reason to be optimistic or pessimistic and therefore might select an alpha of 0.5.

The Hurwicz principle, like the four minimum/maximum principles, also has a few cautions that require the application of common sense. For alpha equal to 0 and 1, the same cautions apply as those for the minimum/maximum principles. An additional caution is illustrated by the following profit matrix, for which we have used an alpha of 0.5. This choice of alpha is not significant. Other alphas could produce similar results.

Alternative	s_1	s_2	s_3	Hurwicz Criterion
A	100	100	100	100
B	0	0	220	110

The Hurwicz principle of choice says B is the alternative to be used. Even an optimistic investor would take alternative A because of the uncertainty on which state of nature will prevail.

25.3.4 Equal Likelihood (Laplace) Principle

The equal likelihood, or Laplace, principle has commonsense appeal. If an estimate of the relative likelihoods of various states of nature cannot be estimated, assume that each has the same probability. Thus, if there are two states of nature, the likelihood or probability of each state is 0.5; if there are three, it is 0.33; and if there are four, it is 0.25.

For the sample matrix, which has four states of nature, the Laplace criterion (L) gives

$$L_1 = (25 + 18 + 28 + 17) \times 0.25 = 22.0$$

$$L_2 = (23 + 22 + 22 + 23) \times 0.25 = 22.5$$

$$L_3 = (24 + 27 + 15 + 24) \times 0.25 = 22.5$$

$$L_4 = (16 + 19 + 24 + 22) \times 0.25 = 20.3$$

$$L_5 = (17 + 20 + 24 + 25) \times 0.25 = 21.5$$

For costs, the minimum value would be selected, in this case, alternative 4 at $20.3 million; for revenues, the maximum value would be selected, in this case, alternatives 2 or 3 at $22.5 million.

If, for any of the principles of choice, the same value is obtained for more than one alternative, as it was for alternatives 2 and 3, we have to look elsewhere. This would include the irreducibles and the dispersion. Since we do not have a probability distribution under assumed uncertainty, the variance is not available as a measure of dispersion; however, the range is. For alternative 2, the range is $1 million (23 − 22) and for alternative 3, $12 million (27 − 15). Thus, alternative 2 is far less risky than alternative 3 and would be selected, assuming the irreducibles were not a factor.

The Laplace principle does not share the cautions that we expressed when we were discussing the other principles. It has column linearity, and it includes the outcomes from all of the states of nature in its evaluation.

25.3.5 Minimax Regret (Savage) Principle

The minimax regret, or Savage, principle is a rather sophisticated principle, in which we first construct a regret matrix and select the minimum of the maximum regrets. This is not as recondite as it first sounds.

Take a look at the first column in the sample matrix (the column for state s_1) that follows. The dollar figures represent profits.

Alternative	s_1	Regret	Regret Computations
A_1	25	0	25 − 25 = 0
A_2	23	2	25 − 23 = 2
A_3	24	1	25 − 24 = 1
A_4	16	9	25 − 16 = 9
A_5	17	8	25 − 17 = 8

The highest profit under state s_1 is 25. If alternative A_2 were selected but state s_1 actually came to pass (which we do not know will happen but which could happen), there would be a regret of 2 (25 − 23) for not having picked A_1. This figure is the difference between the maximum estimated outcome from s_1, namely, $25,000,000, less the estimated outcome from the alternative that was selected, namely, $23,000,000. The remaining regrets in this tabulation are calculated in the same way, and the process is repeated for the other states of nature to produce the following regret matrix.

Alternative	States of Nature				Maximum Regret
	s_1	s_2	s_3	s_4	
A_1	0	9	0	8	9
A_2	2	5	6	2	6
A_3	1	0	13	1	13
A_4	9	8	4	3	9
A_5	8	7	4	0	8

The regret principle favors alternative 2, the minimax value of the maximum regrets, namely, $6 million. Theoretically, it is the loss in profit (the regret) that will make you suffer the least when you later find out that you picked the wrong alternative.

The regret matrix for costs will differ from that for profits. The minimum of the maximum regrets for the five alternatives also favors A_2.

25.4 COMPARISON OF ALTERNATIVES

For the sample matrix, the outcomes for all of the principles of choice under uncertainty are tabulated as follows:

Principle	Cost Matrix	Profit Matrix
Minimax	A_2	—
Maximin	—	A_2
Minimin	A_3	—
Maximax	—	A_1
Hurwicz (alpha = 0.4)	A_4	A_2
Equal likelihood (Laplace)	A_4	A_2, A_3
Minimax regret (Savage)	A_2	A_2

The tabulation brings us back to the questions that we asked earlier in the chapter; namely, which principles shall we apply and, if the answers we get differ, which answer do we accept?

The minimax and maximin principles are for realists, although some decision makers would argue that they are too pessimistic (this does not include your authors). The minimin and maximax principles are for rampant optimists but do have the advantage of at least establishing limits on how low costs might go or how high profits might rise. The equal likelihood principle has appeal but is too simplistic. This leaves the Hurwicz principle and the Savage principle.

If a consensus on the coefficient of optimism is reached (possibly with the help of the Delphi or a similar technique), the Hurwicz criterion is an excellent choice, since, at its extremes (alphas of 0 and 1), it embraces several of the other principles. The results obtained with the Hurwicz principle should be compared with those obtained with the Savage principle for a final decision based on monetary considerations alone.

It is, of course, sound to apply more than one principle to see how often an alternative is favored. For the preceding example, A_2 is a clear winner for both costs and profits.

25.5 SUMMARY

In this chapter, we distinguish between uncertainty analysis and risk analysis. Under uncertainty, we cannot estimate the probabilities of possible outcomes. Therefore, we cannot apply probability theory to the capital selection process, as we did under risk analysis.

Under uncertainty, the first task for the analyst is to identify the scenarios or states of nature that could have an impact on the capital investment under review. The second task is to prepare meaningful cash flow estimates for each scenario and to set these up into a cost or a profit matrix.

Once these two tasks are accomplished, certain principles of choice have been designed to help the decision-making process. These include

- Minimax/maximin for realists and conservatives
- Minimin/maximax for way-out optimists
- Hurwicz for a balanced approach
- Equal likelihood (Laplace) for those who feel uncertainty is too abstruse to do anything but treat each state of nature equally
- Regret (Savage) for those who would like to rue about what might have been

These principles were applied to five alternatives and four states of nature, for which the estimated costs (EUACs) or profits (positive AWs) were arranged in a matrix.

Of the principles reviewed herein, the Hurwicz principle and the Savage principle are the most sophisticated. The Hurwicz principle relies on a coefficient of optimism that should represent a consensus of the best and most experienced minds on what the future might bring. The Savage principle tells us how we can minimize the disappointment if the future doesn't bring what we expected.

The ultimate selection, no matter what the principle or principles of choice, is, of course, the responsibility of the decision maker. He or she would do well to look at both the Hurwicz and Savage principles.

SUGGESTED READINGS

1. James L. Riggs and Thomas M. West, *Engineering Economics*, 3rd ed. (New York: McGraw-Hill, 1986). Chapter 25, pages 773–781, has one of the best discussions of uncertainty in current engineering economic texts.
2. G. A. Fleischer, *Engineering Economy, Capital Allocation Theory* (Belmont, CA: Wadsworth, 1984). Chapter 8, pages 286–292, are good examples of the author's penchant for mathematics in presenting uncertainty and other engineering economy topics.

PROBLEMS

In the problems that follow, the matrices should be routinely checked for dominance and the alternatives should be taken as mutually exclusive.

25-1 Estimated costs for four alternatives and four states of nature are given in the following cost matrix. There is no reasonable way of estimating the probability of occurrence of the four states.

Alternative	S_1	S_2	S_3	S_4
a_1	20	10	16	17
a_2	19	16	9	10
a_3	12	13	15	11
a_4	5	21	14	10

Which alternative should be chosen for the following principles of choice?
a) Minimax
b) Minimin
c) Hurwicz with alpha equal to 0.35
d) Savage (regret)
e) Laplace (equal likelihood)

25-2 The following matrix is a profit matrix, with five alternatives and five states of nature.

Alternative	S_1	S_2	S_3	S_4	S_5
a_1	23	18	13	16	10
a_2	21	13	13	16	17
a_3	6	4	15	16	20
a_4	12	18	20	16	16
a_5	16	16	14	16	14

Which alternatives should be selected under the following principles?
a) Maximin
b) Maximax
c) Hurwicz with alpha of 0.45
d) Savage
e) Laplace

25-3 Consider the following cost matrix, with four alternatives and three states of nature.

Alternative	S_1	S_2	S_3
a_1	240	100	20
a_2	120	120	120
a_3	140	100	120
a_4	40	− 100	500

What is the preferred alternative for the following principles of choice?
a) Minimax
b) Minimin
c) Savage
d) Laplace

25-4 Consider the following profit matrix:

Alternative	s_1	s_2	s_3	s_4
a_1	3	3	3	3
a_2	2	6	2	1
a_3	2	5	2	2
a_4	1	4	2	5
a_5	4	5	4	1

After checking for dominance, fill in the following tabulation. For Hurwicz, use an alpha of 0.4. Then circle your choice.

Alternative	Maximin	Maximax	Hurwicz	Regret	Laplace
a_1					
a_2					
a_3					
a_4					
a_5					

25-5 Rework Problem 25-4, assuming the matrix represents costs. Fill in the following tabulation, and then circle your choice. For Hurwicz, again use an alpha of 0.4.

Alternative	Minimax	Minimin	Hurwicz	Regret	Laplace
a_1					
a_2					
a_3					
a_4					
a_5					

25-6 Comment on what you have learned from Problems 25-1 through 25-5 and particularly from Problem 25-4.

25-7 Consider the following rather simple profit matrices, each of which has two alternatives and two states of nature.

a)

Alternative	s_1	s_2
a_1	3	110
a_2	3	3

Which principle of choice, if any, would you use to help you make a decision?

b)

Alternative	s_1	s_2
a_1	2 •	110
a_2	3	3

On which principle of choice—maximin or maximax—would you base your selection? Why?

c)

	Original Matrix		Revised Matrix	
Alternative	s_1	s_2	s_1	s_2
a_1	2	6	5	6
a_2	5	3	8	3

There was an error in the estimates of the original matrix. The estimates for s_1 should be three units higher for each alternative, as shown in the revised matrix. Compare the value of the maximin principle for both the original and revised matrices. What does this comparison tell you about this principle of choice?

25-8 The highway construction industry is weather-sensitive. Although weather records go back 75–100 years (and more), this is of no help to you in forecasting what the weather might be during the next one to three years. A major highway is to be built through mountainous terrain. Four routes are being considered. The states of nature range from mild winters to severe winters and dry summers to wet summers, and they affect the routes in different ways. A matrix of the estimated gross profit that a highway contractor might realize is given in the following tabulation. The figures are millions of dollars.

Alternative	s_1	s_2	s_3	s_4
Route A	12	10	15	13
Route B	10	13	11	14
Route C	14	14	14	11
Route D	12	12	13	12

Which route would a prospective highway contractor prefer, based on the following rules?
a) Maximin
b) Maximax
c) Laplace
d) Given the following probabilities, which alternative should be chosen under the expectation principle $P(s_1) = 0.25$, $P(s_2) = 0.15$, $P(s_3) = 0.40$, or $P(s_4) = 0.20$?
e) Which would be chosen under the expectation-variance principle?

25-9 Take the matrix of Problem 25-8, and multiply the figures by 10. This gives a rough approximation of the first costs of the highway project.

Which route would the government entity that is going to finance this project prefer, based on the following principles of choice?
a) Minimax
b) Minimin
c) Laplace

25-10 The following three alternatives are present in many situations:

a_1 Expand for the short-term future (two to four years), for which estimates are reasonably reliable.

a_2 Expand for the long-term future (five years and more) for which the best forecasts are, at best, educated guesses.

a_3 Expand for the short-term but provide for the long-term in the expansion plans.

Assume that your firm has to expand one of its facilities, say a warehouse. Its needs for the next two or three years can be estimated quite accurately. After that, the forecasts are a bit hazy, but they do indicate that much more space might be needed, without any clear indication as to when except during the next four to ten years. Three choices are available: (1) build a one-story warehouse that will serve for at least three years and possibly longer, (2) build a three-story warehouse now, or (3) build a one-story warehouse but design the foundations and the steel structure for possible future needs. The estimated costs in millions of dollars are as follows:

One-story warehouse	$6.0
Three-story warehouse	$18.0
One-story warehouse designed for future	
addition of two stories	$8.0

Identify the states of nature, and make a selection based on an MARR of 10% and on the following principles of choice:
a) Minimax
b) Minimin
c) Laplace

25-11 Consider the following matrix:

Alternative	s_1	s_2	s_3	s_4	s_5
a_1	−12	10	6	−9	8
a_2	8	−6	−7	7	6
a_3	4	5	6	5	4
a_4	10	15	−14	9	−11

a) Assume that the matrix is a profit matrix, and apply the Hurwicz principle to determine the effect of the degree of optimism on the choice of the preferred alternative. For your answer, sketch a graph that is similar to that of Figure 25.1 and interpret the results.

b) Repeat the above exercise, assuming the matrix is a cost matrix. Could you use the same sketch as the one you drew for (a)? What, if anything, would you change?

25-12 Another situation with which many businesses are familiar is the inability to forecast demand for products or services. Assume that there is a new product or an old product in a new area. Demand could vary anywhere from 0–2,000 units weekly. Up to 2,000 units could be produced, but it would only pay to do so in lots of 500 units. There are, therefore, five alternatives: 0, 500, 1,000, 1,500, and 2,000 units. For demand, you arbitrarily set up five states of nature, assuming demands of 0, 500, 1,000, 1,500, and 2,000 units, respectively. The product can be sold for $10. Cost of sales is $2.80 per unit, and weekly operating expenses are $2,500, regardless of how much is produced. Set up the matrix and show the results for the following principals of choice:

a) Maximin

b) Maximax

c) Savage

d) Equal likelihood

25-13 The American Red Cross has prepared the matrix that follows for the estimated costs of hurricane disasters for four different recovery plans in a certain hurricane-prone area. Class 1 hurricanes are the least severe, and class 4 hurricanes are the most severe that can reasonably be expected in the area.

Alternative	Class 1	Class 2	Class 3	Class 4
Plan A	8	11	13	16
Plan B	10	11	12	13
Plan C	10	10	13	14
Plan D	6	8	11	20

Which plan would be selected by the American Red cross under the following principles?

a) Minimin

b) Minimax

c) Hurwicz with an alpha of 0.4

d) Savage

e) Regret

25-14 Two alternatives are under consideration; namely, expand an existing warehouse (a_1) or build a new one (a_2). The vice-president of production is faced with three possible future events, namely, (1) no change in current output except for anticipated growth (s_1); (2) a new product, X, for which new space is required (s_2); or a new product, Y, for which new space is required (s_3). The following matrix was prepared for him. The figures are equivalent uniform annual costs.

Alternative	s_1	s_2	s_3
a_1	280	600	600
a_2	400	500	500

a) Which alternative would be selected under the Laplace principle of choice?

b) The vice-president of finance reviews the results (as she should) and notes the conclusion. However, she sees only two states of nature, with which she arrives at a different decision using the equal likelihood principle. Is she right? Justify your answer.

SUMMARY OF PART III

We suggest that you review the summaries of Parts I and II before you read the summary of Part III. Every "reader bite" in the three summaries should mean something to you. If they don't, you should go back into the text.

1. In Part III, we left deterministic analysis for risk analysis. In the former, cash flow and other estimates were treated as single-valued; in the latter, they were treated as multivalued.

2. Estimates fall into three types—conceptual, factor, and detailed. The first and second types are used in preliminary studies. The third and the more refined of the second type are used in definitive studies.

3. Each estimate should be accompanied by a range that sets the limits within which it may fall. The ranges for conceptual estimates are higher than those for factor estimates, and those for factor estimates are higher than those for detailed estimates.

4. Estimates are based on current costs and conditions, and are then modified or adjusted to what might happen in the future with regard to inflation, productivity gains (or losses), and technological innovation (or possible obsolescence).

5. Sensitivity analysis serves as a bridge between deterministic analysis, on the one hand, and risk analysis based on probability estimates, on the other hand.

6. With sensitivity analysis, figures of merit are calculated, not only for the base estimates, but also for the minimum and maximum values of the ranges for these estimates. This is usually done by letting one cash flow or other parameter vary while all other parameters are held at their base value.

7. Iso-quant graphs are often used to present the results of a sensitivity analysis. In such graphs, two key variables are paired—one as the abscissa and the other as the ordinate. Lines are then drawn, for each of which the figure of merit is a constant (hence, the name).

8. Risk analysis for the capital selection process is grounded on the theory of probability as applied to random experiments.

9. A random experiment is one that has the possibility of more than one outcome. Which outcome will occur is not known.

10. Investments in capital projects are random experiments, since the outcomes will not be known until the life cycle is completed.

11. The probability that any one of all of the possible outcomes—the present worths, the IRRs, and so on—will occur is 1, that is, is taken as a complete certainty. The probability that none of the outcomes will occur is taken as 0.

12. The possible outcomes (or random variables) of a random experiment can be structured into a probability distribution. Such distributions are discrete or continuous. For discrete distributions, the random variable is countable. For continuous distributions, it is not, since, by definition, it can take an infinite number of values between any two limits, no matter how close they are.

13. For countable (discrete) distributions, a probability is assigned to each outcome. The result is known as a probability mass function $P(x)$. The sum of the probabilities of all of the outcomes is 1.

14. For noncountable (continuous) distributions, a function $f(x)$ is defined for the random variable x. The area under a graph of $f(x)$ as ordinate versus the random variable as abscissa is 1. The area between any two values of x is the probability of x falling within these two values. The function $f(x)$ is known as the probability density function.

15. The random variables for the selection process, for example, planning horizons and cash flows, are continuous. However, they can be treated discretely by breaking the continuous density function into class intervals and letting the midpoint of each interval serve as a discrete value of the variable.

16. Probability distributions have traits or characteristics that fall into two groups—measures of central tendency and measures of dispersion.

17. The most important measure of central tendency is the mean, and the most important measure of dispersion is the variance or its square root, the standard deviation. The greater is the variance, the greater the risk.

18. There are several continuous probability distributions into which the random variables for the selection process can be fitted. These include the uniform, the normal (including the standard normal), the triangular, and the beta.

19. The normal or bell-shaped distribution is symmetrical. Random variables for which the base estimate falls half-way between the upper and lower limits of the range are often assumed to take this shape.

20. However, many random variables are skewed. For these, the triangular and the beta distributions can be used to structure a probability density function from three estimates—the most likely value and the minimum and maximum anticipated values. These values are given by the base estimate and its range.

21. There are laws or rules for combining means and variances. Some of these can only be used if the random variables that enter into the selection process are independent, that is, if the value of one variable is not beholden to the value of another. This text does not treat dependent variables.

22. The analytical approach to risk analysis uses decision trees, the laws of the mean, and the laws of variance to obtain the mean and the variance of an investment opportunity by combining the means and the variances of the individual random variables that enter into the analysis. Such analyses are often limited to treating only the key cash flows probabilistically, that is, as random variables. All other variables are treated deterministically.

23. The Monte Carlo method offers another approach to risk analysis. Random numbers are assigned to outcomes for discrete distributions and to ranges of outcomes for continuous distributions. A random number table is then used to obtain values of the random variables for computing figures of merit. This process is, with the help of a computer, repeated hundreds of times or more, that is, until a stable risk profile is obtained.

24. There are certain principles of choice under risk that serve as surrogates for more complete approaches. With these, figures of merit are computed for a set of outcomes for each alternative, and probabilities are assigned to each outcome. The results are usually structured into a matrix.

25. The principles referred to in number 24 include the range and the principles of (a) expectation, which compares means; (b) expectation variance, which compares variances; (c) most probable future, which simply selects the alternative with the highest probability; and (d) aspiration level, which selects alternatives based on the probability of reaching (aspiring to) a specified goal.

26. Under risk analysis, decision makers often have to choose between higher figures of merit (higher means) and lower variances (lower

risks). How one is traded off for the other is an individual choice. Optimists will look at such trade-offs in one way and pessimists, in another.

27. Uncertainty analysis differs from risk analysis in that probabilities cannot be assigned to possible outcomes. The outcomes are referred to as states of nature.

28. Certain principles of choice under uncertainty have been developed to assist decision makers in their selection of an alternative. These include the minimax and maximin principles, the minimin and maximax principles, and the Hurwicz, Laplace, and Savage principles.

29. The Hurwicz and the Savage principles are the more sophisticated of the principles. The Hurwicz principle serves well where a consensus can be reached on a coefficient of optimism.

PART IV
THE SELECTION PROCESS: MULTIATTRIBUTE ANALYSIS

___26

INTRODUCTION TO MULTIATTRIBUTE ANALYSIS

26.1 INTRODUCTION

So far in this text our concern has been almost entirely with monetary attributes leading to profit maximization. Allocating resources under this criterion alone may stifle social needs to such an extent that maximizing profits, or its obverse, minimizing costs, produces short-run gains at the expense of long-run stagnation or losses. Our aim, therefore, should be to "satisfice," rather than "maximize," profits by incorporating the irreducibles into the project selection process.

The irreducibles include such nonmonetary attributes or factors as equity, employee morale, safety, reliability, flexibility, appearance, quality, and many others.

Our objective in Part IV is to show how such nonmonetary attributes are combined with monetary attributes so that we can compare alternatives with both types of attributes in mind. Such comparisons take many forms, ranging from scoring cards to unweighted and weighted factor methods and, ultimately, where it is feasible, to single figures of merit for each alternative.

This chapter serves not only as a general introduction to multiattribute analysis (MAA) but also discusses two topics that were first touched on in Chapter 19 and that are closely allied to MAA—cost effectiveness and equity.

26.2 BACKGROUND

You probably know more about multiattribute analysis than you think. In one way or another, you have been using it all your life. Whenever you considered changing jobs, you and your family looked, not only at salary and other monetary attributes, such as health insurance coverage and the cost of commutation, but also at nonmonetary attributes, such as time spent in commuting, the quality of the neighborhood, the reputation of the school system, the adequacy and convenience of shopping, the recreational facilities available in the community or nearby, and so on. All of these play a part in job selection and in comparing future job opportunities with your current position.

Often you do your best to monetize the nonmonetary factors. You may, for example, argue that the better schools associated with job A are partial compensation for the higher salary offered by job B. In addition, you may use unweighted or weighted scoring techniques, although, when you did so, you may not have known these selection techniques by that name.

> *COMMENT:* If you are married, you and your spouse undoubtedly used multiattribute analysis to select each other. We leave it to you to decide whether the monetary factors were more important than the nonmonetary factors.

In using MAA for your personal affairs, you have often been influenced by "gut feelings" that oppose the analysis you set down on paper. Such feelings or emotions also play a part in business affairs—sometimes for the best and sometimes for the worst. We mention this only because MAA is a highly subjective process. In fact, in our procession through this text, as we move from deterministic monetary models to probabilistic monetary models, and finally to MAA models, our analyses become more and more subjective and therefore more and more influenced by our value systems, biases, and prejudices or, simply put, by "our gut feelings."

26.3 SELECTION OF NONMONETARY ATTRIBUTES

In section 26.2, we talked about attributes as if there were just two classes— those we can monetize and those we cannot. This is an oversimplification. There are actually three that reduce to two as our selection process proceeds. We refer to them in the following terms:

- *Always evaluated*—those that are normally quantified in money terms
- *Sometimes evaluated*—those that could be quantified in money terms
- *Never evaluated*—those that cannot be quantified in money terms

The first class includes all of the factors that are normally evaluated in a deterministic monetary analysis—first costs, revenues, expenses, salvage values, and working capital.

The second class includes factors that could be evaluated in monetary terms if time and cost warranted quantification. Quality is a major factor in profits and can be treated as a monetary or a nonmonetary attribute. So can safety, air pollution, and water pollution if adequate safety and health data are available. Is quantifying these and other attributes, as well as such benefits as parks and other recreational facilities, worth the effort, or should they be treated as nonmonetary factors? The answer depends not only on the availability of data but also on the time and cost required to collect it.

The third class consists of the true irreducibles, that is, those attributes that cannot be monetized and for which attempts to do so, rather than to treat them as nonmonetary, seem unreasonable and far-fetched. Examples include ethics, equity, esthetics, political consequences, social consequences, conservation aspects, national goals,* legal and security considerations, and the value of human life.

This brings us to the first task of the study group on an MAA, namely, to decide which attributes, other than those falling into the first class just mentioned, will be treated as monetary and which will not. The answer depends not only on time and cost but also on how far and how deep the study group intends to go. Some guidelines follow.

- If the nonmonetary factors that are deemed significant favor the alternative with the lowest present worth or other monetary figure of merit, there is no need to proceed further. However, this conclusion should obviously be stated and justified in the study group's recommendation.
- If the choice between two alternatives is close on a monetary basis but significant nonmonetary attributes clearly favor one or the other, let these be the basis for selection. (*See* Example 26.1.)
- Calculate the monetary value that an alternative can support, and then decide whether all or part of this sum should be spent on nonmonetary attributes. (*See* Example 26.2.)
- Carry out an MAA with just two or three of the nonmonetary attributes that could have the greatest influence on the decision process. Then, if the results warrant it, add more.

Two examples that will help illustrate these guidelines follow.

Example 26.1 Make or Buy Should a manufacturing company make or buy a new part? To make the part would require a capital expenditure that has to be annualized, plus direct material, labor, and overhead costs. The estimated production cost is x dollars per unit.

A firm quote is in hand for purchasing the part from an outside vendor for y dollars per unit. Since y is less than x, there is a potential for estimated savings based on the difference in unit costs multiplied by the estimated number of units that will be required in the next two or three years.

---

*The decision of several corporations to reimburse their employees $1,000 for not buying a Japanese car is an example of an attempt to further a national goal (more jobs), which could be quantified if we knew how many employees would do so.

The monetary consequences of making or buying are obvious. However, there are several nonmonetary factors that management must weigh. These are

- *Reliability*. The part is an essential component of a major assembly. If the supply failed, the impact would be substantial.
- *Flexibility*. Since the part is new, there will undoubtedly be design changes that can be handled more expeditiously internally than externally.
- *Experience*. The learning curve may bring the cost of the part down to where making it is as economical as buying it.

The correct decision depends not only on the value of the monetary factor—the savings—but also on at least two important nonmonetary factors—reliability and flexibility.

Example 26.2   The Clubhouse   Your company has decided to relocate its head-quarters. Several sites have been considered. The employees participated in iden-tifying and ranking the nonmonetary factors that they considered important. Each alternative shows a substantial monetary return, that is, a return well above the MARR. Location A is favored by top management because it shows the highest present worth. However, location B is strongly favored by the employees and their families because of better recreational and shopping facilities. A survey of the employees indicates that a clubhouse, baseball diamond, tennis courts, and possibly an outdoor swimming pool or indoor gymnasium would do much toward reducing the advantages of B over A, from their viewpoint.

Employee morale is an important attribute, which can be treated as a monetary factor by attempting to estimate the cost of absenteeism, labor turnover, and other tangible signs of disaffection and unrest. However, a monetary evaluation would be difficult, if not impossible, to make in this situation.

This brings us to the following question: "Should management use all or part of the difference in present worth between locations A and B as a measure of what could be spent to show its employees that 'it cares'?" The answer is a subjective one. Let us hope that your company does the right thing.

Today, corporations are well aware that nonmonetary attributes have to be considered in profit maximization studies.

Many corporations have prepared lists of attributes that either cannot be, or are not usually, monetized. Examples are safety, reliability, flexibility, adaptability, uniqueness, ease of operation, quality of output, appearance, style, and others. These lists should be culled to determine which attributes are significant for a particular study. There will seldom be more than 12–15 attributes, and these can usually be narrowed down to no more than 4–6. Because of the subjective nature of MAA, this list, whether it is short or long, must be reviewed and accepted by those who have a stake in the ultimate outcome of the study.

Cost-effective analysis is a technique that is often used when only one nonmonetary attribute is brought into the selection process. This is our next topic.

26.4 COST-EFFECTIVE ANALYSIS

Studies dealing with cost effectiveness are widely used in the public sector to compare alternatives dealing with health, safety, infrastructure, recreation, education, and defense. They are also used in the private sector to deal with the same topics but on a more localized scale. All such studies share two characteristics:

1. A nonmonetary attribute that serves as a measure of effectiveness
2. A monetary attribute, that is, an estimated cost or saving, to reach given levels of effectiveness

The nonmonetary attribute is usually a benefit or a disbenefit that cannot realistically be costed. Examples from both the public and private sectors follow.

Health—cost expenditures for measurable impacts, such as reductions in infant mortality, in the incidence of a particular disease, and in the number of smog-free days per year

Safety—cost expenditures that can be matched against lives saved and accident reduction

Infrastructure—cost expenditures for rural roads and electrification based on the population benefited by such improvements

Recreation—cost expenditures for parks and other recreational facilities based on estimates of user participation

Education—cost expenditures for training facilities matched against employment gains by trainees

Defense—cost expenditures matched against improved reliability and effectiveness

In each example, the nonmonetary attribute is measurable. If it were not, we could not compare cost effectiveness. Examples 26.1 and 26.2 were not cost-effective studies, because we did not have viable measures of effectiveness.

Alternatives in a cost-effective analysis are compared and ranked using cost-effective indices, in which C is the cost attribute usually expressed as a discounted cash flow and E is a measure of effectiveness. The index takes two forms as shown below.

$$\text{Index} = \text{C/E} = \frac{\text{Discounted cash flow}}{\text{Measure of effectiveness}} \tag{26.1}$$

$$\text{Index} = \text{E/C} = \frac{\text{Measure of effectiveness}}{\text{Discounted cash flow}} \tag{26.2}$$

Example 26.3 uses cost-effective indices for a study to reduce fatalities at a dangerous highway intersection.

*Example 26.3   Highway Intersection** The number of cars passing through the highway intersection under review averages 5,000 daily. The number of occupants in each car averages 1.25. The total exposures to risk are therefore approximately 2,250,000 annually (5,000 × 1.25 × 365 days, rounded). Fatalities over the past few years have averaged 100 for every 1 million exposures, or about 225 per year.

Two proposals for reducing accidents are under consideration. One is an overpass costing an estimated $20 million, and the other is an underpass costing an estimated $30 million. Statistics for similar highway improvements made during the past decade indicate that the fatality rate will be reduced to about 10 per 1 million exposures, or about 22–23 per year. In round numbers, an estimated 200 lives will be saved annually.

The above estimates are summarized as follows:

Alternative	E, Lives Saved Annually	C, Cost of Improvement
Overpass	200	$20 million
Underpass	200	$30 million

The monetary factor, C, is the first cost. The nonmonetary factor, E, is the measure of effectiveness—the estimated number of lives saved.

The two cost-effective indices defined by equations (26.1) and (26.2) are easily calculated.

Alternative	C/E, Cost per Life Saved	E/C, Lives Saved per Million Dollars
Overpass	$100,000	10
Underpass	150,000	6.7

Rank ordering, based on cost effectiveness only, favors the overpass, with which 10 lives will be saved for every $1 million of capital expenditure, compared to only 6.7 lives with the underpass.

Cost-effective indices are also used for incremental analysis. Suppose in the preceding example that the underpass would have saved an estimated 210 lives compared to 200 for the overpass. The values of C/E and E/C for the incremental lives saved and the incremental first cost are as follows:

$$C/E = \$10,000,000/10 = \$1,000,000 \text{ per life}$$

$$E/C = 10/\$10 \text{ million} = 1 \text{ life per } \$1,000,000$$

---

*Adapted with permission from *Cost Analysis for Capital Investment Decisions*, Chapter 16, Example 16.2, page 263. (4)

Should the community spend an additional $10,000,000 to save an additional 10 lives? As mentioned in Chapter 19, there is no flat yes or no answer to this question, but, certainly, one question that should be asked is, "Can $10,000,000 be spent effectively elsewhere and possibly save many more lives than just 10?"

In most studies relating to highway safety, the more money that is spent on a capital improvement, the more lives saved. However, the incremental cost of saving just one more life usually rises exponentially. Since the resources of federal, state, and local governments are limited, voters (informed, we hope) have to agree on how much to spend and where to spend it.

In real-life situations, there are often more than two options. Therefore, we have to cull those that are not feasible and those that are dominated by others. This is done with the help of a chart in which effectiveness is plotted against cost and the maximum allowable cost (the budget constraint) and the minimum acceptable or mandatory effectiveness are identified. Such a chart is used in Example 26.4.

Example 26.4 Chemical Pollution There is considerable evidence that the use of chlorofluorocarbons (CFCs) presents a health hazard to life by depleting the earth's protective ozone layer and exacerbating the "greenhouse" effect. A search for acceptable substitutes has produced six candidates, which are referred to as options A through F in what follows. The maximum acceptable cost for producing an option has been set at no more than 4.5 times the cost of producing CFC. Effectiveness is based on laboratory tests, in which each candidate reacts with ozone. Candidates must show at least 50% less ozone depletion than an equivalent amount of CFC. The measure of effectiveness for any candidate is then the difference between the depletion shown by CFC, which is arbitrarily set at unity, and that shown by a candidate. The data on costs and effectiveness are summarized in the following table and mapped on Figure 26.1.

Alternative (1)	Depletion (2)	Effectiveness, E (3) = 1 − (2)	Relative Cost, C (4)
CFC	1.00	0.00	1.00
A	0.90	0.10	1.50
B	0.50	0.50	1.50
C	0.01	0.99	5.00
D	0.30	0.70	2.00
E	0.15	0.85	4.00
F	0.15	0.85	3.00

Figure 26.1 clearly shows the budget constraints and the measure of effectiveness that has to be attained. Alternative A can be eliminated from the study, since its measure of effectiveness is less than 0.5. Similarly, alternative C is eliminated because of its high cost. A comparison of alternatives E and F indicates that F

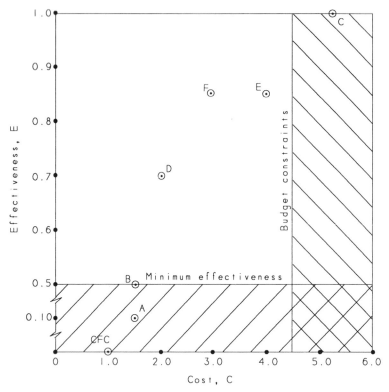

Figure 26.1. Cost-effective analysis.

dominates E, since it is lower in cost for the same effectiveness. This leaves alternatives B, D, and F. The cost-effective indices for these are tabulated below. As shown, the E/C for the do-nothing alternative (CFC) is zero.

Alternative	E	C	E/C
CFC	0.00	1.0	0.00
B	0.50	1.5	0.33
D	0.70	2.0	0.35
F	0.85	3.0	0.28

For alternatives B and D, the cost-effective index is about one-third; for D, it is somewhat lower. However, before we select alternative B, which, shows the lowest cost, we need to make an incremental analysis. This is done as follows:

	ΔE	ΔC	ΔE/ΔC
D versus B	0.20	0.50	0.40
F versus D	0.15	1.00	0.15

Do the incremental costs of alternatives D and F have utility; that is, would taxpayers seriously consider spending additional sums to reduce contaminants below the level offered by B? This question can be rephrased as follows: "Do the higher costs of alternatives D and F have any serious disutility; that is, is the resulting increase in taxation too burdensome?" There are, again, no pat answers. The answers depend not only on available funding but also on public awareness of what is at stake.

26.5 QUALITY ECONOMICS

We mentioned earlier that quality can be treated as a monetary or non-monetary attribute. If it is the only nonmonetary attribute in a study, it can be handled in a cost-effective analysis as a measure of effectiveness, against which the net expenses or savings for improving quality can be compared. In such studies, the set of options consists of raising the level of quality in successive steps, say from 100 rejects per 1,000 units to 10 rejects per 1,000 units, to 1 reject per 1,000 units, and so on, to whatever level of quality is currently attainable based on state-of-the-art process equipment and inspection techniques.

The classical approach to quality economics defines a cost-of-quality (COQ) for which all costs for quality improvement are monetized. These costs consist of conformance costs and nonconformance costs, as defined below.

Conformance Costs	Nonconformance Costs
Appraisal costs	External failure costs
Inspection	Warranty costs
Testing	Returned materials
Evaluating	Field service costs
Prevention costs	Insurance and legal liability costs
Quality planning	Internal failure costs
Process improvement	Scrap
Employee training	Rework and retest
Capital expenditures	Downtime
Cost accounting	Yield losses
	Disposal costs

A category for cost accounting is included under conformable costs, since quality control cannot be conducted without a cost accounting system that identifies the cost categories just listed. The objective of such control is to determine whether higher conformance costs have lowered nonconformance costs. Thus, quality economics involves a trade-off between increasing one set of costs in order to decrease another set.

The preceding discussion is a very simple overview of quality economics. Because of its importance to industrial competitiveness, many sophisticated approaches to this topic have been developed. One of your authors has written extensively on this topic, as you can see from the Suggested Readings at the end of the chapter. An example on quality control follows.

Example 26.5   Quality Control   A manufacturer of transistors has performed a study on the cost effectiveness of improving the quality of its production process. The current level of defects is 15 per 1,000 pieces. The study reveals ten distinct technologies that provide different levels of improvement. The costs associated with these technologies are as follows:

Option	Defects per 1,000 Parts	Cost, $ (millions)
1	6	$5.9
2	1	7.0
3	2	6.3
4	3	6.2
5	6	5.2
6	9	4.5
7	5	5.3
8	4	5.5
9	11	3.0
10	4	6.0

The budget constraint is $5.9 million. The maximum acceptable number of defects is 6. With these facts and figures, we now proceed as we did in Example 26.4.

- Options 6 and 9 are discarded because they do not satisfy the effectiveness criterion.
- Options 2, 3, 4, and 10 are discarded because they do not meet the budget constraint.
- Option 1 is discarded because it has the same effectiveness as option 5 but costs more; that is, option 5 dominates option 1.

This leaves us with options 5, 7, and 8. The cost-effective indices for these options are given below. The level of effectiveness, E, is the difference between the current defect rate of 15 and what each of the three options are expected to do. The costs, C, come from the preceding tabulation.

Option	E	C	$\Delta C/\Delta E$
5	$(15 - 6) = 9$	5.2	0.58
7	$(15 - 5) = 10$	5.3	0.53
8	$(15 - 4) = 11$	5.5	0.50

Thus, the cost of reducing the defect rate by 1 item per 1,000 pieces varies from an estimated $500,000 for option 8 to $580,000 for option 5. Options 7 and 8 look even better if we compare incremental costs and measures of effectiveness with option 5. Thus, for option 7, an incremental reduction of 1 defect per 1,000 pieces costs only $100,000 [(5.3 − 5.2)/(10 − 9)], and, for option 8, an incremental reduction of 2 defects per 1,000 pieces (compared to option 5) costs only $150,000 per defect [(5.5 − 5.2)/(11 − 9)]. Both of these C/E ratios are substantially lower than those for the options themselves.

The manufacturer must now choose one of the options or decide to do nothing. In this instance, the incremental costs are rather small for the reduction in defects gained. This favors option 7 or 8 over option 5.

There is one more topic to cover—equity—before we head into analyses in which more than one nonmonetary attribute is involved.

26.6 EQUITY

Economic analysis is mute on the subject of equity. MAA has difficulty in absorbing it into its list of nonmonetary attributes because it is the most subjective of all such attributes. Consider the following two scenarios, which are by no means untypical. For each, we assume that all benefits and disbenefits can be monetized and that the only important nonmonetary attribute is equity.

- The benefit-cost ratio is greater than 1. However, the benefits to a relatively small and wealthy group are greater than the disbenefits to a relatively large and poor group. Should the project proceed?
- The benefit-cost ratio is less than 1, because the disbenefits to a relatively small and wealthy group are greater than the benefits to a relatively large and poor group. Should the project be turned down?

Consider, for example, a dam for flood protection and power generation. The population upstream from the proposed site will lose their homes and businesses. The economic disbenefits to them may far outweigh the cash payments that they can expect from the state through its exercise of eminent domain. The population downstream will, on the other hand, be benefited, not only by access to cheaper power, but also by lower flood insurance and less flood damage, whether it is recoverable by insurance or not. Any number of scenarios is now possible, of which two were described.

Another common scenario in which questions of equity arise are highlighted in Example 26.6.

Example 26.6 Equity Investments by city and other local governments often have an impact on one population center more than on other centers. An administration facility for an important city service is to be built. The project has been approved, and several sites are now under review. One alternative is to locate it in a decayed area. This will result in a shift of income within city limits. The net annual benefits to the poor area and the net annual disbenefits to other areas are estimated as follows:

	Population Affected	Net Annual Benefit	
		Total	Per Capita
Proposed site	100,000	$10,000,000	$100
Other areas	1,900,000	−4,000,000	−2
Total or average	2,000,000	$ 6,000,000	$ 3

   Benefit-cost analysis would approve the site, since the total benefit is positive, in spite of the fact that 95% of the population would suffer a disbenefit. This, however, would not in itself prove that the project was inequitable. The benefit to the population in the poorer area is $100 per capita, while the disbenefit to the population in the wealthier area is $2 per capita. Under our assumptions, the utility of $100 per capita is far greater than the disutility of $2 per capita.

We leave the subject of equity for you to ponder as we turn to Chapter 27, in which more than one nonmonetary attribute is introduced into the selection process for capital projects.

26.7 SUMMARY

In this introductory chapter on multiattribute analysis, we divide attributes into three categories: (1) those that are always monetized, (2) those that may or may not be monetized, and (3) those that cannot be monetized. The first category includes all of the attributes that we use in carrying out deterministic and risk analyses. The second category includes attributes such as quality, safety, health hazards, and employee morale, which can be monetized if there is an adequate data base and if time and cost warrant quantification. The third category includes such attributes as ethics, esthetics, and the value of human life, which cannot be monetized.
   A study group handling a multiattribute analysis must identify the nonmonetary attributes to be included in its study and, for those that fall into the second category, which of these will be monetized.
   Cost-effective analysis is an effective tool for comparing various options for maximizing a desirable nonmonetary attribute or for minimizing an undesirable one. The analysis is carried out by computing a cost-effective index for which E is a measure of effectiveness (lives saved, defects reduced, etc.) and C is the estimated cost of improving the effectiveness. The index is expressed either as the ratio E/C or C/E and is computed not only for each option under review but also incrementally. In carrying out such analyses, a budget constraint and a minimum acceptable improvement in effectiveness is usually specified.
   Quality can be treated as a monetary or a nonmonetary attribute. For the latter, cost-effective analysis is used. The measure of effectiveness is a re-

duction in the number of defects. The measure of cost is the net cash flow (or net present value) of the conformable and nonconformable costs. This net can be positive or negative, depending on whether the increase in conformable costs is greater or less than the resulting reduction in nonconformable costs.

Economic analysis is mute on the subject of whether or not a proposed venture is equitable. Equity is a difficult nonmonetary attribute to absorb into a multiattribute analysis, because it is the most subjective of all such attributes. If, for a proposed venture, monetary benefits to the few exceed the monetary disbenefits to the many, benefit-cost analysis will, without the intrusion of equity, say yes. If monetary benefits to the many are less than monetary disbenefits to the few, benefit-cost analysis will say no.

SUGGESTED READINGS

1. John R. Canada and William G. Sullivan, *Economic and Multiattribute Evaluation of Advanced Manufacturing Systems* (Englewood Cliffs, NJ: Prentice-Hall, 1989). This text explores how economic and noneconomic factors are combined for making decisions for advanced manufacturing systems. The approach and technique can be used in many applications.

2. John R. Canada, *Annotated Bibliography on Justification of Computer Integrated Manufacturing Systems*, The Engineering Economist, Winter 1986, pp. 137–150. This is an extensive bibliography of articles and books on Computer Integrated Manufacturing (CIM). Multiattribute analysis plays an important part in justifying such systems.

3. William G. Sullivan, *Models IEs Can Use to Include Strategic, Non-monetary Factors in Automation Decisions*, Industrial Engineering, March 1986, pp. 42–50. This article provides a series of models that bring non-monetary factors into investment decisions, particularly those dealing with CIM.

4. Hans J. Lang, *Cost Analysis for Capital Investment Decisions*, 1989, Marcel Dekker, Inc., New York.

Quality Economics References

5. Developing Economic and Non-economic Incentives to Select Among Technical Alternatives, *The Engineering Economist*, Vol. 34, Issue 4, Summer 1989, pp. 275–290.

6. Economics of Quality: Choosing Among Preventive Alternatives, *The International Journal of Quality and Reliability Management*, MCB University Press (England), Vol. 7, Issue 3, 1990, pp. 13–26.

7. Donald N. Merino, "Cost of Quality in R&D: Economics of Quality," American Society of Engineering Management, 11th Annual Meeting Proceedings, October 16, 1990, pp. 192–196.

8. Donald N. Merino, "Optimizing the Cost of Quality Using Quality Economic Models," 1991 American Society of Engineering Education Annual Conference Proceedings, June 17, 1991, Session No. 1242.

9. Donald N. Merino, "Cost of Quality." *Engineering Management Journal* 3: 3 (September 1991): 8–12.

PROBLEMS

Attributes

26-1 There's a well-known saying, "The best is the enemy of the good." Relate this saying to the difference between "maximizing" and "satisficing". (NOTE: Refer to the introduction to this chapter.)

26-2 In choosing a spouse, what attributes would you (or did you) select to make your decision. Would your list include both monetary and nonmonetary attributes? How would you rank the attributes? How would you weight them?

26-3 Think back on your first job or on a recent job change. What monetary and non-monetary attributes did you consider? How did you rank them to arrive at a decision? Did you weight them and, if so, how?

26-4 Set down the important attributes you would consider in buying a car for your personal use. How would you rank them? How would you weight them?

26-5 Salvage value is a monetary attribute which is often taken as equal to zero. Cite examples where the assumption is not a good one.

26-6 Another monetary attribute which is often neglected is working capital. Cite examples where this could introduce substantial errors into the selection process.

26-7 How does a customer's perception of an attribute such as quality impact a product's price and market share?

26-8 You are the manager of a corporate research and development department. What attributes do you look for in decisions on which drugs to develop?

26-9 A list of attributes follows.
Comfort
Commutation time
Education
Effectiveness
Efficiency
Esthetics
Flexibility
Noise pollution
Periodic maintenance
Quality
Reliability
Reputation
Routine maintenance

Set-up time
Storage capacity for inventory
Training
Urban crowding
User friendliness
Waiting time

a) Which can be treated as monetary attributes?

b) Which as either monetary or non-monetary?

c) Which as non-monetary only?

26-10 Your company has formed a Quality Improvement Team (QIT). One of its assignments is to examine the accounts payable process in which the Purchasing and Accounting Departments are the major players.

a) List the attributes you need to consider in examining an accounts payable system.

b) Rank these attributes in order of importance.

c) Discuss "maximizing" versus "satisficing" for some of the attributes identified by you.

Cost Effectiveness

26-11 You are considering several methods of commuting to work. The cost and the comfort and convenience index (CCI) you assign to each method are given below. The CCI is on a scale of 1 to 10 with 10 being the best. Your budget for commutation is a maximum expenditure of $18 per week.

Alternative	Weekly cost	Index
Driving	$20	2
Car pool	5	4
Train	14	8
Bus	16	5

a) Which alternatives are feasible?

b) Which alternatives dominate others?

c) Which alternative do you choose? Why?

26-12 Six electrical substation designs are under review for the power supply to a pharmaceutical company. The selection will be based on a maximum annual cost of $13,000 and a maximum hazard rate of 32.00. The hazard rate is determined by the following equation.

$$\text{Hazard rate} = e^{300,000q}$$

The costs and values of q for the six options are tabulated below.

Option	Annual cost	q (10^{-5})
A	$12,000	1.14
B	16,200	1.09
C	9,100	1.17
D	15,000	1.07
E	12,000	0.99
F	14,200	1.22

a) Construct a diagram of effectiveness versus cost showing the feasible and infeasible regions.

b) Which plans are infeasible and why?

c) Which plans dominate others?

d) Which plan is optimum?

26-13 The first cost, EUAC, and effectiveness of five plans and of the do-nothing alternative are summarized below. The dollar figures are in thousands. The EUAC includes the first cost and O&M costs over the life cycle.

Plan	First Cost	EUAC	Effectiveness
Existing	0	0	0
1	$1000	$1200	0.9
2	300	320	0.3
3	500	550	0.5
4	600	860	0.7
5	450	675	0.3

The first cost cannot exceed $600,000 and the effectiveness must be at least 0.3.

a) Which plans are infeasible and why?

b) Construct a diagram of effectiveness versus EUAC.

c) Which plans are dominated?

d) What is your selection based on a non-incremental analysis?

e) What is your selection based on an incremental analysis?

26-14 The ABA Machine Corporation has two studies under review—one for a new automatic lathe and the other for a new milling machine. Instead of using a multiattribute analysis in which the monetary and nonmonetary factors are combined, ABA has prepared such analyses for the nonmonetary factors alone (you will see how this is done in Chapter 27) and used the resulting figures of merit as measures of effectiveness. The nonmonetary factors considered were equipment flexibility, reliability, ease of maintenance, reputation of vendors for prompt and efficient service, and others. The EUAC and the effectiveness of five options for the lathe and five options for the milling machine gave the following results. The dollar figures are in thousands.

Lathe			Milling Machine		
Option	EUAC	Effectiveness	Option	EUAC	Effectiveness
A	$200	4	A	$300	10
B	300	15	B	400	7
C	500	10	C	100	12
D	600	18	D	900	15
E	800	20	E	500	10

The minimum effectiveness for the lathe and milling machine are 8 and 9 respectively and the maximum EUACs are $700,000 and $600,000 respectively.

a) Draw cost-effective diagrams for the lathe and the milling machine.

b) Check for feasibility and dominance to produce a set of feasible alternatives for each machine.

c) Make a selection for each machine based on a nonincremental analysis.

d) Does your selection change for an incremental analysis? Explain.

26-15 There are six mutually exclusive projects under consideration by your state Environmental Protection Agency for the disposal of low level radioactive wastes. The EUAC and the effectiveness of each plan are tabulated below. The effectiveness is based on a multiattribute analysis which included such nonmonetary attributes as earthquake hazards, the risk of ground water pollution, and public opposition.

Project	EUAC	Effectiveness
A	$2,500,000	6
B	3,400,000	12
C	4,100,000	15
D	4,800,000	13
E	5,700,000	18
F	6,500,000	21

Because of budget constraints, the maximum allowable cost is $6,000,000. The minimum acceptable level of effectiveness was set at 13.

a) Draw a cost-effective diagram for this study showing the feasible and infeasible regions.

b) Delete the projects which are infeasible or are dominated by others.

c) Make a selection and justify your answer.

26-16 You are the Associate Director of Planning for the Regional Water Authority. You are evaluating a number of plans for improving the quality of the water. The results are given in the following table. The cost figures are in millions of dollars.

Plan	Effectiveness, E	Initial Cost	Total Cost, C $(-PW)$	E/C
Existing	0	0	0	—
A	10	2	4	2.5
B	20	3	10	2.0
C	30	3	15	2.0
D	35	5	25	1.4
E	40	5	30	1.3
F	50	6	30	1.7
G	50	7	40	1.25
H	60	8	25	2.4
I	65	9	20	3.35
J	65	9	30	2.2

The effectiveness is the estimated reduction in parts per million (ppm) of the contaminants for which the state has mandated a reduction of at least 25 ppm within the next three years. The figure of merit is the ratio E/C, the reduction in ppm per million dollars of total cost. This cost is expressed as a present worth that includes both the first cost and the O&M costs. The initial cost must not exceed $8.5 million.

a) Draw a cost-effective diagram showing the feasible and infeasible regions.

b) Identify the members of the set of alternatives which are feasible and which are not dominated by other alternatives.

c) Make a selection and defend it based on an incremental analysis if needed.

Equity

26-17 A new dam for flood control is under review. The population affected and the estimated benefits are given below. The upstream population will have to relocate. The downstream population will benefit from lower insurance rates and less repairs due to flood damage.

	Population	Present Worth
Upstream of dam	1,000	$-9,000,000
Downstream of dam	100,000	10,000,000
	101,000	$1,000,000

Should the dam be built? Justify your answer. (NOTE: Your answer could be, "It depends . . ." If so, explain what it depends on.)

26-18 Would your answer to Problem 26-17 change if the area to be flooded above the dam was owned by a single owner who would suffer an estimated loss of $9 million? This estimate was based on the difference between the appraised value of the land and what he or she has been offered by the government under its power of eminent domain.

26-19 Assume the same situation as in Problem 26-18 except that the estimated loss to the lone owner is $12,000,000. For the entire population, that is, both upstream and downstream, the net benefit would then be a minus $2 million.

___27

MULTIATTRIBUTE ANALYSIS TECHNIQUES

27.1 INTRODUCTION

In this chapter, we present several approaches to carrying out a multiattribute analysis for ranking and for selecting a capital project investment opportunity. We assume that the opportunity has been identified, that alternatives have been selected, and that a deterministic analysis and, if deemed necessary, a risk analysis have been completed.

The deterministic analysis has produced figures of merit, such as the present or annual worth or the IRR. The alternatives remaining in the study have satisfied these financial criteria. The risk analysis has produced variances. The trade-off between risk and net worth has been resolved, and only those alternatives remain for which the risk is within bounds.

What we have left is a set of alternatives, for each of which there is one monetary attribute—the figure of merit just mentioned—and, at times, another—the variance. It is now necessary to bring the nonmonetary attributes into the selection process. These were, or should have been, identified early in the selection process, that is, at the time the set of alternatives was assembled.

We begin with the sequential elimination of alternatives and attributes, and from there we move on to graphical techniques, such as score cards and polar charts. Next, we discuss how attributes are culled, ranked, and weighted. This leads to the concept of utility and how this concept is used in the more sophisticated approaches to multiattribute analysis.

27.2 SEQUENTIAL ELIMINATION METHODS

Sequential elimination methods are best described with the help of a matrix of the type shown in Figure 27.1. The attributes, both monetary and non-monetary, are identified by subscripts ranging from 1 to M, with j representing any particular attribute. The alternatives are represented by subscripts ranging from 1 to N, with i representing any particular alternative. The small square marked A_{ij} is the jth attribute for the ith alternative. Matrices such as Figure 27.1 are usually supplemented with additional columns listing preferences and standards (minimum requirements), and we will follow this practice in our examples.

A matrix is obviously a convenient tool for weeding out alternatives and attributes for relevancy and dominance. If any attribute—monetary or non-monetary—is the same for all alternatives or has very little bearing on any of them, it can be culled for lack of relevancy. Any alternative that cannot satisfy specified standards is also removed, as are those that are dominated on all counts (or at least on all of the important monetary and nonmonetary attributes) by others.

COMMENT: You will recall that we warned you several times in Parts II and III not to be too hasty when you are applying dominance on the basis of monetary consequences only. In many building projects—mu-

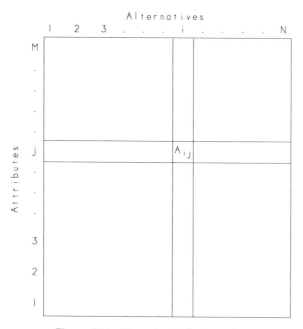

Figure 27.1. Alternative/attribute matrix.

seums, churches, corporate headquarters, and academic centers at major universities—nonmonetary attributes such as style, esthetics, and modernity often outweigh the monetary. For some machine tool and process line installations, flexibility in switching from one operation or part or product to another may be the most important single attribute.

The weeding-out process is demonstrated in Example 27.1.

Example 27.1 New Machine Tool Facility   The attributes and the value of their outcomes, for four alternatives for a study on a new machine tool installation, are shown in the following tabulation. The attributes are identified by the letters A, B, C, D, and E, and the alternatives by A_1, A_2, A_3, and A_4.

		Alternatives and the Value of Their Outcomes					
Attributes		A_1	A_2	A_3	A_4	Preferred	Required
A	Present worth*	$60	$70	$85	$75	$90	$0
B	Flexibility	Best	Worst	Good	Fair	Best	Fair
C	Reliability	3	3.5	5	5	10	3.5
D	Quality	6	5	6	8	10	7
E	Appearance	Good	Good	Good	Good	Best	Fair

*In thousands of dollars.

There is one monetary attribute, the present worth, and four nonmonetary attributes. For two of these—flexibility and appearance—the "value" of the attribute is expressed verbally. For the remaining two—reliability and quality—it is expressed numerically, using a weighting system of 0–10. This system will be discussed later. There are also columns for "preferred" and for the minimum requirement.

A check on relevance eliminates attribute E, since it rates "good" for all alternatives. Dominance eliminates alternative A_2, since, for every attribute, alternatives A_3 and A_4 are better than A_2.

We are left with three alternatives and four attributes. Sequential elimination is now applied in one or the other of several ways. The first way is to restrict (constrain) our choice to those that satisfy the minimum requirement of at least one attribute. This elimination method is called "disjunctive constraint," the adjective *disjunctive* indicating that we look at each attribute separately. By this test, all three alternatives remain in the selection process. A_1 satisfies two of the attributes; A_3, three; and A_4, all four, as you can easily verify.

A second way is to restrict our choice only to those that satisfy the minimum stated requirements for all attributes. This elimination method is obviously more severe and is called "conjunctive constraint." Only A_4 remains.

Do disjunctive and conjunctive constraint make sense? The answer is that it depends. We have not weighted each attribute against the others, but, even without weighting, an attribute such as flexibility may be of such importance to one or more decision makers that it outweighs the standards or requirements that were set for present worth, reliability, and quality. This may be highly unlikely but it does happen. Furthermore, in many instances, it is important to decision makers to portray matrices with all of the irrelevances and dominated alternatives in place. Decision makers are best advised if they know "what was left out" as well as "what was left in."

If we accept disjunctive constraint as our elimination method, we are faced with a selection from one of three alternatives—A_1, A_3, or A_4. We can now proceed in two ways.

The first is called "lexicography" or "lexicographic ordering." These big words hide a simple elimination method that was named after the way in which you search for words in a dictionary. The attribute of greatest importance is selected. If this is present worth, the selection is A_3; if flexibility, A_1; if reliability, A_3 and A_4; and if quality, A_4. For reliability, A_3 and A_4 have the same rating. You therefore proceed in the same way with the next most important attribute. If this is quality, you select A_4 because its rating for this attribute is higher than A_3.

Still another way to proceed is called "elimination of aspects." We look at each attribute and eliminate those alternatives that do not meet its requirement. For attributes A and B, none of the three remaining alternatives is disqualified. For attributes C and D, A_1 is disqualified. We are left with A_3 and A_4, from which a selection based on lexicographic ordering can then be made. This gives us A_4, as it did earlier.

If these elimination procedures and the fancy names they have spawned leave you a bit confused, go through this section of the chapter again to convince yourself that the procedures represent an orderly way of focusing judgment and applying common sense. If you and your study group can reach a decision based on these methods, do so; if not, continue with the methods that will be described.

27.3 GRAPHICAL TECHNIQUES FOR MULTIATTRIBUTE ANALYSIS

The best known of the graphical techniques are score cards and polar graphs. Their advantage is that they are "user friendly" or "user understandable" to decision makers, although there is some question about whether this is so for polar graphs. Their disadvantage is that they do not weigh the relative importance of the attributes. (There are, however, instances in which this disadvantage becomes an advantage due to the often highly subjective, that is, partisan nature of attribute weighting.)

27.3.1 Score Cards

Many of us are familiar with the score cards used by *Consumer Reports* for rating the frequency of repairs and the trouble spots of automobiles (1). A sample resembling such a card is given in Figure 27.2. The cards list 17 trouble spots or attributes, of which 5 are shown, in alphabetical order, plus a trouble index and a cost-of-repair index. The symbols shown, represent ratings from best to worst. There is no attempt to rank or to weight the trouble spots.

Score cards come in a wide variety of sizes, shapes, symbols, and colors. These include shaded circles, transparent color-coded overlays, and many others.

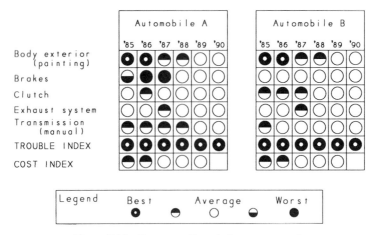

Figure 27.2. *Consumer Reports* type score card.

Shaded Circles. The use of shaded circles produces score cards that re-semble those of *Consumer Reports*. A fully shaded circle represents "excep-tional," "excellent," or "best"; an unshaded circle represents "poor," "worst," or "unacceptable"; and the 90°, 180°, and 270° shadings represent "below average," "average," and "above average," respectively, or similar phrasing that takes us from the worst to the best.

Transparent Color-coded Overlays. For the matrix in Example 27.1, green, yellow, red, and black might be used. Black would wipe out alternative 2, which was dominated by A_3 and A_4, and attribute E, which was irrelevant. Green would represent "best" and possibly "good"; red, the "worst"; and yellow, "average" or "fair." An overlay for the matrix in Example 27.1 is illustrated (without color, unfortunately) in Figure 27.3.

Other Score Cards. Other types of score cards include putting a box around the "best" and "worst" designation for each attribute, using a solid line for the "best" and a dotted line for the "worst." For attribute A of the matrix in Example 27.1, the highest present worth, $85,000, would be boxed in with a solid line and the lowest, $60,000, with a dotted line. A_3 and A_4 would each have two boxes with solid lines. If the two attributes, reliability and quality for A_4, are considered more important than the two attributes, present worth and quality for A_3, and if the relatively small difference in present worth between A_3 and A_4 is not considered significant, A_4 would be selected.

Matrices with geometric figures enclosing the outcomes can also be used. A typical scheme might show a circle for "best," a triangle for "satisfactory" or "average," and a square for "worst."

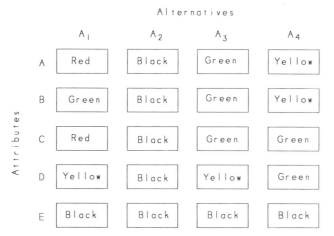

Figure 27.3. Overlay for matrix of Example 27.1.

27.3.2 Polar Graphs

A circle is drawn. Rays extend out from its center—one for each attribute. The angles between adjacent rays are equal. Thus, if there are M attributes, each ray is separated from its adjacent rays by an angle equal to $360°/M$.

Figure 27.4 is a polar graph for the three remaining alternatives and the four remaining attributes of the matrix of Example 27.1. The preference for each attribute is on the periphery of the circle. For attribute B, for example, the preference is "best." The ratings are marked along each ray. For A_4, the value for attribute B is "fair," which is arbitrarily shown at the midpoint of the ray, and the rating for A_3, which is "good," is shown half-way between "best" and "fair." The other attributes have numbers attached to them and are located to scale, as shown. The attributes for each alternative are connected by lines that form a polygon. The sizes and shapes of the polygons are compared. The choice between A_3 and A_4 would be close and would depend on which of the attributes mean more to the decision maker. Alternative 1 is clearly the loser if we look at size alone, but it is the winner if reliability dominates the decision process.

Other versions of polar graphs have the scales on each ray running in the opposite direction so that the smaller and the more concentrated the polygon around the center of the circle, the better the alternative.

Score cards and polar graphs are sometimes used to compare nonmonetary attributes only. If these attributes look better for alternative I than for alternative II, this may outweigh a favorable monetary consequence for alternative II.

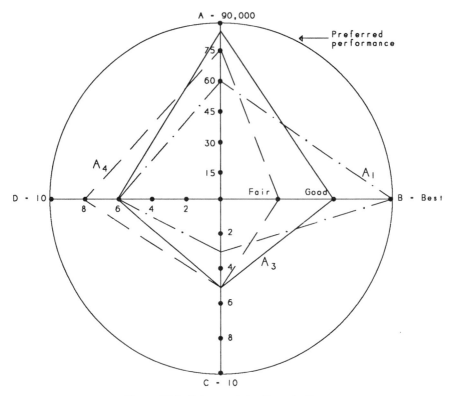

Figure 27.4. Polar graph for Example 27.1.

27.4 RANKING THE ATTRIBUTES

You will recall that we touched on ranking when we picked the most important and next most important attributes for lexicographic ordering. However, we now have to learn how to proceed in a more formal manner.

Ranking is carried out by comparing pairs of attributes. For M attributes, $M(M - 1)/2$ pairs have to be compared. Thus, ranking from two to six attributes gives the following number of combinations:

Number of Attributes	Number of Pairs to be Compared
2	1
3	3
4	6
5	10
6	15

A preferred ranking methodology is carried out in Example 27.2.

Example 27.2   Ranking Attributes   There are five attributes—A, B, C, D, and E—in a particular study. You, the decision maker, have looked at them two at a time and have come up with the following preferences for each of the ten pairs.

1. A < B	6. B > D
2. A > C	7. B > E
3. A > D	8. C = D
4. A > E	9. C < E
5. B > C	10. D < E

The symbol > means "is preferred to"; the symbol < means "is not preferred to"; and the symbol = means "is equally preferred to." If we rewrite all of the combinations, using only the symbols > and =, we have

A > C	B > A	C = D	E > C
A > D	B > C		E > D
A > E	B > D		
	B > E		

B is preferred to all of the other attributes; A is preferred to three of the others; E is preferred to two of the others; and, with regard to C and D, neither outranks the other. The ranking is then

$$B > A > E > C = D$$

In Example 27.2, we implied that the ranking had been done by one decision maker, who happened to be you. More than one person should take part in this task, and they should be allowed to state their preferences. For an important project, the Delphi technique should be used; that is, each person should be allowed to work independently. When the individual rankings are compared, they will usually differ. A consensus is then reached, which presumably has the imprint and the approval of the decision maker.

We close this section by reminding you that ranking attributes is subjective. The topic to follow—weighting the attributes—is even more so. Ranking is also not cast in stone. The weighting methodology described in the next section may require some revision to the preliminary rankings.

27.5   WEIGHTING THE ATTRIBUTES

When we rank, we perform ordinal scaling—what comes first, second, third, and so on. However, ranking does not tell us how close or how far away the first choice is to the second, the second to the third, and the second and third taken together to the first. For this we turn to weighting.

There are two ways to weight attributes—from the top down and from the bottom up. We illustrate these methods in Examples 27.3 and 27.4.

Example 27.3   Weighting Attributes from the Top Down   Assume that you head a study group. Your task is to contact the decision maker and other key players to determine how each would weight the attributes of a proposed investment in a capital project. There are five attributes, for which we use the ranking given in Example 27.2:

$$B > A > E > C = D$$

At a meeting with the key players, you ask each to give a weight of 100 to attribute B and to weight the other attributes in proportion. The individual results are compared, and, after much debate and discussion, the following consensus is reached:

Attribute	Relative Weight
B	100
A	70
E	40
D	30
C	20

One result of your meeting is that attribute C, which was ranked as "equally preferred to" D, has moved below D. Further discussions to check for consistency are led by you by asking such questions as the following:

1. Does the group agree that $(A + E)$, for which the weight is 110 $(70 + 40)$, carries more weight than B alone, for which the weight is 100? The answer is yes, and the weights for A and E stay as is.
2. Is $(E + D)$, with a total weight of 70, equal in preference to A, which has the same weight? This time the answer is no, and the group decides to reduce the weight of D by 10.
3. Is there a preference as between C and D, for each of which the rating is now 20? The group decides that the weight of C should be reduced to 15.

The final weights and their normalized counterparts are tabulated below.

Attribute	Final Weights	Normalized Weights
B	100	41
A	70	28
E	40	17
D	20	8
C	15	6
	Total 245	100

The normalized weights give the relative standing of each attribute based on a total weight of 100 for all attributes.

So much for the top-down approach. Some practitioners of MAA find that more consistent results are obtained with the bottom-up approach.

Example 27.4 Weighting Attributes from the Bottom Up In this approach, you ask each member of the group to apply a weight of 10 (or 100) to the lowest-ranking attribute and use ratios to work up toward the highest ranking. On this basis, C and D would be ranked 10, although the group consensus might again show a higher rating for D after the weighting was completed.

The consensus for this approach and the resulting normalized weights are given in the following tabulation.

Attribute	Final Weights	Normalized Weights
B	60	41
A	40	28
E	25	17
D	10	7
C	10	7
	Total 145	100

You should not expect this approach to give you exactly the same results as the top-down approach. One is no more correct than the other. The one to use is the one that the people you work with are accustomed to and find the most comfortable. If you are in doubt, average the two.

COMMENT: There are several formula methods for weighting that make a mechanical exercise out of this important decision process. None of these is as satisfactory as the procedures we have described. If you are interested in such methods, you should turn to the References and Suggested Reading at the end of this chapter.

Now that we know how to weight attributes, we have to find out how to introduce the weights into the selection process.

27.6 SCALING

Just weighting the attributes won't do. We can't apply weights if the present worth is expressed in dollars, the flexibility in words, and the reliability and quality in numbers for which no units are given. We have to find a common basis. This is done with a technique that we refer to as "scaling." All of the attributes are assigned a number on a common scale, which can range from 0 to 1 or from 0 to 10 or from 0 to 100, or even 1,000. The choice is ours. We use a scale of 0–10 in Example 27.5.

Example 27.5 Scaling Each attribute has a range of outcomes. Consider once again the ranges for the machine tool installation of Example 27.1. For convenience, these ranges are tabulated below for alternatives A_1, A_3, and A_4. Alternative A_2 is not included, since it was dominated by A_3 and A_4. Neither is attribute E since it was irrelevant.

Attribute	Description	Range of Outcomes	Preferred Value
A	Present worth	\$60,000–\$85,000	\$90,000
B	Flexibility	Fair to best	Best
C	Reliability	3–5	10
D	Quality	6–8	10

We now ask, "Where on a scale of 0–10 do the outcomes for each attribute fall." If the output is expressed in words, one of the simplest ways to get answers is to ask the key players such questions as "On a scale of 0–10, where do we put a rating of 'fair' for flexibility?" The answer might be 5 or even somewhat greater, since 5 may have been given as a minimum acceptable value and, in the minds of some members of the group, might therefore rate a 6 or 7. This approach to scaling often works. Where no backup data are available, it may be the only approach. Any attribute for which no definite numbers can be assigned—for example, ethics, esthetics, appearance, modernity—can be scaled in this way.

For attributes whose outcomes are measured in numbers, we can proceed otherwise. Consider the present worth. The preferred value is \$90,000, which we arbitrarily give the maximum value of 10. (Why do we say *arbitrarily*? We could have given a 10 to the highest value of the present worth, namely \$85,000. The choice is again ours.) The minimum requirement is 0, which just returns the MARR. We give it a value of 0 on the scale. The scale reading of the present worth for the three alternatives is then

$$A_1: \quad (\$60,000/\$90,000) \times 10 = 6.8$$

$$A_3: \quad (\$85,000/\$90,000) \times 10 = 9.4$$

$$A_4: \quad (\$75,000/\$90,000) \times 10 = 8.3$$

For flexibility, the consensus was to give "best" a 10, the minimum requirement "fair" a 5, and "good" a rating of 7.5.

COMMENT: Scale readings for attributes expressed verbally should generally be limited to single digits. However, a reading half-way between any two adjacent digits is often used.

For reliability and quality, the outcomes shown in Example 27.1 have already been converted to scale readings, as you probably surmised. These readings were obtained as follows.

For reliability, the measure of value was the mean time between failures. Estimates of the mean time for A_1, A_3, and A_4 are given in the following tabulation, together with the position that each alternative was given on an interval scale.

	Mean Time Between Failures, hrs.	Position on Scale
Poor	≤ 400	0
A_1	460	3
A_3 and A_4	500	5
Best	≥ 600	10

The positions on the scale were calculated as follows:

$$\text{Position} = \frac{\text{Alternative} - \text{Poor}}{\text{Best} - \text{Poor}} \times 10 \qquad (27.1)$$

With this formula, an alternative with 400 hours or less between failures would have a weight of 0 on the interval scale, and an alternative with 600 hours or more would have a value of 10.

For the three alternatives, the position on the scale is computed as follows:

$$\text{For } A_1: [(460 - 400)/(600 - 400)] \times 10 = 3$$

$$\text{For } A_3 \text{ and } A_4: [(600 - 500)/(600 - 400)] \times 10 = 5.$$

A similar procedure was used for quality to produce the ratings shown on the matrix of Example 27.1. The data on which the scaling was based are given in the first column, below.

	Rejects per 10,000 Units	Log	Position on Scale
Poor	> 100	2	0
A_1 and A_3	25	1.4	6
A_4	15	1.2	8
Best	< 10	1	10

For this attribute, the study group suggested a logarithmic scale for interpolation, since this was judged to be more realistic than interpolating linearly between the number of rejects per 10,000 units of production.

Applying Equation 27.1, we get the following positions on the interval scale.

$$\text{For } A_1 \text{ and } A_3 \: [(1.4 - 2)/(1 - 2)] \times 10 = 6$$

$$\text{For } A_4 \: [(1.2 - 2)/(1 - 2)] \times 10 = 8$$

A recapitulation of the scale positions for the four attributes is given in the following tabulation.

	Alternatives		
Attributes	A_1	A_3	A_4
A Present worth	6.8	9.4	8.3
B Flexibility	10	7.5	5
C Reliability	3	5	5
D Quality	6	6	8

Our next step, which we could have done earlier, is to weight the attributes themselves. How this is done was illustrated in Example 27.3 using the top-down approach and in Example 27.4 using the bottom-up approach. We assume that the four attributes of Example 27.1 have been weighted and that a consensus has been reached with the following results:

Attribute	Weight
A Present worth	40
B Flexibility	25
C Reliability	20
D Quality	15
Total	100

We now have everything we need to calculate figures of merit that incorporate both monetary and nonmonetary attributes.

Example 27.6   Combined Figures of Merit   Combined figures of merit for A_1, A_3, and A_4 are computed with the help of Table 27.1
   The scale positions come from Example 27.5. The attribute weights were given earlier. The outcome is the product of the scale position times the attribute weight divided by 10. Thus, for alternative A_1, the outcome for attribute A is $(40 \times 6.8)/10$ equals 27.2. Division by 10 would not have been necessary if we had used a scale of 0–1 instead of 0–10. However, most of us can think more clearly if we

TABLE 27.1   Computations for Combined Figures of Merit

		Alternatives					
		A_1		A_3		A_4	
Attribute	Attribute Weight	Scale Position	Outcome	Scale Position	Outcome	Scale Position	Outcome
A	40	6.8	27.2	9.4	37.6	8.3	33.2
B	25	10	25.0	7.5	18.8	5	12.5
C	20	3	6.0	5	10.0	5	10.0
D	15	6	9.0	6	9.0	8	12.0
	100		67.2		75.4		67.7

are asked, "On a scale of 0–10, what is. . . .?" than "On a scale of 0–1, what is. . . .?"

The figures of merit that now include both monetary and nonmonetary attributes are in the last line of Table 27.1. A_3 leads with 75.4 points out of a possible 100. A_1 and A_4 are too close to name either one as second or third. Both are in second place. A decision between the two would have to be made on the basis of which of the attributes are more important to the decision maker. This is where lexicographic ordering might come into play.

We now leave interval scaling to go to evaluation ratings based on utility. For this effort, we first need to explain what we mean by "utility." Two synonyms you might keep in mind for this term are "worthwhileness" and "satisfaction."

27.7 UTILITY

Utility is not only a fascinating topic but also a very subjective one. Compare the satisfaction or utility of having an extra pair of shoes if you own only one pair with having an extra pair if you already have nine pairs. Most of us would agree that the utility u_2 of a second pair is greater than the utility u_{10} of a tenth pair; that is,

$$u_2 > u_{10}$$

Similarly, what is the utility of 10 rejects per 10,000 units of production compared to 20 rejects per 10,000 units. For most manufacturers,

$$u_{10} > u_{20}$$

Last, what is the utility of "best" versus "fair"?

$$u \text{ (best)} > u \text{ (fair)}$$

We could go much further with such questions and use the answers to develop a utility profile or function for each attribute in a given study. Consider, for example, the following two relationships:

$$u \text{ (best)} > u \text{ (good)}$$

$$u \text{ (good)} > u \text{ (fair)}$$

Is the difference between the utilities of "best" and "good" greater than, less than, or equal to the difference between the utilities of "good" and "fair"? The answer is probably "less than," since, for most attributes (but by no means all), the jump from "fair" to "good" is seen as greater than the jump from "good" to "best."

COMMENT: Go back to shoes for a moment. For most of us, the difference in utility between a first and a second pair of shoes is greater than the difference between a ninth and a tenth pair. Imelda Marcos might not agree with such an evaluation. For her, the difference between the 6,000th pair and the 5,999th pair might have more utility than the difference between her 10th and 9th pair. As we said, utility evaluations are subjective.

The preceding questions and answers make it clear that there is such a thing as a utility function, u, for any attribute. How we quantify this function to bring it into the selection process is our next topic.

27.7.1 The Utility Function

For any attribute, there is a worst outcome, to which a utility of 0 is assigned, and a best possible outcome, to which a utility of 1 or 10 or 100 is assigned. (We will generally use 10.) What is the shape of u between 0 and 10? This depends on the attribute and on the decision maker.

Consider the attribute, present worth, in Example 27.1. Let u equal 0 for a present worth of 0 and 10 for a present worth of $90,000. (This is again arbitrary. We could have made u equal to 10 for the highest present worth, which is $85,000.) Are the values of u for present worths between 0 and $90,000 given by the straight line in Figure 27.5? If so, then the value of u is the same as the scale readings that we computed in Example 27.5. This linear correspondence may make sense for some attributes, but it may be nonsense for others. For most of us, the utility of $100, if we have nothing in our pocket, is greater than the utility of $100, if we have $900 in our pocket. It therefore seems reasonable to sketch a utility curve for present worth that resembles the concave downward curve in Figure 27.5. In this curve, the first $10,000 of present worth is given a u of 2.5. The next $10,000 has a u of 2.0 $(4.5 - 2.5)$. The u of the last $10,000 is about 0.3 and of the next to the last, about 0.5.

Consider next the attribute of flexibility, for which the scale readings range from "fair" to "best." "Fair" has a reading of 5; "good," of 7.5; and "best," of 10. If we use the scale readings as measures of utility, we would, as shown in Figure 27.6, get a straight line, as we did with the present worth. However, for this attribute, a straight line may be reasonable, as it often is for attributes whose outcomes are not directly measurable. Our judgments of utility or satisfaction are bound up in the answers we give to "Where on a scale of 0–10. . . .?" questions. You can see this from the placement of the verbal outcomes along the abscissa of Figure 27.6.

Let's step away from Example 27.1 and ask how we would handle the quality of schooling as an attribute in a job relocation problem. Assume that, for you, a reputation of "fair" is not good enough. You personally would give "fair" a utility of 0. "Best" would get a u of 10, but "good" would get a u of only 5. In short, "good" would only give you half the satisfaction of

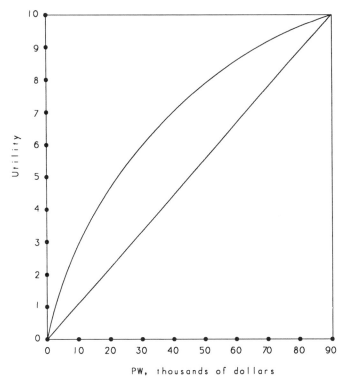

Figure 27.5. Utility functions for PW.

"best." The shape of the utility function would resemble the letter S, as in Figure 27.7. We could also show the function as 0 from "fair" to just before reaching "good," jump up to 5 at "good," and continue concave downward up to 10 for "best."

There are also utility functions that are concave upward. This is particularly true for attributes that are concerned with appearance, esthetics, and greed. This may be the case with Imelda Marcos and her shoes. As mentioned, for her, the satisfaction of adding one more pair of shoes to 5,999 pairs may be greater than adding one more pair to 10 pairs.

Most of what we have just said is summed up in Figure 27.8. The abscissa is the output expressed as a reading on a scale of 0–10. The ordinate is the utility, with 10 as the best possible outcome. Four shapes are shown, into one of which a utility function can usually be fitted.

Assume now that we have prepared utility curves for each attribute of ˙ Example 27.5. We read the utility of the outcome from the curves and replace the scale readings in Table 27.1 with these values. For alternate A_1, for example, for which the present worth was \$60,000, you would use a value of $u = 8.5$ (see Figure 27.5) for present worth instead of the value we previously calculated, namely, 6.8.

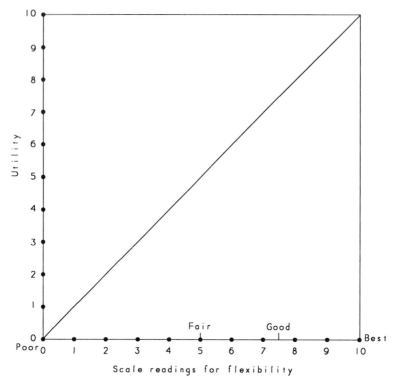

Figure 27.6. Utility functions for flexibility.

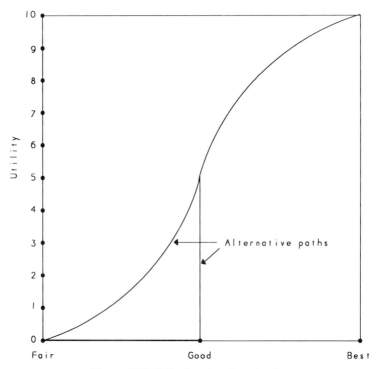

Figure 27.7. Utility functions for schooling.

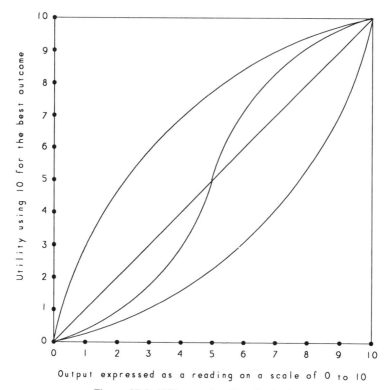

Figure 27.8. Utility as a function of output.

This concludes our discussion of utility theory for the time being. We come back to it in Chapter 28 when we compare the utility of lotteries (business ventures) with the utility of certainties. For now, we apply evaluation ratings based on utility estimates to the selection of a capital project opportunity.

27.8 MULTIATTRIBUTE ANALYSIS

A multiattribute analysis proceeds in an orderly series of steps, which feed back to each other as the analysis proceeds. The steps are described in the following list.

1. Identify the decision makers and other key players.
2. Select the alternatives.
3. Identify the attributes—monetary and nonmonetary.
4. Prepare a deterministic analysis (including sensitivity analysis) for the monetary attributes.
5. Prepare a risk analysis, if needed.

6. Proceed with a multiattribute analysis:
   a) Rank the attributes.
   b) Weight the attributes and normalize them (make the total weight equal 100).
   c) Assign utility values to the outcomes of each attribute.
   d) Compute a combined figure of merit.
7. Rank the figures of merit, and make a selection.

These steps are applied to a corporate headquarters relocation problem in Example 27.7.

Example 27.7   Corporate Headquarters Relocation* Your company is located in the center of a major city and will build a new headquarters in one of the adjoining suburbs. The do-nothing alternative is no longer an option, since the present headquarters have been sold. Top management and a small supporting staff will continue to occupy rental space there.

You have been put in charge of a study team to find a new location within a reasonable distance from the current headquarters. This has been defined as no more than 1½ hours away by automobile or other commute.

Step 1—Identify the decision makers. The prime decision makers are obviously top management, but the employees should also play a part in the decision-making process. A responsible management cannot neglect their interests. The employees have chosen a committee to represent them. You and your study group are to meet with this committee weekly. In addition, top management will review your progress at weekly executive committee sessions.

Step 2—Identify the attributes. Sometimes this is Step 3. Step 3 then becomes Step 2, as it does in this example. No matter which step comes first, the two are closely tied together and feed back on each other. A list of the important monetary and nonmonetary attributes that your group has identified follows.

Monetary	Nonmonetary
Cost of land	Infrastructure, if any, to be furnished
Cost of headquarters	by local government
Operating expenses	Availability and cost of housing
Nonoperating expenses	Public transportation
Preferential tax treatment	Commutation time
Cost of commutation	Availability of office personnel
	Schools
	Shopping facilities
	Recreational facilities

All of the monetary attributes represent corporate expenditures, except commutation. All of the nonmonetary items refer to the employees, except for infrastructure and availability of office personnel.

---

*Adapted with permission from Hans J. Lang, *Cost Analysis for Capital Investment Decisions*, Chapter 17, Example 17.4, page 277. See References at the end of this chapter.

Step 3—Select the alternatives. Your company has looked at many sites. You have been beseeched by many chambers of commerce to look at many more. With input from management and the employees, six sites have been selected that satisfy the budget constraints, have been approved by the executive committee, and are not objectionable to the employees' committee. However, two of these have been culled. One site was plagued with zoning problems, and a second site was discarded because of poor soil conditions, which would have required extensive and expensive piling. Four alternatives are left.

The employee committee has concluded that, for these sites, only three nonmonetary attributes are relevant—housing, schooling, and recreational facilities. Public transportation, commutation time, and shopping facilities show no significant differences.

Your study group has also advised management that they have found no significant differences in the availability of skilled office help. Therefore, this attribute also becomes irrelevant.

Step 4—Prepare a deterministic analysis. This analysis was carried out with an MARR of 8% and a 30-year life. All of the monetary attributes were combined into an equivalent uniform annual worth and expressed as a reduction from the EUAC of the current location. The results of the analysis are tabulated below.

Site	Reduction in EUAC, Thousands
1	$4,000
2	10,000
3	3,000
4	6,000

Step 5—Proceed with a risk analysis, if needed. This project does not require a risk analysis based on probability estimates. We assume that a sensitivity analysis based on the ranges of the estimates for the major variables was carried out under Step 4.

Step 6—Proceed with a multiattribute analysis. Two analyses have to be prepared—one for management and one for the employees. The raw data gathered by the study group for the three nonmonetary attributes of the employees are summarized as follows:

Attribute	Corporate Relocation Alternatives			
	Site 1	Site 2	Site 3	Site 4
Housing	Good	Fair	Good	Fair
Schooling	Fair	Good	Excellent	Good
Recreational facilities	Best	Fair	Good	Good

For schooling, housing, and recreational facilities, "fair" stands for adequate, "good" for satisfactory, and "excellent" for best.

Step 6a)—Rank the attributes. The ranking of attributes, in order of decreasing importance, by management and the employees follows.

Management Ranking	Employee Ranking
Monetary attribute	Housing
Employee morale	Schooling
Infrastructure	Recreational facilities
	Monetary attribute

The monetary attribute under employee ranking refers to the reduction in EUAC mentioned earlier. If employees sensed that the company was in serious trouble and had to do everything possible to reduce costs, they might rank the corporate monetary consequences much higher, since their livelihood would depend on the success of the corporation. Furthermore, just as management should keep the interests of the employees in mind, so should the employees keep those of management in mind.

Step 6b)—Weight the attributes. For weighting, you have asked management to assign 100 to the lowest item on their ranking list and to weight all other attributes as multiples of 100. You advise the employees' group to do the same for their list. The results are summarized below.

Attribute	Management Weighting	
	Absolute	Normalized
Monetary	1200	71
Employee morale	400	23
Infrastructure	100	6
Total	1700	100

Attribute	Employee Weighting	
	Absolute	Normalized
Housing	1200	44
Schooling	1000	37
Recreation	400	15
Monetary	100	4
Total	2700	100

The management weights tell you that the infrastructure is of minor significance in this study and that management rates employee morale four times higher than the infrastructure and the monetary attributes three times higher than employee morale. For the employees, the monetary consequences are the least important. Recreational facilities come next. Housing is rated slightly higher than schooling, but both are rated far higher than the other two attributes.

Step 6c)—Assign utility values to the outcomes. You begin with the employees. Your first chore is to explain the meaning of utility to them and apply it to the monetary attribute. With your help, they conclude that, for them, the monetary attribute plays such a small part that its utility is proportional to the values of the EUACs. A utility of 0 is assigned to an EUAC of 0, and a utility of 10 to an EUAC of \$10 million (*see* Step 4). The utility values are thus directly proportional to the EUACs, as shown in Table 27.2.

TABLE 27.2 Employee Matrix for Utility Evaluations

Attribute	Utilities			
	Site 1	Site 2	Site 3	Site 4
Housing	8	5	9	7
Schooling	3	7	10	9
Recreational facilities	9	5	7	8
Monetary	4	10	3	6

The utility functions for schooling, housing, and recreation are similar in that each is expressed in words. A curve for housing is shown in Figure 27.9. The distances "poor/fair," "fair/good," and "good/best" are equally spaced. For housing, the employees agree on a 5 for "fair," an 8 for "good," and a 10 for "best." The jump from fair to good therefore has a utility of 3 (8 − 5) and from good to best, a utility of 2 (10 − 8). This could be, among other reasons, because the group sees "best" as beyond its means and therefore subjectively moves "good" closer to "best."

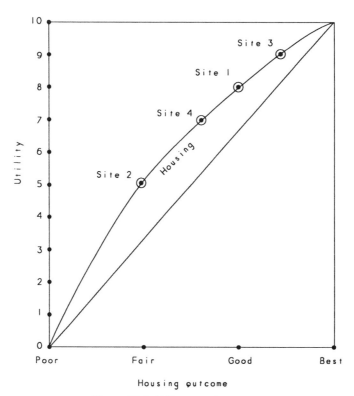

Figure 27.9. Utility curve for housing.

Sketching a utility curve helps to refine the differences among the four sites. The employee group, which had given sites 1 and 3 a rating of "good" for housing now agrees that site 3 should be higher on the curve than site 1. After more discussion, site 1 is left at a rating of 8 but site 3 is moved to 9. Similarly, the group agrees that site 4 is somewhere between "fair" and "good" and agree on a utility value of 7.

Similar curves are prepared for schooling and recreational facilities, and similar discussions are held. The results for all of the attributes, including schooling and recreational facilities, are in Table 27.2.

The preparation of the utility matrix for management is carried out in the same way. For employee concerns, you recommend—and management agrees—to give site 3 a value of 10 and the other three sites a value of 0. This is on the magnanimous side. (Why?) The differences in the infrastructure needs at each site proved to be small. After further review, the study group therefore decided to treat this attribute as irrelevant.

The monetary attribute looms large with management, as it should. The utility function accepted by management is shown in Figure 27.10. The readings from this curve are posted in Table 27.3.

Step 6d)—Compute a combined figure of merit. The utility values from the matrices in Step 6c) are multiplied by the normalized weights from Step 6b) to

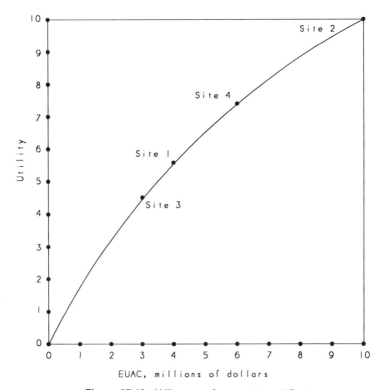

Figure 27.10. Utility curve for monetary attribute.

TABLE 27.3 Management Matrix for Utility Evaluations

	Utilities			
Attribute	Site 1	Site 2	Site 3	Site 4
Monetary	5.5	10	4.5	7.5
Employee morale	0	0	10	0

construct new matrices with which combined figures of merit for management and the employees are calculated. For the employees, the results are shown in Table 27.4.

Make sure that you understand where the figures from this table come from. If you don't, go back to Example 27.5 and reread it. [*Hint*: The figure of 35 for housing under site 1 is its utility for this site (8) times the normalized weight (44) rounded to two significant figures after dividing by 10.] The employees obviously favor site 3, with site 4 as a good second choice. For them, sites 1 and 2 are poor third choices.

For management, the results are shown in Table 27.5.

As expected, site 2 shows the highest figure of merit, because of the high weight and high value of the monetary attribute. Site 3 comes next but only because of the rather unusual treatment by management of the utility of employee morale.

Step 7—Make the decision. Finally, all that is needed for making a recommendation is at hand. Management favors site 2; the employees favor site 3. Management must decide which way to go. If management suspected that employee morale would be adversely affected by the selection of site 2, the weighting for this attribute might be increased and the entire exercise gone through again. However, management, quite rightly, is not going to give up the decided cost advantage of site 2 without good reason. The four sites are, after all, in the same metropolitan area. The employees had agreed that each site was at least acceptable. Those who want the advantages of site 3 can relocate there, even if this means there are certain disadvantages.

If you have followed our progress through Example 27.7, you should have no difficulty in understanding how a multiattribute analysis is carried out for any number of alternatives, any number of attributes, and more than one involved group.

TABLE 27.4 Employee Matrix for Combined Figures of Merit

	Figures of Merit			
Attribute	Site 1	Site 2	Site 3	Site 4
Housing	35	22	40	31
Schooling	11	26	37	33
Recreational facilities	14	8	11	12
Monetary	2	4	1	2
Total	62	60	89	78

TABLE 27.5   Management Matrix for Combined Figures of Merit

Attribute	Figures of Merit			
	Site 1	Site 2	Site 3	Site 4
Monetary	39	71	32	53
Employees	0	0	23	0
Total	39	71	55	53

27.9   SUMMARY

This chapter covered the basic techniques of multiattribute analysis. These included sequential elimination, graphical techniques, and the more sophisticated approaches, which require the ranking and weighting of attributes and the assignment of utility values to their outcomes. With these inputs, a combined figure of merit is computed that incorporates both monetary and nonmonetary effects.

There are four common sequential elimination methods. The first is disjunctive constraint, in which an alternative has to satisfy the minimum requirement of at least one attribute. The second is conjunctive constraint, in which an alternative has to satisfy the minimum requirement of all attributes. With both constraints, more than one alternative may remain viable. If so, a third method, called "lexicographic ordering," is applied. The fourth method is "elimination by aspects." Each attribute is looked at individually, and those alternatives that do not meet its requirements are eliminated.

The graphical techniques include score cards and polar graphs. Their advantage is that they are user friendly. Their disadvantage is that all attributes are treated equally as to their importance in the selection process.

The more sophisticated approach to multiattribute analysis usually involves four steps. The first step is ranking the attributes. This is done using ordinal scaling.

The second step is weighting the attributes. Either a top-down or a bottom-up approach is used.

The third step is to assign a utility value to the outcomes of each attribute. These values are obtained by sketching or eyeballing a utility function versus output. The shape of the function is derived through discussions with those involved in the decision-making process with regard to the satisfaction or utility that each outcome gives them.

The fourth step is to compute figures of merit for each alternative, which now reflect the influence of both the monetary and nonmonetary attributes. This is done by multiplying the utility values of the outcomes by the weights of their attributes. The resulting products are added together to obtain a combined figure of merit for each alternative.

REFERENCES

1. *Consumer Reports*, published monthly by Consumers Union. The repair records of automobiles are an annual feature, which usually appears in the April issue.
2. Hans J. Lang, *Cost Analysis for Capital Investment Decisions* (New York: Marcel Dekker, 1989). Example 27.7 was adapted from this text.

SUGGESTED READING

1. John R. Canada and William G. Sullivan, *Economic and Multiattribute Evaluation of Advanced Manufacturing Systems* (Englewood Cliffs, NJ: Prentice-Hall, 1989). An excellent text, whether your interest is advanced manufacturing systems or not. Chapter 8 covers the basic techniques of multiattribute decision analysis.

PROBLEMS

Sequential Elimination Methods

27-1 You have been asked to analyze and recommend an alternative for a new computer installation which is to be used for order entry. Your analysis is summarized in the following table. The cost savings are expressed in thousands of dollars per year. Expansibility and reliability are rated on a scale of 0 to 10.

		Alternatives and the Value of their Outcomes					
Attributes		1	2	3	4	Preferred	Required
A.	Cost savings	20	60	−10	35	60	0
B.	User friendly	good	fair	worst	best	best	good
C.	Expansibility	6	4	3	8	10	4
D.	Reliability	6	4	4	8	10	6
E.	Serviceability	good	good	good	good	best	fair

a) Which alternatives dominate others?

b) Using disjunctive constraint which alternative(s), if any, would you eliminate?

c) Should all the attributes be used in this selection process, that is, are they all relevant?

d) Which alternatives satisfy all the stated requirements, that is, meet the conjunctive constraint?

e) Which alternative would you choose? Why?

27-2   For the tabulation in Problem 27-1 assume that the attributes are listed in their order of importance, that is, A > B > C > D > E. Determine which attributes remain after applying (a) lexicography and (b) elimination by aspects.

27-3   Suppose the order of importance for the attributes in Problem 27-1 was B > D > C > A > E. What attributes remain after applying (a) lexicography and (b) elimination by aspects.

27-4   Select a personal situation in which you had to make a decision, for example, your choice of college, your first job, a change of jobs, and so on. Construct a matrix such as Figure 27.1 listing the attributes and the alternatives which you had identified as important to your decision. Assign a numeric or verbal rating to each alternative for each attribute based on your best recollection of the conditions with which you were faced at the time you made your selection. Apply the following decision-assisting tools to your matrix.

a) Disjunctive constraint

b) Conjunctive constraint

c) Dominance

d) Lexicography after first ranking the attributes in what you consider their order of importance.

e) Elimination of aspects

f) Compare the decision you made with the above sequential elimination methods.

27-5   The following ratings show how four attributes satisfy two alternatives. The ratings are on a scale of 0 to 100.

| | Alternative | |
Attribute	1	2
A	75	60
B	40	100
C	70	70
D	65	60

Assume the attributes are ranked A > B > C > D and that 50 is the minimum acceptable rating for each attribute. What would be your selection based on (a) lexicography and (b) elimination by aspects.

27-6   In the text, we question whether selections based on disjunctive and conjunctive constraints make sense. Explain, with examples if possible, when they do and when they don't.

Graphical Techniques for Multiattribute Analyses

27-7 What are the advantages and disadvantages of graphical techniques?

27-8 Draw a polar graph for Alternatives A_1, A_2, and A_4 of Problem 27-4. How does the graph illustrate dominance?

27-9 The text mentions that polar graphs are also drawn with the scales on the rays reversed from those shown in Figure 27.1. Redo Example 27-1 and Figure 27.1 in this way.

27-10 Redo the polar graph of Problem 27-8 with the scales running in the reverse direction. Which type of polar graph presentation do you prefer and why?

Ranking and Weighting the Attributes

27-11 You are considering four attributes—A, B, C, and D—in connection with a study for replacing a machine tool in the maintenance shop. This requires six pair-wise comparisons (Why only 6?) for which the results are listed below.

1. $A > B$
2. $A < C$
3. $A > D$
4. $B < C$
5. $B > D$
6. $C > D$

What is the rank order of the attributes based on the above results?

27-12 Five attributes—A, B, C, D, E—are under review for selecting one of four A/E firms that have bid on redesigning the office space of your firm. The results of the ten pair-wise comparisons (Why 10 and only 10?) is given below.

1. $A < B$
2. $A > C$
3. $A < D$
4. $A = E$
5. $B > C$
6. $B < D$
7. $B > E$
8. $C < D$
9. $C < E$
10. $D > E$

Rank order the attributes based on the preferences shown above.

27-13 You have the responsibility of getting the executive committee of your firm to weight five attributes—V, W, X, Y, Z—for a study on expanding robotic manufacturing facilities. The preliminary results of your efforts are shown below.

Attribute	Relative Weight
X	100
W	80
V	70
Y	40
Z	20

a) What kind of questions would you ask before you normalized the weights?

b) If the weights stay as shown after your questioning, normalize them for a base of 100.

27-14 At a conference on concurrent engineering, you assembled a group of experts that came up with the following rankings for four attributes. The rankings were based on the bottoms-up approach with 10 arbitrarily assigned to the attribute which, by consensus, ranked the lowest.

Attributes	Weights
Multi-functional teams	25
Simultaneous activities	20
Life cycle costs	15
Systems approach	10
Total	70

a) What questions, if any, would you ask before you normalized the weights?

b) If the weights stay as shown, normalize them for a base of 100.

27-15 In the text and in Problems 27-7 to 27-14, we rank attributes using pair-wise comparisons and then weight the rankings. Could we rank and weight alternatives in this way without first ranking and weighting attributes. If so, why don't we do it? If not, why not?

27-16 DWM Company is in the process of choosing an injection molding system to make plastic parts. The three attributes which the study group has selected for comparing alternatives are cost savings (annual worth), product quality, and flexibility in changing from the production of one part to another. The attributes have been weighted and the scale position of each attribute for each alternative has been de-

termined. The results are tabulated below for the three alternatives—
A_1, A_2, and A_3—which are still in the selection process.

Attribute	Weight of Attribute	Scale Position			Maximum Scale Position
		A_1	A_2	A_3	
Cost saving	50	30	40	25	50
Quality	30	10	7	3	10
Flexibility	20	4	5	3	10

Calculate a combined figure of merit for each alternative which includes all three attributes.

27-17 Why do we use a scale of 0 to 10 or of 0 to 100 for weighting more
frequently than a scale of 0 to 1. (Note: See Problem 27-24 for why
a scale of 0 to 1 is more convenient for expressing utility functions
mathematically.)

Utility

27-18 What do you think Imelda Marco's utility curve for shoes (or the
utility curve of anyone who has 6000 pairs of shoes) might look like?
What does the utility curve of an avid art collector, say a collector of
rare Chinese vases, look like?

27-19 In Example 27.7, why does the text say it was magnanimous for top
management to give Site 3 a rating of 10 and the other 3 sites a rating
of 0?

27-20 Refer to Example 27.7 and draw the utility curve for recreation for
the employees?

27-21 Redraw Figure 27.6 using equal spacing between the verbal outcomes.
What is now the shape of the utility curve?

Multiattribute Analysis

27-22 Perform a multiattribute analysis from the employer's viewpoint for
the corporate relocation alternatives in Example 27.7.

27-23 Three alternative sites are being considered for a satellite distribution
center. The attributes to be included in the study have been identified,
ranked, and weighted. The results, together with the value of each
attribute for each alternative, are given in the following tabulation.
The present worth of the costs is in thousands of dollars.

Attribute	Attribute Weight	Scale Values		
		Site I	Site II	Site III
1. PW of costs	0.55	$750	$850	$650
2. Availability of labor	0.30	fair	excellent	good
3. Miles to central warehouse	0.10	900	750	1100
4. Community attitude*	0.05	8	9	7

*Based on a scale of 0 to 10

Sketch the utility curve for each attribute and complete the evaluation to arrive at a combined figure of merit for each site.

27-24 Refer to Figure 27.8. We could have drawn this figure using the range 0 to 1 instead of 0 to 10 for normalizing both the outputs on the abscissa and the utility values on the ordinate. This simplifies the expression of utility, u, as a function of output, x. Assume that this has been done for comparing two competing technologies—System I and System II. The value of the outputs for three nonmonetary attributes on a scale of 0 to 1 and the functional relation between u and x are given below.

Attributes	Attribute Weights	Options		Utility Curves
		System I	System II	
Maintainability	0.5	0.5	0.7	$u = x$
Flexibility	0.2	0.7	0.4	$u = x^{0.5}$
User friendliness	0.3	0.6	0.9	$u = x^2$

a) Modify Equation 27.1 to normalize output for a scale of 0 to 1 rather than 0 to 10.

b) Compute a combined figure of merit for each alternative for the data in the above tabulation.

c) How would you combine these figures of merit with figures of merit for a monetary attribute to come up with a combined figure of merit for each alternative?

27-25 In this chapter, we used one monetary attribute in the examples and problems. However, we could also have used the variance of the monetary attribute as still another attribute. Explain how you would incorporate variance into an MAA. How would you rank it? How would you weight it? How could you introduce risk without calculating variances?

____28
MULTIATTRIBUTE ANALYSIS: AHP AND RISK PREFERENCE

28.1 INTRODUCTION

This chapter has two main objectives. The first is to introduce you to the analytical hierarchy process (AHP), which represents a different approach to multiattribute analysis than the approaches we discussed in Chapter 27. The second is to cover an attribute that we have so far excluded from our analyses, namely, risk preference.

The AHP method was developed by Thomas Saaty (1)(2). It lets us set up complex problems involving attributes, subattributes, sub-subattributes, and so on, in an orderly, structured manner. It is not intended to replace the methods presented in Chapter 27 but, rather, to extend them for a more refined evaluation of the two or three alternatives that received the highest ratings. This is particularly worthwhile if such ratings are close.

The second topic—risk preference—is not usually included in discussions of multiattribute analysis. However, there are advantages in doing so. As mentioned, it introduces an attribute to which we have so far payed only cursory attention—the risk preference of investors. These preferences are shaped by two factors—the risk propensity of investors and their ability to accept the losses that risk entails. One or both factors may result in decisions that run counter to what our analyses show.

28.2 THE ANALYTICAL HIERARCHY PROCESS

The analytical hierarchy process is based on erecting a multilevel structure of attributes and alternatives. At the top of the structure—level 1—is the objective of the analysis; what Saaty calls "the focus." The alternatives are at the bottom level of the structure. The attributes, subattributes, and so on, lie between the focus and the alternatives. A structure containing just four levels would thus be built up as follows:

> Level 1   The objective
> Level 2   The attributes
> Level 3   The subattributes
> Level 4   The alternatives

A four-level hierarchy is shown in Figure 28.1. The attributes are identified by F_1, F_2 . . ., the subattributes by F_{12}, F_{21}, . . ., and the alternatives by A_1, A_2. . . . The letter F stands for "factor," which is often used as a synonym for "attribute." We will use both terms from here on. Any item in Figure 28.1 is referred to as an "element." Level 1 has one element. The other levels have more than one element. If they did not, there would be no need for a multiattribute analysis.

There are occasions when three levels will do and others when four levels are not enough. No matter how many levels are used, it is important that the hierarchy be maintained, that is, that a factor (attribute) and a subfactor, or a subfactor and a sub-subfactor not be shown at the same level.

In order to construct a hierarchy, it is necessary to have identified the alternatives and the factors. In what follows, we assume that this has been

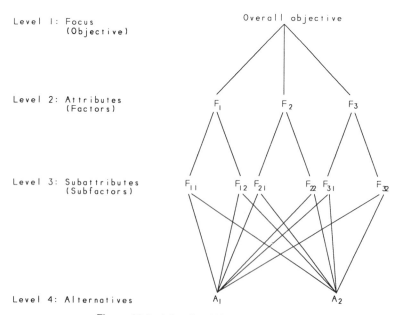

Figure 28.1. A four-level hierarchy for the AHP.

done for a three-level hierarchy (no subfactors) and that such a hierarchy has been constructed. From that point on, we proceed as follows:

Step 1 Weight the factors (attributes).
Step 2 Weight the alternatives with respect to each factor.
Step 3 Weight the alternatives.

The three steps may seem confusing, but each proceeds logically from the first to the next. We think we can convince you that this is so as we work our way through several problems.

28.3 WEIGHTING THE FACTORS (ATTRIBUTES)

Weighting for the analytical hierarchy process (AHP) is done differently than in Chapter 27. There we used scaling and utility values. Here we make pairwise comparisons of elements within a given level to determine what each element contributes to the level above it. For level 2, for example, we pair the factors to see what each contributes to level 1, the objective.

If we had four levels, we would also weight the subfactors (level 3) for their importance to the factors (level 2) with which they are associated. It is easy to see that this methodology could be extended to any number of levels between the lowest level (the alternatives) and the upper level (the focus or objective).

As mentioned, the weighting is done using paired comparisons that are conveniently represented in the form of a matrix. The weights usually consist of numbers on a scale of 1–9, as illustrated in Table 28.1.

The numbers 2, 4, 6, and 8 can be used to reduce the gap between "importance" in ratings. Thus, 8 might be assigned to a rating of "very much more important," lying halfway between "much more important" and "most important."

Consider any two factors, F_x and F_y. If F_y is "clearly more important" than F_x, then the relative importance of F_y as compared to F_x is, by Table 28.1, equal to 5. Conversely, the relative importance of F_x as compared to F_y is the reciprocal of 5, that is, $\frac{1}{5}$. This suggests a second table, such as Table 28.2.

TABLE 28.1 Weighting Scale for "More Important Than"

Importance of Any Factor (Attribute) in Comparison with Any Other Factor	Scale
Equally important	1
A little more important	3
Clearly more important	5
Much more important	7
Most important	9

TABLE 28.2 Weighting Scale for "Less Important Than"

Importance of Any Factor (Attribute) in Comparison with Any Other Factor	Scale
Equally important	1
A little less important	$\frac{1}{3}$
Clearly less important	$\frac{1}{5}$
Much less important	$\frac{1}{7}$
Least important	$\frac{1}{9}$

How we use Tables 28.1 and 28.2 is illustrated in Example 28.1, in which we expand on the corporate site relocation problem of Example 27.7.

Example 28.1 Weighting the Attributes The employees in the corporate reloca-tion problem of Example 27.7 were concerned with four attributes—monetary (the savings in EUAC of their employer due to relocation), recreational facilities, hous-ing, and schooling—and four alternatives—sites 1, 2, 3, and 4. The three-level hierarchy is shown in Figure 28.2. For the time being, concentrate on the structure and forget about the numbers shown on the rays to and from the elements.

For Step 1 of the AHP methodology, we take each attribute, give it a rating of 1, and then compare the other attributes with it by using Tables 28.1 and 28.2. The easiest way to make such comparisons is with the help of a matrix, such as Table 28.3.

To prepare such matrices, first put 1's in the diagonal for which the rows match the columns, since every attribute is "equally important" to itself. Thus, for row 1, put a 1 under column F_1; for row 2, put a 1 under column F_2, and so on. Next, let the employee spokespersons say how important the monetary attribute is com-pared to recreational facilities. They agree that monetary is $\frac{1}{3}$ as important or, conversely, that recreational facilities is three times more important. A $\frac{1}{3}$ goes in row 1 under column F_2 and a 3 goes in row 2 under column F_1. Schooling and housing are rated as 9 times more important than monetary, so a 9 gets put in rows 3 and 4 under column F_1 and $\frac{1}{9}$ gets put in row 1 under columns F_3 and F_4. We continue in this way, remembering that the numbers above the diagonal are re-ciprocals of the numbers below the diagonal. In other words, if you have answers to the paired comparisons above the diagonal, you can immediately fill in the numbers below the diagonal, or the other way round. This reciprocal relationship means that you don't need both Tables 28.1 and 28.2; either one will do. However, having them both is helpful in resolving inconsistent answers (which we will discuss later) on the relative importance or unimportance of paired comparisons.

The matrix is now normalized; that is, the totals in Table 28.3 are set equal to 1.00 (10 and 100 could also be used), and the decimal equivalents are revalued proportionately. The results are given in Table 28.4.

The "Average" column gives the "priority weights" of the factors. Housing ranks first. Schooling comes next. Recreational facilities and monetary are far

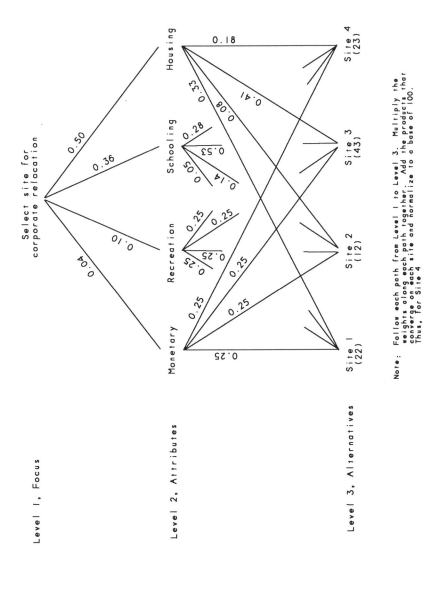

Figure 28.2. Hierarchy for corporate relocation.

TABLE 28.3   Matrix of Paired Comparisons for Factors

		F_1	F_2	F_3	F_4	Decimals			
						F_1	F_2	F_3	F_4
F_1	Monetary	1	⅓	⅑	⅑	1	0.33	0.11	0.11
F_2	Recreational facilities	3	1	⅕	⅕	3	1	0.2	0.2
F_3	Schooling	9	5	1	½	9	5	1	0.5
F_4	Housing	9	5	2	1	9	5	2	1
					Total	22	11.33	3.31	1.81

behind. These weights, normalized to a base of 100, are compared in the tabulation which follows with the results obtained in Example 27.7 by using utility values:

		AHP (Example 28.1)	Utility Values (Example 27.7)
F_1	Monetary	4	4
F_2	Recreational facilities	10	15
F_3	Schooling	36	37
F_4	Housing	50	44
	Total	100	100

The correspondence between the two approaches is good. Which is correct? They both are. Which should you use? The one with which you can obtain the better responses. Some people may feel more comfortable answering "more important than" and "less important than" questions than answering questions on utility evaluations. However, this is only a surmise. A common approach is to use utility values and, if the top two or three contenders are close, to follow up with AHP.

This completes Step 1, the weighting of the factors. We now have to follow a similar procedure for Step 2.

TABLE 28.4   Normalized Matrix for Factors

		F_1	F_2	F_3	F_4	Row Total	Average (Total/4)
F_1	Monetary	0.05	0.03	0.03	0.06	0.17	0.04
F_2	Recreational facilities	0.13	0.09	0.06	0.11	0.39	0.10
F_3	Schooling	0.41	0.44	0.30	0.28	1.43	0.36
F_4	Housing	0.41	0.44	0.61	0.55	2.01	0.50
	Total	1.00	1.00	1.00	1.00	4.00	1.00

28.4 WEIGHTING FACTOR CONTRIBUTIONS TO EACH ALTERNATIVE

Does factor F_x contribute more or less to alternative A_x than to alternative A_y? This is the type of question that we have to ask regarding the contribution of each factor to each alternative. How we proceed is shown in Example 28.2.

Example 28.2 Weighting Factor Contributions There are four factors to consider. Therefore, we need four matrices to set down the results of paired comparisons for each factor. For each matrix, the employees are again asked questions based on the rating scales of Tables 28.1 and 28.2. The answers received on schooling appear in Table 28.5.

Schooling at site 1 is "clearly less important" ("clearly poorer") than schooling at site 2. Therefore, a rating of $\frac{1}{5}$ for site 1 is put under column A_2 and a rating of 5 is put in row 2 under column A_1. Similarly, schooling at site 1 is "least important" compared to site 3 and is "clearly less important" than site 4. The respective ratings in row 1 under columns A_3 and A_4 are, therefore, $\frac{1}{9}$ and $\frac{1}{5}$, and the ratings in rows 3 and 4 under column A_1 are 9 and 5, respectively. The remaining blanks in rows 2, 3, and 4 are arrived at in the same way.

The totals in the matrix of Table 28.5 are normalized in Table 28.6 to a base of 1.

Site 3 is preferred for schooling. Site 4 comes next. The results are the same as in Example 27.7 for ordinal scaling but, as shown in Table 28.7, substantially different with regard to weighting.

The utility values come from Table 27.4 and, like the weights for AHP, have been normalized to a base of 100.

How do we explain the differences between the two approaches? Sites 2, 3, and 4 are much closer together in Example 27.7 than in Example 28.1. We said in the introduction that the AHP is often used to compare the top two or three alternatives that receive the highest ratings and is particularly valuable if these ratings are close. The difference between a rating of 31 and 35 using utility values has grown into a difference between a rating of 28 and 53 for AHP.

Matrices for monetary, housing, and recreation are prepared in the same way. The results, including schooling, are given in Table 28.8.

How did we get 0.25 for all four sites for both F_1 and F_2? We decided (quite arbitrarily) that, since these two factors carry so little weight compared to the other

TABLE 28.5 Matrix of Alternatives for Factor F_3: Schooling

		A_1	A_2	A_3	A_4	Decimals A_1	A_2	A_3	A_4
A_1	Site 1	1	$\frac{1}{5}$	$\frac{1}{9}$	$\frac{1}{5}$	1	0.20	0.11	0.20
A_2	Site 2	5	1	$\frac{1}{5}$	$\frac{1}{3}$	5	1	0.2	0.33
A_3	Site 3	9	5	1	2	9	5	1	2
A_4	Site 4	5	3	$\frac{1}{2}$	1	5	3	0.5	1
					Total	20	9.20	1.81	3.53

TABLE 28.6   Normalized Matrix for Factor F₃: Schooling

		A₁	A₂	A₃	A₄	Total	Average (Total/4)
A₁	Site 1	0.05	0.02	0.06	0.06	0.19	0.05
A₂	Site 2	0.25	0.11	0.11	0.09	0.56	0.14
A₃	Site 3	0.45	0.54	0.55	0.57	2.12	0.53
A₄	Site 4	0.25	0.32	0.28	0.28	1.13	0.28
	Total	1.00	1.00	1.00	1.00	4.00	1.00

TABLE 28.7   Weightings for F₃: Schooling

		AHP (Example 28.1)	Utility Values (Example 27.7)
A₁	Site 1	5	10
A₂	Site 2	14	24
A₃	Site 3	53	35
A₄	Site 4	28	31
	Total	100	100

TABLE 28.8   Normalized Weightings for Factors F₁, F₂, F₃, and F₄

		F₁ Monetary	F₂ Recreation	F₃ Schooling	F₄ Housing
A₁	Site 1	0.25	0.25	0.05	0.33
A₂	Site 2	0.25	0.25	0.14	0.08
A₃	Site 3	0.25	0.25	0.53	0.41
A₄	Site 4	0.25	0.25	0.28	0.18
	Total	1.00	1.00	1.00	1.00

TABLE 28.9   Matrix for Factor F₄: Housing

		A₁	A₂	A₃	A₄	Average (Normalized)
A₁	Site 1	1	3	1	2	0.33
A₂	Site 2	⅓	1	⅕	⅓	0.08
A₃	Site 3	1	5	1	3	0.41
A₄	Site 4	½	3	⅓	1	0.18
	Total	2.83	12	2.53	6.33	1.00

TABLE 28.10   Weightings for F_4: Housing

		AHP (Example 28.2)	Utility Values (Example 27.7)
A_1	Site 1	33	28
A_2	Site 2	8	17
A_3	Site 3	41	31
A_4	Site 4	18	24
	Total	100	100

two factors (*see* Table 28.4), we might as well give each site an equal rating. For four sites, this rating would have to be 1.00/4, or 0.25, for each site. For schooling, the values shown come from Table 28.6. For housing, we used the matrix in Table 28.9.

The priority weights in the last column of Table 28.9 are compared with those for utility evaluations (*see* Example 27.7) in Table 28.10. The utility values, like those for schooling, come from Table 27.4 and are normalized to a base of 100. The ordinal scaling is identical for both methodologies. The spread of the weightings differs substantially, as it did for schooling.

This concludes Step 2. We now have everything we need to proceed with Step 3.

28.5   WEIGHTING THE ALTERNATIVES

Step 3 is easy. All we need to do is take the normalized weights in Table 28.8 and apply them against the normalized weights in Table 28.4 multiplied by 100. The computations follow.

Site 1: $4(0.25) + 10(0.25) + 36(0.05) + 50(0.33) = 21.8$

Site 2: $4(0.25) + 10(0.25) + 36(0.14) + 50(0.08) = 12.5$

Site 3: $4(0.25) + 10(0.25) + 36(0.53) + 50(0.41) = 43.1$

Site 4: $4(0.25) + 10(0.25) + 36(0.28) + 50(0.18) = 22.6$

The figures within parentheses are the matrix of Table 28.8. Those outside the parentheses are the priority weights in Table 28.4 multiplied by 100.

Site 3 is a clear winner for the site relocation, as far as the employees are concerned. Site 4 comes next, followed by sites 1 and 2.

The differences between these ratings and those for the utility evaluations are compared in the following tabulation. Both sets of figures have been normalized to a base of 100 and have been rounded as shown.

		AHP (Example 28.2)	Utility Values (Example 27.7)
A_1	Site 1	22	21.5
A_2	Site 2	12	20.5
A_3	Site 3	43	31
A_4	Site 4	23	27
	Total	100	100

Site 3 is ahead, and site 4 comes in next for both methodologies. The small difference in the utility values of sites 1 and 2 (21.5 versus 20.5) is accentuated under AHP.

Everything we did in applying AHP to the corporate relocation problem is shown in Figure 28.2. Note the resemblance of this figure to a tree diagram and to the probability distributions of Part III. The numbers on the rays from Level 1 to Level 2 are the priority weights from the last column of Table 28.4. The weights of the four sets of rays from Level 2 to Level 3 are from Table 28.8. The sum of the weights of all of the rays coming from any given element total 1. To get the figures of merit for the alternatives, we follow each path from Level 1 to Level 3, multiply the weights along each path together, and add the resulting products of the rays that converge on each site. Thus, for site 4,

$$\text{Figure of merit} = [(0.04 \times 0.25) + (0.10 \times 0.25) +$$
$$(0.36 \times 0.28) + (0.50 \times 0.19)] \times 100$$
$$= 23$$

Many of you will find it convenient to have such a figure at hand as you carry out a multiattribute analysis using the analytical hierarchy process.

28.6 CONSISTENCY RATIO

Inconsistencies will crop up when you are making paired comparisons. The more attributes and the more alternatives there are, the greater the probability that this will occur. A rather blatant example is to have someone tell you that they prefer A to B, B to C, and C to D and, after more reflection, tell you that they really prefer D to A (it happens).

There is a way of checking paired comparisons for consistency. For the factors in Table 28.3, the consistency ratio is 0.03, which is considered acceptable, as is any ratio of 0.10 or less. For how this ratio is calculated, see Appendix 28A.

28.7 ANOTHER APPLICATION OF AHP

Concurrent engineering has been adopted by many manufacturing companies to reduce the time for putting a new product on the market. It differs from conventional or traditional engineering in that engineering, design, testing, and initial production all overlap with engineering in constant attendance throughout the entire process to correct mistakes, solve problems, improve designs, and do whatever else has to be done to move toward steady production as quickly as possible. In Example 28.3, we apply what we have learned about AHP to a comparison of traditional and concurrent engineering.

Example 28.3   Traditional Versus Concurrent Engineering   A manufacturing company has decided to enter into a new market with a product line that differs from its present lines. A new production facility has to be built as quickly as possible, since there are strong indications that other companies are planning to manufacture competitive products. The company decides to compare traditional and concurrent engineering, using AHP.

A four-level hierarchy is used to help solve this problem. The attributes and subattributes have been identified and are shown in Figure 28.3. The two alternatives are traditional engineering (TE) and concurrent engineering (CE).

Notice how the hierarchy is drawn. There are no rays crossing other rays, as there were in Figure 28.2. This figure is now a tree diagram, like those we used in solving probability problems in Part III. Compare, for example, Figure 22.5 with Figure 28.3.

The second level in Figure 28.3 indicates two attributes—strategic considerations (A_1) and operational considerations (A_2) that support the strategy. The strategic considerations attribute breaks down into two subattributes—market share (A_{11}) and competition (A_{12}). The operational considerations attribute is made up of four subattributes—quality (A_{21}), flexibility (A_{22}), reliability (A_{23}), and cost savings (A_{24}).

For the contribution of the attributes of Level 2 to the objective of Level 1, the following matrix was accepted by the management committee:

	A_1	A_2	Priority Weights
A_1 Strategy	1	3	0.75
A_2 Operations	⅓	1	0.25
		Total	1.00

As shown, the committee felt that strategy was a "little more important" than operations, and A_1 therefore rated a 3 as compared with A_2.

COMMENT: Note how AHP accentuates differences. Being a "little more important" gave strategy a priority weight three times greater than that of operations (0.75 versus 0.25). This is the reason AHP is effective in comparing alternatives that are close together based on utility evaluations. It is also the

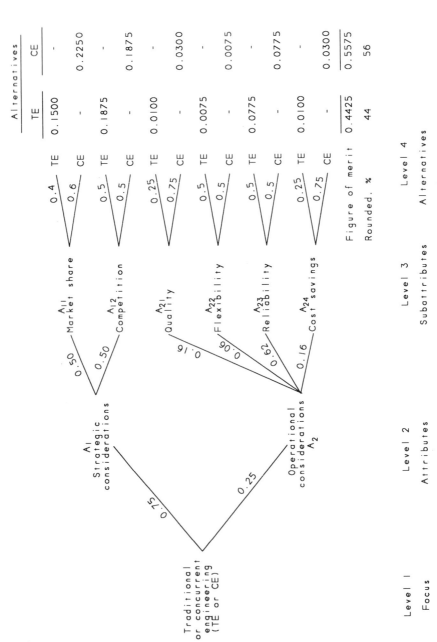

Figure 28.3. Hierarchy for traditional versus concurrent engineering.

TABLE 28.11   Matrix for Operational Subattributes

	F_{21}	F_{22}	F_{23}	F_{24}	Priority Weights
F_{21} Quality	1	3	⅓	½	0.16
F_{22} Flexibility	⅓	1	⅑	½	0.06
F_{23} Reliability	3	9	1	7	0.62
F_{24} Cost savings	2	2	⅐	1	0.16
Total	6.33	15	1.58	9	1.00

reason that we have to be careful in interpreting the results of studies based on AHP.

For operations, the paired comparisons shown in Table 28.11 were used to arrive at priority weights.

The priority weights for the attributes and subattributes are shown on Figure 28.3. With the attributes, we move from Level 1 to Level 2, and, with the subattributes, we move from Level 2 to Level 3. We are not going to spend any time in going from Level 3 to Level 4. You will have to accept the weights shown in Figure 28.3.

All you have to do now is use the multiplication rule to arrive at the weights in the two columns on the right side of Figure 28.3. For the path from Level 1 to A_1, A_{11}, and TE, for example, the combined weight is 0.15:

$$0.75 \times 0.50 \times 0.4 = 0.15$$

Adding together all of the paths that lead to one or the other of the two alternatives gives a figure of merit for traditional engineering (TE) of 44, as compared with 56 for concurrent engineering (CE).

This concludes our discussion of the AHP. We now turn to risk preference.

28.8   INTRODUCTION TO RISK PREFERENCE

Risk preference obviously depends not only on an investor's attitude toward risk but also on his or her resources. We know that the utility of a dollar is higher for a poor man than for a rich one. Similarly, the utility of $100,000 for a small corporation is higher than the utility of the same sum for a large corporation.

Consider the situation in Example 28.4.

Example 28.4   Resources and Risk Preference   Suppose you had the opportunity to place a bet with a 90% probability of winning $250,000 or a 10% probability of losing $500,000. The expected value of not betting is, of course, zero, and the expected value of betting is $175,000, as shown in the following equation.

$$\text{E[Betting]} = \$250,000 \times 0.90 - \$500,000 \times 0.10 = \$175,000$$

The expected value criterion tells you to bet. For a bet of this size, whether you bet or not may have little to do with your risk propensity. It may depend, rather, on your ability to absorb a loss of $500,000. However, your risk propensity might show up if the sums involved were smaller, say a gain of $250 or a loss of $500. Many of us can tolerate a loss of $500. If so, whether we accept such a bet or not depends not so much on our resources as on our attitude toward taking risks.

There are many instances in which the expected value criterion will not be accepted by decision makers. These fall into two broad categories:

1. Those in which a small cost will avoid a large loss
2. Those in which a small cost may bring a substantial gain

Consider insurance. The expected value of "not insuring" is lower than the expected value of "insuring." If it were not, the insurance companies would go broke. Their cash receipts from your insurance payments and millions of others have to be greater than the cash disbursements for insurance claims. Example 28.5 illustrates the expected value of insurance from your viewpoint.

Example 28.5   Fire Insurance on Your Home   The expected value of not insuring is the probability of losing your house to fire multiplied by the value of the house. If this probability is 1/1,000 in any given year and your house is worth $200,000, the expected value of not insuring is

$$\text{E[Not insuring]} = -\$200,000(0.001) = -\$200/\text{year}$$

The expected value of insurance is the cost of the insurance, say $500 annually:

$$\text{E[Insuring]} = -\$500/\text{year}$$

The expected value of not insuring is $+\$300$ greater than the expected value of insuring. The expected value criterion tells you not to insure. You do, nevertheless, because it makes good sense.

The obverse of this situation is a lottery in which a small loss can bring a large gain. The expected value of not gambling is zero. The expected value of gambling is the product of the prize times the probability of winning less your stake. This value has to be less than zero, or the gambling houses would be bankrupt. The expected value criterion breaks down again. This time, you waive it, not because it makes good sense to do so, but because your gut feelings say you are going to win.

Insurance and gambling are lotteries. So are business ventures. Investors do not know how their investments will turn out. They do know that, the riskier the investment, the lower the probability that the investment will meet its stated goals. One could cite numerous examples of commercial and man-ufacturing facilities that were completed but never operated or operated at far below their planned capacity because markets had disappeared, prices had fallen, raw material costs had increased, experienced management had gone elsewhere, taxes had increased, or legal and environmental restrictions had imposed conditions that were not expected at the time that the decision to proceed was made.

Investors differ in their risk preference, that is, in the amount of risk they are willing to accept. One measure of the difference is their "certainty equiv-alent," which we will examine in the next section.

28.9 CERTAINTY EQUIVALENT

A certainty equivalent is a certain cash sum that is as desirable (but not more so) as a given risky investment. By saying it is "as desirable but not more so," we are saying that the utility of the certain sum is the same as the utility of the lottery represented by the risky investment. In short,

$$u(\text{certain sum}) = u(\text{lottery}) \tag{28.1}$$

A lottery will have a "best" possible outcome, to which we assign a utility value of 10, and a "worst" possible outcome, to which we assign a utility value of 0. If the probabilities of the "best" and "worst" outcomes are p and $(1 - p)$, respectively, then the utility of the lottery is

$$u(\text{lottery}) = p \times 10 + (1 - p) \times 0 = 10p \tag{28.2}$$

This is, by equation (28.1), also the utility of whatever certain sum an investor will accept in lieu of the lottery. The size of this sum depends on the risk propensity of the investor.

Assume that two decision makers are faced with the choice of a certain sum X or of a lottery in which there is an equal chance of winning $5 million or losing $2 million. The expected value of the lottery is $1.5 million, as shown in the following equation:

$$\text{E[Lottery]} = 5 \times 0.5 - 2 \times 0.5 = 1.5 \ (\$1.5 \text{ million})$$

One of the decision makers is risk-prone or at least less risk-averse than the other. What are the respective values of X? The greater the preference or, rather, the tolerance for risk, the higher the X. In other words, for any given investment (read "lottery," which most investments in capital projects are), the certainty equivalent for the most risk-averse investor is the lowest and for the least risk-averse investor, the highest. For both investors, it is probably, but not necessarily, less than the expected value of $1,500,000. Example 28.6 follows.

Example 28.6   Risk Preference   Your firm is a well-known engineering contractor. It has been asked to express interest in bidding a fixed price (lump sum) on a petrochemical complex. Conceptual estimates for the complex were prepared by the owner. You, in your capacity as head of the contractor's cost engineering department, have had a chance to review these estimates and agree that they are reasonable. The fixed-price bids prepared by your firm and its competitors will therefore be within this range. Your preliminary estimate of the profit that your firm might earn on a project of this size is $5 million after taxes.

The cost of preparing a fixed-price bid is high. You estimate that the preproposal costs (costs up to and including the cost of preparing the proposal) and the post-proposal costs (costs after submitting the proposal up to the time an award is made) could run to $1,500,000. Since proposal costs are a business expense, there will be an offset due to reduced income tax payments. You estimate that the net effect of bidding is a cash outflow of $1,000,000.

The sales department expects that three or four bidders will be on the owner's bid list but assesses the chances of obtaining the award as closer to 50% than 25–33% because of your firm's knowledge of the processes involved and its experience in working in the foreign location where the facility is to be built. However, the estimated net cash outflow for bidding of $1,000,000 is a concern, particularly since your financial officer has advised that your firm could shortly be faced with a cash flow problem.

The expected value of not bidding is zero. For a possible gain of $5 million with a probability of 0.5 and a possible loss of $1 million with a probability of 0.5, the expected value of bidding is $2 million as shown by the following equation.

$$E[\text{Bidding}] = 5.0 \times 0.5 - 1.0 + 0.5 = 2 \ (\$2 \text{ million})$$

The utility of being awarded the contract is 10 and of losing it is 0. The utility of the lottery (the bidding process) is, by equation (28.2), equal to 5:

$$u(\text{bid}) = 10 \times 0.5 = 5$$

A Far Eastern engineering contractor with much experience in the location where the facility is to be built is attempting to get on the list of bidders. It has a strong engineering staff but little experience with the engineering and design of several of the petrochemical processes. For this reason, it has asked your firm to bid with it as its subcontractor for the conceptual engineering work and much of the detail engineering for these processes. Your firm will be paid its bidding costs plus a fee of $1,250,000, whether the contractor is successful or not. In addition, the earnings on the engineering and design work could produce a like amount.

The Far Eastern contractor's motivation in offering you $1,250,000 is sound. It could remove a substantial competitor from the bid list, and its chances of at least getting on the list are much enhanced (almost a certainty). What does your firm do?

The choice is between a lottery, which is a gamble, and a certainty, which is not. The certainty would bring in at least $750,000 after taxes (about two-thirds of the fee) and much more if the Far Eastern bidder is awarded the contract. It would also ease or remove your firm's cash flow problem.

The utility graph of Figure 28.4 illustrates the choices. The expected value line of the lottery and its expected value are shown. The utility value of the lottery is

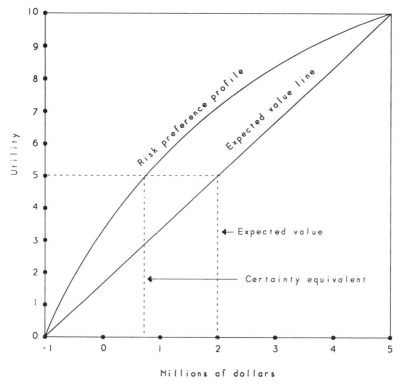

Figure 28.4. Utility graph for Example 28.6.

5, which is also the utility of the certainty equivalent [see equation (28.1)]. If your firm accepts its competitor's offer to be its subcontractor, its certainty equivalent is $750,000 after taxes.

We have three points for sketching the risk preference profile of your firm under current conditions. This profile is the concave-downward curve shown in Figure 28.4. Often, more points for sketching such a profile are obtained by asking such questions as, "What would the certainty equivalent be for an expected value of $4 million?" If the answer is $3 million, the answer is consistent with the curve as drawn; if not, more questions are asked until a curve is obtained that gives reasonably consistent answers. We would expect such a curve to have the shape shown.

Figure 28.4 also gives us the opportunity to compare the risk propensity of investors. In this figure, the further to the left we move on the horizontal line for a utility of 5, the more risk-averse the investor is. Thus, an investor who would accept a certain sum of $500,000 is more risk-averse than the investor of our example. His profile would be more concave, that is, would depart more from the expected value line.

The risk preference profile is concave upward for a risk-prone investor. If, in our example, such an investor would require $3 million to prevent him or her from bidding, the certainty equivalent for a utility of 5 would be to the right of the expected value.

This concludes our discussion of the application of utility theory to risk preference. We have done little more than scratch the surface of utility theory. However, we believe that we have taken you as far as it is currently necessary to go for making decisions on selecting capital projects.

28.10   SUMMARY

Chapter 28 concludes Part IV on multiattribute analysis. Its major topics are the analytical hierarchy process (AHP) and the risk preference of investors.

AHP is based on erecting a multilevel structure that is focused on an objective or goal and can be presented as a tree diagram leading from the goal to the alternatives through one or more levels of attributes. The attributes include both monetary and nonmonetary consequences.

For a three-level structure, AHP first weights the attributes for their contribution to the goal and then weights each attribute for its contribution to the alternatives. The weights are used to compute a figure of merit for each alternative. For structures with more than three levels, a similar process is followed, except that we now deal not only with attributes but also with subattributes, sub-subattributes, and so on.

The weighting is carried out by pairing comparisons with the help of "more important" and "less important" scales. This weighting methodology is particularly helpful in accentuating differences between alternatives where other evaluation methods, such as utility values, give close results.

Risk preference is an extension of utility theory. Investments in capital projects are treated as lotteries, which is what most of them really are. The utility of a lottery is its best value, which is arbitrarily assigned a 1 or 10 or 100, multiplied by the probability of attaining that value [equation (28.2)]. For every lottery, there is presumably a certainty equivalent, that is, a certain sum that an investor will accept in lieu of the lottery and for which the utility value is therefore the same as that of the lottery [equation (28.1)].

Investors differ in their tolerance for risk. For a given investment, risk-averse investors will have lower certainty equivalents than risk-prone investors. This concept is important to the selection process for capital projects because it introduces still another subjective element into this process, namely, the risk tolerance or preference of investors.

REFERENCES

1. Thomas L. Saaty, *The Analytical Hierarchy Process* (New York: McGraw-Hill, 1980). This and the following reference are the basic texts on AHP.
2. Thomas L. Saaty, *Decision Making for Leaders* (Belmont, CA: Wadsworth Publishing Company, 1982).

SUGGESTED READING

1. John R. Canada and William G. Sullivan, *Economic and Multiattribute Evaluation of Advanced Manufacturing Systems* (Englewood Cliffs, NJ: Prentice Hall, 1989). Chapter 10 of this text gives an excellent presentation of the AHP method, which goes further than ours. One of the authors (Canada) has suggested a weighting system that differs from, but is not necessarily any better than, Saaty's. You will find it in the problem set.

PROBLEMS

The Analytical Hierarchy Process

28-1 Sketch Figure 28.1 so that it resembles Figure 28.4, that is, so that there are no rays crossing other rays. Suppose one of the subattributes in this figure was involved with all three of the attributes. How would you draw the figure to eliminate rays crossing?

28-2 Use the AHP method to analyze the corporate relocation problem of Example 27.7 from the manager's viewpoint. You will find everything you need in that example to make intelligent guesses on the answers you would get from the managers to questions based on Tables 28.1 and 28.2. Go through the entire procedure that we followed in Examples 28.1 and 28.2.

28-3 Normalize the utility values of Table 27.4 in Example 27.7, using a base of 100, and check the comparisons between the utility and the AHP methods in Examples 28.1 and 28.2.

28-4 Check the priority weights and the consistency ratio of the matrix for schooling in Table 28.6. What do you do if the consistency ratio is higher than 0.10?

28-5 Check the priority weights and the consistency ratio of the matrix for housing in Table 28.9.

28-6 Check the priority weights and the consistency ratio for the matrix in Table 28.11.

28-7 Go to Figure 28-3 and set up the matrices for the rays from Level 3 to Level 4.

28-8 Fill in the missing numbers in the following matrices, in which the attributes are identified as A, B, C, and D.

	A	B		A	B		A	B		A	B
A	1							½			
B		1			1					⅕	

	A	B	C		A	B	C		A	B	C
A		2	⅓				2			1	1
B			⅕		5						1
C						⅓					

	A	B	C	D		A	B	C	D
A		7						5	
B			2			3			
C	3							2	9
D	5	2	⅓			⅑	¼		

28-9 Pick a topic from your personal or working experience that involved at least four attributes and at least three alternatives. Perform a complete analysis of this topic, using the AHP method. Your analysis should include a hierarchy in the form of a tree diagram, matrices, and priority weight computations. Record the priority weights on the tree diagram, and calculate the figure of merit for each alternative, using the multiplication rule as we did for probability distributions.

28-10 In all of the examples on the AHP method, we had one monetary factor and several nonmonetary factors. None of the monetary factors included the variance. Could this factor be brought into the AHP method? If so, how? Is there a better method of doing so?

28-11 Consider any problem to be solved by the AHP method. Let the alternatives be X, Y, and Z, and let the attributes be A, B, C, and D. There are subattributes for each attribute. How many matrices would you need to obtain priority weights for a tree diagram? Set up the matrices (without weightings, of course) to show how they would be structured.

28-12 Suppose there are three attributes, of which two have subattributes. Would you show the attribute that has no subattributes on Level 2 or 3? Does it make any difference?

28-13 We have said repeatedly that the AHP method accentuates differences between alternatives. Canada (one of the authors of the Suggested Reading) has suggested an alternative scale that substitutes 1, 1.5, 2, 2.5, and 3 for Saaty's scale of 1, 3, 5, 7, and 9. Rework the matrix in Table 28.4, using Canada's preference ratings, and compare the results with the utility value approach of Example 27.7. Comment on your findings.

28-14 Refer to Problem 28-13. Do the same for the matrices of Tables 28.6, 28.9, and 28.11.

Risk Preference

28-15   You tell your wealthy old aunt that you are going to wager $25 on a state lottery. She is violently against betting of any kind and will bribe you to keep you from doing so. You feel especially lucky. This is your winning day for the big jackpot! What is your certainty equivalent for this situation?

28-16   You sketched the risk profile of the investor in Example 28.6, using just three points, namely, (0,0), (0.75,5), and (5,10). You now want to refine this sketch, and so you ask what certain sum would be accepted in lieu of the lottery if its expected value was (a) $2.5 million and (b) $1.5 million. What would the answers have to be for consistency with the curve as drawn?

28-17   Conditions have changed. Your firm in Example 28-6 has received a substantial settlement on a lawsuit and no longer has a cash flow problem. What would happen to its certainty equivalent? Why?

28-18   If you own a house, check how much fire insurance costs you and ask your insurance agent about the risk of loss (he or she may know). Then check the expectcd value of insuring versus not insuring.

28-19   How would you, or rather how could you, incorporate risk preference into the AHP method? Is this the best way to handle this attribute? If not, what would you suggest?

APPENDIX 28A   CONSISTENCY RATIOS

The method described below is an algorithm for approximating the consistency of a set of pair-wise comparisons. It defines a consistency ratio (CR) as a fraction for which the numerator is a consistency index (CI) and the denominator is a random index (RI). Thus,

$$\text{CR} = \text{CI/RI} \qquad (28A.1)$$

To get the consistency index (CI) of a set of paired comparisons, the first step is to compute the product of two matrices, which we refer to as **P** and **Q** in what follows. This product is matrix **R**. Matrix **P** is a square matrix (it has the same number of rows as columns) of order 4, such as those in Tables 28.3, 28.5, and 28.9. Matrix **Q** is a column matrix (it has only one column) of the respective priority weights. For the pair-wise comparisons of Table 28.3 and the priority weights of Table 28.4, the value of **R** is computed as follows:

$$
\begin{array}{ccccc}
\mathbf{P} & \times & \mathbf{Q} & = & \mathbf{R} \\
\begin{bmatrix} 1 & 0.33 & 0.11 & 0.11 \\ 3 & 1 & 0.2 & 0.2 \\ 9 & 5 & 1 & 0.5 \\ 9 & 5 & 2 & 1 \end{bmatrix} & \times & \begin{bmatrix} 0.04 \\ 0.10 \\ 0.36 \\ 0.50 \end{bmatrix} & = & \begin{bmatrix} 0.17 \\ 0.39 \\ 1.47 \\ 2.08 \end{bmatrix}
\end{array}
$$

You may have forgotten how to compute the product of a square matrix by a column matrix with the same number of rows. Just take the first row of **P** and multiply it by the elements of **Q**:

$$1(0.04) + 0.33(0.10) + 0.11(0.36) + 0.11(0.50) = 0.17$$

We will let you do the same for rows 2, 3, and 4.

The next step is to divide each element of **R** by the corresponding element in **Q** and average the results.

	R/Q	
0.17/0.04	=	4.25
0.39/0.10	=	3.90
1.47/0.36	=	4.08
2.08/0.50	=	4.16
Total		16.39
Average		4.10

The average is a characteristic or eigenvalue. Call it lambda (λ). The consistency index (CI) for a square matrix of order N (in our case 4) is then

$$CI = (\lambda - N)/(N - 1) = (4.10 - 4)/(4 - 1) = 0.03$$

For the denominator of the CR, we use the random index approximations of Saaty. These are based on a large number of simulations, for which the "pairing" of "paired comparison" was done randomly. The values of RI for matrices ranging in size from 1 to 10 are as follows:

N	1	2	3	4	5	6	7	8	9	10
RI	0.00	0.00	0.58	0.90	1.12	1.24	1.32	1.41	1.45	1.49

For our example, N equals 4 and RI equals 0.90. The consistency ratio is therefore

$$CR = CI/RI = 0.03/0.90 = 0.03$$

Saaty says that a CR of 0.10 is acceptable. Anything higher should prompt a review of the paired comparisons.

SUMMARY OF PART IV

This is our last opportunity to suggest that you review the "reader bites" in the previous part summaries before you proceed with this summary. If any of these bites leave you with an empty feeling, go back into the text.

1. So far we have dealt only with monetary attributes, such as net cash flow, present worth, annual worth, IRR, and BCR. Multiattribute analysis (MAA) brings nonmonetary attributes into the decision-making process. These include equity, ethics, esthetics, morale, quality, flexibility, reliability, maintainability, cleaner air, cleaner water, and many more.

2. There are attributes such as quality, safety, employee morale, and pollution that, if sufficient data are available, can be monetized. However, such attributes are often treated as nonmonetary when the cost of data gathering is excessive or might prove to be futile.

3. All of the attributes that are to take part in the decision-making process should be identified initially. Some nonmonetary attributes may be so important that their absence or presence in any given option may preclude it from becoming a candidate for a set of MEAs.

4. Cost-effective analysis (CEA) is often used when only one nonmonetary attribute is brought into the selection process. This attribute is usually a benefit or disbenefit whose effectiveness is measurable but which cannot realistically be assigned a monetary value. Typical examples are lives saved and cleaner air and water.

5. A cost-effective index measures the effectiveness of increasing a non-monetized benefit or decreasing a nonmonetized disbenefit by comparing it with the cost of doing so. The index is expressed as the ratio of cost (C) to effectiveness (E) or its reciprocal.

6. Equity is a nonmonetary attribute that is often neglected in cost studies. It deals with whether the distribution of the benefits and disbenefits among those affected by a proposed capital investment is equitable.

7. Several methodologies have been developed for carrying out multiattribute analyses for situations in which more than one (often many) nonmonetary attributes are involved. The simplest of these are sequential elimination and graphical techniques, such as score cards and polar graphs.

8. The more sophisticated methodologies involve the ranking and weighting of the alternatives that are to take part in a multiattribute analysis. The weights are used to compute figure of merits for each alternative, which encompass both monetary and nonmonetary attributes.

9. Ranking attributes is done by examining a pair of attributes at a time and coming up with a preferred selection from each pair. This method of "pairing comparisons" produces ordinal ranking (first, second, third, and so on). However, it does not produce weights for judging attributes quantitatively.

10. Weighting of attributes is done from the "top down" or from the "bottom up." For top-down weighting, the highest ranking attribute is assigned a rating, such as 100 or 1,000, and the other attributes are compared with it. For bottom-up weighting, the lower ranking attribute

is assigned a rating such as 10 or 100, and the other attributes are weighted accordingly.

11. For expressing the contribution or importance of each attribute to each alternative, utility values can also be used. A utility profile is prepared for each attribute by assigning a value of 10 (1 or 100 also are used) to the best possible outcome and a value of 0 to the worst possible outcome. In this way, the attributes are assigned a value on a common scale. If this were not done, a combined figure of merit based on the relative importance of each attribute could not be computed.

12. The analytical hierarchy process is so-called because it sets up a structure or a hierarchy starting with the objective at Level 1 and ending with the alternatives at a level determined by the number of intermediate levels of attributes (also called factors), subattributes, and so on.

13. For AHP, a rating system based on assigning relative weights of 1–9 to the importance of an attribute is used. The ratings are obtained by "pairing comparisons" and by setting up the results in a matrix.

14. Such matrices are prepared first for the importance (weightings) of the attributes (Level 2 in the hierarchy) to the objective (Level 1); next, for the importance of the subattributes to the attributes; and, finally, to the level just before the alternatives for the contribution of that level to each alternative.

15. The priority weights obtained from the normalized matrices are best portrayed on a tree diagram, in which the weights substitute for the probabilities used on tree diagrams for risk analysis.

16. Most investments in capital projects resemble lotteries in that the outcome is not known. The risk preference of investors can therefore be a significant factor in the selection process.

17. Risk preference refers to the tolerance an investor has for accepting risk. Some investors have more tolerance (are less risk-averse) than others. The tolerance, at any given time, depends not only on the personality traits of the investor but also on the resources available for absorbing a loss.

18. The tolerance can be expressed as a certainty equivalent. This is the certain sum that has the same utility value to an investor as the expected value of the lottery (read investment) in which he or she may participate.

The completion of Part IV also gives us the opportunity to look briefly at the text as a whole.

PART I: THE BASICS

In Part I, we presented the basics of engineering economy. These included cash flow patterns; discrete and continuous cash flow conventions; nominal, effective, periodic, and continuous interest rates; equations for the time value of money, with which any cash flow at any point in time (or over any period of time) can be converted to an equivalent present worth, a future worth, or an annual worth; the internal rate of return and its surrogate, the external rate of return; and, finally, the benefit-cost ratio.

PART II: ECONOMIC (DETERMINISTIC) ANALYSIS

The major topics of Part II included ranking—first for technological exclusivity and then for financial exclusivity; funding with owner and creditor financing and leasing; the selection of the MARR; the treatment of assets that are up for retirement or replacement; depreciation and other noncash expenses that affect income taxes and must therefore be included in after-tax analyses; public and multipurpose projects and regulated industries; and equivalent rates of return for simplifying the impact of inflation and other cash flow effects, which can be treated as geometric gradients. Part II wound up with a critique of the discounted cash flow methodology, which concluded that nothing currently available is any better or, if properly used, as effective for making decisions related to the selection of capital projects.

PART III: RISK ANALYSIS

In Part III, we left single-valued (deterministic) cash flow estimates for multivalued estimates. The major topics included cash flow estimates and their ranges; sensitivity analysis to determine what happens to figures of merit as cash flow and other estimates are varied from their minimum to their maximum anticipated values; discrete probability distributions and mass functions; continuous probability distributions and density functions; the mean value and variance of probability distributions; the variance and its square root, the standard deviation, as measures of risk; the triangular and beta distributions for simulating continuous probability distributions; and a simulation technique known as the Monte Carlo method. Part III dwelt at length on how raw data, which are always discrete, are structured into first discrete and/or continuous probability distributions for computing the means (expected values) and variances of cash flows and other variables. Part III concluded with a chapter on uncertainty analysis for situations in which probability assessments cannot be made.

PART IV: MULTIATTRIBUTE ANALYSIS

In Part IV, we finally reached multiattribute analysis for incorporating nonmonetary attributes into the decision-making process both qualitatively (ordinal ranking) and quantitatively (weighting). The leading topics were utility values, the analytical hierarchy process, and the risk preference of investors.

We hope that you have enjoyed our text or, if you didn't, that you have at least learned something and are now able to critique economy studies for the proper allocation of capital spending and, if need be, carry out such studies yourself.

APPENDIX A
NOTATION

A	Assets
A	Cash flow occurring uniformly at the end of every period for a specific number of periods
A_j	Cash flow for period j
AC	Annual cost
A/E	Architect/Engineer
AHP	Analytical hierarchy process
ANSI	American National Standards Institute
AW	Annual worth
B	Benefits
B	Rate base for the first year of operation
B_j	Rate base for year j
BCA	Benefit-cost analysis
BCR	Benefit-cost ratio
C	Cost
C_j	Cash disbursement
CAPM	Capital asset pricing model
CC	Capitalized cost
C/E	Cost-effective ratios
CEO	Chief executive officer
CFO	Chief financial officer
CPI	Consumer price index
CR	Capital recovery
CVP	Cost-volume-profit analysis

D	Disbenefits
D	Depreciation expense
D_j	Depreciation expense for period j
DB	Declining balance
DCF	Discounted cash flow
DCF-ROR	Discounted cash flow rate of return
E	Equity
$E[x]$	Expected value of x
EOM	End-of-month
EOP	End-of-period
EOQ	End-of-quarter
EOY	End-of-year
ERR	External rate of return
EUAC	Equivalent uniform annual cost
F	Equivalent future value
FC	Fixed cost
FTZ	Formula time zone
FV	Future value
FW	Future worth
f	Rate of inflation
$f(x)$	Probability density function of x
G	Arithmetic gradient
GNP	Gross national product
g	Geometric gradient
H	Upper bound for beta distribution
H	Hurwicz criterion
I	Interest payments
I	Fair return to lender
I	Initial cost
I_j	Interest in year j
IBL	Inside battery limits
IRR	Internal rate of return
IRR_{eq}	Equivalent internal rate of return
IRS	Internal Revenue Service
ITC	Investment tax credit
i	Effective interest rate per interest period
i_b	Interest on debt
i_c	Return on common stock
i_{eq}	Equivalent rate of return
i_M	Effective interest rate per subperiod
i_p	Return on preferred stock

L	Liability
L	Lower bound for beta distribution
L	Laplace criterion
LCM	Lowest common multiple
M	Number of compounding periods per year
M	Most likely value for beta distribution
MAA	Multiattribute analysis
MACRS	Modified accelerated cost recovery system
MAPI	Machinery and Allied Products Institute
MARR	Minimum attractive rate of return
MEAs	Mutually exclusive alternatives
N	Number of compounding periods
N*	Payback period
NFV	Net future value
NIAT	Net income after taxes
NIBT	Net income before taxes
NPV	Net present value
NPW	Net present worth
O&M	Operating & maintenance costs
OBL	Outside battery limits
OMB	Office of Management and Budget
OOM	Order of magnitude
P	Return to preferred stockholders
P	Initial investment
P	Equivalent present value of future cash flow
P	Loan principal
P_j	Return to preferred stockholder in year j
$P(x)$	Probability of x
PERT	Program Review Evaluation Technique
PI	Profitability index
PPI	Producers Price Index
PTZ	Problem time zone
PV	Present value
PW	Present worth
R	Receipts
R	Revenues
R_j	Permitted revenue
ROAI	Return on average investment
ROI	Return on investment
r	Nominal interest rate per period
r_b	Ratio share of debt

r_c	Ratio share of common stock
r_p	Ratio share of preferred stock
S	Net salvage value of capital investment
SYD	Sum-of-the-years digits depreciation
T	Income taxes
T_j	Income taxes for period j
TLA	Technical limits analysis
t	Combined income tax return
t_f	Federal tax rate
t_l	Local tax rate
t_s	State tax rate
$V[x]$	Variance of x
VC	Variable Costs
α	Alpha, coefficient of optimism
λ	Eigenvalue
Σ	Sigma, summation
σ	Sigma, standard deviation
μ	Mu, expected value, mean
τ	Tau, levelized income taxes

DISCRETE INTEREST
COMPOUNDING TABLES

The Tables in this Appendix are from *Advanced Engineering Economics* by Chan S. Park and Gunter P. Sharp-Bette, copyright 1990 by John Wiley & Sons, Inc. They are reproduced here by permission of John Wiley & Sons, Inc.

0.5% *Interest Rate Factors*

	Single Payment		Equal-Payment Series				Uniform
	Compound Amount Factor,	Present-Worth Factor,	Compound Amount Factor,	Sinking-Fund Factor,	Present-Worth Factor,	Capital Recovery Factor,	Gradient Series Factor,
N	$(F/P, i, N)$	$(P/F, i, N)$	$(F/A, i, N)$	$(A/F, i, N)$	$(P/A, i, N)$	$(A/P, i, N)$	$(A/G, i, N)$
1	1.00500	0.9950249	1.00000	1.0000000	0.9950249	1.0050000	0.0000000
2	1.01003	0.9900745	2.00500	0.4987531	1.9850994	0.5037531	0.4987531
3	1.01508	0.9851488	3.01502	0.3316722	2.9702481	0.3366722	0.9966750
4	1.02015	0.9802475	4.03010	0.2481328	3.9504957	0.2531328	1.4937656
5	1.02525	0.9753707	5.05025	0.1980100	4.9258663	0.2030100	1.9900250
6	1.03038	0.9705181	6.07550	0.1645955	5.8963844	0.1695955	2.4854532
7	1.03553	0.9656896	7.10588	0.1407285	6.8620740	0.1457285	2.9800502
8	1.04071	0.9608852	8.14141	0.1228289	7.8229592	0.1278289	3.4738161
9	1.04591	0.9561047	9.18212	0.1089074	8.7790639	0.1139074	3.9667509
10	1.05114	0.9513479	10.22803	0.0977706	9.7304119	0.1027706	4.4588545
11	1.05640	0.9466149	11.27917	0.0886590	10.6770267	0.0936590	4.9501271
12	1.06168	0.9419053	12.33556	0.0810664	11.6189321	0.0860664	5.4405687
13	1.06699	0.9372192	13.39724	0.0746422	12.5561513	0.0796422	5.9301793
14	1.07232	0.9325565	14.46423	0.0691361	13.4887078	0.0741361	6.4189591
15	1.07768	0.9279169	15.53655	0.0643644	14.4166246	0.0693644	6.9069079
16	1.08307	0.9233004	16.61423	0.0601894	15.3399250	0.0651894	7.3940260
17	1.08849	0.9187068	17.69730	0.0565058	16.2586319	0.0615058	7.8803134
18	1.09393	0.9141362	18.78579	0.0532317	17.1727680	0.0582317	8.3657701
19	1.09940	0.9095882	19.87972	0.0503025	18.0823562	0.0553025	8.8503962
20	1.10490	0.9050629	20.97912	0.0476665	18.9874191	0.0526665	9.3341918
21	1.11042	0.9005601	22.08401	0.0452816	19.8879793	0.0502816	9.8171570
22	1.11597	0.8960797	23.19443	0.0431138	20.7840590	0.0481138	10.2992918
23	1.12155	0.8916216	24.31040	0.0411347	21.6756806	0.0461347	10.7805964
24	1.12716	0.8871857	25.43196	0.0393206	22.5628662	0.0443206	11.2610708
25	1.13280	0.8827718	26.55912	0.0376519	23.4456380	0.0426519	11.7407151
26	1.13846	0.8783799	27.69191	0.0361116	24.3240179	0.0411116	12.2195295
27	1.14415	0.8740099	28.83037	0.0346856	25.1980278	0.0396856	12.6975140
28	1.14987	0.8696616	29.97452	0.0333617	26.0676894	0.0383617	13.1746688
29	1.15562	0.8653349	31.12439	0.0321291	26.9330242	0.0371291	13.6509939
30	1.16140	0.8610297	32.28002	0.0309789	27.7940540	0.0359789	14.1264895
31	1.16721	0.8567460	33.44142	0.0299030	28.6508000	0.0349030	14.6011557
32	1.17304	0.8524836	34.60862	0.0288945	29.5032835	0.0338945	15.0749927
33	1.17891	0.8482424	35.78167	0.0279473	30.3515259	0.0329473	15.5480005
34	1.18480	0.8440223	36.96058	0.0270559	31.1955482	0.0320559	16.0201792
35	1.19073	0.8398231	38.14538	0.0262155	32.0353713	0.0312155	16.4915292
36	1.19668	0.8356449	39.33610	0.0254219	32.8710162	0.0304219	16.9620503
37	1.20266	0.8314875	40.53279	0.0246714	33.7025037	0.0296714	17.4317430
38	1.20868	0.8273507	41.73545	0.0239604	34.5298544	0.0289604	17.9006071
39	1.21472	0.8232346	42.94413	0.0232861	35.3530890	0.0282861	18.3686430
40	1.22079	0.8191389	44.15885	0.0226455	36.1722279	0.0276455	18.8358508
42	1.23303	0.8110085	46.60654	0.0214562	37.7982999	0.0264562	19.7677827
48	1.27049	0.7870984	54.09783	0.0184850	42.5803178	0.0234850	22.5437211
50	1.28323	0.7792861	56.64516	0.0176538	44.1427863	0.0226538	23.4624199
60	1.34885	0.7413722	69.77003	0.0143328	51.7255608	0.0193328	28.0063816
70	1.41783	0.7053029	83.56611	0.0119666	58.9394176	0.0169666	32.4679615
72	1.43204	0.6983024	86.40886	0.0115729	60.3395139	0.0165729	33.3504143
75	1.45363	0.6879318	90.72650	0.0110221	62.4136454	0.0160221	34.6679396
80	1.49034	0.6709885	98.06771	0.0101970	65.8023054	0.0151970	36.8474249
90	1.56655	0.6383435	113.31094	0.0088253	72.3312996	0.0138253	41.1450768
100	1.64667	0.6072868	129.33370	0.0077319	78.5426448	0.0127319	45.3612613

1% *Interest Rate Factors*

| | Single Payment | | Equal-Payment Series | | | | Uniform |
| | Compound Amount Factor, | Present-Worth Factor, | Compound Amount Factor, | Sinking-Fund Factor, | Present-Worth Factor, | Capital Recovery Factor, | Gradient Series Factor, |
N	(F/P, i, N)	(P/F, i, N)	(F/A, i, N)	(A/F, i, N)	(P/A, i, N)	(A/P, i, N)	(A/G, i, N)
1	1.01000	0.9900990	1.00000	1.0000000	0.9900990	1.0100000	0.0000000
2	1.02010	0.9802960	2.01000	0.4975124	1.9703951	0.5075124	0.4975124
3	1.03030	0.9705901	3.03010	0.3300221	2.9409852	0.3400221	0.9933666
4	1.04060	0.9609803	4.06040	0.2462811	3.9019656	0.2562811	1.4875624
5	1.05101	0.9514657	5.10101	0.1960398	4.8534312	0.2060398	1.9801002
6	1.06152	0.9420452	6.15202	0.1625484	5.7954765	0.1725484	2.4709800
7	1.07214	0.9327181	7.21354	0.1386283	6.7281945	0.1486283	2.9602020
8	1.08286	0.9234832	8.28567	0.1206903	7.6516778	0.1306903	3.4477664
9	1.09369	0.9143398	9.36853	0.1067404	8.5660176	0.1167404	3.9336734
10	1.10462	0.9052870	10.46221	0.0955821	9.4713045	0.1055821	4.4179234
11	1.11567	0.8963237	11.56683	0.0864541	10.3676282	0.0964541	4.9005167
12	1.12683	0.8874492	12.68250	0.0788488	11.2550775	0.0888488	5.3814536
13	1.13809	0.8786626	13.80933	0.0724148	12.1337401	0.0824148	5.8607344
14	1.14947	0.8699630	14.94742	0.0669012	13.0037030	0.0769012	6.3383597
15	1.16097	0.8613495	16.09690	0.0621238	13.8650525	0.0721238	6.8143297
16	1.17258	0.8528213	17.25786	0.0579446	14.7178738	0.0679446	7.2886451
17	1.18430	0.8443775	18.43044	0.0542581	15.5622513	0.0642581	7.7613063
18	1.19615	0.8360173	19.61475	0.0509820	16.3982686	0.0609820	8.2323138
19	1.20811	0.8277399	20.81090	0.0480518	17.2260085	0.0580518	8.7016682
20	1.22019	0.8195445	22.01900	0.0454153	18.0455530	0.0554153	9.1693702
21	1.23239	0.8114302	23.23919	0.0430308	18.8569831	0.0530308	9.6354204
22	1.24472	0.8033962	24.47159	0.0408637	19.6603793	0.0508637	10.0998193
23	1.25716	0.7954418	25.71630	0.0388858	20.4558211	0.0488858	10.5625679
24	1.26973	0.7875661	26.97346	0.0370735	21.2433873	0.0470735	11.0236667
25	1.28243	0.7797684	28.24320	0.0354068	22.0231557	0.0454068	11.4831165
26	1.29526	0.7720480	29.52563	0.0338689	22.7952037	0.0438689	11.9409182
27	1.30821	0.7644039	30.82089	0.0324455	23.5596076	0.0424455	12.3970725
28	1.32129	0.7568356	32.12910	0.0311244	24.3164432	0.0411244	12.8515804
29	1.33450	0.7493421	33.45039	0.0298950	25.0657853	0.0398950	13.3044427
30	1.34785	0.7419229	34.78489	0.0287481	25.8077082	0.0387481	13.7556604
31	1.36133	0.7345771	36.13274	0.0276757	26.5422854	0.0376757	14.2052343
32	1.37494	0.7273041	37.49407	0.0266709	27.2695895	0.0366709	14.6531656
33	1.38869	0.7201031	38.86901	0.0257274	27.9896925	0.0357274	15.0994552
34	1.40258	0.7129733	40.25770	0.0248400	28.7026659	0.0348400	15.5441042
35	1.41660	0.7059142	41.66028	0.0240037	29.4085801	0.0340037	15.9871136
36	1.43077	0.6989249	43.07688	0.0232143	30.1075050	0.0332143	16.4284847
37	1.44508	0.6920049	44.50765	0.0224680	30.7995099	0.0324680	16.8682184
38	1.45953	0.6851534	45.95272	0.0217615	31.4846633	0.0317615	17.3063161
39	1.47412	0.6783697	47.41225	0.0210916	32.1630330	0.0310916	17.7427789
40	1.48886	0.6716531	48.88637	0.0204556	32.8346861	0.0304556	18.1776081
42	1.51879	0.6584189	51.87899	0.0192756	34.1581081	0.0292756	19.0423707
48	1.61223	0.6202604	61.22261	0.0163338	37.9739595	0.0263338	21.5975899
50	1.64463	0.6080388	64.46318	0.0155127	39.1961175	0.0255127	22.4363454
60	1.81670	0.5504496	81.66967	0.0122444	44.9550384	0.0222444	26.5333139
70	2.00676	0.4983149	100.67634	0.0099328	50.1685143	0.0199328	30.4702553
72	2.04710	0.4884961	104.70993	0.0095502	51.1503915	0.0195502	31.2386140
75	2.10913	0.4741295	110.91285	0.0090161	52.5870512	0.0190161	32.3793391
80	2.21672	0.4511179	121.67152	0.0082189	54.8882061	0.0182189	34.2491991
90	2.44863	0.4083912	144.86327	0.0069031	59.1608815	0.0169031	37.8724493
100	2.70481	0.3697112	170.48138	0.0058657	63.0288788	0.0158657	41.3425687

2% *Interest Rate Factors*

	Single Payment		Equal-Payment Series				Uniform
	Compound Amount Factor,	Present-Worth Factor,	Compound Amount Factor,	Sinking-Fund Factor,	Present-Worth Factor,	Capital Recovery Factor,	Gradient Series Factor,
N	$(F/P, i, N)$	$(P/F, i, N)$	$(F/A, i, N)$	$(A/F, i, N)$	$(P/A, i, N)$	$(A/P, i, N)$	$(A/G, i, N)$
1	1.02000	0.9803922	1.00000	1.0000000	0.9803922	1.0200000	0.0000000
2	1.04040	0.9611688	2.02000	0.4950495	1.9415609	0.5150495	0.4950495
3	1.06121	0.9423223	3.06040	0.3267547	2.8838833	0.3467547	0.9867991
4	1.08243	0.9238454	4.12161	0.2426238	3.8077287	0.2626238	1.4752495
5	1.10408	0.9057308	5.20404	0.1921584	4.7134595	0.2121584	1.9604015
6	1.12616	0.8879714	6.30812	0.1585258	5.6014309	0.1785258	2.4422563
7	1.14869	0.8705602	7.43428	0.1345120	6.4719911	0.1545120	2.9208154
8	1.17166	0.8534904	8.58297	0.1165098	7.3254814	0.1365098	3.3960803
9	1.19509	0.8367553	9.75463	0.1025154	8.1622367	0.1225154	3.8680532
10	1.21899	0.8203483	10.94972	0.0913265	8.9825850	0.1113265	4.3367361
11	1.24337	0.8042630	12.16872	0.0821779	9.7868480	0.1021779	4.8021314
12	1.26824	0.7884932	13.41209	0.0745596	10.5753412	0.0945596	5.2642420
13	1.29361	0.7730325	14.68033	0.0681184	11.3483737	0.0881184	5.7230708
14	1.31948	0.7578750	15.97394	0.0626020	12.1062488	0.0826020	6.1786209
15	1.34587	0.7430147	17.29342	0.0578255	12.8492635	0.0778255	6.6308958
16	1.37279	0.7284458	18.63929	0.0536501	13.5777093	0.0736501	7.0798993
17	1.40024	0.7141626	20.01207	0.0499698	14.2918719	0.0699698	7.5256353
18	1.42825	0.7001594	21.41231	0.0467021	14.9920313	0.0667021	7.9681081
19	1.45681	0.6864308	22.84056	0.0437818	15.6784620	0.0637818	8.4073220
20	1.48595	0.6729713	24.29737	0.0411567	16.3514333	0.0611567	8.8432819
21	1.51567	0.6597758	25.78332	0.0387848	17.0112092	0.0587848	9.2759926
22	1.54598	0.6468390	27.29898	0.0366314	17.6580482	0.0566314	9.7054594
23	1.57690	0.6341559	28.84496	0.0346681	18.2922041	0.0546681	10.1316878
24	1.60844	0.6217215	30.42186	0.0328711	18.9139256	0.0528711	10.5546833
25	1.64061	0.6095309	32.03030	0.0312204	19.5234565	0.0512204	10.9744520
26	1.67342	0.5975793	33.67091	0.0296992	20.1210358	0.0496992	11.3910000
27	1.70689	0.5858620	35.34432	0.0282931	20.7068978	0.0482931	11.8043337
28	1.74102	0.5743746	37.05121	0.0269897	21.2812724	0.0469897	12.2144597
29	1.77584	0.5631123	38.79223	0.0257784	21.8443847	0.0457784	12.6213850
30	1.81136	0.5520709	40.56808	0.0246649	22.3964556	0.0446649	13.0251166
31	1.84759	0.5412460	42.37944	0.0235963	22.9377015	0.0435963	13.4256618
32	1.88454	0.5306333	44.22703	0.0226106	23.4683348	0.0426106	13.8230283
33	1.92223	0.5202287	46.11157	0.0216865	23.9885636	0.0416865	14.2172237
34	1.96068	0.5100282	48.03380	0.0208187	24.4985917	0.0408187	14.6082562
35	1.99989	0.5000276	49.99448	0.0200022	24.9986193	0.0400022	14.9961339
36	2.03989	0.4902232	51.99437	0.0192329	25.4888425	0.0392329	15.3808653
37	2.08069	0.4806109	54.03425	0.0185068	25.9694534	0.0385068	15.7624591
38	2.12230	0.4711872	56.11494	0.0178206	26.4406406	0.0378206	16.1409241
39	2.16474	0.4619482	58.23724	0.0171711	26.9025888	0.0371711	16.5162694
40	2.20804	0.4528904	60.40198	0.0165557	27.3554792	0.0365557	16.8885044
42	2.29724	0.4353041	64.86222	0.0154173	28.2347936	0.0354173	17.6236815
48	2.58707	0.3865376	79.35352	0.0126018	30.6731196	0.0326018	19.7555947
50	2.69159	0.3715279	84.57940	0.0118232	31.4236059	0.0318232	20.4419757
60	3.28103	0.3047823	114.05154	0.0087680	34.7608867	0.0287680	23.6961025
70	3.99956	0.2500276	149.97791	0.0066676	37.4986193	0.0266676	26.6632301
72	4.16114	0.2403187	158.05702	0.0063268	37.9840631	0.0263268	27.2234094
75	4.41584	0.2264577	170.79177	0.0058551	38.6771143	0.0258551	28.0434389
80	4.87544	0.2051097	193.77196	0.0051607	39.7445136	0.0251607	29.3571782
90	5.94313	0.1682614	247.15666	0.0040460	41.5869292	0.0240460	31.7929241
100	7.24465	0.1380330	312.23231	0.0032027	43.0983516	0.0232027	33.9862823

3% Interest Rate Factors

	Single Payment		Equal-Payment Series				Uniform
N	Compound Amount Factor, (F/P, i, N)	Present-Worth Factor, (P/F, i, N)	Compound Amount Factor, (F/A, i, N)	Sinking-Fund Factor, (A/F, i, N)	Present-Worth Factor, (P/A, i, N)	Capital Recovery Factor, (A/P, i, N)	Gradient Series Factor, (A/G, i, N)
1	1.03000	0.9708738	1.00000	1.0000000	0.9708738	1.0300000	0.0000000
2	1.06090	0.9425959	2.03000	0.4926108	1.9134697	0.5226108	0.4926108
3	1.09273	0.9151417	3.09090	0.3235304	2.8286114	0.3535304	0.9802970
4	1.12551	0.8884870	4.18363	0.2390270	3.7170984	0.2690270	1.4630606
5	1.15927	0.8626088	5.30914	0.1883546	4.5797072	0.2183546	1.9409048
6	1.19405	0.8374843	6.46841	0.1545975	5.4171914	0.1845975	2.4138332
7	1.22987	0.8130915	7.66246	0.1305064	6.2302830	0.1605064	2.8818508
8	1.26677	0.7894092	8.89234	0.1124564	7.0196922	0.1424564	3.3449630
9	1.30477	0.7664167	10.15911	0.0984339	7.7861089	0.1284339	3.8031762
10	1.34392	0.7440939	11.46388	0.0872305	8.5302028	0.1172305	4.2564978
11	1.38423	0.7224213	12.80780	0.0780774	9.2526241	0.1080774	4.7049358
12	1.42576	0.7013799	14.19203	0.0704621	9.9540040	0.1004621	5.1484991
13	1.46853	0.6809513	15.61779	0.0640295	10.6349553	0.0940295	5.5871976
14	1.51259	0.6611178	17.08632	0.0585263	11.2960731	0.0885263	6.0210418
15	1.55797	0.6418619	18.59891	0.0537666	11.9379351	0.0837666	6.4500431
16	1.60471	0.6231669	20.15688	0.0496108	12.5611020	0.0796108	6.8742137
17	1.65285	0.6050164	21.76159	0.0459525	13.1661185	0.0759525	7.2935667
18	1.70243	0.5873946	23.41444	0.0427087	13.7535131	0.0727087	7.7081158
19	1.75351	0.5702860	25.11687	0.0398139	14.3237991	0.0698139	8.1178756
20	1.80611	0.5536758	26.87037	0.0372157	14.8774749	0.0672157	8.5228616
21	1.86029	0.5375493	28.67649	0.0348718	15.4150241	0.0648718	8.9230888
22	1.91610	0.5218925	30.53678	0.0327474	15.9369166	0.0627474	9.3185772
23	1.97359	0.5066917	32.45288	0.0308139	16.4436084	0.0608139	9.7093413
24	2.03279	0.4919337	34.42647	0.0290474	16.9355421	0.0590474	10.0954006
25	2.09378	0.4776056	36.45926	0.0274279	17.4131477	0.0574279	10.4767741
26	2.15659	0.4636947	38.55304	0.0259383	17.8768424	0.0559383	10.8534818
27	2.22129	0.4501891	40.70963	0.0245642	18.3270315	0.0545642	11.2255440
28	2.28793	0.4370768	42.93092	0.0232932	18.7641082	0.0532932	11.5929821
29	2.35657	0.4243464	45.21885	0.0221147	19.1884546	0.0521147	11.9558179
30	2.42726	0.4119868	47.57542	0.0210193	19.6004413	0.0510193	12.3140740
31	2.50008	0.3999871	50.00268	0.0199989	20.0004285	0.0499989	12.6677736
32	2.57508	0.3883370	52.50276	0.0190466	20.3887655	0.0490466	13.0169405
33	2.65234	0.3770262	55.07784	0.0181561	20.7657918	0.0481561	13.3615992
34	2.73191	0.3660449	57.73018	0.0173220	21.1318367	0.0473220	13.7017749
35	2.81386	0.3553834	60.46208	0.0165393	21.4872201	0.0465393	14.0374932
36	2.89828	0.3450324	63.27594	0.0158038	21.8322525	0.0458038	14.3687803
37	2.98523	0.3349829	66.17422	0.0151116	22.1672354	0.0451116	14.6956632
38	3.07478	0.3252262	69.15945	0.0144593	22.4924616	0.0444593	15.0181692
39	3.16703	0.3157535	72.23423	0.0138439	22.8082151	0.0438439	15.3363262
40	3.26204	0.3065568	75.40126	0.0132624	23.1147720	0.0432624	15.6501628
42	3.46070	0.2889592	82.02320	0.0121917	23.7013592	0.0421917	16.2649910
48	4.13225	0.2419988	104.40840	0.0095778	25.2667066	0.0395778	18.0088952
50	4.38391	0.2281071	112.79687	0.0088655	25.7297640	0.0388655	18.5575093
60	5.89160	0.1697331	163.05344	0.0061330	27.6755637	0.0361330	21.0674159
70	7.91782	0.1262974	230.59406	0.0043366	29.1234214	0.0343366	23.2145415
72	8.40002	0.1190474	246.66724	0.0040540	29.3650875	0.0340540	23.6036263
75	9.17893	0.1089452	272.63086	0.0036680	29.7018263	0.0336680	24.1634248
80	10.64089	0.0939771	321.36302	0.0031117	30.2007634	0.0331117	25.0353447
90	14.30047	0.0699278	443.34890	0.0022556	31.0024071	0.0322556	26.5666537
100	19.21863	0.0520328	607.28773	0.0016467	31.5989053	0.0316467	27.8444470

4% *Interest Rate Factors*

	Single Payment		Equal-Payment Series				Uniform Gradient Series
N	Compound Amount Factor, (F/P, i, N)	Present-Worth Factor, (P/F, i, N)	Compound Amount Factor, (F/A, i, N)	Sinking-Fund Factor, (A/F, i, N)	Present-Worth Factor, (P/A, i, N)	Capital Recovery Factor, (A/P, i, N)	Uniform Gradient Series Factor, (A/G, i, N)
1	1.04000	0.9615385	1.00000	1.0000000	0.9615385	1.0400000	0.0000000
2	1.08160	0.9245562	2.04000	0.4901961	1.8860947	0.5301961	0.4901961
3	1.12486	0.8889964	3.12160	0.3203485	2.7750910	0.3603485	0.9738596
4	1.16986	0.8548042	4.24646	0.2354900	3.6298952	0.2754900	1.4509955
5	1.21665	0.8219271	5.41632	0.1846271	4.4518223	0.2246271	1.9216108
6	1.26532	0.7903145	6.63298	0.1507619	5.2421369	0.1907619	2.3857146
7	1.31593	0.7599178	7.89829	0.1266096	6.0020547	0.1666096	2.8433179
8	1.36857	0.7306902	9.21423	0.1085278	6.7327449	0.1485278	3.2944336
9	1.42331	0.7025867	10.58280	0.0944930	7.4353316	0.1344930	3.7390766
10	1.48024	0.6755642	12.00611	0.0832909	8.1108958	0.1232909	4.1772639
11	1.53945	0.6495809	13.48635	0.0741490	8.7604767	0.1141490	4.6090142
12	1.60103	0.6245970	15.02581	0.0665522	9.3850738	0.1065522	5.0343482
13	1.66507	0.6005741	16.62684	0.0601437	9.9856478	0.1001437	5.4532885
14	1.73168	0.5774751	18.29191	0.0546690	10.5631229	0.0946690	5.8658594
15	1.80094	0.5552645	20.02359	0.0499411	11.1183874	0.0899411	6.2720874
16	1.87298	0.5339082	21.82453	0.0458200	11.6522956	0.0858200	6.6720003
17	1.94790	0.5133732	23.69751	0.0421985	12.1656689	0.0821985	7.0656281
18	2.02582	0.4936281	25.64541	0.0389933	12.6592970	0.0789933	7.4530023
19	2.10685	0.4746424	27.67123	0.0361386	13.1339394	0.0761386	7.8341563
20	2.19112	0.4563869	29.77808	0.0335818	13.5903263	0.0735818	8.2091248
21	2.27877	0.4388336	31.96920	0.0312801	14.0291599	0.0712801	8.5779447
22	2.36992	0.4219554	34.24797	0.0291988	14.4511153	0.0691988	8.9406539
23	2.46472	0.4057263	36.61789	0.0273091	14.8568417	0.0673091	9.2972923
24	2.56330	0.3901215	39.08260	0.0255868	15.2469631	0.0655868	9.6479012
25	2.66584	0.3751168	41.64591	0.0240120	15.6220799	0.0640120	9.9925233
26	2.77247	0.3606892	44.31174	0.0225674	15.9827692	0.0625674	10.3312027
27	2.88337	0.3468166	47.08421	0.0212385	16.3295857	0.0612385	10.6639851
28	2.99870	0.3334775	49.96758	0.0200130	16.6630632	0.0600130	10.9909173
29	3.11865	0.3206514	52.96629	0.0188799	16.9837146	0.0588799	11.3120477
30	3.24340	0.3083187	56.08494	0.0178301	17.2920333	0.0578301	11.6274256
31	3.37313	0.2964603	59.32834	0.0168554	17.5884936	0.0568554	11.9371019
32	3.50806	0.2850579	62.70147	0.0159486	17.8735515	0.0559486	12.2411282
33	3.64838	0.2740942	66.20953	0.0151036	18.1476457	0.0551036	12.5395576
34	3.79432	0.2635521	69.85791	0.0143148	18.4111978	0.0543148	12.8324442
35	3.94609	0.2534155	73.65222	0.0135773	18.6646132	0.0535773	13.1198429
36	4.10393	0.2436687	77.59831	0.0128869	18.9082820	0.0528869	13.4018098
37	4.26809	0.2342968	81.70225	0.0122396	19.1425788	0.0522396	13.6784019
38	4.43881	0.2252854	85.97034	0.0116319	19.3678642	0.0516319	13.9496768
39	4.61637	0.2166206	90.40915	0.0110608	19.5844848	0.0510608	14.2156933
40	4.80102	0.2082890	95.02552	0.0105235	19.7927739	0.0505235	14.4765107
42	5.19278	0.1925749	104.81960	0.0095402	20.1856267	0.0495402	14.9827893
48	6.57053	0.1521948	139.26321	0.0071806	21.1951309	0.0471806	16.3832229
50	7.10668	0.1407126	152.66708	0.0065502	21.4821846	0.0465502	16.8122494
60	10.51963	0.0950604	237.99069	0.0042018	22.6234900	0.0442018	18.6972323
70	15.57162	0.0642194	364.29046	0.0027451	23.3945150	0.0427451	20.1961410
72	16.84226	0.0593744	396.05656	0.0025249	23.5156388	0.0425249	20.4551946
75	18.94525	0.0527837	448.63137	0.0022290	23.6804083	0.0422290	20.8206221
80	23.04980	0.0433843	551.24498	0.0018141	23.9153918	0.0418141	21.3718490
90	34.11933	0.0293089	827.98333	0.0012078	24.2672776	0.0412078	22.2825540
100	50.50495	0.0198000	1237.62370	0.0008080	24.5049990	0.0408080	22.9799999

5% *Interest Rate Factors*

	Single Payment		Equal-Payment Series				Uniform
N	Compound Amount Factor, (F/P, i, N)	Present-Worth Factor, (P/F, i, N)	Compound Amount Factor, (F/A, i, N)	Sinking-Fund Factor, (A/F, i, N)	Present-Worth Factor, (P/A, i, N)	Capital Recovery Factor, (A/P, i, N)	Gradient Series Factor, (A/G, i, N)
1	1.05000	0.9523810	1.00000	1.0000000	0.9523810	1.0500000	0.0000000
2	1.10250	0.9070295	2.05000	0.4878049	1.8594104	0.5378049	0.4878049
3	1.15763	0.8638376	3.15250	0.3172086	2.7232480	0.3672086	0.9674861
4	1.21551	0.8227025	4.31013	0.2320118	3.5459505	0.2820118	1.4390534
5	1.27628	0.7835262	5.52563	0.1809748	4.3294767	0.2309748	1.9025202
6	1.34010	0.7462154	6.80191	0.1470175	5.0756921	0.1970175	2.3579038
7	1.40710	0.7106813	8.14201	0.1228198	5.7863734	0.1728198	2.8052254
8	1.47746	0.6768394	9.54911	0.1047218	6.4632128	0.1547218	3.2445098
9	1.55133	0.6446089	11.02656	0.0906901	7.1078217	0.1406901	3.6757856
10	1.62889	0.6139133	12.57789	0.0795046	7.7217349	0.1295046	4.0990850
11	1.71034	0.5846793	14.20679	0.0703888	8.3064142	0.1203889	4.5144439
12	1.79586	0.5568374	15.91713	0.0628254	8.8632516	0.1128254	4.9219016
13	1.88565	0.5303214	17.71298	0.0564558	9.3935730	0.1064558	5.3215011
14	1.97993	0.5050680	19.59863	0.0510240	9.8986409	0.1010240	5.7132886
15	2.07893	0.4810171	21.57856	0.0463423	10.3796580	0.0963423	6.0973137
16	2.18287	0.4581115	23.65749	0.0422699	10.8377696	0.0922699	6.4736294
17	2.29202	0.4362967	25.84037	0.0386991	11.2740662	0.0886991	6.8422918
18	2.40662	0.4155207	28.13238	0.0355462	11.6895869	0.0855462	7.2033600
19	2.52695	0.3957340	30.53900	0.0327450	12.0853209	0.0827450	7.5568961
20	2.65330	0.3768895	33.06595	0.0302426	12.4622103	0.0802426	7.9029651
21	2.78596	0.3589424	35.71925	0.0279961	12.8211527	0.0779961	8.2416350
22	2.92526	0.3418499	38.50521	0.0259705	13.1630026	0.0759705	8.5729762
23	3.07152	0.3255713	41.43048	0.0241368	13.4885739	0.0741368	8.8970619
24	3.22510	0.3100679	44.50200	0.0224709	13.7986418	0.0724709	9.2139676
25	3.38635	0.2953028	47.72710	0.0209525	14.0939446	0.0709525	9.5237714
26	3.55567	0.2812407	51.11345	0.0195643	14.3751853	0.0695643	9.8265533
27	3.73346	0.2678483	54.66913	0.0182919	14.6430336	0.0682919	10.1223957
28	3.92013	0.2550936	58.40258	0.0171225	14.8981273	0.0671225	10.4113830
29	4.11614	0.2429463	62.32271	0.0160455	15.1410736	0.0660455	10.6936014
30	4.32194	0.2313774	66.43885	0.0150514	15.3724510	0.0650514	10.9691390
31	4.53804	0.2203595	70.76079	0.0141321	15.5928105	0.0641321	11.2380854
32	4.76494	0.2098662	75.29883	0.0132804	15.8026767	0.0632804	11.5005319
33	5.00319	0.1998725	80.06377	0.0124900	16.0025492	0.0624900	11.7565711
34	5.25335	0.1903548	85.06696	0.0117554	16.1929040	0.0617554	12.0062971
35	5.51602	0.1812903	90.32031	0.0110717	16.3741943	0.0610717	12.2498049
36	5.79182	0.1726574	95.83632	0.0104345	16.5468517	0.0604345	12.4871909
37	6.08141	0.1644356	101.62814	0.0098398	16.7112873	0.0598398	12.7185521
38	6.38548	0.1566054	107.70955	0.0092842	16.8678927	0.0592842	12.9439866
39	6.70475	0.1491480	114.09502	0.0087646	17.0170407	0.0587646	13.1635931
40	7.03999	0.1420457	120.79977	0.0082782	17.1590864	0.0582782	13.3774711
42	7.76159	0.1288396	135.23175	0.0073947	17.4232076	0.0573947	13.7884410
48	10.40127	0.0961421	188.02539	0.0053184	18.0771578	0.0553184	14.8943066
50	11.46740	0.0872037	209.34800	0.0047767	18.2559255	0.0547767	15.2232645
60	18.67919	0.0535355	353.58372	0.0028282	18.9292895	0.0528282	16.6061786
70	30.42643	0.0328662	588.52851	0.0016992	19.3426766	0.0516992	17.6211858
72	33.54513	0.0298106	650.90268	0.0015363	19.4037883	0.0515363	17.7876877
75	38.83269	0.0257515	756.65372	0.0013216	19.4849700	0.0513216	18.0175872
80	49.56144	0.0201770	971.22882	0.0010296	19.5964605	0.0510296	18.3526024
90	80.73037	0.0123869	1594.60730	0.0006271	19.7522617	0.0506271	18.8711954
100	131.50126	0.0076045	2610.02516	0.0003831	19.8479102	0.0503831	19.2337239

6% *Interest Rate Factors*

	Single Payment		Equal-Payment Series				Uniform
	Compound Amount Factor,	Present-Worth Factor,	Compound Amount Factor,	Sinking-Fund Factor,	Present-Worth Factor,	Capital Recovery Factor,	Gradient Series Factor,
N	$(F/P, i, N)$	$(P/F, i, N)$	$(F/A, i, N)$	$(A/F, i, N)$	$(P/A, i, N)$	$(A/P, i, N)$	$(A/G, i, N)$
1	1.06000	0.9433962	1.00000	1.0000000	0.9433962	1.0600000	0.0000000
2	1.12360	0.8899964	2.06000	0.4854369	1.8333927	0.5454369	0.4854369
3	1.19102	0.8396193	3.18360	0.3141098	2.6730119	0.3741098	0.9611760
4	1.26248	0.7920937	4.37462	0.2285915	3.4651056	0.2885915	1.4272338
5	1.33823	0.7472582	5.63709	0.1773964	4.2123638	0.2373964	1.8836333
6	1.41852	0.7049605	6.97532	0.1433626	4.9173243	0.2033626	2.3304038
7	1.50363	0.6650571	8.39384	0.1191350	5.5823814	0.1791350	2.7675812
8	1.59385	0.6274124	9.89747	0.1010359	6.2097938	0.1610359	3.1952076
9	1.68948	0.5918985	11.49132	0.0870222	6.8016923	0.1470222	3.6133314
10	1.79085	0.5583948	13.18079	0.0758680	7.3600871	0.1358680	4.0220070
11	1.89830	0.5267875	14.97164	0.0667929	7.8868746	0.1267929	4.4212947
12	2.01220	0.4969694	16.86994	0.0592770	8.3838439	0.1192770	4.8112608
13	2.13293	0.4688390	18.88214	0.0529601	8.8526830	0.1129601	5.1919772
14	2.26090	0.4423010	21.01507	0.0475849	9.2949839	0.1075849	5.5635212
15	2.39656	0.4172651	23.27597	0.0429628	9.7122490	0.1029628	5.9259757
16	2.54035	0.3936463	25.67253	0.0389651	10.1058953	0.0989521	6.2794284
17	2.69277	0.3713644	28.21288	0.0354448	10.4772597	0.0954448	6.6239721
18	2.85434	0.3503438	30.90565	0.0323565	10.8276035	0.0923565	6.9597045
19	3.02560	0.3305130	33.75999	0.0296209	11.1581165	0.0896209	7.2867276
20	3.20714	0.3118047	36.78559	0.0271846	11.4699212	0.0871846	7.6051477
21	3.39956	0.2941554	39.99273	0.0250045	11.7640766	0.0850045	7.9150753
22	3.60354	0.2775051	43.39229	0.0230456	12.0415817	0.0830456	8.2166249
23	3.81975	0.2617973	46.99583	0.0212785	12.3033790	0.0812785	8.5099142
24	4.04893	0.2469785	50.81558	0.0196790	12.5503575	0.0796790	8.7950647
25	4.29187	0.2329986	54.86451	0.0182267	12.7833562	0.0782267	9.0722007
26	4.54938	0.2198100	59.15638	0.0169043	13.0031662	0.0769043	9.3414498
27	4.82235	0.2073680	63.70577	0.0156972	13.2105341	0.0756972	9.6029418
28	5.11169	0.1956301	68.52811	0.0145926	13.4061643	0.0745926	9.8568093
29	5.41839	0.1845567	73.63980	0.0135796	13.5907210	0.0735796	10.1031868
30	5.74349	0.1741101	79.05819	0.0126489	13.7648312	0.0726489	10.3422109
31	6.08810	0.1642548	84.80168	0.0117922	13.9290860	0.0717922	10.5740199
32	6.45339	0.1549574	90.88978	0.0110023	14.0840434	0.0710023	10.7987534
33	6.84059	0.1461862	97.34316	0.0102729	14.2302296	0.0702729	11.0165524
34	7.25103	0.1379115	104.18375	0.0095984	14.3681411	0.0695984	11.2275589
35	7.68609	0.1301052	111.43478	0.0089739	14.4982464	0.0689739	11.4319156
36	8.14725	0.1227408	119.12087	0.0083948	14.6209871	0.0683948	11.6297658
37	8.63609	0.1157932	127.26812	0.0078574	14.7367803	0.0678574	11.8212531
38	9.15425	0.1092389	135.90421	0.0073581	14.8460192	0.0673581	12.0065215
39	9.70351	0.1030555	145.05846	0.0068938	14.9490747	0.0668938	12.1857146
40	10.28572	0.0972222	154.76197	0.0064615	15.0462969	0.0664615	12.3589761
42	11.55703	0.0865274	175.95054	0.0056834	15.2245433	0.0656834	12.6882760
48	16.39387	0.0609984	256.56453	0.0038977	15.6500266	0.0638977	13.5485427
50	18.42015	0.0542884	290.33590	0.0034443	15.7618606	0.0634443	13.7964280
60	32.98769	0.0303143	533.12818	0.0018757	16.1614277	0.0618757	14.7909452
70	59.07593	0.0169274	967.93217	0.0010331	16.3845439	0.0610331	15.4613480
72	66.37772	0.0150653	1089.62859	0.0009177	16.4155784	0.0609177	15.5653740
75	79.05692	0.0126491	1300.94868	0.0007687	16.4558481	0.0607687	15.7058294
80	105.79599	0.0094522	1746.59989	0.0005725	16.5091308	0.0605725	15.9032787
90	189.46451	0.0052780	3141.07519	0.0003184	16.5786994	0.0603184	16.1891232
100	339.30208	0.0029472	5638.36806	0.0001774	16.6175462	0.0601774	16.3710725

7% *Interest Rate Factors*

	Single Payment		Equal-Payment Series				Uniform
N	Compound Amount Factor, $(F/P, i, N)$	Present-Worth Factor, $(P/F, i, N)$	Compound Amount Factor, $(F/A, i, N)$	Sinking-Fund Factor, $(A/F, i, N)$	Present-Worth Factor, $(P/A, i, N)$	Capital Recovery Factor, $(A/P, i, N)$	Gradient Series Factor, $(A/G, i, N)$
1	1.07000	0.9345794	1.00000	1.0000000	0.9345794	1.0700000	0.0000000
2	1.14490	0.8734387	2.07000	0.4830918	1.8080182	0.5530918	0.4830918
3	1.22504	0.8162979	3.21490	0.3110517	2.6243160	0.3810517	0.9549286
4	1.31080	0.7628952	4.43994	0.2252281	3.3872113	0.2952281	1.4155362
5	1.40255	0.7129862	5.75074	0.1738907	4.1001974	0.2438907	1.8649504
6	1.50073	0.6663422	7.15329	0.1397958	4.7665397	0.2097958	2.3032172
7	1.60578	0.6227497	8.65402	0.1155532	5.3892894	0.1855532	2.7303923
8	1.71819	0.5820091	10.25980	0.0974678	5.9712985	0.1674678	3.1465414
9	1.83846	0.5439337	11.97799	0.0834865	6.5152322	0.1534865	3.5517396
10	1.96715	0.5083493	13.81645	0.0723775	7.0235815	0.1423775	3.9460710
11	2.10485	0.4750928	15.78360	0.0633569	7.4986743	0.1333569	4.3296292
12	2.25219	0.4440120	17.88845	0.0559020	7.9426863	0.1259020	4.7025162
13	2.40985	0.4149644	20.14064	0.0496508	8.3576507	0.1196508	5.0648425
14	2.57853	0.3878172	22.55049	0.0443449	8.7454680	0.1143449	5.4167266
15	2.75903	0.3624460	25.12902	0.0397946	9.1079140	0.1097946	5.7582947
16	2.95216	0.3387346	27.88805	0.0358576	9.4466486	0.1058576	6.0896805
17	3.15882	0.3165744	30.84022	0.0324252	9.7632230	0.1024252	6.4110245
18	3.37993	0.2958639	33.99903	0.0294126	10.0590869	0.0994126	6.7224739
19	3.61653	0.2765083	37.37896	0.0267530	10.3355952	0.0967530	7.0241817
20	3.86968	0.2584190	40.99549	0.0243929	10.5940142	0.0943929	7.3163069
21	4.14056	0.2415131	44.86518	0.0222890	10.8355273	0.0922890	7.5990138
22	4.43040	0.2257132	49.00574	0.0204058	11.0612405	0.0904058	7.8724713
23	4.74053	0.2109469	53.43614	0.0187139	11.2721874	0.0887139	8.1368528
24	5.07237	0.1971466	58.17667	0.0171890	11.4693340	0.0871890	8.3923357
25	5.42743	0.1842492	63.24904	0.0158105	11.6535832	0.0858105	8.6391010
26	5.80735	0.1721955	68.67647	0.0145610	11.8257787	0.0845610	8.8773325
27	6.21387	0.1609304	74.48382	0.0134257	11.9867090	0.0834257	9.1072169
28	6.64884	0.1504022	80.69769	0.0123919	12.1371113	0.0823919	9.3289430
29	7.11426	0.1405628	87.34653	0.0114487	12.2776741	0.0814487	9.5427014
30	7.61226	0.1313671	94.46079	0.0105864	12.4090412	0.0805864	9.7486842
31	8.14511	0.1227730	102.07304	0.0097969	12.5318142	0.0797969	9.9470844
32	8.71527	0.1147411	110.21815	0.0090729	12.6465553	0.0790729	10.1380958
33	9.32534	0.1072347	118.93343	0.0084081	12.7537900	0.0784081	10.3219121
34	9.97811	0.1002193	128.25876	0.0077967	12.8540094	0.0777967	10.4987272
35	10.67658	0.0936629	138.23688	0.0072340	12.9476723	0.0772340	10.6687345
36	11.42394	0.0875355	148.91346	0.0067153	13.0352078	0.0767153	10.8321264
37	12.22362	0.0818088	160.33740	0.0062368	13.1170166	0.0762368	10.9890946
38	13.07927	0.0764569	172.56102	0.0057951	13.1934735	0.0757951	11.1398292
39	13.99482	0.0714550	185.64029	0.0053868	13.2649285	0.0753868	11.2845185
40	14.97446	0.0667804	199.63511	0.0050091	13.3317088	0.0750091	11.4233492
42	17.14426	0.0583286	230.63224	0.0043359	13.4524490	0.0743359	11.6841699
48	25.72891	0.0388668	353.27009	0.0028307	13.7304744	0.0728307	12.3446661
50	29.45703	0.0339478	406.52893	0.0024598	13.8007463	0.0724598	12.5286789
60	57.94643	0.0172573	813.52038	0.0012292	14.0391812	0.0712292	13.2320924
70	113.98939	0.0087727	1614.13417	0.0006195	14.1603893	0.0706195	13.6661871
72	130.50646	0.0076625	1850.09222	0.0005405	14.1762506	0.0705405	13.7297574
75	159.87602	0.0062548	2269.65742	0.0004406	14.1963593	0.0704406	13.8136481
80	224.23439	0.0044596	3189.06268	0.0003136	14.2220054	0.0703136	13.9273466
90	441.10298	0.0022670	6287.18543	0.0001591	14.2533279	0.0701591	14.0812167
100	867.71633	0.0011525	12381.66179	0.0000808	14.2692507	0.0700808	14.1703363

8% *Interest Rate Factors*

	Single Payment		Equal-Payment Series				Uniform
	Compound Amount Factor,	Present-Worth Factor,	Compound Amount Factor,	Sinking-Fund Factor,	Present-Worth Factor,	Capital Recovery Factor,	Gradient Series Factor,
N	(F/P, i, N)	(P/F, i, N)	(F/A, i, N)	(A/F, i, N)	(P/A, i, N)	(A/P, i, N)	(A/G, i, N)
1	1.08000	0.9259259	1.00000	1.0000000	0.9259259	1.0800000	0.0000000
2	1.16640	0.8573388	2.08000	0.4807692	1.7832647	0.5607692	0.4807692
3	1.25971	0.7938322	3.24640	0.3080335	2.5770970	0.3880335	0.9487432
4	1.36049	0.7350299	4.50611	0.2219208	3.3121268	0.3019208	1.4039598
5	1.46933	0.6805832	5.86660	0.1704565	3.9927100	0.2504565	1.8464716
6	1.58687	0.6301696	7.33593	0.1363154	4.6228797	0.2163154	2.2763460
7	1.71382	0.5834904	8.92280	0.1120724	5.2063701	0.1920724	2.6936649
8	1.85093	0.5402689	10.63663	0.0940148	5.7466389	0.1740148	3.0985239
9	1.99900	0.5002490	12.48756	0.0800797	6.2468879	0.1600797	3.4910327
10	2.15892	0.4631935	14.48656	0.0690295	6.7100814	0.1490295	3.8713139
11	2.33164	0.4288829	16.64549	0.0600763	7.1389643	0.1400763	4.2395030
12	2.51817	0.3971138	18.97713	0.0526950	7.5360780	0.1326950	4.5957475
13	2.71962	0.3676979	21.49530	0.0465218	7.9037759	0.1265218	4.9402067
14	2.93719	0.3404610	24.21492	0.0412969	8.2442370	0.1212969	5.2730508
15	3.17217	0.3152417	27.15211	0.0368295	8.5594787	0.1168295	5.5944603
16	3.42594	0.2918905	30.32428	0.0329769	8.8513692	0.1129769	5.9046256
17	3.70002	0.2702690	33.75023	0.0296294	9.1216381	0.1096294	6.2037458
18	3.99602	0.2502490	37.45024	0.0267021	9.3718871	0.1067021	6.4920284
19	4.31570	0.2317121	41.44626	0.0241276	9.6035992	0.1041276	6.7696885
20	4.66096	0.2145482	45.76196	0.0218522	9.8181474	0.1018522	7.0369478
21	5.03383	0.1986557	50.42292	0.0198323	10.0168032	0.0998323	7.2940343
22	5.43654	0.1839405	55.45676	0.0180321	10.2007437	0.0980321	7.5411812
23	5.87146	0.1703153	60.89330	0.0164222	10.3710589	0.0964222	7.7786264
24	6.34118	0.1576993	66.76476	0.0149780	10.5287583	0.0949780	8.0066115
25	6.84848	0.1460179	73.10594	0.0136788	10.6747762	0.0936788	8.2253815
26	7.39635	0.1352018	79.95442	0.0125071	10.8099780	0.0925071	8.4351838
27	7.98806	0.1251868	87.35077	0.0114481	10.9351648	0.0914481	8.6362675
28	8.62711	0.1159137	95.33883	0.0104889	11.0510785	0.0904889	8.8288830
29	9.31727	0.1073275	103.96594	0.0096185	11.1584060	0.0896185	9.0132810
30	10.06266	0.0993773	113.28321	0.0088274	11.2577833	0.0888274	9.1897125
31	10.86767	0.0920160	123.34587	0.0081073	11.3497994	0.0881073	9.3584274
32	11.73708	0.0852000	134.21354	0.0074508	11.4349994	0.0874508	9.5196747
33	12.67605	0.0788889	145.95062	0.0068516	11.5138884	0.0868516	9.6737016
34	13.69013	0.0730453	158.62667	0.0063041	11.5869337	0.0863041	9.8207532
35	14.78534	0.0676345	172.31680	0.0058033	11.6545682	0.0858033	9.9610718
36	15.96817	0.0626246	187.10215	0.0053447	11.7171928	0.0853447	10.0948967
37	17.24563	0.0579857	203.07032	0.0049244	11.7751785	0.0849244	10.2224638
38	18.62528	0.0536905	220.31595	0.0045389	11.8288690	0.0845389	10.3440053
39	20.11530	0.0497134	238.94122	0.0041851	11.8785824	0.0841851	10.4597493
40	21.72452	0.0460309	259.05652	0.0038602	11.9246133	0.0838602	10.5699192
42	25.33948	0.0394641	304.24352	0.0032868	12.0066987	0.0832868	10.7744086
48	40.21057	0.0248691	490.13216	0.0020403	12.1891365	0.0820403	11.2758404
50	46.90161	0.0213212	573.77016	0.0017429	12.2334846	0.0817429	11.4107136
60	101.25706	0.0098759	1253.21330	0.0007979	12.3765518	0.0807979	11.9015384
70	218.60641	0.0045744	2720.08007	0.0003676	12.4428196	0.0803676	12.1783183
72	254.98251	0.0039218	3174.78140	0.0003150	12.4509770	0.0803150	12.2165159
75	321.20453	0.0031133	4002.55662	0.0002498	12.4610840	0.0802498	12.2657747
80	471.95483	0.0021188	5886.93543	0.0001699	12.4735144	0.0801699	12.3301323
90	1018.91509	0.0009814	12723.93862	0.0000786	12.4877320	0.0800786	12.4115840
100	2199.76126	0.0004546	27484.51570	0.0000364	12.4943176	0.0800364	12.4545198

9% *Interest Rate Factors*

	Single Payment		Equal-Payment Series				Uniform
N	Compound Amount Factor, (F/P, i, N)	Present-Worth Factor, (P/F, i, N)	Compound Amount Factor, (F/A, i, N)	Sinking-Fund Factor, (A/F, i, N)	Present-Worth Factor, (P/A, i, N)	Capital Recovery Factor, (A/P, i, N)	Gradient Series Factor, (A/G, i, N)
1	1.09000	0.9174312	1.00000	1.0000000	0.9174312	1.0900000	0.0000000
2	1.18810	0.8416800	2.09000	0.4784689	1.7591112	0.5684689	0.4784689
3	1.29503	0.7721835	3.27810	0.3050548	2.5312947	0.3950548	0.9426192
4	1.41158	0.7084252	4.57313	0.2186687	3.2397199	0.3086687	1.3925039
5	1.53862	0.6499314	5.98471	0.1670925	3.8896513	0.2570925	1.8281968
6	1.67710	0.5962673	7.52333	0.1329198	4.4859186	0.2229198	2.2497922
7	1.82804	0.5470342	9.20043	0.1086905	5.0329528	0.1986905	2.6574042
8	1.99256	0.5018663	11.02847	0.0906744	5.5348191	0.1806744	3.0511664
9	2.17189	0.4604278	13.02104	0.0767988	5.9952469	0.1667988	3.4312309
10	2.36736	0.4224108	15.19293	0.0658201	6.4176577	0.1558201	3.7977678
11	2.58043	0.3875329	17.56029	0.0569467	6.8051906	0.1469467	4.1509642
12	2.81266	0.3555347	20.14072	0.0496607	7.1607253	0.1396607	4.4910233
13	3.06580	0.3261786	22.95338	0.0435666	7.4869039	0.1335666	4.8181636
14	3.34173	0.2992465	26.01919	0.0384332	7.7861504	0.1284332	5.1326175
15	3.64248	0.2745380	29.36092	0.0340589	8.0606884	0.1240589	5.4346307
16	3.97031	0.2518698	33.00340	0.0302999	8.3125582	0.1202999	5.7244605
17	4.32763	0.2310732	36.97370	0.0270462	8.5436314	0.1170462	6.0023753
18	4.71712	0.2119937	41.30134	0.0242123	8.7556251	0.1142123	6.2686530
19	5.14166	0.1944897	46.01846	0.0217304	8.9501148	0.1117304	6.5235800
20	5.60441	0.1784309	51.16012	0.0195465	9.1285457	0.1095465	6.7674500
21	6.10881	0.1636981	56.76453	0.0176166	9.2922437	0.1076166	7.0005630
22	6.65860	0.1501817	62.87334	0.0159050	9.4424254	0.1059050	7.2232239
23	7.25787	0.1377814	69.53194	0.0143819	9.5802068	0.1043819	7.4357418
24	7.91108	0.1264049	76.78981	0.0130226	9.7066118	0.1030226	7.6384283
25	8.62308	0.1159678	84.70090	0.0118063	9.8225796	0.1018063	7.8315971
26	9.39916	0.1063925	93.32398	0.0107154	9.9289721	0.1007154	8.0155627
27	10.24508	0.0976078	102.72313	0.0097349	10.0265799	0.0997349	8.1906395
28	11.16714	0.0895484	112.96822	0.0088520	10.1161284	0.0988520	8.3571408
29	12.17218	0.0821545	124.13536	0.0080557	10.1982829	0.0980557	8.5153783
30	13.26768	0.0753711	136.30754	0.0073364	10.2736540	0.0973364	8.6656606
31	14.46177	0.0691478	149.57522	0.0066856	10.3428019	0.0966856	8.8082935
32	15.76333	0.0634384	164.03699	0.0060962	10.4062403	0.0960962	8.9435783
33	17.18203	0.0582003	179.80032	0.0055617	10.4644406	0.0955617	9.0718118
34	18.72841	0.0533948	196.98234	0.0050766	10.5178354	0.0950766	9.1932855
35	20.41397	0.0489861	215.71075	0.0046358	10.5668215	0.0946358	9.3082854
36	22.25123	0.0449413	236.12472	0.0042350	10.6117628	0.0942350	9.4170911
37	24.25384	0.0412306	258.37595	0.0038703	10.6529934	0.0938703	9.5199757
38	26.43668	0.0378262	282.62978	0.0035382	10.6908196	0.0935382	9.6172055
39	28.81598	0.0347030	309.06646	0.0032356	10.7255226	0.0932356	9.7090394
40	31.40942	0.0318376	337.88245	0.0029596	10.7573602	0.0929596	9.7957292
42	37.31753	0.0267971	403.52813	0.0024781	10.8133660	0.0924781	9.9546449
48	62.58524	0.0159782	684.28041	0.0014614	10.9335755	0.0914614	10.3317035
50	74.35752	0.0134485	815.08356	0.0012269	10.9616829	0.0912269	10.4295177
60	176.03129	0.0056808	1944.79213	0.0005142	11.0479910	0.0905142	10.7683153
70	416.73009	0.0023996	4619.22318	0.0002165	11.0844485	0.0902165	10.9427326
72	495.11702	0.0020197	5490.18906	0.0001821	11.0886697	0.0901821	10.9653966
75	641.19089	0.0015596	7113.23215	0.0001406	11.0937822	0.0901406	10.9939586
80	986.55167	0.0010136	10950.57409	0.0000913	11.0998485	0.0900913	11.0299383
90	2335.52658	0.0004282	25939.18425	0.0000386	11.1063537	0.0900386	11.0725594
100	5529.04079	0.0001809	61422.67546	0.0000163	11.1091015	0.0900163	11.0930215

10% Interest Rate Factors

	Single Payment		Equal-Payment Series				Uniform
N	Compound Amount Factor, (F/P, i, N)	Present-Worth Factor, (P/F, i, N)	Compound Amount Factor, (F/A, i, N)	Sinking-Fund Factor, (A/F, i, N)	Present-Worth Factor, (P/A, i, N)	Capital Recovery Factor, (A/P, i, N)	Gradient Series Factor, (A/G, i, N)
1	1.10000	0.9090909	1.00000	1.0000000	0.9090909	1.1000000	0.0000000
2	1.21000	0.8264463	2.10000	0.4761905	1.7355372	0.5761905	0.4761905
3	1.33100	0.7513148	3.31000	0.3021148	2.4868520	0.4021148	0.9365559
4	1.46410	0.6830135	4.64100	0.2154708	3.1698654	0.3154708	1.3811679
5	1.61051	0.6209213	6.10510	0.1637975	3.7907868	0.2637975	1.8101260
6	1.77156	0.5644739	7.71561	0.1296074	4.3552607	0.2296074	2.2235572
7	1.94872	0.5131581	9.48717	0.1054055	4.8684188	0.2054055	2.6216150
8	2.14359	0.4665074	11.43589	0.0874440	5.3349262	0.1874440	3.0044786
9	2.35795	0.4240976	13.57948	0.0736405	5.7590238	0.1736405	3.3723515
10	2.59374	0.3855433	15.93742	0.0627454	6.1445671	0.1627454	3.7254605
11	2.85312	0.3504939	18.53117	0.0539631	6.4950610	0.1539631	4.0640544
12	3.13843	0.3186308	21.38428	0.0467633	6.8136918	0.1467633	4.3884022
13	3.45227	0.2896644	24.52271	0.0407785	7.1033562	0.1407785	4.6987919
14	3.79750	0.2633313	27.97498	0.0357462	7.3666875	0.1357462	4.9955287
15	4.17725	0.2393920	31.77248	0.0314738	7.6060795	0.1314738	5.2789335
16	4.59497	0.2176291	35.94973	0.0278166	7.8237086	0.1278166	5.5493407
17	5.05447	0.1978447	40.54470	0.0246641	8.0215533	0.1246641	5.8070972
18	5.55992	0.1798588	45.59917	0.0219302	8.2014121	0.1219302	6.0525600
19	6.11591	0.1635080	51.15909	0.0195469	8.3649201	0.1195469	6.2860950
20	6.72750	0.1486436	57.27500	0.0174596	8.5135637	0.1174596	6.5080750
21	7.40025	0.1351306	64.00250	0.0156244	8.6486943	0.1156244	6.7188781
22	8.14027	0.1228460	71.40275	0.0140051	8.7715403	0.1140051	6.9188862
23	8.95430	0.1116782	79.54302	0.0125718	8.8832184	0.1125718	7.1084831
24	9.84973	0.1015256	88.49733	0.0112998	8.9847440	0.1112998	7.2880537
25	10.83471	0.0922960	98.34706	0.0101681	9.0770400	0.1101681	7.4579820
26	11.91818	0.0839055	109.18177	0.0091590	9.1609455	0.1091590	7.6186500
27	13.10999	0.0762777	121.09994	0.0082576	9.2372232	0.1082576	7.7704366
28	14.42099	0.0693433	134.20994	0.0074510	9.3065665	0.1074510	7.9137163
29	15.86309	0.0630394	148.63093	0.0067281	9.3696059	0.1067281	8.0488583
30	17.44940	0.0573086	164.49402	0.0060792	9.4269145	0.1060792	8.1762255
31	19.19434	0.0520987	181.94342	0.0054962	9.4790132	0.1054962	8.2961737
32	21.11378	0.0473624	201.13777	0.0049717	9.5263756	0.1049717	8.4090507
33	23.22515	0.0430568	222.25154	0.0044994	9.5694324	0.1044994	8.5151959
34	25.54767	0.0391425	245.47670	0.0040737	9.6085749	0.1040737	8.6149398
35	28.10244	0.0355841	271.02437	0.0036897	9.6441590	0.1036897	8.7086032
36	30.91268	0.0323492	299.12681	0.0033431	9.6765082	0.1033431	8.7964970
37	34.00395	0.0294083	330.03949	0.0030299	9.7059165	0.1030299	8.8789220
38	37.40434	0.0267349	364.04343	0.0027469	9.7326514	0.1027469	8.9561685
39	41.14478	0.0243044	401.44778	0.0024910	9.7569558	0.1024910	9.0285162
40	45.25926	0.0220949	442.59256	0.0022594	9.7790507	0.1022594	9.0962342
42	54.76370	0.0182603	537.63699	0.0018600	9.8173973	0.1018600	9.2188038
48	97.01723	0.0103074	960.17234	0.0010415	9.8969255	0.1010415	9.5000897
50	117.39085	0.0085186	1163.90853	0.0008592	9.9148145	0.1008592	9.5704130
60	304.48164	0.0032843	3034.81640	0.0003295	9.9671573	0.1003295	9.8022945
70	789.74696	0.0012662	7887.46957	0.0001268	9.9873377	0.1001268	9.9112516
72	955.59382	0.0010465	9545.93818	0.0001048	9.9895353	0.1001048	9.9245753
75	1271.89537	0.0007862	12708.95371	0.0000787	9.9921377	0.1000787	9.9409865
80	2048.40021	0.0004882	20474.00215	0.0000488	9.9951181	0.1000488	9.9609261
90	5313.02261	0.0001882	53120.22612	0.0000188	9.9981178	0.1000188	9.9830573
100	13780.61234	0.0000726	137796.12340	0.0000073	9.9992743	0.1000073	9.9927429

12% *Interest Rate Factors*

	Single Payment		Equal-Payment Series				Uniform Gradient Series Factor,
N	Compound Amount Factor, (F/P, i, N)	Present-Worth Factor, (P/F, i, N)	Compound Amount Factor, (F/A, i, N)	Sinking-Fund Factor, (A/F, i, N)	Present-Worth Factor, (P/A, i, N)	Capital Recovery Factor, (A/P, i, N)	(A/G, i, N)
1	1.12000	0.8928571	1.00000	1.0000000	0.8928571	1.1200000	0.0000000
2	1.25440	0.7971939	2.12000	0.4716981	1.6900510	0.5916981	0.4716981
3	1.40493	0.7117802	3.37440	0.2963490	2.4018313	0.4163490	0.9246088
4	1.57352	0.6355181	4.77933	0.2092344	3.0373493	0.3292344	1.3588521
5	1.76234	0.5674269	6.35285	0.1574097	3.6047762	0.2774097	1.7745945
6	1.97382	0.5066311	8.11519	0.1232257	4.1114073	0.2432257	2.1720474
7	2.21068	0.4523492	10.08901	0.0991177	4.5637565	0.2191177	2.5514654
8	2.47596	0.4038832	12.29969	0.0813028	4.9676398	0.2013028	2.9131439
9	2.77308	0.3606100	14.77566	0.0676789	5.3282498	0.1876789	3.2574167
10	3.10585	0.3219732	17.54874	0.0569842	5.6502230	0.1769842	3.5846530
11	3.47855	0.2874761	20.65458	0.0484154	5.9376991	0.1684154	3.8952546
12	3.89598	0.2566751	24.13313	0.0414368	6.1943742	0.1614368	4.1896526
13	4.36349	0.2291742	28.02911	0.0356772	6.4235484	0.1556772	4.4683039
14	4.88711	0.2046198	32.39260	0.0308712	6.6281682	0.1508712	4.7316880
15	5.47357	0.1826963	37.27971	0.0268242	6.8108645	0.1468242	4.9803034
16	6.13039	0.1631217	42.75328	0.0233900	6.9739862	0.1433900	5.2146643
17	6.86604	0.1456443	48.88367	0.0204567	7.1196305	0.1404567	5.4352969
18	7.68997	0.1300396	55.74971	0.0179373	7.2496701	0.1379373	5.6427366
19	8.61276	0.1161068	63.43968	0.0157630	7.3657769	0.1357630	5.8375242
20	9.64629	0.1036668	72.05244	0.0138788	7.4694436	0.1338788	6.0202033
21	10.80385	0.0925596	81.69874	0.0122401	7.5620032	0.1322401	6.1913173
22	12.10031	0.0826425	92.50258	0.0108105	7.6446457	0.1308105	6.3514067
23	13.55235	0.0737880	104.60289	0.0095600	7.7184337	0.1295600	6.5010067
24	15.17863	0.0658821	118.15524	0.0084634	7.7843158	0.1284634	6.6406450
25	17.00006	0.0588233	133.33387	0.0075000	7.8431391	0.1275000	6.7708396
26	19.04007	0.0525208	150.33393	0.0066519	7.8956599	0.1266519	6.8920974
27	21.32488	0.0468936	169.37401	0.0059041	7.9425535	0.1259041	7.0049123
28	23.88387	0.0418693	190.69889	0.0052439	7.9844228	0.1252439	7.1097639
29	26.74993	0.0373833	214.58275	0.0046602	8.0218060	0.1246602	7.2071167
30	29.95992	0.0333779	241.33268	0.0041437	8.0551840	0.1241437	7.2974189
31	33.55511	0.0298017	271.29261	0.0036861	8.0849857	0.1236861	7.3811020
32	37.58173	0.0266087	304.84772	0.0032803	8.1115944	0.1232803	7.4585796
33	42.09153	0.0237577	342.42945	0.0029203	8.1353521	0.1229203	7.5302482
34	47.14252	0.0212123	384.52098	0.0026006	8.1565644	0.1226006	7.5964858
35	52.79962	0.0189395	431.66350	0.0023166	8.1755039	0.1223166	7.6576527
36	59.13557	0.0169103	484.46312	0.0020641	8.1924142	0.1220641	7.7140911
37	66.23184	0.0150985	543.59869	0.0018396	8.2075127	0.1218396	7.7661257
38	74.17966	0.0134808	609.83053	0.0016398	8.2209935	0.1216398	7.8140634
39	83.08122	0.0120364	684.01020	0.0014620	8.2330299	0.1214620	7.8581942
40	93.05097	0.0107468	767.09142˙	0.0013036	8.2437767	0.1213036	7.8987915
42	116.72314	0.0085673	964.35948	0.0010370	8.2619393	0.1210370	7.9703981
48	230.39078	0.0043405	1911.58980	0.0005231	8.2971629	0.1205231	8.1240834
50	289.00219	0.0034602	2400.01825	0.0004167	8.3044985	0.1204167	8.1597235
60	897.59693	0.0011141	7471.64111	0.0001338	8.3240493	0.1201338	8.2664136
70	2787.79983	0.0003587	23223.33190	0.0000431	8.3303441	0.1200431	8.3082149
72	3497.01610	0.0002860	29133.46753	0.0000343	8.3309503	0.1200343	8.3127385
75	4913.05584	0.0002035	40933.79867	0.0000244	8.3316372	0.1200244	8.3180648
80	8658.48310	0.0001155	72145.69250	0.0000139	8.3323709	0.1200139	8.3240928
90	26891.93422	0.0000372	224091.11853	0.0000045	8.3330235	0.1200045	8.3299865
100	83522.26573	0.0000120	696010.54772	0.0000014	8.3332336	0.1200014	8.3321360

15% Interest Rate Factors

	Single Payment		Equal-Payment Series				Uniform
N	Compound Amount Factor, (F/P, i, N)	Present-Worth Factor, (P/F, i, N)	Compound Amount Factor, (F/A, i, N)	Sinking-Fund Factor, (A/F, i, N)	Present-Worth Factor, (P/A, i, N)	Capital Recovery Factor, (A/P, i, N)	Gradient Series Factor, (A/G, i, N)
1	1.15000	0.8695652	1.00000	1.0000000	0.8695652	1.1500000	0.0000000
2	1.32250	0.7561437	2.15000	0.4651163	1.6257089	0.6151163	0.4651163
3	1.52088	0.6575162	3.47250	0.2879770	2.2832251	0.4379770	0.9071274
4	1.74901	0.5717532	4.99338	0.2002654	2.8549784	0.3502654	1.3262573
5	2.01136	0.4971767	6.74238	0.1483156	3.3521551	0.2983156	1.7228149
6	2.31306	0.4323276	8.75374	0.1142369	3.7844827	0.2642369	2.0971904
7	2.66002	0.3759370	11.06680	0.0903604	4.1604197	0.2403604	2.4498497
8	3.05902	0.3269018	13.72682	0.0728501	4.4873215	0.2228501	2.7813286
9	3.51788	0.2842624	16.78584	0.0595740	4.7715839	0.2095740	3.0922258
10	4.04556	0.2471847	20.30372	0.0492521	5.0187686	0.1992521	3.3831958
11	4.65239	0.2149432	24.34928	0.0410690	5.2337118	0.1910690	3.6549412
12	5.35025	0.1869072	29.00167	0.0344808	5.4206190	0.1844808	3.9082046
13	6.15279	0.1625280	34.35192	0.0291105	5.5831470	0.1791105	4.1437604
14	7.07571	0.1413287	40.50471	0.0246885	5.7244756	0.1746885	4.3624076
15	8.13706	0.1228945	47.58041	0.0210171	5.8473701	0.1710171	4.5649614
16	9.35762	0.1068648	55.71747	0.0179477	5.9542349	0.1679477	4.7522463
17	10.76126	0.0929259	65.07509	0.0153669	6.0471608	0.1653669	4.9250889
18	12.37545	0.0808051	75.83636	0.0131863	6.1279659	0.1631863	5.0843122
19	14.23177	0.0702653	88.21181	0.0113364	6.1982312	0.1613364	5.2307289
20	16.36654	0.0611003	102.44358	0.0097615	6.2593315	0.1597615	5.3651373
21	18.82152	0.0531307	118.81012	0.0084168	6.3124622	0.1584168	5.4883159
22	21.64475	0.0462006	137.63164	0.0072658	6.3586627	0.1572658	5.6010202
23	24.89146	0.0401744	159.27638	0.0062784	6.3988372	0.1562784	5.7039795
24	28.62518	0.0349343	184.16784	0.0054298	6.4337714	0.1554298	5.7978939
25	32.91895	0.0303776	212.79302	0.0046994	6.4641491	0.1546994	5.8834329
26	37.85680	0.0264153	245.71197	0.0040698	6.4905644	0.1540698	5.9612337
27	43.53531	0.0229699	283.56877	0.0035265	6.5135343	0.1535265	6.0319000
28	50.06561	0.0199738	327.10408	0.0030571	6.5335081	0.1530571	6.0960022
29	57.57545	0.0173685	377.16969	0.0026513	6.5508766	0.1526513	6.1540766
30	66.21177	0.0151031	434.74515	0.0023002	6.5659796	0.1523002	6.2066270
31	76.14354	0.0131331	500.95692	0.0019962	6.5791127	0.1519962	6.2541229
32	87.56507	0.0114201	577.10046	0.0017328	6.5905328	0.1517328	6.2970025
33	100.69983	0.0099305	664.66552	0.0015045	6.6004633	0.1515045	6.3356731
34	115.80480	0.0086352	765.36535	0.0013066	6.6090985	0.1513066	6.3705118
35	133.17552	0.0075089	881.17016	0.0011349	6.6166074	0.1511349	6.4018673
36	153.15185	0.0065295	1014.34568	0.0009859	6.6231369	0.1509859	6.4300609
37	176.12463	0.0056778	1167.49753	0.0008565	6.6288147	0.1508565	6.4553886
38	202.54332	0.0049372	1343.62216	0.0007443	6.6337519	0.1507443	6.4781216
39	232.92482	0.0042932	1546.16549	0.0006468	6.6380451	0.1506468	6.4985087
40	267.86355	0.0037332	1779.09031	0.0005621	6.6417784	0.1505621	6.5167773
42	354.24954	0.0028229	2354.99693	0.0004246	6.6478475	0.1504246	6.5477705
48	819.40071	0.0012204	5456.00475	0.0001833	6.6585306	0.1501833	6.6080157
50	1083.65744	0.0009228	7217.71628	0.0001385	6.6605147	0.1501385	6.6204840

18% *Interest Rate Factors*

	Single Payment		Equal-Payment Series				Uniform
N	Compound Amount Factor, (F/P, i, N)	Present-Worth Factor, (P/F, i, N)	Compound Amount Factor, (F/A, i, N)	Sinking-Fund Factor, (A/F, i, N)	Present-Worth Factor, (P/A, i, N)	Capital Recovery Factor, (A/P, i, N)	Gradient Series Factor, (A/G, i, N)
1	1.18000	0.8474576	1.00000	1.0000000	0.8474576	1.1800000	0.0000000
2	1.39240	0.7181844	2.18000	0.4587156	1.5656421	0.6387156	0.4587156
3	1.64303	0.6086309	3.57240	0.2799239	2.1742729	0.4599239	0.8901579
4	1.93878	0.5157889	5.21543	0.1917387	2.6900618	0.3717387	1.2946962
5	2.28776	0.4371092	7.15421	0.1397778	3.1271710	0.3197778	1.6728377
6	2.69955	0.3704315	9.44197	0.1059101	3.4976026	0.2859101	2.0252179
7	3.18547	0.3139250	12.14152	0.0823620	3.8115276	0.2623620	2.3525889
8	3.75886	0.2660382	15.32700	0.0652444	4.0775658	0.2452444	2.6558063
9	4.43545	0.2254561	19.08585	0.0523948	4.3030218	0.2323948	2.9358144
10	5.23384	0.1910645	23.52131	0.0425146	4.4940863	0.2225146	3.1936310
11	6.17593	0.1619190	28.75514	0.0347764	4.6560053	0.2147764	3.4303320
12	7.28759	0.1372195	34.93107	0.0286278	4.7932249	0.2086278	3.6470350
13	8.59936	0.1162877	42.21866	0.0236862	4.9095126	0.2036862	3.8448850
14	10.14724	0.0985489	50.81802	0.0196781	5.0080615	0.1996781	4.0250399
15	11.97375	0.0835160	60.96527	0.0164028	5.0915776	0.1964028	4.1886570
16	14.12902	0.0707763	72.93901	0.0137101	5.1623539	0.1937101	4.3368814
17	16.67225	0.0599799	87.06804	0.0114853	5.2223338	0.1914853	4.4708355
18	19.67325	0.0508304	103.74028	0.0096395	5.2731642	0.1896395	4.5916099
19	23.21444	0.0430766	123.41353	0.0081028	5.3162409	0.1881028	4.7002559
20	27.39303	0.0365056	146.62797	0.0068200	5.3527465	0.1868200	4.7977799
21	32.32378	0.0309370	174.02100	0.0057464	5.3836835	0.1857464	4.8851384
22	38.14206	0.0262178	206.34479	0.0048463	5.4099012	0.1848463	4.9632352
23	45.00763	0.0222185	244.48685	0.0040902	5.4321197	0.1840902	5.0329189
24	53.10901	0.0188292	289.49448	0.0034543	5.4509489	0.1834543	5.0949826
25	62.66863	0.0159569	342.60349	0.0029188	5.4669058	0.1829188	5.1501630
26	73.94898	0.0135228	405.27211	0.0024675	5.4804287	0.1824675	5.1991421
27	87.25980	0.0114600	479.22109	0.0020867	5.4918887	0.1820867	5.2425476
28	102.96656	0.0097119	566.48089	0.0017653	5.5016006	0.1817653	5.2809557
29	121.50054	0.0082304	669.44745	0.0014938	5.5098310	0.1814938	5.3148927
30	143.37064	0.0069749	790.94799	0.0012643	5.5168060	0.1812643	5.3448380
31	169.17735	0.0059110	934.31863	0.0010703	5.5227169	0.1810703	5.3712263
32	199.62928	0.0050093	1103.49598	0.0009062	5.5277262	0.1809062	5.3944514
33	235.56255	0.0042452	1303.12526	0.0007674	5.5319713	0.1807674	5.4148681
34	277.96381	0.0035976	1538.68781	0.0006499	5.5355689	0.1806499	5.4327958
35	327.99729	0.0030488	1816.65161	0.0005505	5.5386177	0.1805505	5.4485210
36	387.03680	0.0025837	2144.64890	0.0004663	5.5412015	0.1804663	5.4623002
37	456.70343	0.0021896	2531.68570	0.0003950	5.5433911	0.1803950	5.4743624
38	538.91004	0.0018556	2988.38913	0.0003346	5.5452467	0.1803346	5.4849118
39	635.91385	0.0015725	3527.29918	0.0002835	5.5468192	0.1802835	5.4941299
40	750.37834	0.0013327	4163.21303	0.0002402	5.5481519	0.1802402	5.5021780
42	1044.82681	0.0009571	5799.03782	0.0001724	5.5502384	0.1801724	5.5153190
48	2820.56655	0.0003545	15664.25859	0.0000638	5.5535859	0.1800638	5.5385317
50	3927.35686	0.0002546	21813.09367	0.0000458	5.5541410	0.1800458	5.5428211

20% *Interest Rate Factors*

	Single Payment		Equal-Payment Series				Uniform
	Compound Amount Factor,	Present-Worth Factor,	Compound Amount Factor,	Sinking-Fund Factor,	Present-Worth Factor,	Capital Recovery Factor,	Gradient Series Factor,
N	$(F/P, i, N)$	$(P/F, i, N)$	$(F/A, i, N)$	$(A/F, i, N)$	$(P/A, i, N)$	$(A/P, i, N)$	$(A/G, i, N)$
1	1.20000	0.8333333	1.00000	1.0000000	0.8333333	1.2000000	0.0000000
2	1.44000	0.6944444	2.20000	0.4545455	1.5277778	0.6545455	0.4545455
3	1.72800	0.5787037	3.64000	0.2747253	2.1064815	0.4747253	0.8791209
4	2.07360	0.4822531	5.36800	0.1862891	2.5887346	0.3862891	1.2742176
5	2.48832	0.4018776	7.44160	0.1343797	2.9906121	0.3343797	1.6405074
6	2.98598	0.3348980	9.92992	0.1007057	3.3255101	0.3007057	1.9788276
7	3.58318	0.2790816	12.91590	0.0774239	3.6045918	0.2774239	2.2901626
8	4.29982	0.2325680	16.49908	0.0606094	3.8371598	0.2606094	2.5756231
9	5.15978	0.1938067	20.79890	0.0480795	4.0309665	0.2480795	2.8364242
10	6.19174	0.1615056	25.95868	0.0385228	4.1924721	0.2385228	3.0738622
11	7.43008	0.1345880	32.15042	0.0311038	4.3270601	0.2311038	3.2892913
12	8.91610	0.1121567	39.58050	0.0252650	4.4392167	0.2252650	3.4841021
13	10.69932	0.0934639	48.49660	0.0206200	4.5326806	0.2206200	3.6596999
14	12.83918	0.0778866	59.19592	0.0168931	4.6105672	0.2168931	3.8174861
15	15.40702	0.0649055	72.03511	0.0138821	4.6754726	0.2138821	3.9588410
16	18.48843	0.0540879	87.44213	0.0114361	4.7295605	0.2114361	4.0851092
17	22.18611	0.0450732	105.93056	0.0094401	4.7746338	0.2094401	4.1975875
18	26.62333	0.0375610	128.11667	0.0078054	4.8121948	0.2078054	4.2975153
19	31.94800	0.0313009	154.74000	0.0064625	4.8434957	0.2064625	4.3860669
20	38.33760	0.0260841	186.68800	0.0053565	4.8695797	0.2053565	4.4643469
21	46.00512	0.0217367	225.02560	0.0044439	4.8913164	0.2044439	4.5333864
22	55.20614	0.0181139	271.03072	0.0036896	4.9094304	0.2036896	4.5941419
23	66.24737	0.0150949	326.23686	0.0030653	4.9245253	0.2030653	4.6474954
24	79.49685	0.0125791	392.48424	0.0025479	4.9371044	0.2025479	4.6942552
25	95.39622	0.0104826	471.98108	0.0021187	4.9475870	0.2021187	4.7351589
26	114.47546	0.0087355	567.37730	0.0017625	4.9563225	0.2017625	4.7708756
27	137.37055	0.0072796	681.85276	0.0014666	4.9636021	0.2014666	4.8020100
28	164.84466	0.0060663	819.22331	0.0012207	4.9696684	0.2012207	4.8291064
29	197.81359	0.0050553	984.06797	0.0010162	4.9747237	0.2010162	4.8526525
30	237.37631	0.0042127	1181.88157	0.0008461	4.9789364	0.2008461	4.8730387
31	284.85158	0.0035106	1419.25788	0.0007046	4.9824470	0.2007046	4.8907880
32	341.82189	0.0029255	1704.10946	0.0005868	4.9853725	0.2005868	4.9061093
33	410.18627	0.0024379	2045.93135	0.0004888	4.9878104	0.2004888	4.9193521
34	492.22352	0.0020316	2456.11762	0.0004071	4.9898420	0.2004071	4.9307851
35	590.66823	0.0016930	2948.34115	0.0003392	4.9915350	0.2003392	4.9406446
36	708.80187	0.0014108	3539.00937	0.0002826	4.9929458	0.2002826	4.9491383
37	850.56225	0.0011757	4247.81125	0.0002354	4.9941215	0.2002354	4.9564482
38	1020.67470	0.0009797	5098.37350	0.0001961	4.9951013	0.2001961	4.9627332
39	1224.80964	0.0008165	6119.04820	0.0001634	4.9959177	0.2001634	4.9681323
40	1469.77157	0.0006804	7343.85784	0.0001362	4.9965981	0.2001362	4.9727664
42	2116.47106	0.0004725	10577.35529	0.0000945	4.9976376	0.2000945	4.9801463
48	6319.74872	0.0001582	31593.74358	0.0000317	4.9992088	0.2000317	4.9924036
50	9100.43815	0.0001099	45497.19075	0.0000220	4.9994506	0.2000220	4.9945052

25% *Interest Rate Factors*

	Single Payment		Equal-Payment Series				Uniform Gradient Series
N	Compound Amount Factor, (F/P, i, N)	Present-Worth Factor, (P/F, i, N)	Compound Amount Factor, (F/A, i, N)	Sinking-Fund Factor, (A/F, i, N)	Present-Worth Factor, (P/A, i, N)	Capital Recovery Factor, (A/P, i, N)	Factor, (A/G, i, N)
1	1.25000	0.8000000	1.00000	1.0000000	0.8000000	1.2500000	0.0000000
2	1.56250	0.6400000	2.25000	0.4444444	1.4400000	0.6944444	0.4444444
3	1.95313	0.5120000	3.81250	0.2622951	1.9520000	0.5122951	0.8524590
4	2.44141	0.4096000	5.76563	0.1734417	2.3616000	0.4234417	1.2249322
5	3.05176	0.3276800	8.20703	0.1218467	2.6892800	0.3718467	1.5630652
6	3.81470	0.2621440	11.25879	0.0888195	2.9514240	0.3388195	1.8683320
7	4.76837	0.2097152	15.07349	0.0663417	3.1611392	0.3163417	2.1424337
8	5.96046	0.1677722	19.84186	0.0503985	3.3289114	0.3003985	2.3872478
9	7.45058	0.1342177	25.80232	0.0387562	3.4631291	0.2887562	2.6047768
10	9.31323	0.1073742	33.25290	0.0300726	3.5705033	0.2800726	2.7970975
11	11.64153	0.0858993	42.56613	0.0234929	3.6564026	0.2734929	2.9663143
12	14.55192	0.0687195	54.20766	0.0184476	3.7251221	0.2684476	3.1145163
13	18.18989	0.0549756	68.75958	0.0145434	3.7800977	0.2645434	3.2437417
14	22.73737	0.0439805	86.94947	0.0115009	3.8240781	0.2615009	3.3559478
15	28.42171	0.0351844	109.68684	0.0091169	3.8592625	0.2591169	3.4529882
16	35.52714	0.0281475	138.10855	0.0072407	3.8874100	0.2572407	3.5365964
17	44.40892	0.0225180	173.63568	0.0057592	3.9099280	0.2557592	3.6083754
18	55.51115	0.0180144	218.04460	0.0045862	3.9279424	0.2545862	3.6697923
19	69.38894	0.0144115	273.55576	0.0036556	3.9423539	0.2536556	3.7221773
20	86.73617	0.0115292	342.94470	0.0029159	3.9538831	0.2529159	3.7667262
21	108.42022	0.0092234	429.68087	0.0023273	3.9631065	0.2523273	3.8045061
22	135.52527	0.0073787	538.10109	0.0018584	3.9704852	0.2518584	3.8364620
23	169.40659	0.0059030	673.62636	0.0014845	3.9763882	0.2514845	3.8634258
24	211.75824	0.0047224	843.03295	0.0011862	3.9811105	0.2511862	3.8861254
25	264.69780	0.0037779	1054.79118	0.0009481	3.9848884	0.2509481	3.9051945
26	330.87225	0.0030223	1319.48898	0.0007579	3.9879107	0.2507579	3.9211816
27	413.59031	0.0024179	1650.36123	0.0006059	3.9903286	0.2506059	3.9345598
28	516.98788	0.0019343	2063.95153	0.0004845	3.9922629	0.2504845	3.9457352
29	646.23485	0.0015474	2580.93941	0.0003875	3.9938103	0.2503875	3.9550551
30	807.79357	0.0012379	3227.17427	0.0003099	3.9950482	0.2503099	3.9628158
31	1009.74196	0.0009904	4034.96783	0.0002478	3.9960386	0.2502478	3.9692687
32	1262.17745	0.0007923	5044.70979	0.0001982	3.9968309	0.2501982	3.9746269
33	1577.72181	0.0006338	6306.88724	0.0001586	3.9974647	0.2501586	3.9790705
34	1972.15226	0.0005071	7884.60905	0.0001268	3.9979718	0.2501268	3.9827512
35	2465.19033	0.0004056	9856.76132	0.0001015	3.9983774	0.2501015	3.9857966
36	3081.48791	0.0003245	12321.95164	0.0000812	3.9987019	0.2500812	3.9883135
37	3851.85989	0.0002596	15403.43956	0.0000649	3.9989615	0.2500649	3.9903918
38	4814.82486	0.0002077	19255.29944	0.0000519	3.9991692	0.2500519	3.9921061
39	6018.53108	0.0001662	24070.12430	0.0000415	3.9993354	0.2500415	3.9935189
40	7523.16385	0.0001329	30088.65538	0.0000332	3.9994683	0.2500332	3.9946824
42	11754.94351	0.0000851	47015.77403	0.0000213	3.9996597	0.2500213	3.9964267
48	44841.55086	0.0000223	179362.20343	0.0000056	3.9999108	0.2500056	3.9989295
50	70064.92322	0.0000143	280255.69286	0.0000036	3.9999429	0.2500036	3.9992864

30% *Interest Rate Factors*

	Single Payment		Equal-Payment Series				Uniform
N	Compound Amount Factor, (F/P, i, N)	Present-Worth Factor, (P/F, i, N)	Compound Amount Factor, (F/A, i, N)	Sinking-Fund Factor, (A/F, i, N)	Present-Worth Factor, (P/A, i, N)	Capital Recovery Factor, (A/P, i, N)	Gradient Series Factor, (A/G, i, N)
1	1.30000	0.7692308	1.00000	1.0000000	0.7692308	1.3000000	0.0000000
2	1.69000	0.5917160	2.30000	0.4347826	1.3609467	0.7347826	0.4347826
3	2.19700	0.4551661	3.99000	0.2506266	1.8161129	0.5506266	0.8270677
4	2.85610	0.3501278	6.18700	0.1616292	2.1662407	0.4616292	1.1782770
5	3.71293	0.2693291	9.04310	0.1105815	2.4355698	0.4105815	1.4903075
6	4.82681	0.2071762	12.75603	0.0783943	2.6427460	0.3783943	1.7654474
7	6.27485	0.1593663	17.58284	0.0568736	2.8021123	0.3568736	2.0062818
8	8.15731	0.1225895	23.85769	0.0419152	2.9247018	0.3419152	2.2155945
9	10.60450	0.0942996	32.01500	0.0312354	3.0190013	0.3312354	2.3962725
10	13.78585	0.0725382	42.61950	0.0234634	3.0915395	0.3234634	2.5512187
11	17.92160	0.0557986	56.40535	0.0177288	3.1473381	0.3177288	2.6832768
12	23.29809	0.0429220	74.32695	0.0134541	3.1902601	0.3134541	2.7951705
13	30.28751	0.0330169	97.62504	0.0102433	3.2232770	0.3102433	2.8894581
14	39.37376	0.0253976	127.91255	0.0078178	3.2486746	0.3078178	2.9685007
15	51.18589	0.0195366	167.28631	0.0059778	3.2682112	0.3059778	3.0344446
16	66.54166	0.0150282	218.47220	0.0045772	3.2832394	0.3045772	3.0892138
17	86.50416	0.0115601	285.01386	0.0035086	3.2947995	0.3035086	3.1345126
18	112.45541	0.0088924	371.51802	0.0026917	3.3036920	0.3026917	3.1718338
19	146.19203	0.0068403	483.97343	0.0020662	3.3105323	0.3020662	3.2024722
20	190.04964	0.0052618	630.16546	0.0015869	3.3157941	0.3015869	3.2275410
21	247.06453	0.0040475	820.21510	0.0012192	3.3198416	0.3012192	3.2479899
22	321.18389	0.0031135	1067.27963	0.0009370	3.3229551	0.3009370	3.2646228
23	417.53905	0.0023950	1388.46351	0.0007202	3.3253500	0.3007202	3.2781164
24	542.80077	0.0018423	1806.00257	0.0005537	3.3271923	0.3005537	3.2890366
25	705.64100	0.0014172	2348.80334	0.0004257	3.3286095	0.3004257	3.2978543
26	917.33330	0.0010901	3054.44434	0.0003274	3.3296996	0.3003274	3.3049594
27	1192.53329	0.0008386	3971.77764	0.0002518	3.3305382	0.3002518	3.3106735
28	1550.29328	0.0006450	5164.31093	0.0001936	3.3311832	0.3001936	3.3152606
29	2015.38126	0.0004962	6714.60421	0.0001489	3.3316794	0.3001489	3.3189369
30	2619.99564	0.0003817	8729.98548	0.0001145	3.3320611	0.3001145	3.3218786
31	3405.99434	0.0002936	11349.98112	0.0000881	3.3323547	0.3000881	3.3242291
32	4427.79264	0.0002258	14755.97546	0.0000678	3.3325805	0.3000678	3.3261046
33	5756.13043	0.0001737	19183.76810	0.0000521	3.3327542	0.3000521	3.3275993
34	7482.96956	0.0001336	24939.89853	0.0000401	3.3328879	0.3000401	3.3287891
35	9727.86043	0.0001028	32422.86808	0.0000308	3.3329907	0.3000308	3.3297350
36	12646.21855	0.0000791	42150.72851	0.0000237	3.3330697	0.3000237	3.3304864
37	16440.08412	0.0000608	54796.94706	0.0000182	3.3331306	0.3000182	3.3310826
38	21372.10935	0.0000468	71237.03118	0.0000140	3.3331774	0.3000140	3.3315552
39	27783.74216	0.0000360	92609.14053	0.0000108	3.3332134	0.3000108	3.3319296
40	36118.86481	0.0000277	120392.88269	0.0000083	3.3332410	0.3000083	3.3322258

40% *Interest Rate Factors*

	Single Payment		Equal-Payment Series				Uniform Gradient Series
N	Compound Amount Factor, $(F/P, i, N)$	Present-Worth Factor, $(P/F, i, N)$	Compound Amount Factor, $(F/A, i, N)$	Sinking-Fund Factor, $(A/F, i, N)$	Present-Worth Factor, $(P/A, i, N)$	Capital Recovery Factor, $(A/P, i, N)$	Factor, $(A/G, i, N)$
1	1.40000	0.7142857	1.00000	1.0000000	0.7142857	1.4000000	0.0000000
2	1.96000	0.5102041	2.40000	0.4166667	1.2244898	0.8166667	0.4166667
3	2.74400	0.3644315	4.36000	0.2293578	1.5889213	0.6293578	0.7798165
4	3.84160	0.2603082	7.10400	0.1407658	1.8492295	0.5407658	1.0923423
5	5.37824	0.1859344	10.94560	0.0913609	2.0351639	0.4913609	1.3579886
6	7.52954	0.1328103	16.32384	0.0612601	2.1679742	0.4612601	1.5810986
7	10.54135	0.0948645	23.85338	0.0419228	2.2628387	0.4419228	1.7663512
8	14.75789	0.0677604	34.39473	0.0290742	2.3305991	0.4290742	1.9185155
9	20.66105	0.0484003	49.15262	0.0203448	2.3789994	0.4203448	2.0422421
10	28.92547	0.0345716	69.81366	0.0143238	2.4135710	0.4143238	2.1419039
11	40.49565	0.0246940	98.73913	0.0101277	2.4382650	0.4101277	2.2214883
12	56.69391	0.0176386	139.23478	0.0071821	2.4559036	0.4071821	2.2845366
13	79.37148	0.0125990	195.92869	0.0051039	2.4685025	0.4051039	2.3341233
14	111.12007	0.0089993	275.30017	0.0036324	2.4775018	0.4036324	2.3728660
15	155.56810	0.0064281	386.42024	0.0025879	2.4839299	0.4025879	2.4029554
16	217.79533	0.0045915	541.98833	0.0018451	2.4885213	0.4018451	2.4261977
17	304.91347	0.0032796	759.78367	0.0013162	2.4918010	0.4013162	2.4440630
18	426.87885	0.0023426	1064.69714	0.0009392	2.4941435	0.4009392	2.4577345
19	597.63040	0.0016733	1491.57599	0.0006704	2.4958168	0.4006704	2.4681545
20	836.68255	0.0011952	2089.20639	0.0004787	2.4970120	0.4004787	2.4760675
21	1171.35558	0.0008537	2925.88894	0.0003418	2.4978657	0.4003418	2.4820567
22	1639.89781	0.0006098	4097.24452	0.0002441	2.4984755	0.4002441	2.4865763
23	2295.85693	0.0004356	5737.14232	0.0001743	2.4989111	0.4001743	2.4899776
24	3214.19970	0.0003111	8032.99925	0.0001245	2.4992222	0.4001245	2.4925308
25	4499.87958	0.0002222	11247.19895	0.0000889	2.4994444	0.4000889	2.4944431
26	6299.83141	0.0001587	15747.07853	0.0000635	2.4996032	0.4000635	2.4958723
27	8819.76398	0.0001134	22046.90994	0.0000454	2.4997165	0.4000454	2.4969383
28	12347.66957	0.0000810	30866.67392	0.0000324	2.4997975	0.4000324	2.4977322
29	17286.73740	0.0000578	43214.34349	0.0000231	2.4998554	0.4000231	2.4983223
30	24201.43236	0.0000413	60501.08089	0.0000165	2.4998967	0.4000165	2.4987604
31	33882.00530	0.0000295	84702.51324	0.0000118	2.4999262	0.4000118	2.4990850
32	47434.80742	0.0000211	118584.51854	0.0000084	2.4999473	0.4000084	2.4993254
33	66408.73038	0.0000151	166019.32596	0.0000060	2.4999624	0.4000060	2.4995031
34	92972.22254	0.0000108	232428.05634	0.0000043	2.4999731	0.4000043	2.4996343
35	130161.11155	0.0000077	325400.27888	0.0000031	2.4999808	0.4000031	2.4997311

50% Interest Rate Factors

	Single Payment		Equal-Payment Series				Uniform
	Compound Amount Factor,	Present-Worth Factor,	Compound Amount Factor,	Sinking-Fund Factor,	Present-Worth Factor,	Capital Recovery Factor,	Gradient Series Factor,
N	(F/P, i, N)	(P/F, i, N)	(F/A, i, N)	(A/F, i, N)	(P/A, i, N)	(A/P, i, N)	(A/G, i, N)
1	1.50000	0.6666667	1.00000	1.0000000	0.6666667	1.5000000	0.0000000
2	2.25000	0.4444444	2.50000	0.4000000	1.1111111	0.9000000	0.4000000
3	3.37500	0.2962963	4.75000	0.2105263	1.4074074	0.7105263	0.7368421
4	5.06250	0.1975309	8.12500	0.1230769	1.6049383	0.6230769	1.0153846
5	7.59375	0.1316872	13.18750	0.0758294	1.7366255	0.5758294	1.2417062
6	11.39063	0.0877915	20.78125	0.0481203	1.8244170	0.5481203	1.4225564
7	17.08594	0.0585277	32.17188	0.0310831	1.8829447	0.5310831	1.5648373
8	25.62891	0.0390184	49.25781	0.0203013	1.9219631	0.5203013	1.6751784
9	38.44336	0.0260123	74.88672	0.0133535	1.9479754	0.5133535	1.7596370
10	57.66504	0.0173415	113.33008	0.0088238	1.9653169	0.5088238	1.8235243
11	86.49756	0.0115610	170.99512	0.0058481	1.9768780	0.5058481	1.8713414
12	129.74634	0.0077073	257.49268	0.0038836	1.9845853	0.5038836	1.9067935
13	194.61951	0.0051382	387.23901	0.0025824	1.9897235	0.5025824	1.9328580
14	291.92926	0.0034255	581.85852	0.0017186	1.9931490	0.5017186	1.9518783
15	437.89389	0.0022837	873.78778	0.0011444	1.9954327	0.5011444	1.9656667
16	656.84084	0.0015224	1311.68167	0.0007624	1.9969551	0.5007624	1.9756038
17	985.26125	0.0010150	1968.52251	0.0005080	1.9979701	0.5005080	1.9827282
18	1477.89188	0.0006766	2953.78376	0.0003385	1.9986467	0.5003385	1.9878122
19	2216.83782	0.0004511	4431.67564	0.0002256	1.9990978	0.5002256	1.9914254
20	3325.25673	0.0003007	6648.51346	0.0001504	1.9993985	0.5001504	1.9939836
21	4987.88510	0.0002005	9973.77019	0.0001003	1.9995990	0.5001003	1.9957890
22	7481.82764	0.0001337	14961.65529	0.0000668	1.9997327	0.5000668	1.9970591
23	11222.74146	0.0000891	22443.48293	0.0000446	1.9998218	0.5000446	1.9979504
24	16834.11220	0.0000594	33666.22439	0.0000297	1.9998812	0.5000297	1.9985742
25	25251.16829	0.0000396	50500.33659	0.0000198	1.9999208	0.5000198	1.9990099
26	37876.75244	0.0000264	75751.50488	0.0000132	1.9999472	0.5000132	1.9993135
27	56815.12866	0.0000176	113628.25732	0.0000088	1.9999648	0.5000088	1.9995248
28	85222.69299	0.0000117	170443.38598	0.0000059	1.9999765	0.5000059	1.9996714
29	127834.03949	0.0000078	255666.07898	0.0000039	1.9999844	0.5000039	1.9997731
30	191751.05923	0.0000052	383500.11847	0.0000026	1.9999896	0.5000026	1.9998435

RATE TABLES FOR GEOMETRIC GRADIENTS

DISCRETE COMPOUNDING							I= 5%
Uniform series present worth factor							(P/A,I,g,N)

N	g=2%	g=3%	g=4%	g=5%	g=6%	g=8%	g=10%	g=15%
1	0.9524	0.9524	0.9524	0.9524	0.9524	0.9524	0.9524	0.9524
2	1.8776	1.8866	1.8957	1.9048	1.9138	1.9320	1.9501	1.9955
3	2.7763	2.8031	2.8300	2.8571	2.8844	2.9396	2.9954	3.1379
4	3.6493	3.7021	3.7554	3.8095	3.8643	3.9759	4.0904	4.3891
5	4.4975	4.5839	4.6721	4.7619	4.8535	5.0419	5.2375	5.7595
6	5.3213	5.4490	5.5799	5.7143	5.8521	6.1383	6.4393	7.2604
7	6.1217	6.2976	6.4792	6.6667	6.8602	7.2661	7.6983	8.9043
8	6.8992	7.1300	7.3699	7.6190	7.8779	8.4261	9.0173	10.7047
9	7.6544	7.9466	8.2521	8.5714	8.9053	9.6192	10.3991	12.6765
10	8.3881	8.7476	9.1258	9.5238	9.9425	10.8464	11.8467	14.8362
11	9.1008	9.5334	9.9913	10.4762	10.9896	12.1087	13.3632	17.2016
12	9.7932	10.3041	10.8485	11.4286	12.0466	13.4070	14.9519	19.7922
13	10.4658	11.0603	11.6976	12.3810	13.1137	14.7425	16.6163	22.6295
14	11.1191	11.8020	12.5386	13.3333	14.1910	16.1161	18.3599	25.7371
15	11.7538	12.5296	13.3715	14.2857	15.2785	17.5289	20.1866	29.1407
16	12.3704	13.2433	14.1966	15.2381	16.3764	18.9821	22.1002	32.8683
17	12.9693	13.9434	15.0137	16.1905	17.4848	20.4769	24.1050	36.9510
18	13.5511	14.6302	15.8231	17.1429	18.6037	22.0143	26.2052	41.4226
19	14.1163	15.3039	16.6248	18.0952	19.7332	23.5956	28.4055	46.3200
20	14.6654	15.9648	17.4189	19.0476	20.8736	25.2222	30.7105	51.6838
21	15.1988	16.6131	18.2054	20.0000	22.0247	26.8952	33.1253	57.5584
22	15.7169	17.2490	18.9844	20.9524	23.1869	28.6160	35.6550	63.9925
23	16.2202	17.8728	19.7559	21.9048	24.3601	30.3860	38.3053	71.0394
24	16.7092	18.4848	20.5202	22.8571	25.5445	32.2066	41.0817	78.7575
25	17.1842	19.0851	21.2771	23.8095	26.7401	34.0791	43.9904	87.2106
26	17.6456	19.6739	22.0269	24.7619	27.9472	36.0052	47.0375	96.4687
27	18.0938	20.2516	22.7695	25.7143	29.1657	37.9863	50.2298	106.6086
28	18.5292	20.8182	23.5050	26.6667	30.3959	40.0240	53.5741	117.7142
29	18.9522	21.3741	24.2335	27.6190	31.6377	42.1199	57.0776	129.8774
30	19.3631	21.9193	24.9551	28.5714	32.8914	44.2757	60.7480	143.1991
31	19.7622	22.4542	25.6698	29.5238	34.1571	46.4931	64.5931	157.7895
32	20.1500	22.9789	26.3777	30.4762	35.4348	48.7739	68.6213	173.7695
33	20.5266	23.4936	27.0789	31.4286	36.7246	51.1198	72.8414	191.2713
34	20.8925	23.9984	27.7734	32.3810	38.0267	53.5328	77.2624	210.4400
35	21.2480	24.4937	28.4612	33.3333	39.3413	56.0146	81.8940	231.4343
40	22.8786	26.8321	31.8036	38.0952	46.1042	69.5291	108.5776	370.4886
45	24.2892	28.9561	34.9898	42.8571	53.1953	85.0878	142.2491	589.6314
50	25.5094	30.8854	38.0271	47.6190	60.6306	102.9998	184.7384	934.9897
55	26.5651	32.6378	40.9225	52.3810	68.4268	123.6212	238.3546	1479.2574
60	27.4783	34.2295	43.6826	57.1429	76.6013	147.3617	306.0117	2336.9967
65	28.2683	35.6753	46.3138	61.9048	85.1726	174.6930	391.3866	3688.7517
70	28.9517	36.9886	48.8221	66.6667	94.1599	206.1585	499.1191	5819.0515
80	30.0543	39.2650	53.4925	76.1905	113.4643	284.0874	806.6104	14467.1576
90	30.8794	41.1431	57.7367	85.7143	134.6880	387.3737	1296.2390	35945.7801
100	31.4969	42.6926	61.5936	95.2381	158.0219	524.2687	2075.8906	89290.5489

DISCRETE COMPOUNDING							I= 8%
Uniform series present worth factor							(P/A, i,g,N)
N	g=2%	g=3%	g=4%	g=5%	g=6%	g=8%	g=10%	g=15%
1	0.9259	0.9259	0.9259	0.9259	0.9259	0.9259	0.9259	0.9259
2	1.8004	1.8090	1.8176	1.8261	1.8347	1.8519	1.8690	1.9119
3	2.6263	2.6512	2.6762	2.7013	2.7267	2.7778	2.8295	2.9617
4	3.4063	3.4543	3.5030	3.5522	3.6021	3.7037	3.8079	4.0796
5	4.1430	4.2204	4.2992	4.3795	4.4613	4.6296	4.8043	5.2699
6	4.8388	4.9509	5.0659	5.1837	5.3046	5.5556	5.8192	6.5374
7	5.4959	5.6476	5.8042	5.9657	6.1323	6.4815	6.8529	7.8871
8	6.1165	6.3121	6.5151	6.7259	6.9447	7.4074	7.9057	9.3242
9	6.7026	6.9458	7.1997	7.4650	7.7420	8.3333	8.9780	10.8545
10	7.2562	7.5501	7.8590	8.1836	8.5246	9.2593	10.0702	12.4839
11	7.7790	8.1265	8.4939	8.8822	9.2926	10.1852	11.1826	14.2190
12	8.2727	8.6762	9.1052	9.5614	10.0465	11.1111	12.3157	16.0665
13	8.7391	9.2005	9.6939	10.2217	10.7863	12.0370	13.4696	18.0338
14	9.1795	9.7004	10.2608	10.8637	11.5125	12.9630	14.6450	20.1286
15	9.5954	10.1773	10.8067	11.4878	12.2252	13.8889	15.8421	22.3592
16	9.9883	10.6320	11.3324	12.0947	12.9248	14.8148	17.0614	24.7343
17	10.3593	11.0657	11.8386	12.6846	13.6114	15.7407	18.3033	27.2634
18	10.7097	11.4794	12.3260	13.2582	14.2852	16.6667	19.5682	29.9564
19	11.0407	11.8738	12.7954	13.8158	14.9466	17.5926	20.8565	32.8239
20	11.3532	12.2500	13.2475	14.3580	15.5957	18.5185	22.1687	35.8773
21	11.6484	12.6088	13.6827	14.8851	16.2329	19.4444	23.5051	39.1286
22	11.9272	12.9510	14.1019	15.3975	16.8582	20.3704	24.8663	42.5906
23	12.1905	13.2774	14.5055	15.8958	17.4719	21.2963	26.2527	46.2771
24	12.4392	13.5886	14.8942	16.3801	18.0743	22.2222	27.6648	50.2024
25	12.6740	13.8854	15.2685	16.8511	18.6655	23.1481	29.1031	54.3822
26	12.8958	14.1685	15.6289	17.3089	19.2458	24.0741	30.5679	58.8329
27	13.1053	14.4385	15.9760	17.7540	19.8153	25.0000	32.0599	63.5721
28	13.3032	14.6960	16.3102	18.1868	20.3743	25.9259	33.5796	68.6184
29	13.4900	14.9415	16.6321	18.6075	20.9229	26.8519	35.1273	73.9919
30	13.6665	15.1757	16.9420	19.0166	21.4614	27.7778	36.7038	79.7136
31	13.8332	15.3990	17.2404	19.4143	21.9899	28.7037	38.3094	85.8061
32	13.9906	15.6121	17.5278	19.8009	22.5086	29.6296	39.9447	92.2935
33	14.1393	15.8152	17.8046	20.1768	23.0177	30.5556	41.6104	99.2015
34	14.2797	16.0089	18.0711	20.5423	23.5173	31.4815	43.3069	106.5571
35	14.4123	16.1937	18.3277	20.8976	24.0078	32.4074	45.0348	114.3895
40	14.9727	16.9969	19.4751	22.5314	26.3269	37.0370	54.1663	161.8573
45	15.3938	17.6306	20.4252	23.9506	28.4392	41.6667	64.1752	226.8357
50	15.7102	18.1306	21.2119	25.1834	30.3630	46.2963	75.1459	315.7844
55	15.9480	18.5251	21.8633	26.2541	32.1151	50.9259	87.1706	437.5459
60	16.1266	18.8363	22.4027	27.1842	33.7109	55.5556	100.3508	604.2248
65	16.2609	19.0819	22.8494	27.9921	35.1643	60.1852	114.7974	832.3907
70	16.3617	19.2756	23.2192	28.6939	36.4881	64.8148	130.6322	1144.7262
80	16.4945	19.5491	23.7790	29.8329	38.7917	74.0741	167.0123	2157.5589
90	16.5695	19.7193	24.1629	30.6923	40.7026	83.3333	210.7196	4055.4818
100	16.6118	19.8253	24.4260	31.3407	42.2878	92.5926	263.2297	7611.9539

DISCRETE COMPOUNDING							I= 10%
Uniform series present worth factor							(P/A, i,g,N)

N	g=2%	g=3%	g=4%	g=5%	g=6%	g=8%	g=10%	g=15%
1	0.9091	0.9091	0.9091	0.9091	0.9091	0.9091	0.9091	0.9091
2	1.7521	1.7603	1.7686	1.7769	1.7851	1.8017	1.8182	1.8595
3	2.5337	2.5574	2.5812	2.6052	2.6293	2.6780	2.7273	2.8531
4	3.2586	3.3037	3.3495	3.3959	3.4428	3.5384	3.6364	3.8919
5	3.9307	4.0026	4.0759	4.1506	4.2267	4.3831	4.5455	4.9779
6	4.5539	4.6570	4.7627	4.8710	4.9821	5.2125	5.4545	6.1133
7	5.1318	5.2697	5.4120	5.5587	5.7100	6.0269	6.3636	7.3002
8	5.6677	5.8435	6.0259	6.2151	6.4115	6.8264	7.2727	8.5411
9	6.1646	6.3807	6.6063	6.8417	7.0874	7.6113	8.1818	9.8385
10	6.6253	6.8837	7.1550	7.4398	7.7388	8.3820	9.0909	11.1948
11	7.0526	7.3548	7.6738	8.0107	8.3664	9.1387	10.0000	12.6127
12	7.4487	7.7958	8.1644	8.5557	8.9713	9.8817	10.9091	14.0951
13	7.8161	8.2088	8.6281	9.0759	9.5542	10.6111	11.8182	15.6449
14	8.1568	8.5955	9.0666	9.5724	10.1158	11.3273	12.7273	17.2651
15	8.4726	8.9576	9.4811	10.0464	10.6571	12.0304	13.6364	18.9590
16	8.7655	9.2967	9.8731	10.4989	11.1786	12.7208	14.5455	20.7298
17	9.0371	9.6142	10.2436	10.9307	11.6812	13.3986	15.4545	22.5812
18	9.2890	9.9115	10.5940	11.3430	12.1656	14.0640	16.3636	24.5167
19	9.5225	10.1898	10.9252	11.7365	12.6323	14.7174	17.2727	26.5402
20	9.7390	10.4505	11.2384	12.1121	13.0820	15.3589	18.1818	28.6556
21	9.9398	10.6945	11.5345	12.4706	13.5154	15.9888	19.0909	30.8672
22	10.1260	10.9231	11.8144	12.8129	13.9330	16.6071	20.0000	33.1794
23	10.2987	11.1370	12.0791	13.1396	14.3354	17.2143	20.9091	35.5966
24	10.4588	11.3374	12.3293	13.4514	14.7232	17.8104	21.8182	38.1238
25	10.6072	11.5250	12.5659	13.7491	15.0969	18.3957	22.7273	40.7658
26	10.7449	11.7007	12.7896	14.0332	15.4570	18.9703	23.6364	43.5278
27	10.8725	11.8652	13.0011	14.3044	15.8041	19.5345	24.5455	46.4155
28	10.9909	12.0192	13.2010	14.5633	16.1385	20.0884	25.4545	49.4343
29	11.1006	12.1635	13.3900	14.8104	16.4607	20.6322	26.3636	52.5905
30	11.2024	12.2985	13.5688	15.0463	16.7712	21.1662	27.2727	55.8900
31	11.2968	12.4250	13.7377	15.2715	17.0704	21.6904	28.1818	59.3396
32	11.3843	12.5434	13.8975	15.4864	17.3588	22.2052	29.0909	62.9459
33	11.4654	12.6543	14.0485	15.6916	17.6367	22.7105	30.0000	66.7162
34	11.5407	12.7581	14.1913	15.8874	17.9044	23.2067	30.9091	70.6578
35	11.6104	12.8553	14.3264	16.0744	18.1624	23.6938	31.8182	74.7786
40	11.8902	13.2561	14.8987	16.8890	19.3184	25.9999	36.3636	98.3685
45	12.0819	13.5446	15.3311	17.5347	20.2790	28.1038	40.9091	127.8298
50	12.2134	13.7522	15.6577	18.0463	21.0772	30.0233	45.4545	164.6238
55	12.3035	13.9017	15.9044	18.4517	21.7404	31.7745	50.0000	210.5757
60	12.3653	14.0093	16.0908	18.7731	22.2915	33.3722	54.5455	267.9647
65	12.4077	14.0867	16.2317	19.0277	22.7494	34.8299	59.0909	339.6376
70	12.4367	14.1425	16.3380	19.2295	23.1299	36.1597	63.6364	429.1494
80	12.4702	14.2115	16.4791	19.5161	23.7088	38.4799	72.7273	680.5553
90	12.4860	14.2473	16.5596	19.6961	24.1085	40.4112	81.8182	1072.6824
100	12.4934	14.2658	16.6056	19.8092	24.3845	42.0186	90.9091	1684.2979

DISCRETE COMPOUNDING							I= 15%
Uniform series present worth factor							(P/A I,g,N)
N	g=2%	g=3%	g=4%	g=5%	g=6%	g=8%	g=10%	g=15%
1	0.8696	0.8696	0.8696	0.8696	0.8696	0.8696	0.8696	0.8696
2	1.6408	1.6484	1.6560	1.6635	1.6711	1.6862	1.7013	1.7391
3	2.3249	2.3460	2.3671	2.3884	2.4099	2.4531	2.4969	2.6087
4	2.9317	2.9707	3.0103	3.0503	3.0908	3.1734	3.2579	3.4783
5	3.4698	3.5303	3.5919	3.6546	3.7185	3.8498	3.9858	4.3478
6	3.9471	4.0315	4.1179	4.2064	4.2971	4.4850	4.6821	5.2174
7	4.3705	4.4804	4.5936	4.7102	4.8303	5.0816	5.3481	6.0870
8	4.7460	4.8824	5.0237	5.1702	5.3219	5.6418	5.9851	6.9565
9	5.0791	5.2425	5.4128	5.5902	5.7749	6.1680	6.5945	7.8261
10	5.3745	5.5650	5.7646	5.9736	6.1926	6.6621	7.1773	8.6957
11	5.6365	5.8539	6.0828	6.3237	6.5775	7.1261	7.7348	9.5652
12	5.8689	6.1126	6.3705	6.6434	6.9323	7.5619	8.2681	10.4348
13	6.0750	6.3444	6.6307	6.9353	7.2593	7.9712	8.7782	11.3043
14	6.2578	6.5519	6.8660	7.2018	7.5608	8.3556	9.2661	12.1739
15	6.4200	6.7378	7.0789	7.4451	7.8386	8.7165	9.7328	13.0435
16	6.5638	6.9043	7.2713	7.6673	8.0947	9.0555	10.1792	13.9130
17	6.6914	7.0534	7.4454	7.8701	8.3308	9.3739	10.6062	14.7826
18	6.8045	7.1870	7.6028	8.0553	8.5484	9.6729	11.0146	15.6522
19	6.9049	7.3066	7.7451	8.2244	8.7489	9.9537	11.4053	16.5217
20	6.9939	7.4137	7.8738	8.3788	8.9338	10.2173	11.7790	17.3913
21	7.0729	7.5097	7.9903	8.5198	9.1042	10.4650	12.1364	18.2609
22	7.1429	7.5956	8.0955	8.6485	9.2613	10.6976	12.4783	19.1304
23	7.2050	7.6726	8.1907	8.7660	9.4060	10.9160	12.8053	20.0000
24	7.2601	7.7415	8.2768	8.8733	9.5395	11.1211	13.1181	20.8696
25	7.3089	7.8033	8.3547	8.9713	9.6625	11.3137	13.4173	21.7391
26	7.3523	7.8586	8.4251	9.0608	9.7759	11.4946	13.7035	22.6087
27	7.3907	7.9081	8.4888	9.1424	9.8803	11.6645	13.9773	23.4783
28	7.4248	7.9525	8.5464	9.2170	9.9767	11.8241	14.2392	24.3478
29	7.4550	7.9922	8.5985	9.2851	10.0655	11.9739	14.4896	25.2174
30	7.4819	8.0278	8.6456	9.3473	10.1473	12.1146	14.7292	26.0870
31	7.5057	8.0597	8.6882	9.4040	10.2227	12.2468	14.9584	26.9565
32	7.5268	8.0883	8.7267	9.4558	10.2922	12.3709	15.1776	27.8261
33	7.5455	8.1138	8.7615	9.5032	10.3563	12.4874	15.3873	28.6957
34	7.5621	8.1367	8.7930	9.5464	10.4154	12.5969	15.5878	29.5652
35	7.5768	8.1573	8.8215	9.5858	10.4698	12.6997	15.7796	30.4348
40	7.6289	8.2319	8.9280	9.7372	10.6845	13.1271	16.6207	34.7826
45	7.6575	8.2748	8.9923	9.8332	10.8272	13.4393	17.2942	39.1304
50	7.6732	8.2996	9.0313	9.8942	10.9222	13.6674	17.8334	43.4783
55	7.6818	8.3139	9.0548	9.9329	10.9855	13.8340	18.2652	47.8261
60	7.6866	8.3221	9.0691	9.9574	11.0275	13.9558	18.6109	52.1739
65	7.6891	8.3269	9.0777	9.9730	11.0555	14.0447	18.8878	56.5217
70	7.6906	8.3296	9.0829	9.9828	11.0741	14.1096	19.1094	60.8696
80	7.6918	8.3321	9.0880	9.9931	11.0947	14.1917	19.4290	69.5652
90	7.6922	8.3329	9.0898	9.9972	11.1039	14.2356	19.6339	78.2609
100	7.6923	8.3332	9.0905	9.9989	11.1079	14.2590	19.7653	86.9565

CONTINUOUS CASH FLOW FACTORS

Nominal rate, r percent	$\dfrac{i}{\ln(1+i)}$	$\dfrac{\ln(1+i)}{i}$	$\dfrac{i}{(1+i)\ln(1+i)}$
5%	1.025	0.976	0.976
6%	1.030	0.971	0.969
7%	1.035	0.967	0.967
8%	1.040	0.962	0.963
9%	1.044	0.958	0.958
10%	1.049	0.953	0.954
12%	1.059	0.944	0.945
15%	1.073	0.932	0.933
18%	1.088	0.920	0.922
20%	1.091	0.912	0.914
25%	1.120	0.893	0.896
30%	1.143	0.875	0.880
35%	1.167	0.857	0.864
40%	1.189	0.841	0.849
45%	1.211	0.826	0.835
50%	1.233	0.811	0.822
60%	1.277	0.873	0.798

RANDOM NUMBERS

26368	06447	88540	23204	18765	03561	27526	81389	88555	05548
58059	80346	02155	35271	31656	56581	00662	32263	41285	96241
80932	26123	05017	45159	22116	38156	79042	07821	59242	84418
09882	23399	01220	96754	31931	74281	63991	78799	15857	99935
13062	60330	28172	71426	46666	30572	39094	42140	00773	45604
60695	20317	72854	54286	08168	60341	43418	72306	09762	30101
00676	60879	28434	65424	24619	39012	78069	15186	46328	91641
95945	21773	58925	26661	36147	96784	42557	17176	48205	49666
98816	73668	03119	07718	72193	73197	39601	63750	65729	65322
59411	33515	77047	29242	58858	35551	02313	15084	24910	21112
91257	61654	47485	72539	98710	91529	87626	26004	94725	24905
06472	67278	69506	75303	64736	25014	06065	00580	02247	41696
32439	29390	56282	54562	17375	71571	65745	95925	39036	07832
05560	67631	90523	29033	64687	91961	31101	72332	68090	17929
76548	65201	38577	13146	28402	24027	68710	88041	71402	80195
82695	21030	12230	62701	23949	41554	75567	99314	73755	15717
59603	03879	08684	82847	93768	05439	69367	25881	07876	01934
82561	61030	80591	78175	68982	57110	84018	13329	69991	11473
81362	88253	00230	56588	81880	67064	73359	72099	53105	25933
43005	49553	78218	57879	74082	59754	82593	35928	29368	73292
26577	78416	79692	74873	98936	91349	94436	80522	94522	34635
24397	48514	83144	94181	64451	27926	36134	38953	85518	59139
93911	99066	78857	90599	08068	74402	60066	86245	34646	81380
92004	02543	72483	55011	00273	42882	65873	82370	11100	89039
42253	73554	09444	18321	94631	62999	51669	28231	08979	53046

This table was prepared on a DOS based AT&T 386SX with a clock cycle of 16MHz. To produce these numbers the random number generating function in Microsoft Excel Version 3.0 was used.

RANDOM DEVIATES FOR NORMAL DISTRIBUTIONS

-0.22	-0.80	-0.39	-0.22	0.11	0.16	0.04	-0.03	-1.29	1.31
-1.33	-0.52	0.68	0.13	0.08	0.40	0.98	0.60	0.19	1.79
0.40	0.22	-0.35	1.16	-0.90	-0.19	-1.02	1.00	1.10	1.43
-0.74	-1.55	-0.83	-0.23	-0.46	1.72	-0.49	0.65	0.65	0.10
-0.24	-0.06	-0.08	-1.13	-1.24	0.81	-1.49	-0.05	0.46	1.98
1.28	0.23	0.21	-1.03	0.57	1.26	-1.32	-0.99	-0.19	0.30
-0.45	-0.42	0.44	1.02	-0.37	-2.01	-0.43	-0.72	0.02	-1.02
-0.28	0.29	0.94	-0.05	1.95	2.76	1.38	-0.08	-0.78	1.86
0.89	-2.15	0.63	-0.35	1.57	2.26	-1.95	-1.49	-1.05	0.45
-1.64	-0.75	1.06	0.05	2.34	-1.69	0.41	0.18	2.45	0.51
-0.47	0.08	-0.64	1.92	0.05	-1.01	-1.06	-0.57	0.63	-0.70
0.19	-0.35	0.77	0.95	-0.99	1.15	-3.16	0.91	-0.22	-0.83
-0.38	0.16	-0.84	-1.53	-0.43	-0.03	-1.24	-0.26	-0.19	0.17
0.44	0.23	0.20	2.19	-0.07	0.32	-0.94	0.55	0.09	1.22
1.22	0.07	-1.87	-0.30	1.48	0.16	-1.70	0.49	0.13	-0.15
-0.45	1.16	1.26	0.28	-1.15	-0.32	-0.56	-0.35	-0.47	-1.88
-1.76	-0.03	-0.66	-2.26	0.46	-0.13	0.76	-0.43	-0.77	1.13
-0.41	-1.96	-0.75	0.36	0.83	1.25	0.93	0.36	-0.43	0.86
-1.69	-1.56	-2.76	0.11	0.50	0.06	-0.67	0.86	1.00	0.06
-0.02	-0.78	1.12	0.34	-0.40	-0.40	-1.33	0.97	-0.11	-0.04
-2.14	0.73	-0.78	2.36	-0.75	0.31	-0.52	1.41	-0.62	-1.60
2.73	-1.70	-0.72	-0.05	0.29	-0.20	0.17	0.40	1.17	-1.93
0.90	-1.50	1.83	0.09	1.82	-2.34	0.33	1.51	-1.10	0.26
-0.05	1.10	1.28	-0.19	0.81	-0.57	-0.06	-0.54	-0.86	0.97
-0.46	-1.94	0.36	-1.16	0.40	-0.71	1.46	0.55	0.50	-0.79

This table was prepared using the formula $(0.5 - x)*12$ where 'x' was the mean of twelve random numbers generated with values between 0 and 1.

ANSWERS TO SELECTED PROBLEMS

CHAPTER 1

1-3   (a) yes (b) no (c) no (d) yes (e) no (f) no (g) no (h) yes
(i) no (j) no

CHAPTER 2

2-3   (a) no (b) no (c) yes (d) no (e) yes (f) no

2-5

Account	Statement	Classification
Cash	Balance sheet	Asset
Salaries expense	Income statement	Expense
Salaries payable	Balance sheet	Liability
Retained earnings	Balance sheet	Equity
Sales	Income statement	Revenue
Depreciation expense	Income statement	Expense
Gains and losses on disposal of assets	Income statement	—
Paid-in capital	Balance sheet	Equity
Accumulated depreciation	Balance sheet	Contra-asset
Prepaid rent	Balance sheet	Asset
Contract advance	Balance sheet	Liability
Accounts payable	Balance sheet	Liability
Office equipment	Balance sheet	Asset
Land	Balance sheet	Asset
Buildings	Balance sheet	Asset

Process machinery	Balance sheet	Asset
Accounts receivable	Balance sheet	Asset

2-12   (a) F (b) O (c) I (d) NC (e) NC (f) O (g) F (h) O
(i) NC (j) F (k) O (l) NC (m) O

2-13   (a) Prepaid rent $12,000
                Cash $12,000
        (b) Rent Expense $ 1,000
                Prepaid rent $ 1,000

2-15   Net income, $4662.   Total assets, $91,000

2-17   Date of purchase:
            Fixed assets (computer) $100,000
                Cash $100,000
        End of year adjusting entry:
            Depreciation expense $ 25,000
                Accumulated depreciation $ 25,000

2-19   Annual depreciation expense, $25,000
        Sold for $30,000:
            Cash $30,000
            Accumulated depreciation   75,000
                Fixed assets (computer) $100,000
                Gain on disposal   5,000
        Sold for $15,000:
            Cash $15,000
            Accumulated depreciation   75,000
            Loss on disposal   10,000
                Fixed assets (computer) $100,000

2-20 $52,000

2-21   Difference between ending and beginning balances of accounts.
            Accounts receivable $10,000
            Equipment   50,000
            Notes payable   15,000
            Accounts payable   7,000
            Retained earnings   7,000

CHAPTER 3

3-11   S2
3-13   (a) Machine A   (b) Machine B   (c) 165 fenders
3-15   Method A profit per ton of raw ore, $155
        Method B profit per ton of raw ore, $135

CHAPTER 4

4-1   3.5 years
4-3   Pegasus, 3.5 years.   Zeus, 4.5 years

4-5   A, 4.6 years.   B, 4 years
4-7   I, 2.125 years.   II, 2.250 years
4-9   Alternative A
4-11 $5000
4-13   (a) A, 3.3 years. B, 6.7 years   (b) A, 8.2%. B, 10.9%
       (c) A, 16.4%. B, 21.8%

CHAPTER 5

5-1 $3,207; $3315; $3,319; $3319
5-3   29.61%
5-5   (a) 3.03%   (b) 12%   (c) 12.68%   (d) 12.75%
5-9 $818
5-11   0.52%; 6.38%; $3,394
5-15 $2,525.04
5-17   11.52 years

CHAPTER 6

6-19   PW = $53,681; $52,064;
6-21   AW = $5,000 + 500($A/G$, i, 8)
6-23 $26,380
6-25 $198
6-27 $4,780
6-29   −$1,089,245
6-31   (a) $25,654
6-35   −$11,176
6-37   (a) 11 years   (b) $500   (c) 500 (P/A, i, 11) + 100(A/G, i, 11)(P/A, i, 11)
6-39 $3,689

CHAPTER 7

7-1   PW = P; FW = $P(F/P, i, N)$; AW = $P(A/P, i, N)$
7-3   PW = $A(P/F, i, 3)$; FW = A($F/P, i,$ N − 3); AW = PW($A/P, i, N$)
7-5   AW = $A(1 + i)$
7-7   PW = $2A + A(P/A, i,$ N − 1); AW = PW($A/P, i, N$)
7-9   Formula for PW of geometric gradient in Table 6.2 multiplied by (1 + i) and by (A/P, i, N)
7-11   (a) $1,130   (b) $313   (c) $4051.5   (d) $313.7; $4,051.3
7-13 $44,482; $7,579
7-15   (b) −$8,981; −$10,811   (c) −$39,866; −$47990   (d) Alternate A
7-17   EUAC(A) = −$8,016; EUAC(B) = −$8,196; PW(A) = −$37,474; PW(B) = −$38,318; Choose machine A.

7-19   (a) \$1,146/month   (b) Interest portion Year 1—\$800; Year 2—\$797
        Principal portion Year 1—\$346; Year 2—\$349
7-21   (a) \$610/month for the dealer: \$529/month for the bank

CHAPTER 8

8-1   (a) AW(A) = − \$11,836; AW(B) = − \$1,696; Choose Product B
        (b) −\$59,180; −\$8,480   (c) −\$59,180; −\$8,480
8-3   \$14,000,000; \$27,000,000
8-5   \$715,800
8-7   \$2,842
8-9   \$5,669; − \$669
8-11   PW-cost for A = \$55,056. For B = \$52,856
8-13   \$3.65/car
8-15   \$452.5

CHAPTER 9

9-1   (a) B, E, F; \$100,000   (b) E
9-3   2.3%/month
9-5   (b) 12.73%
9-7   (b) 12.06%; 11.83%   (c) 11.23%   (d) Alternative B
9-9   No, IRR = 4%
9-11   Yes, IRR > MARR
9-13   9%; 3%; 3.5%; 2.3% Do not choose any alternatives.

CHAPTER 10

10-1   3 roots; 1 root
10-3   (a) 2 roots   (b) 1 root   (c) IRR = 290%
10-5   (a) 3 roots, 1 root   (b) 8.8%   (c) 8.9%
10-7   (a) 2   (b) 23.8%   (c) 17.6%
10-9   (a) 1.379%   (b) 4.1%

CHAPTER 11

11-3   It will never get there; 6%
11-5   1.71
11-7   1.36; 1.5
11-9   (b) 3.48
11-11   0.953; 0.943

11-13   X
11-15 $5.76/trip; B is still the preferred choice
11-17 $5.76
11-19   (a) E 1.5, W 0.942
11-21   About 7 years
11-23   (a) Y

CHAPTER 12

12-3   A, B, AY, AZ, BY, BZ
12-7   (a) $58,000; $23,000   (b) $94,000   (c) $51,300
12-11   (a) $140,000; $180,000; $220,000; $155,000   (b) $133,063;
        $172,452; $210,750; $143,228
12-13   (a) None   (b) B, C
12-15   (c) C > B > A > 0 > D PW   C >B > A > 0 > D IRR
12-17   IRR 24.2%; 25%; 25%; 22.8%
        Incremental IRR ranking 3 > 2 > 4 > 1 > 0
12-23   (a) BOOM $18,250; WHACK $20,375; THUD $16,500
12-25   (c) NPW C > B > A; IRR C > B > A B/C C > B > A
12-27   1.21; 1.25; 1.25; 1.14;
        Incremental BCR ranking 3 > 2 > 4 > 1 > 0
12-31 $AW_1 = -\$145,297$; $AW_2 = -\$131,865$; $AW_3 = -\$127,910$
        (b) 40%   (c) 17%   (d) Recommend 3

CHAPTER 13

13-3   0, A, B, AB = 4; 0, A, B, C, AB, AC, BC, ABC = 8
13-5   (a) 128   (b) 48   (c) 72
13-7   (a) A, B, C, D   (b) A, B, D
13-9   (a) 3.33%; 8.07%; 18.85%; 11.95%; 19.68%   (b) E1, P1
13-11   (a) 18   (c) E1, P1   (d) M2, E2, P1   (e) M2, E1, P1
13-13   (a) 256   (b) 144   (c) 72
13-15   (b) A; D   (c) 32
13-17   (a) A, D, G, H   (b) A, D, G, H   (c) A, G, H

CHAPTER 14

14-3   24.6%
14-7   (a) $1,650,000   (b) 22.3%   (c) $4,752,000   (d) 74.2%
14-13   11.28%
14-17   6.97%
14-21   11.16%

14-23 $1,197
14-27   Lease PW = --$1,682
14-29   (a) 50 days   (b) yes
14-30   (a) $42,740   (b) $7,123   (c) Interest payment year five $1,378

CHAPTER 15

15-3   (a) $1,950
15-5   (a) $23,817
15-7   (b) 2 years
15-9   4 years
15-11   4 years
15-13   Keep defender
15-15   S > $217,255
15-17   8 years
15-19   (a) New building $8800. Old building $4110
15-21   Replace at EOY 1
15-23   Replace at EOY 2

CHAPTER 16

16-11   SL $30,000 first year. MACRS $16,667 first year
16-15   7.7%
16-23 $333,333
16-25   Cost $33,300. Percentage $20,000
16-27   (a) $14,516   (b) $15,954   (c) 19.6%
16-29 $15,098
16-31   (b) EUAC $586.9
16-33   (a) $44,300   (b) 17.3%
16-35 $5,044
16-37   (a) $5,910   (b) 15.1%
16-39 $3,062

CHAPTER 17

17-4   3.5 million crossings; $7 million; $2.75 million
17-10   (a) 0.4   (b) 4
17-13 $150
17-19   (a) 1.56   (b) 2.8; 2.1; 1   (c) 1.8; 1.3; 1
17-21   (a) 2.08   (b) 3.1; 3.3; 2; 1.7; 6; 1.75   (c) 2.5; 2.4; 1.7; 1.4; 3.0; 1.7
17-25   11.8%
17-27   (a) $300,000,000   (b) $289,000,000   (c) $201,000,000

17-29   a; aP
17-31   (a) 0.038   (b) 0.038   (c) $754,000
17-35   (a) 0.0486   (b) 0.1275   (c) 21.6%
17-37   (a) $50,000,000   (b) $120   (c) $60,000,000   (d) $60,000,000

CHAPTER 18

18-3   (a) 8.15%   (b) 1.71%
18-5   (a) 12.16%   (b) 1.93%   (c) 11.15
18-7   (a) $2,313.72   (b) 11.25% per year
18-13   10.25%
18-15   (a) $4,510   (b) $4,510
18-17   (a) $1,573   (b) $3,114   (c) $6,474
18-19   AW = ($-$55,975; $-$58,440) PW = ($-$279,427; $-$291,732)
18-23 $-$40,800, $-$35,200

CHAPTER 19

19-7   Yes, PW < $500,000

CHAPTER 20

20-13   (a) $14,410,000   (b) $15,680,000
20-15 $57,810,000
20-17   0.65
20-25   (a) $24,000   (b) $44,000   (c) $46,222
20-27   (a) $222,222   (b) $333,333
20-31   (a) Plant should remain open   (b) $45
20-33   Higher

CHAPTER 21

21-3   15.6%; 14.7%; 13.0%
21-13   (a) $50,410
21-17   (a) 1.21   (b) 0.253   (c) 2.360
21-19   Revenue ($698,148; $-$337,856), Initial cost ($780,205; $-$569,841)
21-21   (a) $283,000; 14.55%   (b) $983,441   (c) $213,440; $318,441; 13.54%;
         16.36%
21-25   Life ($49,227; $14,955) Net Cash Flow ($60,952; $7,976) MARR
         ($24,846; $46,455)
21-27   Decrease in Annual Savings >50.5%

CHAPTER 22

22-7   3; 0; 7.8; 2.36
22-9   (a) 0.001   (b) 0.5
22-11   (a) 7/18   (b) 1/2   (c) 1/36   (d) 1/4
22-13   (a) 1/4   (b) 1/2   (c) 3/13   (d) 3/51   (e) 3/52
22-15   1/3
22-17   3.5; 2.917; 1.71; 2, 3, 4, 5; 2/3
22-19 $75,500,000; $110,400,000
22-21 $64.25
22-25 $74.5
22-27   (a) 10.60   (b) 37.54; 6.13
22-31   (a) 0.96; $2.30; $2,208/1000 ft^3
22-33   (a) 1, 2, 3, 4, 5   (c) 2.667; 2.22; 1.49

CHAPTER 23

23-1   (a) $25.78 million   (b) $2.278 million
23-5   (a) $2,252,000; $259,000   (b) $2,257,000; $264,000
23-11 $0; 3 × 10^{12}; $1,732,000. $3,000,000; 8.333 × 10^{12}; $2,887,000
23-15   (a) 0.5   (b) 0.5   (c) 0.841   (e) 0.659   (f) 0.791   (g) 0.347
23-17   91
23-19   0
23-21   0.009043 to the right
23-25   Choose A$_2$
23-27   (a) A$_2$ (b) A$_4$ (c) A$_2$ (d) A$_3$ orA$_4$

CHAPTER 24

24-7   26.33; 4; 2
24-9   (a) $3,440; $36,200; $53,600   (b) 10.1%; 16.8%; 20.0%
        (c) $101,000; $20,200: $1670, 11.5 years   (d) $33,860; 16.8%
24-11   Not quite but excusable
24-23 $142,000
24-27   (a) 5.61; 0.694

CHAPTER 25

25-1   (a) a$_3$ (b) a$_4$ (c) a$_3$ (d) a$_3$ (e) a$_4$
25-3   (a) a$_2$ (b) a$_4$ (c) a$_1$, a$_3$ (d) a$_1$, a$_2$, a$_3$
25-5   (a) a$_1$ (b) a$_2$, a$_4$, a$_5$ (c) a$_1$ (d) a$_1$, a$_3$, a$_4$ (e) a$_1$, a$_4$
25-7   (a) None   (b) Maximax

25-9   (a) D   (b) A, D   (c) B
25-13   (a) D   (b) B   (c) B   (d) A

CHAPTER 26

26-11   (a) Train, bus, car pool   (b) Train > bus > driving   (c) Car pool
26-13   (a) 1   (c) 5   (d) 2   (e) 3
26-15   (b) A, B, D, F   (c) E
26-16   (b) C, H   (c) H

CHAPTER 27

27-1   (a) 4 > 1   (b) 3   (c) E   (d) 1, 4   (e) 4
27-3   (a) 4   (b) 4
27-5   (a) None   (b) 2
27-11   C > A > B > D
27-13   (b) 32, 26, 23, 13, 6
27-23   23, 51, 26 (Answers can vary somewhat depending on how utility
         curves are drawn.)

CHAPTER 28

28-11   Five plus number of subattributes
28-13   Priority weights, $F_1 = 12$, $F_2 = 18$, $F_3 = 35$, $F_4 = 35$
28-16   (a) $1.1 million   (b) $0.333 million

INDEX